The Emergence of Philosophy of Religion

THE
EMERGENCE
OF PHILOSOPHY
OF RELIGION

by
James Collins

Yale University Press, New Haven & London

To My Students in Philosophy
Across the Years

Preface

In the course of doing some previous work on the problem of God in modern philosophy, I found myself constantly being brought up short at the border line separating that problem from the related one of the modern philosophical conceptions of religion. Although the specific investigation of theories of God required me to maintain a working distinction between the two issues, I began to realize that there was a much closer set of ties between them than I had originally supposed. What particularly impressed me was the insistence on the part of many modern philosophers that their inquiry into our knowledge of God was only part of a larger inquiry into the religious relationship between man and God. Questions began to arise in my mind about the modifications which would have to be introduced into our understanding of the modern philosophical views on man and God, in the light of the unifying context supplied by the theory of religion. Prompted by such considerations, I launched into the present research and quickly found that the topic was worth pursuing for its own sake, and not simply as a means for grasping something else in modern philosophy. It was clearly impossible to try to do justice to the complexity and variety of modern philosophical doctrines on religion, without making them the central focus of a distinct historical study. The present book developed out of my attempt to meet this situation and bring out the import of some major approaches to religion made in the modern philosophical tradition.

In every age, philosophers have taken an intense interest in the meaning of religion and its role in our personal and social existence. Modern philosophers are no exception to this general concern, but their response is made in accord with their distinctive historical condition. Unlike the Greek, Roman, and Oriental philosophers of the ancient world, they are marked by the historical experience gained from the tradition of Jewish and Christian religious thought and practice. And yet they are also unlike the Fathers of the Church in being professional philosophers, and unlike the medieval Schoolmen in not combining their philosophical competence with that of the theologian. The modern philosophers approach the problem of religion in terms of their own unique historical configuration: they are professional philosophers, treating religion initially in the forms specified by the Jewish and Christian scriptural and institutional sources, but doing so in a philosophical spirit which is not itself a minister to some theological purpose. Without overlooking the particular religious conditions under which they come to the issues, they nevertheless seek out the properly human significance of religion as it can be grasped and lived cooperatively by all men. These are the qualifications which they place upon the philosophical study of religion and which in turn affect any contemporary work which we ourselves may do in this area.

This book concentrates upon the emergence of the philosophy of religion as a full-blown modern discipline. It is hazardous to specify any chronological limits for a process which has so many continuing factors bound up with it, but some working landmarks do help to identify the process and discern the direction it is taking. The crucial hundred years for the explicit and systematic development of the philosophy of religion reach from about 1730 to 1830. These dates are significant, since they embrace a period extending from Hume's early reflections on religious issues to Hegel's last lectures on the philosophy of religion. The three central thinkers are Hume, Kant, and Hegel. They lay the classical foundations for the modern philosophical theories of religion. To understand their conceptions of religion is to grasp the great points of reference, with respect to which the earlier probings gain an orientation and the later theories secure a philosophical basis. With them, the philosophy of religion comes of age and takes its place among the basic parts of philosophy.

Something is sacrificed, and something gained, by restricting our investigation to the positions of Hume, Kant, and Hegel. The losses come from not considering the vital context furnished by earlier modern theories of religion, by other contemporary positions, and by the impact of Hume, Kant, and Hegel upon the subsequent course of modern philosophical speculation on religion. Essential preparatory work was done throughout the seventeenth century. Skeptics used the theological controversies and religious wars to call into question the humane value of religion. Spinoza treated biblical religion as a human achievement that develops in stages, requires positive comparison with other human religions, and submits to ultimate purification and rectification by philosophical truth. Herbert of Cherbury specified the basic tenets of natural religion; Locke and the deists found the interpretative norm of religious statements in philosophy; and Leibniz looked upon philosophical principles as a harmonizing center for securing the religious unification and organization of the whole world and all its particular religions. Philosophy of religion springs from this well-nourished soil. Moreover, notable contributions were made by the Enlightenment leaders and Rousseau during the century dominated by our three classical philosophers of religion. In addition, the full implications of the doctrines of Hume, Kant, and Hegel could not be realized until they had been developed and reworked by the nineteenth-century theories of religion flowing from this watershed. These many relations deserve to be given a thorough examination on their own merits.

What warrants the limitations placed upon the present study, however, is the need for a detailed presentation of the philosophies of religion of the three classical thinkers. Usually, their views on religion are treated as dispensable appendixes to their main doctrines. But from the standpoints of Hume, Kant, and Hegel themselves, their theories of religion are much more central to their philosophical enterprise and crucial for our understanding of its full nature. There is no really effective way of showing the intimate relationship and importance of the topic of religion in their thought, except by closely analyzing how it is developed within the specific doctrinal frameworks. The involvement of the position on religion with basic points in methodology, metaphysics, theory of man, and ethics can only be manifested by actually tracing out some major links. The presence of these determinate links within the total philosophical effort is also what constitutes the decisive difference between a thinker who draws some conclusions about religion and one who develops a thoroughgoing philosophy of religion. Hence it is necessary to trace out the specific arguments and internal connections which lead to the gradual constitution of a theory of religion within the philosophies of Hume, Kant, and Hegel. Only after we view this internally governed emergence from several aspects are we in a position to grasp the import and rigor of the classical modern philosophies of religion. This is the only safe basis for evaluating these theories and attaining some new, yet philosophically responsible, views of our own on the meaning and truth of religion.

A remark must be made about the last two chapters. They record two distinct, but not entirely unrelated, conclusions which I have drawn from the investigation. The purpose of Chapter 9 is to bring together the convergent historical findings concerning the issues jointly faced by Hume, Kant, and Hegel. There is a much higher degree of intellectual continuity between them on the problem of religion than exists between most major philosophers. Just as Hume recapitulates many earlier modern notions of religion and subjects them to criticism, so also Kant is a critical reader of Hume, and Hegel a critical reader of both his predecessors. This common fund of inquiry leads to a rather broad consensus about defining the basic problems in philosophy of religion, even though each thinker treats them in accord with his own method and thus reaches his distinctive interpretation of religion. These jointly defined questions and determinate methodological differences enable us to discern the nature of the classical modern approach in philosophy of religion. The historical aim of the present study is to contribute something toward reaching this understanding. An examination of the interwoven pattern of problems explored by our three classical sources will show what it means in practice to philosophize on religion in the modern spirit.

Chapter 10 is exploratory in nature. It inquires about the significant differences in philosophy of religion which can result from a sustained attempt, on the part of realistic theism, to deal with the problems raised in classical modern philosophy of religion. Such a meeting results in some modifications in both these currents of thought. There are some helpful conceptions of religion in the theistic tradition of Augustine, Aquinas, and Newman, but they are not likely to remain unchanged by being rethought within the context of modern philosophical inquiries into the meaning of religion. My own view is that the resources of realism and theism on this question can only be released through a radical acceptance of the method of integrative analysis and experiential inference. This method is intended to develop a realistic theory of religion in a distinctively philosophical manner and within the limits of the statements thus warranted. At the same time, if a realistic theism is carried to completion in a philosophically established theory of religion, it will also have some definite repercussions upon the modern philosophical conceptions of religion. The effect of such a reconsideration of the classical problems is, at the very least, to widen the range of effective positions open to inquirers in the philosophy of religion.

In the last chapter, therefore, the methodological consequences of joining realistic theism with the modern mode of philosophizing on religion are weighed. It is toward achieving such a new position in the philosophy of religion that all the critical reflections in this book are directed. My working standpoint is that of an open religious humanism, developed on the basis of a realistic theism.

This book is the outgrowth of the second series of St. Thomas More Lectures, which I delivered in Yale University in 1963. My stay there was made memorable by the warm hospitality of Rev. James Healy, as well as by the probing conversation of Yale's philosophers. The task of writing the book was greatly aided by the John Simon Guggenheim Foundation, which granted me a Fellowship for the academic year 1963-64. The entire research has also been substantially supported by Saint Louis University, at the recommendation of the then chairman of the Philosophy Department, Rev. William L. Wade, S. J. In my own way, I have tried to profit by a series of discussions with Rev. George P. Klubertanz, S. J., present chairman of the Philosophy Department, concerning some philosophical approaches to religion.

James Collins

Normandy, Missouri
July, 1966

Contents

The Emergence of Philosophy of Religion

I

Hume:
The Naturalizing of
Religious Belief

Like the other two philosophers studied in this volume, David Hume was a Christian believer in his childhood and always kept in mind his personal experience of religious living. His family gave strong support to Scottish Calvinism and brought him up in the full rigor of early eighteenth-century predestinarian doctrine and Sabbath devotions.[1] As he later admitted to the shamelessly inquisitive James Boswell, he was personally religious as a youth and indeed was scrupulous about examining his conscience for any signs of pride or infidelity.

Difficulties on the latter score commenced, however, as soon as he began searching for reasonable arguments to support the doctrines he had been taught. The skepticism which gradually stole over him ran counter to his early religious inclination, and perhaps even to the condition of his reason. Hume singled out the reading of Locke and Clarke as the beginning of his loss of Christian faith, since he found their rational defenses of that position inconclusive. His questionings increased with a study of Bayle's account of the ancient naturalists, who seemed to combine atheism and virtuous living very nicely, as well as with his initiation by Fénelon, Malebranche, and Bayle himself to the dialectical rigors of the problem of evil and that of demonstrating God's existence.

Although there was no dramatic repudiation of his early stand, Hume's religious belief steadily eroded under pressure from his philosophical re-

1. Hume's religious background is described in J. Y. T. Greig, *David Hume* (New York, 1931), pp. 36–48, 61–62; Ernest C. Mossner, *The Life of David Hume* (Austin, 1954), pp. 32–34, 64–65; and N. K. Smith's Introduction to his edition of Hume, *Dialogues Concerning Natural Religion* (Indianapolis, Bobbs-Merrill, 1963), pp. 1–44.

flections and was accompanied by severe emotional disturbances. This slow but irreversible process left him thereafter personally a stranger to what he termed the grim realm of religious devotion, but his intellectual interest never slackened in the plan of trying to understand the forces which lead people to acts of religious belief and devotion.

Hume's speculations on religion were sharpened not only by his reading of theological, philosophical, and devotional treatises in the Christian tradition but also by extensive conversation and correspondence with believers on religious topics. Even during his early retreat at Descartes' old college of La Flèche, he walked the grounds with a Jesuit father and discussed the question of miracles and the Gospel. The radical thoughts which he then formulated on miracles, religious belief, and morality were intended for his first work, A *Treatise of Human Nature*, but were cautiously removed lest they impede the chances of its favorable reception. These critical views were more incisively restated and included, however, in An *Enquiry Concerning Human Understanding*, where they earned him the public reputation of being an infidel.

Hume became the target of considerable abuse from the more conservative wing of the English and Scottish clergy, who prevented him from ever obtaining a university teaching post. Yet he chose his own friends in Edinburgh chiefly from among the liberal clergy, who remained his companions and defenders. He kept them informed about his religious studies, which culminated, shortly after 1750, in the composition of his two main works on the subject: *The Natural History of Religion* (published in 1757) and *Dialogues Concerning Natural Religion*. Portions of the latter manuscript circulated among his friends for twenty years, stimulating their discussion and letters. During the last year of his life Hume revised the *Dialogues* and took the greatest care to insure its posthumous publication (1779). Thus, from his youthful memoranda down to his mature treatises and his deathbed interview with Boswell, he showed a steady concern with the problems centering around religious belief and practice, especially in their relationships to human knowledge and moral conduct.

THE PHILOSOPHICAL TREATMENT OF RELIGION

Hume begins one of his essays on religion with the abrupt declaration that "every enquiry, which regards religion, is of the utmost importance." [2]

2. Hume, *The Natural History of Religion*, ed. H. E. Root (London, Black, 1956), p. 21.

Far from being a conventional encomium, this remark accurately reflects the place assigned to religious questions in his thought, where they are never very far from the center. Since he does not suppose that his method of philosophical analysis requires all problems to be flattened out to a dead level, Hume is not reluctant to establish a theoretical and practical ranking among his various subjects of investigation. He finds some good grounds, both in the intrinsic aims of his philosophy and in the probable social consequences of his work, for recognizing the importance of the philosophical study of religion.

In order to determine the basis for this evaluation, we must bear in mind that Hume was a moral philosopher in the capacious eighteenth-century sense of a thinker concerned primarily about the meaning of man and the possibilities of reshaping his existence in new ways. Throughout a long lifetime of work, Hume remained remarkably faithful to a youthful resolve to make human nature his principal study and the source of every really significant truth for his own philosophy. Hence what he once referred to in a letter as his primary concern for "our knowledge of human nature from experience" provided not only the main subject matter of his analysis but also the norm for deciding upon the relative importance of a topic.[3] Because of the close relevance of a study of religion for deepening our understanding of human nature and perhaps for practically redirecting its tendencies, Hume was bound to include such a study among the more essential tasks in philosophy.

In the introductory pages of A *Treatise of Human Nature*, he stressed the relevance of his inquiry for those remote areas of knowledge that might seem to remain unaffected: mathematics, physics or natural philosophy, and natural religion. The Humean science of man must be extended into these areas if only because it considers the nature and limits of human experience and the knowing powers used in their scientific elaboration. Drawing an optimistic draft upon the future, Hume then added:

> It is impossible to tell what changes and improvements we might make in these sciences were we thoroughly acquainted with the extent and force of human understanding, and could explain the nature of the ideas we employ, and of the operations we perform in our reasonings. And these improvements are the more to be hoped for in natural religion, as it is not content with instructing us in the nature of

3. J. Y. T. Greig, ed., *The Letters of David Hume* (2 vols. Oxford, Clarendon Press, 1932), 1, 349.

superior powers, but carries its views farther, to their disposition towards us, and our duties towards them; and consequently we ourselves
are not only the beings, that reason, but also one of the objects,
concerning which we reason.[4]

A philosophy based on the experimental study of man has definite implications to be worked out for natural religion, not only because the latter
relies upon the human understanding and passions, but also because it is
essentially a relational discipline, one of whose poles is man himself.
Because religion dwells upon the God-man relationship, its very subject
matter involves man most intimately and responds to changes in our
conception of human nature.

Thus the minimal meaning for the importance of a philosophical inquiry into religion is that this inquiry is relevant for the empirical study
of man. This bearing is of a reciprocal sort. When Hume is thinking
about such particular doctrines as God's goodness and providence, he
emphasizes the effect which his independent philosophical account of our
limited experience and knowledge has upon the claims of religion to
convey knowledge concerning these doctrines. In this case, philosophical
relevance is achieved by working out the restrictive implications of Hume's
theory of knowledge and of passions for some common religious beliefs.
Yet when he attempts to penetrate into the structure of the religious
attitude itself, he recognizes that his findings here constitute a further
insight into the nature and dynamic tendencies of man. To study religion
is not only to examine some topics traditionally labeled as religious in import, but also to examine those springs in human nature itself from which
the religious attitude and its interpretations of our existence rise. In this
stronger sense, then, the study of religion is philosophically relevant by
reason of its own direct contributions to our apprehension of man's
makeup and aspirations.

Hume challenges the common opinion that this twofold minimal relevance can be expanded to the maximal point of claiming that the entire
fabric of morality and human society depends upon an understanding and
acceptance of some religious convictions. He is content to defend the
philosophical importance of the study of religion at the minimal level of
a demonstrable connection between this study and our grasp of human
reality. He treats the crucial problem of religion and morality in a way

4. Hume, A *Treatise of Human Nature*, ed. L. A. Selby-Bigge (Oxford, Clarendon
Press, 1946), p. xix. Hume's spelling and capitalization are modernized throughout the
present work.

that asserts the independence of morality from religion and hence refuses to base the latter's philosophical importance upon any contribution it supposedly makes toward morality.

One theme which sounds clearly through the pages of Hume, and which will be strongly reaffirmed by the other classical modern philosophers of religion, is that religion must be treated with the *same* method, principles, and sources of evidence used in the rest of one's philosophy. The philosopher has no business in making an exception here or in regarding the region of religion as privileged. He will, to be sure, have to make some adaptations to the problems arising in this region, but he will be modifying his common procedures and not suspending or subverting them.

In Hume's case, this means remaining loyal to his general approach to all human phenomena. As he observes in one of those revealing testimonies which enliven his correspondence, his approach to man is that of the anatomist rather than the painter.[5] His procedure in any philosophical matter bears a closer resemblance to Leonardo da Vinci's anatomical and architectural drawings than to his full-fleshed portraits, such as *The Musician* or the *Virgin of the Rocks*. It is in the same anatomizing spirit that Hume launches upon his study of man's religious attitude and activities.

Hume treats the beliefs, strivings, and practical actions of the religious man as an order of complex phenomena. This order can only be clarified and understood by submission to analysis in terms of his general theory about human perceptions, associations, and passions. To anatomize the religious phenomena is to discern at their heart the same steady forces of association which shape our judgments, passional attachments, and activities in all other areas of human life. And to accept this anatomy lesson as the only philosophically reliable approach is Hume's way of insuring impartiality in his treatment of religion: what his common method yields here is the only report on religion which can be incorporated into his philosophy of man.

Since the aim of this philosophy is to introduce the experimental, Newtonian method into moral or humane subjects, a philosophical treatment of religion requires the orderly use of the two phases of the experimental method: resolutive analysis and compositive synthesis. In the first phase, religion is taken as a complex human phenomenon which must be resolved analytically into its component factors in our experience. For Hume's purpose, it is necessary to clear up the ambiguity which results from taking the religious complexus to mean a particular body of teach-

5. *Letters*, 1, 32–33.

ings at one time and a characteristic human outlook at another. Both meanings can be retained, as long as a definite order is firmly maintained between them. There is a cognitive aspect of religion expressible eventually in a complex system of propositions, but this aspect is an outgrowth of some basic human attitudes and hence draws sustenance from some steady forces operating within human nature itself. This human basis retains a controlling power over all doctrinal expressions of religion.

Resolutive analysis applies to religious teachings, therefore, chiefly by way of tracing them back to their sources in a sustaining human attitude. It then deals with the complex religious attitude itself by reducing it to certain component passional and cognitive principles, working within human nature. Thus the real bearer of the complex religious phenomenon is the concrete religious believer himself. Just as the Newtonian scientist resolves a complex physical body into its particulate structure and binding forces, so the Humean analyst of religion resolves the given religious beliefs of men into the believer's elementary passions, perceptions, and forces of association.

Yet, in the second phase, Hume is well aware that the experimental method in both physical and human subjects is twofold, that the initial analysis must provide the materials for a new composition or synthesis of the elements thus distinguished. The compositive phase of the method is required not only to provide a verifying check upon the adequacy of the analytic components but also, and more importantly, to secure a proper understanding of the initial phenomena. This latter point is strongly urged by the tradition of Bacon, Hobbes, and Newton. If we are not strict creators of reality, we can become the next best thing, namely, analytic minds which learn about physical and human phenomena by resolving them into their constitutive factors and then remaking these things, through a synthesis of the analytic results.

Hume's intent is to prolong this common method into the area of religion and thus gain some philosophical understanding of religious belief. The application of the two stages of experimental inquiry is fairly straightforward. Religious believers themselves are the concrete subjects furnishing the complex matter for analysis. A resolutive scrutiny of the religious attitudes of men leads Hume back to the passional drives of fear and hope, along with a lively concern to know the causes of events affecting our human welfare. These drives and concerns are the elementary roots of religious belief, as far as an internal philosophical analysis can determine. By recomposing them in a likely way, Hume seeks to furnish a probable account of the genesis and import of the religious beliefs of the broad majority of men. Since religious belief is a peculiarly human phenomenon, there is even more hope here than in the case of physical phenomena that a philosophical reconstitution will furnish a likely story, which comes satisfactorily close to disclosing the real structure and basis of this complex aspect of man.

Nevertheless, the whole project is confronted with a formidable obstacle as soon as the experimental method is specified more closely within the Humean framework. In its referential character, religion finds its reality not as a separate entity but precisely as a relational bond between men and God. Although the human aspect of religion permits Hume to include it within his broadly conceived moral philosophy, its reference to the reality of God raises a special difficulty for a phenomenalist type of philosophy of man. If philosophical analysis and inference are brought to a radical halt at the boundary of our own perceptions and objects in perception, then there is no methodical path for moving towards the distinct reality of God. The God-pole in the religious relationship is removed in principle from investigation, and thus the plan for a philosophy of religion is apparently frustrated by the limits set upon knowledge by the general philosophy of Hume.

In Hume's view, this objection is not quite fatal. It can be reduced to two difficulties, only one of which need be faced at the outset of his study of religion. The religious attitude involves a belief about a reality distinct from the immanent life of our perceptions, passions, and beliefs, taken as human acts; it also involves belief about a reality which is distinct not only from the sphere of human acts but also from the entire physical world. The latter assertion specifies and extends the former, and hence can be postponed until there is question about the particular arguments for the being and nature of God. The former assertion concerns, however, transphenomenal realities in general. Here, religious conviction joins the wider company of beliefs entertained about the various modes of being which remain distinct from our intraperceptual life, and yet with which we still claim to have some determinate relations.

A parallel can be drawn, therefore, between this aspect of the religious problem and the problem of the external world.[6] Both of them concern the way in which a phenomenalist philosophy can deal with a relational situation, one of whose presumed terms is a reality existing apart from

6. See *Treatise*, pp. 187–218.

human perceptual life and the objects and relations immanent to it. Although his method does not permit Hume to determine the very being of a world existing apart from objects in perception, it does enable him to examine the components and genesis of our human belief in such a world. Within the limits of his philosophy of human nature, he can specify the grounds in perception and association for accepting the permanence and independence of the external world. Similarly, he can give a determinate account of those passional and perceptual factors which lead men to believe in a powerful, minded being existing independently of ourselves and our intraperceptual objects and relations. Thus a philosophy of religion is possible as a portion of the Humean study of man's ways of believing and acting.

Nonetheless, Hume frankly admits that, in practice, there are some severe handicaps for the project of prolonging his general method into the sphere of religion. Whether these difficulties be inherent in the investigation itself, or amenable to gradual changes in social life and philosophical procedures, he considers them to be serious enough for explicit mention. They arise from four main sources: the social context for religious inquiry, its descriptive materials, the available criteria, and the appropriate literary form.

During relaxed moments, Hume permitted himself to dream about the ideal *social milieu* for investigating problems in the philosophy of religion. He was intrigued by the genial setting for Cicero's dialogue on the nature of the gods and, had he been familiar with them, would doubtless have approved of the open and friendly religious discussions held at St. Augustine's farm at Cassiciacum and Petrarch's country home. It was in this spirit of honest inquiry that Hume proposed a revival of "the happy times, when Atticus and Cassius the Epicureans, Cicero the Academic, and Brutus the Stoic, could, all of them, live in unreserved friendship together, and were insensible to all those distinctions, except so far as they furnished agreeable matter to discourse and conversation." [7]

The harsh fact was, however, that the social circumstances of Hume's own day prevented any calm, pluralist discussion of the nature and bases of religious belief. Even in the universities, men seemed to lose their mutual respect and dedication to the search after truth as soon as religious topics were introduced. There was no institutional arrangement affording relief from the atmosphere of incessant, bitter warfare surrounding the

7. *Letters*, 1, 173.

controversies of orthodox divines, deists, and freethinkers in the eighteenth-century circles frequented by Hume.

The lack of a social framework for a philosophical, rather than a controversial, treatment of religion deeply affected Hume's own approach. It led him constantly to battle for the emergent life and autonomous standing of philosophy of religion, and thus to introduce into it an insistently polemical edge of satire and exaggeration, intended to counterbalance any received opinions in religion. When he did make the rare encounter with a reasonable and humane believer, such as the minister and moral philosopher Richard Price, he expressed honest amazement at receiving a firm but courteous criticism. Price's forthright reply remains a model for theists who engage in the philosophical discussion of religion.

> I am not, I hope, inclined to dislike any person merely for a difference in opinion however great; or to connect worth of character and God's favour with any particular set of sentiments. It is one of my most fixed and favourite principles which I endeavour often to inculcate, that nothing is fundamental besides a faithful desire to find out and to practise truth and right.[8]

Such a principle was seldom observed in practice by any of the parties to the religious disputes at the time, and Hume remained frustrated in his search for regular social channels of philosophical discussion of religion.

There is a definite connection between the problem of social context and that of *descriptive materials* in the philosophical study of religion. The analysis of belief in causal connections and an external world is a simple undertaking for Hume, by comparison with the analysis of religious beliefs and their interpretant principles. In this zone, "nothing is pure and entirely of a piece." [9] For religion makes us aware of that intermingling of misery and happiness, foolishness and wisdom, which constitutes human existence and gives it a thoroughly ambiguous look. On this point, Hume's testimony agrees with that of Pascal and Kierkegaard. There is no other level of human inquiry into our experience where the play of the passions can so strongly influence our position, and where our leading ideas are open to such diverse developments. It is above all in the philosophy of religion, then, that we need the aid of other minds and the corrective guidance of free discussion of the cross currents.

8. R. Klibansky and E. C. Mossner, eds., *New Letters of David Hume* (Oxford, Clarendon Press, 1954), p. xix.

9. *Natural History*, p. 74.

Hume likens his own inquiry in this field to that of a stranger groping around in a foreign land, where he can recognize no familiar landmarks. For one thing, he does not place his trust in any church as providing an authoritative account of the nature of religion. Hume, as a philosopher of religion, accepts no guideline from any religious institution, but assumes full responsibility for his interpretation of the relevant phenomena. Furthermore, he feels that in this pioneer enterprise he cannot draw upon any adequate sorting and analysis of the vast empirical materials on the religious life of men. His inductive sources are rather severely limited to his own religious upbringing in Scotland, his more worldly observation of religious conditions in Britain and France, his very thorough study both of the classical Roman accounts of religions and those found in Bayle, and his desultory acquaintance with tales of explorers and missionaries. Hume experienced the unenviable predicament of trying to develop an empirical theory of religion without having the means of control over the whole field of materials, control now available in comparative religion.

Are there not some *ready criteria*, however, whereby the individual inquirer can judge adequately for himself in the religious domain? Hume poses this question as a genuine difficulty, thus parting company with both the freethinkers and the orthodox apologists of his century who thought that there was nothing easier than to reach a clearcut conclusion on the claims of religion. He does not find the same definite criteria available here as in the areas of ethics, political theory, and natural philosophy. At least in these latter areas, we have some firm negative control over our speculation. We know that our moral argument is somehow defective if it runs contrary to constant human sentiments, and that our political or scientific reasoning is faulty if it collides with some matters of fact.

But Hume notes that the metaphysical and theological treatments of religion in this day cannot be checked independently by the criteria of sentiment and matter of fact, and hence that they furnish no reasonable determination of the issues. Even his own suggestion that "nothing there [in metaphysics and theology] can correct bad reasoning but good reasoning: and sophistry must be opposed by syllogism," does not really alleviate the situation.[10] For even after we feed the metaphysical and theological treatises to the bonfire, we may still have grounds for giving assent to statements on religion. The validity of such statements cannot be deter-

10. *Letters*, 1, 151.

mined simply by the canons of formal reasoning, since religious belief is not confined to formal assertions but does somehow concern itself with matters of fact and human sentiment. Yet the reference of religious assertions back to the world of human fact and passion is more devious than in the case of natural and moral philosophy.

Hume was quite familiar with the appeal of Montaigne and the fideistic skeptics to sentiment as the way to choose between the various creeds and churches. But he remained unconvinced and offered two telling objections. His first point was that "certainly this were a very convenient way, and what a philosopher would be very pleased to comply with, if he could distinguish sentiment from education." [11] In such a plastic nature as that of man, it is very difficult to make this distinction and hence to show that one has the warrant of common human sentiment behind his particular religious stand, rather than a family or regional prejudice of a vivid and heartwarming sort. Religious sentiment is continually reshaped by our education and other prevailing cultural influences.

Hume's second criticism concerned those who justified their choice of a particular religious confession on the general principle that truth in religious matters lies beyond our human capacity, and hence we must consult our traditions, upbringing, and present convenience. This provoked his wry observation that "such a conduct is founded on the most universal and determined scepticism, joined to a little indolence. For more curiosity and research gives a direct opposite turn from the same principles." Prolonged research and reflection may very well lead a man to conclude that, in religious questions where reason is apparently impotent and where assent is determined by contingent and often divergent traditional circumstances, the reasonable and prudent thing is to withhold one's assent entirely from all particular forms of religion.

Hume's purpose in raising these two objections against the powerful standpoint of fideistic skepticism is neither to underplay the role of sentiment in determining religious convictions nor to ward off a determined skeptical analysis of these convictions. Rather, he seeks to move the discussion of religion beyond a vague general recognition of the predominant role of sentiment in determining religious assent. A specific analysis of the

11. This and the next quotation are from ibid., 1, pp. 151, 152. As a young man, Hume read widely in French fideistic and freethinking skepticism, whose history is traced by Richard Popkin, *The History of Scepticism from Erasmus to Descartes* (New York, 1960); J. S. Spink, *French Free-Thought from Gassendi to Voltaire* (London, 1960); and R. A. Watson, *The Downfall of Cartesianism* (Hague, Nijhoff, 1966).

relevant sentiments must be made, their connection with the basic drives of human nature ascertained, and the bearing of this connection shown for a philosophical assessment of the validity of religious beliefs.

Whereas the fideists took comfort in Descartes' sharp distinction between the search for truth and the conduct of life, Hume's new breed of religious skeptic insists that both theory and practice are intimately affected by the outcome of an empirical analysis of religion, especially in the case of the philosophically minded inquirers themselves. Their religious attitude and moral conduct must be determined, not lazily by their nurse and prince, but by their own mature inspection of man the believing animal.

Due to the perplexities stemming from the social context, descriptive content, and criteria for a philosophical inquiry into religion, Hume regarded the question of its proper *literary form* as being much more than a matter of taste and external embellishment. True to the British philosophical tradition reaching from Bacon to Berkeley, he was very sensitive about adopting a style appropriate to the content and method of his thought. In treating religion, he used the essay form in the *Natural History of Religion*, which probes into some actual religious phenomena and their passional roots. But he continued to search for a more adequate medium, especially when his analysis had to move from the human passions underlying our religious beliefs to the complex object of those beliefs, namely, the man-God relationship. Here, he had to give fitting expression to the tension generated by using his own method, centered around the internal nature of man, to study the religious relationship with its transcendent reference to God.

In order to represent a situation fraught with many difficulties, obscurities, and controversies, Hume turned to the dialogue, producing one of the most supple philosophical examples of this form in his *Dialogues Concerning Natural Religion*. And lest the point be lost upon us, he devoted the entire introductory statement in that work to asking about what literary instrument a philosopher should employ in studying the nature of religion.[12]

Despite its use by Malebranche, Berkeley, and Diderot, the philosophical dialogue was largely an anachronism by the mid-eighteenth century, an embarrassing attempt to recall the spontaneity of ancient philosophical

12. *Dialogues*, pp. 127–28. Hume remarks that a philosophical dialogue should really be composed by two people in order to eliminate nonsense and straw men, as well as to secure vivacity and variety in the argument. *Letters*, 1, 153–55.

discussions. Hume attributed its decline to the widespread acceptance of the rationalistic ideal of close analysis, mathematical clarity and economy, and system building. A philosophical book shaped according to this standard would have to state its ultimate aim at the very outset, take the most direct and objectively ordered path of argument, and thus develop a system impersonally, without bothering to prepare individual minds for the various turns of discussion. Usually, the gains in precision and systematic order did outweigh any inconvenience which cultured men might feel from the lack of concern for their personal preparation for following the argument. But Hume also admitted the need to adapt his reasoning to the subject under investigation, without sacrificing his ultimate loyalty to accuracy and close inspection. Sometimes, these latter qualities in philosophical inquiry can only be achieved by using a literary form quite different from the geometrical mold of Spinoza's *Ethics* and even the more informal, yet impersonal, economy governing the essays of Locke and Hume himself.

Even in an age of analysis and intellectual rigor, there is room for a well-executed philosophical dialogue. If the subject of inquiry is vitally important to us as personal agents, and yet if it shares in that mixed condition of certainty and uncertainty, clarity and obscurity, which marks so many basic human issues, then it is best explored through the resources of the dialogue. As Hume points out, the problem of natural religion is precisely of this kind. It engages us individually and socially in a radical way; it usually involves some steady assurance about the reality of God together with considerable perplexity about His nature and dealings with our world; and thus it affords proper matter for intelligent disagreement and continual groping on the part of searching minds. The philosophical inquiry into religion flourishes in an atmosphere of fruitful conversation, permitting an interplay of opposing views and a gradual development of common argument through the work of several participants. On these grounds, Hume justifies the dialogue as the best instrument for capturing the spirit of a genuinely philosophical examination of man in his religious aspect.

Some philosophically significant points emerge from this defense of the dialogal approach in the philosophy of religion. Although Hume intends a rigorous execution of his project of prolonging the experimental study of human nature into the domain of religion, he does not think that this can be done in a perfectly uniform and wooden way. Just as he must make some methodic adjustments in passing from ideal relations to matters of fact or existence, so must he respect the difference between the order of speculation and that of action, where the religious reality lies. Furthermore, Hume specifies the precise reason why a philosopher cannot afford to ignore the difficulties of inquiry into religion when he remarks that it takes "time, reflection and study" before the religious states of soul can be unraveled, the relevant features of our experience identified, and the various arguments fully developed and understood by believers and skeptics alike.[13] The use of dialogue in preparatory analyses, in following out the byways of thought, and in preparing the transitions and lines of continuity, is not a waste of time but rather the most appropriate form for securing a just course of reasoning which really penetrates the life of religious convictions and practices.

Thus the appreciation of a dialogal method in philosophy of religion is no monopoly of such recent personalist thinkers as Martin Buber and Gabriel Marcel. In Hume, we find the roots for an empirical and naturalist employment of this method as a means for respecting both the particular subject matter and the general, but adaptable, canons of an analytic theory of human nature. His actual employment of dialogal thinking has a skeptical flavor, insofar as it works out at length the difficulties in the design argument and other intellectual defenses of theism. But it also aims at securing some common ground for the philosophical theist and the skeptic concerning the working limits in our knowledge of God.

One final implication of the Humean rehabilitation of the dialogue in the philosophy of religion can be drawn out. The purpose of a philosophical dialogue is not to compound obscurity but to illuminate it and dispel the shadows as much as possible; the purpose is not to wallow in uncertainty but to recognize it, discover its basis, and perhaps set some limits upon it. Hume distinguishes between a preanalytic and a postanalytic form of obscurity and uncertainty. The former kind is found in the religious assent of nonreflective minds, as well as in the popular philosophies which seek merely to paint in more vivid colors the prevailing beliefs. These varieties of preanalytic obscurity and uncertainty can be removed through patient philosophical work in the area of religion.

Yet even after making a careful analysis of religious assents and attitudes, Hume finds that there is some residual, postanalytic obscurity and uncertainty. He does not claim that the extension of his philosophy of man to religion will bring the latter into the noonday brightness of

13. *Dialogues*, p. 154.

Holbach's and Voltaire's theories about our religious beliefs. His modest hope is to establish some points of orientation for understanding and evaluating man's religious life. This must be done moderately, within the limits set by Humean phenomenalism and by the actual situation of those who believe in a groping way, even after the lessons of philosophical criticism have sunk home to them.

MEANINGS OF NATURAL RELIGION

Even a preliminary reading of Hume's pages on religion brings out the fact that he is employing the key term "natural religion" in several distinct, although perhaps related, senses. Closer attention to the text shows that this is not a flagrant case of equivocal usage, however, but that Hume is aware of moving from one sense to another in accord with the shifts in his argument. He is not the victim of multiple uses of this term but their master, insofar as he sees that his own account of religion must be developed in relation to several current meanings. However, he does not take the trouble to list formally these several senses of "natural religion" and to explain the procedure whereby he orders them for treatment within his own philosophical framework. For understanding why he feels confident about the soundness and inclusiveness of his philosophy of religion, it will be helpful for us to determine what these various meanings are and how they are ordered within the Humean critique.

At no time during the long history of human discussion on religion was there a more luxuriant and tangled growth of meanings than during the hundred years extending from Descartes' death in 1650 to Hume's composition of his two major writings on religion in 1751–55. Even if we confine ourselves to the French and British treatments of natural religion during this century, we are unlikely to capture all the outstanding conceptions.[14]

14. A. O. Lovejoy and G. Boas, *Primitivism and Related Ideas in Antiquity* (Baltimore, 1935), p. 456, distinguish these classically based meanings for "natural religion": acquired solely by the light of nature or without the aid of revelation; derived from a study of external, physical nature and its design; containing self-evident and immutable truths; finding its God in the universe as a whole; that religious meaning which is known always, everywhere, and by all men; existing in the primitive age of mankind and hence as old as creation itself. For the connotation found in British theology and science, cf. C. E. Raven, *Natural Religion and Christian Theology* (2 vols. London, 1953), especially vol. 1, chap. 1, and H. Metzger, *Attraction universelle et religion naturelle chez quelques commentateurs anglais de Newton* (3 vols. Paris, 1938). In *Natural History*, p. 68 n., Hume himself refers to the work done by his countryman and friend, Chevalier Andrew Ramsay, *The Philosophical Principles of Natural and*

Using Hume's own writings as a basis of relevance, however, we can at least specify which conceptions of natural religion are sufficiently prominent and challenging to warrant some attention in his theory of religion. Without being an exhaustive enumeration, the following six ways of using "natural religion" are among the important senses accepted in his day and dealt with in his essays and dialogues on religion. The Cambridge Platonist, Ralph Cudworth, had indeed referred to the rational analysis of religion as a "philosophy of religion." But Hume's custom of referring simply to his studies in "natural religion" is the more common usage at the time and, moreover, has the advantage of indicating a rich deposit of meanings.

Natural Theology. Especially in academic quarters, people spoke almost synonymously about natural religion and natural theology. The philosophical arguments establishing the existence and attributes of God, including His providential activity, were regarded as constituting the rational defense of religion. It was necessary only to relate the philosophical doctrine on God to a practical conception of man in order to show the bond between man and God, and thus establish the duty of religious worship. Insofar as religion had an intellectual aspect determined on philosophically ascertainable grounds, it made sense to equate natural religion with philosophical or natural theology. Whether the latter could be developed apart from revealed faith and whether it could have any real bearing upon salvation within the Christian scheme were further questions, upon which the educated men of the age were divided in line with their theological differences. Nevertheless, in both Protestant and Catholic schools, some rational arguments were proposed for the existence and nature of God, and this argumentation constituted one identifiable sense of "natural religion."

During the century prior to the composition of Hume's *Dialogues*, however, the content of this argumentation underwent a drastic change. In philosophy handbooks used in mid-seventeenth-century classrooms, the sections on natural theology were usually summaries and simplified schemes based upon the works of the medieval and Renaissance Schoolmen. There was heavy dependence upon the logical and physical principles of Aristotle, along with use of the metaphysical terminology and problems of the Schoolmen. But the impact of the Cartesian revolution in thought

---

Revealed Religion (2 vols. Glasgow, 1748–49), who regarded natural religion as original, universal, and also historically variable.

made itself felt even in the textbooks of Catholic and Protestant Scholasticism, so that during the second half of the seventeenth century, various compromise ways were sought to introduce the new approaches to God even into the university manuals of philosophy.[15] There were some strange blendings of the older Scholastic proofs and the newer Cartesian ones.

Yet these adjustments failed to satisfy either the skeptical critics of natural theology or those thoroughly modern theists who saw the need for reconstructing the whole of natural theology in a radical way. When Hume looked for typical presentations of this discipline, he consulted such innovators as Malebranche, Fénelon, and Clarke, all of whom were convinced of the need for a thorough reconstitution of natural theology along rationalist lines. Such thinkers recognized, moreover, that the transformations in natural theology were not confined to the speculative metaphysical order, since they entailed a shift in that practical aspect of natural theology which was one with natural religion.

The Design Argument.   The winds of change also helped to bring to the fore the design argument, a reflective development of which constituted one of the principal meanings of natural religion. Two historical factors conspired to give this argument a special formulation and prominence in Great Britain during the years 1650–1750. First, the drift of philosophical discussion on the continent during these years insured the decline of the older natural theology found in the School manuals, without awarding any clearcut victory to the new rationalist types of metaphysics and natural theology over skeptical criticism. Since there was no metaphysical common ground upon which to build a solid theory of God and man's religious bond with Him, it seemed more prudent to many theists to separate the intellectual defense of their belief completely from the endless uncertainties of metaphysical dispute.

That such a separation of theism from metaphysics was feasible, in terms of another type of evidence and argument leading toward God, was the point warmly urged by Boyle, Newton, and other believing scientists during the later seventeenth century. Their confidence supplied the sec-

15. Although this blending of Scholastic and modern thought is not yet fully investigated, the following studies bring out some aspects: Max Wundt, *Die deutsche Schulmetaphysik des 17. Jahrhunderts* (Tübingen, 1939); P. Dibon, *La Philosophie néerlandaise au siècle d'or*, 1 (2 vols. Amsterdam, 1954–   ); W. T. Costello, *The Scholastic Curriculum at Early Seventeenth-Century Cambridge* (Cambridge, 1958).

ond historical factor favoring reduction of the intellectual aspect of natural religion to a study of the scientifically ascertained patterns in nature.[16]
William Derham, and other Boylean Lecturers at Oxford, sought to
strengthen natural religion by sloughing off risky metaphysical assumptions and narrowing the scope and method of natural theology. They
reduced it in practice to a study of the scientific evidences of design in
the visible world and an inference to its divine designer, having the
requisite attributes for producing the structured world described in physicotheology—not to mention the specialized areas of astrotheology, bronto-
theology, and hydrotheology!

The design argument with which Hume was familiar contains two distinct levels of meaning. The persistent bottom layer consists of mankind's
agelong meditation upon the orderly phenomena in nature, together with
the idea of an ordering mind which is responsible for the unity of nature
and to which we owe a religious response. This is the ordinary argument
from order which Hume and most cultivated people consulted in the
Stoic form, as propounded in Cicero's dialogues.

As a second layer peculiar to the modern period, however, is the intention to make the study of natural order a substitute for any metaphysical
theology, as well as to shape it according to the method, data, and limitations of the current scientific study of natural phenomena. It is this
substitutional and wholly *phenomenalized* approach to the visible world
which constitutes the design argument in the specifically modern sense.
Hume himself was well aware of these two distinct components in the
theism of the design argument. But he judged that the substitutional and
phenomenalizing intention now effectively dominates every traditional
effort to conceive of natural religion as a meditation on God's traces in
our universe.

God's Natural and Moral Attributes. Within this design-oriented approach to natural religion, there is a crucial distinction between the two
classes of divine attributes which can be inductively established: the natural and the moral attributes of God. When we determine the being,
knowledge, and power of God, we are concerned only with His natural
attributes, or those aspects of His reality which are required to shape the

16. On the role of natural religion in achieving a convergence of modern science
with religious belief, consult R. S. Westfall's *Science and Religion in Seventeenth-
Century England* (New Haven, 1958) and John Dillenberger's *Protestant Thought and
Natural Science* (New York, 1960), pp. 104–62.

world but which do not, by themselves, have any moral significance. They do not assure us that the divine reality is a loving and caring God. In order to penetrate to Him as a morally concerned personal reality, we must also establish the specifically moral attributes of goodness and justice, mercy and providence.

The import of this distinction for natural religion is systematically developed by Samuel Clarke, Newton's theological champion against Leibniz.[17] Natural religion cannot rest solely upon an affirmation of God's natural attributes, since then He may just as well be regarded as an amoral being who remains unconcerned about our welfare, and hence who does not deserve our response of religious respect and worship. The design argument cannot be fully relevant to natural religion until it shows the explicit grounds in our world for affirming the moral, as well as the natural, attributes of God.

As far as Hume was concerned, this emphasis upon the moral nature of God considerably sharpened the issue of natural religion. It showed that the problem of evil is not an afterthought or a mere skeptical exercise, but is at the heart of the attempt to make a distinctively religious interpretation of the study of design in the natural world. Those who sought to stop short at the natural attributes of God were sometimes polemically called "naturalists," not in the sense that they denied any reality beyond nature, but that they did not specifically attribute to God those qualities of personal moral goodness which are required for eliciting a religious response from men toward the powerful divine reality, existing distinct from nature.[18] From a more skeptical standpoint, the function of the

17. In the Leibniz-Clarke exchange of papers in 1715–16, Leibniz's very first sentence is that "natural religion itself, seems to decay (in England) very much," presumably as a result of Newton's natural philosophy. Clarke replies that "Christianity presupposes the truth of natural religion," while the Newtonian experimental philosophy has consequences which "confirm, establish, vindicate against all objections, those great and fundamental truths of natural religion." H. G. Alexander, ed., *The Leibniz-Clarke Correspondence* (New York, Philosophical Library, 1956), pp. 6, 11, 12. The distinction between God's natural and moral attributes is prominent in the theory of God and natural religion developed by Clarke in his two series of Boylean Lectures (delivered in 1704–05): *A Demonstration of the Being and Attributes of God* (London, 1705) and *A Discourse Concerning the Unchangeable Obligations of Natural Religion, and the Truth and Certainty of the Christian Revelation* (London, 1706). These volumes are bound together in a facsimile reproduction (Stuttgart, 1964).

18. In *Hume's Philosophy of Human Nature* (London, Methuen, 1932), p. 291, John Laird quotes the definition of naturalism proposed by Hume's enemy, Bishop

problem of evil was to suggest that the traditional religious response to nature, along with the very meaning of natural religion, was due for re-examination in the light of empirical difficulties which might prevent one from affirming the moral attributes as confidently as the natural attributes of God.

Religion and Morality.   To meet this situation, a fourth prominent mean-ing of natural religion is proposed by such British moralists as Price and Clarke, Joseph Butler, and William Wollaston.[19] They frequently urge a more intimate relating of natural religion with morality, so that the two may reinforce each other or even show their fundamental identity.

There are three main lines of reasoning involved in this proposed con-solidation of morality and religion. (a) One basic meaning is that we can neither understand the meaning of the divine moral attributes nor find sufficient evidence for their actual presence in God, until we reflect upon ourselves as moral agents and study the relationships involved in moral life. Religion finds its natural intellectual basis in a study of order within man's moral life.

(b) Stemming from this is the further point that the obligation to religion is among the primary relationships toward which we are impelled

---

Warburton: "the belief of a God, the creator and physical preserver, but not moral governor of the world." Although Hume is a religious naturalist in the sense of reducing to zero the philosophical validity of any belief in the divine moral governance of the world, John Passmore is right in maintaining nevertheless that Hume is not a religious naturalist in the Pope-Beattie sense of trusting in our unerring, God-given, "natural" instincts; see Passmore, *Hume's Intentions* (London, 1952), pp. 146–47.

19. Their views on morality and natural religion can be conveniently consulted in the collection edited by L. A. Selby-Bigge, *British Moralists* (2 vols. bound in one. Indianapolis, 1964), 1, 244 (Butler); 2, 22–23, 50–51 (Clarke), 161 (Price), 374–75, 384 (Wollaston). Shaftesbury formulated the question of the interrelationship of morality and religion in a provocative manner, which influenced the entire British development of the problem:

If we are told a man is religious, we still ask, "What are his morals?" But if we hear at first that he has honest moral principles, and is a man of natural justice and good temper, we seldom think of the other question, "Whether he be re-ligious and devout?" This has given occasion to inquire "what honesty or virtue is, considered by itself, and in what manner it is influenced by religion; how far religion necessarily implies virtue; and whether it be a true saying that it is im-possible for an atheist to be virtuous, or share any real degree of honesty or merit." (*Characteristics of Men, Manners, Opinions, Times,* ed. J. M. Robertson [2 vols. bound in one. Indianapolis, Bobbs-Merrill, 1964], 1, 238).

as moral agents, and hence that religion is natural insofar as it is a moral duty for men. Given the distinction between moral good and evil and the human search for happiness, our active search for fulfillment ought to culminate in a religious adherence to God, as the ultimate standard of moral good and the source of permanent happiness. (c) Conversely, morality requires a religious basis in order to direct our actions effectively. Religious conviction enables the moral agent to recognize that the good of man is found concretely only in interpersonal relations, and that his highest good consists most concretely in his individual and social relations with the personal God. This reciprocal dependence and close union between morality and religion furnish the content for what Hume regards as one of the most important and most contestable meanings of natural religion.

The Reasonableness of Christianity. During Hume's century, the treatment of natural religion invariably included some major reference to Christianity. To determine the content and validity of natural religion entailed showing in some way its relation with Christianity, thus determining the sense in which the latter is reasonable or not. The implications of natural religion for Christianity were understood in two quite different ways by the British deists and the orthodox divines.[20]

For the former, natural religion consisted of our assent to a basic group of truths attainable by our own reasoning power, together with the minimal moral and religious practices common to all men who accept the core truths. With a few variations from author to author, these truths concerned the existence of God as the supremely perfect being, our duty to worship Him, and our ability and obligation to lead virtuous lives (whether or not there be any sanctions in an afterlife). Such deists as Toland, Woolston, and Tindal occupied themselves more with discussion about these fundamental principles of natural religion, along with their moral and institutional implications, than with a detailed establishment of their validity. They assumed quite readily that the basic propositions in natural religion are obvious to anyone using his own reason.

Their main conclusion concerning Christianity was that its intrinsic reasonableness extends no farther than the central principles of natural

20. This debate can still be followed profitably with the help of two older works: Leslie Stephen, *English Thought in the Eighteenth Century* (3d ed. 2 vols. New York, 1949), 1, 91–343 (culminating in Hume), and John Orr, *English Deism: Its Roots and Its Fruits* (Grand Rapids, 1934).

religion. Everything else, affirmed by way of creed and rite over and above
these principles, consists of a positive, contingent surplus whose demands
upon the believer are either disputable or fraudulent. Thus the deistic
conception of natural religion favored a reductionist approach to Christianity, accepting only what we can learn about the religious relationship
from our study of design in nature and moral virtues in man. The Christian message was held to be essentially nonmysterious and as old as the
creation of man, the reasoning animal. Only in the sense of being a
"republication of nature," or a social restatement of the truths of natural
religion open to all men, did revelation serve any useful human function.
It did not announce any universal religious truths beyond our naturally
ascertainable ones, and did not provide any salvation and practical means
beyond those obtainable through natural moral reflection and virtuous
action.

Many of the Christian writers consulted by Hume welcomed the notion
of natural religion, not as another religious position set alongside of their
own or as a reductive basis for Christian doctrine and practice, but rather
as a defense of the reasonable grounds for accepting God and acting
virtuously. But there was considerable disagreement among them about
how to prevent the deistic closure of natural religion against a distinct
revelation.[21] The more orthodox wing of the Scottish clergy held the
traditional Calvinist position that the aid of faith is already required in
order to see God's presence in nature and society, at least if that knowledge is to lead to any saving religious relationship with Him.

For his part, the Anglican Bishop Butler welcomed the reflective philosophical study of man and nature as a striking way to exhibit the conformity between the human methods of moral and scientific investigation
and the message of faith. From the similarities between the Newtonian
view of nature, the outlook of natural religion and moral conscience, and
the Christian revelation, he argued to a system of analogies rather than
a single reductive basis in natural religion. But Clarke and other rationalistic theologians rivaled the deists in claiming that the basic tenets of
natural religion can be fully demonstrated by accurate, obvious, and
mathematically cogent reasons. Indeed, they went a further step by using

21. Hume respected the attempt at reaching an overarching synthesis in Joseph
Butler's *The Analogy of Religion Natural and Revealed to the Constitution and Course
of Nature* (1736), but was compelled by his own theory of knowledge and human
nature to introduce cleavages where Butler proposed analogies. See A. Jeffner, *Butler and
Hume on Religion* (Stockholm, 1966).

the same kind of reasoning to demonstrate the truth of revealed Christian doctrine, as a complex conclusion derived deductively from an analysis of the content of natural religion and the testimony of Scriptural miracles.

Natural Reason and Faith. Natural religion sometimes carried with it an epistemological connotation, derived from the long Western discussion of faith and reason.[22] It was taken to mean that kind of knowledge about the bond of man with God which we can gain from our own cognitive powers, studying the realms of nature and man without the aid of any special revelation or light of supernatural faith. In the modern era, this conception of natural religion was strongly influenced by the Cartesian aim of developing a human philosophical wisdom about man, God, and their practical relations, independently of the supernatural wisdom of revealed faith. Whether or not a natural religion was intended to culminate in acceptance of the further principles of Christian faith, it was considered as having an autonomous basis. The historical context of the Jewish and Christian religious traditions was required, however, in order to make significant the abstractive and autonomizing act which energizes this meaning of natural religion.

Hume's books and letters show his close familiarity with all these interpretations of natural religion. He does not passively retain the given framework and merely choose one privileged meaning as his own. Instead, he appeals to the actual situation of plural, and often conflicting, interpretations in order to argue that the question of natural religion must be radically reformulated and perhaps resolved from a fresh philosophical perspective. His practical procedure is a firm and skillfully executed one, involving three steps. First, he reduces the six prevailing usages to three main problem areas; then he shows that the scope of these areas is incomplete, in the light of a crucial distinction; and finally, he clarifies his own notion of what an adequate philosophy of religion can be expected to accomplish. The main lines of his empirical philosophy of religion become more firm and visible to us, in the process of his achieving some intellectual control over these current meanings of natural religion.

The first two ways of understanding natural religion (as natural theol-

22. The historical stages in this problem are examined from different standpoints by E. G. Bewkes and J. C. Keene, *The Western Heritage of Faith and Reason* (rev. ed. New York, 1963); Etienne Gilson, *History of Christian Philosophy in the Middle Ages* (New York, 1955); Richard Kroner, *Speculation and Revelation in the History of Philosophy* (3 vols. Philadelphia, 1956–61).

ogy and reflection on design) can be grouped together as comprising the
speculative type of intellectual justification of religion. Natural theology
and the design argument seek to supply a speculative basis for our knowledge of God and thus for the object of our religious faith and worship.
Hence, one major problem area around which Hume organizes his
Dialogues is that of the speculative arguments for theism, considered not
merely as an abstract philosophical position but as an intellectual ingredient in man's religious life.

The second problem area concerns the *practical* considerations which
also contribute toward the intellectual justification of religion. This class
includes the next two prominent meanings for natural religion, namely,
those which rest upon the distinction between the natural and moral
attributes of God and upon the relation between morality and religion.
Locke had recommended his demonstration of the existence of an eternal,
immaterial, creative mind as "being so fundamental a truth, and of that
consequence, that all religion and genuine morality depend thereon." [23]
But the function of Hume's second major problem area is to jar the traditional assurances at this point and thus sharpen the issue of God, morality,
and religion.

Finally, the two interpretations of natural religion in terms of the
problem of Christianity and the use of unaided reason constitute the
third problem area: the relation between philosophy of religion and faith
in a divine *revelation*. Hume often refers to his own standpoint as being
that of "mere natural and unassisted reason," indicating thereby that he
is elaborating his philosophy of religion entirely apart from commitment,
through an act of faith, to the truth of Christian revelation.[24] In elaborating his theory of natural religion, Hume methodically abstains from
sharing in the conviction of the community of believers in Christ, sacred
history, and the various credal statements. Although the Scottish philosopher of religion cannot ignore this religious tradition, he must treat it
in a factual way as making a claim to truth and certitude which he himself does not use as a norm, in his analyses of religious phenomena and
assertions. None of the human aspects of religious existence are excluded
from investigation, and yet they are studied by a mind which does not
give any philosophically operative, antecedent assent to a revelational

23. John Locke, *An Essay Concerning Human Understanding*, ed. A. C. Fraser (2
vols. New York, Dover Press, 1959), 2, 311–12.

24. Hume, *An Inquiry Concerning Human Understanding*, ed. C. W. Hendel (New
York, Liberal Arts Press, 1955), p. 111. This book is referred to here as *Inquiry*.

truth claim, or even to the customary value judgment about the humane worth and moral significance of Christian ideas and practices.

By defining his philosophical position on Christianity and natural religion in this specific way, Hume is able to maintain a certain distance between himself and the philosophical arguments and religious beliefs under analysis. This detachment of his philosophical inquiry from any systematic commitment to the truth of everyday theism and the several claims to revelation is consonant with the motto guiding his religious studies: "Keep sober and remember to be skeptical." [25] Nevertheless, this attitude does not induce him to revoke or weaken his judgment about the capital importance of the philosophical study of religion. Disengagement from the assent of Christian faith does not lead him to become disengaged from the philosophical search for the truth concerning the problems raised by Christianity and other modes of human religious existence.

Having marked out the three main problem areas within which the several current treatments of natural religion fall, Hume is then able to show that they fail to supply a comprehensive framework for the philosophical inquiry into religion. For this inquiry recognizes that "there are two questions in particular, which challenge our attention, to wit, that concerning its [religion's] foundation in reason, and that concerning its origin in human nature." [26] Even a preliminary look at these two questions brings out the one-sidedness of the prevailing approaches to natural religion. The first two problem areas deal with our speculative and practical inferences to God. Together, they comprise the attempt to give an intellectual validation of religious beliefs, and thus correspond to Hume's first question concerning the rational foundation of religion. Moreover, the third area is proportioned to the standpoint taken in the first two areas. The problem of revelation and philosophy of religion is usually confined to the relation between faith and reason, taking the latter in the sense of the speculative and practical arguments for theism.

All three problem areas are thus centered around the *grounds in reason for* our religious belief, without giving due weight to its *origin in human nature*. An empirically adequate philosophy of religion must study religious

25. For the Greek original of this sentence from Epicharmus, see E. C. Mossner, "Hume's Early Memoranda, 1729–1740: The Complete Text," *Journal of the History of Ideas*, 9 (1948), 503, and *Letters*, 1, 173.

26. *Natural History*, p. 21.

belief and action in their dynamic human sources, as well as in the light of formal argumentation. Indeed, since the question of origin has been systematically slighted in the usual problem areas, it must be given a special development and emphasis within a theory of religion dedicated to uncovering the footing in human nature for all our beliefs and modes of acting.

In trying to come to a philosophically adequate judgment about the nature, grounds, and human worth of religion, Hume adheres closely to his own precept laid down in the *Treatise.* "In every judgment, which we can form concerning probability, as well as concerning knowledge, we ought always to correct the first judgment, derived from the nature of the object, by another judgment derived from the nature of the understanding." [27] This procedural rule means that, in inquiries concerned with matter of fact as well as with ideal relations, there must be not only a logical analysis directed toward the object of belief but also a psychological study focusing upon all the conditions on the part of the mind which does the judging and believing. The three conventional problem areas in the theory of natural religion furnish only an object-directed, logical analysis of religion's foundation in reason and its objective argumentation. This approach must be integrated with the more decisive analysis of religious tendencies in the human self.

With this ordering of the inquiry held firmly before him, Hume hopes to attain both descriptive and normative results in a well-balanced conception of religion. The descriptive aim will be to obtain a more accurate and determinate understanding of religious belief in its rooting in our human inclinations, its mode of seeking objective evidence, and its relation with the order of moral judgments. On the normative side, there is a leading question which cannot be evaded by anyone who takes seriously the findings of the descriptive analysis. What ought to be the minimal, philosophically controlled position of a reflective mind concerning religious belief and its influence on our moral life? Whereas a Sir Thomas Browne had tried to elaborate—in all its baroque richness— the *religio medici,* Hume now seeks to determine the very spare basis for the *religio philosophi.* He wants to find out whether any critically sifted religious assent still remains possible for, and perhaps required of, the remorseless philosopher of human nature who is also a practical man in our world.

27. *Treatise,* pp. 181–82.

PASSIONAL ANALYSIS OF RELIGION

The distinction between religion's origin in human nature and its foundation in reason helps Hume to organize his entire treatment of the subject. The *Natural History* is devoted mainly to the former aspect of the problem and the *Dialogues* to the latter, although there is no airtight separation of the issues. The emphasis in the *Natural History* is placed upon a study of the human passions which give internal shape to the religious attitude, but the relevance of this analysis for an appraisal of the rational proofs is also duly noted. Conversely, the *Dialogues* focuses upon the main kinds of formal theistic argumentation, without ever losing from sight those human drives which direct and sustain the work of reason in its religious search after God.

We are familiar today with the contrast drawn, by analytic philosophers and historians of science, between the suggesting reasons and the supporting reasons for a scientific hypothesis.[28] The grounds upon which a scientist is originally led to conceive and formulate a new scientific conception remain logically, and often psychologically, distinct from those which bear out and validate his concept. This distinction does not imply that the suggesting and the supporting reasons are in any necessary opposition to each other, or that the latter are mere rationalizations concealing the real motives of assent. But it does point up the need for having two distinct phases in the investigation of any major human conception. In this way, we can distinguish the sense in which the genetic or suggesting grounds of a belief are "reasons" from the rationality proper to the evidentially supporting arguments for that belief, and can determine the precise relationship between the two sets of considerations in the particular case.

Although Hume was by no means the first to use a similar distinction in the area of religion, he did formulate it sharply and recommend it as a principal logical tool for developing an experimental philosophy of religion. It offered him the polemical advantage of shifting religious discussion out of the familiar, single track of the rationalistic natural theologies and the design argument and into the more complicated, double-

28. Antony Flew, *Hume's Philosophy of Belief* (New York, 1961), pp. 96–98, remarks that questions about validity need not be the irreconcilable rivals of questions about origins. On suggesting and confirming reasons in science, consult N. R. Hanson's *Patterns of Discovery* (Cambridge, 1958).

grooved analysis of human passions, taken along with the rationally formulated evidences. The effect of this shift was to achieve a thorough relativizing of the search for a rational foundation of religion, so that it could no longer be interpreted and properly evaluated apart from a view of the human passional genesis of religious belief.[29] Henceforth, the a priori proofs and the evidences of design could comprise only one portion of the grounds for religious assent, and indeed, as far as most believers were concerned, the less germinal and compelling portion.

To examine the origins in human nature for religious belief is to develop the "natural history" of religion. In using this term to characterize his naturalization of religious belief, Hume underlined his solidarity with his skeptical, scientific, and philosophical sources, as well as his aim of unifying them in a comprehensive naturalistic theory of religion.[30] Bayle had taught him to look always for the passions and unspoken grounds prompting a religious conviction, for the inclining forces within man himself which are more powerful and persuasive than the adduced reasons for belief. And from the scientific tradition of Fontenelle and Buffon, he had learned to look upon the various religious creeds and rites as so many flora and fauna in the vast forest of human experience and its modes. His British predecessors in philosophy, from Francis Bacon onward, had advocated applying the same genetic and descriptive method in the study of man and his range of convictions as is used in the study of bodies, in their mechanical, chemical, or biological properties. In principle, they exempted no aspect of human experience and no sphere of human theory and belief, including that on religious matters. Thus Hume had considerable encouragement from his sources to launch out as a natural historian of religion.

Perhaps the boldest attempt made in previous English philosophy to treat religion as a thoroughly human phenomenon, open to investigation by the natural historian, was the chapter devoted to religion in the first part of Hobbes' *Leviathan.* Hobbes began bluntly with this declaration:

29. "The first ideas of religion arose not from a contemplation of the works of nature, but from a concern with regard to the events of life, and from the incessant hopes and fears, which actuate the human mind" (*Natural History,* p. 27).

30. Frank E. Manuel, *The Eighteenth Century Confronts the Gods* (Cambridge, 1959), pp. 168–83, situates Hume's *Natural History* within the tendency in his century to describe the birth of the gods from some conception of a primitive mentality, to objectivize religion as one more problem concerning man's views and works, and thus to achieve a naturalistic reduction of religious mystery to anthropology.

"Seeing there are no signs, nor fruit of *religion*, but in man only; there is no cause to doubt, but that the seed of *religion*, is also only in man." [31] With very quick strokes, he then sketched out his resolution of religion into its composite principles or seeds in human nature.

Hobbesian man is basically curious about the causes of events he sees, especially those affecting his own welfare. He supposes that some cause must be present wherever he observes a beginning of a train of events; and his memory and foresight of the consequence of events lead him to dwell anxiously, and with constant solicitude, upon whatever cause he imagines or hears from authority to be responsible for his own woe and well-being.

> This perpetual fear, always accompanying mankind in the ignorance of causes, as it were in the dark, must needs have for object something. And therefore when there is nothing to be seen, there is nothing to accuse, either of their good, or evil fortune, but some *power*, or agent *invisible:* in which sense perhaps it was, that some of the old poets said, that the gods were at first created by human fear: which spoken of the gods, that is to say, of the many gods of the Gentiles, is very true. But the acknowledging of one God, eternal, infinite and omnipotent, may more easily be derived, from the desire men have to know the causes of natural bodies, and their several virtues, and operations; than from the fear of what was to befall them in time to come. . . . From the propagation of religion, it is not hard to understand the causes of the resolution of the same into its first seeds, or principles; which are only an opinion of a deity, and powers invisible, and supernatural; that can never be so abolished out of human nature, but that new religions may again be made to spring out of them, by the culture of such men, as for such purpose are in reputation.

Although he did not develop in detail this theory about the genesis of religion and relate it to specific arguments for God's existence, Hobbes set the example of making a resolutive analysis of religious belief into some constant human tendencies. And the particular tendencies in man to which he appealed—the perpetual fear of natural forces, the search for causes under conditions of ignorance, the supposition of invisible yet

31. Thomas Hobbes, *Leviathan*, ed. Michael Oakeshott (Oxford, Blackwell, 1946), p. 69. The next text is taken from ibid., pp. 70–71, 77.

accessible power above the natural world, the split between belief of many gods as arising from anxiety, and belief in the one God as coming from causal study of the bodily universe—all these points indicated to Hume the shape which a solidly grounded natural history of religion is likely to assume.

Upon perceiving man's situation in this visible, changing world, why do religious minded people give their lively practical assent to the conception of a supramundane power, with which they are somehow bound? For an answer, Hume turns to the workings of nature within us. In this context, "nature" refers neither to the course of external bodily events nor to some static internal structure, supposed for a formal definition of man. Rather, it signifies the silent but steady and powerful operation of the passions and laws of association within human life, an operation which determines us to judge and believe just as much as to breathe and to feel.[32] Fundamentally, our understanding is determined in its religious belief and religious response to the human situation by the powerful workings of our passional tendencies, in summoning up ideas and establishing associative links among them. Thus Hume's natural history of religion consists of a naturalization of religious belief in function of the *passional* determinants of the understanding, along with its acts of practical assent to some supernal power affecting human well-being.

Next, Hume must decide whether to regard religion in its passional basis as being an original instinctual drive of our nature, similar to self-love, or else as a derivative state depending on some more fundamental passions. The issue is not just a factual one that can be settled by a direct inspection of the acts of religious believing. It concerns the explanatory pattern within which the facts of religious belief are to be viewed. If religion is regarded as a primary impulse of our nature, then it is an analytically irreducible element in explanation, comparable to gravity and the laws of association. The latter can function as principles in explanation, but they are not themselves the proper subjects of explanation in terms of anything more basic and general, as far as Newtonian natural philosophy and Humean philosophy of human nature are concerned.

If Hume were to consider the passional aspect of religion as a primary impulse of man, then he would have to treat it as an analytically irreducible principle. It could figure in the explanation of other phenomena,

32. *Treatise*, p. 183.

but could not itself be subjected to any penetrating genetic analysis. But he wants to do more than register the combination of a religious impulse with other irreducible factors in perception. He seeks to understand religion by uncovering its own natural history in the human soul. To do so he is obliged to regard it as a composite and relatively derivative aspect of our passional life.

Many philosophical advantages accrue from treating religious belief as a complex human reality, furnishing a proper subject of investigation. Hume would agree with Hobbes and Vico that we know only what we can somehow make.[33] By locating religion among the complex subjects open to analysis, Hume gains access not only to a speculative understanding of it but also to a practical understanding of the basis for inducing changes in the religious order. If religion were a primary impulse and an analytic irreducible, nothing much could be done about it. It would be a given factor simply present in our nature, an irreformable tendency of man which has no history and holds out no possibility of being transformed. Yet when the experimental philosopher of religion consults his actual sources in persons having religious beliefs, he finds that this religious reality is complex, carries with it the traces of a development, and lies open to some sort of critical reform.

Hume never loses sight of the practical and normative aim of his inquiry into religion, both as regards the religion befitting a philosopher and as regards the broader social repercussions of his analysis of the origins of religion in human nature. There is an explanatory analogue in Hume's practical treatment of justice and the belief in social obligation.[34] The

33. Vico argues bluntly that philosophers should transfer more of their energies from the physical world, which they did not make, to the world of human affairs or "civil world, which, since men had made it, men could hope to know." Vico's "new science" is designed to study the religious convictions of men in their crude human beginnings, not merely in their more refined statements.

> We must start from some notion of God such as even the most savage, wild and monstrous men do not lack. That notion we show to be this: that man, fallen into despair of all the succors of nature, desires something superior to save him. But something superior to nature is God, and this is the light that God has shed on all men. (T. G. Bergin and M. H. Fisch, eds., *The New Science of Giambattista Vico* [Ithaca, Cornell University Press, 1948], pp. 85, 89).

34. Justice is artificial or conventional, in the sense that it is not a non-derivative tendency but a human achievement which supposes the use of reason and some social union and sense of public utility among men. It is a natural virtue, however, insofar as it is a nonarbitrary and absolutely necessary work of man, something common to

latter closely resembles religious belief in being in the practical order, involving a valuational complex of passions and assents of the understanding, and thus being adapted to resolutive analysis. Neither religion nor justice is natural to man, in the restricted sense of being part of his original equipment or natural propensity, prior to any play of the passions, association, and interpretation. Thus Hume can take an experimental approach toward these beliefs, by searching out the specific passions and lines of association which lead men to accept them and shape living actions often by their standard.

Although human justice is artificial by comparison with the original propensities of man, it is a natural trait in the sense of following necessarily upon a certain reflective use of our mind and thus being present, in some degree, in all men and social conditions. Hume does not concede a similar universality to religion, since its actual forms can be variously modified, held in check by skeptical counterbalance, and even repudiated by some peoples. "The first religious principles must be secondary; such as may easily be perverted by various accidents and causes, and whose operation too, in some cases, may, by an extraordinary concurrence of circumstances, be altogether prevented." [35] Nevertheless, the religious attitude does spring directly from some passional tendencies which themselves are basic, permanent, and pervasive among men. In the degree that the proper principles and operations of religion usually do follow in a fairly steady and universal way (but with many modal variations and some exceptions), religion is natural to man in a somewhat weaker sense than is justice.

From the standpoint of the religious theist, "the universal propensity to believe in invisible, intelligent power, if not an original instinct, being at least a general attendant of human nature, may be considered as a

---

and inseparable from his social life. In a somewhat weaker sense—since it need not be actually operative in every human society as a condition for achieving the latter's common temporal interest—religion is natural in its human foundation in our needs and inclinations. It is artificial in being dependent on the actual operation of the human passions and mind, under widely varying conditions. *Treatise,* p. 484; *An Inquiry Concerning the Principles of Morals,* ed. Charles W. Hendel (New York, 1957), pp. 122–24.

35. This quotation and the next one are from *Natural History,* pp. 21, 75. Taken together, they require us to make a distinction between the specific inclination toward religious belief, the passional principles from which this propensity arises in man, and the actual forms of belief found in the various religions shaped by diverse historical circumstances.

kind of mark or stamp, which the divine workman has set upon his work." This broad meaning for the naturalness of religion, as being rooted in some permanent primary drives of human nature, is not intended by Hume in a eulogistic sense. He himself cannot make the theistic supposition of a divine workman at the outset of his inquiry, and at no subsequent moment will he deny that our natural instincts are fallible, sometimes deceptive, and always man-centered. These traits of our active nature are inevitably communicated to our natural religious beliefs. To establish—even in a highly qualified sense—that religion is natural to man, therefore, carries with it no guarantee about the human worth and philosophical soundness of any religious conviction. It establishes only the human provenance of our religious principles and actions, but their source in the human heart is notorious for yielding both good fruit and bad.

Hume's anatomizing of precisely those fundamental human passions responsible for the first birth of religious phenomena depends upon a twofold act of abstraction: from Biblical man and from scientifically acculturated man. The philosopher of religion must begin by abstaining from any believing use of the Biblical account of the condition of the first man in paradise. Since reason must remain unassisted by any assent to revelation or a special religious tradition, it is guided by the image of a barbarous animal rather than by that of the noble Miltonic Adam.

> ADAM, rising at once, in paradise, and in the full perfection of his faculties, would naturally, as represented by MILTON, be astonished at the glorious appearances of nature, the heavens, the air, the earth, his own organs and members; and would be led to ask, whence this wonderful scene arose. But a barbarous, necessitous animal (such as a man is on the first origin of society), pressed by such numerous wants and passions, has no leisure to admire the regular face of nature, or make enquiries concerning the cause of those objects, to which from his infancy he has been gradually accustomed.[36]

Abstraction must, however, be made not only from the faith and poetry behind the Biblical account but also from the present advanced state of social organization, culture, and scientific understanding of the

36. Ibid., p. 24. M. Fox, "Religion and Human Nature in the Philosophy of David Hume," in *Process and Divinity*, ed. W. L. Reese and E. Freeman (La Salle, Ill., 1964), pp. 561–77, locates Hume's main critique of religion in his reductive comparison between man and other animals. But man remains a distinctively self-civilizing animal.

world, to reach the human condition proper for an analysis of the origin of religion in human nature. We have to imagine how the world and his own situation may well look to a man whose mind is unillumined by a special revelation, whose daily living does not rest upon any technical control over natural forces, and whose moments of wonderment and reflection come only in fits and starts, without the benefit of any leisurely tradition of philosophical reflection and scientific generalization on the nature of things.

That which Hume arrives at in this way is not what we regard today as primitive man, reached through a time journey provisioned by anthropology and comparative religion, but philosophically primitivized man. Using the hints furnished by fables, histories, and sailors' reports as priming materials, he takes an inward path into the living self, in search of those analytically irreducible tendencies which we may suppose to be steadily operative, even apart from the supports of civilization. When man is directly exposed to the disasters and benefits resulting from wind and tide, soil and sun, and yet does not have the aid of any comforting message from God or any scientific instruments of control and generalization, he is forced back upon those basic resources of passion and understanding without which he would not even be human. Concern for his own existence is the underlying drive. Unlike the case of other animals, however, this concern is mingled in man with a sense of his own ignorance, a stubborn desire to understand the happenings which overwhelm him, and an anxious look for causal powers which will relieve the ignorance and tame the happenings in his own favor.

For Humean primitivized man, religion is the child of fear and hope, these characteristics being the primary passional sources of human religious belief and action. Religion rests most basically upon fear, in the sense that it is called into being and constantly sustained by our concern about the uncertainty and fragility of human existence, which is under the steady pressure of natural events always threatening disaster. Even in this analytically reconstructed original condition of man, however, Hume recognizes the presence of some interpretation on the part of concrete reason. The fear which gives rise to the religious attitude is not stark terror, but has a certain imaginative and meditative dimension suited to an enduring condition of human life. Human existential fear involves a conception of natural events as being the manifestation of power exerted by some agencies which are unseen, but which are not altogether unlike ourselves, since they use power along with some intelligent purpose.

Whatever the philosophical difficulties about the logical justification for power and causal connection, man in his natural passional condition thinks and fears in terms of some intelligent powers, which he holds responsible for the events upon which his welfare depends so utterly. However exalted and awesome they may be, these powers are somehow personal, somehow concerned with man's welfare and open to propitiation by his religious acts.

Given the passional dynamics of religious belief, Hume can now sharpen his theory of religion on its genetic side. There is a vague, but permanent and unifying, content underlying all the theological variations and conflicts in religious history. "The only point of theology, in which we shall find a consent of mankind almost universal, is, that there is invisible, intelligent power in the world." [37] This is Hume's considered reply to the efforts of rationalistic apologists and deists alike to specify a common basis of natural religion. Their emphasis upon common consent to the idea of God is stated too sharply and speculatively, as exemplified in the writings of Herbert of Cherbury and Ralph Cudworth. At the heart of passionally anatomized religious belief lies a hazier, yet stubbornly persistent, affirmation that man can relate himself to a presence which is invisible, mindful, and powerful.

Because religious belief is born of a practical synthesis between imagination and the passions, Hume concludes that the original form of religion must be some sort of animism and polytheism, and that thereafter religious beliefs must alternate forever between polytheism and monotheism. In a key text, he sets forth this theory of the genetic primacy of polytheism and the perpetual alternation in religious beliefs.

> The unknown causes are still appealed to on every emergence; and in this general appearance or confused image, are the perpetual objects of human hopes and fears, wishes and apprehensions. By degrees, the active imagination of men, uneasy in this abstract conception of objects, about which it is incessantly employed, begins to render them more particular, and to clothe them in shapes more suitable to its natural comprehension. It represents them to be sensible, intelligent beings, like mankind; actuated by love and hatred, and flexible by gifts and entreaties, by prayers and sacrifices. Hence the origin of religion: And hence the origin of idolatry or polytheism. But the same anxious concern for happiness, which begets the idea

37. Ibid., p. 32.

of these invisible, intelligent powers, allows not mankind to remain long in the first simple conception of them, as powerful, but limited beings; masters of human fate, but slaves to destiny and the course of nature. Men's exaggerated praises and compliments still swell their idea upon them; and elevating their deities to the utmost bounds of perfection, at last beget the attributes of unity and infinity, simplicity and spirituality. . . . The feeble apprehensions of men cannot be satisfied with conceiving their deity as a pure spirit and perfect intelligence; and yet their natural terrors keep them from imputing to him the least shadow of limitation and imperfection. They fluctuate between these opposite sentiments. The same infirmity still drags them downwards, from an omnipotent and spiritual deity, to a limited and corporeal one, and from a corporeal and limited deity to a statue or visible representation. The same endeavour at elevation still pushes them upwards, from the statue or material image to the invisible power; and from the invisible power to an infinitely perfect deity, the creator and sovereign of the universe.[38]

The forms and cycles of religious belief are thus determined jointly by our imperious search for happiness and our reliance upon the images of concrete intelligence to express the objects of that search and the practical modes of getting related to them. In the human realm the religious life is a restless tension between acknowledging invisible power and seeking its presence in sensible shapes, between worshipping the familiar but all too human gods and striving toward the one spiritual God, who nevertheless seems to tire our power of apprehension and elude our desire for intimate possession. Men of faith are the prisoners of a manic cycle of depression and exaltation, in their search for a religious view which satisfies and yet purifies them.

The long passage just taken from the Natural History is a high point in Hume's passional analysis of religion. It sets forth his thesis about the polytheistic basis of religious belief, the birth of monotheism from polytheism, and the subsequent fluctuation between the polytheistic and the

38. Natural History, pp. 47–48. Hume supposes that there is an evolutionary law of "the natural progress of human thought" (ibid., p. 24) which requires us to move from a cruder to a more refined notion of God, and hence which forces us to start with polytheism rather than monotheism, due to the very perfection of the latter view of God.

monotheistic tendencies in religion. Hume regards this thesis as the strongest part of his explanation, but he also admits that it involves certain difficulties which are significant for his general theory of religion. The difficulties center around the three issues of transcendence, the integration of passion and understanding, and the distinction between a genetic and a pragmatic evaluation. A brief indication of how these issues are implicated in the general dialectic of polytheism and monotheism will help us to grasp the evaluative implications of Hume's passional conception of religion.

Polytheism and monotheism. Hume pictures our everyday religious sentiments as being in a constant oscillation between polytheistic and theistic (monotheistic) conceptions of divine power and presence. What he refers to as "this alternate revolution of human sentiments" is a tidal flux and reflux, going from an animistic reverence for the sensible forces in nature to a unification of power in the one God, and then back again to more concrete manifestations of divinity in various mediators and intercessors, in an endless cycle.[39] He does not stop to argue the theological point about whether these plural manifestations and means of access to divinity can rightly be called many gods, once the belief in the one God has become widespread. Hume's chief concern here is to state that, in terms of constant human phenomena, the aboriginal religious principle must be polytheism and the subsequent story of popular religion must be told through the tidal metaphor. Since he is very sparing elsewhere in the use of the word "must," its twofold use here is specially significant.

The necessity in question is not of an absolute and essential sort, which Hume confines to the ideal relations studied in logic and mathematics. Since religious belief lies in the factual and existential order, the necessity involved in the theory of religion is a high probability based upon a study of human tendencies toward belief, a consideration of historical developments, and an elimination of some alternate explanations. The polemical intent of eliminating the deistic account of the core rational religion of mankind also leads Hume to make some incisive negations. All these considerations add up to a necessity, in the sense of a very likely explanation of religion's origin and growth within human nature.

Hume's argument turns around the key distinction between popular religious belief (both polytheistic and monotheistic) and speculative the-

39. Ibid., p. 48.

ism, or natural religion in the first two senses previously designated (natural theology and the design argument). His passional theory of religion maintains: first, that the popular religious attitude cannot rest originally upon a speculatively argued theism, and secondly, that a popular religious monotheism cannot depend essentially upon a speculatively established theism at any time in the fluxing life of religious man. Whatever may be the historical conformity between the affirmations of popular theism and philosophico-scientific theism, it only shows the dependence of the latter upon the former.

There are three major obstacles against supposing that men are motivated by a speculative study of physical nature in their initial religious gropings, or that popular religion is ever fundamentally influenced by such a study. First, the subjective disposition required for an intellectually founded theism is a pure love of speculative truth, including a capacity for sustained inference leading from nature to its author. This speculative frame of mind does not suit the pragmatic concerns of most men, whether at the outset of human history or at any subsequent moment. If they had to rely upon the strength of their speculative curiosity and inferential power for enkindling religious belief, they would never feel its warming presence within them. Second, the unified conception of nature, forming one part of the analogy by which theists infer a unique maker of things, can only be elaborated under conditions of civilization and a certain freedom from immediate wants. Hume appeals to cultural history just enough at this point to establish the slow growth of civilization and the absence of leisure from the lives of most men, although they may be religious.

Finally, and most decisively in his eyes, the real evidence for a nature-based theism is not automatically made available, even when civilized men do experience a speculative love of truth and even when scientists and philosophers achieve a unified conception of nature. Hume regards as a piece of forced pleading on the part of Clarke, Derham, and other Boylean Lecturers that it is quite easy and obvious to view nature as a well-designed machine, requiring a divine maker. The evidential basis for such a notion of nature supposes the development of the philosophical theory of atomism, the modern scientific theory of the corpuscular structure of bodies, and the mathematics needed to express universal mechanical laws. Quite literally, man in his original condition is ignorant of general physical causes, mechanical models, and a universal system of physical laws and corpuscular structures. Yet he does not wait until this ignorance is cleared away before developing his original religious convictions. And even after the philosophical and scientific conception of the world machine has been transformed into a popular image, he does not draw his primary religious inspiration from it, as the apologists for speculative theism pretend.

Moreover, the same considerations which favor the distinction between popular religious theism and philosophical theism also favor the view that, within popular religious belief, the monotheistic component cannot be primary. In the absence of the speculative motive and the philosophical and scientific analyses of nature, the first impetus toward religious belief cannot come from the objective study of nature as a whole, and hence cannot be monotheistic.[40] Our propensity to believe in a religious way is aroused by passions in the *plural*, and is directed toward the many sorts of events and forces which powerfully affect our existence. Hence the very structure of religious belief, as originating in the many passions of man and their manifold relations with particular objects and forces, dictates that the primary religious outlook be polytheistic.

Hume is not thereby denying that intelligence is operative in forming our fundamental religious response. But he does deny that its contribution is altogether primary, independent of the passional inclinations and interests, and operative in everyday religion in the abstract way in which it functions in the thinking of those philosophical theists who argue from design in nature or from metaphysical principles. This leads him to conclude that the monotheistic aspect of popular religion arises in human nature as a prolongation of man's passional drives, and thus as a subsequent refinement of the animistic and polytheistic groundwork.

Because this dialectic requires popular religious theism to develop out of the passional materials furnished by fear and hope, rather than from a speculative study of the rational evidences for design in nature, monotheism is presented by Hume as being the offspring of flattery, terror, and the desire for pragmatic control over the power governing all visible happenings. That there is one God, infinite and perfect in every respect and benevolent toward men, is a popularly held religious belief only because of its agreement with our common desire to adulate power, our fear of

---

40. Hume deliberately stresses the affective origins of religion, in order to reorient the Enlightenment view of religion away from a foundation in the theologically and scientifically described world to one in the life world of humanly significant events, as matching our hopes and fears. In this respect, his naturalization of religion is not a scientific "naturizing" but a "hominizing" process, that is, a centering of religion around man, with his passional and environing interests.

denying any honorific attribute to the center of power, and our cunning search for the ritual means of favorably disposing the forces which bring us weal or woe. Later on, we may adjust this passionally generated theism to the monotheistic doctrine reached by reflective arguments. But our popular theism always remains independently based in the passional life of man, and retains its uneasy polar fluctuation with the polytheistic view which underlies all our religious sentiments. It is in this precise sense that Humean reason remains the slave of the passions in the religious sphere, just as it does in the spheres of morality and esthetic appreciation.

Transcendence. Although Hume's method commits him to find the origin of religion within human nature and its passions, it does not oblige him to limit the significance of religious belief to man and his context in nature. Instead, he recognizes that man comes to religion under the pressure of some deepseated tendencies, which are thoroughly human in origin and which nevertheless reach out beyond man and his natural context in their active intention. We do not find full satisfaction in the relations which we set up between ourselves, within the human community, and between man and the rest of the visible world. This discrepancy between what human nature seeks and what it provides for itself through social interchanges and action upon the environment calls forth the religious response, which never gets completely eliminated by skeptical criticism and technological progress.

Hume is careful to note that the sheer recognition of power in the world is not enough to constitute the religious attitude. For the latter to be realized in its distinctively human mode, we must give a threefold response to the presence of superior power. First, men must relate themselves to it as agents, through some practical striving, and not merely as theoretical observers. Next, the relationship must be suffused with a personal quality, by conceiving or imagining the superior power in a personal form. Thus animism and polytheism bear witness to the religious effort at establishing a personal communion with the divine. Thirdly, the development of the religious attitude requires men to feel deeply the tension between affirming a superior power beyond nature and seeking to relate oneself practically to it, in function of various symbolic forms and actions. The latter are needed to sustain the imagination, but they are not adequate for expressing our sense of the divine and quenching our thirst for happiness.

Our religious striving must be practical and personally ordered, but it must also contain a definite strain of transcendence. Monotheism embodies that moment in religious awareness which finally realizes that men are searching after a superior, concerned, powerful reality which is immanent in the world but not as a component of nature, which is personal and one, but in a way somehow transcending the limited configuration of sensible things.

Hume is now faced with the difficulty of joining his theory about the passional origin of religion with his stress upon the fact of religious transcendence. The desires, imagery, and language of religious existence clearly indicate that it is "almost impossible for the mind of men to rest, like those of beasts, in that narrow circle of objects, which are the subject of daily conversation and action." [41] And the practical nature of the religious nisus requires that there be an adequate passional basis for becoming concerned about a reality which transcends our everyday talk and activity.

> It must necessarily, indeed, be allowed, that, in order to carry men's intention beyond that present course of things, or lead them into any inference concerning invisible intelligent power, they must be actuated by some passion, which prompts their thought and reflection; some motive, which urges their first enquiry. But what passion shall we here have recourse to, for explaining an effect of such mighty consequence? [42]

This mighty passion cannot be any special religious instinct or any speculative love of truth. Religion develops from the workings of the ordinary passions of man. Yet the results are extraordinary, when the transcending impetus which sustains the religious attitude is compared with the usual immanent objects of these passions.

In his general theory of the passions, Hume treats hope and fear as direct passions arising from our joy, grief, and imaginative concern over objects which affect our happiness. They follow directly upon our experiences of pleasure and pain, disposing us to action in regard to the particular, temporal, sensible circumstances which determine our pleasure and pain. Neither in origin nor in object do these basic passions ordinarily tend to surpass the experienced conditions of daily life. Man is also moved by the indirect passions, which are expressed in various forms of

41. *Treatise*, p. 271.
42. *Natural History*, p. 28. See *Treatise*, pp. 439–48, on the direct passions of hope and fear.

flattery, adulation, and service. Some intervening idea is required for
their development, but the causes and objects of these passions usually
concern only the contingent materials and outcomes of human actions, as
they affect the individual and human society.

There is something incommensurate, therefore, between the human
origin and thoroughly this-worldly significance of the direct and indirect
passions involved in religion and the transcendent reference which they
nevertheless provoke in the religious believer. Human passions express not
only their exciting causes and objects in sense experience but also the
relationship of our operative human nature to this world, including a certain incommensurateness on man's part. Hope and fear are direct passional acts of man, not only insofar as he confronts situations but also
insofar as he constantly seeks a happiness with which he cannot merely
coalesce. His passional relationship with the world is deeply marked by
an awareness of the vulnerability and transiency of his own existence,
along with his desire for a permanent and satisfying condition of soul.
Hence the added reach of transcendence found in religious fear and hope
stems from the rooting of these passions in human nature, with its
quenchless and perilous search for happiness.

On this point, Hume is not so very far removed from the company of
Augustine, Pascal, and Malebranche. They all trace the source of religious
transcendence back to the restless quest of the human soul for a con-
summately powerful good, present in all the processes of life and yet
surpassing all the goods of the visible world.

Religious integration of passion and understanding. For most religious
thinkers who focus upon the human search for a surpassing and permanent
good, moreover, the religious tendency does not signify a brute drive but
an impulse permeated with intelligence. In his own critical way, Hume
agrees that the passions forming the basis of a religious response are not
isolated, but work along with some concrete mode of intelligence. In
stressing the passional component in religious belief, his purpose is not
to eliminate the understanding entirely but to distinguish the religious
use of the understanding from other uses, and thus to avoid a sheerly
intellectualist view of the genesis of religion.

Whereas the Newtonian divines regarded the religious response as an
intellectual inference from the scientific description of the order and
uniform laws in the universe, Hume points out that the popular mind is
religiously aroused by the disorders and crises in life. Those who come to

theism by the ordinary paths of belief "are never led into that opinion by any process of argument, but by a certain train of thinking, more suitable to their genius and capacity." [43] Judged by purely theoretical standards, the actual path followed by believers seems irrational and superstitious, but it is not entirely blind and lacking in an experienced foundation. For the religious response does embody some personal reflection upon man's situation in this world.

Hume often refers to the distinctive train of thinking involved in everyday religious conviction as "imagination." It is a concrete mode of thought, not theoretically motivated but integrated with, and adapted very closely to, man's passions and practical needs. Within the practico-passional context of our actual existence and needs, we do use our concrete intelligence or imagination to reflect nonscientifically upon our natural condition and to make informal inferences and symbolic expressions. Religious belief is not a mere fiction but a steady, forcible judgment reaching out beyond the experienced domain, through a synthesis of all these factors in our imagination and sentiment. In his critique of causality, Hume questions the evidential validity of transempirical causal inferences, whether they be made formally or informally. But in his theory of religion, he recognizes that the simple models of associative thinking used in his epistemology cannot entirely dissolve or render cognitively meaningless the characteristic religious train of thinking. Our concrete intelligence insures the abiding presence of a transcendent cognitive meaning in religious belief.

Ultimately, it is this passional-cognitive complexity of ordinary religious thinking which accounts for the alternation between polytheism and monotheism. In this insight, Hume anticipates Freud on the need for a joint contribution of both the happiness principle and the reality principle to the growth of religious belief.[44] Out of the happiness principle, or the operation of the passions in relating man to a world of changing satisfactions, there develops the outlook of animism and polytheism. And from the operation of the reality principle, or the search after causal knowledge of the powers which shape the natural world and human existence, comes the tendency toward a monotheistic conception of God and our religious relationship with Him. Hence there is a dual trend in

43. *Natural History*, p. 42.
44. Sigmund Freud, *The Future of an Illusion* (New York, 1957), p. 54, does not deny the possible presence of a reality value in religious doctrines, although he maintains that we cannot judge about it on the basis of his method.

the religious train of thinking: sometimes it places a polytheistic emphasis upon the multiple sources of happiness and danger in the universe, and sometimes it stresses the monotheistic unification of power and intelligence in the divine mind.

Hume sometimes distinguished between these two functions of religious intelligence by calling the former a mode of "the heart," or imagination in the narrower sense, and the latter a mode of "judgment." [45] From this functional standpoint, there must be a perpetual alternation of views in the mind of the everyday believer. Judgment suggests the conception of a powerful and invisible reality; imagination or the heart seeks to overcome the indefiniteness of this conception by referring it to various sensible manifestations and symbolic objects of worship; and judgment works again to rectify the crudeness of the myths and images by directing worship toward a transcendent, perfect, yet personal reality. As far as Hume could see, there were no ordinary means available for liberating us from a ceaseless religious fluctuation between the onesided deliverances of polytheistic imagination and monotheistic judgment. Neither popular religion nor natural theology could rise above the situation. It would take a revelation from God or a skeptical critique, devised formally by the human philosopher of religion, to break out from this circle. Whether liberation could be achieved in such a way as to secure a more firmly grounded religious integration of passion and intelligence was the question which pointed Hume toward his own theory of the philosopher's religion.

Genetic and pragmatic evaluation. In the later sections of the *Natural History*, there is a significant shift of viewpoint. Instead of continuing to delve further into the springs of religious belief afforded by human nature, Hume now turns his attention to a comparison between the several actual forms of religion, grouped roughly into the polytheistic and the monotheistic varieties. His purpose is not to make a comparative theological analysis, but rather to complete the natural history approach to religion by considering its fruits as well as its seeds in man. It is necessary to study not only the passional origins of religion but also the states of soul which are the steady effects of the play of religiously qualified passions. Only in this way can the passional analysis of religion yield its full

45. *Natural History*, p. 67.

contribution toward an understanding of human nature in empirical terms.

There are some interesting implications here for Hume's methodology. The precept of tracing our ideas back to their original impressions weights his experimental philosophy heavily on the genetic side, but the emphasis is not placed exclusively there. This can be seen clearly in his philosophy of religion, which requires both a genetic analysis of the passional sources and a consequential study of how these sources variously compose together to shape the actual characters of religious men and their ways of acting. Hume deliberately seeks to avoid the genetic fallacy of totally explaining religion, and thus in effect explaining it away, in terms of its passional sources. The genetic approach is neither exhaustive on the descriptive side nor fully decisive for an evaluation of the worth of the religious spirit in man. William James once complained that classical British empiricism is too retrospective in its concerns and not sufficiently oriented in a forward-looking direction. This criticism is not entirely just, for Hume does give a prospective view of religious experience, even though he lays greater stress upon the theme of its passional origins. Both the genetic and the pragmatic aspects of religion must be included within Hume's program of the naturalization of religion.

That is why the passional analysis in the *Natural History* culminates with a reflection upon the fruits of the religious spirit in our individual lives and social history. A frank self-interrogation about the practical impact of religious belief and striving will lead anyone to conclude that the consequences in human action are essentially ambiguous. For every humanly ennobling gift of the religious spirit mentioned in St. Paul's litany, Hume offers a matching quality of inhumane conduct which also claims to have a religious basis. Out of the religious treasury of mankind come forth both courage and dispiritedness, both wisdom and absurdity about the divine reality, both a precept of love for neighbor and a policy of intolerance and oppression. This practical ambiguity becomes most acute and menacing for the welfare of humanity in the case of the most developed form of religious belief and practice: monotheism.

Abstractly considered, the effect of theism upon our conduct should be salutary, in human terms as well as religious. "As that system supposes one sole deity, the perfection of reason and goodness, it should, if justly prosecuted, banish every thing frivolous, unreasonable, or inhuman from religious worship, and set before men the most illustrious example, as

well as the most commanding motives, of justice and benevolence." [46]
But the sad fact is that, in practice, the theistic vision of life becomes
obscured by motives of power, which tend to identify the divine truth
and majesty with the interests of a particular religious party. The step
is very short from monotheism to a monolithic consolidation of all religious thought in a single system of theology, and of all religious values
in a single official way of life.

What measures can be taken to avoid such a disastrous step and to
relieve social life of the underlying religious ambiguity? This is the lingering question with which Hume hopes we will close our reading of the
Natural History. Its highly practical character indicates that the passional
approach to religion embodies a movement from genetic description to
pragmatic evaluation. But once the evaluative level is reached, it disposes
us to consider some possibilities which lie beyond the horizon framed by
a restricted study of the grounds in human nature for religious belief. We
are left wondering whether the situation of practical ambiguity can be
fundamentally modified by introducing the resources of the rational
evidence for God's existence and the moral implications of such evidence.
Hume now invites us to weigh the intellectual factor in religion and to
determine its worth for assuring the humane quality of human conduct,
insofar as it responds to religious motivations.

46. Ibid., p. 49.

2

Hume on the Philosopher's Religion

In terms of the cardinal distinction governing Hume's entire theory of religion, he must now turn from considering the origins of religious conviction in our active human nature to a scrutiny of the grounds in reasoned argument backing up such conviction. He does not abandon his passional findings on religion, but rather establishes their relevance for understanding and appraising the different modes of philosophical theology. In a general way, Hume seeks to show that the distance is not as great as is usually supposed between the workings of concrete religious imagination—within the context of popular religious belief—and the workings of abstract intelligence in the prevailing philosophical theories of God. There is a greater formalization achieved in the latter instance, but not a greater amount of evidence to show a strong basis in experience for the claims of theism.

On every question, especially on religious ones, Hume admits that he is much quicker to raise doubts than to reach any certainties. His habitual stance is that of the keen-eyed critic, who can point out the defects and blind spots in other people's positions on religion more easily than he can define and defend his own. And yet every step in his persistent inquiry into religious belief and action helps to determine and clarify his own stand, as being distinct from the views under criticism and grounded in a more reflective awareness of the human conditions which shape it.

At the end of his intellectual pilgrimage to the shrines of believing mankind, Hume does have the courage to state his own religious conviction. It turns around the culminating distinction between popular theism (with its accompanying explication and defense in theological and philosophical terms) and *philosophical theism*. The latter is a severely retrenched affirmation, which nevertheless persists in the midst of all the critical discussions. It constitutes what Hume believes himself to be permitted to hold concerning a divine powerful minded reality, within the very restricted boundaries set for all existential inference and belief by his own conception of human nature and its relation with the natural world. Most significantly for the philosophy of religion, this minimal probable belief in God is also the maximal expansion of religion within the Humean philosophical context. The residual position in the theory of God is here proposed as being the sole philosophically legitimated act of religion for the reflective person.

RELIGION AND RATIONAL ARGUMENTATION

In the *Dialogues,* Hume examines the cogency of the main types of reasoning used to defend the monotheistic conception of God's existence and attributes. His strictures against the current theistic proofs and his many alternate proposals to theism are among the best known parts of his philosophy, the parts which come most readily to mind whenever he is called "the great infidel." However, his critique of the theism of his day is usually studied in isolation, as a set of speculative objections against a metaphysical approach to God and any rational basis for natural theology. This is a valid but incomplete account of what Hume is doing. For what sometimes goes unnoticed is the broad context in the philosophy of religion for his entire investigation of the theistic proofs. They are the subject matter for some "dialogues concerning natural religion," precisely because these proofs constitute the rational validation of religion and fulfill two of the meanings already assigned for natural religion (as natural theology and as a view of nature in the light of the design argument).

Apart from reference to its religious context, indeed, the *Dialogues* has an unaccountably lopsided and random appearance. It does not make a thorough and balanced examination of the major kinds of theistic arguments, considered in detail and in the intrinsic basis on which they rest in their historical development. Instead, it concentrates upon two popular arguments, the a priori one and that which appeals to design in nature. And even these two proofs are given a very uneven treatment, by the standards of any speculative treatise in natural theology. For Hume compresses his study of the a priori approach into a single brief section, whereas he deals in a leisurely way with various aspects of the design argument throughout the work. Even the location of the section on the a priori argument is somewhat odd, since it appears in the latter part of the dialogues, at an intermediate point where it can neither serve any foundational role nor function as the culmination of theistic reflection.

What would be questionable peculiarities, from the standpoint of a speculative critique of natural theology, are nevertheless quite appropriate to the execution of Hume's actual aim. He is examining those rational approaches which are most favored by apologists for religion in his own day. He receives confirmation from Clarke on the one side and from Bayle on the other that religious believers actually look for the rational foundations of their faith in the two places marked by the a priori argument and that from design.[1] Moreover, Hume knows from his own circle of acquaintances, as well as from a reading of current theistic literature, that these two types of reasoning are not equally influential in shaping the religious mind, when it seeks some rational validation of its convictions. The "high priori" road winds through a very rarefied plateau, at an intellectual height that most believers find impossible to reach and that does not sustain for very long even those who succeed in mounting to it.

Despite the speculative importance of a priori reasoning about God and the incisiveness of his own criticism, therefore, Hume displaces discussion of it from the center of his treatment of the relation between rational argumentation and religious faith. In the concrete, the men of faith with whom Hume is acquainted are more deeply moved by the traditional appeal to order in nature and especially by the design argument, which seeks to capitalize on the growing prestige of natural science and the Newtonian natural philosophy. For this reason, the design argument holds center stage in Hume's investigation of the grounds in reason for theistic religious faith, whereas the a priori proof is viewed as a refuge to which some believers may retreat but where they cannot find the chief intellectual buttress for their religion.

In the history of modern philosophy, it is a safe rule to suppose that every major thinker establishes his own meaning for the *a priori argument* for God's existence. The philosophers are not really following a standard dictionary definition, which gets its final philosophical formulation in Kant. In the *Dialogues*, its Humean meaning is determined partly by the desire of orthodox minds to escape from some inconveniences in the

1. See A. Leroy, *La Critique et la religion chez David Hume* (Paris, 1930), pp. 113–34, on the conflation of abstract a priori reasons and a posteriori argumentation in the theistic proofs of Clarke and Wollaston.

design argument, and partly by the actual text of Clarke's Boylean lectures on the existence and attributes of God.

The appeal to design is not entirely satisfactory to modern theists, once its limitations are brought out. Hume drives home the point that ordinary believers feel uneasy when they are told that, in this scientific age, they must regard their conception of God as a hypothesis which is subject to tests for its degree of probability, and must affirm about God only what they can infer from a contemplation of the natural world. On the contrary, they view their religious assent to God as a strong commitment of a nonhypothetical sort, which cannot be treated impersonally as a hypothesis brought up for testing. When it is further suggested that from a study of our finite world and its conflicting phenomena the only just inference may be to one or several gods of a limited nature, they are more likely to question the value of the design argument itself than to surrender their credal acceptance of the one, all perfect God and creator.

It is at this juncture that the rationalistic revision of natural theology sometimes exerts an appeal upon believers, even when they cannot really follow the argumentation itself. They are drawn to the a priori argument on the strength of its supposed consequences for religion. It claims to supply a rational certitude which will silence the doubts and difficulties of skepticism, and will give philosophical standing to religious convictions concerning the unity and infinity of the divine nature.

Demea, the spokesman in Hume's *Dialogues* for the deists and rationalistic divines, forges a meaning for "that simple and sublime argument *a priori*" which meets this crisis in the intellectual defense of religion.[2] His reasoning is a priori, in several related senses. It furnishes a demonstration, rather than a high probability, about God as a necessarily existent being. It proceeds from axiomatic first principles, not from an inductive study of the experienced world. And it claims that to deny the conclusion concerning the necessarily existent being is also to deny the principles of contradiction, causality, and reason-for-existence. The reasoning itself is supposed to have the coercive strength and certitude of a mathematical proof, since it arrives at an understanding of God's very reason for existing, and thus at the essential definition from which His existence follows with complete necessity.[3] The conclusion that there is a

2. *Dialogues*, p. 188.
3. Ibid., pp. 188, 189. Hume is summarizing the first three propositions in Clarke's *Being and Attributes of God*, pp. 18–33.

God follows with perfect necessity, since we have applied the proper principles, excluded all other possibilities, and thus arrived at the essential nature of that being which must itself exist, in order to be the cause required for explaining all other existing things and rescuing all statements from absurdity.

Confronted with the awesome claims made for this a priori reasoning, the other two participants in the dialogue (Cleanthes, the proponent of the design argument, and the skeptical Philo) join forces for making a two-pronged reply. They make an epistemological criticism of it, drawing upon Hume's study of causality and imagination, and then they bring out its religious irrelevance. Although they regard the former criticism as speculatively decisive, they also find it necessary to add the latter point in order to remain closely connected with the main issue of the whole discussion, which concerns the foundation in reason for our religious belief.

In a purely logical criticism of the a priori approach, it would be sufficient for Hume to raise difficulties against a transphenomenal use of causality, and to suggest that the psychological necessity in human thinking does not apply to the divine existence itself. Within the context of his study of natural religion, however, he must also offer a distinctive criticism of a priori reasoning from the standpoint of its religious inefficacy. Hence he is careful to have Cleanthes declare that the argument "seems to me so obviously ill-grounded, and at the same time of so little consequence to the cause of true piety and religion, that I shall myself venture to show the fallacy of it." [4] Exposing its fallacious nature does nothing to shake religious belief, since the latter is not really based upon this species of abstract and metaphysical argumentation.

Sometimes, believers are eager to accept such an argument, doing so mainly because of a mistaken notion that all our convictions must be homogeneous. They think it is necessary to bring their independently grounded religious conviction into line with the mathematical pattern of knowledge. Philo is explicit on this point in motivation.

> The argument *a priori* has seldom been found very convincing, except to people of a metaphysical head, who have accustomed themselves to abstract reasoning, and who finding from mathematics, that the understanding frequently leads to truth, through obscurity, and contrary to first appearances, have transferred the same habit of thinking to subjects where it ought not to have place. Other people, even of

4. *Dialogues*, p. 189.

good sense and the best inclined to religion, feel always some defi-
ciency in such arguments, though they are not perhaps able to explain
distinctly where it lies. A certain proof, that men ever did, and ever
will, derive their religion from other sources than from this species
of reasoning.[5]

Religious belief does not really suspend itself until some a priori demonstration of God's existence is found, and hence criticism of the demonstration does not really undermine popular religious belief and the natural
train of informal reasoning which it encompasses. The effective sources of
religion are not located in any a priori demonstrations but in human
passions.

Hume's treatment of the *design argument* is much more intricate and
sinuous, as befits a path of reasoning which gripped religious minds at all
intellectual levels, during the pre-evolutionary period in modern science.
He sets an example for subsequent philosophers of religion by acknowledging the design argument to be the strongest speculative proof offered for
theism. It incorporates many features of our ordinary inference from
natural order to God; it remains open to the scientific findings being made
about the material world; and in starting from a study of experienced
natural things, it establishes a footing in the existential order for an
existential conclusion about God, the maker of nature.

Yet each of these sound points is pushed beyond the proper limits by
Cleanthes, who makes explicit the unspoken assumptions and long-range
religious consequences of design-based theism. The exaggerated claims
made by Cleanthes for the design argument elicit some countervailing
exaggerations on the part of the skeptical Philo. The upshot is that Philo
applies to the design approach the same double criticism previously made
by Cleanthes against the a priori proof: it is intellectually ill-grounded
and, in the precise form of philosophical reasoning proposed by the
design theorists, is inconsequential for religious believers. Certainly, Hume
did not want attention to be concentrated so exclusively upon the first
part of this criticism as to let the second part go unnoticed. For grasping
the emergence of the philosophy of religion, it is important to see the
religious focus of the entire issue.

Within the strategy of the dialogue, Philo does not simply criticize the
design argument. He criticizes it precisely as the bearer of Cleanthes' dual
assertion that it has the same evidential force as our everyday and scien-

5. Ibid., pp. 191–92.

tific reasoning, and that it is the sole and sufficient way of establishing all the truths of theology, natural and revealed.[6] Cleanthes is convinced that only by sustaining this dual claim can he establish the rational foundations of religion, and halt the inroads of modern religious skepticism. In this project, he appeals to "the judicious sentiment of Mr. Locke," which recommends itself to believers who witness the failure of the a priori argument and the growing skepticism about the possibility of making any intellectual defense of religion. The design argument is proposed here, not in isolation, but quite pointedly within a tissue of claims about its homogeneity with other types of reasoning and its unique power for giving a rational validation to natural and revealed theology.

When the proof from design is thus qualified, Philo (and on this topic he is clearly Hume's own representative in the religious dialogue) refers to it rather guardedly and distantly as "your hypothesis of experimental theism," "your principles, that the religious system can be proved by experience, and by experience alone," and "the experimental argument; and this, you say too, is the sole theological argument." These cautious expressions are warranted, since Cleanthes is not simply repeating the agelong appeal to order in nature, an appeal which usually allows room for several other proofs and for several ways of knowing.

In the *Dialogues*, Cleanthes stands as the symbol for the tendency which Hume observed among many Newtonian theists of his day toward noetic reductionism. They sought to identify the reasoning involved in the design argument with the interpretation of experience by common sense and physical science, and then to reduce all the other meanings of natural religion and natural theology to a design-based theism. This specifically reductionist sort of experimental theism is vulnerable to criticism twice over, both on epistemological and on specifically religious grounds.

Philo presses home the *epistemological* criticism on several fronts, all of them connected in some way with the use of analogy. Whether we look at the practice of ordinary men, the history of science, or the philo-

6. Ibid., pp. 137, 138, 143. The qualifying phrases quoted at the beginning of the next paragraph are taken from ibid., pp. 164, n. 1, and 165. Hume's remark about Locke probably refers to *An Essay Concerning Human Understanding*, IV, xviii–xix (Fraser ed. 2, 415–41), on how reason must judge whether a particular religious doctrine is really a divine revelation or not. This principle disposed both deists and Christian rationalists to concentrate upon the rational character of religion and its objective grounds of assent, as described by John Yolton, *John Locke and the Way of Ideas* (Oxford, 1956). Hume undercuts both parties to the discussion by calling attention to the power of the passions and habits in determining matters of religious assent.

sophical implications of phenomenalism, the same lesson is taught that the modes of analogical reasoning are many, and that there is something peculiar about the mode employed in the design argument. We can use analogy with some confidence in our everyday reasoning, because we have had some experience already with the kind of objects under comparison, and can check our inference about a particular case by the past experience of that kind of object. The analogy is regarded as reliable because of a conformity with what we call our common sense or summed-up experience, and because of our assurance that the class of objects under investigation does come within our range of experience.

Similar conditions hold for the use of analogy by the astronomers, who brought about the gradual acceptance of the Copernican system.[7] The hypothesis of the moving earth came to be seen as having the support of resemblances drawn from the satellite moons which move around Jupiter and Saturn. Galileo was able to gain acceptance for his hypothesis about a common matter for all heavenly bodies, when he exhibited that the moon and the planets are similar to the earth in figure, density, surface irregularities, and other observable traits. The experienced likenesses in the class of objects under investigation permitted him to use an argument from analogy, as something distinct from a wild guess or a fictitious comparison.

Philo is now ready to show that these conditions for the use of analogy are not fulfilled in the design argument. Hence it is not fundamentally identical with our everyday and scientific analogies, and does not enjoy any logical advantage over them. In the design argument, it is not simply a case of arguing from like effects to like causes in some degree. The real task is to show that the natural world must be construed as a crafted effect at all, in the sense of being the outcome of a making process somewhat similar to the process of making on the part of the intelligent human maker. The very aboriginality and uniqueness of the cosmogonic making process prevent it from belonging in a wider class of makings which men can experience, and hence prevent the design analogy from having that experiential basis required for a sound analogical argument in everyday life and scientific inquiry. We do not have the experience of the origin of the world or of many worlds in the making, and hence we do not have the proper warrant for calling the design argument an argument from

7. That Cleanthes' position closely expresses the actual views of two prominent Newtonian theists, George Cheyne and especially Colin Maclaurin, is established by R. H. Hurlbutt, *Hume, Newton, and the Design Argument* (Lincoln, 1965).

experience, let alone for assigning it any logical advantage over the experientially controlled types of analogy.

Hume questions the real religious value of a cosmic analogy by noting some features of our experience which suggest a different analogy than the theistic one of the supreme maker and his handiwork.[8] If we want to express the permanent power at the heart of the universe, then perhaps we should use the old Stoic theory of the soul of the world, a fully immanent principle rather than a transcendent one. And to characterize the life of this indwelling principle, we can imagine it (with Robinet) as being a great vegetative soul with a natural reproductive power, in relation to which the order of mind and intelligence is a peripheral offshoot. It may not even be too extreme to accept Diderot's figure of the cosmic spider, endlessly spinning worlds out of its own vitals and then casting them off indifferently from itself. Certainly, the massive lack of concern in natural processes for the moral qualities and quandaries of men lends some plausibility to this comparison.

Hume's stream of nontheistic suggestions is intended to bring out the lack of theoretical rigor in the use of analogy by the theologians of design. When an analogical argument is used in design theism, it moves beyond the region where the familiar checks of sense and the experienced world can operate. Hence the theology of design is affected even by palpably fanciful counterhypotheses, as long as the latter can point to some puzzling aspect of our experience and then make an imaginative use of analogy for a nontheistic explanation.

As a direct consequence of this unsettling technique, Cleanthes is provoked into making some concessions, thus drawing some explicit conclusions from his design argument that he might otherwise never have done. These points are not merely logical clarifications in the speculative order; they directly affect our personal relationship to the God attained through design argumentation, and hence they have a practical religious significance. Philo is not reluctant to underline this latter meaning and thus to establish his major contention about the *religious* inadequacy of a natural theology governed by the design approach.

This decisive turn of the dialogue hinges around three topics: a revised rule of analogy, an admission of divine finitude, and a restriction placed on the divine attributes. With their aid, Hume is able to mount a subtle religious critique of design-based theism.

8. *Dialogues*, pp. 165–87.

Revised Rule of Analogy. Although Cleanthes is stung by the skeptical use of analogy in favor of nontheistic conceptions of the divine principle, he shares too much in common with skepticism to appeal to a more metaphysical theory of analogy and causality. His claim that the design argument finds its footing squarely in the scientific description of physical phenomena rules out any nonphenomenalistic analysis of the structure of finite beings and their causal relations, which might provide a rigorous control over analogical inferences to the divine maker. The only way open to Cleanthes for meeting the objection against our having any experience of a divine making is to deflect our attention from knowledge of the causal relation and the making process, and concentrate it exclusively upon a revision of the rule of analogy itself.

In its new formulation, it is reducible to this concise maxim: "the liker the better." [9] This means that the more resemblance we suppose to hold between man the maker and God the maker, the stronger the basis of analogy and the more conclusive the design argument. Taking the rule of analogy in this sense, Cleanthes treats the divine attributes of power and intelligence as being fundamentally the same perfections found in man, but realized in God in an expanded degree and heightened form. We know the nature of these attributes, since they are traits of ourselves as makers, and hence we know the nature of the designing mind which made the elements of the world. Cleanthes carries his reasoning to the bitter conclusion that the divine mind is like the human mind, and hence that we must conceive the divine exemplar ideas as being many, really composed, changing, and successive. The traditional attributes of simplicity, immutability, and eternity must then be sacrificed. Within a noncausal framework, they cannot apply to the God reached through this analogical argument from experience.

Philo makes the inevitable comment that "you have run into *anthropomorphism,* the better to preserve a conformity to common experience." [10] But this conformity is also gained at the cost of claiming to enjoy a greater insight into the divine nature than men do in fact possess. The use of analogy in the design argument leads only to an imaginative expansion of our conception of human practical intelligence, as well as to a suppression of all mystery concerning the being of God and our relation to Him. This leads to the paradoxical result that the more plausible the

9. Ibid., p. 166.
10. Ibid., p. 186.

theistic hypothesis is made by Cleanthes' brand of analogy, the more it ceases to be specifically and properly a religious sort of hypothesis and a rational defense of the human religious attitude toward God.

Hume presses home the objection that the revised rule of analogy is a desperate expedient, which violates the descriptive traits of religion. Our religious relation to God is marked by the groping darkness in which we approach Him, by the transcendence of His own reality to all our concepts thereof, and by the contrast between His way of being and that of things within the natural, temporal order. Philo sometimes draws an ironical contrast between the "mystics" (who accept these religious traits, along with the traditional attributes of simplicity and immutability) and the "anthropomorphites" bred upon the design argument. Yet he does agree that the former remain closer to everyman's religious spirit by preserving the mystery and difficulty of theism, and that the latter tend to dissipate the faith which they seek to found in a rational way.

Admission of Divine Finitude. This same conclusion is reached from a somewhat different angle, when Philo draws out the further consequence that none of the divine maker's attributes can be regarded as infinite or even as perfect in some respect.[11] The Newtonian theists interpret analogy and experimental proof in such a fashion that the inferred cause must be proportioned exactly to the effects which we experience. Since all the objects of our experience are limited in their being and attributes, the design argument can lead only to a finite deity having limited attributes. And in view of the mixed quality of everything in our experience, it is doubtful whether the asserted attributes of the cosmic maker can be treated as complete and perfect, even within their limited kind.

Philo is quick to bring out some uncomfortable dialectical implications about the divine nature. A design theism cannot, for instance, rule out the possibility that our world comes from a bungling but improving deity, a maker who does better with every try at producing world after world. Indeed, there is no analogical and experimental way of settling a controversy about whether the divine knowledge and power displayed in nature belong to a youthful deity, one in the prime of life, or one who is now on the wane. These temporal and biological designations do make some sense within the frame of design argumentation, since we can point to particular aspects of our worldly experience as a plausible ground for

11. *Dialogues*, pp. 166–69.

conceiving the maker analogy in any one of these ways. But it is doubtful whether such a deity can evoke our sustained religious response.

Demea, representing here the ordinary religious mind, is deeply disturbed by the unsatisfactory religious consequences of the reductionist theory of design. He exclaims that it must be a very slight religious life

> which can be erected on so tottering a foundation. While we are uncertain, whether there is one Deity or many; whether the Deity or Deities, to whom we owe our existence, be perfect or imperfect, subordinate or supreme, dead or alive; what trust or confidence can we repose in them? What devotion or worship address to them? What veneration or obedience pay them? To all the purposes of life, the [design-based] theory of religion becomes altogether useless: And even with regard to speculative consequences, its uncertainty, according to you, must render it totally precarious and unsatisfactory.[12]

The project of basing all theology and religion on the design argument fails to meet the norm of religious trust and acts of worship. We need not respect and worship a cosmic craftsman, who may be only a component within nature and subject to a stronger power and broader course of events. Either religious belief has no foundation in reason or else it must find a more solid and appropriate one than a concentration upon physical design and the maker analogy can yield.

Restriction of Divine Attributes. Finally, the uselessness of the design-based theory of religion for the purposes of human life can be shown in terms of the distinction between God's natural and moral attributes. A practically helpful theory of religion should be able to establish something about the moral as well as the natural attributes, since both kinds are included within the meaning of natural religion. Cleanthes recognizes this to be a fair test of the adequacy of his reconstruction of all the truths of religion and theology. One of his objections against the a priori approach is, indeed, that it centers too exclusively on metaphysics and abstract reasoning to do justice to the moral reality of God. Hence he is willing to sacrifice the demonstrative sort of reasoning and the natural attribute of divine infinity in order to preserve a footing in what he calls the "human analogy," or our common moral experience, as a basis of attributing moral qualities to God. But his moralizing effort comes to grief on the shoals of the problem of evil.

12. Ibid., p. 170.

The long analysis of evil in the *Dialogues* is not a detached logical critique of theodicy, but an integral part of Hume's assessment of the philosophical validation of popular religious belief. Its purpose is to show quite concretely that the Newtonian divines cannot justify God's moral attributes by the method of analogy and the proof from design. Consequently, Hume does not make a full-scale study of evil in all its metaphysical, psychological, and moral dimensions, but confines himself to the design and analogy aspects presented by Dr. Clarke, Bishop Butler, and Archbishop King.[13] Their common religious aim accounts for the peculiar conditions under which the Humean analysis of evil labors.

There are three chief restrictions within which Cleanthes works out his religious interpretation of evil. First, he accepts no help from the a priori proof of God's being and the doctrine that God is infinite in power and knowledge. Second, he wants to face the problem of evil in a bare way, as it were, or without fortifying his mind beforehand with the aids of faith and revelation concerning a benevolent, providential God. His judgment on evil is to be drawn exclusively from a study of the phenomena in nature, as befits an experimental theism. And finally, he refuses to accept the stress which most believers and skeptics lay upon disorder and disaster in nature, as well as upon the weakness and misery of mankind. "The only method of supporting divine benevolence (and it is what I willingly embrace) is to deny absolutely the misery and wickedness of man." [14] The rule of human analogy requires him to maintain that the liker man is to a condition of present felicity, the better it goes for inferring the benevolence of God.

It is Hume's considered opinion, on the contrary, that when the question of evil is treated under these three conditions, one can never establish the goodness of God (in any sense corresponding to what we know as human moral goodness) or His other moral attributes. He is specially roused by Cleanthes' third point, which would require us to maintain the predominant happiness of men in this life. This runs contrary to everyone's feeling and experience, that is, it seeks futilely to controvert the main authority

---

13. Hume describes theodicies as "all the fruitless industry to account for the ill appearances of nature and save the honor of the gods, while we must acknowledge the reality of that evil and disorder with which the world so much abounds" (*Inquiry*, p. 148). The great modern source of theodicy reasoning is G. W. Leibniz's *Theodicy* (New Haven, 1952), and the basic opposition to it is formulated in Pierre Bayle's *Historical and Critical Dictionary*, ed. R. H. Popkin (Indianapolis, 1965), pp. 144–53, 166–93, 213–54.

14. *Dialogues*, p. 200.

to which all our opinions must defer. It is not a question of nicely balancing off the misery against the happiness, and concluding that the latter
weights down the scale of human life. When men cry out against evil,
they are asking in effect why there is any misery at all in a world produced by a powerful God, who is also presumed to be benevolent toward
us, as a human father would be toward his sons.

As far as our bare reason can determine from searching the face of
nature and human history, the evils uncovered by that search are not
necessary and unavoidable, as Cleanthes and the theistic apologists claim.
Hence it does not facilitate their case to shift from infinite power and
goodness to a defense of the moral attributes of a finite deity, who is
very wise and benevolent in a limited way. Even such a deity could have
matured and disciplined us otherwise than by pain, by subjection of our
carefully rationed powers to the sting of necessity, by the administration
of general laws which grind down the individual man, and by the clash
between various lines of force in our universe.

Hume also distinguishes between the operation of reconciling an otherwise well-grounded theory of a morally qualified God with our experience
of the world, and that of establishing the moral reality of God in the first
instance from a study of our experienced world.[15] Experimental theism
cannot merely show some consistency and compatibility between the
religious hypothesis and our world, but must actually establish the right
to include any moral attributes within that hypothesis, and do so exclusively from an examination of the natural phenomena commonly available
to us.

David Hume is keenly aware of the difference which the acknowledged
presence of religious knowledge would make in treating the problem of
evil and the divine moral attributes. He constantly qualifies his criticism
of natural religion by stipulating that his arguments suppose that we are
drawing upon no antecedent conviction about the good Lord, that we do
not know beforehand or in any a priori way about His moral goodness
and providence, and that we are not trying to reconcile with the fact of
evil some knowledge of God gained otherwise than from the direct study
of natural phenomena. Within the *Dialogues*, these exclusions are justified by the conditions laid down by Cleanthes for developing his experimental theism, and by Philo's own conviction that originally the real case
with man is that he "is not antecedently convinced of a supreme intelli-

15. *Dialogues*, pp. 201–05.

gence, benevolent, and powerful, but is left to gather such a belief from the appearances of things." [16] Thus the Humean topic of natural religion, as embracing the natural and moral attributes of God in the face of our experience of evil, is always systematically treated apart from the actual operation of religious faith and revelation.[17]

The claim of experimental theism to give a rational foundation to all the truths of religion, natural and revealed, has now been shown to be very shaky. If revealed truths are regarded deistically as restatements of natural ones, then the weakness of Cleanthes' attempt to establish the moral attributes of God is visited upon revealed doctrine itself. And if revealed truths are regarded as being somehow distinct from and superior to the philosophical theory of God and religion, then the philosopher of religion must still demand some "tolerable reasons" for accepting the teachings as true. This is usually the place where miracles are cited, and in this respect the topic of miracle is relevant for the Humean philosophy of religion.

Hume's main treatment of miracle occurs in a section which (in somewhat different form) was excised from the original draft of the *Treatise*, out of regard for Joseph Butler's religious sensibilities. As it stands in the first *Inquiry*, this section seems to be a purely speculative essay in epistemology. Nevertheless, Hume remarks several times there that he is considering miracles only insofar as they are used in support of some religious system, and hence insofar as they are taken to back up the claim of a particular doctrine to be truly revealed by God. From this functional standpoint, his theory of miracle is a component in his philosophy of religion, being closely related to the question of whether we can draw upon any revealed source for the truth of the moral attributes of God.

This context explains some of the peculiarities in his approach, which

16. Ibid., p. 205. Philo remarks in passing that "what I have said concerning natural evil will apply to moral, with little or no variation" (Ibid., p. 212). Although this physicalistic assumption suits Hume's aim of separating religion from morality, it does not give sufficient weight to a personal religious view of the moral self and evil, such as Kant will propose.

17. Hume's essay "On the Immortality of the Soul," in *Essays Moral, Political and Literary*, pp. 597, 604, appeals to faith, the gospel, and revelation as the real sources of the conviction of the human soul's immortality. For the paradoxical use made of Hume by Hamann and Kierkegaard to preserve the complete transcendence of Christian faith beyond a philosophical natural religion and a natural morality, see Philip Merlan, "From Hume to Hamann," *Personalist*, 32 (1951), 11–18, and Richard Popkin, "Hume and Kierkegaard," *Journal of Religion*, 31 (1951), 274–81.

is as noteworthy for what it does not treat as for what it does. Hume refrains systematically from the first level question of whether miracles can or do occur, confining himself to whether we can ever know through experience and an experientially dependent reason that a miracle has occurred. The former question would require a metaphysical theory of causality and a doctrine on God which are not at his disposal, and it would also plunge him into a detailed study of religious scriptures at a more particular and historical level than is set by his analysis of natural religion.

Another feature of his treatment is that it depends upon a seemingly offhand definition of miracle as a violation of the laws of nature, *"a transgression of a law of nature by a particular volition of the Deity, or by the interposition of some invisible agent."* [18] In point of fact, however, this violational meaning of miracle is the one commonly found in contemporary works of apologetics, which try to fit it into the context of a theism based on the design argument. Even though it does not rest on a comparative study of other conceptions of miracle, Hume's definition has the virtue of reflecting the current religious thinking of design-based theists.

Within these limits, defined by his own philosophy of religion and the contemporary situation in religious apologetics, Hume concentrates upon the conditions for human knowledge of miracle. The claim to have such knowledge depends upon some testimony of eyewitnesses or of historians, so that the question of miracle becomes equivalently that of the trustworthiness of witnesses claiming to report the occurrence of a violation of a law of nature. Yet human experience and rational inference are based upon the firm and unalterable character of the common course of nature. And anything we may know in a philosophical way about God and His particular volitions is garnered solely from our experience of His productions in the usual course of nature. Hence there is no warrant in human experience, custom, and experientially tutored reason for accepting as probable or trustworthy a report about a violation of the laws of nature.

To lend credence to such a report would be to introduce a domestic

---

18. *Inquiry*, p. 123, n. 7. This definition reflects the contemporary theological discussions of miracle, such as Clarke's *Obligations of Natural Religion*, pp. 349–68. Flew argues that a nomological universal law of nature serves in principle "as a criterion of exclusion, which must rule out a range of logical possibilities as impossible in fact" (*Hume's Philosophy of Belief*, p. 208). But Hume himself is compelled, not by the logic of nomological laws of nature, but by his antecedent theory of causality and his separation of religion from morality, to establish an opposition in principle between scientific explanation and religious openness to miracle.

conflict within our view of experience, the only effect of which would be to dissolve every effort at giving religion a foundation in experiential reason. To include acceptance of miracle among the requirements for the intellectual defense of popular religion would be to annihilate religious belief, insofar as it does spring from our experience and does seek a rational clarification.[19] The appeal of particular religions to miracle is thus self-destructive. Within the defined meaning of miracle, therefore, no rational basis has been found for the popular religious conviction about the moral goodness, benevolence, and providential action of God.

Hume cannot complete his evaluation and set forth the minimal religious faith of the philosopher, however, until he investigates one prominent meaning for natural religion which still remains. Although his skeptical questioning has brought the intellectual defenders of religion to a standstill on other grounds, there is still the practico-moral way of giving religion a basis in reason. This differs from the problem of whether or not to apply the moral attributes to God, since it is concerned mainly with the role of God and religious belief in shaping the moral outlook of man himself. Yet the difficulties encountered in trying to establish the inference to the moral reality of God inevitably weaken, by anticipation, the project of showing the relevance of God and religious belief to the moral character and decisions of man.

RELIGION AND MORALITY

Whenever Hume treated religion in his books or correspondence, he included a separate discussion of its relation with morality. He was consciously engaged in calling into question the venerable position that their relation ought to be an intimate one, and that morality cannot flourish without the support of religion. This assumption had come increasingly under attack after the middle of the seventeenth century, providing a receptive climate for Hume's own attempt to sever the traditional bond. There was a strong current of criticism about the effect of religion upon morality and social life made by Bayle from the skeptical quarter, by Sprat as spokesman for many scientists in the Royal Society, by Locke in his political appeal for toleration, and finally by the French Encyclopedists.[20] Not all of these critics were antireligious, but they did agree in

19. *Inquiry*, p. 137.
20. The best systematic presentation of seventeenth-century criticism is made by Arnold Toynbee, *An Historian's Approach to Religion* (New York, 1956), pp. 155–210.

opposing an established religion in the state. They stressed the inhumane consequences of religious wars, of civilly enforced religious observances, and of moral codes dependent upon particular religious creeds and moral theologies.

The eighteenth century challenged, on a broader scale than ever before, the argument for religion drawn from the disastrous consequences which would follow for public and private morality, were religion to be repudiated or relegated to the nonofficial zone of our lives. There was a growing consensus among critical minds that these consequences would not in fact follow, since we could draw upon sufficient resources within human nature itself for moral action and social decision, entirely apart from religious aids, goals, and sanctions.[21]

Hume was fully sympathetic toward the ideal of a secularized morality and civilization, but he felt that some closer philosophical reasoning was still required in order to show that the separation of religion and morality can be achieved, without injury to man's nature and order of values. In other words, the philosophical groundwork for the secularization of civilized moral living had to be supplied by his own experimental philosophy of man and its study of the relationship between religion and morality. Hence this problem became a major topic in the modern philosophies of religion.

Hume's first move is to distinguish between the religion-morality relationship at the given factual level and at the level of principle. In the order of tangled historical fact, there is the closest union between what men regard as their religious belief and their moral conviction. Whether this mutual influence is beneficial or deleterious for human development cannot be decided, however, solely by reporting on the actual cases and adding up the consequences. Hume consistently refuses to restrict his experimental philosophy of man to a descriptive function. He seeks out the principles of belief and action, and thus admits that his philosophy has a normative and reforming function to perform. He believes enough in the power of ideas to quote La Rochefoucauld's maxim that "a wind, though it extinguishes a candle, blows up a fire." [22] Whatever the con-

---

21. This consensus is examined briefly by Charles W. Hendel, "The Eighteenth Century as an Age of Ethical Crisis," *Ethics*, 72 (1962), 202–14, and more in detail in two books by L. G. Crocker: *An Age of Crisis* and *Nature and Culture* (Baltimore, 1959 and 1963).

22. *Letters*, 2, 316. Hume takes a complex attitude toward the actual effect of his theory of religion. As far as the popular mind is concerned, "every thing remains

temporary opposition to his ideas on religion and morality, their rooting in the springs of human belief and action assure them an eventual revolutionary effect on the general convictions and historical institutions of men.

Viewed in relation to the active principles in human nature, religion and morality are distinct and even disparate in their respective bases and ultimate references, their motivations and consequences for human existence. Hume expresses the core of his thesis nowhere more succinctly than in a frank and sympathetic letter to the Scottish writer on moral sentiments and professor of moral philosophy at Glasgow, Francis Hutcheson. The latter had been charged with heresy for teaching that our standard of moral goodness is the promotion of the happiness of others, and hence that we could know the norm of good and evil without, and prior to, a knowledge of God. Hume sharpens the issue and indicates his own position.

> I wish from my heart, I could avoid concluding, that since morality, according to your opinion as well as mine, is determined merely by sentiment, it regards only human nature and human life. This has been often urged against you, and the consequences are very momentous. . . . If morality were determined by reason, that is the same to all rational beings: but nothing but experience can assure us, that the sentiments are the same. What experience have we with regard to superior beings? How can we ascribe to them any sentiments at all? They have implanted those sentiments in us for the conduct of life like our bodily sensations, which they possess not themselves.[23]

---

precisely as before" (*Treatise*, p. 251) in the sense that popular religious assent was not originally based on philosophical arguments and hence will not be immediately affected by criticism of a formally philosophical sort. Nevertheless, Hume recognizes that anyone who has digested his skeptical arguments in religion will be profoundly and permanently affected: "He will be found different" (*Dialogues*, p. 134). And in the long run, Hume hopes that his theory of man and religion will not only produce a total alteration in philosophy but will be embodied in general cultural forms, which will at last affect even the religious views of ordinary believers. His remarks about the social impact of Francis Hutcheson's moral philosophy also embody his wishes for his own philosophy. "I must own I am pleased to see such philosophy and such instructive morals to have once set their foot in the schools. I hope they will next go into the world, and then into the churches" (*Letters*, 1, 48).

23. *Letters*, 1, 40. Hume thinks that mystics transfer to God the moral sentiments found in their hearts, somewhat in the manner that the blind Scottish poet, Thomas Blacklock, supplies nonvisual imagery in order to use visual words meaningfully; see *Letters*, 1, 201.

If morality were based on some law of abstract reason, then it would have a universal significance and could be attributed in some way to God as well as man. Since we do conceive of mind or reason as belonging to God, there could be some community shared between God and man in regard to a reason-based morality. But Hutcheson and Hume sought the foundation of morality in our common human sentiments of approbation and disapprobation, in such fashion that the rational factor which intervenes is not abstract, universal reason, but a concrete reason thoroughly restricted to the operations and range of human sentiments.

Within a broadly theistic frame of reference, we may hold that our moral sentiments come ultimately from God, but they do so in the same way as do our sensations. In neither case does the causal admission of an ultimate divine origin warrant us to infer that God Himself possesses the qualities in question, whether sensations or sentiments. Only our experience could justify this inference concerning the being of God, and our experience does not encompass any direct acquaintance with a just, merciful, and provident God. Hence we have no natural and philosophical grounds for attributing moral sentiments to God, or for supposing that human moral sentiments include a significant reference of our moral conduct toward God, as the proponents of religion usually insist.

Thus, the difficulty which Hume had previously urged against the attribution of moral qualities to God is now expanded to apply to the view that human moral sentiments and duties depend upon some controlling religious belief, and involve some religious ordering of our everyday actions. Since we cannot discover any moral community of being between ourselves and God, we cannot regard the God-man relationship as the basis of morality or the proper source of any definite implications for influencing our moral judgments. We must rely upon the immanent human sources of moral conduct, rather than upon natural religious belief or a special religious revelation from God concerning His own reality and His ways with man.

Hume systematically reinforces this position concerning the mutual exclusion of the spheres of religion and morality by drawing the results of several independent lines of investigation into a common focus. He now makes explicit the convergent bearing upon the present issue of four points: the critique of speculative theism, the basis and range of the moral sentiments, the motivation of moral duties, and the observable effect of religious belief upon everyday attitudes. From every side, he adduces evidence against regarding the union of morality and religion as a truly beneficial state of affairs for man.

From his previous dissection of the weaknesses in *speculative theism*, Hume concludes that any attempt to base morality upon this intellectual argumentation would be disastrous. Natural theology is theoretically uncertain, because it tries to transcend experience with the help of principles which cannot be so stretched, without losing their ability to guide us concerning the real order. And it is useless in practical affairs, because of its failure to show the relevance of its discourse about the divine nature for our daily conduct.[24] Our moral life cannot afford to wait upon the efforts of natural theology to clarify its principles and shore up its arguments for God. Men must have some commonly available principles and grounds for moral judgment, quite apart from the sinuous arguments and controversies which form the tissue of natural theology. In point of fact, men do arrive constantly at their moral decisions and do mold their moral characters without knowledge of, or reliance upon, the several formal ways of establishing theism. Moral life does not await the outcome of theistic speculations in philosophy, or even the outcome of the agelong struggle between natural theology and skepticism.

There are both negative and positive grounds for maintaining the strictly *intra-human basis and range* of our moral sentiments. Hume regards the text in his first *Inquiry*, where he dissolves any necessary, rationally grounded connection between the design argument and morality, as being one of his most radical negative statements on the religious question. For here he breaks away from those moralists who would identify natural religion with morality. From the moral standpoint, there is no good reason for making this identification or for making the fate of morality hinge upon that of religion and design-based theism.

The issue is presented in terms of an imaginary speech of Epicurus to the Athenian people, in which he bases his preference of virtue over vice upon a direct examination of the course of events and our founded human experience, rather than upon an appeal to design, providence, and a system of sanctions in the other world.

> You tell me, indeed, that this disposition of things proceeds from intelligence and design. But whatever it proceeds from, the disposition itself, on which depends our happiness or misery, and consequently our conduct and deportment in life, is still the same. It is still open for me, as well as you, to regulate my behavior by my experience of past events. . . . The course of nature lies open to my contemplation as well as to theirs. The experienced train of events is

24. Cf. *Inquiry*, p. 151.

the great standard by which we all regulate our conduct. Nothing else can be appealed to in the field or in the senate. Nothing else ought ever to be heard of in the school or in the closet. . . . Nor have the political interests of society any connection with the philosophical disputes concerning metaphysics and religion.[25]

Both individual and social morality rest upon our human reflection on the steady disposition of things as they affect our happiness. There is no need to transcend the design in nature, since we can base our moral decisions upon those bonds between our sentiments, actions, and conditions of happiness which come within our direct experience and the constant testimony of human history.

The passions upon which our moral judgment rests arise from, and fundamentally concern only, our human condition of earthbound existence. The inner sentiments nourishing our moral convictions are wholly limited in origin and meaning to man's temporal situation, his drive for self-preservation, and the visible social circumstances which characterize his relations with other men. Moral reason is determined only by human nature and human life, as thus circumscribed. Not only in origin but also in norm and range of meaning, our moral convictions are in principle strictly confined to the course of nature, understood in this humane and purely this-worldly sense. This is an autonomous and self-sealed region, in respect to which any religious reference of our moral judgment to the norm of a powerful divine mind and its intentions for man must be regarded as an intrusion upon, and subversion of, the principles of moral living.

To strengthen the mutual isolation between the structures of morality and religion, Hume next makes a systematic contrast between the *duties and motivations* involved in these respective spheres. Moral obligation arises from the inclination of our own nature and the habitual connections established among the passions by individuals and social institutions. Virtuous conduct is prompted by these inclinations, and concerns itself only with the duties we owe to ourselves and to the society of men. In performing our moral duties, we feel that we are satisfying the demands of our own nature and the requirements of human social living, without invoking any other norms or motives. "The moral obligation, in our apprehension, removes all pretension to religious merit; and the virtuous con-

25. *Inquiry*, pp. 149, 151, 155.

duct is deemed no more than what we owe to society and to ourselves." [26]
This is a thoroughly nonreligious, secular obligation resting upon a feeling
of the internal bonds among men, a moral obligation which includes no
reference to God and which remains in force regardless of our belief
concerning God and religious teachings.

In pressing the argument for an independent morality, Hume does move
from defending its autonomy to showing its sharp contrast with *everyday
religious attitudes*. Hume portrays the religious agent as defining his
grounds of conduct by way of an opposition to the human sense of moral
obligation. The ordinary believer seeks to specify his religious actions as
those which are done for God's sake, without any reference to those
common moral motives concerning ourselves and our fellowmen.

> He considers not, that the most genuine method of serving the divin-
> ity is by promoting the happiness of his creatures. He still looks out
> for some more immediate service of the supreme Being, in order to
> allay those terrors, with which he is haunted. And any practice, rec-
> ommended to him, which either serves to no purpose in life, or offers
> the strongest violence to his natural inclinations; that practice he will
> the more readily embrace, on account of those very circumstances,
> which should make him absolutely reject it. It seems the more purely
> religious, because it proceeds from no mixture of any other motive
> or consideration.[27]

In drawing this rather severe portrait of the religious mind, Hume makes
use of the Jansenist and Quietist treatises of spirituality which interpret
the purity of religious motives to mean their opposition to all our human
inclinations and social interests.

As Hume describes him, the everyday religious believer is caught up in
an inhuman logic, in his effort to achieve a distinctively religious obligation and mode of conduct. The believer tries to achieve the religious
integrity of his actions, by construing their reference to God to mean
that they can include no other motives or considerations. The guarantee

26. *Natural History*, p. 72.
27. Ibid. Latent in this text is the possibility that a genuine religious service of God
may include the aim of furthering our human happiness, and thus include a moral
imperative toward mankind. But for religion to become a steady, effective principle of
conduct, there must be some historical revealed faith to stimulate our senses and
imagination, not merely the abstract natural religion of the deists and orthodox rationalists. See "The Sceptic," in *Essays Moral, Political and Literary*, pp. 169–70.

of the purity and merit of religious actions lies in their exclusion of any reference to man and any modes of satisfaction desired by the individual and civil society. The quest for religiously sanctioned meritorious conduct leads the believer to surrender his reliance on his own moral reflection and courage, his self-respect and regard for humanity. By the very nature of the case, therefore, an antithesis is generated between the conditions for moral integrity and those for religious service.

Taking religion as commonly found in the world and in popular works of spirituality, then, Hume concludes that its ultimate tendency is to "weaken extremely men's attachment to the natural motives of justice and humanity." [28] It diverts precious human attention and energy away from the great moral enterprises, concerned with happiness and social power in this life. Its stress upon the salvation of the individual dilutes the sympathy and responsibility which he should feel for other men, as well as the practice of the ordinary virtues required in human society. And Hume infers from his own experience with the Scottish kirk that religious emphasis upon themes of terror and melancholy, in connection with the divine will, tends to demoralize and render the individual unfit for making useful contributions and achieving a happy life in this world.

Because religious motives make an unfamiliar supernatural reference, they operate upon our actions only by fits and starts. And yet religion demands an attitude of steady devotion from believers. Thus it generates in them either a hypocritical discrepancy between their inner sentiments and their visible actions, or else an excessive meditation upon precisely those images of terror and strained relationship with God which unfit men for a steady moral engagement in human society. Hence in social and political affairs, Hume agrees with Bayle that "the utmost a wise magistrate can propose with regard to popular religions, is, as far as possible, to make a saving game of it, and to prevent their pernicious consequences with regard to society." The most prudent policy is to reduce the actual influence of popular religions to a safe minimum, both in individual lives and in the social order.

There remains a meaningful distinction, nevertheless, between severely restricting religion's scope in regard to morality and public power and

28. This and the following text are drawn from *Dialogues*, pp. 222, 223, where there are strong echoes of Bayle's plea for religious toleration in the neutral state. John B. Stewart, *The Moral and Political Philosophy of David Hume* (New York, 1963), pp. 277–87, notes that Hume recommends toleration as the best policy for preventing a division of the state along religious lines.

outrightly suppressing religion. In refusing to identify morality with natural religion, Hume approves of divesting particular religions and their laws of any civil sanction, yet without advocating the total uprooting of religion from the human mind. That he does not go to this extreme is indicated by several features of his treatment of the principles of morality and religion. He carefully qualifies the antithesis between them to signify only that there are disastrous moral consequences entailed by popular religion, which is equated with superstition and excessive practical zeal. This still leaves undetermined the nature of the philosopher's religion, and its relationship to private and public morality.

Furthermore, along with Edward Gibbon and the pagan observers of Christianity, Hume admits in several passages that popular religion often enkindles hope and charity in the souls of believers.[29] In its actual operation, then, popular religion does not always entail the antihumane consequences predicted by Hume. Religious melancholy is not unrelieved by hope, and religious preoccupation with the individual's salvation does not entirely shut out a loving concern for the condition of other people. Lest he concede too much at this point and thus blunt his own view of the essential properties of popular religion, however, Hume usually adds that these constructive and morally acceptable traits are generated somewhere outside of the religious principle, and are then incorporated into its working expression. It is not entirely clear whether the borrowing of these traits violates the nature and dynamism of popular religion or realizes some of its other potentialities, about which Hume remains silent in his determination to distinguish as emphatically as possible between morality and popular religion.

There is one last complication in this topic. Toward the end of the *Dialogues*, Cleanthes declares: "The proper office of religion is to regulate the heart of men, humanize their conduct, infuse the spirit of temperance, order, and obedience; and as its operation is silent, and only enforces the motives of morality and justice, it is in danger of being overlooked, and confounded with these other motives." To which cautious support of religion as a reinforcement for morality, Philo replies: "And so will all religion . . . except the philosophical and rational kind." [30]

29. See the ironical references in *Letters*, 1, 20–21, 189.

30. This exchange of views is made in *Dialogues*, p. 220. Hume also speaks informally about

the salutary consequences which result from true and genuine piety. The proper office of religion is to reform men's lives, to purify their hearts, to enforce all

The two reasons for Philo's failure to agree enthusiastically with Cleanthes are revealing. One reason rests on the distinction, discussed in the previous chapter, between the minimal and the maximal grounds for regarding the topic of religion as being philosophically important. Hume himself operates on the minimal basis of religion's close connection with human nature, without requiring that this connection be interpreted in a maximal way as signifying some indispensable contribution of religion to morality itself. His second point is that the contingent beneficial influence of popular religion furnishes no reliable principle for determining the nature of the philosopher's religion. We must now give separate consideration to this latter concept.

"THE PRIMARY PRINCIPLES OF GENUINE THEISM AND RELIGION"

The net result of Hume's treatment of natural religion might appear as entirely negative. His relentless critique would seem to be aimed at depriving religion of any reliable human basis, and thus at extirpating it from the human heart. Yet in point of fact, he never drew the latter conclusion, and had to bear some ridicule from his enlightened friends in France for failing to take this step.[31] His actual intent was not nihilistic, but rather a more complex effort to transfer the meaning and grounds of natural religion from their supposed basis in natural theology to the basis uncovered by his own theory of human nature. He sought to develop a philosophical theism which would specify, at the same time, the minimal religious belief open to the cautious philosopher of human experience. His revaluation of religion was brought to a climax with the threefold

---

moral duties, and to secure obedience to the laws and civil magistrate. While it pursues these useful purposes, its operations, though infinitely valuable, are secret and silent, and seldom come under the cognisance of history. (Draft Preface for vol. 2 of *History of Great Britain Under the House of Stuart*, quoted in Greig, *David Hume*, p. 217).

Hume cautions us, however, that he sometimes employs the word "religion" in its common usage, which really includes three distinct factors: prayer and devotion, morality, and speculative assent to the proposition about God's existence (*New Letters*, p. 13). He regards these components as being distinct from each other and not necessarily entailing each other. His reformed philosophical usage of "religion" is confined solely to the speculative assent to the proposition about God's existence.

31. Ibid., p. 72, n. 4. See Mossner's *Life of David Hume*, pp. 483–87, comparing Holbach's dogmatic atheism with Hume's moderate skepticism.

positive work of acknowledging the distinctive nature of religious assent, determining the philosophical meaning of theism and religion, and indicating the residual mystery involved in religious belief.

Distinctive Religious Assent.   Hume's critique of speculative and moral theology is a rigorous, yet indispensable, way of showing that religious belief has an intrinsic structure which resists reduction to natural theology, design speculation, and moral principles. Religious belief does not depend essentially upon a priori demonstration, upon the pious glosses made on Newtonian natural philosophy, or even upon moral reasoning and its consequences. It is a distinctive and irreducible response of human nature to man's situation in the world, a response which is evoked by our deepest passions of hope and fear, and which persists despite the fortunes of social institutions and theological systems.

In terms of the Humean analysis of perceptions, religious belief can be classed along with other complex ideas involving an imaginative synthesis of many strains of meaning. If nothing more than a complex idea, however, it could perhaps be dissolved or at least rendered quite ineffective by analysis into its components. This end might be achieved by showing that the simple ideas and impressions from which it is formed do not derive directly from any experience of a divine reality, and do not even provide a demonstrative basis for inferring anything about this reality.

But we are concerned here with a complex idea which is also a belief.[32] What is crucial for the religious mind is its way of entertaining and interpreting the impressions and ideas which comprise our experience of the changing, visible world. The mind does not meet this situation passively, and merely for the sake of registering and conforming with it. The encounter is an active one, since man comes to grips with the world through the mediation of his concrete intelligence, working along with his hopes and fears. From this integration of our worldly experience with our human aspirations for happiness, we have the natural propensity to believe in a powerful, minded cause of the world to which we can gain access through prayer and cultic acts. Thus religious belief is sufficiently complex to include the strong impressions of reflection which express our passional response to the world, together with that lifting up of the human heart to a superior power, in which it puts its trust.

It is axiomatic with Hume that no natural propensity is infallibly

---

32. See C. W. Hendel, *Studies in the Philosophy of David Hume* (new ed. Indianapolis, 1963), p. 439.

reliable and beyond philosophical criticism, even when we feel its powerful tug within ourselves. Hence his act of rebasing religion upon a natural propensity to seek divine aid, in coping with the world and achieving happiness beyond the world's satisfactions and terrors, is not intended to make religious belief immune to criticism. Indeed, there is no other effective way for him to bring to light one further aspect of religious belief than by submitting it to as radical and persistent a skeptical inspection as his philosophy can devise. Only after he submits it to this treatment, can he establish experientially that religious belief remains vital in some form, even in a skeptically disciplined mind. Even after undergoing the skeptical cleansing, some belief in God remains and is not diminished as much as might reasonably be expected.

To Holbach and other atheistic friends of Hume, the reasonable expectation was that, upon exposure of the frailties and fallacies involved in natural theology and upon presentation of an areligious moral humanism as the social ideal, religious belief would shrivel up and disappear. It was freely predicted that this result would follow at least for those honest minds who gave sufficient time, study, and reflection to the problem of the intellectual standing of theism. But Hume's own experience ran counter to this prediction, even though he did not care to give any comfort to the proponents of traditional theism and the institutional forms of religion.[33] One's assent to God's reality may be deprived of many customary supports in argument, without thereby being annihilated or reduced merely to an uncommonly stubborn social custom, destined for eventual disappearance.

Its persistence may perhaps be interpreted abstractly as a sign of the totally noncognitive basis of religious belief, but this view does not do justice to Hume's complex study of the passional sources of belief. The skeptically educated person may still find himself passionately inquiring

33. All our inference [from design in nature to God] is founded on the similitude of the works of nature to the usual effects of the mind. Otherwise they must appear a mere chaos. The only difficulty is, why the other dissimilitudes do not weaken the argument. And indeed it would seem from experience and feeling, that they do not weaken it so much as we might naturally expect. A theory to solve this would be very acceptable. (*Letters*, 1, 157)

In the Introduction to his edition of Hume's *Dialogues*, pp. 73–74, N. K. Smith suggests the explanation that we require time and reflection before we can grasp the force of skeptical objections. But Hume's point is that neither the experience of evil nor the lesson of skepticism entirely eliminates a postcritical residual belief in a divine mind beyond nature.

about the orderly aspects of the natural world, believing that they indicate the powerful presence of some transnatural mind, and assenting to the reality of this powerful superior mind, even across the chastening experience of skeptical objections. Unlike the natural theologians and proponents of the proof from design, he will not claim to have demonstrative, scientific knowledge about God. But he will recognize some grounds within his own questioning nature, and within the visible world, for believing in the divine reality and power.

A man who has been formed by Hume's philosophy of human nature finds it impossible to remain either an untroubled dogmatist in religious matters or an untroubled skeptic, whose judgment is permanently neutralized and deprived of theistic belief. He gives a cautious and highly qualified assent to the religious reference of human life, not as being a religious hypothesis established on purely scientific and impersonal grounds, but as a belief generated by his own passionate search for happiness and his anxious scrutiny of the aspects of design in nature which are open to our ordinary experience, philosophical speculation, or scientific research. "A purpose, an intention, or design strikes everywhere the most careless, the most stupid thinker; and no man can be so hardened in absurd systems, as at all times to reject it." [34] Although this belief cannot be converted into a metaphysically or scientifically demonstrated certitude, and cannot insure any moral qualities in God or in human conduct, it does constitute a characteristic mode of human response to our existence in this world. Religious belief discloses something permanent about the nature of the human mind and its environing being.

Philosophical Reform of Theism and Religion. When Hume maintains that the conscientious philosopher can never be quite the same for having reflected upon the Humean theory of religion, he means to say more than that a skeptical disciplining of the mind permits no return to the naive immediate condition of religious belief. His further point is that the mind which reflects comprehensively upon both the propensity to believe and the limits placed upon the grounds of belief by skeptical challenge will emerge with a transformed view of theism and religion themselves, in their minimal yet viable human meanings. This accounts for Hume's careful procedure of suggesting that his critique enables the religious mind to subordinate both popular belief and skeptical suspension of

34. *Dialogues*, p. 214.

assent to a new, philosophically valid position concerning man's relation to God.

Thus the entire investigation of the passional basis of religion in the *Natural History* is ordered toward the discovery of "the primary principles of genuine theism and religion." [35] And at two dramatic turns in the discussion in the *Dialogues*, similar qualifications are duly entered, distinguishing Hume's minimal theism from more luxuriant growths. Before plunging into his criticism of the use made of the principle of analogy by incautious Newtonians, Philo remarks:

> All the new discoveries in astronomy, which prove the immense grandeur and magnificence of the works of nature, are so many additional arguments for a Deity, according to the true system of theism: But according to your hypothesis of experimental theism, they become so many objections, by removing the effect still farther from all resemblance to the effect of human art and contrivance.[36]

Hence the inconveniences of the appeal to analogy, as incorporated within an experimental theism that claims to be giving scientific proof of a religious hypothesis, cannot properly be charged against a theistic philosophy employing analogy and design apart from the scientizing model of proof.

An even more striking differentiation is made at the very end of the *Dialogues*, after Philo has ruthlessly spelled out the opposition between morality and a religion of the superstitious or enthusiastic sort.

> True religion, I allow, has no such pernicious consequences: But we must treat of religion, as it has commonly been found in the world; nor have I any thing to do with that speculative tenet of theism, which, as it is a species of philosophy, must partake of the beneficial influence of that principle, and at the same time must lie under a like inconvenience, of being always confined to very few persons.

The philosopher of religion cannot remain satisfied with the popular forms of religion. He tries to determine a true conception of religion guided by a speculatively sound tenet of theism, which can survive the most severe skeptical questioning and also be compatible with a morality unfounded in religion and unoriented toward it.

35. *Natural History*, p. 21.
36. This quotation and the next are from *Dialogues*, pp. 165, 223.

Just as we found it advisable in the last chapter to make a critical review of the several Humean meanings for "natural religion," so will we find it helpful now to sort out Hume's different uses of the term "theism." As the following table indicates, he makes a close correlation between the forms of theism and those of religion.

POPULAR THEISM	
Religious monotheism	*Realm of popular religion and its intellectual reflections*
Satellite religious theology, dependent on religious monotheism	
Uncritical philosophical theism, based on the a priori, design, and moral arguments for God	
CRITICAL PHILOSOPHICAL THEISM	
"Genuine theism," or the probable speculative assent to God within Hume's framework of philosophy	*Realm of the philosopher's religion, regulated by critical theism*
"True religion," or the purified religious response to God which confines itself within the speculative limits of Hume's doctrine on God and human belief	

Hume's entire analysis of the various theories about God and the modes of religion is ordered toward achieving the passage of reflective minds from popular theism to his own critical position, and thus from popular religious belief to his own philosophical kind.

In its broad generic usage, theism is equivalent in Hume's writings to *religious monotheism*. This is the most prominent meaning found in his theory on the passional sources of religion, where the representative theistic outlook is being distinguished from polytheism and animism. In this descriptive and genetic context, theism is the popular religious way of expressing belief in the one supreme God. It is not so much a theoretical content as a practical affirmation of the uniqueness of the divine reality and the corresponding restriction of human worship to the one God.

Both polytheism and monotheism, but especially the latter, lead eventually to a relatively *abstract theology*, justifying the original religious belief and reconciling it with discordant features in everyday experience.[37] Having resolutely placed aside every claim about the truth of a revela-

37. *Natural History*, pp. 53–65.

tion, Hume views these theologies solely as refinements of the passional
drives in man, as intellectual reflections of the original alternation between polytheistic and monotheistic religious outlooks. Their sole function is to reformulate the religious state of soul in abstract terms and to
provide it with a justifying framework, adapted to the general level of
cultural understanding and explanatory concepts. In every historical period, then, popular theism includes both the monotheistic religious belief
and its satellite religious theology. The theological system which reflects
popular monotheistic religion belongs to the working connotation of
"theism," as Hume employs the term.

The next major meaning of theism is furnished by the main arguments
used to develop a natural theology, or philosophical theory of God and
of man's bond with Him. They constitute the *uncritical philosophical
theism* whose various forms are examined in the *Dialogues*. Hume's
interest in this type of theism is not confined to his formal study of the
principles of reasoning employed in the a priori metaphysical theory of
God, the design argument of experimental theism—one mode of uncritical philosophical theism—and the moral approach. He realizes that
his criticism will not entirely remove these natural theologies from the
scene, and hence he is obliged to look beyond the formal arguments to
their other sources of support. His aim is to suggest a broader sense in
which this kind of theism is uncritical.

In the face of skeptical objections, Hume accounts for the continued
popularity of the several philosophies of God by the hypothesis that they
are covertly allied with, and dependent upon, popular religious theism.
Although the natural theologians claim to be elaborating a doctrine on
God purely from the evidence available to natural reason, apart from
the commitment of faith and religious practice, they are in fact engaged
in defending a set of theses about God which harmonize with, and in the
final analysis derive from, popular religious theism. Whether they are
aware of it or not, their philosophizing is really a form of abstract apology
for monotheistic religion, and derives its vitality and definite direction
from this subterranean basis.[38] It is little wonder, then, that such a
typical philosophical theology as Samuel Clarke's should turn out to be
only a restatement, in rationalistic language, of the dogmatic theological
treatise on the one God and of some other tenets in the Christian creed.
Hume regards such a defense of philosophical theism as being radically
uncritical as it is allied with some form of Christian theology.

38. Ibid., p. 54.

It is only by contrast with these popular meanings of theism that Hume can now give a definite sense to his own normative kind of theism. His *critical philosophical theism* is monotheistic, but it does not derive merely from the process of a dialectical refining of polytheism under the pressure of fear and adulation. It takes into account the intellectual developments of mankind, especially the work of philosophers in achieving a unified view of nature, and the work of modern scientists in conceiving the unity of nature in terms of mechanical and organic models. In the wake of these interpretations of our direct experience of the world, it is likely that there is one supreme mind shaping the forces of nature. This likelihood is tempered, but not destroyed, by considering the contrary evidences of counterpurpose, evil, and randomness in the world. The genuine theism which Hume seeks is speculative rather than moral, and is a posteriori or experiential rather than a priori in its speculation.

The core of human reflection on nature can be recovered and integrated within a critical theistic framework by relating it methodically to three points, which the Newtonians tend to ignore. First, there is a gulf between the scientific evidence showing the presence of order *in* nature and the theistic interpretation of that evidence, as manifesting an order or design established *for* nature by a powerful mind existing apart from nature. Second, the inference required to bridge this gulf is not based solely on physical principles but draws strength and direction from man's passional drives, the transcending movement of his being toward happiness, and the propensity to believe in an ordering power shaping all natural events and human situations. And finally, the theoretical basis of the inference lies in the principle of analogy, which alone cannot prove the existence of the divine maker and His attributes. This does not preclude the use of the analogy between the universe and a work of art, but it does require the thinker to include an explicit statement of the weaknesses in analogical reasoning and the purely probable character of any conclusions about God to which it leads us. In a functional definition, then, Hume's genuine philosophical theist is one who constantly bears in mind that these three qualifications essentially condition his acceptance of the idea of a powerful maker of the universe.

The truly critical philosophical theist is not governed by the aim of reaching a compromise between popular theism and skepticism, since his theory is determined by his own experiential approach to human nature. Nevertheless, his minimal position does enable him to stress the common features in both the popular and the skeptical approaches to God.

On the specific issue of the analogy between God and an intelligent human artisan, "the theist allows, that the original intelligence is very different from human reason: The atheist allows, that the original principle of order bears some remote analogy to it." [39]

Hume does not conclude that there should be a featureless amalgamation of the two viewpoints, even though he uncovers their tendency toward a minimal convergence. But he does require his critical theism to incorporate the best features in each position and transcend their weaknesses. It stresses the differences between the divine mind and human reason, without suppressing every assent to the former's reality, as is done in atheism. Hume's philosophical approach to God also acknowledges the role of the natural propensity to believe in a transcendent ordering principle, without surrendering the rational function of tracing that propensity to its human sources and rigorously limiting its influence upon our study of order in the world—a discipline which theists are usually reluctant to embrace.

The last and perhaps most difficult task of this philosophical reform of theism is to determine its precise relationship with religion. Each of Hume's steps in criticism of the ordinary meanings of natural religion is a contribution to this end. If religion is understood in the six meanings which come under his investigation, then his philosophical theism involves a reform of the connotation of religion itself and leads to a new view of what is philosophically warranted in this sphere.

That Hume's critical revision of theism as a speculative tenet is closely correlated with a revision of the meaning of religion is evident from his treatment of the problem of morality and religion. The purpose of his criticism is not only to cut the ground from under the project of regulating a philosophy of God by its supposed bond with our moral life, but also to prepare the way for a sharply retrenched conception of religion itself. Natural theology must be restricted to the bare probable inference to the existence of a powerful mind as the principle of order in nature, and religion must be restricted to a speculative assent to the conclusion about God and His natural attributes. We make no commitment to His moral attributes, and draw no moral consequences for our conduct from the speculative assent given to His existence and natural attributes of mind, power, and ordering activity.

Hume is gradually bringing about an equivalence between his reformed philosophical theism and a philosophically reformed conception of reli-

39. *Dialogues*, p. 218.

gion. He does not want the latter to realize itself in human life beyond the boundaries set in a critical way by the former. The *philosopher's mode of religion* is precisely that which confines itself deliberately to the act of giving a probable speculative assent to an ordering cosmic mind, while scrupulously refraining from drawing any practical consequences, on religious grounds, about what we should do or avoid doing in daily life. "To know God, says Seneca, is to worship him. All other worship is indeed absurd, superstitious, and even impious." [40] Our natural propensity to believe becomes "true religion," only when it accepts this discipline of confining itself to the probable inference and the purely speculative assent contained in Hume's genuine theism. Thus the transition from popular religion to philosophically accredited religion turns out to be the same as that from uncritical forms of theism to a critically warranted philosophical theism.

The Humean religion is itself a species or application of the philosophy of human nature and nothing more. Hume is under no illusions that his rarefied notion of genuine theism and religion will ever become widely accepted. A philosophically reformed religion is viable only for a few reflective minds. He is also aware that even the most critical philosopher is a man who remains vulnerable, in the religious order as well as elsewhere, to the buffeting waves of unrestrained skepticism and to counter-waves of unrestrained belief. Hence he requires only that the plain philosophical assent of religious knowledge and worship be given at those times when the inquiring mind actually considers the entire human context for the theistic inference and actually entertains the resultant proposition about God.

Hume's philosophical theism can be best described as an ever-renewed effort to bring into a unified reflection all the relevant forces in human nature, and all the critical principles in theistic reasoning, required for understanding and disciplining religious belief. Such an effort is complex, difficult to achieve and hold in focus, and unfitted for becoming a habitual principle of thought and action. And yet its purifying influence is necessary in any aspiration to a philosophically grounded religious attitude.

The Mystery of Religious Belief. Hume also realizes that his notion of a philosophically retrenched religion will leave a feeling of dissatisfaction in everyone, whether philosopher or ordinary believer. This is due to the

40. Ibid., p. 226. Hence in *New Letters*, p. 11, Hume classifies as atheistic those who think that God can be moved by prayers and sacrifices to perform acts of particular providence in their own favor.

fact that the propensity toward religious belief arises from some mighty passions, which themselves are ordered toward action and the shaping of human conduct. Yet philosophical criticism imposes such restrictions upon the cognitive content of this belief that the conscientious inquirer cannot permit it to function as a practical principle, governing his moral judgment and conduct. By the nature of the religious situation, then, there is a disproportion and tension between our aspirations toward transcendence and religious action and our ability to validate them in terms of a rational reflection upon experience and human nature.

Out of this unavoidable tension springs our human desire for some direct communication from God Himself, some good word revealing Him to be morally concerned about our welfare and providentially engaged in furnishing us with definite supernatural means of achieving salvation. We have a natural desire for receiving a revelation from God, so that we may participate somehow in His eternal life and power, and thus overcome the limits of a philosophically reformed theism and religion. The search for the revealing God is made understandable and cast into sharper relief by the very restrictions which Hume places upon a philosophical theism and religious assent.

After outlining the highly circumscribed religious assent permitted by the experimental philosophy of human nature, Philo brings the *Dialogues* to a conclusion with these enigmatic words.

> But believe me, CLEANTHES, the most natural sentiment, which a well-disposed mind will feel on this occasion, is a longing desire and expectation, that Heaven would be pleased to dissipate, at least alleviate, this profound ignorance, by affording some more particular revelation to mankind, and making discoveries of the nature, attributes, and operation of the divine object of our Faith. A person, seasoned with a just sense of the imperfections of natural reason, will fly to revealed truth with the greatest avidity: While the haughty dogmatist, persuaded that he can erect a complete system of theology by the mere help of philosophy, disdains any farther aid, and rejects this adventitious instructor. To be a philosophical sceptic is, in a man of letters, the first and most essential step towards being a sound, believing Christian.[41]

41. *Dialogues*, pp. 227–28. For a study of Hume's pervasive irony, culminating in his attitude toward religion, see J. V. Price, *The Ironic Hume* (Austin, University of Texas Press, 1966).

One point in this much disputed text is unequivocal: a design-based theism cannot make good on its claim to establish all the truths of theology, natural and revealed. To see its failure on this score is a condition for looking for religious truths which do come from divine revelation and not from philosophical speculation. In this sense, the skeptical critique of natural theology and Newtonian theism clears the air for any believer seeking to enlarge his religious faith beyond the minimum permitted by Hume's critical theism. He will have to look directly to the revealing presence of God and the correlative act of faith rather than to human reasoning, whose incapacity to inform about the moral nature and providential will of God is emphasized by Hume.

There is an ironical overtone in this passage, however, when it is pressed to mean that a skeptical reconsideration of theism not only removes confusions and unwarranted claims but positively inclines the inquirer to accept some specific doctrines as being revealed, and some means of grace as being truly given to us by God. Hume's philosophy provides no grounds for maintaining that our expectation of a divine revelation can be known to be actually fulfilled. His critique of miracle is intended to remove the main avenue whereby such a conclusion could be reached, in terms that are compatible with a philosophy based upon the events experienced in the course of nature and human testimony. Hume is not continuing the strategy of Pascal and fideistic skeptics, who stress the weakness of human reason and the narrowness of human experience in order to prepare for the acceptance of faith on a supernatural basis.[42] Nor is he simply a forerunner of Hamann and Kierkegaard, who prepare for faith by stressing its paradoxical and transcendent relationship with philosophical reason.

Rather, he is drawing another and more uncomfortable lesson here from the fideists' view that supernatural faith contravenes our natural understanding, that its accompanying miracles violate the course of visible nature and the common experience of mankind, and that human nature is inclined by its passions in a counterdirection to the life of grace. His

---

42. In *David Hume* (Paris, 1953), pp. 308–09, A. Leroy remarks that Hume's religious skepticism differs from that of the Christian fideists on three counts: it is not directed toward arousing an act of supernatural faith; it does not abase human reason and experience in order to make way for revelation; and it does not keep religion and philosophy entirely apart, as it allows for a philosophical species of religion. Leroy goes on to identify the latter with a sincere and forceful manner of moral reflection and adherence to moral obligations, but Hume keeps his philosophical religion rigidly distinct in principle from morality.

inference is that, on this reckoning, the order of supernatural faith is un-
connected with, and totally disruptive of, that human nature which it
claims to heal and elevate. This is a faith which remains both unassimilable to the principles of natural belief and antagonistic toward them.
Thus there can be no knowable conception of how to relate man with
the purported revelation, no way of conceiving a harmony between the
natural propensity toward religious belief and supernatural faith, and no
way of reconciling the assent to such a message with human understanding, experience, and religious aspiration. Such a Christian religion seems
to Hume to be actively annihilative of the very principles in man which
could make its acceptance a humanly perfective act.

He is driven back, therefore, to his own philosophy of human nature
for his final evaluation of religious belief. Surveying his entire analysis of
man's religious life, Hume asks himself one question: "Who can explain
the heart of man?" and gives a modest reply. "The whole is a riddle, an
enigma, an inexplicable mystery." [43] Whenever Hume mentions mystery
in a religious context, his words carry several connotations. At the lowest
level, they have the value of social insurance—whenever he deems it
advisable to carry some—against the tempers raised by his treatment of
religious topics. In addition, the mention of mystery conveys a note of
irony, especially when Hume combines a remark about how revelation
transcends our reason with a piece of advice to the prudent philosopher
about escaping from religious controversies to the region of cool analysis
of human phenomena. The implication is that supernatural faith transcends human reason by contradicting it, not by elevating and perfecting
it. But there is a third level of significance usually found in Hume's talk
about religious mystery, namely, that some aspects of human nature can
be adumbrated, but not fathomed, by his analysis of religion.

Hume succeeds in hominizing religion, that is, rooting it in the tenden-

43. *Dialogues*, p. 221; *Natural History*, p. 76. R. J. Butler, "Natural Belief and the
Enigma of Hume," *Archiv für Geschichte der Philosophie*, 42 (1960), 90–100, locates the enigma in our expansion of natural belief about design in nature into a
belief about a designing mind for nature, since the expansion is not a regular inference
but a broadening of our way of looking at the world. Another aspect of the mystery
of natural religious belief is, however, that it deeply affects our self-experience and
our conception of human nature, even after Hume systematically reduces its scope.
James Noxon, "Hume's Agnosticism," *Philosophical Review*, 73 (1964), 248–61,
argues that Hume himself reaches complete agnosticism early in his career and thereafter is simply explaining the phenomenon of other people's religious belief. But the
religious problem is never completely objectified and settled for him.

cies of human passion and understanding. And yet in trying to explore religion's meaning and basis in man, "we are like foreigners in a strange country." [44] For it makes us taste directly of our mixed condition of being, where light and darkness constantly intermingle and where the human response is always one of groping, combined with firm assent. Religious belief is a fitting act of our concrete understanding, which does not usually attain to the sunlight of essential definitions and ideal connections, but which must be content to operate in "that glimmering light, with which we are environed" in our exploration of the world of existential fact.[45] Under the actual conditions of persistent, postanalytical obscurity and uncertainty, our passional and imaginative self requires religious belief as one mode of interpreting this world of human events and natural order. Although the philosopher must subject the religious interpretation to severe criticism in regard to its cognitive evidences and principles of inference, it is purified rather than eradicated by the examination.

Fundamentally, the mystery of religious belief means for Hume its function of disclosing, in a concrete way, the drive of the human self toward transcendence. Both the human and the divine poles of the religious relationship tend to elude the dominant concepts of Hume's philosophy, and thus to emphasize an unfathomable aspect of reality which is being concretely symbolized, although not analytically understood, by the religious man. Religion gives convergent importance to man considered as a unified personal self, at a level not constituted entirely by the forces of custom; it orients the human self toward God considered also as an active personal agent, who harmonizes the real forces in nature with the real tendencies and aspirations of our human nature; and thereby it calls attention to some aspects in nature and man which involve a real causal efficacy and a real continuity in time and action.[46]

On all these points, Hume encounters difficulties in his general philosophy of human nature that prevent him from making a thorough pene-

44. *Dialogues*, p. 135.
45. *Natural History*, p. 65.
46. Gilles Deleuze, *Empirisme et subjectivité: Essai sur la nature humaine selon Hume* (Paris, 1953), pp. 72–78, points the path toward Kant by suggesting that there is a regulative cognitive function for the Humean conception of religion, since it enables us to think of God as the source of the finality or harmony between the habits and inferences of man and the course of physical nature. This may throw some light on Hume's obscure reference to "a kind of pre-established harmony between the course of nature and the succession of our ideas," as well as to "the ordinary wisdom of nature" (*Inquiry*, pp. 67, 68).

tration of the personal, mutually active, and causally efficacious traits of the religious relationship. And yet he also acknowledges that the religious tendency in man keeps these aspects alive and meaningful for our passional life and our concrete imagery. Themes which seem to become dissolved by skeptical criticism in the Humean theory of knowledge are nevertheless quickened again, at least in a descriptive way, in the Humean theory of religion and what it signifies about the interpretative mind of man. A zone of mystery remains after the anatomist has completed his charts.

Hume concludes all of his essays about religion on a peculiar note of internal frustration, of discord between what religion demands and what his philosophy will permit it to achieve in human life. He readily concedes that the religious tendency in man searches for more than his philosophy of human nature considers to be reasonable and realizable through individual human resources. Men stand ready to welcome and respond to the revealing, saving presence of God. The hopeful expectation of religious initiative from the revealing God will be diversely interpreted by the Humean philosopher of human nature and by the man of supernatural faith. The former will regard it as a longing for which there is no rational evidence of its being fulfilled, or even fulfillable, within the horizon of human experience and history. The latter will feel challenged to show how the further reach of religious faith can be related meaningfully and perfectively to the nature and historical experience of man. Thus Hume leaves us with an ambivalence concerning the sense in which religious belief directs man not only toward the transcendence of God but also toward an expectation of His personal nearness, in a revealed truth and way of living. The various strands in the religious condition of men do not get interwoven into a neat and comprehensive pattern. In their resistance to such integration consists the ultimate mystery of religion for Hume.[47]

47. G. J. Nathan, "Hume's Immanent God," in *Hume: A Collection of Critical Essays*, ed. V. C. Chappell (New York, 1966), pp. 396–423, argues for an identification of nature with God, as an internal impersonal principle of order and rationality immanent in the universe. But this converts Hume's skeptical counterhypotheses into dogmatic theses.

3

The Kantian Reversal of Speculative Theology

Immanuel Kant always expressed gratitude for his moral and religious upbringing at home. From his Pietist parents, he learned that the religious spirit brings an unfailing note of joy and tranquillity into daily life, especially when it is based upon a careful performance of duties and an attitude of forbearance toward other men. In addition, his mother opened his mind and sensibility to the religious significance of the natural world, when it is approached in the context of faith in the creative and provident God. These religious values remained with him, even after his schooling in the Pietist center at Königsberg made him disaffected with Pietism, as a stern regimen of life and an intellectual system in compromise with rationalism. In his maturity, Kant withdrew entirely from the public expression of religion in official services and prayers, because they presented an occasion for hypocrisy and neglect of moral obligations in this world. But he neither withdrew his assent from a personal theism free from these defects nor ceased to investigate the intellectual problems of religion, insofar as they were touched by his own philosophical ideas.

One of the indelible lessons which he learned during his precritical period was that his philosophical questioning was bound to affect religion and theology, as well as the areas of natural science, metaphysics, and ethics.[1] Kant's early writings touched upon such religiously sensitive issues

1. A general view of Kant's philosophy of religion as constituting the climax of his practical philosophy is furnished in Friedrich Delekat's *Immanuel Kant* (Heidelberg, 1963), pp. 340–78, as well as in the Introductions by T. M. Greene and J. R. Silber to Kant's *Religion Within the Limits of Reason Alone*, trans. T. M. Greene and H. H. Hudson (rev. Torchbook ed. New York, Harper, 1960). This book will be referred to as *Religion*.

as the basis of proof for demonstrating God's existence, the tension between mechanism and teleology in the study of natural order, the manner in which the divine power and goodness and glory can be manifested in nature, and the question of whether disasters such as the Lisbon earthquake can shake the belief in providence and optimism. He found himself in close agreement with Rousseau on the need for a foundation of religion upon the moral personality. Just as he sought to transfer the model of philosophical reasoning from pure mathematics to Newtonian natural philosophy, so also did he seek to transfer the natural basis of religious convictions from metaphysical and physical reasoning to the soil of our personal, moral life. This latter transition was reinforced by the summer lectures on Oriental religions which Kant delivered throughout his teaching career. He found that he could best understand these religions by considering the moral qualities and relationships which they fostered or hindered in man.

During the tremendously productive decade of 1780–90, which saw the publication of the three *Critiques*, the problem of the intellectual foundations of natural religion was never far from the center of Kant's mind. He read Hamann's manuscript translation of Hume's *Dialogues* in 1780, and was sufficiently impressed by the force of Hume's criticism of the design argument to follow a similar line of objection in the final version of the *Critique of Pure Reason*. The section in that *Critique* dealing with the dialectical difficulties in all forms of speculative theology made a threefold contribution to the Kantian theory of religion. It removed the speculative claims to demonstrate the divine existence; it called attention to the distinctive task of determining a coherent meaning for the idea of God, or the divine attributes; and it prepared the way for the transition from a speculative to a practical foundation of the whole theory of God. This refounding was achieved in the *Critique of Practical Reason,* one of whose major aims was to regulate our religious relationship by the requirements of moral theism. The religious use of purposive judgment was considered in the *Critique of Judgment,* which placed some strict limits upon the efforts to discern God's beneficent presence in nature.

Throughout the same decade, Kant gave a regular series of lectures on natural religion or the philosophical theory of religion. He sketched in popular form the several types of philosophical theology and his own criticism of the arguments for God's existence contained therein. To the theologians who attended his course, he suggested that his critical theory of religion entailed a more rigorous interpretation of revealed religion itself. At a more technical level, Kant filled his manuscript notebooks with detailed commentaries on the sections in Alexander Baumgarten's *Metaphysics* dealing with the existence and attributes of God. In the midst of these commentaries, he inserted a very long analysis of J. A. Eberhard's widely used manual, *Preparation for Natural Theology*, which synthesized the state of university opinion around 1781 on the philosophical study of God and religion. The editors of the Prussian Academy edition of Kant's writings have added to the evidence of his preoccupation with such issues by gathering together a broad selection of Kant's private reflections on religion, including the annotations in his Luther Bible.

Thus Kant had served a long apprenticeship before issuing his main work in the philosophy of religion: *Religion Within the Limits of Reason Alone* (1793). In preparation for his discussion of good and evil, natural and revealed religion, and morality and revelation, he did more than consult his own previous writings and his old Königsberg catechism. He also drew upon the theological manuals of his Pietist teacher, F. A. Schultz, and especially upon the twelve-volume *Foundation for the True Religion* by the Swiss Calvinist theologian, J. F. Stapfer. Kant found their emphasis upon moral sincerity, the struggle with evil, and personal rebirth, much more congenial to his own view of religion than the historical-philological approach, which was then being taken by his theological colleagues in the German universities. In all his discussions with the theological and ecclesiastical establishment, Kant found it advisable (as did Hamann and Kierkegaard, under similar circumstances) to focus even more explicitly on the personal act of belief and its practical fruit.

Despite the difficulties raised by official censors, Kant persisted in religious inquiries throughout his last years. His provocatively titled essay, *On the Failure of All Philosophical Attempts in Theodicy* (1791), helped to break the dialectical stalemate between Leibniz and Hume by transferring the focus of attention from the divine attributes, taken as deductive premises, to the experienced manner in which religious men do endure evil and retain a sincere faith in the good God. *The End of All Things* (1794) represented Kant's main contribution to philosophical eschatology, with a special stress upon the religious importance of love and hope. At the end of *The Metaphysics of Morals* (1797), he pointed out that the older ethical treatment of religion, as a set of duties owed in justice to God, would have to be transformed in the light of his critical reconstruction of ethics. The educational implications of his approach were explored in the first part of *The Strife of the Faculties* (1798), where he defended the freedom of philosophy to make its own examination of the meaning of religion and revelational sources against any encroachments from either the state or the theological faculty. And in those last manuscript annotations which we now call the *Opus Postumum*, the aged Kant continued to raise the most radical questions on the nature and human worth of religion, always looking for more satisfactory leads than he himself had been able to furnish in his great critical writings.

A WORLDLY THEORY OF RELIGION

Kant subscribes firmly to the maxim that a person's theory of religion is determined by his conception of the nature, aim, and method of philosophy. In one respect, his own conception fits into the tradition of those philosophers who, from Plato to Wittgenstein, regard their task as a therapeutic one. The intellectual malady to be cured by philosophy is variously described by these thinkers. Kant gives it the dramatic name of "cyclopism," a term which frequently appears when he is discussing the meaning of philosophy and the state of mind and soul for which philosophy provides the soundest therapy.[2]

Cyclopism is a disease of civilized men, who find that they can make notable advances in knowledge and the control of nature only by concentrating all of their energy and skill upon particular fields of research. Specialization of studies is the intellectual condition making possible the scientific, social, and artistic explorations which constitute the peculiar glory of the modern mind. As in the case of every other instrument of human progress, however, there is a serious risk involved in specialized research and activity, although men gladly accept it in view of the continued release of creativity in modern societies. The danger is that the total dedication of mind required for making any significant advances in one area will quite unfit the participating researchers for appreciating other approaches and other kinds of generalization. They are apt to dry up the vision in "the other eye," the one which should keep them aware of, and sympathetic toward, the viewpoint of others and the common concerns of humanity.

There is not the slightest trace of intellectual Ludditism discoverable in Kant's diagnosis of the cyclopic attitude. He does not recommend any

2. Kant, *Introduction to Logic*, trans. T. K. Abbott (New York, Philosophical Library, 1963), p. 36.

slackening in the pace of scientific investigation and technological control, social development and creativity in the arts. Rather, his purpose is to show, as relevantly to our culture as possible, the need and distinctive function for philosophy. In modern cultural terms, its work is to over-come cyclopism by securing the presence of another line of vision, which will always seek out the convergent human significance in our particular perspectives.

In each mode of experience, the philosopher must ask: What is its bearing upon man and his life in our natural world? This key question sets the condition under which a theory of religion is elaborated within the Kantian framework. Like every other human activity, religion can engage our energies and interests in a cyclopic fashion, so that we tend to get lost in it and become insensitive to the methods and values of other human occupations. Here as everywhere else, the duty of the philosopher is to inquire about the general human significance of religion, along with the specific means of integrating it with our other modern concerns and achievements. Kant will propose a critical theory of religion, in order to bring the religious outlook into an intelligible relationship with his other major interpretations of experience through science, morality, and art.

He draws a basic contrast between the impersonally developed school philosophy of the Wolffian systematizers and his own worldly philosophy, or mundane wisdom.[3] The school philosophy fails to respect the vital concern of all our reasoning with the elucidation of man's own condition. But Kantian philosophy acquires its worldly character precisely from the constitutive question directed against cyclopism: How does a particular area of experience and intellectual achievement bear upon man and his relation with the world? Only by accepting this complex specification of itself as a study of man-in-the-natural-world, can philosophy avoid the two extremes of rhapsody (a purely subjectivist sort of humanism, without the discipline of the natural sciences) and school thinking (an objectivism centered upon an abstract system or upon the scientific world, at the expense of what is distinctively human). It is not surprising that Jaspers and Heidegger—the existentialist philosophers for whom the theme of man in the world looms so large—have been careful readers of Kant, in

3. Kant, *Critique of Pure Reason*, trans. N. K. Smith (New York, Macmillan, 1933), A 838–39:B 866–67 (pp. 657–58); *Logic*, pp. 14–15. The importance of this contrast for the theory of religion is noted by Johannes Franken, *Kritische Philosophie und dialektische Theologie* (Amsterdam, 1952), pp. 211–27.

whom this theme is not peripheral but the founding principle of philosophical inquiry itself.

Kant is quite aware of the pejorative overtones of the term "worldly."
We may reproach someone for having too worldly an outlook or range
of interests, meaning thereby that he excludes from his mind any concern about his relationship with God or spiritual values. Or a man may
speak with relish about his worldly outlook, namely, his knowledgeable-
ness in the ways of men and his regard for the values and pursuits of our
temporal life alone. In these normative moral usages, there is an implied
opposition between the worldly attitude and a religious one which does
care about a set of values beyond our visible, temporal situation.

Nevertheless, Kant firmly rejects any opposition in principle between
the worldly and the religious, insisting rather upon the requirement that
the religious order of values build itself upon the soil of worldly concerns.
He is no passive victim of ordinary linguistic usage, but exercises the
philosopher's right to criticize and reform the living language. Man's relations with the world do not exclude his bond with a divine reality, as long
as the latter can be brought into a meaningful and evidenced connection
with our central worldly experience. It is in and through our basic commitment to the man-and-world situation that we must work out the
reality and order of religious values, as far as a human conception of religion is concerned.

A world-oriented philosophy is both a science and a wisdom, or rather,
it follows the scientific account of man's natural relations to the point
where we must make some moral reflection upon the ultimate ends of
reason in human life, and thus attain to wisdom. Such a philosophy is
internally shaped by the *conspectus cosmicus,* the mundane orientation
which insures it to be "the science of the relation of all knowledge to the
essential ends of human reason (*teleologia rationis humanae*)." [4] This

---

4. *Pure Reason,* A 839:B 867 (pp. 657–58). Robert McRae, *The Problem of the
Unity of the Sciences: Bacon to Kant* (Toronto, 1961), pp. 123–43, studies the Kantian
concept of the *conspectus cosmicus,* the unifying perspective for natural and moral
knowledge. Kant maintains the necessary relationship between a scientific and a
sapiential meaning for philosophy (especially in the operational sense of philosophizing) in *Logic,* pp. 16–17; *Critique of Practical Reason,* trans. L. W. Beck, in *Critique
of Practical Reason and Other Writings in Moral Philosophy* (Chicago, University
of Chicago Press, 1949), p. 243; *Opus Postumum,* Prussian Academy edition of
Gesammelte Schriften (24 vols. Berlin, Walter de Gruyter, 1902–66), 21, 128. All
German source references to Kant will be made by volume and page to this edition,
with the four exceptions subsequently to be noted of the books edited by Lehmann

teleological concern for the whole vocation of man not only distinguishes Kant's worldly philosophy decisively from every school philosophy, but essentially opens it up toward the study of morality and religion. The latter topics are not extrinsic additions, but are necessary components in a philosophy intending to make a reflective examination of man in his entire relational reality and many-sided vocation.

Since mundanity contains a religious aspect, capable of being given some sort of philosophical treatment, the philosophy of religion is a worldly enterprise. In stressing the mundane character of all philosophical inquiry into religion, Kant is not moved by any theological or anti-theological considerations. His concern is simply to secure a philosophically legitimate approach to religion, one that agrees with his attack upon cyclopism and the school spirit in all areas of human life. Within the context of a *Weltweisheit* or *conspectus cosmicus*, Kant is able to infuse his theory of religion with the spirit of his entire philosophy. Just as his theory about the world remains incomplete until it becomes integrated with a moral and religious humanism, so also in a reciprocal way his analysis of religious. life must be in conformity with his general account of our scientific knowledge of the natural world. His theory of religion is worldly, not in any morally deordinate sense, but in the epistemological sense that man can approach God only across the experienced reality of nature, and in accord with those human powers and limitations brought to light in our scientific, moral, and esthetic activities in the natural world.

This reciprocal continuity is underlined by Kant in three strategic places: the first *Critique*, the popular lectures on logic, and a letter to his friend, the theologian Stäudlin, written shortly after the *Religion* book was issued and hence at the conclusion of the critical enterprise itself.[5] The common theme of these passages is that Kant's critical investigations hinge around three fundamental questions posed by man to himself and

---

(*Enzyklopädie*), Noack (*Religion innerhalb*), Pölitz (*Religionslehre*), and Reich (*Streit*).

5. *Pure Reason*, A 804-06:B 832-34 (pp. 635-36); *Logic*, p. 15; *Letter to C. F. Stäudlin*, May 4, 1793, where Kant remarks about his recently published *Religion Within the Limits of Reason Alone* (1793): "In this book I have proceeded conscientiously and with genuine respect for the Christian religion but also with a befitting candor, concealing nothing but rather presenting openly the way in which I believe that a possible union of Christianity with the purest practical reason is possible." Kant, *Philosophical Correspondence*, 1759-99, trans. A. Zweig (Chicago, University of Chicago Press, 1967), p. 205. See J.-L. Bruch's general analysis, *La Philosophie religieuse de Kant* (Paris, 1968).

about himself, and that Kant's philosophy attempts to furnish specific replies to these questions.

First, what can I know? This is a question in theory of knowledge and metaphysics, and is treated mainly in the *Critique of Pure Reason*. Secondly, what ought I to do? Here the moral issues are raised, and the Kantian solutions are proposed in the *Critique of Practical Reason* and other ethical writings. Finally, what may I hope? This is a purposive and religious type of inquiry, which Kant begins in the *Critique of Judgment*, continues in his briefer writings on the meaning of history, and brings to a climax in *Religion Within the Limits of Reason Alone*. Kant adds that the three main critical questions can be summed up in the comprehensive question: What is man? For the problems of knowledge, obligation, and hope are issues which arise originally from man's activities and relationships in the world.

Under the influences of phenomenology and existentialism, Kantian scholars today are inclined to emphasize the unifying question about man, since this brings out the need for developing a philosophical anthropology. Such an anthropology is only as sound, however, as the guiding principles and specific evidences advanced in the three major areas of study. A chief function of the Kantian theory of religion is to focus attention upon the third question just mentioned, the question of hope, which is often glided over as being only of secondary interest for the philosopher of man.

Kant himself regards the theme of hope as central to his critical work. The critical philosopher cannot remain content with isolated analyses of our speculative knowledge of nature and our practical moral life, but must seek some principles for the practical unification of the two zones of nature and moral freedom. He does not do so by further multiplying the domains of being, beyond those of nature and moral freedom. Instead, he seeks to specify the reflective principles whereby an intrinsic union of these two aspects of human experience can be realized. The efforts at achieving this reflective union constitute what Kant calls the dimension of hope, or the aim of fulfilling the ultimate ends of reason within the limiting conditions of human existence. It is within this region that the philosophy of religion makes its unique contribution.

Kant tells Stäudlin that the Kantian theory of religion completes the project of examining the interpretative means of relating nature with human freedom, and thus caps the critical and transcendental philosophy as a whole. Along with the organic, esthetic, and historical modes of unifying our experience, the religious interpretation of human existence gives us the reflective grounds of hoping for the practical realization of human values in the world of nature. The religious reference of man to God is the ultimate act in our search for a human wisdom, which is practically fulfilling as well as theoretically true to our condition in nature. Hence the philosophical theory of religion plays a culminating, hope-bearing role in Kant's worldly philosophy.

The schema concerning the three basic questions in critical philosophy can be misleading to someone who concludes that Kant deals with one question separately and completely, before passing on to the next. His actual practice is a constant interweaving of these three primary themes, even when the requirements of analysis and exposition compel their development in a certain sequence. Although the question of hope in its religious mode is postponed until last in the formal exposition, its active presence can be detected in all of Kant's previous critical investigations into knowledge and morality. To the degree that these investigations become unified around man and the ultimate practical ends of reason, they lead by their own impetus into the philosophical study of religion. A grasp of the gradual preparation of Kant's position on religion, in terms of his discussion of the limits of human knowledge and the nature of moral action, is essential for appreciating the religious import of his philosophical work as a whole.

A guide to the religious themes in Kant's critical philosophy is furnished by a very broad division of the kinds of theology proposed in his *Lectures on the Philosophical Theory of Religion*.[6]

6. *Vorlesungen über die philosophische Religionslehre*, ed. K. H. L. Pölitz (Leipzig, 1817), pp. 11–12. This work has to be used with some caution, since the text is not directly by Kant but is based on a student notebook preserved by D. Rink. My policy is to use only those teachings which can be corroborated and modified by Kant's direct writings. A critical study of the Pölitz text and two other sets of students' notes for Kant's lectures on natural theology and religion (probably based on the course of 1783–84, although it was also given again in 1786–87) is made by Kurt Beyer, *Untersuchungen zu Kants Vorlesungen über die philosophische Religionslehre* (Halle, 1937). Pölitz also edited Kant's *Vorlesungen über die Metaphysik* (Erfurt, 1821; reprint, Darmstadt, 1964), the last section of which (pp. 262–343) deals with rational theology. On the development of Kant's philosophy of religion prior to *Religion*, consult Hermann Noack's Introduction to his edition of *Die Religion innerhalb der Grenzen der blossen Vernunft* (7th ed. Hamburg, Meiner, 1961), pp. xi–xlvi, and Bernhard Jansen's *Die Religionsphilosophie Kants* (Berlin, 1929), pp. 1–63. Vol. 28 of the German Academy ed. of Kant will contain accurate texts of the religion and metaphysics lectures: *Vorlesungen über Metaphysik und Rationaltheologie*.

I. THEOLOGY: Any orderly knowledge concerning God

    Archetypal theology: God's own self-knowledge: Divine theology

    Ectypal theology: Derived human knowledge about God: Human or natural theology in the broadest sense, consisting of these kinds:

        Empirical theology of revelation

        Rational theology of human reason

II. RELIGION: Man's practical bond with God through belief and action, applying the kinds of human or natural theology to the man-God relationship

This working outline provides a clue to the main divisions in Kant's philosophical theory of religion, corresponding as it does to the main kinds of ectypal theology or derived human knowledge about God and man's relationship with Him. It also enables us to discern his grand strategy of delay, as he takes up the topics in a well-considered order.

Kant draws a rough distinction between the reality of religion itself, which is a practical faith and ordering of our life toward God, and theology, or a systematic knowledge of God drawn from various sources. All such knowledge, insofar as it is brought to a reflective and systematically organized condition, constitutes some sort of human theology or theory concerning God. Taken in this most general sense, then, natural theology includes all those knowledges about God (whether revelatory or not) which can be distinguished from God's own self-knowledge and hence which are thoroughly human, in being fitted to our own understanding and capacity for action.

Kant then proposes a fundamental division in the area of human or natural theology, a distinction which serves him well as a working frame of reference for treating theological matters throughout his critical philosophy. His underlying contrast is between the empirical or revelatory knowledge of God and the rational kinds of theology. We can best understand the peculiar meanings which "empirical" and "rational" have in this primary division by considering two contemporary positions, which help to determine Kant's usage at this point.

The first contribution is made by Wolff, who distinguishes systematically between historical knowledge and philosophical knowledge.[7] Historical knowledge is a grasp of the facts, or the things which occur, obtained through the senses and some experience of the occurrences. Philosophical knowledge moves on from a reception of the facts to an under-

7. Christian Wolff, *Preliminary Discourse on Philosophy in General*, trans. R. J. Blackwell (Indianapolis, 1963), pp. 3–7.

standing of their sufficient reasons and intelligible connections, obtained through the use of our own reasoning power. There is a similarity between Wolffian historical knowledge and Kantian empirical theology, insofar as the latter signifies a doctrine on God based upon a message, received under the revelational conditions of sense experience and historical circumstances. Likewise, Kant's notion of rational theology bears a likeness to Wolffian philosophical knowledge, insofar as it is a theory about God resulting from the active investigations of our own reason and its principles of method and evidence.

The second relevant point is that all parties in the Enlightenment debate over religion agreed in making a rough distinction between the positive religion of revelation and the natural religion of reason. Positive religion is empirical, in the sense of being bound up with particular contingent circumstances, of coming through some historical process, and of requiring the believer to have an attitude of docile reception. For its part, the rationality of natural religion does not mean that reason is used to elaborate a conception of religion to the complete exclusion of sense experience and history, but only that the latter factors are kept in a subordinate place. Within a rational theology, these sources are always subjected to the critical standards set by human reason, acting upon its own initiative. Kant incorporates these various considerations into his basic meaning for an empirical theology of revelation and a rational theology proper to philosophy itself.

For his long-range purposes, however, it was advisable to postpone as long as possible any formal discussion of the differences between the empirical and rational kinds of theology. The problem of revelation and reason had to be delayed until Kant could determine, in accord with his own philosophical principles, the competence of reason itself in gaining some knowledge about God. Hence his notion of religion could not attain philosophical maturity until after his examination of the speculative and moral forms of rational theology.

THEORIES OF GOD AND THE EXISTENTIAL PROOFS

Kant's best known contribution to the philosophy of God is found in that section of the first *Critique* where he examines the nest of dialectical arguments for God's existence. Pure speculative reason becomes entangled and confused in its efforts to show the reality of the unconditioned ideal, which underlies all its activities. Because Kant seeks to make an exhaustive classification of theoretical arguments for God and then to expose their inherent deficiencies, his treatment of speculative theology is often regarded as being purely negative and he himself is dubbed "the shatterer of all things," in Moses Mendelssohn's famous phrase. From this perspective, his subsequent attempt to supply a moral basis for belief in God is judged to be either an unfortunate weakening of his critical intelligence or an accommodation to the conventions and wishes of the common man.

Yet when the section in question is restored to its actual context, supported at every stage by preparatory analyses and clarifying reflections, this interpretation is found to be oversimplified. A merely refutational approach to speculative theology runs counter to the actual thrust of his inquiries concerning God and religion. The working attitude behind these lifelong inquiries is embodied in two striking, general remarks of Kant's concerning the human intention of giving proofs of God's existence.

Writing nearly twenty years before the first *Critique* was published, Kant concluded one of his critical studies on the basis of proof for a demonstration of God's existence with this sentence: "It is absolutely necessary to *convince* oneself of the existence of God, but it is not as necessary that one should *demonstrate* it." [8] The two words we have underlined help to bring home a capital point which Kant observed. Evidential conviction is more than a peculiar persuasion on the individual's part, but not every well-evidenced conviction is based upon a formal speculative demonstration. Men do feel obliged to furnish some evidence supporting their conviction that God exists, but they do not confuse the conviction and its evidential support with the further project of giving a strict demonstration in form. Their theistic conviction and its supporting grounds remain independent of any theoretical efforts at demonstrating God's existence, and do not rise or fall in correlation with such efforts, as Locke had supposed. Hence a believing philosopher can engage in radical criticism of the speculative demonstrations, without undermining his religious conviction.

Toward the end of the first *Critique*, Kant adds another observation which can serve as a guiding thread in following his account of the speculative proofs. In order to distinguish as clearly as possible between an

8. *The Only Possible Argument for a Demonstration of the Existence of God,* in G. Rabel, *Kant* (New York, Oxford University Press, 1963), p. 58. On the objective validity of reasonable conviction, as distinct from subjective persuasion, see *Pure Reason.* A 820:B 848 (p. 645).

impersonal speculative proof and a moral certainty about God, he advises that a linguistic caution always be observed.

> I must not even say, '*It is* morally certain that there is a God, etc.,' but '*I am* morally certain, etc.' In other words, belief in a God and in another world is so interwoven with my moral sentiment that as there is little danger of my losing the latter, there is equally little cause for fear that the former can ever be taken from me.[9]

It is inappropriate to impose the impersonal mode of discourse upon a statement of theistic certainty. The latter is essentially personal, since it is out of a concrete reflection upon my own moral life that I draw my theistic conviction. My belief in God is defensible and can undergo philosophical scrutiny, but only on condition that I retain the first-personal mode of discourse in which its evidence arises and its certainty is grasped. Kant is severe with the speculative proofs of God's existence precisely because they wash out the personal language and grounding of theistic conviction.

Classification of Theories on God. We are familiar with Kant's reduction of all speculative proofs of God's existence to the ontological, cosmological, and physicotheological arguments. But his intent is not confined to an analysis and criticism of these arguments, narrowly construed as attempting nothing more than proof of the existence of God. Each of these proofs belongs within the wider framework of a unified theory of God, including doctrines on His nature and activity, as well as His existence. For a comprehensive treatment which goes to the heart of the entire speculative doctrine on God, then, Kant refers the three kinds of argument concerning God's existence to the three dominant kinds of speculative *theories* about the divine reality. This relationship is crucially important for his philosophy of religion, which incorporates something in the theories of God without accepting the fallacious proofs.

For determining the representative ways of developing the doctrine on God, he does not ransack the remoter history of philosophy or deal with ideal possibilities in theological construction. Kant takes the speculative paths of theorizing about God as he finds them in the widely used school manuals of Baumgarten and Eberhard, supplemented by a consideration

9. *Pure Reason*, A 829:B 857 (p. 650). On the epistemological problem of the I-form of discourse, see Jaakko Hintikka, *Knowledge and Belief* (Ithaca, 1962), pp. 19–20, 110–15.

of the contemporary theological literature to which they in turn refer the reader.[10] These approaches constitute the living claim to have a speculative doctrine on God, as far as he is concerned, and his task is to order them for purposes of his own analysis and criticism. His manuscript notes are filled with repeated attempts to achieve a specific classification of the rational or nonrevelatory theories on God which will be not only descriptively adequate but also philosophically illuminating and fruitful. Kant does not disdain the use of diagrams, and it may be helpful for us also to offer another one which synthesizes his several tries.

RATIONAL THEOLOGIES (THEORIES ON GOD)

INFORMAL

PHILOSOPHICAL

Speculative
- Transcendental: (1) *Ontotheology*
- Natural
  - Metaphysical: (2) *Cosmotheology*
  - Physical: (3) *Physicotheology*

Moral: (4) *Ethicotheology* (*moral theology, moral theism*)

Even in this bare form, the outline brings to focus some major questions in Kant's philosophy of religion.

The diagram clearly indicates that the classical treatment of speculative proofs of God's existence in the first *Critique* is properly concerned with formal philosophical argumentation, rather than with our informal

10. Kant's ready sources of information on current university presentations of natural theology are A. G. Baumgarten, *Metaphysica* (4th ed. Halle, 1757) and J. A. Eberhard, *Vorbereitung zur natürlichen Theologie* (Halle, 1781), the latter being a teachers' manual. Baumgarten's text and Kant's comments are gathered in the Prussian Academy edition under the title, *Erläuterungen zu A. G. Baumgartens Metaphysica*, 17, 5–226; Kant's other metaphysical reflections are organized under the Baumgarten divisions as *Reflexionen zur Metaphysik*, 17, 227–745, and vol. 18 in entirety. The text of Eberhard and Kant's accompanying comments in his personal copy are printed in the midst of *Reflexionen*, 18, 489–606. My outline of the kinds of theology is based on *Pure Reason*, A 631–32:B 659–60 (pp. 525–26); *Religionslehre*, pp. 11–12; *Reflexionen*, 17, 421, 595, 18, 196–97. It is subject to three qualifications imposed by Kant's actual usage. Kant uses "speculative theology" to designate either a dogmatic, uncritical study of God or a reformed critical study of Him made in full awareness of the regulative limits of human experience and in conjunction with a basis taken in moral theism. "Transcendental theology" is sometimes used in a generic sense to cover all speculative theology, insofar as all of the latter's existential proofs are seen to be logically reducible to the ontological argument and thus to ontotheology. Although Kant usually reserves "empirical theology" for a doctrine on God based on faith in a historical revelation, he sometimes applies the term to physicotheology itself, insofar as it makes use of empirically determined evidence.

thoughts about God. Kant refers to the latter as the way of ordinary non-scientific reason to God, and adds that informal reflections are always cultivated by the believer, whether or not he becomes involved in a critique of the philosophical theories. The importance of this personally developed belief in God will be seen later on, when Kant discusses the existential sources in man for the moral idea of God and for the conviction about His existence.

The contrast between transcendental theology and natural theology is a striking indication of how Kant is striving to master the speculative approaches to God and ultimately subordinate them to the moral way. The transcendental approach seeks to develop the entire doctrine on the existence and nature of God out of an analysis of the idea of the most real and perfect being. It proceeds entirely from the essential necessity of rational principles and concepts, without requiring any intrinsic dependence upon human experience and the world. The total doctrine on God resulting from such a method is an ontotheology, or theory of God based upon the intrinsic rational necessities in the notion of being, taken in an unconditioned way.

As for the ontological proof of God's existence, it is only one moment within the whole system of ontotheology, and indeed is regarded as a subsequent moment in the full analysis of the notion of unconditioned or most real being. Divine existence follows almost as a matter of course, once the essential nature of God is ideally defined. The procedure of ontotheology also has an imperialistic quality, such that if its theoretical claims are allowed, it then proceeds to regard all other ways in theology as being so many deducible inferences from its own ontological principles.

Invariably, when using the term "natural theology," Kant notes the anomalies associated with its usage in his own day.[11] We have already met with its broadest Kantian meaning, as designating any organized knowledge about God (whether revelatory or not) which belongs in a human theology, taken in counterdistinction only to God's own self-knowledge. Within this broadest meaning of natural theology, we can distinguish between two main types of speculative, philosophical inquiry into the being and attributes of God: transcendental and natural theology, taken in a more specific sense. Since transcendental theology makes no pretense at being an empirical approach to God, Kant does not regard it as a type of natural theology, in the more restricted sense. He reserves

11. *Practical Reason*, p. 240; *Reflexionen*, 18, 60, 566.

that usage for those two routes to God which do depend, in some basic phase of reasoning, upon the idea of nature and the world of natural experience. Cosmotheology and physicotheology are the two parts of this restricted meaning for natural theology.

Cosmotheology makes a metaphysical analysis of the contrast between contingency and necessity, which are features of experience in general and of a world taken in a general way. From these features, it leads by the conceptual necessity of the sufficient reasons involved in them to the unqualifiedly necessary being of God. For its part, physicotheology stays closer to our particular physical world and to specific aspects in our experience of ordered nature. It argues from the designed, particular features in the scientifically describable world to a divine maker operating with an intelligent plan. In its distinctive and restricted Kantian usage, therefore, a natural theology is a philosophical theory of God which proceeds in some a posteriori way from evidence furnished by the natural world and human experience of nature.

What remains in the division of rational theologies is moral theism.[12] Taken as an inference to God on the basis of man's moral life, it has no rightful place in Hume, who orients morality and theism in opposite directions. And in the Wolffian tradition, the appeal to man's desire for God and his search for a highest good has only a minor function to fill, as an appendix to the main arguments in natural theology. In his lectures on the philosophy of religion and his commentary on Eberhard's manual for teachers of philosophical theology, Kant observes that his predecessors had failed to set off a moral theism sufficiently from the other parts of philosophical theology and to notice its uniquely important contribution. His own plan is to show that moral theology (taken as a doctrine on God reached through a study of our moral existence, not as a form of ethics) is both autonomous and controlling in the entire field of philosophizing about God.

Criticism of the Existential Demonstrations. A critically informed philosophical theology has a twofold task. It must make a negative assessment of the speculative proofs for failing to reckon with the limits of reason and human experience, and must then salvage in a positive way whatever

12. Of moral theism, Kant remarks: "This is the genuine theology, which serves as the fundament of religion" (*Religionslehre*, p. 16). Whereas Eberhard gives only the speculative proofs of God's existence, Kant inserts his own section on moral theism as the fundament of all theology, as well as of religion (*Reflexionen*, 18, 579–80).

sound gleams of theological method and meaning remain in the speculative doctrines on God. The delicacy of this operation becomes manifest when the treatment of speculative theology in the first *Critique* is viewed in terms of Kant's gradually developing philosophy of religion. Within this framework, the criticism is seen to be both more severely controlled and more penetrating than would be possible in a program of wholesale elimination of speculations concerning God.

The proper objects of Kant's attack are the three kinds of speculative proofs of God's existence, not the three kinds of speculative theology taken in an unqualified way. The three speculative theologies are deeply affected by his criticism of the existential demonstrations, of course, but only in the manner and degree that these demonstrations function within the theological systems. For instance, the criticism of the ontological argument does not destroy everything about the ontotheological approach to God. It does force us to look upon ontotheology itself as being an existentially *non*demonstrative body of thought. Whether anything significant for theological reflection remains in such a transformed, de-existentialized ontotheology remains an open question, and is left for the more positive phase in the Kantian critical theology to determine. Similarly, the undermining of the claim to have existential demonstrations of God in the cosmotheological and physicotheological arguments affects the entire structure of cosmotheology and physicotheology quite profoundly, but the precise nature of the modifications in these theological systems is not determined simply by undermining the existential arguments themselves. For Kant strongly suspects that there may be some corrective functions and positive meanings contained in these theological systems which survive the criticism, and which will receive their genuine ordering from a moral principle rather than a speculative demonstration.[13]

He does not introduce such qualifications in order to whittle down in the slightest degree the rigorous conclusions reached in his criticism of the speculative proofs for God's existence. Judged by the standards of apodictic speculative knowledge, the proofs fail to satisfy the Kantian conditions for demonstration in the existential order. The ontological proof is defective, since it fails to make the anthropological reference to the nature and scope of human knowledge, a reference required in any

13. *Pure Reason*, A 639–42:B 667–70 (pp. 530–31). For the epistemological arguments showing that the speculative proofs as such do not satisfy the Kantian requirements for knowledge, see James Collins, *God in Modern Philosophy* (Chicago, 1959), pp. 163–86.

genuine argument in a human philosophy of God. Due to this defect, it simply stipulates that existence is a perfection of the most real and perfect being, without inquiring whether we can know about any existence other than one which is proportioned to the context of our limited world of spatial-temporal events and qualities. Any plausibility in the onto-logical proof derives from our making an undetected fusion between humanly contrived essential definitions and the divine mind itself, con-sidered as the realizing principle of existing perfections.

The cosmological argument founders, in turn, when it seeks to show that the necessary being required by our mind is the unique and in-finitely real God. It becomes involved in the dilemma of either falling back upon the ontological standpoint, and thus remaining in the concep-tual order, or else distinguishing between logical and real necessity in respect to the objects of human inference. As soon as the epistemological question is raised, a critical mind can see that we do not possess the human cognitive resources for making a valid distinction, on speculative grounds alone, between logical and real necessity, logical and real possi-bility, in the case of an unconditioned being which is inferred to exist apart from sensible conditions. For our speculative human way of grasping the distinction depends upon a reference to sense experience. And even the physicotheological argument fails to reach the existent reality of God. Either it stops short at a finite maker or else it moves from this cosmic demiurge to the infinite God, by relying upon the same ideal connection which vitiates the other two proofs in their existential claim.

These criticisms remain fully operative when Kant turns to consider the problem of religion. Indeed, the remarkable thing about his theory of religion is its complete refusal to tamper with the critical conclusion that there are, and in principle can be, no speculative demonstrations of God's existence. The Kantian philosophy of religion never weakens or revokes this judgment upon all speculative proofs of God's existence, but accepts it as a working premise essentially conditioning all our inquiries into morality and religion. Such inquiries do not extend or supplement a meta-physical demonstration that God exists: they are a substitute elaborated by men in its absence. The *substitutional* function deeply marks the entire course and procedure of Kant's philosophy of religion.

The speculative proofs are criticized from both the epistemological and religious standpoints. Kant is just as careful as Hume to establish their religious deficiencies, along with their defects in the order of demonstra-tive knowledge. As his epistemological criticism contains a general attack upon the project of giving a speculative proof of God's existence, then a special analysis of the weaknesses in the individual arguments, so his religious critique is carried out at both the general and the specific levels. His general objection is that, if a speculative demonstration were really achieved, it would destroy the grounds for a moral and religious bond with God. And at the level of the particular kinds of proof, he shows that they fall far short of presenting us with a religiously available God, and may indeed direct our minds away from the God of theistic religion.

Kant's general religious critique is intimately connected with his epistemology. It consists in showing that, on the hypothesis that the speculative arguments did conform with his own standards of demonstrative knowledge, they would lead to a view of God inconsistent with theistic religion.[14] For if the proofs were genuine speculative demonstrations, they would attain to the only sort of object consistent with the limits of our speculative reason and experience, namely, a phenomenal object or law. God would then have to be conceived either as being Himself a phenomenal reality, open to our sensible experience, or else as being the purely immanent law of the space-time universe. Such a meaning for God runs counter to religious belief in a divine reality which is invisible, spiritual, and transcendingly distinct in its own being from the structure of the universe. Moreover, a speculatively demonstrated God would have to submit to phenomenal conditions not only in His existence but also in His activity. His actions would be totally subject to the determinism governing the phenomenal world, and hence would be limited in their scope to making modifications in the already present continuum of events. In other words, such a God would not be the free, creative principle for which the religious man is searching.

This conclusion is then applied in detail to the particular kinds of argument, taken precisely as claims to give demonstrative knowledge of God's existence. Kant makes the religious bearing of his specific criticisms unmistakably clear. The arguments are so structured that, if they were to establish some existent reality, they could not bring out its identity with the living God acknowledged in our religious worship.

The most perfect and infinite being at which the ontological argument arrives is, at bottom, a morally indifferent and religiously useless concept.[15] Although the rationalist theologians attempt to derive all the

14. *Critique of Judgment*, trans. J. H. Bernard (New York, Hafner, 1951), pp. 310–11; *Religionslehre*, p. 148.
15. Ibid., p. 15.

attributes of God from this indeterminate principle, they do so in a purely conceptual way and without making any legitimating, anthropological reference to human experience and our human mode of reasoning. This failure to refer to man's actual situation is not only an epistemological fault but also a religious one. For this school-philosophy approach achieves an impersonal necessity of systematic inference, but at the price of divorcing its object from human concerns and hence also from the grounds of religious relevance.

Whatever the metaphysicians may argue concerning a purely ideal existence unrelated to our lives in any fundamental way, the religious mind is convinced of its worthlessness for belief. Our religious assent is reserved for a divine reality arrived at by following through the implications of our own experience and striving. And should the ontotheologian seek to achieve human relevance by coalescing the divine and human minds, he would at the same time destroy the basis of distinction required for a theistic sort of religious relationship. This point will be the nub of Hegel's quarrel with Kant over the validity and religious significance of the ontological argument. Hegel will try to restore the religious quality of the proof, but in doing so he will have to merge the human and the divine spirit in a nontheistic bond.

Kant always found the cosmological argument quite elusive and epistemologically troublesome, forcing him to return to a critical analysis of it repeatedly during his last years.[16] The source of the difficulty showed up even in his classificatory schemata. In the division of rational theologies already given, cosmotheology was located along with physicotheology as a part of natural theology, in its proper and restricted sense. But when Kant came to classify the proofs of God's existence, he assigned the cosmological argument sometimes to natural theology and sometimes to transcendental theology. The former view is justified by the appeal that this proof makes to experience and a natural world, in their general traits of contingency and necessity. But the very generality of the cosmotheological analysis of contingency and necessity makes its actual connection with our experienced world a very tenuous one, maintained only long enough to obtain some conceptual definitions and reasons. The argument swiftly centers upon the notion of a necessary being, whose further qualities and relationship with the one, infinite God can be ascertained only by using

16. See the reformulations of his criticism made in the 1790s: *Reflexionen*, 18, 634–48.

the ontological ideal of the most real and perfect being. Taken in this light, the cosmological argument is akin to the ontological one, and hence belongs in transcendental theology.

From the religious standpoint, Kant adds that the epistemological ambivalence of this approach to God makes it a dubious support for religious conviction. When the cosmological argument is considered in its transcendental aspect, it shares in the drawbacks of the ontological proof for the religious mind. The paradox of the cosmological proof is that when centered upon a real being, it cannot assure us that this necessary being is divine, and when it seeks to establish the latter point it abandons the religious terrain of a God who is pertinent to real existence and human concerns.

Kant's praise of the physicotheological proof as being the oldest, clearest, and most accordant with reason is well-known. He expresses his esteem, however, at the same time that he absorbs and reaffirms Hume's stringent criticism of the proof as a philosophical argument. This mixed evaluation reflects the quite special place accorded to the design proof by the contemporary religious mind. If possible, the popularity of the physicotheological line of reasoning to God had increased with its transfer from England to Germany, where the mid-eighteenth century witnessed an astounding proliferation of supporting literature. The Hamburg physicotheologians ransacked every aspect of nature for a reflection of some divine attribute, a clue to the existence of a wise and powerful mind, whose transcendent majesty is signified by the visible world.[17] Kant acknowledges the actual religious relevance of this proof, in contrast to the other speculative approaches, and nevertheless criticizes it on both epistemological and religious grounds. His criticism has a broader cultural resonance, due to the alliance established by many contemporary believers between the religious and scientific views of the universe.

Kant maintains rather bluntly that, to the extent in which the physicotheological proof is regarded as a strict demonstration and a rational basis of belief, it is neither physical nor theological. It is neither good science nor good philosophy, but only a confusing attempt at mixing the two modes of thought. To establish any demonstrative conclusion about God,

17. The pre-Kantian apologetic use of scientific findings is studied by Wolfgang Philipp, *Das Werden der Aufklärung in theologiegeschichtlicher Sicht* (Göttingen, 1957). The impact of the physicotheological approach can be gauged by the detailed arguments, divisions, and bibliography supplied by Eberhard to philosophy teachers; cf. Kant's *Reflexionen*, 18, 566–79.

it must use the findings of the natural sciences and our ordinary experience of the world in a special way, which is not legitimized directly by the scientific and ordinary modes of thinking as such. An epistemological justification would have to be given for inferring something about the spiritual being of God from the sense evidence, for using the causal principle to reach an existent that transcends the experienced world, and for applying the analogy of an intelligent maker beyond the human sphere. In their headlong eagerness to exploit the wonders and adaptations in nature, the physicotheologians fail to perform these basic tasks and hence fail to show that their inferences from the scientifically described world do indeed demonstrate God's existence. They leave their reasoning exposed to Hume's alternative suggestions about a finite, bungling, and perhaps malevolent artisan of the cosmos.

In this nonrigorous and vulnerable condition, the physicotheological proof also fails to supply a sound theological basis for a religious outlook. Kant points out three defects which prevent it from giving strong intellectual support to religion.[18] The fundamental objection is that the cosmic designer is not shown to exist precisely as transcending the realm of visible nature, and hence as demanding a worshipful religious response from us. When Kant states that the physicotheological proof must eventually subordinate itself to the other two speculative proofs, his criticism has a religious as well as an epistemological edge. In trying to identify the cosmic artisan ontologically with the infinite, transcendent God, the partisans of design not only compromise the existential character of their inference but also remove it from the range of meaningful religious response.

The second religiously pertinent flaw is that an argument based on the particular designs in our world yields only a contingent and quite arbitrary conception of the cosmic designer's will. This accounts for the note of insecure fear and terror which Hume presumed to be always characteristic of the religious believer, in his relation to God. Kant traces it back to a theological confusion between basing one's knowledge of God's being upon a study of nature and using such a study to confirm and exhibit one's

18. "Physico-theology is therefore unable to give any determinate concept of the supreme cause of the world, and cannot therefore serve as the foundation of a [moral] theology which is itself in turn to form the basis of religion" (*Pure Reason,* A 628:B 656 [p. 523]); cf. *Religionslehre,* pp. 128–30; *Reflexionen,* 18, 421, 447 (on the inadequacy of the physicotheological inference to establish the divine attributes required for religion: unity, wisdom, and goodness).

independent belief in God. If one has prior assurances from moral experience or from revelation about the moral quality of the divine will, then one is unlikely to identify that will with a terrifying natural power.

A final indication of the religious inadequacy of using physicotheology to furnish a demonstrative foundation of theism is seen in its concentration upon the evidence of physical nature, at the expense of the witness of our moral life. Although the physicotheologian speaks about the providence and benevolence of God, he interprets these properties in the light of physical order and adaptation. He does not strictly show that these properties must be taken in the moral connotation indispensable for establishing a humane religious relationship with God.

Taken by itself, a study of design in nature suggests in an indeterminate way the presence of a mind which is not transcendent, wise, or morally adequate to be the God of our religious awe and worship. On this point, Kant and Hume are in firm agreement. But whereas Hume concludes that the philosophically responsible form of religion is now brought to a dead halt, Kant reaches the much more cautious conclusion that there is something faulty in the prevalent view that the physicotheological and other speculative proofs can supply demonstrative foundations for religion.

TRANSREGULATIVE ANALYSIS OF THE IDEA OF GOD

Throughout his critique of the speculative proofs, Kant is careful not to overstate his case by declaring speculative theology to be entirely invalid and useless for the philosophy of religion. He does not advocate a shift of venue to the moral order which would simply abandon the entire body of speculative thought about God. Kant is able to salvage the content of the speculative idea of God by applying to it the clarifying distinction between a constitutive use and a regulative use of the ideas of pure reason. Although we cannot correctly use the idea of God to constitute a metaphysical knowledge of the unconditioned being, we can rightly use it in a regulative way as an ideal encouragement for the scientific investigator. With the aid of the idea of the wise, just, ordering mind of God, the researcher can buoy up his assurance that our world is intelligible for the human mind, and that always more inclusive and unified explanations of natural phenomena can be attained in our scientific theories.

But the speculative idea of God is useful not only for scientific explanation but also for the theory of religion. The positive task of philosophical theology is to determine this religious significance, thus achieving the transition from a critique of theology to a critical theology which is in the service of morality and theistic religious conviction. The theology so oriented is *transregulative* in its approach to the idea of God and the entire theory of God. Its major responsibility is to achieve the transition from a purely regulative use of the idea of God in theoretical philosophy to the practical, constitutive use that establishes the moral and religious meaning of God. The transregulative approach to the theory of God does not seek to reach any metaphysical truths about Him, but it does ascertain which theoretical elements are sound enough to be carried along into the moral and religious view of God.

The ground for making this transregulative appraisal is skillfully prepared in the *Critique of Pure Reason,* at the end of the very section in which the speculative proofs of God's existence are dissected. Kant enables us to anticipate a whole range of positive functions which will be performed by a nondemonstrative speculative theology, or transcendental theology in the reformed sense, once it becomes assimilated within moral theism.

> Thus, while for the merely speculative employment of reason the supreme being remains a mere *ideal,* it is yet *an ideal without a flaw,* a concept which completes and crowns the whole of human knowledge. Its objective reality cannot indeed be proved, but also cannot be disproved, by merely speculative reason. If, then, there should be a moral theology that can make good this deficiency, transcendental theology, which before was problematic only, will prove itself indispensable in determining the concept of this supreme being and in constantly testing reason, which is so often deceived by sensibility, and which is frequently out of harmony with its own idea. . . . [Speculatively used reason] is yet of very great utility in *correcting* any knowledge of this being which may be derived from other sources, in making it consistent with itself and with every point of view from which intelligible objects may be regarded, and in freeing it from everything incompatible with the concept of an original being and from all admixture of empirical limitations.[19]

This text constitutes a charter for the legitimate role of speculative theology within Kant's moral-religious theory of God.

In Kant's hands, the very meaning and status of a speculative theology undergo a profound transformation. It is deautonomized, in that it ceases

19. *Pure Reason,* A 640–41:B 668–69 (pp. 530–31).

to be taken as a self-founded body of dogmatic knowledge, leading directly to the reality of God and governing our religious relationship to Him. A reversal in perspectives takes place, so that now the critically aware mind comes to view the entire theoretical approach to God as a development made out of a fundamental moral and religious belief in Him, rather than the converse relationship. This does not mean that the speculative investigation becomes a servile instrument, however, pandering to a set of religious prejudgments. It has its own distinctive tasks and its own kind of integrity to maintain, within the whole context of man's living relationship with the God he seeks.

Kant's salvaging operation goes far enough to include even the main lines of reasoning toward God's existence, as long as they are not treated as speculative demonstrations. Although they are not the basis of speculative theology, they do have an incitive role in this area. Their function is to keep our minds always alive to the unique importance of the existential question about God, and always dissatisfied with a purely ideal analysis of the divine essence. Kant's critical principles rule out any valid existential demonstrations in speculative theology, but they do not rule out the existential question itself, the search for some kind of existential conviction about the real being of God. The traditional proofs are carriers of the legitimate human aim of distinguishing between mere logical possibility and existential truth in our religious statements.

When Kant says that the idea of God is an inevitable and intrinsically coherent idea of pure reason in its speculative as well as practical aspects, he does not intend to reinstate a theory of innatism. The idea of God is not a ready-made part of our human constitution, residing in—but in no sense developed by—our reason. It is precisely in his theory of religion that Kant indicates how to avoid what empiricist philosophers from Locke to William James have castigated as a blocklike, innate idea of God. For it is in this portion of his philosophy that Kant justifies the several kinds of theology, by relating them to the progressive development of human reason.

Although the moral and religious conception of God is ultimate in the purposive order, it does not (and cannot) stand alone in the mind of the mature human person. The mature mind must use all its reflective powers in the search for God, examining all the modalities of experience in a speculative, as well as a practical, way for their disclosures concerning the divine reality. When philosophers reflect upon these theistic paths in order to test and organize the evidence, they are able to bring out the internal development in the theistic conception of the divine reality. This they do in a formal way in the several kinds of speculative theology, as well as in moral theism.

A major task of the philosopher of religion is to present these modes of theology as gradual stages in the intellectual elaboration of the idea of God found in theistic religion. Kant makes a careful correlation between the needs of the human mind for several modes of intellectual search after God and the resultant kinds of theology, as well as between the dominant notions of divine activity in relation to the world and the corresponding kinds of human religious relationships.[20]

NEEDS OF HUMAN REASON	KINDS OF THEOLOGY	GOD AS AGENT	MODES OF RELIGION
Necessary logical ideal for speculation	Onto-theology	Underived being as primal cause	Deism
Necessary hypothesis of nature and experience in general	Cosmo-theology	First Mover, Author of nature	Indeterminate natural theism
Analogous principle for our ordered world	Physico-theology	Living author of nature, Architect of world	Determinate natural theism
Moral-religious principle of ethical order and happiness	Moral theology	Creator, World ruler, and lawgiver	Religion of moral theism

The religious reorientation of the three kinds of speculative theology is consummated when they are firmly embedded in this matrix of human intentional meanings and religious attitudes. We make the definitive passage from an *isolational* school philosophy to a *situational* worldly philosophy of religion through the act of relating the several modes of philosophical theology to their source in the living tendencies of our mind, and to their goal in the religious ordination of our whole being.

Kant introduces the important notion of *completional concepts* (*Begriffe der Vollendung*), in order to facilitate this situational religious view of human theology.[21] Each particular kind of theology is an objective,

20. Ibid., A 631–32:B 659–60 (pp. 525–26); *Religionslehre*, pp. 11–16; *Reflexionen*, 17, 595.

21. *Reflexionen*, 18, 489–90. In his moral philosophy, Kant draws upon the experience of law and freedom in order to give completion to the categories of modality (possibility, existence, necessity). In his theory of religion, he draws upon the moral search for the highest good in order to give completion to the categories of relation

doctrinal development of a rational line of inquiry, expressed in a summary concept which seeks for evidential completion. The speculative and practical needs of human reason are embodied in these completional concepts, together with the corresponding doctrinal efforts at discovering and testing the available evidence.

Thus ontotheology is essentially regulated by the rational concept of completeness of determination of a thing, in respect to all possible predicates. It culminates in a view of God as the most real being, the most inclusive subject of all perfections, and the primal cause of all other things. In cosmotheology and physicotheology, the entire investigation is activated by the rational concept of completeness in the order of causal explanation, or derivation of real beings. These two parts of natural theology specify God's causality, both in respect to any natural system of beings and in respect to our particular world and its adaptive design. Finally, in moral theism the underlying completional concept is that of a unified community of relationships between God and the world, with special stress upon our practical moral aims and search for happiness. Here, God is specified in terms of an embracing system of ends and hence as the highest good, satisfying all the speculative and practical tendencies of man.

The theory of completional concepts advances Kant's philosophy of religion through its unifying power. The completional principles are not isolated from each other but stand in a complementary relationship: all are needed to advance the quest of our mind for an adequate theistic interpretation. Consequently, the several kinds of theology are not separate, competing explanations but distinct phases in a common theological work. A critique is needed to determine these relationships, so that the weakness of one way will be provided for by another, and so that the unique contributions of each form of theology will be recognized and brought into synthesis with the rest.

The continuity in theological reasoning is further advanced by referring the kinds of theology to their respective views on God's agency. It is not sufficient for Kant to invoke his restriction of causality to phenomenal objects as a criticism of causal demonstrations of God's existence. He must also reckon with the positive presence of some notion of divine

---

(substance, cause, community). He establishes a close correspondence between these relational categories and the three main completional concepts which function in moral and speculative theology (perfection, causal origination, happiness), in order to gain an objective practical meaning of God.

agency in most human theories on God and most religious attitudes, quite apart from any claim to demonstrative causal knowledge of God. In his theory of the categories, he recognizes that the general meaning of causality is not confined intrinsically to the particular schematized form of causal relations among phenomenal objects in the spatio-temporal world. And in his theory of religion, he has the opportunity to analyze a progressive development of the meaning of causality, in terms of the several theological conceptions of divine power and agency.

Although causality is treated in an unschematized way in rational theology, it is not deprived of all determinate structure and significant distinctions.[22] Within ontotheology, for instance, causality has the quite minimal but definite meaning of a relation of determining order between the most real being and other things, which share in various degrees in the perfections of God. Kant appeals to German usage here, since to call God a cause in the broadest sense is to designate Him as the *Ur-sache*, the primal reality in the order of determinate perfections. Cosmotheology adds the more definite note of God as the first mover and authoring source of nature, and of whatever belongs in experience. The causal derivation is now viewed as the active use of power, issuing forth in a natural order of beings. This conception is further specified in physicotheology, which uses the analogy of the human maker to bring out the role of purposive intelligence and living will in the divine causal agency.

The meaning of divine causality is now on the verge of its religious connotation, but it still lacks an explicit reference to the total production of all beings through a creative act and the personal relating of God to ourselves. Kant regards creativity and personal recognition as the decisively religious traits in our causal thinking about God. These notes are furnished chiefly by moral theism, since it is through reflecting on our practical human relationship with God, in its completely dependent and yet inviolably personal character, that we realize the full and proper meaning of the causal agency of God. All of the other meanings of divine causality are intrinsically ordered to this moral-religious meaning. They are so many stages in the purposive search of human reason for the full significance of God's causal power.

The most proper analogue for divine power is not to be found in an ideal determination of predicates or in a fashioning of natural materials, but in the life of personal influence and friendly aid toward the good. Here is the definite moral-religious equivalent of the schematic determination of the causal category. The controlled reference achieved in moral

22. *Judgment*, pp. 336–38; *Reflexionen*, 18, 420–26, 496–500.

theism is not intended for speculative knowledge of God's activity, but it does aid our moral and religious understanding of how we stand related to the living creator and moral lawgiver.

As an instance of how the various types of reflection on God converge upon a common religious meaning, Kant's choice of causality is carefully made. For he agrees with Hobbes and Bayle, Hume and Rousseau, that the religious attitude is our human response to the power and agency of God. There need be nothing craven and terror-ridden about a religious relation aroused by the power of God, however, provided that the various meanings of divine agency are distinguished and viewed synoptically in their progression toward the moral significance of God's causal power. Only if a man insists on basing his religious attitude upon some single, isolated aspect of divine causal power, unordered toward a free and personal moral relationship, are his religious conceptions bound to be one-sided and superstitious. By tearing the fabric and order of causal meanings, he only frustrates the dynamism of his human search for God.

All the shortcomings in natural religion already catalogued by Hume are traceable to its exclusive correlation with physicotheology, which fails to subordinate itself to the evidence and conviction provided only by moral theism.[23] Hence Kant regards religious deism and the varieties of nature-based theism as incomplete, preliminary forms of religious life. They have forgotten their origin in, and teleological orientation toward, the religion of the moral theist. If the moral theist is at all reflective and philosophical, he must appreciate and incorporate the religious values arising from the pursuit of the deistic God above the world and the theistic God present in the order of nature. But he cannot stop at either of these stagings, because he cannot forget that their completional goal is found only in the personal practical relation of man with a morally concerned, personal creator. Thus, even in a study of Kant's transregulative reversal of speculative theology, we must take explicit account of his moral theism, which furnishes the living center for mankind's religious reflection and action.

THE HIDDEN GOD AND OUR PREDICATIONS

Kant prolongs his revaluation of speculative theology beyond the proofs of God's existence into the vast forest of predications made about God's nature and attributes. Quite apart from the claims made for exis-

23. "The moral ground of proof of the Being of God, properly speaking, does not merely *complete* and render perfect the physicoteleological proof, but it is a special proof that *supplies* the conviction which is wanting in the latter" (*Judgment*, p. 331).

tential demonstration, he still finds it necessary to give a meaningful account of the rich and persistent efforts of speculative minds, down the ages, to think about the divine nature. Some interpretation is required in this area, not only because the theory of divine names helps to manifest the meaning of God in human experience, but also because the critical stand one takes toward such a theory palpably affects one's position on religion and moral theism. Nothing less is at stake than the proper order to be established between religious belief and the long tradition of speculative reflections on the nature and attributes of God.

Kant has in mind specifically the intellectual predicament of those believers who draw their religious convictions from the Jewish and Christian traditions. Such people must accept a complex position, holding both that God is exalted above us and hidden from our gaze and also that we must meditate upon the mystery of His being, seeking Him out with our mind as well as our heart. Kant retains the tension between the hidden God and the God who somehow manifests Himself and His ways in our experience and for our reflective understanding. His unique blending of the themes of mystery and manifestation is not confined to his moral and religious treatments of God, however, but is already observable in his approach to the speculative doctrine on the nature and attributes of God.

What are the speculative theologians doing, in that vast portion of their philosophical treatise on God which is devoted to His nature and attributes? Kant is sure about one negative point: they are not piercing the barrier of the mystery of God, and converting His hidden reality into something essentially known and demonstrated through humanly apprehended sufficient reasons. His assurance on this score is derived in part from his epistemological limitation of speculative knowledge to phenomenal objects and the constituting principles of consciousness in general. Kant's negative assurance is also derived from the fact that the rationalistic claims, made in natural theology, run counter to the theistic religious conviction which his own philosophy of religion seeks to analyze, not dissolve. At least part of the problem of a speculative philosophy of God is set by the stubborn religious belief that God remains unknown in His own being, even when we may discover true things to say about Him in our philosophy. A constant testimony of the theistic religious tradition— *Natura divina est imperscrutabilis*: the divine nature is unsearchable by us—is one to which the philosophical theories on God must learn to adjust.[24]

24. *Reflexionen*, 18, 713–14; cf. 485–86, on God as both concealing and revealing Himself in the three revelational modes of moral reason, history, and nature. Kant's

There is no stairway of sufficient reasons enabling us to obtain a demonstrated knowledge of the divine nature and an essential insight into the attributes. One need not make an extravagant claim of having such insight, however, in order to do justice to the persistent meditations of religious minds upon the reality of God and His ways with men. Kant even suggests that there can be some speculative reasoning concerning God which avoids the rationalistic extravagance, and makes no violation of the unsearchable being of God.

By respecting the following three critical rules, a philosopher can make some legitimate investigation of the divine reality. First, if he draws materials for analysis from the statements of religious believers, he cannot regard them as yielding knowledge in the same sense in which the statements of physicists yield knowledge about the physical world. Any findings which bear upon the transphenomenal being of God do so in a manner that is distinct from the reference of our perceptions and concepts to the phenomenal objects in experience.

Secondly, the philosopher of God must keep before his mind the crucial distinction between the nature (*Natur*) of God and the idea and essence (*Idee und Wesen*) of God.[25] The former remains a mystery to us. In Locke's and Hume's metaphor, we cannot drop the plumb line of our understanding far enough to reach the divine nature in its own being. But we can develop an idea of God which truly expresses what He means in and for human experience, and we can regard this objectively as a doctrine on the divine essence. The chapters in the natural theology books dealing with the "nature and attributes of God" are, in fact, concerned about our idea of God, as stated in the objective systematic form of a

---

views on the hidden God, the sublime and holy one whom we must trust and hold in awe, are compared with Rudolf Otto's conception of the holy by Herman Schmalenbach, *Kants Religion* (Berlin, 1929), pp. 51–61, and are studied in their biblical and aesthetic origins by Werner Schultz, *Kant als Philosoph des Protestantismus* (Hamburg, 1961), pp. 27–32, 83–87. Schultz rejects the usual designation of Kant as "the philosopher of Protestantism," because Kant assimilates God to the categorical imperative, as well as attributes our belief in God and our religious rebirth to the power of human practical reason. Yet Schultz fails to give due weight to Kant's distinction between the being of God and our idea of God (only the latter being assimilated to the moral imperative), as well as to Kant's consistent refusal to claim that the philosophical explanation of theistic belief and religious orientation is exhaustive.

25. The significance of this distinction for religion is noted in *Reflexionen*, 18, 713, and in *Vorarbeiten zum Streit der Fakultäten*, 23, 438. The moral and religious requirement of qualifying the divine nature by the specifically moral predicates of will and freedom is stressed in *Reflexionen*, 17, 339, 607–08.

doctrine on the divine essence. Thirdly, the theory about the human conception of the divine essence is not entirely arbitrary and devoid of any reference to God's own reality. Even though we cannot directly apprehend God in His own nature, we can still study the relational presence of God in man's moral life and the experienced world.

In replying to Hume's objection that a theism operating under such conditions leads inevitably to anthropomorphism, Kant introduces a distinction between types of anthropomorphism whose import runs through his entire philosophy, from the theory of knowledge to that of religion. All of our philosophizing is anthropomorphic, in the general and undifferentiated sense that we examine the problems which concern men, and do so with the aid of our own minds and the lode of meaning mined from our own experience. We need not infer, however, that the meanings drawn from our experience are significant only for the human component in our experience. This inference is not permitted to transform the investigation of nature into a study of human subjectivity alone, and it should not be permitted to transform the theory of God and religion into a study of human consciousness alone.

In analyzing the more specific human approaches to God and the religious relationship, Kant finds it helpful to distinguish between a dogmatic-constitutive anthropomorphism and a symbolic-regulative anthropomorphism.[26] The difference lies in two ways of interpreting our theistic predications. They can be regarded as directly grasping and specifying the reality of God, so that our categories give us strict knowledge of God's existence and nature, in their divine actuality. This is the standpoint of a *dogmatic* anthropomorphism, which makes a constitutive theoretical use of our concepts and predications about God, and thus confuses our idea of God with the divine reality itself. Since this view supposes that our human statements about God apply literally to Him, in much the same way that our categories apply to the physical world, its effect upon the mind is to dispel a conviction in God's transcendence and hiddenness, and hence to misread the religious attitude itself. Kant agrees with Hume that this sort of anthropomorphism is unavoidable, as long as one seeks a demonstrative speculative knowledge of God upon which to erect our religious beliefs. But it can be effectively avoided by any reflective person who grasps the import of Kant's critique of speculative theology, and

26. *Prolegomena To Any Future Metaphysics*, trans. P. G. Lucas (New York, 1953), pp. 122–28; *Pure Reason*, A 697–701:B 725–29 (pp. 566–69); *Religion*, pp. 156–57; *Reflexionen*, 18, 439, 503.

accepts the three conditions mentioned above for interpreting all human speculations about God.

Acceptance of these heuristic conditions enables the careful philosopher of God and religion to escape from dogmatic anthropomorphism. But he must persevere in his unreserved acceptance of the human condition, without trying to escape from it in the course of his speculative and practical reflections on religious issues. Kant asks us to acknowledge *symbolic* anthropomorphism, not as our dire fate but as the fitting expression of our human situation in reality, whenever we engage in the search for God. Symbolic anthropomorphism is a freely developed and accepted principle for interpreting what men do in their speculative and practical investigations concerning God. We do not try to penetrate into the hidden being of God Himself—who always remains *Deus absconditus*—but only to fathom some of His relationships with us, some of His ways of manifesting the divine reality in natural process and human moral freedom.

Once we grasp the moral grounding of the idea of God, we can avoid any sort of dogmatic-constitutive use of this idea, whether for speculative or for practical religious purposes.[27] Thus the Kantian reversal of speculative theology includes a passage from the dogmatic-constitutive to the symbolic-regulative kind of anthropomorphism. When this transition is made in our understanding of the interpretative uses of the meaning of God in our experience, the term "anthropomorphism" ceases to carry the weight of a palmary objection. Instead, it conveys a straightforward description of how man carries on his ordinary reflections concerning God and achieves practical relationships with Him.

As for the specifying term "symbolic," it is similarly compounded of several elements whose full significance is brought out only gradually by Kant, as he moves from the speculative to the practical phases in his theory of religion. We use the directly apprehended human meanings in our experience to intimate, for ourselves and others, something about our relationship to the holy reality of God, without pretending to penetrate that reality through a direct experience or vision. The problem of religious symbolism is approached by Kant at the most general level of the interpretative act of the mind involved in trying to make do with what our ordinary experience affords us, in order to express the significance of man's opening toward the divine presence and saving acts.

27. In discussing the theoretical, regulative use of the idea of God (*Pure Reason*, A 670–704:B 698–732 [pp. 550–70]), Kant includes in its content the moral attributes of wisdom and providence, will and purpose so as to stress the practical basis of all theistic predication.

The first task of a philosophical study of the symbolic thinking, acting, and discoursing involved in religion is to inspect the originative human meanings found in the signifying process. The purpose of this anthropological reference is not to make a psychological reduction, but simply to gain control over the direct human meanings and then to observe the modifications which religious belief and practice introduce into the fundamental senses of words and acts. After the tension between the directly experienced sense and that which is appropriate to a religious attitude is descriptively ascertained, the next step is to inquire whether the inferred and adjusted usage of the religious symbolism is justified. At this point of searching for the human evidence behind our reference of meanings and acts to the divine reality, Kant's symbolic anthropomorphism achieves its distinctive philosophical form, and might more properly be called a *symbolizing theism*. The intent of this symbolizing theism is to stress simultaneously the altogether human basis of all our means of discourse and enactment concerning God and also the religious striving and import of many traits in our existence.

By the nature of the investigation, a symbolizing theism makes a deliberate use of analogy in all its predications concerning God and the religious reference of human life. Kant recognizes the broad need for analogical thinking in the theory of God and religion, without permitting himself to reinstate any transcendent metaphysical basis for it. He is led to this broad recognition of religious analogy from his criticism of Wolff and Hume. The former makes extreme claims for the competence of philosophical reason in natural theology, precisely because his method is fundamentally univocal in its reliance on essential definitions and sufficient reasons, which reach even into the hidden being of God's nature. As for Hume, he represents the other extreme of so contracting the scope of our moral reason that we have no definite guidance in moral experience for our statements on God and religion. Hence he oscillates, in a condition of equivocal discourse, between the popular conception of religion and his own philosophical minimum.

In discussing the theistic use of analogy, Kant consults the current manuals of speculative theology used in the German universities. He is not much interested in the elaborate internal division of the kinds of analogy proposed by these sources. For his purpose, it is sufficient to mark off a theistic analogy, which involves a search after the nonquantitative and nonfinite meaning of God, from a mathematical analogy based on definite proportions between quantities and figures. Of far greater importance to him is the venerable tradition of the three ways of making predications about God: by negation, by eminence, and by causality.[28]

Kant reduces the way of causality, as used in the rationalistic natural theologies, to that of ground-and-consequent. He then criticizes the latter, as it supposes the presence of some sufficient reason in God which we can grasp and use as a principle of predication—a supposition contrary to Kant's own stress on the hidden God. Hence he agrees with Baumgarten in substituting the way of analogy for that of causality. This does not rule out the attribution to God of predicates expressing various aspects of causality. As Kant's correlation between the kinds of theology and the kinds of divine agency has already shown, he is prepared to think about God in terms of the causal model and various causal predicates. But he does not permit causality to serve as a strict mode of *inference to* God and as a governing *principle of predication about* Him. We can make causal predications about God, but we cannot legitimate these predications by means of a causal inference, or elucidate them through a causally specified way of interpreting all predication. Hence the way of analogy is a substitute for that of causality, in the Kantian theory of the theistic ways of predication.

Kant's meaning for analogous predication in rational theology is bound up with his distinction between interpreting a statement according to the standard of physical truth and according to that of humane significance. Whereas the former standard is inappropriate in regard to the non-phenomenal reality of God, the latter is proper to the case of theistic and religious discourse. Kant refers to the theistic way of speaking about God, through an analogy with our own moral and natural reality, as an *argumentum ad modulum humanitatis, secundum assumta humanae naturae, non hominis singularis*.[29] That is, the argument in a symbolizing, analogi-

---

28. *Religionslehre*, pp. 46–50; *Reflexionen*, 18, 554–55. The latter text is from Kant's commentary on the chapter in Eberhard's *Vorbereitung* that discusses the three ways of predication. Erich Adickes, the editor of the *Reflexionen*, notes here that Kant explicitly agrees with Baumgarten in substituting the way of analogy for that of causality, which Eberhard associates with negation and eminence. Kant makes his substitution quite clear: "Thirdly, the way of causality or better, as in Baumgarten, the way of analogy" (*Reflexionen*, 18, 554, n. to l. 10).

29. *Reflexionen*, 18, 88. This is the sense in which Kant maintains that man himself is the analogous principle for determining the meaning of the idea of God (*Opus Postumum*, 21, 47) and hence that "*we create a God for ourselves*" (*Religion*, p. 157) in the process of developing a symbolizing moral theism. Whereas causality cannot serve as a way of proof but only as a schema of thinking about God, the way of

cal theism is not drawn from the peculiarities of the individual man, but rests on the common traits of the human nature we all share and experience.

This moral-existential base in man does not provide us with a strict schema or speculative type of objective determinant of meaning, in the manner of our categorial thinking about natural objects. But it does furnish a norm of moral objectivity and humane relevance for our discourse about God. In this sense, Kant allows that there is an analogous schema furnished by the likeness between the idea of God and our reflection upon human nature in its moral aims and natural relations. This moral-religious schema gives a determinate meaning and practical objectivity to theistic inference and to the religious ordination of our existence toward God.

Yet even the way of analogy cannot be used exclusively in our thought and discourse about God. If it were made the sole rule of predication, our idea of God might simply be a magnified likeness of our image of human nature. The result would be a triumph of dogmatic anthropomorphism in the most general and objectionable sense. To avoid this outcome, Kant deliberately combines analogy with the other two ways of predication: negation and eminence.

But how can the human mind be prodded into making a systematic use of the ways of negation and eminence, in order to purge and elevate our concept of God as much as possible and thus achieve a nonidolatrous sort of analogy between man and God? Kant's methodological answer to this question is provided by the mutual relationship between the three kinds of speculative theology. Their main function does not lie in the order of existential demonstration, but rather in the essential order of predications, where they are concerned with developing and purifying the intrinsic components in our idea of God. By performing these functions, the speculative theologies together constitute an indispensable prolegomenon to the practical philosophy of God.

Ontotheology has both a negative and a positive task in the Kantian theory of the divine attributes.[30] Negatively, it must purge out any general dogmatic anthropomorphism which may result from conceiving of God

---

human analogy is both a schema of predication and a basis of proof for the moral inference to God. The human religious task of fashioning within oneself a moral ideal of God, as a way of opening one's practical life to God's own reality, is examined by Joseph de Finance, *Essai sur l'agir humain* (Rome, 1962), pp. 309–27.

30. *Religionslehre*, pp. 86–88; *Reflexionen*, 18, 209.

in terms of the properties drawn from our experience of the physical world and ourselves. A transcendental theology keeps us critically aware of the incommensurability between the most real and perfect being and all the attributes derived from finite sources. On the positive side, this ontological approach in theology assures an inner consistency and connectedness among those attributes which are included in the idea of God. Whereas the ideal character of ontotheology is a handicap in existential demonstration, it is an asset in the complex work of purging our idea of God of all univocal uses and incoherencies. It urges on the mind to submit all proposed divine properties to the ways of negation and eminence, so that their attribution will not destroy the transcendent reality of God.

There is a genuine need, however, for the other two types of speculative theology. They help to remedy a defect in the ontological predicates, which specify our idea of God only in a highly metaphysical and indeterminate way. It would be no defect in a purely theoretical approach to God to speak of Him mainly as the most real and perfect being, but our human idea of God is ultimately ordered to a practical assent and a religious relationship. For such a purpose, the presence of God to our experienced world and His relevance to our personal life of intelligence and the use of power must also be incorporated into the idea of God. Cosmotheology and physicotheology supply these more determinate natural and psychological predicates, which make the idea of God more determinately related to human experience.[31] Hence they use the analogical modes of predication to deepen the ordination of that idea toward our eventual moral assent and religious response to God.

The Kantian way of analogy is not simply a theoretical procedure for blending likenesses with basic differences, in our predications about God. It is also a distinctive religious searching out of the order of nature and human experience for those meanings which manifest God's free, purposive mind and personal agency. In particular, physicotheology is cultivated by our mind in order to find a more concrete way of envisioning

---

31. Ibid., *18*, 431–32, 445. The psychological perfections or *realitates* of understanding and will cannot validly be incorporated into the idea of God, however, unless God's own incomprehensible being is acknowledged as a safeguard against dogmatic anthropomorphism. Ontotheology can aid us here by requiring predication through negation and eminence, and thus counterbalancing the adaptation of physicotheology to an artisan deity. In this sense, Kant holds that the ontological *predicates* are tacitly but properly understood as a condition for the valid theistic application of the psychological ones, quite to the contrary of the invalidating effect of the ontological *argument* on the other proofs.

the divine perfections and exhibiting God's powerful, living presence in the natural world we inhabit. This theology is not the generative source and basis of a theistic belief in God. But it is an effective means whereby the believing mind can make the question of God relevant to nature, scrutinize nature for the marks of God, and thus prepare the path for a religious response to Him involving an ordering of all natural existents.

A reciprocity is operative in speculative theology between the *natural* and *psychological* predicates, signifying perfections drawn from the order of nature and purposive human intelligence, and the *ontological* predicates derived from an essential analysis of the notion of the most real, perfect, and necessary being. The former set of predicates encourages the use of the way of analogy, in which there is some room for likeness and relationship between ourselves and God. And the latter set generates the need to use the ways of negation and eminence, so that the otherness and transcendence of God will be preserved in an idea of His unbounded perfection. Thus the work of speculative theology is to achieve a constant tension among the several attributes and modes of predicating them, so that we can attain as worthy an idea of God as is possible in the order of direct speculation.

Yet even such an accomplishment remains insufficient for the ultimate purposes of a religious response to God, until it submits to a critical reinterpretation. Kant is prepared to show, for instance, that physicotheology is more precisely construed as a physico*teleology*, which makes a regulative use of the idea of purpose, but not a metaphysically constitutive use.[32] Therefore, the analogical predications which a physicoteleology makes about the intelligence and will of God are intrinsically subject to the limiting conditions set forth in Kant's own third *Critique*. Not even the religious form of teleological judgment can penetrate the internal structure of the divine purposive workings in the world.

Even after speculative theology synthesizes the ontological and natural

---

32. "Physicotheology is a misunderstood physical teleology, only serviceable as a preparation (propaedeutic) for theology, and it is only adequate to this design by the aid of a foreign principle on which it can rely, and not in itself, as its name seems to indicate" (*Judgment*, p. 292; see pp. 286–304, 329–34; *Reflexionen*, 18, 719, 723–24). Only after a "foreign principle" is found in the nonspeculative argument of moral theism, can the study of traces of an ordering mind in nature acquire a determinate theistic significance. Thus Kant makes a twofold philosophical reduction: physicotheology to physicoteleology, and then the latter to moral theism or moral teleology. In the case of believers, their revealed faith constitutes another kind of "foreign principle" used in the religious interpretation of nature.

predicates about God, it still has one last service to render humanity. It must point beyond itself to moral and religious theism, of which it is only the instrument and philosophical preparation.[33] We can gauge just how profoundly this reordering of speculative to moral theology affects the school doctrine on the attributes of God, by observing the two key changes which Kant himself introduces into the theory of divine names. These modifications concern the divine infinity and wisdom.

Among the ontological attributes, he is quite dissatisfied with the prominence given to the infinity of God. The meaning which this note usually summons up in our minds is closely associated with the image of vast spatial stretches and durations of time. Kant seeks to correct the misleading imagery of cosmic vastness by subordinating infinity to the more closely religious thought of divine *allsufficiency*.[34] Kant dwells upon the frequent references in St. Paul to the allsufficient God, who is from eternity and to eternity, and in whom men will find their own true sufficiency of life. This thought conveys something of God's majesty and power, His complete otherness from all dependent beings, and the steadfast eternal good which He offers to men in their search for happiness. Since these aspects of God are specially significant for establishing a religious bond with Him, Kant places the emphasis upon the ontological attribute of allsufficiency, rather than upon infinity as the favorite note stressed in the rationalist ontologies.

He makes a similar, religiously motivated revaluation of the attributes found in natural theology, especially the so-called psychological predicates of life, intelligence, and will which physicotheology assigns to God. To think of God as a living, purposive, free maker of ourselves and the visible universe does indeed mark a further determination of the conception of God. It makes the meaning of unconditioned perfection and actuality more proportioned to human religious apprehension. Yet Kant questions whether *wisdom* should be counted among God's natural attributes, established in a purely theoretical way. Hume had agreed with the Wolffians on the ability of speculative theology to show that the divine

33. "The concept of God is one which belongs originally not to physics, i.e., to speculative reason, but to morals" (*Practical Reason*, p. 242).

34. Kant shifted the emphasis from infinity to allsufficiency during his early years and retained it throughout his critical writings. See *Der einzig mögliche Beweisgrund zu einer Demonstration des Daseins Gottes*, 2, 151–54; Horst-Günter Redmann, *Gott und Welt: Die Schöpfungstheologie der vorkritischen Periode Kants* (Göttingen, 1962), pp. 68–72, 150–59.

mind is wise, and hence that wisdom belongs among the natural attributes of God. But Kant observes that some practical and moral meaning is ordinarily assigned to our concept of wisdom.[35] We do not concede that someone is really wise, until we are sure that he uses his mind, will, and power in a good way and for morally consonant ends.

Similarly, in a theistic analogy it is not enough to infer God's wisdom from physical order or from the sheer presence of mind and will in Him. The question of the practical use of divine intelligence and will remains, and this is not just a matter of exercising these powers but of using them well in respect to the moral welfare of man and the destiny of the universe. Hence the attribute of divine wisdom belongs properly among God's moral and religious attributes, rather than among the theoretico-psychological ones. Its function is to specify all the natural attributes in a religious manner, and thus to lead the inquirer after wisdom from a speculative to a moral and religious consideration of God.

---

35. *Practical Reason*, p. 233; *Judgment*, p. 291; *Über das Misslingen aller philosophischen Versuche in der Theodicee*, 8, 256. Kant's operative distinction here is between the artistic wisdom of a cosmic demiurge, arrived at in a physicoteleology, and the moral wisdom of the transcendent, provident God to which we are led by moral theism. His behind-the-scenes sharpening of this issue can be traced in *Reflexionen*, 17, 173–74, 744, 18, 452–53; *Opus Postumum*, 21, 120. The modern philosophical treatment of wisdom is examined by James Collins, *The Lure of Wisdom* (Milwaukee, 1962).

4

Kant's Moral Radication of Religion

The net effect of Kant's Copernican revolution in the speculative theory of God is to prevent any direct passage from transcendental and natural theology to the religious conception of God. Such a passage cannot be made on a purely speculative basis, due to the radical dependency of every speculative view of God upon the dynamism of our moral life. Hence Kant stands for the essential need to insert the moral interval into every well-constructed philosophy of religion. In contradistinction to the attempt of a theological ethics to deduce our moral and religious duties from a metaphysical theory of God and man, he undertakes to develop an ethicotheology or morally based account of our relations with God. In the Kantian philosophy of religion, this means that the act of religious faith must agree with the general pattern set by moral belief, and that the practical religious reference of man to God must draw strength from the active tendencies in human reality and its moral freedom. Only after man's religious assent and action are thoroughly radicated in their practical context can the problem of revealed religion be meaningfully studied in the philosophy of religion.

THE PATH OF MORAL BELIEF IN GOD

In order to develop a disciplined ethicotheology within his critical philosophy, Kant carefully adapts his general theory of moral belief to the specific case of the assent to God. He directs attention to four special points of relevance: the role of practical interest, the plural ways of affirming an invisible powerful reality, the meaning of moral orientation, and the synthesis of objectivity and freedom in theistic moral belief. Taken together, these aspects of his theory of belief compel Kant to attach an indelible moral qualification to every assent to God and every practical response of the religious man, as well as to every theological doctrine pertaining to these matters.

Practical Interest. One way to appreciate the practical context for the philosophy of religion is to notice the pervasive presence of interest and its ultimately practical character. We never approach the question of God's existence, nature, and significance for man in a purely detached and unconcerned way. Even when we propound the difficulties from a speculative standpoint, we are responding to an interest of reason in maintaining the integrity and critical limitation of its concepts and modes of inference. Both the reasonings involved in theism and the active responses toward which they lead are big with value significance for man.

A consequence of Kant's general theory about the interest aspect in all human inquiries is that the inquiry about God always involves, at least implicitly, a practical current of interest.

> Every interest is ultimately practical, even that of speculative reason being only conditional and reaching perfection only in practical use. . . . Everything in the end verges toward the practical, and it is in this tendency of all theory and all speculation in respect to their employment that the practical value of our knowledge consists.[1]

In its origin as well as its goal, the speculative doctrine on God is instrumental to the fulfillment of our practical interests, as searching personal agents. Hence all the components in our speculative idea of God can be integrated, in principle, with the moral meaning of God and the practical religious tendencies of our active life. Interest is the binding thread for achieving a personal religious synthesis of man's several ways of inquiring about, and actively searching for, God.

Dynamic Plurality. This position is reinforced when Kant directly inspects the dynamic plurality of human ways of arriving at the religious conviction that there are invisible powers, belonging to a divine order of reality. In pursuing the genetic question about the basic religious

1. *Practical Reason*, p. 225; *Logic*, pp. 77-78.

belief in a powerful spiritual reality, he offers a reformed version of Hume's natural history of religion. Our several cognitive powers must be brought into play to generate the belief, and their modes of operation can lead either to some onesided and conflicting religious attitudes or else to a complex unification around the adequate standard of the religion of moral theism. There are four basic correlations between the cognitive bases of assent and the resulting religious positions.[2]

A. WAYS OF IMAGINATION
> Concrete imagining: idolatrous superstition
> Intuitive vision: enthusiastic fanaticism

B. WAYS OF REASON
> Speculative proof: metaphysical theologism
> Moral belief: moral theism

The kind of natural history of religion which Kant proposes at this point is based upon this analytic correlation between the cognitive operations of human nature and the dominant religious attitudes at any stage in human history, rather than upon a comparative empirical study of the actual religions of mankind.

Men first come to their belief in unseen, powerful reality along the path of concrete imagining and myth. They are impressed by the surplus of power manifested in both the periodic and the violent aspects of nature, as well as in human society. Men become convinced of the reality of invisible ruling powers, which are held to be many and personal. These are the gods of nature and the city. They are not regarded as total creators of the natural world, but rather as natural beings who have superior power and who can respond, for our woe or weal, to human supplications. Religious myths grope toward a meaning of the divine that will actively relate it to particular sensible things, as well as to the forces moving in nature and human society. A superstitious religious attitude is readily generated by this imaginative approach, although it never stifles the fundamental search after something sacred which will aid man.

This inclination within us to seek out the divine order of reality is never satisfied with the mere affirmation of non-moral power, however

---

2. *Reflexionen*, 18, 511–13; cf. pp. 598–601, containing the section in Eberhard's *Vorbereitung* entitled "Natural History of Religion." By 1759, both French and German translations of Hume's *Four Dissertations*, containing the *Natural History of Religion*, were published.

exalted its mythic presentation and its influence in practical life. Kant maintains that men seek to develop the moral aspect of religion, as soon as their practical reason begins to reflect upon the human relationship with the divine. Quite early in mankind's religious quest, the germ of moral reflection becomes operative beyond the imaginative representation of sacred power. Such reflection inclines people, however vaguely, to envisage the divine power as residing in a personal God, who is the law-giver and the defender of standards of just treatment among men. Thus, even before men engage in formal theological speculations about the one God, their practical moral impetus enables them to make a pre-liminary passage from polytheism to a moral monotheism.

In its initial condition, moral theism is quite vulnerable to speculative objections and practical reversions to polytheism. With the growth of the sciences and their logical methods, however, men have tried to remedy this weakness by placing theism upon a speculative footing. They have treated religion as though it were a practical consequence drawn from independent metaphysical reasonings about God, and hence as though it were essentially dependent upon the validity of speculative demonstra-tions in natural theology. Yet this metaphysical theologism has never been able to sustain its own claims and reasonings in rigorous fashion, so that its long-range influence upon our human acceptance of spiritual reality has been unsettling rather than stabilizing. As a result of intel-lectual controversies, religious believers tend again to subordinate the way of reason to that of imagination, either by adopting a more sophisticated form of superstition or by claiming to have some intuition or vision of the divine. The descent from speculative proof to visionary enthusiasm in religious matters is swift, and often goes undetected. And when people eventually do recognize this fluctuation between pretended speculative proof and pretended spiritual vision, their adherence to God is funda-mentally shaken. Skepticism in religious questions is a protective response against the conflict between the ways of imagination and that of specu-lative theological reason.

To overcome fanaticism and enthusiastic dreaming in religion, one can-not appeal to still further speculative demonstrations, since it was the strain placed upon us by the overclaims made for such demonstrations which led to the visionary attitude. Instead, Kant recommends that the distinctive resources of moral belief be freed from subordination to theologism and be integrated, instead, with a critique of knowledge and a reflective understanding of human history and cultural growth.

Kant makes a decisive contrast between the *precritical* and the modern *critico-historical* condition of moral theism. Modern culture opens up some fresh possibilities of the spirit for a moral theism which becomes allied with the critical outlook and an awareness of human historicity.[3] A critically and historically mature moral theism supplies the corrective against the distorting factors in our religious response to God. With the aid of a critical theory of knowledge, it shows that the demand to gain speculative demonstrations about God is unwarranted and oversteps the limits of human reason. Once this demand is systematically removed, the human mind is also relieved of the pressure to overcompensate by means of an intuitive vision of spiritual reality. And the powerful tendency toward a superstitious view of the divine is thereby remedied. Religious superstition is undermined partly by taking account of the scientific conception of natural forces, partly by seeing man the social agent in the light of different historical contexts for social power, and partly by following the critical rule of distinguishing between the subjective conditions of human knowing and the divine reality itself.

In making his epistemological correlation between ways of cognition and religious standpoints, Kant does not intend to add another chapter to those empirical descriptions of religions which he so much enjoyed reading. His intent is the philosophical one of showing a path out of the perpetual flux and alternation to which Hume had doomed the ordinary religious mind. Kant breaks loose from the Humean alternating cycle of monotheism and polytheism, by shifting the emphasis from these objective contents of belief to the cognitive modes of reaching our conviction in the sacred, spiritual presence of the divine. Moral theism escapes from a religious cyclic reflux in the degree that our moral belief in God becomes critically reflective and historically aware of its foundation in human reality. This puts us in possession of a religious monotheism which maintains a personal, morally responsible relation with God, and hence which uproots polytheism along with superstition and fanaticism.

In terms of the relationship between reason, experience, and assent to God, Kant is now able to give an epistemological account of these aberrant religious attitudes.[4] The superstitious mind seeks to conform belief

3. Kant's essay, *What Is Enlightenment?* trans. L. W. Beck, in *Writings in Moral Philosophy*, pp. 286–92, illustrates the critico-historical approach to moral theism.

4. *Practical Reason*, p. 238; *Religion*, pp. 78, 162–63; *Lectures on Ethics*, trans. Louis Infield (New York, 1963), pp. 87–89; *Der Streit der Fakultäten*, ed. Klaus Reich (Hamburg, 1959), pp. 52–59, where a correlation is made respectively between

in God to the conditions of sense experience, apart from a rational purification of the act and object of worship. To the extent that religious people seek God in visible forms and human content, the tendency toward idolatry still remains strong. Conversely, the fanatical or enthusiastic type of believer is fascinated by the ideal of divinity set forth by reason, but refuses to take seriously the limitation placed upon our assertions about God by the limits of human experience. Ideal conceptions and aspirations are considered in isolation from the human mode of reasoning, and hence are treated as immediate apprehensions of divine reality.

Both of these extremes are left behind by the theological rationalist, who does concede the importance of both reason and experience in determining our understanding of God. Religious conviction seems to be strengthened by a metaphysical theologism, until the development of the modern sciences forces men to compare the different kinds of knowledge and thus to take a critical position toward the whole program of gaining philosophical knowledge about God. Criticism of rationalist theology has three possible outcomes. It can provoke a relapse into the fanatical frame of mind; it can generate fideism or else skeptical unbelief; and it can prepare the ground for moral theism itself. The Kantian critique seeks to foster this latter alternative, while at the same time searching the roots of modern religious unbelief.

Kant makes a significant comparison between the epistemological premises of the moral theist and the unbeliever. Their similarity consists in recognizing the mutual determination of reason and experience, in our judgments about reality. But the unbeliever rejects the reality of anything whose existence cannot be strictly proved, in the way that physical objects are given a speculative demonstration through reason and experience. On the contrary, the moral theist incorporates into his investigation the maxim of being ready to accept whatever is necessary for the complete experiential use of reason, in its task of penetrating the structure of human existence and acting in accord with its practical requirements.

The basic disagreement between the unbeliever and the man of moral faith concerns the acceptance of this maxim and its implications, rather than any particular content of a creed. A moral believer is one who is ready to accept the personal spiritual reality of God, as being somehow

---

superstition and orthodoxism, fanaticism and mysticism, criticism and philosophical moderation in religion.

required for the full understanding of our human reality and its practical tendency, even though God's existence is not shown in the same way that an object is scientifically established as being real.

Adoption of the maxim concerning realities which are not in the modality of physical objects and speculatively demonstrable conclusions, depends upon a widening of experience and an opening of the mind to belief. Anticipating Hegel on the need for a broader view of experience, Kant argues explicitly for a twofold meaning for the nonchimerical, experiential use of reason: physical and pure.[5] The *physical* experiential use of reason consists in determining the objects and necessary conditions for our experience of the physical world. And the pure or adequately *humane* experiential use of reason consists in a determination of whatever conditions are required for human experience in its entire range. They include not only our relationship to physical objects but also our grasp of ourselves, as free and morally obligated agents, and our quest of the divine.

Just as Kant correlates the physical experiential use of reason with *knowledge*, so does he correlate the humane use with *belief* in realities bearing upon human experience, but not presented as constitutive principles of sensible objects. The direct contrast between knowledge and belief is more fundamental for Kant's theory of religion than is the trichotomy he sometimes makes between knowledge, opinion, and belief.[6] This classical trichotomy is useful mainly to show that the opinionative state of mind is entirely lacking in certitude, whereas belief does provide a subjective principle of certitude, and knowledge provides both a subjective and an objective principle of certitude. But the threefold division can be misleading, if it suggests that belief is only a high grade of opinion on its way toward becoming knowledge, or that certitude is only half-realized in belief and finds its full, homogeneous realization only in knowledge.

The belief concerned with the assent to God and the religious ordering of life is different in kind from opinion and knowledge. It is not an instance of opinion, since it involves some certitude about the reality of God and the religious bond. Yet it is not a case of halting theoretical knowledge, since it is not an assent concerning physical objects and their a priori principles. Kant regards theistic belief, not as a weaker grade of knowledge, but as a distinctive cognition which is in principle *nontrans-*

---

5. *Reflexionen*, 18, 506–11; *Judgment*, pp. 324–25, on dogmatic unbelief.
6. *Pure Reason*, A 820–31:B 848–59 (pp. 645–52); *Practical Reason*, pp. 229, 243–47; *Logic*, pp. 56–64; *Judgment*, pp. 318–25.

formable into the objective order of knowledge and opinion. That it draws its certitude from a subjective source alone does not imply that it enjoys only a half-share in the same certitudinal basis found in knowledge. The subjectivity of theistic belief means its adaptation to the real conditions which shape the moral life of the free, human person or subject.

To believe is to accept as certain and true, and hence to assent to, those realities which are implicated in our moral freedom and obligation, but which are not available in our intuition or our objective speculative demonstration. We cannot dictate the mode of disclosure to God's transcendent reality, and hence our cognitive response to His presence must adapt itself to God's manner of becoming relevant to human experience. Theistic moral belief is the proportionate human way of attaining some certitudinal conviction about the spiritual, presential act of God and our religious relationship with Him.

Orientation in Thought.   Because the act of believing is not a step along the path of speculative knowledge but a cognitive way of its own, it requires a distinctive disposition of the mind, operating under a distinctive maxim of reason. Kant employs the ordinary word "orientation" in a technical sense to designate this opening of the human mind to the act of believing and its rational rule.[7] A modern person, alive to the challenges of skepticism and naturalism in religious matters, must engage in a deliberate process of reflection and gradual orientation in order to believe, at least to believe in an intellectually defensible manner.

As illuminating the nature of religious belief, Kant specifies the four steps in the preparatory reflection quite closely. First, we must make sure that the subject of the search does not fall within the scope of knowledge and opinion, in the sense of being open in principle to sense intuition, to demonstration through some a priori principle, or to ascertainment in the manner of a historical fact. Next, the conscientious mind must reflect sufficiently upon the religious meaning in question to certify that it contains no contradictions and survives the speculative tests for internal consistency. Thirdly, its coherence with what we do know and experience has to be established, by bringing the concept of what is to be believed into some determinate relationship with man and his world. Analogies and the corrective modes of predication through negation and emi-

7. *What Is Orientation in Thinking?* trans. L. W. Beck, in *Writings on Moral Philosophy,* pp. 293–305.

nence can be used at this point, as long as the developed meanings on God and religion are not confused with a demonstrative inference.

In fact, the fourth and final preparatory step consists in making a comparison between the limits of human knowledge and the drive of our reason to increase its cognitive act, so that it may somehow include the divine reality lying beyond the range of objective knowledge as such. Once we recognize this discrepancy between what we can know and what we seek to cognize in some other fashion, our reason necessarily generates the feeling of a cognitive need for relying upon some act of faith. Although reason itself does not feel, it brings this feeling of a need before itself as a means of clarifying its own impulse toward the believing mode of cognition.

The inquiring mind orients itself toward belief, when it accepts the rule of guiding its practical assent by the implications of the need of reason, insofar as that need is shown to spring from some conditions required for the humane experiential use of reason. Orientation occurs in the act of adopting the maxim of the right of this need of reason to serve as the grounding principle in man's acceptance of some divine reality through the mode of rational belief. This is the positive sense in which Kant holds that belief rests upon a subjective principle of certainty. That is, it depends on a reflective awareness of a need for faith on the part of the active personal subject. Although religious believers do not ordinarily follow through the explicit stages in orientation as a prelude to their act of believing, Kant maintains that there is always some minimal reflection present in moral belief, as distinct from the way of imagination. This nucleus of reflective consideration of man's situation constitutes our informal, yet reasonable, knowledge of God. It can be developed into a deliberate orienting of the mind toward the attitude of belief, and should be so developed in the atmosphere of modern criticism.

There is the ready objection that man's religious orientation leads to uncontrolled, wishful thinking. In reply, Kant shows the distinction between *moral* belief, whereby we assent to God and interpret our lives in a religious sense, and other types of belief. The main variants are *pragmatic* belief and *doctrinal* belief, the former involving a practical judgment, and the latter a theoretical judgment, for which the individual inquirer alone stands warrant. Their common feature is that the judgment concerns contingent needs and ends of man, which can be sought after by means of wishes, hypothetical ideas, probabilities, and shifting instrumental relationships.

On the contrary, rational moral belief is genuinely present only when the believing assent is determined by some necessary human need or end of practical reason, that is, by something which is implicated in the very structure of man's free moral agency. Not what we wish to judge or what seems probable, but what we must judge in regard to the human condition of being free agents under law and in search of happiness, constitutes the determining principle of theistic moral belief. The task of moral philosophy and its continuation in the theory of religion is precisely to test the claim of specific candidates for moral belief, by finding out whether or not they do involve the necessary practical relationship to human moral action required for determining the assent of moral belief.

Kant contrasts the stable and certain (but not physically objective) assent found in moral belief with the impermanent and shaky character of the pragmatic and doctrinal forms of belief. For his theory of religion, there is a significant contrast between the direct founding of moral belief in the requirements of moral life and the dependent nature of all theoretical, doctrinal beliefs concerning God. The latter do not enjoy a direct rooting in any speculative demonstration of God's existence, but stand in an instrumental relationship to moral belief in God. Theoretical doctrinal beliefs concerning God help in explicating the meaning of moral theism and in preparing for its intellectual analysis and defense. They constitute an organon of our moral belief in God, but they cannot serve as its fundament.

Thus the Kantian reversal and reorientation of speculative theology reach down to the very acts of mind whereby we adhere to the ideas and reasonings about God in the speculative order. Doctrinal belief is the proportionate intellectual mode of adherence to the statements made in speculative theology. This latter discipline remains radically subordinate to moral theism, as reflected in the intrinsic subordination of all modes of doctrinal belief to moral belief. To attempt to build a moral and religious theory of God upon the supposed demonstrations in speculative theology is to run counter to the proper order obtaining between moral and doctrinal belief.

Moral Objectivity and Freedom.   Kant adds one final strand in his epistemological approach to moral theism: the tension between moral objectivity and freedom in our theistic reflection. It may be asked whether we can affirm the objective reality of the God in whom we have moral faith. Kant offers a reply in three parts. First, he denies that moral belief affirms anything to be real and objective, in the same way in which the objects and a priori conditions of our physical knowledge are real and objective. This denial conforms with the distinction between knowing and believing, and strengthens the position that to know God, in the sense of treating Him as an objective entity or law of the sensible world, would destroy our intended meaning and lead to idolatry in religion.

Secondly, however, Kant is careful to build up, in the Preface to his *Critique of Practical Reason*, a valid moral meaning for the real and the objective which applies here.[8] Something has moral reality and objectivity insofar as it is a component of human freedom and moral law, or is necessarily related in some way with man's condition as a moral agent in the natural world. Thus freedom itself is affirmed to be objectively real, as constituting man's mode of responsible action under law. The judgment can be made in a universal and necessary way (and hence objectively) that, as moral agents under law, men are free. Since the belief in God rests on an inference made from our moral situation, and expresses an implication inherent in that situation as shared by all men, this belief also affirms a real and objective truth in the moral order. The believer opens himself to an active being, who is the real and steadfast source of power and moral good, even though God is not an object in the world.

There is a third qualification which Kant attaches to the meaning of a real object of moral belief, and this note is crucial for catching the religious significance of the problem. Even when we keep God distinct from objects and laws in nature, there is the danger of taking His objective reality to mean that belief in Him is an impersonal truth, which we can all be coerced into accepting. This view rests on a confusion between the content affirmed in belief and the act of believing. The former can be shared by all men, but each one of us must make his own personal act of orienting toward, and believing in, God.

The act of believing is a free, personal response. It is not identical with the conclusion necessarily arrived at in a demonstration, since the spheres of belief and demonstrative knowledge remain distinct. It is free also in the sense that the believer's assent cannot be determined solely by impersonal considerations drawn from the object, apart from all reference to the inquirer's own interests and needs. Indeed, theistic belief springs into existence in the inquirer's mind only when he makes a personal discovery of the involvement of God in his own moral situation. The need of reason for such moral belief in God is necessarily founded in our

8. *Practical Reason*, pp. 118-20. See B. Rousset, *La Doctrine kantienne de l'objectivité* (Paris, 1967).

common humanity, but the believing act itself is a personal fruit of freedom on each believer's part.

In order to emphasize the freedom and personal basis of belief in God, Kant remarks that the key word for the moral theist is not *crede* but *credo*.[9] My primary task is not to issue a command binding upon someone else's act of belief, but rather to assume responsibility for my own act of believing and relating my self-reality to God. Religious belief does have a social aspect, but this aspect is humanely realized only by respecting the grounding of belief in a free, personal act of reflection and commitment. In this sense, Kant is ready to adopt Hamann's vivid maxim that I must make the descent into the hell of self-knowledge, as the first condition for orienting myself and humanity toward God, in the religious relationship. The way in which I conceive of religion will depend upon what I discover in exploring my own moral selfhood, grasped in its interpersonal relations with other men in the world of nature and history.

RELIGION AND THE MINIMUM OF THEOLOGY

Whenever Kant discusses religion, he makes use of the minimal working definition of it as "the recognition of all duties as divine commands." [10] It is an active relating of morality or our moral freedom to God, considered precisely as the highest underived personal good and the author of moral commands. At first glance, this description seems to involve a futile attempt to compress the burgeoning religious movement of spirit within the tight confines of the moral order. There are many instances, indeed, where Kant does take too hasty a look at religious reality, and pass too narrow a judgment upon it by reference to this touchstone. But the intent of his definition of religion is to achieve not a facile moral reductionism but a pithy focus for a whole series of converging investigations. It merely demarcates the meaning of religion functioning within Kant's pure practical philosophy.

9. *Streit*, p. 12; *Vorarbeiten zur Religion innerhalb der Grenzen der blossen Vernunft*, 23, 109. See *Streit*, p. 53, for Kant's reference to Hamann.

10. *Practical Reason*, p. 232. Cf. *Judgment*, p. 311; *Religion*, p. 142; *The Doctrine of Virtue*, trans. M. J. Gregor (New York, 1964), pp. 106, 162–63. This definition serves a paradigmatic function for Kant's philosophical discussion of the nature of religion, somewhat similar to the paradigm of reasonableness in religious discussion recommended by Basil Mitchell, "The Justification of Religious Belief," *Philosophical Quarterly*, 11, (1961), 213–26, and John King-Farlow, "Justification of Religious Belief," *Philosophical Quarterly*, 12 (1962), 261–63.

He explicitly notes that this conception of religion disturbs the usual order of topics found in the school manuals in practical philosophy.[11] There, religion is usually treated as one specific type of moral duty, that which we owe to God. But for Kantian morality, the religious disposition is a habitual way of viewing all our moral duties, a referring of them all to our idea of God and hence a treatment of them all as though they are divine commands. This is the formal aspect of religion, as distinct from the material aspect of religion which singles out certain specific duties owed to God.

As far as Kant's pure, practical philosophy is concerned, the formal and general aspect of religion is alone decisive: it introduces a fresh perspective into all phases of our moral life by viewing our obligations in the light of the religious meaning for God. This affects the philosophical order of treating religion within an ethical framework. It does not figure as one of the particular internal topics in special ethics, but is postponed to a position of generality and culmination for the entire range of moral duties.

The advantage of such an approach is to establish a paradigm for Kant's basic description of religion. Whatever else religion may turn out to be—or to be held to be—among men, the perspective within which it can be reasonably investigated by the critically formed philosopher is set by the cumulative tendencies of our moral existence toward a religious relationship. Kant distinguishes between religion as an objective content of *doctrine* and as a subjective *attitude or disposition* of mind and heart.[12] Both elements are required in a full study of religion. Nevertheless, he gives the primacy to the latter, because it strengthens the need for an operational and practical conception of religion. In its subjective or dispositional character, religion is an active relating of our moral freedom to God, viewed as the source of moral commands. Although the philosopher may not be able to specify the particular doctrinal content of religion in its full range, he can certainly determine the human religious attitude in which all theological doctrines must be rooted.

11. *Lectures on Ethics*, pp. 78–79.

12. All religion is objectively a doctrine embodied in a credal statement and subjectively a disposition to regard all duties as divine commands (*Reflexionen*, 18, 485). This distinction is ultimately governed by the fundamental one between philosophy as a doctrine and as a disposition for philosophizing (*Opus Postumum*, 21, 80, 119; *Vorlesungen über philosophische Enzyklopädie*, ed. Gerhard Lehmann [Berlin, Akademie-Verlag, 1961], p. 38 [cf. pp. 18, 82]).

Kant found it necessary to give his own meaning to the widespread eighteenth-century search for the *minimum of theology*. Hume and the deists understood it to mean the quest for an irreducible set of doctrines on God, and man's relations with Him, which recommends itself to natural reason, and which constitutes the philosopher's religion. Although he accepted the ideal of some irreducible theistic doctrines, Kant did not simply identify the acceptance of them with religion. This would make religion a highly theoretical and abstruse affair, in which only those of a philosophical cast of mind could genuinely participate. Even after a critical purification of doctrines, religion is a matter of the mind's disposition and the heart's practical response, bound up closely with the moral concerns which all men can appreciate and act upon. Kant repudiated the Humean split between popular and philosophical religion, since Rousseau taught him that religious reform can be carried on at the heart of every man's religious life, without segregating the religious position of the philosopher from that given in everyday belief.

More specifically, the question of the minimum of theology arises as soon as we inquire about the kind and amount of knowledge of God required, in order that there may be a religious referring of our moral duties.[13] Kant distinguishes between three uses to which human theological knowledge can be put: for the development of the life of virtue, for the basic religious response of hope-fear-love of God, and for engaging in ecclesial services.

First, the minimum of theology refers to that sort of understanding of God required in pure practical philosophy and for cultivation of the moral virtues. This is the same as the amount of theological understanding needed for having the formal aspect of religion, that is, the viewing of all moral duties as if they are divine commands. To maintain this reference, it is necessary to have the coherent meaning for God found in His moral attributes, along with those speculatively determined attributes which both agree with and help to clarify the moral ones.

13. *Reflexionen*, 18, 498–99, 516, 523. Kant makes the following correlation between the three theological modes and three acts of the mind: (1) the theological minimum of our idea of God is sustained by an act of moral and speculative opinion; (2) the assent to God's actual existence upon which our religious orientation depends is itself an act of moral belief, as distinct from even a well-founded opinion; (3) the theological grasp of the revealing God and His message is achieved through an empirico-historical act of knowing, which the believers in revelation regard as an act of supernatural faith. On the doctrinal content of the first two acts of theological apprehension, see *Pure Reason*, A 631–42:B 659–70, A 805–19:B 833–48 (pp. 525–31, 636–44); *Practical Reason*, pp. 240–43.

In addition, the moral theist must also grasp the real possibility that God may exist. In the purely speculative treatment of God, we do not yet have the grounds for distinguishing between the logical and the real possibility of God's existence. The only way in which these modes of possibility are distinguished speculatively is by reference to the capacity of an object to become integrated into the space-time context. But this criterion holds good solely for phenomenal, sensuous objects and does not apply to the divine existence. It is only in the moral order that we discover a way of distinguishing logical and real possibility in regard to noumenal or spiritual realities: through their connection with man's moral freedom and the conditions for its reasonable exercise. In pure, practical philosophy it is enough to refer our duties to the idea of God compounded of our coherent moral and speculative meaning for the divine essence and the real possibility of the divine existence, in virtue of some as yet undetermined link with our freedom.

Secondly, something more is required in our understanding of God if we wish to foster a direct religious response to God and not simply make an interpretation of moral duties as divine commands. In the developing religious attitude, the emphasis of human action moves from taking a theistic view of duties to responding in hope and fear and love to the divine reality itself. This direct religious response to God must grow out of the moral basis, but it must do so by expanding the theological minimum. What is chiefly required is the conviction in the truth of God's actual existence, not just the conviction in the real moral possibility that God may exist. Kant has to specify those aspects of our moral life which do lead us to moral belief in God's existence and to the religious attitude of godliness, where virtue is joined with piety toward God. This task leads him to the very boundaries of the philosophy of religion.

Third, and finally, this discipline cannot itself take the further step of furnishing the maximum theological knowledge required in order to justify becoming a member of a visible church and participating in its rites and sacraments. One can only take that step on the basis of having a revealed faith in God and receiving a message from Him. The philosopher of religion grounds himself properly in the first two types of theological understanding (the moral meaning of God and the moral belief in His existence). But he must study at least those subjective reasons in human nature that incline men toward the transition to the third, or maximal, interpretation of our knowledge of God and our practical religious bond. It is in this sense that Kant situates the philosophy of religion in the zone of transition and interaction between the first two meanings of theological conviction and the third one. Its complex object of study is that ethical and speculative doctrine on God, which is both necessarily implied by man's moral situation and required for his religious belief and practice.

Yet the very fidelity of this complex position to the working meaning of the religious disposition, as defined by Kant, seems to inject an alien factor into his ethics and thus to disrupt, rather than secure, the close relationship between morality and religion. For in an ethics stressing the moral autonomy and self-legislation of man, there would seem to be no room left for a referring of our moral freedom to God, and no ground discoverable for considering God as the source of moral commands. Indeed, one might even regard the religious reference as an invasion of heteronomy into the very citadel of moral freedom, as a surrender of responsibility for making one's own determination of obligation and imposition of duty. Kant appears to be working at cross purposes with himself when he joins a religious understanding of God with his ethical system.

This difficulty educates us to see that the question of the foundation of morality does not comprise the whole of Kant's ethics and does not even, by itself alone, give us full access to his interpretation of moral life. What the philosopher of religion must learn to do is to distinguish firmly between *foundational* and *implicational* issues, and then to establish the proper order between them. His task is not to determine a theological foundation for moral judgments, but to determine the implications concerning God and religion which must be drawn from our basic moral judgments and principles themselves. We cannot infer from the autonomy of the basic moral principles that man's moral life is so sealed up in the realm of pure practical reason that it permits no further references of moral activity to be made. There are implications of man's moral situation which have to be followed out, as they point toward religious belief and action. Thereby, we gain a critical basis for ascertaining the religious attitude which is proportioned to the human moral condition.

THE MORAL INDICATORS OF RELIGION

Although the foundational and implicational problems in ethics differ, the evidences for resolving them are found together in the most basic features of moral life. The fact that theistic religious beliefs belong among the implications does not hinder them from being grounded in the same moral soil where the foundational principles of morality are also present. Hence it is not surprising that Kant looks for the theistic religious implications in certain aspects of the very same structure of moral autonomy. He bids us take a second look at this judgmental structure, but now for the sake of tracing out the religious implications of its human modality and its practical tendency.

As a guide to such a reflective use of the mind, Kant calls attention to four basic moral indicators of theism and a religious response to God. They concern: the objective practical principle of morality, the subjective practical principle, the feeling of respect, and the distinction between the ground and the object of the moral will. These central features of the moral situation are double-faced: one aspect concerns the foundations of morality, and another concerns the theistic religious implications of human moral existence. The latter side is reflectively apprehended in the moral indicators of the religious, which work together to incline us freely toward a religious belief in God's existence and morally qualified power.

The first moral indicator of the religious is found precisely in Kant's insistent teaching that the only *objective principle* of morality, for a rational agent, is the law itself. Only when the rational agent regulates his action by the pattern of the moral law and for the sake of realizing that pattern, can he succeed in preserving his freedom and at the same time act in a moral way. This objective requirement for the morality of action holds universally for all rational agents, but the moral philosopher must also bring out the characteristic way in which it holds for man, who is that sort of rational agent having a limited, composite, and dependent being. Whereas the objective practical principles of action present themselves to all rational agents as practical laws or patterns of free action, they are related to man in the form of demanding laws or imperative commands.

The imperative character of human moral law contains a twofold disclosure. Its immediate effect upon the reflective mind is to reveal the moral significance of our peculiarly human way of existing, which Kant calls our human condition as "dependent beings." [14] He gives an operational description of human dependence, rather than a metaphysical analysis into general principles of being. Human reality is dependent insofar as it is not purely rational but a composition of reason and sense, rational will and sensuous desire. We are subject to the necessary course

14. *Foundations of the Metaphysics of Morals*, trans. L. W. Beck, in *Writings in Moral Philosophy*, p. 75; cf. p. 96.

of physical nature, to physiological needs, and to the influence of sensuous desires. Our freedom is never unqualifiedly independent of these pressures and attractions, since it must realize itself under conditions where they are strongly influential, and where they can achieve a primacy over rational principles of action. Moral law has the aspect of duty for man, because he must learn to give it disciplined adherence, even in the face of an inward tug in other directions. Kant's stress upon virtue as a pursuit of duty under conditions of conflict is not motivated by any narrow relish for rigorism, but simply by his fidelity to these conditions of human action.

Moral action under an imperative holds a second, and significant disclosure for the theory of religion. As we reflect upon the situation of moral obligation, we can elucidate it by making reference not only to our composite human reality but also to the idea of a completely underived, uncomposed, and independent agent. We become more appreciative of our own moral condition by comparing it to that of God's independent reality, taken also in a moral rather than a metaphysical way. Divine independence or allsufficiency of action means a freedom from the determinism of physical nature, the pressure of physiological needs, and the inclination of sensuous desires. Since there are no countertendencies in the divine reality against the universal rational pattern of action, this pattern does not have an aspect of imperative command and obligation in God's case. For Him, the objective practical principle is moral law as such, without its being humanly qualified as a commanding and restricting law or duty.

This comparison does not warrant any inference about God's actual existence, let alone any metaphysical predications about His nature. Yet it does open up our spirit to appreciate something about God's significance for our moral life. The comparison is not merely a contrast between utterly disparate modes of being. There is some likeness between divine and human reality, since in both modes there is a use of freedom which respects the moral law or pattern of reasonable action. Just as man is not so dependent upon nature and the sensuous order that he cannot achieve the primacy of rational law and hence moral freedom, so the independence and freedom of God are not so alien as to mean a lack of concern for the moral law in any relation between man and God.

Closely bound up with this line of thought is a second moral indicator of the religious relationship, as being implied in the *subjective principle* of morality. The need to distinguish between law and duty in the objective order, suggests that a similar distinction must be made in the subjective order of moral agency. Kant deepens his moral analysis, and also opens up a further point of access to the religious outlook, by distinguishing, in the subjective aspect of moral action, between the holy will and the good will.

In what sense are we reluctant to ascribe a holy will to any man involved in temporal existence, even though we are ready to designate a good will as the subjective principle of his moral action? [15] Kant's reply is that a holy will belongs to a being who need only say "I will," in order to have his action agree with the rational pattern or moral law. The moral will is confronted here with no discrepancy between desire and rational judgment, no attraction away from the universal moral principle, and hence no condition of moral struggle. Such a will is holy, both in its root principle and its entire activity. We dare not claim to have a holy will, because it does not fit our self-experience and our knowledge of the human condition. Hence we reserve the holy will for God, for the all-sufficient personal reality whose will and power of realization are completely in accord with the moral law.

Kant agrees with St. Paul about the chasm which ordinarily spreads out between what I will to do, in the sense of making acknowledgment of the morally upright course, and what I actually do in my conduct of life. A man cannot simply will to do a morally good act and thus be assured of its execution, since his actual choice is not regulated solely by the moral demands of practical reason. The moral composition of human nature consists both of will (*Wille*), in the normative sense of an enduring rational moral demand, and of the power of free choice (*Willkür*), or the ultimate principle of spontaneity underlying our desires and decisions.[16]

However the mystery of moral evil may be explained, our experience of evil assures us that human desires and choices need not conform with the inclination of the morally good will. Hence the characteristic word of the morally concerned man is not "I will" but "I ought." His aim is to bring his desiring and choosing power, or elective will, into conformity with his demanding moral will, but he cannot do this without a constant struggle to affirm the primacy of moral reason and its continued operation as the ordering principle of human action. This is the pregnant sense in

15. *Practical Reason*, pp. 143–44, 188–91.

16. The moral and religious importance of this distinction is shown in J. R. Silber's Introduction to Kant's *Religion*, pp. lxxxiii–lxxxiv, xciv–cvi. See L. W. Beck, *A Commentary on Kant's Critique of Practical Reason* (Chicago, 1960), pp. 176–81.

which the virtuous individual is a man of good will, but not yet a man of holy will.

Yet Kant is very careful not to permit the contrast between the good will and the holy will to harden into a sheer antithesis between morality and holiness. For although man in his striving moral reality cannot pretend to be holy, he is nevertheless attracted by the ideal of holiness as an ultimate, unifying goal of his practical life. He seeks to close the gap between the initial commitment of the good will and its persevering development through character and actions. A participative, human sort of holiness fulfills the tendency of the good will itself to gather up all its intentions, acts, and dispositional trends into a unified human life, fully responsive to the demands of the moral ideal. If the virtuous man cannot simply be holy, in the sense of wiping out the difference between the human and divine ways of being and acting, he can still aim at becoming holy or achieving that practical unification of activity which constitutes the human moral analogue to God's holiness. This effort is strengthened through making a practical religious commitment of oneself to God, the holy one.

What sets off Kant from Spinoza and Hegel on this issue is the theistic nature of the religious reference. As he sees it, holiness becomes practically involved in our moral pattern without making any monistic transfiguration of our temporal existence and moral activity into God's allsufficient being. The holy integration of our moral growth neither turns out to be the same as God's eternal holiness nor constitutes a phase in the unfolding of that holiness. It remains a humanly intended analogue to God's holy power and action, and indeed an analogue whose complete actualization may require some aid from the creative power of God. It is this practical use of analogy, rather than its speculative complications, which is important for Kantian philosophy of religion.

Kant also regards the *feeling of respect* as an irreducible factor in moral life, and a third sure indicator of the religious dimension.[17] He does not permit feelings to serve as the foundation and norm of morality, but he recognizes the distinctive function of the feeling of respect in our moral life. Granted that the sole objective motive of moral action is the impartial rational demand of self-imposed moral law itself, a human moral philosophy must view the moral law not only in itself, but also in relation to the human moral agent. Considered in its influence upon the

17. *Foundations of the Metaphysics of Morals*, p. 62; *Practical Reason*, pp. 181–88; *Orientation in Thinking*, p. 299.

composite reality of man the moral agent, the moral law has a subjective effect and serves as a subjective motive or incentive. Insofar as our sensibility and feelings are affected by the presence of the moral law, we are moved toward moral action by a feeling of respect. It steals over us when we realize that our desiring power becomes a good will only through its unconditioned, and yet free, submission to the moral law, regardless of considerations of personal convenience and self-love.

Respect with an overtone of reverence is a unique, complex feeling. It is a distinctive response of the human subjectivity, analogous to a combination of fear and loving inclination. Respectful awe consists of a morally specified dread and esteem: dread before the obliging force of a moral law to which our self-love must conform, and esteem for that law insofar as it is freely imposed by our own judgment of practical reason. Respect works as the incentive to moral action, because it humbles our pride sufficiently to open us out to the universal commands of moral reason and, at the same time, assures us sufficiently of the worth and power of our moral ideal to incline us toward actually governing our practical choices by its standard. It leads us to appreciate both the good nature of the moral law and the worthwhileness of devoting our lives to achieve its dominance in our world.

Once ethical analysis takes the feeling of respect into account, Kant observes, it is already implicitly at the religious level, already at the point where a religious interpretation of moral life is unavoidable. One task of the theory of religion is to make explicit the religious meaning of respect. This attitude is a sure index of the orienting power of the human spirit, its capacity to rise above our immediate involvements, to compare them with a commonly shared norm, and to redirect our lives toward a spiritual center of worth. Our respect is not directed toward sensible things but toward a common moral law and toward other persons, taken as fellow interpreters of the law. By attending to the social significance of this feeling, we come to realize that the moral person is not isolated, but belongs to a wider interpersonal community. The individual person's moral integrity and autonomy need not be violated by considering him as a member of this community, or by regarding God as the head of the interpersonal moral community which Kant calls the kingdom of ends.

There is continuity, but not identity, between respect for the moral law and reverence for God. The former does not fulfill all the potentialities of the human attitude in question, and the latter is not an act utterly foreign to moral man, one which religion alone demands of the human spirit. This is another instance where Kant looks to our ordinary moral experience for the controlling analogy which will give determinate meaning to discourse about our religious relationship with God. Moral respect provides both a motive and a guide to the religious act of reverence. Men can see how fitting it is to venerate God, once they reflect upon Him as a person related in a definite way to the moral law—in His case as a personal source of command. And they can specify their reverential attitude as a feeling of religious awe, which joins a certain fearful dread with a loving esteem, a sense of God's transcendent holiness with an inclination to share in His goodness.

Kant is sure that morality must lead to religion, because so many of his moral conceptions are already steeped in religious significance. This interpenetration is well-illustrated by his analysis of moral respect, which is essentially what Kierkegaard and Jaspers call a border reality requiring both a moral foundation and a religious explication. This is a good example of how a symbolizing theism uses an experienced moral state to indicate our religious relationship with the holy and hidden God.

For his fourth and final moral indicator, pointing symbolically beyond itself to the religious sphere, Kant reconsiders the distinction between *the ground and the object* of moral will. As far as the foundational phase of his ethics is concerned, the ground of morality cannot be located in any object sought by our voluntary desire, be it happiness, an accruing perfection, or an agreement with the divine will. But his theory of religion forces Kant to take a fresh look at the reality of ends or objects of human action, viewed now from the implicational standpoint.

An ethics based on the autonomy of the moral law is not dispensed, thereby, from examining the relation of moral action to its aims and consequences. The human agent cannot remain morally indifferent to practical outcomes, to the fact that his moral choices and actions do have actual results which affect his own happiness and that of others, and hence which function as objects sought or avoided by his desiring and choosing power. This tension between autonomous freedom and achievable goods bearing on our happiness, or between the ground and the object of moral will, is the benchmark of morality functioning under thoroughly human conditions.

Kant recognizes that man, insofar as he is a finite rational agent, must be in search of a highest good which includes both virtue and a happiness proportionate to it. Using the convenient Latin terminology of the school manuals in order to sharpen his meaning, he explains that the human *summum bonum* has a necessarily complex structure, since it synthesizes virtue, happiness, and a certain reference to God.[18] It is *supremum* in respect to the predominance accorded to virtue; and at least for those who follow out the full implications of the human moral predicament, it is also *finitum seu derivativum,* in being affected by the world and referred to the powerful and morally responsive action of God, who is the underived and originating highest good (*originarium*). Thus the religious reference of morality to God is intrinsic to the moral life itself, whenever the latter is viewed as a human tendency toward the good and a search for happiness.

We can now understand Kant's strong statement that his ethics becomes a positive doctrine on happiness and hope, only at the point where it also becomes a theory of religion.[19] Our search for happiness and our need for hope in the attainability of the highest good do not constitute the foundation for moral judgment. But they are quite relevant, as soon as the order of ethical investigation focuses upon the human conditions for actualizing our moral freedom, and thus for realizing the active tendencies of man within a moral context. Our moral action develops within a physical order which is not specially responsive to the human values of freedom and personal happiness. Also, it occurs within a social order, where neither individual nor group effort can fully assure the realization of the common social good and happiness of men. Yet moral man must neither dilute the strictness of moral duty nor prevent his moral will from seeking, as its permanent object, a highest good that includes moral fidelity along with a proportionately satisfying human happiness.

In this situation, the reflective individual postulates the existence of the morally concerned God. To "postulate" God's existence is not to treat it as a wish, a hypothesis, or a weak probability, but rather to assent in the mode of a moral belief. This assures that God will not function in

18. *Practical Reason,* pp. 214–15. Kant establishes a correlation between *actus arbitrii originarii* and *summum bonum originarium* (the act of the underived elective will and the underived highest good, which is God), as well as between *actus arbitrii derivativi* and *summum bonum finitum seu derivativum* (the act of the derived elective will and the finite or derived highest good, which is that rational beings should be happy in this world insofar as they are not unworthy of being happy, i.e. in proportion to their virtue) (*Reflexionen,* 17, 317, 18, 452, 468).

19.
   Only if religion is added to it [morals] can the hope arise of someday participating in happiness in proportion as we endeavored not to be unworthy of it. . . . When for the sake of this wish the step to religion has been taken—then only can ethics be called a doctrine of happiness, because the hope for it first arises with religion. (*Practical Reason,* pp. 232, 233)

our lives as a speculative entity whose real existence blurs undetectably with our own idea of perfection, or as a cosmic moral computer programmed for calculating the equation between virtue and happiness. Belief in God is an assent to Him precisely as a transcendent and morally concerned person, whose creative power not only originates the orders of nature and morality, but also assures the ultimate achievement of moral ends in the natural and social worlds.

To believe in the existing, morally concerned God is to have a strong basis of hope that our conscientious activity in this world makes some sense. The religious man does not regard as futile or silly his search for happiness in our world and his maintenance of moral integrity therein. Kant does not tamper with either component in this situation of moral action: he does not romantically moralize the order of nature, and he does not despairingly weaken the moral imperative and the drive toward the highest good. Instead, he maintains both nature and morality in their full strength, and then suggests that reflection upon their real tension furnishes the humanly necessary basis for the moral and religious assent to God. The human spirit turns to God primarily as the author of nature and moral order together. It is under this unifying aspect that He becomes the God of our religious hope and desire.

This synoptic look at the four moral indicators of the religious interpretation of life, enables us to characterize more precisely the relationship between Kant's ethics and his theory of religion. His initial working description of religion may strike one as being a narrow *moralization* of the nature of religion. But it is closer to fact to say that, by means of the moral indicators, the theory of religion achieves the *humanization* of Kantian ethics itself. The moral law has religious implications because of its human mode of realization.

The moral indicators also guarantee that our moral and speculative convictions about God will always retain both their foundation in moral life and their ordination primarily toward religion, rather than toward any independent metaphysical or theological system. To assure the moral context, Kant specifies that religion in its subjective, formal aspect consists in the recognition of the sum of moral duties *as if* (*instar, tanquam*) they are divine commands.[20] This qualification is not intended to fictionalize

20. On the as-if qualification, see *The Doctrine of Virtue*, pp. 162–63; *Reflexionen zur Religionsphilosophie*, 19, 646, 650. (Kant's reflections on philosophy of religion, as distinct from his commentaries and preparatory notes on the *Religion* book, are collected in the Prussian Academy edition, 19, 617–51.)

the reference of moral law to God, or to make the formal religious act a sheer stratagem on the part of the practical self. But it does place some definite restrictions upon the religious reference corresponding to the needs of pure practical philosophy.

The qualification is a sharp reminder to the religious believer that his strong adherence to God does not relieve him of dependence upon the moral evidence furnished by the good will and the object of its tendency and action.[21] Hence his religious recognition of God as the source of commands cannot be made in such a way that it destroys, or takes precedence over, the direct relationship between these moral indicators and the intrinsic foundation of duty in moral law itself. To regard moral duties under the aspect of their being divine commands, is not to shift the ground and objective principle of morality, but rather to enlarge our understanding of man's total moral situation enough to see that we also can have a religious incentive and hope for conducting our lives in accord with moral obligation.

By attaching the as-if qualifier to our basic religious assent to God, Kant safeguards the radication of all aspects of the religious relationship in its humane and moral foundation. Our direct response to God is made through the religious attitudes of reverence, love, and respectful fear. But the philosopher of religion must adopt the maxim of treating these components in the religious disposition as proportionate expressions of certain tendencies in human nature and their matching conceptions of the central moral attributes of divine holiness, goodness, and justice.[22] Thus the act of reverence arises from the correlation in man between his lawgiving

21. Hence Kant proposes a formal order of inference to be followed in making the move from morality to religion and even suggests a sort of catechism of questions in the proper sequence. See *The Doctrine of Virtue*, pp. 152–58; *Reflexionen*, 18, 455–56: *Reflexionen zur Religionsphilosophie*, 19, 641–44.

22. *Practical Reason*, pp. 233–34; *Religion*, pp. 60–66, 132 (where a minimal moral interpretation is made of the Trinity and the economy of salvation); *Lectures on Ethics*, p. 97; *Religionslehre*, pp. 133–35; *Reflexionen*, 18, 450. On the strength of this tight correlation between moral attributes of God and human religious attitudes, Kant can claim that "these three [moral] attributes contain everything whereby God is the object of religion, and in conformity to them the metaphysical perfections of themselves arise in reason" (*Practical Reason*, p. 234 n.). This is a stenographic way of stating that moral theism is the basis for all religious approaches to God on the one hand, and for all speculative reflections about Him on the other. But Kant does not agree with d'Alembert, for instance, that every revelational conception of religion beyond the common moral core should be eliminated; cf. Ronald Grimsley, *Jean d'Alembert, 1717–83* (New York, 1963), pp. 197–99.

moral reason and his view of God as the holy source of laws. Similarly, religious love is sustained by the dynamism coming from our desire for happiness and our moral notion of the good Lord, just as our respectful fear arises from the interaction between conscience and the attribution of incorruptible justice to God.

HUMAN TENDENCIES	GOD'S MORAL ATTRIBUTES	RELIGIOUS ATTITUDES
Moral reason as legislative	Holy lawgiver	Reverence
Inclination to happiness	Good provider of happiness	Love
Conscience	Just judge of my actions as moral and worthy of happiness	Respectful fear

Whenever Kant appeals to a "genuine" or "authentic" religious disposition, he means one which respects the full complexity of this context. It is one which sinks its roots into the three practical tendencies on the part of the conscientious man, which turns to God in terms of the three primary attributes constituting our moral idea of His essence, and which synthesizes the responses of reverence, love, and respectful fear.

Is there any need for a further philosophical study of religion? An affirmative answer is implied in what has just been noted about the minimum moral idea of the divine essence. Each of its three constituent attributes conveys an invitation to enter into more intimate communion with God. Hence Kant recognizes that believers not only give a religious interpretation to moral duties but also engage themselves in specifically religious practices and institutions. They expect a message from God about His own nature and workings in the world which will broaden the religious understanding of His attributes and their meaning for religious life. Kant's aim is neither to suppress this human movement beyond the minimum nor to give credence to every maximalizing assertion in the religious sphere. Instead, his next step is to assure some sort of philosophical control on the part of the moral conception of religion over all further human elaborations, and to assign a limit in principle for what can be determined about the religious disposition and doctrines by a critical philosophy of religion.

RELIGION AND REVELATION

In carrying his theory of religion beyond the ideal structural elements implied by pure practical philosophy, Kant is responding to the general tendency in his thought to achieve a close union between the pure rational factors and those of contingent, temporal experience. From his study of methods in the great *Critiques,* he recognizes that two main procedures are available for closing the gap between the minimal principles specified by pure practical reason and the rich texture of actual human religious beliefs and practices. One method is synthetic and progressive. It begins with the pure principles of religion, synthesizes them in various combinations, and works out their latent meanings in order to generate the actual religious phenomena of mankind. The other method is analytic and regressive. It must start with some given religious complexity, discover its inherent structural forms, and finally attain to those essential conditions and principles which inwardly constitute and control the whole range of humanly developed religious attitudes and doctrines.

Kant does not have to hesitate for very long between these two paths in religious inquiry. The first method would be intrinsically more satisfactory and comprehensive, if it were a matter of developing the theory of religion quite apart from any crucial attention to the kind of mind engaged in the inquiry. But since his own investigation of religion is marked by its constant reference to the human conditions governing the inquiry and furnishing the evidence behind every resultant assent, he must take the second path. His main procedure is to make an analytic inspection of religion as an experienced, complex reality among men.[23]

The way of reflective analysis recommends itself to Kant, not only in general terms of method but also as a consequence of his previous work on religion. Just as the pure moral theory of religion helps to humanize ethics, so in turn does that religious theory itself require further humanization by being considered within the experiential context of some historical mode of religion. In the case of a theistic conception of religion, this means in effect that an analytic study must be undertaken of a revelational form of religion, accepted by its believers as a message from God and a way of life leading men toward Him.

On the grounds of both analytic method and the human norm of philosophizing, then, Kant deems it necessary to study some historical and revelational actuality of religion as the human setting and realization of moral theism. This is the underlying reason behind his choice of a rather cumbersome title for his main writing in this area: *Religion Within the Limits of Reason Alone.*[24] He wants to avoid the disadvantages in claiming

23. *Vorarbeiten zur Religion innerhalb,* 23, 94, 115.
24. Cf. *Religion,* p. 11; *Streit,* p. 2 n.

to develop a theory of religion "from" reason alone or simply one "of" reason alone. Such a claim would require use of the synthetic method for the construction of a theory of religion solely from the concepts of reason, and this would remain a sheer ideal to which there may be no corresponding reality in actual human religiousness. It would also place an unduly narrow restriction upon the factors entering into the reconstructed meaning, since it would exclude a consideration of those revelational meanings of religion furnished by some actual religions of mankind.

To signify that, in principle, he excludes no empirical religious materials from his analysis, Kant deliberately incorporates the words "within the limits" into the title of his major work on religion. Yet his approach must also adhere to its critical task of distinguishing between the rational and empirical components in religion, determining the limits of each, and thus ascertaining that content in a revelational religion which can also be known by philosophical reason through its own principles. Kant cites the precedent for this procedure in the traditional theological teaching about the naturally knowable truths which are in fact given through revelation, as well as in the project of his contemporary, theologian J. D. Michaelis, to draw a moral philosophy from the Bible. The philosophy of religion seeks to focus analytically upon that general meaning for religion which is conveyed by some given revelational religion, and yet whose grounding evidence in a relationship to human nature can be grasped in itself by the critical philosophical mind.

Analysis must be made of some revelational form of religion, but it does not fall within the philosopher's competence to limit the theory of religion, in principle, to any one particular revelation. At the descriptive level, there are many claims to have a revealed religion, in the sense of receiving a message from God and embodying it in a historically developing way of life and a written scripture. Through a well-planned reading program, Kant brought himself fully abreast of the translations from Eastern religious sources and the best scholarly studies in comparative religion made during the seventeenth and eighteenth centuries. From these materials he came to a vivid awareness of the actual pluralism of religions of revelation. Kant stated explicitly that he might well have taken his revelational materials from the Rig Veda, the Zendavesta, or the Koran.[25] But the historical and comparative study of religions was not sufficiently advanced in his day to make a thoroughly comparative sort of

25. *Religion innerhalb*, p. xciii.

analysis practicable, or to bring out its distinctive value for a philosophical theory of religion.

In practice, Kant's philosophical interpretation of religion in the revelational mode concentrates mainly upon Christianity and Biblical religion, although he does not exclude, in principle, the other religions and does make some strategic references to their scriptures and teachings. As a reason for this preference, he cites the basic consonance between his conception of the moral life and the religious view of man presented in the Old and New Testaments.[26]

Despite his conflict with particular theological teachings, Kant holds that the religious view of man and God in the Bible is readily susceptible to a moral and religious interpretation, determined by his own ethical principles and concept of religion. What further recommends the Biblical outlook to him is its consistent and integral presentation of man's religious situation. There is a certain wholeness about this account which responds, in a concrete way, to his philosophical search for a unified systematic meaning for religion. Although the Bible conveys its meaning through many kinds of imagery and historical actions, the whole structure hangs together and does not compel the philosopher to make an arbitrary selection of isolated notions.

Nevertheless, Kant finds it necessary to distinguish his own explanation of the relationship between reason and revelation from the three leading positions in the age of Enlightenment: naturalism, reductive rationalism, and reductive supernaturalism.[27] Holbach's *naturalism* gives a simplistic resolution of the problem by denying the reality of any divine being, who has personal existence and power distinct from whatever is present in the totality of nature. It eliminates not only the actuality but also the very possibility of revelation, due to its refusal of the transcendent God. Kant sees that the problem of revelation is not a primary one for naturalism, but is a consequence of its general attack upon theism. Where Kantian philosophy of religion properly joins issue with naturalism is at the fundamental level of the evidence for and against moral theism.

26. Kant's study of the relation between moral religion and biblical revelation aims to show that moral "reason can be found to be not only compatible with Scripture but also at one with it, so that he who follows one (*under guidance of moral concepts*) will not fail to conform to the other" (*Religion*, p. 11). I have italicized the words which Kant puts in parentheses, because they indicate that his entire investigation of Biblical religion is regulated by the principles of his own moral philosophy. Cf. *Streit*, p. 6; *Vorarbeiten zur Religion innerhalb*, 23, 91–94.
27. *Religion*, p. 143.

But Kant is also dissatisfied with the standpoint of Voltaire and the philosophical theists, who admit a personal God and even a kind of revelation from Him, but who identify that revelation exhaustively with whatever can be determined by philosophical reason. This *mere or reductive rationalism* recognizes that the structures which philosophy finds in nature and in reason itself constitute, in some sense, a revelation or manifesting trace of the divine reality and our religious relationship. Yet it arbitrarily restricts the entire meaning of religion to the philosophically elaborated content, and seeks to dispense completely with the historical and institutional aspects of revealed religion. All the drawbacks of a purely synthetic approach to religion are exhibited here. Reductive rationalism is excessively abstract and artificial. It can make no sense out of mankind's constant religious orientation toward mystery and the divine theophany in nature and history, even though its own philosophical concept of religion depends largely upon revelational sources which do have this orientation at their animating center.

Such criticisms of naturalism and reductive rationalism do not, however, drive Kant into the arms of an equally *reductive supernaturalism.* His objection against the university theologians is that they defend Biblical religion either by making it the primary norm of moral reasonableness or by removing it entirely from an independent philosophical evaluation or by enforcing their interpretation of it with civil ordinances. All three methods of defense constitute a threat against the mundane and humane philosophical approach to religion which Kant is trying to develop. If we must first know that an action is a divine command before we can be sure about its moral and religious worth, we cut off the native roots of moral and religious conviction. Man's inspection of the intrinsic evidence in human nature and its relations with the experienced world ceases to be a foundational act. In that case, any harmony between Biblical religion and philosophical reflection is rendered insignificant, because the philosopher's work becomes only that of giving an elaborate echo of the doctrines already determined by Biblical theology. Since philosophers will not docilely accept this echoing role for themselves in the modern world, the Biblical theologians often move in panic toward the other extreme of placing revelational religion entirely beyond the scope of rational reflection.

Kant remains adamantly opposed to *irrationalism* in religion, whether in its ethical minimum or its revelational maximum. From such liberal theologians as Stäudlin, Semler, and Stapfer, he garners arguments aimed at showing, in his own critical reformulation, that the *facta*, or reports made about the historical deeds and sayings involved in revelation, must always contain some general conceptual factors related to moral reason and its belief in God.[28] The presence of a rational element in religion is unavoidable, if the witnesses and the tradition make use of language in proclaiming and clarifying their message. For the linguistic medium implicates the revelation at once in a network of general meanings, which are testable by and communicable to men.

Moreover, the revelation is not made in a cultural vacuum, as though it were a physical happening in a nonhuman universe. It is a message which speaks to our moral reason, in order to elicit a reasonable practical response of a truly human kind. The mature person thus called upon to make a specifically revelational religious orientation has some responsibilities toward himself, in making the response. He must be able to discern a need in the human condition for some divine aid coming in the form of historical revelation, and must compare the message itself with his inner moral ideal of God and a religious relationship.

Hence a revelation intended to affect our actual religious orientation must at least show itself to be a responding realization of man's religious reflections and practical tendencies, whatever else it does. This thought lies behind Kant's strong statement that he could fear, but not love and reverence, a God whom man comes to acknowledge without any disciplined use of practical reason. A revelation proposed solely by appeal to divine power and authority, or to some already constituted set of civil and ecclesiastical ordinances, would not manifest to us the morally good and just God. Hence it could not fulfill our basic need for a religious response compounded of reverence, love, and a morally respectful sort of fear.

To distinguish himself from all these other positions, Kant designates his own standpoint on reason and revelation as a *pure or nonreductive rationalism*. Its most interesting feature is the contention that although

28. Ibid., pp. 144, 157; *Religion innerhalb*, pp. xcii, xcvi; *Religionslehre*, pp. 201–03. Kant's knowledge of current theological sources is exhaustively studied by Josef Bohatec, *Die Religionsphilosophie Kants in der "Religion innerhalb der Grenzen der blossen Vernunft"* (Hamburg, 1938); cf. pp. 42–57 on the contemporary Calvinistic opposition to naturalism and irrationalism in religion. Liselotte Richter, *Immanenz und Transzendenz im nachreformatorischen Gottesbild* (Göttingen, 1955), pp. 118–28, views Kant as the point of convergence for the positive ethicizing and rationalizing tendencies of the Calvinist ethicians, the Wolffian-Pietist systematists, and the neologists or theological rationalists who appeal to practical reason.

the Biblical revelation of Christianity is not naturalistic, it is a form of *religious naturality.*[29] Basically, this means that the Christian revelation speaks a message to man in his practical reason, adapts itself to man's composite temporal nature, and seeks to aid mankind in realizing its common moral good in the social order. The naturality of the revelation does not necessarily eliminate a supernatural principle from religion. But it does assure that the revelational principle is more meaningfully adapted to our moral conception of religion than a reductive supernaturalism allows, and meets our human moral and social needs more creatively than a reductive rationalism dares to concede.

It is no surprise, then, that Kant should feel uneasy about the offhand contrast made by both Hume and the Wolffians between *natural* religion and *revealed* religion. They take this distinction to mean that natural religion concerns what we can know about God and our duty toward Him from reason alone, without the aid of faith, whereas revealed religion is the exclusive way of faith going beyond reason. From what he has uncovered about religion, however, Kant finds both sides of the distinction unsatisfactory. His analysis tends to show that, wherever our religious assent and practice are involved, both faith and reason are present in some sense. Thus an act of belief is essential to the assent given in the pure moral form of religion; on the other hand, practical reason is fully engaged in the assent given to Christian revelation in its moral significance.

Kant recommends his nonreductive rationalism as a decisive way to prevent the mutual estrangement of natural religiousness and revelational faith. He seeks to achieve a philosophically comprehensible relationship between the two through an interpretation of the principle that "there is only *one* (true) religion; but there can be *faiths* of several kinds."[30] It does not signify that the several faiths of mankind are barren of truth, but rather that they participate in a common religious truth which is available to our practical reason. Kant differs from Mendelssohn and the standard reductive rationalism of the Enlightenment, in regarding the plurality of historical faiths as an indispensable means of embodying and developing religious truth under diverse human conditions. The revelational faiths assure the concrete and active presence of moral religion in human history, lest it become embalmed in an abstract set of propositions to which no one gives a living, socially important assent. There may be

29. *Streit,* pp. 40–41, 57–58; *Vorarbeiten zum Streit,* 23, 440.
30. *Religion,* p. 98. On the distinction between pure and applied (natural and revealed) religion, see ibid., pp. 11–12; *Vorarbeiten zur Religion innerhalb,* 23, 96.

other ends served by revelational faiths, but at least this minimal function supposes the mutual relevance of revelation and man's natural religious attitude.

Although for convenience Kant often employs the customary division into natural religion and revealed religion, he does suggest that the first step in rethinking the issue is to make a linguistic reform. It is formally more accurate to use the terms "pure religion" and "applied religion." Pure religion is the basic moral theism of practical reason, leading to the permanent religious disposition of fulfilling all human duties as divine commands. Applied religion is the theistic doctrine and practical attitude, considered as developing under the conditions of a revelation and a faith coming through history. Although many points remain undetermined, this usage does avoid the dilemma of either treating natural religiousness and revelational faith as mutually alien spiritual attitudes or else emptying out the significance and value of the one order, by virtue of its complete translation into the other.

The "purity" of pure moral religion is a property of the analytic method being used by Kant, and does not necessarily entail any existential or genetic claim. It signifies the task of the philosopher of religion to find the evidence for the theistic assent in the principles established by pure practical reason, as well as to find the ground for the religious attitude itself in the human conditions under which we must attempt to realize these pure practical principles.

However, Kant deliberately refrains from making the following over-claims: that mankind must first enter into a historical stage of pure religion and then pass on to revelational religion; that in making his analysis of moral theism, the philosopher of religion uses no revelational sources in history; and that the actual religious believer keeps his pure moral religion in a separate compartment from any revelational commitments he may also hold. Kant confines himself to the methodological point that some cogent evidential basis must be sought within our active human tendencies for the theistic assent and the complex religious response of reverence-love-and-respectful-fear. He is sure that the meaning of religion elaborated by pure practical reason constitutes a unified system, as do all the achievements attained through reflection upon the pure speculative and practical principles of reason. Hence all the developments of religion introduced by revelation and history must be integrated within this unified system, in order to attain valid standing in the philosophy of religion.

The nub of the question is now reached, since revelational religion would seem to be merely a superfluous and insignificant "republication" of the systematic meaning of pure moral religion. This is the inference usually drawn by the deists and other reductive rationalists. Kant meets this objection by bringing out some complexities involved in the concept of an applied religion of revelation and its faith history.

He distinguishes systematically between three meanings, which are usually coalesced in our concrete religious life. Within the actual Christian cultural context of eighteenth-century Europe, the religion of revelation means: a statutory ecclesiastical faith, determined by the creed and practice of a church and reinforced by civil ordinances; a doctrine and practice which are supernatural in their origin, content of truth, and special divine aid to men; and a vehicle or concrete instrument for the realization of moral theism, under human conditions. These are respectively the statutory, the supernatural, and the instrumental senses in which men refer to a religion of revelation. Although the first one is usually employed when someone is asked—"What is your religion?"—its usefulness as an identifying tag cannot conceal its ultimate dependence upon what men think concerning the other two senses. Consequently, Kant postpones any extensive examination of statutory religion of revelation (the ecclesial and civil meanings of religion), until he determines the relationship between the supernatural and the instrumental conceptions of revelation, at least as far as he is able in his philosophical theory of religion.

This last qualification is the capital point in differentiating Kant's non-reductive rationalism. Philosophy of religion treats revelation from the instrumental standpoint only, since its controlling principle is furnished by the relationship shown by moral theism to hold between religion and human reality. There is bound to be a difference in principle, then, between the account of revelational religion arrived at from the instrumental perspective of philosophy, and that arrived at from the supernatural perpective of the theology of revelation. The latter will maintain the centrality of revelational religion, and will refer all elements of human religiousness to a sharing in a supernatural life and truth, as their measure. The only way in which these two interpretations of revelational religion could be perfectly synthesized would be to deny either the irreducibility of the evidence for moral theism or the possibility of the supernatural—and Kant regards neither step as warranted by the human situation.

He states that revelational religion "perhaps may contain something which no philosophy at all can ever grasp with insight [*einsehen*]." [31] A

31. *Religion innerhalb*, p. xcvii.

philosophy of religion developed within the human condition recognizes its limits, does not pretend to overcome them in a dialectical transcendence of human reason, and hence refrains from denying the supernatural. It may even recognize the need for God's supernatural initiative, at the historical moment of introducing mankind to the meanings gathered together in a revelational religion, although thereafter a philosophical analysis and grounding of them can be made. In the practical order and especially in confrontation with evil, the religious man is too strongly aware of the need for some supernatural help to deny its reality, or to confuse it with what his own powers can bring him. A "something more" may be required for the integrity and perfection of human action, although our expectation of receiving divine aid must rest upon our moral hope in the good God, rather than upon any penetration into the divine mystery itself.

In order to preserve the integrity both of his own explanatory philosophical principles and of the divine reality affirmed by his moral theism, Kant places the supernatural aspect of revelation entirely beyond the range of philosophical investigation. It remains totally unassimilable to practical reason and underivable from the moral imperative. It is a mystery which cannot be denied, but also one which cannot be communicated to us, even by God, in the form of a speculative truth or a philosophically known, determinate actuality.[32] The supernatural and the instrumental conceptions of revelation cannot be synthesized, and the Kantian philosophy of religion is confined in principle to the latter.

As far as concerns the philosophical study of religion within the limits of reason alone, revelation can only be regarded as *a process of concretization and humanization*. The process is required, if the meanings involved in the pure moral conception of religion are not to remain "mere empty ideals without objective practical reality."[33] They must be brought down to our human soil, made relevant for the concrete world of human experience and practical effort. In effect, this means that the pure moral view of religion must be radically adapted to our human realm of sensible events, provocative images, and the flow of history. The adaptation is made through the revelational mode of religion, which can therefore be called an "applied" religion, that is, an instrument for giving practical human import to our minimal religious belief.

Revelation achieves this practical realization by interpreting our basic

32. *Religion*, pp. 158, 159.
33. *Religion innerhalb*, p. xciii.

reference to God in terms of three traits of human action: first, its use of
concrete imagery and symbols; secondly, its concern for the temporal and
historical aspect of decisions; and third, its need for a community aiming
at the practical union of men. In the specific case of the Bible and Christian revelation, these concretizing forces work together to mold the human
religious attitude. They are found respectively in the symbols, stories, and
myths of the Biblical narrative; in the theme of God's sacred presence in
history and actual historical events; and in the role assigned to tradition
and the church. Moral theism becomes fully human through these three
adaptive means, operating in the revelational process.

Kant makes a remarkable comparison between this humanizing of basic
theism through revelational religion and his own epistemological doctrine
on the schematizing of the categories. A central topic in his theory of
knowledge concerns the function of the concrete schemata of the imagination. Their work is to achieve a mutual adaptation between the general
categories of the understanding and our sense perceptions. Kant now
suggests the existence of a definite analogy between the task of the
imaginative schemata and that of the religious forms, furnished by revelational religion. Just as the imaginative schemata make the categorial
meanings relevant for the experienced world and thus achieve speculative
knowledge, so do the revelational modes of image-history-community
make our moral theism relevant to the sphere of human action and thus
achieve objective practical value for religious meanings.

The schematizing of religious meanings meets a deepseated human
need. "For man, the invisible needs to be represented through the visible
(the sensuous); yes, what is more, it needs to be accompanied by the
visible in the interest of practicability and, though it is intellectual, must
be made, as it were (according to a certain analogy) perceptual." [34] Our
religious orientation toward the invisible divine reality has to be given a
visible form of expression. Revelational religion performs this incarnational and sacramental function, so that we can permeate our imagery,
our practical decisions, and our historical striving with religious significance.

We can now understand why Kant refuses to locate the philosophy of
religion exclusively within the confines of pure moral religion or exclusively in an exegesis of revelational religion. Instead, the Kantian philosophy of religion finds its defining angle of vision precisely in the *Über-*

34. *Religion*, p. 180 (translation modified). On schematism, see *Pure Reason*, A 137–
47: B 176–87 (pp. 180–87).

schritt, the transitional or in-between reality constituted by the mutual passage back and forth between moral theism and religion in its revelational, sacramental, and historical dimensions. It is only by installing himself in this field of transition and analyzing the schematizing or incarnational process that the philosopher of religion can measure the practical response of man to God, and thus determine the meaning of our religious existence.

The methodological considerations concerning practical reason and revelation govern the twofold experiment which Kant proposes to make, in order to establish the relation between religion and human nature from the philosophical standpoint.[35] First, he will take the Bible and the Christian religious tradition as the given instance of revelational religion used for the analysis. His purpose is not to engage in Scriptural exegesis, by determining the supernatural sense of the Scripture or by arguing that his account is the real intent. This is a task for the theologians, and he does not seek to render their work superfluous. But he does want to determine the analytic moral meaning of religion conveyed through the Bible.

The first experiment is that we read the Bible in the light of a guiding metaphor: the pure religion of moral reason and revelational religion are related as concentric circles, with moral religion as the animating core and revelation as its wider concrete setting. The philosopher of religion will treat of revelation, but only insofar as it ministers to the inner circle of moral-religious insight, by supplying it with a context of imagery, saving acts, and historical direction.

Oriented in this way, we can then make the second and crucial experiment. We can begin our analysis with the Bible, considered only as a historically given constellation of religious meanings. Using our general moral concepts as a normative aid, we can interpret the Scriptural conceptions of religion in order to develop a philosophical view of man's religious life that is both adequate to his experience and faithful to his practical tendencies. The unified conception of religion thus attained will prove to be identical with the content of pure moral religion. By actually making frequent transitions to and from pure moral religion and revela-

35. Ibid., pp. 11–12; see p. 97 on the vehicular or instrumental relationship between natural and revelational religion. Just as Kant proposes the experiment of the antinomies to test the soundness of his epistemology (*Pure Reason,* B xxi [p. 24]), so does he propose the experiment of the concentric circles and an instrumental interpretation of revelation in order to test the soundness of his theory of religion.

tional religion, we can establish the controlling presence of the former and the enriching consonance of the latter.

In proposing these experiments, Kant does not seek to conclude that the supernatural meaning of revelation is absent or reducible, but rather that the philosophically ascertainable meaning for religion is indeed present in the Christian revelational form. If the experiments are repeated for other religions, then the Kantian philosopher of religion can exhibit a universally valid meaning of religion. It holds for men existing under all historical conditions, and hence is the common theme of religious truth which is variously rendered concrete and human in all revelational developments.

5

Kant and the Human Modalities of Religion

Perhaps the controlling influence of Kant's critical philosophy upon his theory of religion can be most readily discerned in his way of handling the topics of evil, the visible church, and the historical nature of religion. For most Enlightenment writers on religion, these topics serve merely as an occasion for polemical thrusts at the established forces of religion. But for Kant they constitute an essential step in the analytical study of the meaning of religion. For they mark the specific points at which the concretizing process is carried on and the revelational form of religion is made directly pertinent to our active life. Just as the analysis of scientific judgments and moral judgments must be made sufficiently determinate to characterize the human conditions and limitations in these areas, so also must the philosophical theory of religion reach into the determinate human modalities of our religious assent and action. Only in this way does Kant gain assurance of dealing critically with religious actuality, even though it also leads him to acknowledge that this actuality is not totally comprehended within his philosophical conception of human religiousness.

EVIL AND THE SPRINGS OF RELIGION

We cannot proceed very far in the investigation of religion without encountering mystery, not in the sense of the plural mysteries of faith or theological doctrines, but as an all-pervasive awareness of the presence of a reality which engages man in action, but which is not open to his direct inspection. Kant's reflections on religion lead him to a twofold mystery, involving the very being and nature of God and the ground of human freedom itself.[1] Since the theistic religious relationship is constituted by the bond between human freedom and God, this existential practical mystery is at the very center of the study of religion and not at its periphery.

Kant is led to acknowledge mystery in God's reality, because of his critical examination of the limits of human knowledge in regard to that which transcends the realms of nature and man. But even within the human order, he finds the ground of freedom to be a reality which eludes our direct gaze and involving some unexpected potencies, in its use for a good or an evil end. The mystery found in our moral life history concerns: the development of a good or an evil basis for particular actions, our capacity to achieve a rebirth of the good principle in a life heretofore dominated by moral evil, and our persistence in the struggle for a permanent orientation toward the good.

Since the above are precisely the aspects of freedom which are also fundamental to the religious life of man, including the revelational mode, the two zones of mystery have their point of intersection in the religious theme of man's combat with evil and the coming of the kingdom of God. The symbols and narrative of revelation on this theme of evil provide an indirect access to the structure of human freedom, thus verifying the need in philosophy of religion for reflection upon the revelational account of man and God in actional unity.

Kant was prompted to attempt a new tack on the question of evil by his considered judgment that, in his own century, the several parties in the discussion of evil had reached a stalemate. He distinguished between three main approaches: the metaphysical, the theological, and that of the theodicists and antitheodicists. Taken either separately or together, their treatment of evil failed to carry conviction, and in general the failure was due to a fragmentation of the human plight which originally generated the entire inquiry. The full situation included the twofold mystery of God's goodness and power and man's freedom, as well as the concrete message of religious revelation concerning the interpenetration of divine power and human freedom in the moral struggle with evil. Yet these primary existential factors were split apart, as a result of the isolated approaches taken by the metaphysicians, the theologians, and the theodicists. Hence Kant proposed that the philosophy of religion should gather

1. *Religion*, pp. 129–38.

together the separate strands of the problem and give it a fresh, integral treatment.

Briefly, but with telling criticism, he pinpointed the cause of the breakdown in each separatist approach to evil. His dispassionate report of Baumgarten's *metaphysical* arguments only underlined their ultimate irrelevance to the issue.[2] One argument takes the dualistic view of attributing evil to matter and the intrinsic laws of natural substances in their interaction, rather than to God. But this only leads Kant to wonder whether rationalistic metaphysicians in the Christian West take seriously the total creation of beings and their operative tendencies by God. The divine creative act extends to the interrelationships and joint activities of finite agents. Another argument grants that God created substances, but points out that evil is a privation rather than a substantial being, and hence does not come within God's responsible causality. The difficulty with this easy reduction of evil to a privation is that it confines the issue to a metaphysical definition of concepts, whereas the bitter presence of evil which troubles theists is an affair of the striving moral will and the active principles of good and evil in the practical order.

Kant's main objection against the *theologians* of his acquaintance was that their abstract doctrine on original sin tends to weaken the volitional conflict.[3] Clearly enough, man's corrupted practical reason and will cannot be used to explain the original emergence of moral evil among us, but neither can their corruption be pushed very far in explaining the growth and present condition of evil. The corruption cannot be urged to the point where men would be deprived of their practical power of reflection and choice, or where the steady demand of the rational will for the conformity of actions with the moral law would be stifled. For in such an extreme, our actions would cease to spring from our own responsible choice and respect for law, and thus would cease to have those qualities of moral good and evil which are being studied. Similarly, an appeal to our sensuous nature as the mainspring of either the original commitment to evil or of evil actions in human history is selfdefeating. Although our sensuous impulses are relevant to the tendency toward evil actions, they cannot by themselves constitute the evil principle without destroying the free human character of the actions whereby evil becomes a power in this world.

2. *Religionslehre*, pp. 164–69; Baumgarten's texts from the *Metaphysica* are given in Kant's *Erläuterungen zu A. G. Baumgartens Metaphysica*, 17, 56, 191.

3. *Religion*, p. 30. The contemporary Calvinist and Pietist positions are described by Bohatec, *Die Religionsphilosophie Kants*, pp. 241–341.

Within the broad ambiance of philosophical *theodicy,* Kant located the theories on evil propounded by Leibniz and the physicotheologians, as well as by Bayle and Hume.[4] His primary criticism was directed against Leibniz's threefold division into metaphysical, physical, and moral evil, which provided the framework for most of the discussion on theodicy. Kant made no objection against distinguishing among different aspects and kinds of evil, to each of which a distinct analysis can be given. But he did object to the illusion that moral evil is only an instance of a wider class, and that the general concepts for understanding and overcoming it have already been determined through a prior investigation.

This view violates the religious testimony to the mystery of moral evil. The religious mind is aware of moral evil's unique and radical quality, and the need to reflect upon it from within the decisive relationship between human freedom and God. The relationship between human freedom and moral good-and-evil furnishes the primary context for the religious interpretation of evil, requiring every metaphysical and physical consideration to remain subordinate and provisional. Hence the philosophy of religion must preserve the original human sense of moral evil, rather than try to view it as the last chapter in an issue already settled from a distance by a cumulative theodicy.

By criticizing the three-stage approach to moral evil, Kant helped to neutralize the modern European movement of theodicy and antitheodicy. Appeals to physical order are essentially subject to all the restrictions that he had already placed around physicotheology. By using purposive concepts of interpretation, we can obtain a view of natural purposes in relation to the human mind, but we do not possess the speculative intuition required for grasping the entire scope of nature, or for deciding the purpose intended by the divine mind for nature as a whole. Moreover, likelihood of the existence of other worlds inhabited by other rational beings prevents us from drawing any cogent conclusions, one way or the other, about the adaptation of the material universe to man and his terrestrial needs.[5] The purposive traces which we can discern in the experienced world are not sufficiently firm, by themselves, to determine anything about the divine wisdom itself, or to make a defensible transition

---

4. The theories on evil proposed in the span from Leibniz to Kant are analyzed by Friedrich Billicsich, *Das Problem des Übels in der Philosophie des Abendlandes* (3 vols. Cologne, 1952–59), 2, 111–251.

5. *Reflexionen,* 18, 213–454.

from regarding God as an artful maker to regarding Him as a morally good and provident Lord.

The logical dilemma urged by Bayle and Hume about there being either a good and weak God or a powerful and malevolent one fails, in its turn, to respect the human conditions of the problem. One major defect is found in its ambiguity concerning the meaning of "good" and "powerful," which terms are taken sometimes in respect to the physical order and sometimes in respect to the moral. Kant challenged the common assumption among the theodicists and their dialectical opponents that one can treat the issue of moral evil primarily by starting with the categories adapted to the physical world's order and disorder, and then applying them with some modifications to the order and disorder in the region of human moral freedom.[6] Furthermore, we cannot suppose ourselves to be made privy somehow to the standard of divine goodness, wisdom, and providence, apart from what we can dimly discern in our own moral experience and our reflection upon religious belief in the revelational form.

In order to more accurately plot the course of philosophy of religion on the question of evil, Kant distinguishes sharply between all the cumulative, doctrinal theodicies and antitheodicies and his own "genuine theodicy." [7] The latter rests on a methodic resolution to approach moral evil first by specifying one's practical philosophy of man, and then by reflecting critically upon the revelational presentation of the matter. What this method of viewing evil really produces is not a literal theodicy, as though God Himself were put on trial and stood in need of justification by us, but rather a *religious anthropodicy*, or reflection upon the grounds which permit the maintenance of man's religious belief in the face of moral evil.

Within the Kantian critical framework, it can be seen that the generative source of the difficulties is moral and religious, rather than physical and metaphysical. Evil becomes an acute question only within the context of our belief in God's three chief moral attributes. In the presence of that belief, we become anguished about the actual condition of the physical world and man. It is not the isolated physical world, but this world viewed religiously as the handiwork of the holy, good, and just God, which makes us troubled by the presence of obstacles and counterforces to the life of virtue and holiness. And it is the same belief in the holy, good, and just

6. *Religionslehre*, pp. 127–34.
7. *Misslingen*, 8, 264, with Job as the prototype of an authentic or lived theodicy. Cf. *Practical Reason*, p. 249; *Reflexionen*, 18, 454, 464–65.

God which makes us religiously troubled about man's active departure from a holy, good, and just life. The problem of evil cannot be detached from the practical relationship between the good Lord and human freedom for the speculative purposes of doctrinal theodicy and its dialectical counterpart.

There are five tenets in Kant's moral anthropology which he weaves together as a specially designed pattern for understanding the human basis of moral evil. First, the metaphysical finitude cited by Leibniz is not a sufficiently determinate and practical ground for the possibility of evil in man. To the speculative awareness of our limits in being must be added the more personal and compelling reminder given by such a natural disaster as the Lisbon earthquake that we are indeed contingent, changing, dependent beings to our very marrow. But even these traits must be brought within a human moral context, before they are significant for grasping the root of evil in our active life. Kant takes the trouble to give the term "human nature" or "nature of man" a thoroughly practico-moral meaning, for this purpose.[8] In its moral operational meaning, human nature signifies the freely chosen antecedent ground of all our actions. Human nature is the self-constituting source of operations in those agents who not only choose but work out a responsible course of action in the temporal world, whose freedom must recognize the demanding quality of the moral law, and who must also satisfy sensuous needs. Moral evil looms as a real possibility for the nature of man, who is a needy, tempted, and morally struggling agent in the natural world.

Kant also finds it helpful to distinguish between two senses of "human act." It can signify either the particular responsible actions of the human person or else his relatively permanent, practical dispositions. The inquiry into moral evil is much more concerned about the dispositional grounds of action than with the particular manifestations in this or that action. What counts most is a man's good or evil character, and this is something radical in his active nature, a settled practical principle in reference to which his transient actions gain their moral quality and order. What sets off moral dispositions from temperament and body cast is that the former are always freely chosen, practical commitments and principles of conduct. One reason why moral evil is involved in a context of practical mystery is that the disposition from which it proceeds is both a radical principle of free acts and itself a work of our impenetrable freedom.

8. See *Religion*, pp. 10, 16–17 ("human nature"), 26–27 ("act").

A third point is that the morally constituted disposition is never simple, but always consists of a complex ordering of our dynamic tendencies. Kant transforms the theoretical statement that man has a composite nature into the practical one that man has three basic tendencies, which he must learn to interweave and integrate toward the unity of his character. To be a man is to be inclined in a powerful, practical way toward integrating our animality or sensuality, our humanity, and our personality.[9] This situation would not be humanly moral, if our power of choice were attracted solely by the sensuous needs or solely by the ideal of rational, law-abiding action, in which our distinctive humanity consists. The choosing agent is humanly marked by his responsiveness to both orders of value, by his constant awareness of the pressures they simultaneously exert upon his will, and by his responsibility for the active and complex relationship between them in which the moral use of power must result.

Kant is now able to state the nature of moral choice and hence the moral meaning of good and evil. At the radical level of the permanent principles of action, we are able to choose between that combination in which the tendency toward humanity is subordinated to the one toward sensuality (the will to evil), and that other combination in which sensuality is subordinately related to the demands of humanity or moral rationality (the will to good). Both courses of action enable man to realize his power of desireful choice, but only the latter one enables him to will in such a way that there is also a fulfillment of his moral personality.

Our moral personality does not consist in the bare ideal of humanity or the isolated rational will to conform with moral law. It has its human realization only in that complex human integration wherein the sensuous tendencies are present, precisely as being subordinated to the moral principle of acting out of regard for the universally binding law. The good man is he whose disposition and actions develop the order of personality, whereas the evil man is he who has freely subordinated his humanity to needs and motives which disintegrate this order. Moral evil consists essentially in a disordering of the practical tendencies in man, in a refusal to accept the primacy of the rational demands, and thus in a powerful asser-

9. *Religion*, pp. 21–23. E. L. Fackenheim, "Kant and Radical Evil," *University of Toronto Quarterly*, 23 (1953–54), 339–53, observes that the moral choice is not that of willing or not willing, but that of willing the primacy of one principle or the other in the moral conflict.

tion of willfulness which nevertheless frustrates the realization of human personality.

As a fourth tenet, Kant, borrowing a phrase from the theologians, remarks that it belongs to moral wisdom to recognize that man is not a *res integra*.[10] He does not find it easy to achieve the order of personality and moral goodness in his life, and indeed he experiences a strong pull in the opposite direction. Disorder fascinates him, the position of the rebel against moral law exhilarates him, and he feels a drive within himself to achieve the values of power apart from any moral regulation. Each individual can verify within himself the accuracy of the theological description of the inordinate or counterordering heart. The inordinate heart is weak, insofar as it constantly mixes moral and nonmoral considerations in order to avoid making the moral law the ruling ground and motive of its action. And it becomes actually perverse, through the free act of reversing the order between selflove and the moral law. Quite apart from any concern for the doctrine of original sin, the theological description of our inner struggle with evil has a realistic ring about it. For Kant, this means that moral and religious warfare is not with theoretical dilemmas, but with powerful inclinations and habituations within our own active nature.

Finally, Kant applies the contribution of moral and religious hope to the problem of evil. The commitment to an evil disposition is permanent in relation to a whole pattern of actions and plans organized around it, but it is not absolutely irrevocable, in the sense of being beyond criticism and the possibility of reform. A human life organized around an evil principle still remains vulnerable, because of the very complexity of the purposive tendencies involved in the evil disposition and its actional unity. As long as the evil in question is that of a morally responsible human agent and not evil in the abstract, there is a deordination but not a complete suppression of the demands of the moral law. The will to respect the moral order is never entirely silenced, as we can experience in the stubborn judgment of an accusing conscience.

Kant does not hesitate here to use the language of immanent teleology, in saying that man is intended for achieving personality in a normative,

---

10. *Religion*, pp. 50–51 n. Kant's discussion of the fragility, impurity, and perversity of the human heart (*Religion*, pp. 24–25) is an instance of his familiarity with, and personal reworking of, the current Calvinist manuals in theology. Paul Ricoeur, *Fallible Man* (Chicago, 1965), pp. 216–24, uses the phenomenology of man's fallibility to move through man's present evil condition of actual deviation back to his primordial fragility and free power to commit himself in evil ways.

moral sense. To be a free human agent is to aim at the maximal realization of the animality-humanity-personality complexus. This comes about only when the principle of personality is effectively respected, that is, when our sensuous needs, self-regarding impulses, and search for happiness are integrated within the order established by the moral will. From this standpoint, evil never ceases to have the ring of a counter principle to this personal order and hence to be exposed to an act of moral reorientation. In the concrete language of religion, to which Kant resorts at this culminating stage in the analysis, the reorientation consists in a change of heart, a rebirth of the self, and a slow reforming of one's entire life.[11]

Kant seeks to penetrate the mystery of personal renewal through a study of the revelational religion of the Bible, using the five philosophical points already mentioned as the basis of interpretation. Insofar as the Biblical message helps to clarify the human meaning of the struggle with evil, it conveys a view of man which is philosophically intelligible and verifiable through controlled analysis. Kant knows what he is looking for, but the significant thing for him is that his expectation is borne out, not only in the particular aspects of revelational religion but also in its general coherence and illuminating power. This is the operational sense in which the instrumental view of revelation strengthens Kant's religious anthropodicy, thus making a verifiable contribution to his philosophy of religion and his understanding of the uses of freedom.

He finds the story of the Fall of man helpful, for instance, on some important issues.[12] That there should be an immediate passage from the state of innocence to that of guilt indicates that an act of freedom is involved at the very outset of moral development. We do not simply drift into an evil disposition, as a consequence of the accretion of many psychological and cultural habits, without any morally responsible decision. Whatever the theological niceties about original sin, its "originality" reinforces the Kantian distinction between particular actions and the constitution of a basic moral disposition. The latter is a radical or original act of freedom, which is not mediated and determined from afar by our metaphysical finitude or by a physical evolution or even by the wearing tide of our daily actions.

11. *Religion*, pp. 42–43, with Biblical citations from Genesis and John. On Kant's philosophical use of the human religious symbols of good and evil, see Paul Ricoeur, "The Symbol: Food for Thought," *Philosophy Today*, 4 (1960), 206–07.

12. *Religion*, pp. 36–39. Kant incorporates an interpretation of Genesis, chaps. 2–6, into his philosophy of history (*Conjectural Beginning of Human History*, in *On History*, ed. L. W. Beck [Indianapolis, Bobbs-Merrill, 1963], pp. 53–68).

That portion of the Bible story, in which the banishment from the garden is tempered by the promise of a savior, holds special interest for Kant. It is a concrete and dramatic way of saying that the principle of moral rationality is never obliterated by an evil disposition, and that we have some solid ground of hoping for the ultimate dominance of moral personality. The Bible account also brings home forcefully the fact that while a choice of evil is made by the individual agent, due to the social solidarity of mankind, the choice affects others. That is why the religious reorientation is also not exclusively an individual affair, but affects humanity itself in its social and historical aspects.

It is sometimes asserted that Kant prefers the God of the Old Testament over the God of the New Testament, but this is not borne out by his actual treatment of religious themes in the Bible. Perhaps it would be more accurate to say that he regards the moral factor in religion as the decisive means whereby the revelational message of the Old Testament is liberated from theocratic politics, and reaches fulfillment in the climactic revelational context of the New Testament.

The main confrontation between Kant's philosophy of religion and the Biblical revelation centers around the New Testament, especially the Gospels and Saint Paul. In submitting the New Testament to interpretation by his moral conception of religion, Kant does not intend to reduce it to the Old Testament, but rather to treat it as the convergent focus for revelational religion as a whole. Here is the best place for verifying his own view of the instrumental relation between revelation and morally based religion. This intention clearly controls his treatment of the Biblical message on the power of evil and the power of good.

The clash between these powers is most vividly represented in the life and teachings of Christ. Kant's interpretation is regulated by the general distinction made in his practical philosophy among the archetypal moral idea, its function as a model, the particular moral examples, and the empirical conditions under which the examples are presented to us. Our practical reason is not completely indeterminate, but is an active tendency toward realizing the order of personality. Deep within ourselves, then, we can find the practical ideal of striving to fulfill our personality, and this is the archetypal idea of humanity acting under universal moral law. When we attend to this idea and accept it as the guiding norm for our choosing will, it serves as the moral model for our life and actions. But since human reality does not consist simply of practical reason contemplating its own best ideal and following it, there is also a real need among men for particular, historical examples of moral living.

Kant appreciates the contribution of examples, and yet he also warns against their abuse.[13] Their positive moral function is to assure the composite human agent that his moral archetype is indeed realizable, under the conditions of action in our world. Nevertheless, Kant does not want our dependence upon examples to become the dominant theme in moral and religious life, thus usurping the primary role of the moral archetype itself. Good examples can lead us astray in three ways. They may narrow down the full meaning contained in the archetypal moral idea, they may replace the moral law itself as the ground of moral action and obligation, or finally, they may tend to orient us toward the particular empirical conditions of a man's life rather than toward the archetypal moral meaning which his life should evoke. Examples must remain instrumental to the main task of realizing the order of personality within oneself and in all mankind. Hence we can use them for purposes of encouragement and emulation, but not for literal imitation.

Kant reformulates the Prologue to St. John's Gospel in terms of his moral conception of religion, and treats the life and teachings of Christ in the light of the above distinctions. From the standpoint of philosophy of religion, the Word of God is the archetypal idea of humanity within us. The aim of the Gospel is to set forth this idea for us in the example of Christ, whose actions convey to us what it means to be a person most pleasing to God. "The *archetype* of such a person is to be sought nowhere but in our own reason," but the life of Christ prompts us to make that search into our own active nature.[14] Meditation upon His life is a powerful means for accepting moral personality as the effective model and norm in our own action.

This is the Christological aspect of the Kantian philosophy of religion. Kant does not want his inquiry into religion to become entangled in the theological metaphysics of the two natures in Christ, or in the particular circumstances of His earthly life, since then His example would divert us from the moral and religious meaning of human existence. Christ does

13. *Practical Reason*, pp. 251–58; *Foundations of the Metaphysics of Morals*, pp. 68–69; *Lectures on Ethics*, pp. 98, 109–10.

14. *Religion*, p. 57. Kant gives a paraphrase of John's opening verses (ibid., pp. 54–55), along with their meaning for moral religion (ibid., pp. 55–60). However, the English translation does not preserve the distinction between *Urbild* and *Vorbild*, archetype and model.

not bring the archetypal idea of a morally and religiously ordered human-ity to us for the first time, but He does provoke us to reflect upon this idea in its full human unity and power. The philosopher of religion must concentrate upon the evoked pattern of goodness and sacrifice that is valid for all men, since this interior model constitutes what Kant deems to be the essential religious attitude open to philosophical investigation.

We are urged by Christ's example to be born again, to undergo an interior practical revolution and change of heart, to put on the new man. Pietism stresses this side of the Christian message. But Kant also criticizes his childhood religion for fostering a *pietas morosa*, a morose religious attitude which dwells upon our human impotence, the aggressive power of evil, and the need for passively awaiting the coming of grace from above.[15] Reading the Bible in the light of his own philosophy of moral freedom, Kant finds other themes which provide a corrective to such quietism. Without becoming involved in the theological intricacies, he defends a *restitutio imaginis dei*, some sort of a restoration of the image of God within us. The Christian message can be proposed in a world where evil flourishes, precisely because no man can completely obliterate the image of God in himself and thus place himself entirely beyond the appeal of religion. The religious theme of the inexpugnable image of God in man supplies a concrete schema for the Kantian moral doctrine on our steady rational will and our archetypal idea of moral personality.

The reflective religious mind also finds profit in the Biblical distinction between the initial reorientation or rebirth of the soul and the slow process of reform, or learning to participate in the divine life. In concrete religious language, a truly faithful man must put his own talent to work and not wrap it away; he must work while there is yet light; he must carry out his stewardship and give an accounting for his entire life, and not merely for the instant of accepting God. The philosophical point is that there must be not only a basic reorientation of our practical dis-position but also a lifelong perseverance in the struggle, under the all too human conditions of criticism, discouragement, and death. The Gospel story encourages us to hold that the moral and religious conquest of evil

---

15. *Reflexionen zur Religionsphilosophie,* 19, 642, where Kant pairs it with a *pietas blandiens,* which dissolves the soul in love and enthusiasm for the good prin-ciple, but which makes virtue and religion rest on overwrought emotions rather than on the good will and the search for the highest good. On *restitutio,* see *Vorarbeiten zur Religion innerhalb,* 23, 110.

does not lie beyond our power of free decision and enduring disposition.

In pondering the Christian revelation, Kant seeks to avoid the two extremes of either displacing the moral imperative from its foundational position or glossing over the weakness of man, through a Promethean exaggeration of his power. He succeeds in reaching a balance through his conception of *godliness*, or the true religious disposition.[16] It has two main functions, which work against the extremes of pietism and limitless activism.

The first function of godliness is to combine piety and virtue, the service of God and the observance of the moral law for its own sake. The difference between a debilitating pietism and authentic godliness lies in the way in which piety and virtue are ordered. If piety is regarded as the end, and morality as a means to it, then the religious attitude is characterized by pietism. Here, the foundational nature of our commitment to the moral law is destroyed, and the possibility is opened up of trying to relate our life religiously to God apart from a basic moral orientation. Godliness supplies a corrective by supporting a functional or means-end relationship between religious piety and morality, such that the former is essentially ordered toward strengthening our moral disposition and the pure moral relationship to God. The moral law remains the foundation and is respected for its own sake, when one's religious disposition is that of godliness. Religion itself benefits from this ordering, since the act of religious rebirth and reform remains a morally responsible relating of man toward God, rather than an act whose moral quality remains doubtful.

But this first function of godliness cannot be the sole one, without implying man can do everything required for his wholeness. If this were the case, the need for a religious ordering of human existence would be negligible, and Kant would be forced to retract his teaching on the weakness and perversity of the human heart and the power of evil. The second important function of godliness is, therefore, to keep us aware of our human limits and to incline us toward a confident trust in God. Here, the philosopher of religion is aided by the message of revelation. Revelational religion insists upon the correlative hiddenness and mercy of God, upon the correlative freedom of man and his reliance upon the divine aid.

This correlation comes out strongly in the letter which Kant wrote to Lavater on evil, happiness, and the Christian faith. Kant acknowledges

16. *Religion*, pp. 170–73, 189; *Lectures on Ethics*, pp. 82–83.

that "I seek in the Gospels not the ground of my faith but its fortification."
Yet he adds that the essential moral spirit of the Gospels is "that righteous-
ness is the sum of all religion and that we ought to seek it with all our might,
having faith (that is, an unconditional trust) that God will then supplement our efforts and supply the good that is not in our power." [17] There
is need for religious trust and even for a certain resignation to the divine
will, and these religious acts are compatible with our own strenuous moral
efforts. Thus godliness brings out the distinctive contribution of religion,
as the unfailing principle of hope in our human lives.

The dual function of godliness is Kant's clue of how to avoid both a
reductive naturalism and a reductive supernaturalism, whenever we try to
overcome evil by good.

> Despite the fall, the injunction that we *ought* to become better men
> resounds unabatedly in our souls; hence this must be within our
> power, even though what *we* are able to do is in itself inadequate
> and though we thereby only render ourselves susceptible of higher,
> and for us inscrutable, assistance. . . . [Practical reason] holds that,
> if in the inscrutable realm of the supernatural there is something
> more [*etwas mehr*] than she can explain to herself, which may yet
> be necessary as a complement to her moral insufficiency, this will
> be, even though unknown, available to her good will. . . . In the
> moral religion (and of all the public religions which have ever existed,
> the Christian alone is moral) it is a basic principle that each must
> do as much as lies in his power to become a better man, and that
> only when he has not buried his inborn talent (Luke 19: 12–16)
> but has made use of his original predisposition to good in order to
> become a better man, can he hope that what is not within his power
> will be supplied through cooperation from above.[18]

The experience of struggling against evil, and yet doing so under an
unrelaxing imperative to become better, is what impels men to supplement their basic moral belief in God with the religious attitude of godliness, or trusting faith in His supernatural cooperation. Godliness does
not enable a man to understand the supernatural or to penetrate into the
mystery of God. We trust in divine help on the basis of our experience

17. *Letter to J. C. Lavater*, after April 28, 1775, in Kant, *Philosophical Correspondence*, pp. 82, 83. Goethe makes a similar correlation between constantly striving man
and God's redeeming help, in *Faust*, II.5.11936-37: "Wer immer strebend sich bemüht/
Den können wir erlösen."
18. *Religion*, pp. 40–41, 47, 48.

of moral man and our acceptance of the moral God, rather than on the basis of some special access to divinity. But godliness does enable us to concentrate upon our own moral responsibilities, while hoping to receive something more of divine aid. Hence in the Kantian philosophy of religion, it constitutes the developed religious disposition proper to the condition of men, striving to realize the laws of freedom in the midst of natural happenings and evil counterlines of conduct.

CHURCH AND ESTABLISHMENT

There is no sharp break between Kant's study of evil and his treatment of the church and history. He agrees with Charron the Christian skeptic and Stäudlin the Christian theologian that every modern inquirer into religion should meditate at length upon the famous warning of Lucretius: "So great the evils to which religion could prompt!" [19] Only by studying the actual forms and works of the religions of mankind can we plumb the capacity of the human heart for good and evil. This means examining religion in those social institutions and historical developments which enable it to achieve visible expression and become a power among men.

Being neither theologian nor comparative historian of religion, Kant finds it important to reaffirm his distinctive philosophical standpoint in making an independent reflection upon religion in the ecclesial form. He must ask why the active predisposition toward the moral conception of religion should realize itself in a social manner, and even in visible ecclesiastical institutions. And from the side of revelational religion, the same question arises in regard to the three meanings of "revelation." Why does revelation signify not only a supernatural origin and content and an instrumental or vehicular relationship to the moral core of religion, but also a statutory ecclesiastical faith? The ecclesial phenomena requiring explanation include a visible organization, statutes, rites, a Scriptural statement, a tradition of learning, and a regional establishment backed up by political ordinances and power. A philosophical analysis must now be brought to bear upon these manifestations of the concrete religious spirit, so as to determine their general human significance. The theory of morality and that of religion are the joint beneficiaries of this phase in the

19. Lucretius, *On the Nature of Things*, I.101, trans. H. A. Munro, in *The Stoic and Epicurean Philosophers*, ed. W. J. Oates (New York, Random House, 1940). p. 71; quoted by Kant in *Religion*, p. 122.

philosophy of religion, since the answer must be sought in some common factor which binds together the moral tendency to religion and the traits of actual religious and churchly life.

Concretely considered, that common link lies in man himself, grasped in terms of a controllable philosophical analysis. The transition from the pure idea of religion to the human modes of referring conduct to God is, in fact, a transition to the realm of the morally good and evil acts of men in the plural and in the social group. Together, men corrupt each other, and together they work out the social conditions for achieving a virtuous and a religiously ordered life.

As Kant observes, a religion of pure moral belief would be sufficient for rational agents who were related to the practical idea of humanity and personality solely through their private freedom and isolated decision. But this is not the case with human beings, who are involved with each other in the spatiotemporal world, and hence who reach their moral and religious decisions together, as fellow citizens in this field of conflicting social powers. Therefore, religion must develop some social forms which take account of the practical mediation of the human community in all our movements toward God or away from Him. Human religion could not consist solely of the mystical flight of "the alone to the Alone," since under more complete analysis even such a relationship would turn out always to have some support from, and some implications for, the wider human community.

Kant seeks the roots of the social character of religion in the very process whereby the moral law itself becomes adapted to human existence.[20] A man is responsible not only for regulating his own conduct by the principle of morality, but also for doing whatever he can toward aiding other men in accepting a similar ground of action. He must share his moral maxim with others, uniting with them in socially effective ways which encourage their own adherence to morality and which lessen their vulnerability to social forces inimical to the moral disposition. This aspect of the moral life is accomplished: (a) through acts of *love*, and (b) through regarding the basic moral imperative as a principle intended for a *community* of human moral agents or persons.

There is a legitimate, indeed necessary, function for love and community dedication in Kant's ethical and religious theory. He stresses duty and moral autonomy so that he may establish a certain order among the

20. *Religion*, pp. 85–89.

principles and incentives of human action, but not so that he may eliminate the values of love and social ties. The philosophy of religion brings to prominence the role of love and social concern in the pure moral idea of religion, as well as in revelational religion. The so-called "material content" or interpersonal reality of ethical and religious life stands forth in this portion of the Kantian philosophy of religion.

Kant defines love succinctly as "the free reception of the will of another person into one's own maxims." [21] It opens us out responsibly to the interior struggle of other men to achieve a virtuous life, including the religious referring of their duties to God. It prompts us to move beyond an ethical and religious "state of nature" in which, parallel to Hobbes' description of the state of nature for political man, each individual would try to pursue his own moral and religious welfare at the expense of others, and without any respect for the common weal of humanity. The presence of love is felt when we recognize that the *summum bonum* is not only morally qualified by the primacy of the moral imperative, but also socially qualified by the joint relation of all men to the practical goal of moral personality.

The social nature of the highest good is already foreshadowed in that formulation of the categorical imperative which bids us treat other men always as fellow members of the kingdom of ends, as persons joined together in the *corpus mysticum* or moral union of virtuous wills. But this rule does not manifest the full significance of the social character of the highest good, because the moral imperative as such concerns what the agent can responsibly accomplish through his own free decision and disposition.

Love is a forceful reminder, however, of our peculiarly human sort of moral interdependence. The highest good is social, in the pregnant sense that moral worth ought to be realized precisely as an interdependent

---

21. *The End of All Things*, in *On History*, p. 82. Elsewhere, Kant offers an equally compact definition of the supreme form of religious love: "To love God is to do as He commands with a willing heart" (*Lectures on Ethics*, p. 36). We must learn to fear God without being fearful, and to love Him without forgetting that human love fulfills the moral law. Religious love of God includes a reverential moral fear, but not Hume's "natural fear," aroused solely by a craven recognition of nonmoral power in nature (*Religion*, p. 163). Kant even reinterprets the theological teaching that God's glory is the final purpose of the universe to mean that God creates personal beings whom He can love and who can love Him in return in a free, personally dignified way (*Reflexionen zur Religionsphilosophie*, 19, 644; *Practical Reason*, pp. 189–91, 233–34).

actional reality among all the members of this living species to which the individual moral agent belongs. And yet, as Kant quietly notes, we cannot guarantee that the ethical commonwealth will ever attain this plenary actualization in our world of changing circumstances and social conflicts.

Kant's correlation between the question about hope and the religious response can now be considerably sharpened. The generating question itself for religion concerns not only what *I* may hope by myself but, more determinately and incisively, what *we* may hope together, as fellow men and bearers of the tendency toward personality. And the proportionate religious response bears upon God precisely as the Lord of the ethical commonwealth, as the common hope for men who are striving together to realize a social good which may not lie entirely within human power.

In the religious perspective, then, God is the powerful moral unifier not only of nature and man (insofar as our supreme good involves a happiness dependent upon the ordering of nature in accord with virtue), but also of man and man (insofar as our supreme good rests upon an ordering of the social will and action of the human community, under the laws of virtue). What unites the moral believers in God is their joint practical conviction that the divine will is good and holy. They believe that, in whatever God wills as a law for man, there is a perfect identity between the true moral duty and the command, between respect for personality and an ordering of men toward the social good. To regard our ethical duties as divine commands in accord with the religious reference of our social life strengthens, therefore, rather than jeopardizes, the primacy of the moral principle and the integrity of personality within the ethical community united under God.

A commonwealth thus united under divine laws constitutes the City of God, or the *invisible church*. Properly considered, it is a union of hearts and wills, a family relationship, a people of God.[22] Kant has deliberate recourse to this traditional familial language, in order to emphasize the interpersonal and moral character of the religious-ecclesial union. In the ideal case—and if men were pure rational agents—this invisible union of the people of God would suffice for realizing the commonwealth of humanity and its moral social good. It has an objective practical reality as an archetypal idea in our moral reason, even though it is never wholly attainable and capable of presentation in our sensible experience.

---

22. *Religion*, pp. 90, 93. The German theological situation during Kant's maturity is analyzed in the fourth volume of Emanuel Hirsch, *Geschichte der neuern evangelischen Theologie* (5 vols. Gütersloh, 1949–54).

Yet men being the composite, experience-bound agents that they are, this moral union of hearts in the invisible church does not, in fact, suffice for the ordering of our practical life. Kant is plainly disappointed by some additional demands men place upon their ecclesial union with God. He agrees with Rousseau's sentiment that there is an inevitable narrowing, and often a debasing, of the archetypal idea of the religious commonwealth in the hands of men in their actual historical condition.

> By reason of a peculiar weakness of human nature, pure faith can never be relied on as much as it deserves, that is, a church cannot be established on it alone. . . . Because of the natural need and desire of all men for something *sensibly tenable,* and for a confirmation of some sort from experience of the highest concepts and grounds of reason (a need which really must be taken into account when the universal *introducing* of a faith is contemplated), some historical ecclesiastical faith or other, usually to be found at hand, must be utilized.[23]

Apart from any evaluative judgment he may wish to pass, however, Kant recognizes that the passage from the pure moral belief in God to a faith involving history and rites and public statutes, i.e. the passage from the invisible to the *visible church,* does respond to a need of our actually constituted human reality.

The schematizing of our religious ideals does not stop with an invisible union of minds, but presses on to a visible union of men in the concrete. Just as the transition from pure moral religion to revelational religion in general meets the human need for relating practical ideas to the conditions of sensible experience and contingent historical happening, so does the transition from the invisible to the visible assembly of the people of God meet the need of human sociality in action. It is not enough for the religious man to orient his dispositional act toward the pure idea of the people of God. He must also strive to give that archetypal idea a practical form, which is relevant to our sensible world and its social forces. Taken at its best, then, a visible church is a determinate social schema enabling men to attain some partial realization of the practical meaning concentrated in the conception of an ethical commonwealth.

There are two chief means usually employed in this schematizing and

23. *Religion,* pp. 94, 100 (translation modified). Kant underlines the word *introduzieren,* because he grants that the worldwide introduction of moral religion may require a supernatural act, even though the message itself has a natural meaning open to determination by our practical reason, once we receive the revealed word.

visibilizing process.[24] First, some message is accepted as revealed word coming from God. It is eventually written down in a sacred Scripture, which then serves as the basis of a creed and an historical tradition of learning and interpretation. Second, the various rites and observances which men practice toward God in addition to the basic moral law are regarded as divine commands, having a statutory force upon our belief and conduct. For the defense and spread of this public religion, it is often reinforced by the laws of the state or political commonwealth. In the European tradition, the visible Christian church in the land becomes the *established* church or statutory religion. The religious establishment looks to the political ruler to determine the *jus circa sacra* in some way that is binding upon all citizens, as well as to maintain the primacy of the theological faculty in the university, when religious matters are in dispute.

The very palpable political and educational consequences of a religious establishment are sufficient indication to Kant that his philosophy of religion is still concerned with the central question of moral good and evil, even when it is investigating the relationship between the invisible and the visible church. He strongly agrees with the religious dissenters and the freethinkers in the Enlightenment that statutory religion infringes upon our intellectual and moral freedom. But this conclusion retains its specifically Kantian meaning in his hands, because it is reached in the light of his reflections upon the church and without abandoning his own theory about the relationship between the visible and the invisible church. That Kant's evaluation of church and establishment is firmly governed by his own principles in the philosophy of religion can be seen in the five following lines of argument.

Servile Religion. Kant feels that the Pietists and other dissenting groups make their strongest case in pointing to the perverse moral effects of an

---

24. Lest his epistemological safeguards be swept away, Kant is careful to distinguish between "the *schematism of analogy*, with which (as a means of explanation) we cannot dispense" in the moral and religious orders, and "a *schematism of objective determination* (for the extension of our knowledge)," which is proper to our theoretical knowledge of nature but which leads to an illusory and injurious anthropomorphism in the religious domain (*Religion*, pp. 58–59 n.). The analogical kind of schematizing makes the meaning of religion more definite by always relating it to our selfhood and personal acts, but the latter kind transforms religious realities into the same kind of objects as are found in the physical world, and thus depersonalize religious meaning by confusing it with a theoretical, nonmoral kind of knowledge. Cf. *Pure Reason*, A 179–81:B 222–24, A 664–66:B 692–94 (pp. 210–12, 546–47); *Practical Reason*, pp. 177–79.

established religion. It transforms the free assent of faith into a servile, coerced, and mercenary act. Our relationship to God beomes either a purely public profession or a favor-currying bond, in which God is treated like any other powerful official, who can be moved by flattery and acts of service which do not require one to become a morally better man. In such an atmosphere, one's moral disposition is reduced to third place, standing well behind a careful observance of the statutes and a careful participation in the visible rites of worship. Thus the proper order is reversed between moral judgment and public religious observances, regarded as divine commands.

Kant is not arguing for religious individualism, in the sense of an abolition of all communal aspects of religion. Rather, the point of his objection is that religious sociality itself suffers in being narrowed down to the visible church and even to the conditions of the establishment. When practical religious life gravitates entirely around public religion, believers tend to forget about their inner commitment and their familial relationship with God and each other. They find it outlandish to refer with the Pietists and Rousseau to the union of hearts,, the kingdom of God, or the people of God.[25] To Kant, this is a sure sign that the invisible church is forgotten, and that the vivifying moral core of religion is dried up. His critique is intended to stir up reflection on this matter, so that the reality and primacy of the invisible union of believers with God can once more shape our religious thought and talk.

The Functional Church.   Since the concrete realization of the religious community depends on the visible church, the latter does have a legitimate function in human religious existence. It makes a positive contribution to our religious life, however, only under three strict conditions. First, its members must be kept vividly aware of its functional role as serving the people of God, as leading beyond itself teleologically to the invisible church. Second, the visible church must really assist believers in a constantly closer approach to actualization of the archetypal principle of the spiritual religious community. And lastly, it must so orient men that they stand ready to affirm their primary citizenship in the ethical commonwealth, living under the laws of the holy God. In short,

25. Rousseau's religious position is presented by Pierre Burgelin, *La Philosophie de l'existence de J.-J. Rousseau* (Paris, 1952), pp. 406–74, and his theological relationship with Kant and Lessing is studied by Karl Barth, *From Rousseau to Ritschl* (London, 1959), pp. 58–196.

Kant establishes as a norm for the visible life of the church an effective ordering of the believers' assent toward the practical idea of humanity-referred-to-God and, underlying even that, toward man's fundamental disposition of adhering to the moral law.

The pathology of religious life consists of a study of violations of this norm and their consequences for human believers. Kant notices some similarities between illusions in metaphysics and those in religion. In neither area does the illusion arise from the unreality of the object, whether it be God Himself or the social union of men with Him. Rather, it is traceable to a failure to consider human limitations and to establish, among the components in a conviction about the object, the order imposed by these limitations upon our thought and action. The specifically religious type of illusion comes from treating the visible and statutory aspects of religion as the essential and highest factors, and from keeping the practical concern for living a better life in a subordinate position.[26] When a religious attitude rests upon this inverted order of values, it produces the reciprocal illusions that God is concerned mainly

26. *Religion*, pp. 156–63. In *The Metaphysical Elements of Justice*, trans. J. Ladd (Indianapolis, 1965), pp. 91–95, 134–37, Kant assigns to the state the right to modify church property foundations which no longer serve our living social intent, and hence which now generate socially harmful illusions. He criticizes the illusions of statutory religion in terms of the moral law and *man's* freedom, whereas Hamann criticizes them in terms of *God's* freedom and initiative in sacred history. These two poles of the constructive criticism of established religion made in eighteenth-century Germany are brought to focus in the following two statements. Kant asks: "Where shall we start, i.e., with a faith in what God has done on our behalf, or with what we are to do to become worthy of God's assistance (whatever this may be)? In answering this question we cannot hesitate in deciding for the second alternative" (*Religion*, p. 108). Hamann brings out the significance, however, of the first alternative for the interpretation of revelational religion:

> The mystery of Christian devotion does not consist of services, sacrifices and vows, which God demands of men, but rather of promises, fulfilments and sacrifices which God has made and achieved for the benefit of men; not of the finest and greatest commandment which he has imposed, but of the supreme good which he has given; not of law-giving and moral teaching which have to do merely with human dispositions and human actions, but of the performance of divine decrees by means of divine acts, works and measures for the salvation of the whole world. (*Golgotha and Scheblimini*, trans. in R. G. Smith, *J. G. Hamann, 1730–1788: A Study in Christian Existence* [New York, Harper, 1960], pp. 229–30)

The integration of man's moral integrity (Kant's theme) with God's free action in sacred history (the stress of Hamann and Kierkegaard) still remains a primary goal for the theory of religion.

with our formal observances, and that we in turn become pleasing to God chiefly through following them.

The practical consequence of this deordinate notion of religious service is to make men superstitious or fanatical in carrying out their religious observances. Religion in its visible ecclesial modes does not necessarily generate these warped habits, but the danger of doing so increases in proportion to the assimilation of visible religion to the civil establishment. Whenever the visible church accepts the status of an established religion, it tends in practice to blur the provisions already specified for control of the humanization of moral religion. To that extent, it breeds a climate favorable to religious illusion and to the sophisticated idolatry of trusting in something other than a morally good course of life to make us pleasing to God.

Religion and Civil Liberty. Kant also urges that, if the political commonwealth is genuinely interested in the welfare of religion, it will observe a self-limitation in its support of a religious establishment and in its demand that the citizens accept a statutory faith. His own philosophical theory of religion can help the state to find some room for manoeuvering on this issue, without making the statesman feel obliged to accept the dire alternative of either imposing an established religion upon everyone, or treating the visible church as an unmitigated obstacle to the religious spirit. For he does not make any wholesale condemnation of the visible churches, but judges each instance functionally by whether or not it fosters religious freedom among men.

One basis for religious freedom in an age of church establishments is found in Kant's earlier theme of the naturality of Christianity, or its embodiment of the natural moral religion of mankind. The moral center of religion cannot be coerced by public law, since it rests upon that moral belief in God and that reference of duties to Him which are free acts of man. Here is a limit that cannot be overstepped by the state, without corrupting the very reality it attempts to establish.

Another basis lies in the relationship between the spiritual conception of the people of God and the visible church. The presence of the latter does not necessarily guarantee its proper ordering toward the former. That ordering is violated when a believer is deprived of his religious freedom, through the civil imposition of some statutory faith. Paradoxically, he cannot adhere in a genuinely religious way to a church and its faith, unless his assent remains free. If his assent is coerced, then his adherence is not religious in nature and the ecclesiastical faith itself is idolatrous rather than religious. Kant does not permit his practical cautiousness to obscure his judgment that the church which chooses establishment above religious freedom is quite literally choosing to make itself something other than authentic religion.

Religion and Academic Freedom. Kant devotes the longest part of *The Strife of the Faculties* to a defense of academic freedom in religious matters. He applies to the university situation his distinction between two legitimate approaches to the Bible: that of the Scriptural exegete and theologian of revelation, and that of the moral philosopher interested in revelational religion. Each approach is governed by a distinctive intention. The theologian seeks to determine the precise sense of the text as conveying a message from the revealing God, whereas the philosopher seeks to disclose the presence of man's basic moral meaning of religion, as verified through an understanding of human reality itself. These different aims insure a rightful difference and independence in the interpretations of religion and the Bible proposed by the theological and philosophical faculties. It also insures that there will be a fruitful and permanent conflict between the two faculties, a conflict which has to be given formal status in the university.

It is in the interest of both religion and philosophy to encourage this academic strife.[27] Otherwise, theology can narrow down to a legalistic repetition of proof texts, without any real interchange between different churches or any appreciation of religion's human meaning. Similarly, the philosophy of religion can become so abstract and involuted that it ceases to concern itself with actual believers and the actual modes of faith. Since some important human values are at stake, the political com-

27. The academic strife has four traits (*Streit*, pp. 27–30). (1) There can be no peaceful settlement out of court, for the historical, logical, and subjective areas of conflict must be publicly examined and adjudicated by critical intelligence. (2) The strife is ceaseless since, as members of the university community, both the Biblical theologian and the philosopher return constantly to their respective sources in revelation and man for further illumination of the great questions in religion. (3) Neither the government nor the people can rightfully intervene to suppress the university discussion of the closely intermingled elements of natural moral religion, sacred history, and symbolic expression. (4) Political power is best used to insure full freedom not only for the theological faculty, which may or may not represent a religious establishment, but also for the philosophical faculty and its distinctive principles and methods. Thus Kant locates the problem of the philosophy of religion squarely within the modern university situation.

monwealth should respect the freedom of religious discussion within the university and the context of learning. Specifically, it should not try to restrict the religious inquiries carried on by the philosophical faculty, even when they fail to agree with the statutory articles of faith supporting an established church.

It is here that the problem of *authority*, which looms so large in theological discussions on revelational religion, also becomes important for Kant, the philosopher and teacher. He is not concerned with determining anything about authority as an issue among the confessional churches and their theologians, since they treat it in relation to the supernatural word of the revealing God. But when the Bible or any other religious source is considered as a contribution to the basic moral meaning of religion, then it comes within the range and perspective of philosophy.

A critical philosophy of man possesses a method of verification and some evidence for determining the human significance of Biblical religion.[28] Since it has the principles for making a critical appraisal and reformulation of our moral idea of God and of the human practical relationship with Him, the philosophy of religion can control its own inquiry. It has proper competence in determining the import and evidential limits of its own statements on religion, and hence enjoys full authority and final authority over the human moral meaning of religion. Philosophical reason is the ultimate exegete for interpreting human experience and revelational sources, not in every respect but in order to determine the constant moral truth of religion, or what Kant calls the "one true religion of humanity." Neither theological faculty, visible church, nor political sovereign can rightfully suppress this authority or prevent it from securing the freedom of philosophical inquiry into religious questions.

The Marks of the Church. Finally, in clarifying the sense in which the spiritual union of wills constitutes the one true church, Kant gives a new lease to the old theological question about the marks of the church. The

---

28. *Streit,* pp. 65–67; *Religion,* pp. 100–05. The philological-doctrinal sort of hermeneutics resolves religious inquiry into a matter of specialized learning and the authentication of documents and artifacts, whereas Kant asks the liberal disciplines in the philosophical faculty to develop a "genuinely authentic" hermeneutics, namely, one which concentrates upon the significance of the revealed message of religion for human practical life.

theological tradition had guided the discussion between the several forms of Christian revelational religion, by specifying that the true church must be one, holy, catholic, and apostolic. These were regarded as the identifying marks of the visible religious community, founded by Christ and continuing to be animated by Him. Kant's philosophical standpoint does not permit him to concern himself with the founding act and historical identity of the visible church of Christ, but it does provoke him into making a distinctively philosophical use of the topic. Within his philosophical ecclesiology, the marks of the true church are those traits which constitute the attitude of pure moral religion, and hence which indicate its presence at the core of this or that particular church faith. They are the broadest characteristics of the invisible church or common structure of religiousness among men. Hence their philosophical function is not to distinguish one visible church from another, but rather to assure the animating presence of the one invisible church, or the basic human meaning for religion, among the various religious groupings of mankind.

In the Kantian ecclesiology, the marks of the true church are: unity, holiness, freedom, and an unchangeable intention.[29] Although there is a partial verbal agreement with the usual theological marks, Kant methodically correlates his set with his epistemological division of the classes of categories (quantity, quality, relation, and modality). This is not a formal gesture toward achieving systematization at any price, but carries out his general principle that the basic categorial principles have more determinate significance than can be captured in the mode of theoretical knowledge. Thus the categories in the class of quantity contain a reserve of meaning, which becomes actualized in the mark of religious unity. The further reach of meaning in the categories of quality is liberated through the trait of religious holiness. A similar function is performed by the note of religious freedom in respect to the categories of relation, and by the mark of religious permanence of intention in respect to the categories of modality.

Taken together, these marks of the church indicate that the religious community achieves a practical objective reality for that portion of the human meaning of the categories which does not attain its fulfillment through purely scientific judgments or through other types of practical judgments and actions. The Kantian theme of the traits of the church is thus a further development of the central critical problem of the categories and their several ways of entering into true judgments concerning

29. *Religion*, p. 93.

humanly attainable reality. Here as elsewhere in his theory of religion, his primary concern is not theological but epistemological and human, within a practical perspective.

Taken separately, the marks of the church are simply a reaffirmation of particular aspects of the pure moral religious attitude so central to Kant's entire analysis. The true church is one, because it consists of those common truths about the religious relating of man to God which can, in principle, be apprehended by all men having the use of practical reason. It is holy, insofar as it rests on the moral ordering of motives, which ought to assure that our wills are referred first of all to morality itself and then to the holy, good, and powerful God. Its freedom specifies that the relationship among religious believers is familial, steering clear of the two extremes of a purely externalized statutory organization and a purely internalized illuminism of the lonely spirit. And its unchangeable intention means that the people of God is constituted fundamentally by the undeviating aim of a community to join minds and hearts together, for the practical task of becoming better men and, only on that basis, men who are pleasing to God.

To the extent that any of these marks are present in a social group, it has some religious characteristics and some participation in the life of the human religious community. In this sense, Kant holds that the nontheistic religions of the East have some rightful claim to be taken as authentic religions. Their moral quality, if not their overt conception of the divine, makes them sharers in the true church or spiritual family of God.[30] The Oriental religions offer one path to the free and holy life. This common religious principle has an implicit theistic significance, based upon the tendency of man's moral predisposition itself toward the living God, whatever the doctrinal interpretation may be.

Like his theological colleagues, Kant regards the mark of *unity* as the decisive and yet the most difficult note to explain. It is not a question of quantitative indivision and, for him, its work is not to point the believer toward any particular Christian church. In order to control its meaning, he equates it here with the two categorial requirements for a morally objective reality: universality and necessity. In the religious context, this

30. Helmuth von Glasenapp, *Kant und die Religionen des Ostens* (Kitzingen, 1954), analyzes Kant's knowledge of Eastern religions. There is a common core of religious belief among men: (1) the world is not ruled solely by physical laws; (2) there is a powerful moral order in the universe; and (3) men must be conscientious in acting in accord with this superior moral order. See the many comparative references to religions other than Judaism and Christianity in *Religion*, pp. 99, 102, 131–32, 161–64, 172–73, 182.

means that the principle of unity is found only where an attitude and a doctrine are universally communicable, in virtue of being founded upon some cogent needs of man and common traits of his practical experience.[31] Because natural moral religion consists of an attitude and a doctrine marked by their human shareability, Kant finds the perfection of unity realized here. Within his philosophy of religion, then, "the one true church" is a designation reserved for the invisible church or assembly of God which is present at the heart of any visible religious community. By identifying unity with universal validity for practical reason, Kant is able to conclude that pure moral religion is the *catholicismus rationalis* sought in the philosophy of religion.

The crucial difficulty is, however, that the visibilizing means needed to give a human incarnation to the practical idea of the one moral religion are also the instruments for making it become particularized and subject to contingent circumstances. In other words, the process of humanizing moral religion is also one of pluralizing its ecclesial and credal forms, and thus of hiding as well as manifesting its unity. The visible churches embody the one invisible church or people of God, but they do so under the particularizing, contingent conditions which also divert the believer away from the principle of unity and the other sacral marks. Hence there is an enduring tension of the religious mind before the two requirements of achieving both the incarnation and the unification of our religious relationship with God.

Kant's perplexity over religious unity was not lessened by consulting such respected students of religion as Rousseau and Hamann, Michaelis and the Biblical philologists in the universities. Rousseau taught that the message of religion should be communicable even to the most unlearned man, by moving his moral disposition. Hamann agreed, and added that the rationalistic and philological presentations of Christianity by the university theologians cannot satisfy this requirement. On the other hand, Michaelis and his scholarly colleagues regarded ordinary believers as intellectual children, who cannot grasp the scientific arguments and the exegetical explanations and hence who remain scientific idiots about the intellectual basis of their faith.

---

31. *Religion*, pp. 143–44; *Religionslehre*, pp. 204–05; *Streit*, p. 46, where the contrast is drawn between the *catholicismus hierarchicus* of established churches and the *catholicismus rationalis* of moral religious belief. In trying to restrict the perfection of religious unity to the latter, Kant assumes that the only universally communicable religious teaching is the one whose evidenced truth is directly grasped by our practical reason.

Because he appreciated certain points in both positions but could not subscribe wholeheartedly to either, Kant was forced to regard Christianity as an essential complexity, made up of both the natural moral religion and a religion of learning and statutes.[32] As natural religion, its moral message can be verified in everyman's experience of the human condition and hence can be known by one's own moral reason, regardless of how it was first announced. As a revelational religion or faith, Christianity has a sacred Scripture and must eventually organize a tradition of commentary on that Scripture through the resources of philology, history, and philosophy. Inevitably, it must use learning in order to fathom and communicate its message as a revelational religion and a visible church.

On the side of the believers, therefore, there must be either a learned public for the theological study of the Christian gospel or a set of statutes to be obeyed by the majority of men, who cannot follow the learned discussions. The mark of unity is obscured by both the learning and the statutes: a religion mediated by learning is not universally communicable to all men, and one mediated by particular statutes is so restricted that it thwarts our reflection upon the common human basis of religion. Thus the complex structure of historical Christianity both favors and hinders the actualization of religious unity among men.

This attempt to reach a critical philosophical meaning for religious unity leads Kant to revise his initial distinction between natural and revelational religion in terms of the *supernatural*.[33] Religion can be:

SUBJECTIVELY SUPERNATURAL:
> The message is given to us in the mode of revelation and sacred history

OBJECTIVELY NATURAL:
> However conveyed, the truth of the message can be known in principle by all men through their own practical reason and reflection on common moral experience

OBJECTIVELY SUPERNATURAL:
> We cannot judge the religious truth through our own reason, but we can convey the message through learning and statutes

32. In *Streit*, pp. 59–69, Kant points out that, although the biblical scholars and theologians of his day commonly regard laymen as idiots in the sciences required for a learned exegesis of the Bible, ordinary men do in fact use the more pertinent resources of their natural moral reason and hearts in pondering the religious meaning of revelation.

33. *Religion*, p. 144; *Reflexionen*, 18, 485; *Vorarbeiten zum Streit*, 23, 440. It is not the possible presence of the objectively supernatural factor, but the proposal of it as a speculative body of knowledge and as a public creed required of all the citizens, which makes established Christianity antinatural.

Christianity cannot be examined philosophically through the simple alternative of its being either natural or supernatural religion, because in fact it realizes all three of the above potentialities. Being a revelational religion with a sacred history, it is subjectively supernatural in regard to our actual mode of access to it. Yet it also survives the Kantian experiment of supposing that its message conveys the pure moral religion, responding to our own reflective study of man's practical condition. Hence Christianity is also the bearer of objectively natural religion, in which respect we can grasp its truth through our own reflective use of reason.

Furthermore, Kant is told by the theologians and the ministers of state for religious affairs and education that Christianity contains an aspect of truth which cannot be determined by philosophical study of the evidence in human reality, and hence which absolutely transcends our use of reason in exploring the evidential grounds of conviction. Although this objectively supernatural doctrine is conveyed by a tradition of learning and by public statutes, neither method of transmission shows to mankind the foundation of the truth of the message in our common human reality. In the measure that Christianity claims to be objectively (rather than just subjectively) supernatural, therefore, it disconnects itself from rational investigation and compels the philosopher of religion to remain silent about it. He can furnish some moral equivalents for the particular mysteries and duties contained in objectively supernatural religion, but in doing so he does not make this aspect of Christianity intelligible in its objective mode of supernaturality.

That Kant is not entirely satisfied with his treatment of the objectively supernatural is indicated by a few fugitive speculations on the relation between learning and religion. He grants that if a religion is revelational and scriptural, it must use the resources of learning. Furthermore, on the hypothesis that all men were learned, learning could be used as a means of transmission accessible to all. In that case, religious faith could be free rather than servile, even though it involved the mediation of history and a learned tradition. Whatever the actual situation, there is no conflict in principle between free religious assent and the role of learning in a religious tradition.

Kant sometimes distinguishes between two functions of theological learning: to clarify the meaning of religion and to communicate the teaching from one generation to the next. In our actual condition of having only a few men learned in the theological field, the function of clarification can be considered separately from that of being the basic means of sharing the belief. Learning serves to clarify the religious message, without becoming the necessary means of communicating it. Kant recognizes that in actual religious life, the message is brought to men through preaching, dialogue, and catechesis.[34] They are the living means for communicating the word of God, which is not conveyed primarily through research and statutory laws. Yet the theologians of his day subordinated preaching, dialogue, and catechesis to a learned theology and an apparatus of church and civil laws. Hence Kant did not clearly recognize, in preaching and catechetical instruction, the principal instruments for the apprehension and communication of the religious word, as well as for the resulting continuity of the religious community in history.

HISTORY AND RELIGION

Although Kant saw that religion in its human mode is quite intimately bound up with history, he did not develop this insight in the same depth as the other themes in his philosophy of religion. There were some epistemological obstacles to making a thorough analysis of the historical nature of religious belief and the religious community. Two striking instances can be cited of how Kant's general difficulties with history affected his treatment of religion. First, in distinguishing between the religion of reason and a historico-revelational religion, he found it convenient sometimes to retain the older Wolffian connotation for historical knowledge. Religious assent in the historical mode is too changeable and confined to particular circumstances to have an intelligible structure and universal validity of its own; it rests upon the slavish receptivity of the mind, rather than upon a free act; and it provides no critical principle for controlling excesses in belief and practice. For Kant, the advantage of such a description of historically based belief was that it facilitated the complete subordination of revelational to rational religion. But the disadvantage was that it seemed to deprive the historical aspect of religion of any positive significance and value in human life.

Kant's own theory of time raised a second hurdle. If time is bound down to the inner form of sensibility and hence to the causal determinism of the phenomenal world, then acts of freedom are somehow timeless in their own noumenal reality and temporal only in the actional consequences following upon them. The moral center of religion has to be preserved from becoming fully temporalized and historicized, lest in

34. *The Doctrine of Virtue*, p. 151; *Religion*, pp. 152–55; *Streit*, pp. 63–68.

the process it lose its rational freedom and primacy over historical revelation. Hence Kant counted among the peculiar weaknesses of man that he should want to relate religious belief to the temporal and historical conditions of existence.

Weakness or not, this concern for having religion in some historical mode is a human trait which Kant considers worthy of special examination.[35] Lessing's conception of history as the process for achieving man's moral and religious education appeals to him. One reason for a long-range development of mankind is that the moral predisposition toward a religious relationship is originally present among mankind in a seed condition. Its full implications for human existence are not grasped at the outset, and hence it must develop in a gradual temporal way and through many historical forms. Kant is sufficiently a man of his times to think that all these developments converge upon the Enlightenment, which earns its name partly because of attaining to maturity concerning religious liberty and the essential significance of moral religion. Where he transcends the Enlightenment, however, is precisely in relating religious liberty to moral law as its foundation, and to historical process as its proper expression.[36] Kant assigns a creative function to those historical modes of revelational religion which have furnished the experiential materials for his moral interpretation of religion.

In fact, his own notion of religiousness supports the historicity of religious existence. This is the common implication of his views on hope and holiness, reform and the struggle between good and evil. The conviction that religion as a human reality must somehow be historical is strongly maintained by Kant, despite the epistemological and moral difficulties already cited.

Religious hope makes a significant addition to our understanding of man, because our moral striving and our religious fidelity are involved in

35. *Religion*, pp. 39 n., 102–03; *Streit*, p. 43; *Pure Reason*, A 835–37:B 863–65 (pp. 655–56).

36. In addition to the essay, *What Is Enlightenment?* see *Reflexionen*, 18, 504–05, and *Religion*, pp. 113–14 and 122–23, on how "the contemporary state of human insight" brings the moral-religious germ of Christianity to its fruition. The philosophical hermeneutics of religion is intended to achieve a "growth in Christian truth," so that a man might become "a Christian *in potentia*, i.e., as far as lay in him" (*Vorarbeiten zum Streit*, 23, 424, 440). Like Kierkegaard, Kant distinguishes sharply between claiming flatly to be a Christian and accepting the name of "Christian" in the demanding sense of trying to become one, and thus to realize the full religious vocation of a man (*Reflexionen zur Religionsphilosophie*, 19, 639).

a peculiarly human sort of duration. It is neither purely noumenal nor purely phenomenal, but a composite ordering and interpenetration of the two. Our religious disposition is freely originated, but it must endure and bear fruit within the temporal world. Men of faith are patient and enduring under religiously significant historical conditions, since the actual referring of their complex reality to God is a temporal act. The religious orientation of their lives does not occur in an instant, and the religious mode of human hope does not flourish outside a context of sacred history.

Similarly, an ahistorical religious attitude would not foster that constant approach toward the moral good and the divine reality in which holiness consists. A morally directed religion neither promises nor provides instant holiness, for this would mean a fraudulent identification with the holy God. Rather, it sets us on the path toward holiness by engaging us in "a continual becoming of a subject pleasing to God." [37] Because there is no moral religiousness without hope and the search after holiness, there is no purely timeless and ahistorical manner in which men can actualize a morally founded religious relationship.

Even in the case of religious outlooks developed apart from a sacred history and an ordinary historical framework, there are some elements which can be related to the human roots of religious historicity. Kant cites the recurrent myths about rebirth and the struggle between good and evil. In his moral interpretation, rebirth is never enough.[38] It is the first act in the drama of religious reorientation, but there are other acts to follow, generating a religious involvement in time and history. Whether the rebirth be viewed as an act of free decision or as a visitation from the life-bringing God, it calls for a further lifetime of reform, which will affect the course of temporal life and thus will have an historical resonance.

That our engagement in the test of temporal fidelity is not a purely individual affair, but involves us in a broader social relationship among all peoples and ages, is the message conveyed in the story of good and evil. Our religious life is drawn up into a universal struggle between the good and the evil, considered as consolidating principles around which are marshalled the social powers and ages of mankind. Hence Kant looks for the archetype of such myths in a conflict between the *kingdom* of good and that of evil. The man of religious faith looks forward expectantly

37. *Religion*, p. 69 n.
38. Ibid., p. 43.

to the triumph of the good, considered precisely as being realized in a kingdom or an abiding social union of men. Whether or not the ultimate triumph of the good community is conceived as taking place in human history, it does involve human history in the issue. The schematizing of moral religion is, at the same stroke, a deepening of human awareness of the social and historical impact of religion.

Kant's reflections on the historicity of religion are regulated by the same bridge-making aim which guides the rest of his theory of religion. His general aim is to discover the religious mode of joining nature and freedom. One special problem is to unify the two main strands in human historical development: the cultural and the moral.[39] In his general conception of history, Kant regards the gradual forging of human culture as the necessary undergirding for every historical growth of the human spirit. This cultural foundation is made firm by the technological and the pragmatic factors in our complex human activity. The technological or civilizing aspect is found in our steady effort to learn more about natural things and to shape our physical environment practically into a world which serves our human uses. But this humanized world of tools and ready materials would be meaningless, unless it were made to enhance the quality of human society. Hence our historical work also includes a pragmatic or self-cultivating side, devoted to the better ordering of interhuman relations.

Through what Leibniz terms the *concordia discors*—the unsocial sociability of men—we find that every step taken in the creation of a humane environment, education, and political order binds us more closely together and makes us more interdependent. And yet the increasing sociality in cultural history does not guarantee any proportionate increase in our moral values and effective freedom. There is no automatic process whereby the cultural enrichment of technological and pragmatic values is simply expanded to include the moral. Often, our moral judgments about a human society are adversely made, despite its high cultural attainments. Some additional, independent evidence must be adduced to show that man in his civilized and cultivated condition is responsive to moral considerations, and hence that morality has a historical as well as an in-

---

39. *Judgment*, pp. 279–84; *Anthropologie in pragmatischer Hinsicht*, 7, 322–25, on the technical, pragmatic, and moral dispositions in human action and history. The problem of synthesizing cultural and moral history is stated by E. L. Fackenheim, "Kant's Concept of History," *Kant-Studien*, 48 (1956–57), 381–98, but the religious contribution to the solution lies beyond the scope of the article.

dividual significance. Moreover, in accord with the systematic requirement that religion be founded upon morality and not the converse, this
evidence must not be sought primarily in religious conviction about history, but in a direct reflection upon the course of cultural history itself.

This is the function of Kant's study of the French Revolution.[40] He
was drawn toward the events, not only because of his sympathy for all
movements advancing intellectual and political liberty, but also because
of the contribution which this particular movement made to his theory
of history. At least in its initial phases, the French Revolution furnished
him with concrete evidence of the drive of the human spirit toward freedom, its generosity and sacrifice in searching for a better way to realize
the moral values of humanity, and the capacity of one particular moral
effort in history to arouse the common sympathy of men who are otherwise widely separated. Here, Kant found experiential testimony that there
is a moral as well as a cultural (technico-pragmatic) history of mankind,
and that the latter can be opened up and referred to the former, through
the free social actions of men.

Once the epistemological ordering of evidence was established, however, Kant was ready to acknowledge the importance of the religious conception of history. A major function of the reflective judgment in its religious modality is to strengthen the bridge between the cultural and the
moral currents of history. It works toward this unification through its own
line of interpretation. For the religious mind, the cultural developments
in technology and civil society do not draw their power solely from "nature," or the unsocial sociability of men with the physical world and each
other, but also from the divine providence which operates in and through
the natural, social condition of mankind.[41]

Similarly, the moral aim displayed in historical acts is sustained both
by human moral freedom and by a religious communion with God. Thus
the interpreting religious mind unifies the cultural and the moral history
of man, by relating both of them to the interworkings of God and man.
The belief in God as the Lord of history, reinforces our conviction on the

40. *An Old Question Raised Again: Is the Human Race Constantly Progressing?*
[Part II of *Streit* in trans.], in *On History*, pp. 142–48.

41. See the several essays in *On History*, pp. 16, 25, 68, 106, for Kant's use of the
idea of providence to interpret history as moving from technico-cultural progress to
the level of moral progress. This is a critical pronoiodicy, or justification of the interpretative idea of providence as manifesting a moral purpose in human history. In this
sense, Kant refers to his own conception of history and its moral-religious purpose as a
"philosophical chiliasm" (*Religion innerhalb*, p. 36).

unity of human history and the opportunity for a free orientation of cultural development to the social moral good of humanity. Kant's moral interpretation of sacred history led him to view it, not as a special course of deeds transpiring in a separate realm, but as an integrative way of looking at the ordinary cultural and moral activities of men.

The peculiar fruit of this integration is to assure that the element of hope, accentuated in Kantian philosophy of religion, will itself have a threefold historical signification. First, whatever the systematic difficulties, the highest good which our moral disposition must promote is not only social but temporal and historical. The moral disposition must be related effectively to this social historical good, without destroying personal freedom. Kant finds in the religious notion of the people of God a concrete expression of the project of combining moral responsibility with an enduring social intent in history.

A second historical aspect of religious hope is the conviction that evil will not have the last word in history, any more than in one's interior decision. As the Hebrew prophets assure us, the Lord of history will achieve the eventual victory of the kingdom of good over that of evil, a victory toward which our historical strivings can contribute. Great social undertakings benefit from such religious encouragement, as well as from the technical analyses and the basic moral evaluation of the action.

The third feature of a historically oriented religious hope is that purposiveness is operating within the sphere of religious developments themselves. Kant distinguishes between the history of the churches and the history of religion.[42] Each of the visible religious communities and churches of mankind has a peculiar career of its own, interacting as one contingent societal entity with the other components in the social situation. The books and university courses devoted to universal church history are, in fact, concerned with joining these separate stories into a coherent pattern. By emphasizing the divisions, heresies, and conflicts among the visible religious communities of believers, however, this universal history belies its name and is really the story of the particularities and scissions of religion in its visible forms. It becomes the story of the "church militant," in the pejorative sense of the arena for domestic battles and estrangements. Hence Kant regards such a universal church history merely as the social phase of Hume's natural history of religion.

But in the light of his own account of the relation between revela-

42. *Religion*, pp. 115–16.

tional and moral religion, Kant discerns another struggle and another meaning of history, insofar as it involves the visible forms of religion. There is a steady, common orientation of all these forms toward the pure moral meaning of religion, a striving to realize the human nucleus of religion under the social and historical conditions of our race. This is another sort of militancy for the visible church: its struggle to fulfill its vocation as the human instrument for the practical idea of a free relationship with God. As distinct from various church histories, the religious history of humanity is the story of the developing teleological relations between the visible church and the invisible church or family of God. Thus the perspective of transition taken by the philosophy of religion has a historical connotation, insofar as it studies the movement from ecclesial to religious history. This perspective constitutes the passage from Hume's natural history of religion to Kant's moral history of religion.

The moral history of religion gives a framework for developing a philosophical *eschatology*. In his essay, *The End of All Things*, Kant briefly outlines the shape of such a discipline. The materials for analysis are drawn from our everyday statements about facing death or passing from time to eternity, as well as from the dogmatic theology of the last things: death, judgment, hell, and heaven. The responsibility of a philosophical eschatology is to interpret these materials as being revelatory of the structure of human nature and the activity of moral reason and will. We do not meditate upon such matters in order to become frightened, demoralized, or insensible to our temporal obligations, but precisely to sharpen our moral awareness and strengthen our moral activities in the world.

Hence Kant searches for both the symbolic significance and the intellectual meaning of the religious orientation of man toward the end of all things. As a symbol, it renders concrete our necessity of standing ready at all times, of always being vigilant about our soul's condition and being conscientious before our divine judge. Its intellectual meaning for reflective moral reason lies in the necessity "really to consider ourselves always as chosen citizens of a divine (ethical) state." [43] This is a normative meaning, because it establishes a definite order between the end of the world considered as the death of the individual, the fulfillment of the physical and cultural cosmos, and as the universal realization of moral ends.

43. Ibid., p. 126; see *The End of All Things*, pp. 73, 77–79. The religious aspect of the latter work is brought out in H. A. Salmony's commentary, *Kants Schrift "Das Ende aller Dinge"* (Zurich, 1962), which relies heavily on Karl Jaspers' philosophy of religion.

Moral realization must be given primacy over the first two meanings of eschatology. The individual has to use his life for moral ends, and has to work for the incorporation of natural and cultural history into the moral history of humanity. He does not do this work alone, however, but as a fellow member of the moral and religious community in which all cosmic, cultural, and ecclesial values find their home. To consider ourselves always in this teleological ordering, is to live by the religious conviction concerning the last day and the divine judgment. This eschatological orientation does not shatter history or postpone its climax interminably, but it does make us aware of history's insistent and always contemporary demands upon all the citizens of the City of God.

BETWEEN ZOROASTER AND JOB

During the last dozen years of his life, Kant sought repeatedly to sum up his position on religion in some concrete, practically influential imagery. He polarized this effort around the two key concepts of wisdom and holiness, in accord with his remark that "the idea of wisdom must underlie philosophy, just as the idea of holiness underlies Christianity." [44] These practical ideals are both generative and consummative: they provoke the best theoretical and practical activities of men, and they also serve to unify these activities in the humanly most significant patterns of achievement and power. In trying to respond to the two sets of demands as fully as possible, we manifest to ourselves the several facets in the whole vocation of man. As a mundane wisdom, philosophy seeks to realize that vocation by joining a theoretical knowledge of the natural world with a practical understanding of man's moral life. And as an attitude and a doctrine concerning man's relation with God, religion enlarges the vocation of man by urging on the good will toward a sharing in the holiness of God.

Can the philosophy of religion succeed in making a perfect synthesis between wisdom and holiness, and thus in rounding off the whole vocation of man within the ultimate ambit of philosophy itself? Kant's ultimately negative answer is inevitable, in view of his basic distinction between our idea of God and the reality of the hidden God of theistic religion. Philosophy does explore the meaning of the idea of God and the human relationship with God, insofar as they belong within the moral world and

44. *Vorlesungen über philosophische Enzyklopädie,* p. 34; cf. *Practical Reason,* pp. 125–26 n., 230–32.

thus come within the proper range of a worldly wisdom. Thus the philosopher of religion does hold a real purchase upon the reality of religion, within the mundane limits set for theoretical and practical reason.

But, though the man of religion belongs thoroughly within the physical and moral world, he nevertheless also attends to, and orients himself toward, the living God Himself. Although there is a broad foundation in human reality for the philosophical study of religion, there is no good reason for claiming that the philosophy of religion exhausts the reality of the religious relationship. When the philosopher of religion comes to the boundaries set by his theory of experience and reason, he does not come at the same stroke to the limits of the religious man's free relationship with God. There is an open personal bond with the holy God which outstrips the range of our philosophical scrutiny.

Kant expresses this residual distinction in principle between the philosopher of religion and the religious man in the concrete figures, respectively, of Zoroaster and Job. He does not propose them as examples to be imitated, but as vivid archetypes which can arouse our reflection and encourage our action along definite paths. Wisdom and holiness are one in God, but in man they remain distinct practical goals to be sought, rather than perfections in our plenary possession. We can represent the lover and pursuer of wisdom, including the philosophical wisdom about religion, in the image of Zoroaster. And we can represent man's religious striving after holiness, a striving which furnishes the materials of analysis for philosophy of religion and yet somehow eludes its grasp, in the image of Job. These figures reflect Kant's study of oriental religions and the Bible, but their main function is to bring into concrete focus his own investigations into human religiousness.

In his *Opus Postumum*, Kant views Zoroaster as a personal archetype for "philosophy in the entirety of its conceptual content gathered together under one principle," and as "the ideal of the physical and also the moral-practical reason united in one sense-object." [45] In its allsufficiency, wisdom

---

45. *Opus Postumum*, 21, 4, 156. Kant adds that the symbol of Zoroaster keeps us aware of the existence of God's independent, originary wisdom, which the philosopher is always striving to realize a likeness of through his own methods and evidences (ibid., 21, 8). For Kant's knowledge of Parsism, see Glasenapp, *Kant und die Religionen des Ostens*, pp. 45–49, 123–27. Voltaire's appeal to Zoroaster is described by René Pomeau, *La Religion de Voltaire* (Paris, 1956), pp. 154–58, whereas Friedrich Nietzsche uses the imaginative figure of Zoroaster as the focus of his own philosophy, as expressed in *Thus Spoke Zarathustra*, trans. R. J. Hollingdale (Baltimore, 1961).

is found only in God, but we can render the human analogon of wisdom perceptible to ourselves in the figure of Zoroaster. He represents the highest standpoint of philosophy, which is a love and quest for a wisdom of the world which is commensurate with the human modes of experience, reason, and will. In him, we can see before us the philosophical ideal of joining theoretical and practical reason, the realm of nature and that of freedom and moral self-knowledge.

By attending to the religious aspect of Zoroaster's wisdom, we are reminded that the unifying synthesis sought in philosophy requires a theory of religion, or a study of the idea of God and the religious referring of our practical life. This theory of religion must be kept functionally subordinate to the general philosophical task of understanding man, who is the living copula, or middle term, welding the sensory and intelligible orders, the physical and moral worlds. But whereas Nietzsche's figure of Zarathustra represents the unity of the universe as an endless circle of becoming, from which God is excluded, Kant's Zoroaster unifies the universe through an open movement of man toward God.

The agelong religious meditation upon man's lowliness and sublimity, his misery and grandeur, attains its philosophical significance through what Kant calls the theme of *mundi incola Homo:* man the indweller of the world.[46] In the symbol of Zoroaster, we can visualize how the philosophy of religion enables man to achieve an ordering of the components in the universe.

MAN'S composite personal being actively interprets	WORLD as unity of physical and moral laws for mundane beings, including man himself IDEA OF GOD founded analogously in human freedom	Bound together as the UNIVERSE by man's whole vocation as indweller of the world and moral theist

It is to man's personal life and reflection that the poles of the universe are kept in meaningful relation. He must cultivate that binocular vision which sees human reality both as one mundane entity along with all other beings in the world, and also as having the unique capacity for moral reflection and decision. The idea of God arising within him is an

46. *Opus Postumum*, 21, 46–47. The religious anthropology of the *Opus Postumum* is related to Kant's earlier doctrines by Georg Antonopoulos, *Der Mensch als Bürger zweier Welten* (Bonn, 1958), pp. 41–51.

orienting principle which, as fully interpreted, directs his active life toward a personal and free God. Yet from the philosophical standpoint, his religious tendency has to be morally disciplined, in order to achieve man's whole vocation as the unifier of nature and freedom within the experienced universe.

We can symbolize moral and religious theism itself through Job, the holy man of God. His figure looms large in Kant's essay *On the Failure of All Philosophical Attempts in Theodicy.* After pointing out the inability of speculative theology and physicotheology to meet the problem of evil, Kant directs our attention toward the genuine, experiential theodicy embodied in the attitude of Job. He is the man of unfeigned moral belief, who admits that God remains a mystery, not only in His own reality but also in His ways with the moral and physical world.

Job's living acceptance of God is decisively religious, because it bears all the marks of *conscientiousness:* a moral basis, honesty about difficulties, simplicity of expression, and a thorough sincerity of faith. His conception of God is shaped by the requirements of the moral good for man, rather than by any physical extrapolations from nature or by metaphysical arguments. The firmness of his assent to the good God is perfectly compatible with a frank avowal of difficulties and doubts, since Job remains a man and does not possess either the vision or the purely spiritual nature of an angel. It is in this Pascalian frame of mind that Kant himself declares in a private annotation: "I do not have at all the ambition to want to be a seraph; my pride is only this, that I am a man." [47] Being bound by a twofold fidelity to God and his own human condition, Job refuses either to flatter God or to deceive himself and others about his own religious wrestling. His speech is simple and straightforward, without any overtones of trying to win God's favor and without glossing over the need for patient endurance, as we hold to a morally good course in our actual world.

Above all, Job is our visible encouragement to strive after sincerity in religion. He silences his critics and in fact becomes pleasing to God, due to his carefulness in measuring his religious profession by what he personally believes and stakes his life upon. The man of religious probity is the one who never permits the question of truth to become detached from that of personal sincerity of belief. He cannot say "I believe in this or that article of faith," without ever looking into his interior forum and becoming aware of his own conviction or lack of it. Job stands there to

47. *Bemerkungen zu den Beobachtungen über das Gefühl des Schönen und Erhabenen,* 20, 47. On Job, see *Misslingen,* 8, 265–67, and Rabel, *Kant,* pp. 233–35.

warn us that only the man who is a personal witness to his religious faith
can really serve as its herald to others. If one tries to proclaim the word
of God to others, without establishing a personal acceptance of it, one is
living in bad faith. This deceitful condition is both unavailing (since it
attempts to conceal a discrepancy from God, the searcher of hearts) and
criminal (since it saps one's own uprightness and tends to corrupt the
faith of others). Whereas for Sartre, bad faith is the essential situation
of the religious believer, for Kant it is the fate of those who refuse to
accept the conditions governing the relationship between religious truth
and religious sincerity on the believer's part.

This is almost the only issue which leads Kant to abandon his dry and
typically low-keyed approach to religion for a warmly emotional stand.
In the midst of his discussion of conscientiousness, he adds the personal
testimony: *mihi hoc religioni,* this is what religion means to me.[48] This
response is elicited from him because, in contemplating the traits of Job—
the conscientious man of God—Kant is also reflecting upon the personal
attitude which alone assures the right ordering between morality and
religion. This is the crux of both the critical and the constructive phases
in his theory of religion, but formulated now as a function of the personal
attitude of the believer. Kant hails its religious importance in this famous
apostrophe:

> O *sincerity!* Thou Astraea, that has fled from earth to heaven, how
> mayest thou (the basis of conscience, and hence of all inner religion)
> be drawn down thence to us again? I can admit, though it is much
> to be deplored, that candor (in speaking the *whole* truth which one
> knows) is not to be found in human nature. But we must be able
> to demand *sincerity* (that *all that one says* be said with truthfulness),
> and indeed if there were in our nature no predisposition to sincerity,
> whose cultivation merely is neglected, the human race must needs be,
> in its own eyes, an object of the deepest contempt.

Thus there is a firm interlocking relationship between human dignity and
our unquenchable inclination toward moral and religious sincerity.

All of Kant's elaborate reservations concerning the visible religious

48. *Opus Postumum,* 21, 81. On religious conscientiousness, see ibid., pp. 25–26;
Misslingen, 8, 267–71; *Vorarbeit zu Über das Misslingen,* 23, 85. The invocation to
sincerity quoted here comes toward the end of *Religion,* p. 178 n. It is reaffirmed in
A. N. Whitehead's remark that "the primary religious virtue is sincerity, a penetrating
sincerity" (*Religion in the Making* [Cleveland, World Publishing, 1960], p. 15).

community stem from his concern lest our personal probity become stunted and displaced, in the course of a social development of religion. If the only means for developing a visible church is through the customary device of a civil establishment of statutory faith and a subordination of personal witness to theological learning, then Kant fears that religious sincerity may flee beyond recall. His critical theory of religion can be understood here as a defense of the religious attitude expressed in the Gospel cry: "Lord, I believe; help thou my unbelief!" [49] There can be no strengthening of the family of God, where this joint avowal of the individual's belief and his need for divine help is divorced from the central proclamation of the religious message.

There is one final lesson to be garnered from meditation upon Job. Not only is he sensitive to his own conscience, but he is also open to the word emanating from God. His personal existence is practically oriented, both to the moral conception of God and to the hidden reality of God's own goodness and power. In his religious attitude, we can detect an abiding recognition of the presence of God as a personal existent who talks with man, and whose living word must be received in obedient trust. Job conveys the meaning of religion as the reverent honoring of a personal transcendent reality, before whom everyone must bow his knee and to whom everyone owes a personal loyalty.[50] In Job's conduct, we hear the invitation to enter into dialogue with God Himself and not with our own moral reason alone. This invitation is correlative with the command to serve God's personal will and not simply our own conception of the good and the obligatory.

49. Mark 9:24, quoted by Kant in *Religion*, p. 178. He reflects upon Job 27:5–6 in *Misslingen*, 8, 267 (see also Rabel, *Kant*, pp. 234–35).

50. In *Opus Postumum*, 21, 26–27, 101, 149, Kant differentiates between a God who is a metaphysical substance, an impersonal law, or a soul of the world, and one who is the living God of religion. The latter is encountered in the *dictamina sacrosancta*, the holy precepts of conscience and our moral life. Only within this ethico-religious context, where "God exists" means that we are in the demanding presence of a holy moral person who has a good will and real power to effect our happiness, does Kant feel it safe to admit that this is an existential (i.e. a moral-religious, not a cosmological or metaphysical) truth, and that it is practically relevant for religion. The religious situation is the one in which our respect for moral law within us leads us to bend our knee in reverence to the existing God, who is present to us as the holy judge of our moral actions. Only within this highly qualified situation does God's own existence become relevant for religion, without leading us to reduce our religious energies to the narrow sphere of the statutory observances enjoined by a publicly established religion.

When the Lord speaks to Job out of a whirlwind, Job's only answer is: "I will lay my hand upon my mouth." [51] This spontaneous gesture of reverent awe signifies that our religious service of love and fear is owed, not only to our moral ideal of God, but to the holy and sublime God Himself. Job's personal center of existence reaches out to the allsufficient personal existence of the good God. In this personal and existential orientation, the idea of God is not sufficient to sustain the religious life, which must nourish itself in some way upon the living God Himself. In the figure of Job, human religiousness begins to move beyond the limits set for moral theism by the Kantian critical philosophy of religion. In the very act of providing materials for the philosophical analysis of religion, the archetypal man of religion intimates that beyond the methodological limits of this analysis there lies a personal relationship with God, about which the careful philosopher of religion must remain silent.

Kant's self-imposed limits are clearly visible in his treatment of prayer as a means of grace. He distinguishes between the spirit of prayer and verbal prayer. The former is a heartfelt interior wish to be well pleasing to God in all our actions, whereas the latter is a statement of that wish in words and formulas. The man engaged in the spirit of prayer is working upon himself, by using the idea of God to quicken his own moral disposition. But the man engaged in verbal prayer is trying to work upon God Himself, by addressing Him as though He were there in person. From the standpoint of pure moral religion, Kant holds that the practice of verbal prayer is a means "of conversing within and really *with oneself,* but ostensibly of speaking the more intelligibly *with God.*" [52] Hence he concludes that it cannot be required as a statutory duty of all citizens, since many men can stimulate their moral disposition without having recourse to this stratagem of making an audible and public address to God.

Kant is doing more here than defending the primacy of interior prayer and the freedom of our life of prayer. He is also restricting the moral conception of prayer to the instrumental use of the idea of God as a means for heightening our moral disposition, as it carries over into our daily actions. From his philosophical standpoint, he criticizes any direct

---

51. Job 39:34. As Philipp notes in *Das Werden der Aufklärung,* pp. 117–18, the Hamburg school of physicotheologians treated Job as the model for anyone seeking to find God's presence in awesome natural happenings. Kant transferred Job's significance to the domain of awesome moral-religious happenings, that is, to religious fidelity in the face of intellectual perplexity and moral evil.

52. *Religion,* p. 185.

personal address to God as being an effort to exploit Him for one's own ends, or as an instance of the fanaticism of pretending to have an intuitive grasp of His presence, or simply as failing to recognize an act of human self-stimulation for what it is. In this respect, there is something unsettling and even scandalous about Job. Insofar as Job's life of prayer involves a conversing with God which remains intact after Kant's criticism is made, it serves as a symbol of the difference persisting between the philosophy of religion and human religiousness.

Kant does not consign us exclusively either to Zoroaster or to Job. His study of religion is closely regulated by the essential aims and limits of his philosophical critique of knowledge and morality. Hence he invites us to mold our philosophical understanding of religion in accord with the critical principles concerning man in the physical and moral worlds. Thus his theory of religion is developed as a part of a mundane philosophical wisdom, but with due regard for two final recommendations. The first point is that we make a direct and nonreductive examination of mankind's revelational modes of religious interpretation for the nature-and-freedom relationship. Kant's concluding counsel is that we respect the unsettling conscientiousness of the religious witness, both when he avows his intellectual and moral difficulties in this world and when he pursues the ideal of holiness by turning toward the life of the holy and eternal God. Those who follow the Kantian approach to religion find themselves engaged, therefore, in a lifelong philosophical reflection upon the field of interplay between Zoroaster and Job, between philosophical wisdom about religion and the autonomous religious wisdom of the holy man of God.

6

Young Hegel's
Struggle with Religion

Because his university education was obtained with the support of the theological foundation at Tübingen (1788–93), Georg Wilhelm Friedrich Hegel received a more thorough and professional grounding in theology than did Hume or Kant.[1] Following the regular course of studies open to the Lutheran seminarians, he was given a degree in philosophy for a thesis on the relationship between moral duties and belief in immortality, and was certified in theology on the basis of a detailed paper on recent church history in his native state of Wurtemberg. His theology teachers belonged to a transitional generation, moving from the Enlightenment toward the Romantic and idealistic eras. They attempted to humanize the highly rationalistic presentation of theological doctrine by introducing Kant's stress upon practical reason and by taking a moralistic approach to the Bible. Hegel felt that their compromise failed to do intellectual justice to any of the components: speculative reason, the moral order, and Biblical revealed religion.

Along with his classmates, the poet Hölderlin and the philosopher Schelling, he opened his soul to the religious conceptions found in Spi-

1. On the development of Hegel's thought on religion, see Karl Rosenkranz, *Georg Wilhelm Friedrich Hegels Leben* (Darmstadt, 1963), pp. 45–60, 94–99; G. E. Müller, *Hegel: Denkgeschichte eines Lebendigen* (Bern, 1959), pp. 42–49, 63–71, 112–29, 228, 358–72; Paul Asveld, *La Pensée religieuse du jeune Hegel* (Louvain, 1953); J. N. Findlay, *Hegel: A Re-Examination* (New York, 1958), pp. 131–43, 341–44; Walter Kaufmann, *Hegel* (New York, 1965), pp. 41–69, 95–100, 160–62, 273–78; G. R. Mure, *The Philosophy of Hegel* (London, 1965), pp. 43–51, 102–09, 194–99. There is a thorough, general analysis of the theory of religion in G. Lasson, *Einführung in Hegels Religionsphilosophie* (Leipzig, 1930); A. Chapelle, *Hegel et la religion*, (3 vols. Paris, 1964-67); R. Vancourt, *La Pensée religieuse de Hegel* (Paris, 1965); and E. L. Fackenheim, *The Religious Dimension in Hegel's Thought* (Bloomington, 1967).

noza, Rousseau, and the Greek poets. From the outset, his search for a living religion of mankind was intertwined with an enthusiasm for the French Revolution and a keen interest in the interrelation of social, economic, political, and religious factors in every cultural situation he studied. Hegel's circle also discussed Kant's second *Critique* and *Religion* book, along with Fichte's *Essay Toward a Critique of All Revelation,* all of which were issued during his student years. It is significant that Hegel's approach to Kantian epistemology was colored by his study of these two books and the *Metaphysics of Morals,* in all of which the moral conception of religion is prominent.

During his apprentice period as a tutor in Bern and Frankfort (1793–1801), young Hegel filled countless manuscript pages and correspondence sheets with efforts to make a philosophical interpretation of his far reaching social and religious researches. (Modern editors have supplied titles for cognate groups of these manuscripts, but the chronological order of the widely separated fragments should be respected.) One group of essays deals broadly with the theme of "Folk Religion and Christianity," in which the humane features of the Greek religious spirit are contrasted favorably with the otherworldly orientation and institutionalism of modern Christianity.

In order to test Kant's claim that at least the essential message of the New Testament can be restated in pure moral terms, Hegel makes the experiment of paraphrasing the main teachings of Jesus. This so-called "Life of Jesus" fails to resolve the issue: it makes Jesus speak as a moral instructor, but at times it introduces some new overtones about infinite reason and the harmony of life, which do not fit into the Kantian religious pattern. It then occurs to Hegel that he should combine the best traits in his image of Greek religion and in the Kantian moral interpretation of the religious bond. He makes this synthesis in the manuscripts on "The Positivity of the Christian Religion," where the Graeco-Kantian standpoint represents the cause of free humanity, in opposition to the Christian restriction of the religious spirit to the contingent, historical, positive aspects of revelation and church organization.

But this solution does not permanently satisfy Hegel, who spends the remainder of his early period remedying its three principal defects. First, in order to explain why men would ever pass from the ideal Greek to the restrictive Christian type of religious life, he develops a series of "Sketches for the Spirit of Judaism," picturing the Jewish religious figures as prototypes of alienated man. Next, he finds that the Greek and Kantian conceptions of religion are too diverse to be simply melded together. While celebrating the Greek esthetic and social outlook on a folk religion in his poem "Eleusis," Hegel also devotes some annotations on "Morality, Love, and Religion" to showing Kant's misunderstanding of the nature of religious love in his attempts to make it a modal implication of moral duty. Thirdly, Hegel comes to realize that his own evolving religious position includes many aspects of the Christian message, which he proceeds to restate more favorably in "The Spirit of Christianity and Its Fate." As a climax to all this underground preparation, Hegel sets down (in 1800) a phenomenological description of the religious attitude, centered around the key concepts of love and life.

After his appointment to a philosophy post at Jena in 1801, however, Hegel saw that the problem of the relationship between religion and philosophy is closely related to that of the possibility of metaphysics. In his very first lecture course on the history of philosophy, he proposed the thesis that the modern epoch is constituted by the definitive passage of the human mind from the ultimacy of religion to that of philosophy, within whose capacious setting the truth and value of the religious attitude are henceforth to be relocated. That is why the "highway of despair" traced out in Hegel's first major work, the *Phenomenology of Spirit* (1807), leads up to the final disillusioning of the human spirit about the objective otherness of the divine principle, worshipped by Christianity and the other religions of mankind.

The systematic consequences of the total incorporation of religion within the philosophy of spirit were spelled out in Hegel's other books and lecture series, all of which contain notable treatments of religion. He suggested that one way to view his *Science of Logic* (1812–16) is as furnishing a theory of God in His eternal essence, before the creation of nature and finite spirit. This is a logical way of treating the same content which is found in the religious soul's meditation upon the internal life of God and the kingdom of the Father. In the *Encyclopedia of the Philosophical Sciences* (1817), Hegel regarded art, religion, and philosophy as progressively more adequate ways of grasping and expressing the spiritual nature of the absolute ground of being. Even in the *Philosophy of Right* (1821), Hegel took the opportunity to clarify the sense in which religion is basic for our organized social life, and also the problem of church and state.

Hegel's Berlin professorship (1818–31) was distinguished by the lecture series which he gave in special fields of philosophy, and which were preserved partly in his own manuscripts and partly in various students' notebooks. During this time, he formally lectured four times on the philosophy of religion, giving his mature teaching on the nature and kinds of religion, especially Christianity as the absolute or revealed religion. Furthermore, it is impossible to appreciate his lecture course on the proofs of God's existence, unless one recognizes that Hegel took this opportunity (in 1829, two years before his death) to recapitulate his doctrine on religion and to assimilate the entire treatment of the theistic proofs within his own account of the activity of the religious mind.

Nor did he overlook the connection of religion with the topics treated in his other lecture series. The discussion of esthetics enabled him to reformulate his ancient theme about the relationship between religious belief and different art forms. In his lectures on the philosophy of history, he noted the great differences between a historical outlook animated by a religious belief in divine providence, and one which lacks this interpretative principle. Finally, there was scarcely a major division in Hegel's series on the history of philosophy in which the problem of religion and philosophy failed to figure. Of particular importance for understanding his view of philosophical development is the role he assigned to Christianity and the Enlightenment, in shaping the modern spirit. To the Christian faith, he attributed that intellectual development in which men have at last become aware of their subjectivity, freedom, and personal dignity. The question which the Enlightenment raised, in its anti-Christian phase, is whether this awareness has now outgrown the forms of Christian faith and worship, and perhaps even outgrown the religious attitude of mankind without reservation. Hegel's speculative theory of religion can be seen as a response made to this challenge, by furnishing us with a patient philosophical analysis of human religiosity.

RELIGION AS A SPUR TO PHILOSOPHY

Hegel was convinced that a philosopher's thinking about the nature and functions of religion directly affected his conception of philosophy itself. It was an artificial procedure to justify the philosophical study of religion on the basis of a preset notion of philosophy, since certain judgments concerning the religious factors in human knowledge and action were already incorporated into that notion. When Hume and Kant appealed to their view of human nature for some implications warranting the philosophical analysis of religion, they were already using some presuppositions about man's religious attitude which it is the business of the philosopher to examine for their own sake. Hence, Hegel's call to the

theologians to come out of their Gothic cathedrals into the light of day
for a study of the rational foundations of their belief was, at the same
time, a call to the philosophers to bring into the light their own latent
assumptions about religion.

Yet he felt strongly that the relationship between philosophy and religion cannot be properly framed in terms of the question-and-answer
schema, which was commonly accepted by both parties to the German
Enlightenment dispute over religion, and which has been more recently
defended by Tillich. The orthodox theologians at Tübingen supposed that
philosophy raises the ultimate questions about human destiny, and that
the answers are supplied by faith and theology. Conversely, the critics
of Christianity claimed that religious faith and theology raise fundamental
questions, the answers to which can be supplied by philosophy alone. But
any such sharp segregation of the source of the questions from that of the
answers overlooked the fact of the close mutual involvement of religion
and philosophy in both phases of the human inquiry into ultimate issues.
Whether Hegel turned to the history of human thought, to his own
intellectual development, or to a systematic explanation, he found that
religion and philosophy were working together both in formulating the
issues and in indicating the direction to take for their resolution.

As a first hint of his own position, Hegel liked to give a distinctive
twist to the maxim of St. Anselm: "It seems careless for us, once we are
established in the faith, not to aim at understanding what we believe." [2]
Religious faith stirs up the subjective energies in the human existent. It
impels him on a lifelong quest for the intellectual grounds of his religious
interpretation of life and for the practical means of bringing his ideal to
realization. Gradually, it dawns on him that the relationship between
religion and philosophy is not precisely an instrumental one, but rather
one of organic maturation. The theoretical and practical truths he once
held on faith can eventually be held through a philosophically motivated
judgment. The act of faith and that of philosophical knowing stand related as the implicit and the explicit stages of a single growth in awareness.

Religion is philosophy grasped in the mode of groping presentiment,

---

2. St. Anselm, *Why God Became Man*, trans. E. R. Fairweather, in *A Scholastic
Miscellany: Anselm to Ockham* (Philadelphia, Westminster Press, 1956), p. 102.
Hegel quotes this sentence twice in *Enzyklopädie der philosophischen Wissenschaften*,
eds. F. Nicolin and O. Pöggeler (6th ed. Hamburg, 1959), pp. 15, 101, with the
purpose of defending a closer relation between believing and knowing than was previously allowed.

whereas philosophy is religion brought to its internal fulfillment and conscious articulation. It is the same person who says the creed as a youth and as an old man. Wisdom comes to him when he recognizes that the aim of his eager religious search for understanding is fully realized in the method and judgments constituting his philosophical knowledge. He sees that philosophy is religion's deeper and truer self, the unfolded truth concerning the certainties of religious faith and practice.

To determine the precise ordering between religion and philosophy is a task set for Hegel's philosophy of religion. He lays down its ground rules in the introductory portion of his Berlin lectures on philosophy of religion.[3] His four rules concern: religion's cultural solidarity, the starting point for a philosophical study of religion, the shift in the scales of knowledge and interest, and the fragmentation of all current views on religion. Unless the philosopher appreciates the problematic situation with which these working rules are designed to cope, he will be unable to make a creative contribution to the modern discussion about religion.

The philosophical examination of religion must respect the general *solidarity* of religion with the other components in human culture, as well as the particular solidarity of this or that religion with its own cultural situation. If religion is intimately bound up (for better or for worse) with our active human nature, then it is bound up with the whole network of cultural forms in which man's nature actually displays itself

---

3. *Vorlesungen über die Philosophie der Religion*, ed. G. Lasson (4 vols. bound in 2, Hamburg, Meiner, 1966), 1, 1–76 (1, 1–85). The primary reference is by vol. and page to the four separately paginated volumes, reprinted unchanged from the original Lasson ed. (4 vols. Leipzig, Meiner, 1925–29). The volume and page numbers within parentheses refer to the approximately corresponding place in the English version, *Lectures on the Philosophy of Religion*, trans. E. B. Speirs and J. B. Sanderson (3 vols. London, Routledge and Kegan Paul, 1962). Lasson gives the text of Hegel's own manuscript in larger print, but runs it in with the text devised by the early editors from various student reports of the lecture course on the philosophy of religion. All direct quotations here will be limited to Hegel's own text of the *Philosophie der Religion*, but citations of longer passages will include his text along with the text devised by the early editors. The editors of the forthcoming, genuinely critical edition of Hegel (Nicolin and Pöggeler) intend to remedy the presentation of the German text, and their solution will permit the eventual appearance of a critically accurate English translation of the course on philosophy of religion and the other courses. The situation is better with Hegel's *Vorlesungen über die Beweise vom Dasein Gottes*, ed. G. Lasson (Hamburg, Meiner, 1966), which he delivered in the summer of 1829. References to the *Beweise* will be accompanied by a parenthetical reference, by page number only, to the English translation, *Lectures on the Proofs of the Existence of God*, which is included at the end of vol. 3 of the Speirs-Sanderson translation of the *Philosophy of Religion*.

and develops. While Hegel widens the notion of human nature beyond the Humean percipient and the Kantian moral subject, to the level of the unified cultural whole, he also finds it necessary to interpret the relation of religion to human nature as being a relation specified at the level of the cultural context. Primary attention must shift from the artificially isolated religious believer to the broad social matrix of religion.

This means that the philosopher must show how this particular religious outlook is adapted to this definite cultural situation. Hegel does not take this rule in a purely relativistic and deterministic sense, since he does not stipulate that the reference to a restricted and changing cultural configuration is the sole and exhaustive way of determining the human worth of a particular religion. Nor does he stipulate that there is a one-way causal influence of the other cultural factors upon religion. But he does question the soundness of the abstract empiricist and moralistic estimates of the religious principle, taken in isolation from an actual historical setting.

Something can next be specified about the proper *starting point* for philosophy of religion. On the negative side, Hegel finds no difficulty in ruling out three common ways of getting the inquiry under way. One inadequate method is that of a universal skeptical suspension of assent which, as applied to the religious sphere, seeks to start entirely from scratch in the study of religion. But the skeptical posture is itself determinately specified by the cultural and religious situation from which it tries to remove. The philosopher of religion does not pretend to evacuate all conceptions of religion and every assent to religious statements, but rather tries to understand them and reform them in the light of his general method and his other knowledges.

Another inadequate approach, one often responsible for the skeptical tactic, is to begin with a given abstract definition of religion and then treat all problems by a deduction of consequences from that privileged definition. But the philosopher is required by his vocation to demand some good reasons for accepting one proposed definition rather than another. He must look with some suspicion upon any postulated notion of religion which is arbitrarily imposed at the outset of the inquiry, rather than slowly arrived at as the fruit of a careful investigation. If religion is really implicated in human nature and the cultural process, then any philosophical analysis of religion must be guided mainly by a view of it that emerges from these sources, and not by one initially laid down in bare and splendid isolation from the human context.

Finally, Hegel refuses to base the inquiry into religion upon some purely private persuasion. He sympathizes with those believers who retreat from the battle between the skeptics and the rationalistic theologians into a zone of private sentiment. But he also points out that their starting point is just as abstract, on the subjective side, as are the skeptical and rationalistic conceptions of religion on the objective side. To build a theory of religion upon a one-sided inner conviction is only to guarantee that the resultant account of religion will remain unbalanced in principle, and incapable of doing justice to the complexity of our religious beliefs and practices.

For positive guidance, Hegel turns to his general procedure in any field of philosophy. Whatever the field of problems, the start can only be made through a gradual penetration into the actual structures and forces present in one's own age and cultural situation. This is not a form of cultural solipsism, since those structures manifest some constant trends and ideals of humanity. To obtain both a theoretical and a practical comprehension of religion, therefore, the philosopher must follow the common maxim: Here is the Rhodes where you must make your jump, here is the America where you must understand and refashion your human reality.

The specific "here" in question is what Hegel often speaks of as "modern times and its religion." [4] The modern world embodies the religious heritage of Greece and the ancient world religions, especially Christianity and its Biblical presentation. But it places a unique stamp upon these human materials by reinterpreting them in the light of the decisive steps taken in the Reformation, the Enlightenment, and the French Revolution, which work together to shape the modern form of man's subjective religious spirit. When religious modernity is understood in this ample sense, there is nothing parochial about requiring the philosophical approach to religion to begin with an assessment of the here-and-now actuality of religious life and the strongest criticisms of that actuality.

Any firm appraisal of the modern condition of religion is also bound to take notice of what Hegel regards as a fateful *shift in the scales* of knowledge and interest. The more our knowledge of, and control over, finite things has increased, the more we have contracted our claims to possess knowledge of God and have apparently shifted our practical interest away from religious values.

> There was a time when one had the interest, the drive, to know about God, to fathom His nature, when the spirit had and found no rest

4. *The Phenomenology of Mind*, trans. J. B. Baillie (2d ed. New York, Macmillan, 1931), p. 86. I introduce modifications into this and the other English translations of Hegel which are used. K. Dove's awaited translation of *Phenomenology* will be issued by Harper and Row.

except in this occupation, when it felt itself unfortunate not to be able to satisfy this need, and regarded all other interests of its knowledge as inferior. Our time has renounced this need and its toils, we have dispensed with them. What Tacitus said of the ancient Germans, that they were *securi adversus deos,* we have again become in respect to knowing: *securi adversus deum.* It no longer grieves our age to know nothing of God. Rather, it is regarded as the supreme insight that this knowledge is not even possible. What the Christian religion, like all religions, declares as the supreme, the absolute command: "You shall know God," this now passes for folly.[5]

We have oriented our social structures, our scientific and artistic projects, and our pursuit of happiness toward the world, so that we know and care more about it than about the pursuit of God. This contraction of our dedication to the divine is even mirrored in the attempt of Schleiermacher and other theologians to push dogma into the background and to center the philosophy of religion upon our human attitude and feeling, rather than upon the being of God as their specifying goal.

Hegel does not underline this shift of existential emphasis toward the finite world in order to bemoan it, but simply in order to characterize more precisely the starting point and task for a relevant philosophy of religion. Its aim is to discern the presence and the power of religion in our very concern with the real world, rather than in any movement of flight away from this world. The great release of subjectivity required for the pursuit of secular knowledge, institutions, and values, arouses in modern man a desire for a living unity which neither this pursuit nor the typical positions on religion can satisfy, and yet which achievement is the essential aim of the human religious quest.

Hegel's final descriptive note concerning the actual context for the study of religion is that the accepted views on the meaning of religion are too

5. *Philosophie der Religion,* 1, 5 (1, 36). Whereas Kant's theory of religion is a function of his wisdom of the world, Hegel regards philosophical wisdom itself as primarily a study of God and religion, with the world considered in relation to man and God:

> Thus God is the one and unique object of philosophy. [Its work is] to occupy itself with Him, to know every thing in Him, to reduce every thing to Him, as well as to derive every particular from Him and justify every thing only insofar as it arises out of Him, maintains itself in its connection with Him, lives and has its soul from His radiation. Therefore philosophy is theology, and occupation with it or rather in it is, as such, worship. (Ibid., 1, 30 [1, 19–20])

fragmented to carry conviction with modern man. Christianity is riven, for instance, by the orthodox establishment, looking for intellectual support in an alliance with civil power, and by the pietist dissenters who rely upon inner feeling and purely private activities. Hegel regards the Enlightenment critique of this divided Christianity as being inevitable and justified. Such critics as Voltaire and Lessing, Diderot and Holbach, have indeed punctured the intellectual claims of the apologists, brought out the incongruities and injustices entailed by the religious establishment in every country, and at least raised a question about the exact significance of the feelings usually labeled as religious. But the result is disappointing, since the enlightened deists keep God too far removed from the world to sustain an effective religion, whereas the materialists do not seem to recognize the divine traits and religious attitudes which they have been obliged to smuggle back into their godless universe. Even such philosophers of religion as Hume and Kant seem determined to treat God as a nonappearing object, and thus to frustrate that religious sense of the presence and power of God which they are supposed to be examining.

Yet Hegel does not draw the pessimistic conclusion that it may be prudent to postpone or eliminate the philosophical inquiry into religion. One must pluck the rose of a philosophically true and adequate conception of religion from the thorns of the present condition of man, without waiting for it to be handed to one painlessly as a gift. The philosopher can no more expect the human circumstances to open up an effortless vision of the significance of religion than he can expect them to reveal the nature of the state to our indolent gaze. In both cases, philosophical reason must penetrate the refractory materials, master the countertendencies in experience, and develop the truth out of the philosophical combat itself.

Hegel's confidence in the outcome of a philosophical interpretation of religion rested not only upon his systematic view of reason, as attaining its ends through a struggle with the antitheses in experience, but also upon his personal history. His own interest in religion served as a constant spur to his philosophical work as a whole. The method of thinking and the metaphysical view of reality which his interest in the nature of religion helped him to formulate, also gave him some access to the meaning of the other aspects of human experience. Because his philosophical method and metaphysics were not developed in complete isolation from man's religious activity, he had some assurance that the meaning and truth of this activity are not closed in principle to his philosophical inquiry.

This open corridor policy between philosophy and religion has led Hegelian scholars to make some sharply opposed estimates of his philosophy, especially in the light of his early or pre-Jena writings. One group echoes Nietzsche's remarks that German "philosophy has been corrupted by theologians' blood. . . . One need merely say 'Tübingen Seminary' to understand what German philosophy is at bottom: an *insidious* theology." [6] Hence we are told to look for the theologian lurking behind Hegel's philosophical manner, to see in his philosophy a laicized theology, and to regard him as the most Christian of all philosophers for having built upon theological concepts. These colorful admonitions serve the good purpose of alerting us to the fundamental role which Hegel's reflections on religion played in the formation and development of his philosophy, as well as to his study of Christian theological doctrines as a means of understanding religious life. In these respects, he challenged the methodic separation of earlier modern philosophy in respect to theology.

Nevertheless, the view of Hegel as a crypto-theologian does not establish itself simply by pointing to his steady concern with religion and theological issues, since the problem is to determine precisely how he was concerned with these matters and how he made them relevant for his philosophical purposes. Even a radical and constant reflection on man's religious attitudes and theological speculations can be conducted in a philosophical way, without supposing that the philosopher is a theologian in lay garb. Hegel does not permit his philosophical reflections on religion and theology to become converted into religious meditations or theological inferences. Religious questions spur on his philosophizing in such a manner that they convince him of the need to use a distinctively philosophical procedure in treating the issues.

Other scholars are impressed with another feature of Hegel's mind: his sharp criticism of the prevalent theological systems and his methodic correlation of religion with the other components in a society. From this angle, it is suggested that he is antitheological rather than theological, and even that he is a forerunner of the Marxian explanation of religion

6. Nietzsche, *The Antichrist*, trans. W. Kaufmann, in *The Portable Nietzsche* (New York, Viking, 1954), p. 576. Asveld, *La Pensée religieuse du jeune Hegel*, p. 2, calls Hegel's mature system "a species of laicized theology" and finds its roots in the early fragments. Similarly, Findlay concludes his *Hegel: A Re-Examination*, p. 354, with the remark that Hegel is "in a sense the most Christian of thinkers." The opposite view of at least the early writings is defended by Walter Kaufmann, "Hegel's Early Antitheological Phase," *Philosophical Review*, 63 (1954), 3–18, whereas the classical case for a Marxist reading is made by Georg Lukács, *Der junge Hegel* (Berlin, 1954).

through its social determinants. Once more, there is considerable merit in pressing the case this far, since it forces us to attend to some features in Hegel's treatment of religion which might otherwise be overlooked. His interest in religion and theology is never passive and uncritical, since he is always trying to bring them within a philosophical perspective and appraise them in terms of his own method and principles. Moreover, his study of religion is always contextual and relational, whether it be in the embryonic form of his early correlation between Christianity and the Roman empire or in the mature systematic reference of religion to our cultural modes of reality.

But just as Hegel's interest in religious phenomena and theological ideas does not make him a theologian, so his sharp criticism of the forms of religion and theology does not make him an antitheologian. The terms "theological" and "antitheological" cannot be used in a normative sense, as the primary criteria for determining the meaning and soundness of his thought. He is primarily neither an apologist for Christianity nor its opponent, since his relationship with it is always that of an independent philosophical interpreter.

It is more precise and just to use the contrasted terms in a descriptive way, but then we find that they can both be applied to him. Hegel's mind is theological, in the sense that it undertakes a strenuous and persistent inspection of religious life and theological propositions. And it is also antitheological, in the sense of striving after a critical evaluation and reformulation of religion—especially Christianity—within his own philosophical and cultural framework. But clearly, this descriptive usage is quite inconclusive about the foundation and philosophical worth of his theory of religion. For determining the latter, we must examine Hegel's actual procedures, without relying upon the facile prejudgment that he is conforming to a theological or an antitheological standard.

CRITIQUE OF RELIGIOUS POSITIVITY

The special importance of Hegel's pre-Jena thought is that it enables us to observe the formative process for his conceptions of both philosophy and religion. His early speculations on religion are notably experimental in temper. Like Pascal before him and Kierkegaard in his own wake, he delights in working out different religious and antireligious viewpoints from within, developing each one in its internal logic to the point where it comes into open conflict with the others, and then searching after a fresh position. These intensely developed explorations of the varieties of religious belief and disbelief provide Hegel with a concrete instance of the essentially dialectical character of all human activity. The youthful Hegel speaks to us now as a Greek enthusiast trying to preserve his religion from Christian corruptions, now as a Kantian Jesus preaching from the second *Critique* and the *Religion Within the Limits of Reason Alone* as his sacred texts, and now as a romantic sensibility striving toward a vital union of the pagan, Christian, and modern religious convictions. He does not stagger headlong from one of these positions to the next, but tries to bring to communicable form the indissolvable kernel of truth in each one. In religious inquiry as elsewhere, he adapts himself to the partiality of all our human convictions, as well as to the philosopher's responsibility of focusing them all together.

Amid all the turns and tentative moves of his early exploration of religion, however, Hegel steadily pursues two major themes: the critique of religious positivity, and the movement beyond moral theism to a new conception of the religious totality. For understanding the foundation of his philosophy of religion and its critical differentiation from other theories, it is necessary to examine carefully the arguments which he assembles on these two themes.

What distinguishes Hegel's treatment of positivity and the relation between morality and religion from the Humean and Kantian approaches is the context furnished by his image of *Greek religion*. He does not pretend that the philosopher's stance toward religion is genuine only when it becomes completely detached from every religious ideal and views them all from an equal critical distance. It is more honest and adequate to begin where one is, to make a start with a critical analysis of one's own vital situation in respect to religious belief. As Hegel expresses his task in a letter to Schelling, "the ideal of youth must transform itself into reflective form and, at the same time, into a system." [7] For Hegel himself, the youthful ideal which animated his reflections and led eventually to a systematic philosophical account of religion is the notion of Greek religion which he shared with his Tübingen friends, Hölderlin and Schelling, as well as with a whole generation of German archeologists and poets. This is the frame of mind in which he feels religiously most at home. He does not try to conceal it or suspend its power with a touch of the skeptical

---

7. *Briefe von und an Hegel,* eds. J. Hoffmeister and R. Flechsig (2d ed. 4 vols. Hamburg, Meiner, 1961), 1, 59. For Hegel's lifelong love affair with the Greeks, see J. G. Gray, *Hegel and Greek Thought* (New York, 1968), and J. Taminiaux, *La Nostalgie de la Grèce à l'aube de l'idéalisme allemand* (Hague, 1967).

wand. It is there to be understood, to be criticized and supplemented by all the other components in our religious thinking and practice, and nevertheless to serve as a seedbed from which can grow a comprehensive theory of religion.

In appealing to the happy serenity of Greek religious rites, Hegel was not the prisoner of a pathetic anachronism. With every step in his philosophical self-education, he realized more fully that he was not reporting on a historical situation and was not advocating a return to some long past and unrecoverable religious condition of man. He called his view of the Greek religious mind a youthful ideal in order to underline the role of imagination in shaping it, the forward practical direction in which it beckoned, and the need which it aroused for critical reflection and systematic elaboration in terms of some as yet unarticulated principles. Hegel's use of a poetic image of the Greek religious spirit did mark out the path which philosophical discussion of religion should follow. It should accept the common human requirement of proceeding from concrete imagery to clarified concepts, from given individual patterns to their universal significance, rather than take the reverse route.

Nevertheless, we may still ask Hegel why he did not start simply with the Lutheran Christianity in which he was raised, and to which he always gave his allegiance. He would probably reply that this allegiance was never intended as a passive subscription to a given historical creed and institution. It was mediated in principle by an act of philosophical reinterpretation, which in turn rested upon his critical use of the ideal of Greek religion. The latter image grew up in his soul, during his student years, as an expression of disappointment in the contemporary symbols of the divine and as a concrete search for a more convincing human way of signifying the sacred aspects of our existence.

These aspects were not being adequately recognized by either the Church establishment or Kantian moral theism. The conventional forms used in the creed, the sacraments, and the acts of worship were deadened by their distant objectivity and association with civil coercion. In his appeal to the starry heavens above and the moral law within, Kant was indeed invoking the living religious symbols of the age, but in the form of a separation between nature and man which also characterized modern man. From Hegel's line of vision, the starry heavens made the sacred too remote and inhuman for man, whereas the moral law made it too exclusively interior and rational to function in the everyday public world.

Thus the sacred signs were failing, either by reason of our locating the sacred in an objective established order, cut off from human desires and decisions, or by reason of our splitting the sacred into the dual realms of extreme transcendence and extreme interiority. Hegel's invocation of the Greek religious genius sought to achieve a closer bond between the objective order and human interiority, between the transcendent and the sacramental aspects of the sacred. In assigning this high religious significance to the Greek strain of experience, Hegel joined company with a distinguished line of German poets and critics, archeologists and philosophers. The attitude of esthetic paganism was attractively developed by Winckelmann and Schiller, Goethe and Hölderlin.

Especially in Hölderlin there was expressed an acute tension between a mood of nostalgia for the natural pieties of Greece, a sense of emptiness and frustration about present religious sensibilities, and a resolute search for a new and quickening presence of divinity among men. His poem *Bread and Wine* embodied this three-tensed ambiguity in the religious symbolism of Greece for the modern mind:

> But we have come too late, my friend. It is true that the gods are still alive, but up there above our heads in another world. There they are endlessly active and seem to care little whether we are alive, so much do the heavenly ones spare us. For a weak vessel cannot always contain them, man can only support divine plenty from time to time. Life henceforward is a dream of them. But bewilderment helps, like slumber, and night and distress make us strong, until enough heroes have grown in the brazen cradle, enough hearts exist, as of old, like those of the heavenly ones. Then they will come thundering. . . . What the song of the ancients prophesied about the children of God —look, it is us, us! It is the fruit of Hesperia! It is miraculously and exactly fulfilled as in men; let him who has tried it, believe! But so much happens, nothing takes effect, for we are heartless, shadows, until our Father Aether is recognized and belongs to each and to all.[8]

In his prose fragment on religion, Hölderlin continued to call for a humanly perceptible religion, adapted to the actual social source of our

8. This prose translation of Hölderlin's *Brot und Wein* is given in *The Penguin Book of German Verse*, ed. L. Forster (rev. ed. Baltimore, Penguin Books, 1959), pp. 300, 302. This poem contains the famous question, "What is the use of poets in a poverty-stricken age?" upon which Heidegger has commented. For Hölderlin's fragment on religion, see his *Sämtliche Werke*, ed. F. Beissner (6 vols. to date. Stuttgart, 1944–62), 4, 287–93. See Henry Hatfield, *Aesthetic Paganism in German Literature from Winckelmann to the Death of Goethe* (Cambridge, 1964), esp. chap. 9, "The Greek Gods and Christ: Hölderlin" (pp. 142–65), on the Hölderlin-Hegel circle.

religious experience. He concluded that a vital religion must have a communal divinity, and must employ both imagination and reason to represent and enrich the basic religious relationship. His view that religious reality is relational, communitarian, and representable only by a mythic synthesis of the intellectual and the imaginative-historical factors was deeply influential for his friends, Schelling and Hegel.

The term "religion" was employed in Hegel's early works in both a broader and a more restricted way. In the broader sense, he hailed the Greeks as a free religious people. They are religious insofar as their entire society is infused with a common social ideal, one which captures the imagination and arouses the unified efforts of the entire people. This meaning for the religious quality could easily be acknowledged by John Dewey. A free, religious people affirms the divine, as being the concrete symbol for a convergence between social purpose and the nourishing forces of human passion and conviction. But whereas Rousseau had dreamed of localizing such a civil religion in the Swiss republics, Hegel and Hölderlin identified it with the Greek heritage functioning throughout Western history. They proposed this ideal as a contemporary means of moving beyond the impasse between purely private piety and ritualized religious conventions.

Hegel also treated Greek religion in a more restricted sense, taking it as one component within the social whole. From this standpoint, he held that the Greek people were constituted by three active internal forces: history, the constitution, and religion.[9] Figuratively, their father was the onrushing temporality and historicity of man, however dimly realized; their mother was the constitution or a public spirit committed to law; and their nurse was religion, aided by the several arts. In calling religion the nurse and friend of the sons of nature, Hegel was attempting to incorporate into his Greek ideal those features of the religious attitude which he missed so keenly in modern religious forms. The latter were notably lacking in intimacy, friendliness, and piety toward man's everyday life.

In painting his bright ikon of Greek religion, Hegel was thus identifying the three general conditions required in any civilization for having religion

9. *Hegels theologische Jugendschriften*, ed. H. Nohl (Tübingen, 1907), pp. 27–28. Nohl's collection of fragments and the Knox-Kroner selected translation (see below, n. 10) are cited here only by general title and page, not by the special editorial titles supplied for the individual papers. These writings are now properly published in vols. 1 and 2 of the historical-critical edition of Hegel's *Gesammelte Werke: Jugendschriften I-II*, ed. F. Nicolin and G. Schüler (Hamburg, Meiner, 1969-).

as a vital component, rather than as an uneasy appendage and burden. Its rites must be a celebration of life rather than a flight from it. Religion must strengthen man's bonds with nature and his social responsibilities, instead of weakening them in a diversionary movement toward another world. And it must learn to enlist the support of imagination and the arts in weaving garlands over the brow of the ever hidden divinity, that is, in giving symbolic religious import to the sensible world and human everyday activities, without claiming the authority to uncover their full truth and actuality. Whatever transformations they underwent in his developed system of thought, these basic requirements always remained operative in Hegel's evaluation of religions and in his ultimate distinction between the religious sphere and philosophy.

More immediately, the young Hegel used them as a handy indicator of the problem of *religious positivity*. There is something prima facie wrong with the modern religious situation, insofar as it discourages a serene and joyous affirmation of this life, separates man from the natural world and temporal social projects, suppresses his natural interest and passions, and coerces assent to its own glib story of how our salvation is won. Hume had declared these traits to be of the essence of religion and hence to indicate the inhumanity of anything beyond his own minimal philosophical interpretation of life. But for Hegel, such traits were essential only to the attitude of religious positivity, without being essential to religion as such. By allowing himself to dream about a Greek religious ideal, free of these dehumanizing characteristics, he affirmed the distinction in principle between religion and its perverting condition of positivity. Hence he could also hope to liberate the meaning of religion from its deformations in modern positivity.

Hegel's idealization of the Greek religious attitude enabled him to sharpen the problem of religious positivity in three ways. First, it brought home the typically modern character of the entire discussion about positive religion. Such a discussion would not make sense outside of the historical context supplied by the Jewish and Christian claims to having divine revelation, by the medieval and modern experience of ecclesiastical institutions and church-state unions, and by the assumptions underlying the Enlightenment critique of the established religions. Since the rise of deism, it had been assumed that there is one universal natural religion and many particular positive religions (or, in Kantian terminology, one religion and many faiths and churches), and that the latter are nonnatural, in the intensive and pejorative sense of being not merely above nature but against it. Yet Hegel's own image of Greek religion did not rest on the abstract notion of a single natural religion for rational humanity. Hence he concluded that the question of positivity is not exhaustively posed in the modern form of regarding particular historical religions as contra-natural deviations.

In the second place, he found that the use of his Greek ideal as a criterion of positivity cut in two directions. Its most obvious polemical use was against the theological tradition which recommends the accept-ance of specific Christian doctrines, as answering the permanent needs and desires of the human spirit. To defend theological doctrines in this way supposes that religious men must everywhere experience a deep sense of sin and personal responsibility before a personal God, that they need salvation precisely from such a condition, and that their desire for happi-ness is specifically one for an eternity beyond this life. Yet as Hegel depicted the Greek religious soul, it was not in fact moved by these specific needs and desires.[10] Hence one could not argue that they are universal and necessary demands of man, and that the Christian message must be accepted simply as meeting them.

But Hegel could not push his conclusion against the theologians beyond this point. His Greek ideal showed that Christianity cannot avoid includ-ing some particular and contingent factors in its message and mode of worship. What it did not show to his satisfaction, however, was the soundness of the deistic verdict that such historical factors are unimpor-tant for man and that everything distinctive about Christian doctrine and worship is an instance of inhumane religious positivity. This conclusion would only follow on the Enlightenment assumption about a universal natural religion, and Hegel was not prepared to grant the ultimacy of this abstract notion.

Thirdly, his adventure with Greek religious sensibility set Hegel think-ing about the conditions required for making a passage from a relatively humane form of religion to a positivity marked by gloom, suspicion to-ward natural life, and restriction of freedom. How could men ever be

10. Hegel saw no need to follow St. Thomas Aquinas and other Christian theo-logians in pitying the Greeks for their comfortless anguish which is supposed to flow from their lack of a religious message assuring them of personal immortality, forgive-ness, and redemption. "Our sympathy is superfluous, since in the Greeks we do not encounter the needs which our [Christian and theistic] practical reason has today when we have learned how to saddle it with plenty of them" (Hegel, *Early Theological Writings*, trans. T. M. Knox and R. Kroner [Chicago, University of Chicago Press, 1948], p. 152).

induced to cast their religious existence into the mold of religious positivity prevailing in modern official Christianity? He found a fruitful clue in the connection between the broader and the more restricted meanings of Greek religion. A people can only be called free and religious in the broad sense, provided that the three internal constituents of their social existence (history, the constitution, and religion) are humanly sound. Alterations in a people's attitude toward temporal change and public life are bound to have a profound effect upon the sort of religious belief and practice which it regards as desirable. This is a more definite statement of the Hegelian position on the correlation between every particular form of religion and its social context.

Thus the transition from the Greek city-state to the despotic Roman empire led to a decline in public-spirited projects, an increase of greed and uncontrolled power on the part of the leaders, and widespread social misery among the people. Men no longer felt at home with the natural world and the state, and they experienced a strong need to project their social ideals beyond this life into a safer region. Once men were culturally altered in their respect for temporal existence and the immanent aims of human society, their attitude toward religion was bound to change in proportion to the social displacements. They asked of religion that it be something other than the pious nurse helping them celebrate daily life. That life had become intolerable for them, and hence they demanded a religion which would safeguard their values apart from the world, and provide them with the solace of a life beyond the present one and its miseries.

If a modern people can scarcely be called free and religious in the sense of Hegel's broadly conceived Grecian ideal, this is not due precisely to the reception of Christianity but rather to its reception into a fractured and alienated humanity. Hegel's reflection upon religion as a component in our social life, and upon the dynamism required to move from one religious condition of mankind to another, is one of the major sources for his general theory of *alienation*. The only way in which he can explain the development of an unfree religious positivity, which is a parasite upon the religious spirit itself as well as upon our basic human interest in life and reason and freedom, is by correlating this religious split with the other social divisions of man from nature and from his fellows in the social body. The estrangement process which operates in the religious sphere to bring forth the forms of positivity, also operates in all other human spheres as a threat to freedom and the reasonable aims of society.

The positivizing of Christian life begins when its message is proposed on some other grounds than those which can be determined by our own theoretical and practical reason and rational freedom.[11] We are asked to accept a religious story with our minds, but not in virtue of what our minds can ascertain through their own searching and free decision. Once the wedge is opened for an act of religious faith motivated by some authority other than man's steady interests and tested insights, the autonomous freedom and immanent teleology of our human powers have been violated in principle. It is then relatively an indifferent matter whether the authoritative basis of religious faith is said to be kept apart from, set in opposition to, or held in harmony with reason. The main point is that religious faith is grounded upon some extrarational principle, which inevitably sets in motion the alienating and positivizing process of splitting apart the unity of man with his world.

Whereas the key word for religion itself as depicted in Hegel's Greek archetype is "reconciliation," that which characterizes the spirit of positivity most accurately is "cleavage." The master cleavage is that between the subjective and the objective in various modes. Hegel does not regard every sort of distinction between the subjective and the objective orders as a cleavage which generates religious positivity, but only that kind which so separates them that the objective can never become incorporated within the reality of the subjective, while the latter can never find its full and proper development in an objective expression. Thus religious positivity is not a simple thing to be identified with a particular church or creed, but always consists in the two correlative forms of an *isolative subjectivity* and an *isolative objectivity*. To the extent that religion submits passively to the dualistic categories generated by these forms, it loses its own authentic urge toward reconciliation and submits to the alienating process of positivity.

Hegel suggests that it is this process, rather than the direct human thrust of religiousness, which accounts for the rigid contrast between this world and the next, the finite and the infinite, the human and the divine. This primordial gap between the human world and God is at the root of the Jewish religious outlook, which Hegel conceives as the antithesis of the Greek ideal.[12] To overcome his insecurity and obtain a measure of

11. *Early Theological Writings*, pp. 71–86, specifies the human conditions for positivizing Christ's life and teaching, in contrast to the autonomy of reason.

12. *Early Theological Writings*, pp. 182–205. The young Hegel's ethical and religious dialectic for Judaism and Christianity is studied by M. C. Wheeler, "The Con-

self-identity and power, Abraham establishes a distance between his community and the world of natural forces, as well as between his community and the rest of mankind. In order to sustain his group in their isolation and encourage them with a sense of having a special alliance with the source of all power in nature and human society, Abraham then visualizes the divine principle as a personal God, existing in the world beyond and yet dominating this world by His laws of nature and moral conduct. Men of faith achieve a union with this all-powerful God by subjugating themselves completely to His rule. Thus the two-worlds outlook is deliberately generated, for the sake of the presumed advantage it gives to the people of God.

Such a relationship of alliance and conspiracy with the divine force is achieved only at the steep price of transforming religious believers into things in the hands of their overlord God. They estrange themselves from their own free self-determination and thus lose their subjective reality. At the same time, they find that the significance of their God shifts in proportion to their own changing self-appraisal. To the degree that religious believers comport themselves as passive things, they also tend to regard the God of their devotion as a remote thing, an object on high. Thus the religious bond turns out to be a relationship between two non-selves, two foreign objects. The actuality of life and subjective freedom has been drained out of both poles in this religious union, reached under the sign of human self-alienation. The logic of Macbeth has asserted itself. Having stepped outside the vital union with nature and mankind, the alienated religious people finds itself dehumanized and its deity reduced to the condition of a baleful object and terrifying threat to all men.

One may perhaps retort that nonetheless a union has been realized between the finite and the infinite, and hence that religious positivity is worth the sacrifice it entails. This objection enables Hegel to sharpen the point that religious positivity is precisely a pseudo-reconciliation, one which achieves a bond only between beings which have had their selfhood depleted and their subjective integrity shredded. Such a union excludes a free and humane relationship, and indeed is found only in the believer's fantasies and not in the actual reality of natural process and human history. Such religious positivity joins men with the divine only by stripping them of the power to bring the divine life effectively into the

cept of Christianity in Hegel," *New Scholasticism*, 31 (1957), 338–63, and Adrian Peperzak, *Le Jeune Hegel et la vision morale du monde* (Hague, 1960), pp. 134–40.

realms of nature and human society. This is not a truly religious integration of the divine and the human, but a transformation of the divine into an alien overlord and of the human into a well-ordered kingdom of puppets.

Hegel might well have concluded his critique of religious positivity with the general verdict that it rests on a tragic self-deception and dehumanization, were it not for two further considerations which complicated the analysis. The first point was that this positivity becomes institutionalized in the established churches of the modern world, only because it serves some very powerful secular interests and is deliberately used as a tool to foster them. And the other point was Hegel's concern lest, in criticizing positivity and its social exploitation, he might also lose sight of some genuine human values which remain even in this distorted form. The first consideration led Hegel to specify the alliance between religious and political servitude more closely, whereas the second one led him to defend against the Enlightenment a certain set of human historical values which the modes of positivity cannot suppress.

Religious Despotism.   What made Hegel approach the question of religious positivity, not with academic detachment but with passionate concern, was precisely its connection with the issue of social and political oppression, especially in the modern world being created in the wake of the French Revolution. Whether or not they intended it, the theologians who presented the religious message uncritically within a perspective of positivity were giving a religious sanction to that conception of man which best served the ends of despotism within modern political society.[13] The theological stress upon man's weakness and incapacity, his need for external authority and direction rather than for trust in his own reason and free decisions, encouraged people to view themselves in the way most advantageous to the established political rulers and economic centers of power.

---

13. Hegel makes this point in a letter to Schelling:
   The philosophers demonstrate this dignity [of humanity], the people will learn to feel it, and not just to claim their rights lowered in the dust, but to embrace them again—to reappropriate them for themselves. Religion and politics have played along under *one* roof. The former has taught what despotism wanted: contempt for the human race, its incapacity for any good, for being anything through itself. (*Briefe*, 1, 24)
Cf. *Early Theological Writings*, pp. 97–98.

Long before Karl Marx propounded his thesis about the opiate function of religion, Hegel had brought out the comfortable understanding reached between religious positivity and the forces of political and social reaction. The chief difference between the two thinkers on this problem was that where Marx thought there was an essential alliance between every form of religion and the despotic state, Hegel restricted the relationship to that form of religious life captured by alienation. Marx thought that religion today was opposed to social freedom and should be rejected, whereas Hegel argued that the oppressiveness came from positivity and called for the complete liberation of the religious spirit itself from the context of positivity and oppressed sighing.

Responsibility for maintaining that context is shared by pietism (subjective religious positivity) and the established church (objective religious positivity). The pietistic advocates of a purely interior and private kind of religion regard the world of social power as morally and religiously indifferent, thus abandoning the effort to tame that power and order it toward humane uses. Political despots take quick advantage of the abandonment of the social world by subjective positivity, by removing all moral and religious checks upon their policies. But they find the objective modes of positivity even more advantageous. The entire ecclesiastical establishment serves as an indirect method for molding and regulating the populace. Men are kept in a condition of dependence and tutelage throughout their entire lifetime, and are discouraged from developing those adult qualities of intelligence and practical initiative which might lead to criticism and modification of the political and social regime. By attaching certain civil advantages to adherence to the established religion, the worldly rulers succeed in corrupting religious life itself and preventing it from looking creatively beyond the given social order.

Hegel becomes especially biting in his treatment of the two favorite means used by the established church to prevent mature reappraisal and dissent: the system of church-sponsored education and that of moral-theological casuistry. Concerning the former instrument of objective positivity, he remarks:

> In any education the child's heart and imagination are affected by the force of early impressions and the power exercised by the example of those persons who are dearest to him and linked with him by elementary natural ties, though reason is not of necessity fettered by these influences. The church, however, not only uses these influ-

ences but in addition educates the child to believe in the faith, i.e., reason and intellect are not so trained as to be led to develop their own native principles or to judge what they hear by their own standards. On the contrary, the ideas and words engraved on imagination and memory are so girt with terrors and placed by commands in such a holy, inviolable, and blinding light that either they dumbfound the laws of reason and intellect by their brilliance and prevent their use, or else they prescribe to reason and intellect laws of another kind. By this legislation *ab extra,* reason and intellect are deprived of freedom, i.e., of the ability to follow the laws native to them and grounded in their nature.[14]

This kind of education is a self-stultifying enterprise, however, since it so debilitates the believer's natural powers that he cannot make a worthy, humane act of religious faith and worship. Furthermore, an education regulated by the demands of an established church unfits the believer for the cultural works in life. Either he cannot engage creatively in the progress of the arts and sciences or else he cannot integrate his achievements in these cultural fields with his profession of faith. Hegel attributes the serious split in the modern world between religion and the creative movements of culture to an alienating ecclesial education.

Hence he takes a sardonic view of the catechism, which is the symbolic instrument of the established church in its educational activities. Whereas in his practical philosophy Kant had admitted the need for a moral catechism containing some basic points about religion, Hegel is sensitive to the danger of thereby stunting the quest for further religious truth and reducing the mystery of religion to a mechanical formula.

> Every church gives out that its own faith is the *non plus ultra* of truth, it starts from this principle and assumes that its faith can be pocketed like money. The faith really is treated like this; every church holds that nothing in the world is so easy to find as truth: the only thing necessary is to memorize one of its catechisms. For the churches it is false to say [with Schiller]:
> 'Tis the earnestness that flinches from no toil
> That alone can catch the gurgle of truth's deep-hid spring.
> The church offers truth in the open market; the stream of ecclesi-

14. Ibid., pp. 115–16.

astical truth gurgles noisily in every street, and any wayfarer may drink his fill of it.[15]

Our sense of the hidden nature of religious truth and the great toil required even to hail it from a distance recoils from the sort of education which presents it as a handy commodity, a thing to be packaged and passed on without rethinking.

There is one more descriptive note whereby Hegel renders the meaning of religious positivity quite specific in reference to his own culture. In his personal life, he resembles Hume in having undergone a crisis of belief induced by an overly scrupulous use of books of moral casuistry and lists of questions for the examination of conscience. Hence whereas Kant had found a legitimate place for casuistry in the gradual particularization of moral doctrine and religious ideals, Hegel views it as the calcifying of moral and religious thought into a comprehensive and automatically applied system of rules of perfection.

There is an authentic echo of his own harrowing experience in his protest against the assumption that all our responsible actions must fit into pre-given niches, that the right decision can be deduced from an omnipresent set of practical principles merely by using the reflex principles of casuistry, and that a man can attain moral wholeness and religious holiness by surrendering his free prudential judgment to "this systematic web woven round him from his youth up." [16] A man who permits his life to be encased in this alienating web is caught up in a bewitched world. The motives he is supposed to assign, the feelings he is supposed to have, the values he is supposed to recognize, are unlike those of anyone he meets on the street and even unlike those he experiences intermittently within himself. To submit to this ultimate instrument of religious positivity is to enter on a downward path, which easily passes from being scrupulous to being hypocritical, and then to a full-blown case of anxiety and despair. What Kierkegaard calls the sickness unto death is already portrayed in

15. Ibid., p. 134. Hegel's assault on religious positivity anticipates by a half-century Søren Kierkegaard's *Attack upon "Christendom,"* 1854–1855 (Princeton, 1944).

16. *Early Theological Writings*, p. 137. Hegel probably draws upon his own early experience in the passage in *Jugendschriften*, pp. 12–16, where he describes the scrupulosity and anxiety raised by one's literal following of rules given in a popular moral guide for youth. Among others, Theodor Haering, *Hegel: Sein Wollen und sein Werk* (2 vols. Leipzig, 1929–38), 1, 279, proposes the questionable thesis that there is a good, as well as a bad, positivity in Hegel's early doctrine.

Hegel's account of the conscientious person who permits his moral judgment to become other-directed.

Historicity of Religion. Given this radical and many-leveled criticism of religious positivity, can anything be salvaged from religion which has developed under this form? The affirmative answer which Hegel gives is sometimes misconstrued as being a belated defense of a "good positivity." What he does defend is the indefeasible core of human religiousness, which cannot be totally won over and corrupted by the several modes of positivity.

One thing which Hegel learned from his analysis was the thoroughly historical nature of religion. When he asked himself why religion is so thoroughly historical, the inescapable answer was that it is a primary need and drive of human nature, which itself is constantly undergoing development and historical reorientation. Religion partakes of the historicity of man's own social being, since it is one of the modes in which man keeps on realizing his own powers and satisfying his own desires through new social forms. If the historical being of man is taken seriously, then the historical character of religion must deeply affect the question of religious positivity. Religion is never abstractly identified with positivity, but becomes positive in some particular way, a way dependent upon certain historical circumstances.

Hegel now saw the central weakness in the treatment of positivity by the deists and freethinkers to be its failure to reckon with the historicity of man and his religious life. This results in an *ignoratio elenchi,* a mistaking of the real issue raised by the growth of positive religions. The Enlightenment critics seek to determine "the truth of religion in *abstraction* from the manners and characteristics of the nations and epochs which believed it, and the answer to *this* question is that religion is empty superstition, deception, and stupidity." [17] But such a question overlooks the concrete historical modes through which alone man can express his religious aims and test their adequacy to his experience. The Enlightenment verdict on the actual religions of man is neat but nevertheless evasive of the genuine difficulties, from which it systematically abstracts. It simply leaves untouched "the problem of showing religion's appropriateness to

17. *Early Theological Writings,* p. 173; the next quotation, ibid. The constructive philosophical results which Hegel obtains from his study of religious positivity are assessed by Günther Rohrmoser, *Subjektivität und Verdinglichung: Theologie und Gesellschaft im Denken des jungen Hegel* (Gütersloh, 1961), pp. 33–37.

[human] nature through all nature's modifications from one century to another." The real task is to examine the meaning and worth of religion in its historical realization throughout mankind's various ages, customs, and new opportunities.

Hegel's patient analysis of the problem of positivity thus hastened the breakdown of the Enlightenment criterion of natural religion. The view that there is only one natural religion and many contranatural positive religions, rested upon a questionable appeal to human nature as a non-historical, atemporal entity. The supposition was that the meaning of human nature is constituted by a few invariant concepts. The criterion for natural religion would then be the restriction of religious belief within the purity of this conceptual definition, whereas any variations and additions would serve to characterize a religion as positive and, ultimately, as opposed to natural religion. In denying that this abstract concept of human nature in its purity can really encompass man's living reality, Hegel was also showing the inadequacy of the entire Enlightenment approach to historical, revelational religion.

In the light of his own ideal of human nature—where man is regarded as being essentially historical in every aspect of his reality and activity—Hegel achieves a new understanding of natural religion. Its naturalness consists in its being an appropriate expression of man's religious needs and feelings, taken concretely within a particular temporal context and historical stage of development. Our historically qualified "human nature itself of necessity needs to recognize a Being who transcends our consciousness of human agency, to make the intuition of that Being's perfection the animating spirit of human life, and to devote time, feelings, and organizations directly to this intuition, independently of aims of other kinds." [18]

The religious exigency of human nature can only be satisfied, therefore, in ways that are inescapably *complex, plural, and historically developing.* In this sense, there can be, and indeed must be, many modes of natural religion. Hence natural religion is not one unchanging, abstract core of concepts, but lives in and through the entire historical pattern of man's many religious beliefs and practices, insofar as they serve to increase his appreciation and search of the divine.

As Hegel envisions it, the actual religious situation in the modern world contains three factors: man's desire for a permanent and comprehensive

18. *Early Theological Writings*, p. 176.

order of divine being, his historically particular and developing modes of expressing that desire, and the forms of positivity into which his alienated condition in definite social situations forces him to fit that desire and those realizations of it. Every religious condition of man must be complex in the sense of combining the first two factors, and it may be complex in the further sense of having the traits of the third. Thus human religious existence must somehow weave together the eternal and the temporal, the universal and the particular, in its interpretation of our life and its ordering of our practice and institutions. But it may also treat the temporal and contingent aspects in a way that confuses them with the eternal and the universal, and that leads believers to make unwarranted claims for the temporal and contingent features. We are always beset with what Paul Tillich characterizes as "the tendency to preserve the holy even when it has become obsolete," and we introduce the element of positivity as soon as we give in to this tendency.[19]

Hence the philosopher of religion must expect to find that our actual religious life is quite a mixed affair. It is both natural and positive together, in a disconcerting union: natural insofar as it blends the permanent with the contingent aspects of human reality, and positive insofar as it tends to confuse and misvalue these aspects, reducing the religious attitude to an idolatry of some fixed objective things or practices. A given religion is likely to be both natural in its adaptation of the divine to the historical actuality of a particular age and people, and also positive in falling short of realizing the full religious potency of human nature.

From his study of religious positivity, therefore, Hegel draws the lesson that human religious life is profoundly ambiguous. He cautions that any religious doctrine or practice can become subjected to positivity, just as any doctrine or practice can be made to surrender a genuine human aspiration and well-founded meaning. It is not the content of the doctrine, but the way in which it is proposed and taken by men, which renders it positivistic. If it is proclaimed on purely external authority, if it undermines our freedom and human dignity, and if it makes claims running counter to our reason and experience, then the doctrine becomes a mode of positivity and breeds practical relations in the same mold. But a philosophy of religion equipped with an adequate critique of positivity

19. Paul Tillich, *Systematic Theology* (3 vols. Chicago, University of Chicago Press, 1951–63), 3, 169. Hegel's twofold criticism of religious positivity and antireligious naturalism foreshadows Tillich's twofold attack on both a "demonization of the holy" and a "reductionist profanization of religion" (ibid., 3, 101–02).

can work toward weakening such deformations and reinterpreting religious beliefs and practices in line with a complex, freedom-ordered ideal of human nature.

Hegel even looks for a salvageable meaning of the vital role of authority in the acceptance of Christianity and other world religions. The acceptance of a religious message on authority rests on "man's natural sense of the good or on his longing for it and presupposes that man looks up to God . . . that man has a natural sense or consciousness of a supersensible world and an obligation to the divine." [20] Hence there is something at the heart of his being which responds to the proposal of a divine revelation, and which opens out to receive it on the presupposition that everything good and noble is divine and comes to us as God's gift. The religious word comes to man under the concrete condition of such a longing and expectation, and in this respect even a revealed religion is natural. Christianity is not a sheer positivistic intrusion upon human nature, and in this sense Hegel agrees with Kant upon its religious naturality. Instead of permitting the appeal to revelation and authority to strengthen the hold of positivity upon believers, however, the philosopher of religion must illuminate the religious opening in man's own being and hence the natural foundation of his assent to the divine message. Such a reference helps to constrict the sphere of positivity and widen that of our own reflective and passionately interested reason.

FROM MORAL THEISM TO THE LIVING WHOLE

The study of positivity left Hegel with one major piece of unfinished business: his evaluation of the Kantian view of religion in the light of a new conception which would be definitively free from positivity. He wanted to show that Kant was not free from this taint, and that the reason lay in Kant's still uncritical acceptance of the customary theistic reading of the Christian religious attitude. A criticism of Kant's moral theism in terms of its inherited religious background thus became unavoidable.

Hölderlin had already hailed Kant as the Moses of the German nation, leading it out of captivity and into the free and lonesome desert land of his own speculation. Hegel agreed enthusiastically about the liberating effect of Kant's moral and religious writings in particular, because of their

20. *Early Theological Writings*, pp. 174, 175.

vindication of human freedom and autonomy. Pushing the metaphor one step further, however, Hegel noted that men cannot wander around in a desert forever with their philosophical Moses, and that someone else must actually conduct them into the promised land of an adequate understanding of the human meaning of religion. Kant himself could not carry off the entire feat, because of an internal contradiction in his position. He was attempting to extend the benefits of freedom into the religious and social orders, but without repudiating the main theological source of positivity in those orders.

The nature of that hindering postulate was described in unmistakable terms by Hegel. Usually, his critique of positivity remained at the general plane of evaluating a religious outlook as a whole and not in its particular doctrines, especially in view of his maxim that positivity is not found in the content of a doctrine but in the way it is taken as applying to man. However, he found it advisable to make a twofold exception in the case of the theistic conception of God and its extension to the orthodox belief in Christ's divinity. When God is conceived as a transcendent, personal power and when Christ's divinity is conceived as setting him apart as God in the theistic sense, then all the consequences of positivity are necessarily visited upon a religious attitude which looks to a divine source for its strength.

> This view becomes glaringly positive if human nature is absolutely severed from the divine, if no mediation between the two is conceded except in one isolated individual [Christ], if all man's consciousness of the good and the divine is degraded to the dull and killing belief in a superior Being [God] altogether alien to man . . . a Being completely outside the world.[21]

Theism and the Nicene doctrine on Christ are not merely matters of doctrinal content, which can be taken either in a positivistic or an antipositivistic sense. They are themselves the isolating principles of interpretation which lead to the entire system of religious positivity in modern Christian belief and practice, and which generate a positivity factor in Kant's philosophical theism.

Hegel's rather repulsive picture of Abraham and the Jewish religion is now applied to Kant himself. Because of his failure to break

21. Ibid., p. 176. Hegel regards university education as the chief social means for awakening us from this killing belief, even though this involves making a break with our upbringing (ibid., p. 328).

with theism, Kant serves as the modern prolongation of the Jewish religious spirit. The only difference which Hegel can detect between the Jews, Puritans, and Shamans criticized by Kant and Kant's own position is "that the former have their lord outside themselves, while the latter carries his lord in himself, yet at the same time is his own slave." [22] Kant merely succeeds in transferring the dehumanizing relationship between alienated man and his objectified deity from the external sphere to the inner forum of moral conscience. He remains the captive of an internal positivity, based on treating the moral law and God as superior things. This introjection of the thingified relation between God and man, within the human breast, does not make it any less deadly and humiliating for man. Hence Kant's theory of religion can only be regarded as a way station in the desert, not as an adequate account of mankind's religious spirit and its goal.

Hegel now strives to make his criticism something philosophically more rigorous than a manipulation of the Moses metaphor and an extension to Kant of his image of the Jewish soul. He does this by analyzing the suppositions which underlie Kant's moral faith in the personal God.

Hegel does not object to having moral faith as an immediate pragmatic context for the religious attitude, but he does find fault with the Kantian theologians who establish an absolute cleavage between moral faith and knowledge. A dualism of this sort supposes that our knowing reason is not absolute in respect to all modes of human cognition, and has competence only in the nonreligious sphere. In this case, however, man is led to surrender every principle of rational control over his religious beliefs. This is the essence of religious positivity. The man of moral faith can no longer justify any act of distinguishing among the proposed doctrines, rejecting certain ones, and accepting others insofar as they remain coherent with his tested rational knowledge.

Hegel's next step is to establish a direct connection between the act of depreciating the rational knowledge-context for the affirmations of moral faith and that of accepting the Kantian form of the moral proof of God's existence. The subjective condition for assenting to the morally qualified, transcendent, personal God is that the believer must regard his rational ideal as being capable of fulfillment only by some being which is foreign to humanity, and set apart from speculative and practical reason. For the nub of the moral proof of theism is to regard man as standing in need of a

22. Ibid., p. 211, which is an evident reference to Kant's *Religion Within the Limits of Reason Alone*, pp. 158–63.

state of happiness, which is both proportionate to his moral worth and yet beyond his own power to attain. Hegel does not deny that man is a needy being, or that his religious ideal is intended by his reason to satisfy his searching interest and need. But he does agree with Schleiermacher that the basic human need for the divine should not be modeled upon a notion of happiness drawn primarily from the order of sensibility, where the empirical self depends upon the initiative taken by some external active source, alien to man's own being.[23] Moral faith in a transcendent God is the religious counterpart of empirical dependence upon some outside source of satisfaction.

Instead of accepting this hedonic exemplar for the man-and-God relationship, Hegel suggests that man is religiously needy in the sense of wanting to discover the reconciling *sameness* of being between his rational ideal and its realizing goal. Man does not stand in need of an estranged, transcendent Other, but of a divine principle which discloses itself as being radically one in actuality with his own rational ideal and tendency. To reinterpret human need in terms of reconciliation within a wider community of being, rather than in terms of dependence on an extrinsic adjuster of empirical happiness and morality, is to reject the premises required for Kant's moral proof of God. Hence it also means rejecting the theistic positivization of religion which relates man, taken as an abjectly dependent suppliant, to an estranged God who serves only as an extrinsic, arbitrary source of benevolence.

With the impetus gained from his criticism of the Kantian moral approach to God, Hegel can now directly press the attack against Kant's theistic conception of religion. The argument proceeds in three stages.[24] The first consists in a criticism of the supposed moral bases of religion, and is aimed at showing that a religious attitude resting on these bases cannot avoid being an instrument of still further human estrangement. The second stage is a constructive countersuggestion that religion is the

---

23. *Jugendschriften*, pp. 233–39. Peperzak, *Le Jeune Hegel*, pp. 110–17, analyzes the inclusion of the Kantian calculus of morality and happiness within Hegel's conception of religious positivity. A somewhat similar objection is raised in a book which Hegel studied carefully: Friedrich Schleiermacher's *On Religion*, trans. John Oman (New York, 1958), pp. 99, 116–17; cf. Louis Dupré, "Toward a Revaluation of Schleiermacher's Philosophy of Religion," *Journal of Religion*, 44 (1964), 97–112.

24. A concentrated reassessment of Kant is made in *Early Theological Writings*, pp. 210–16. On the German idealists' reversal of Kantian moral theism, see X. Tilliette, "Philosophie morale et philosophie religieuse après le criticisme," in *Demitizzazione e morale*, ed. E. Castelli (Rome, 1965), pp. 281–93.

independent expression of love, rather than the dependent expression of the implications of moral duty. This latter argument then leads Hegel to propose his own distinctive view of the living whole, from which he can eventually develop a new metaphysical interpretation and phenomenological treatment of religion.

He invites us to take a closer look at the Kantian moral roots of religion. They expose the thoroughly dualistic way in which human practical life is conceived: as always involving a contrast between the ground and the object of moral action, between the holy will of God and the good will of man, between a divine underived freedom and a human derived freedom, and between the moral imperative and the inclinations of our will. The religion of moral theism cannot rise higher than this systematic fissure between the divine and the human, the moral and the desirable. A religion whose main function is to bridge this gulf can do nothing more for man than ratify these divisions, and console him temporarily for finding no intrinsic way of overcoming them and achieving union with the divine. There is a certain truth in this moralistic notion of religion, but it is only the truth which comes from accepting human self-estrangement as ultimate, and not the truth which flows from the discovery of the principle which assimilates the human to the divine, as the religious spirit in man basically seeks to do.

Hegel explicitly considers and rejects Kant's contention that he does indeed make provision for the kind of religious union proper to man's creaturely being and the corresponding attitude of hope. The two philosophers agree upon the need for a religious unification of life, but they disagree upon its meaning and the way to realize it. Kant maintains that the religious reference of our moral life to God must respect the theistic relationship between rational creatures and the allsufficient God. Hegel retorts that the term "rational creature" is an indefensible juxtaposition of words, since reason cannot regard itself as being a creature, in the sense of being something inferior and foreign to the living divine reality itself.[25] Thus Hegel reads into the meaning of creatureliness a lack of

25. *Early Theological Writings*, p. 215. Hegel has in mind the passage in *Critique of Practical Reason*, p. 191, where Kant interprets the love for God in terms of duty, since "the stage of morality on which man (and so far as we know, every rational creature) stands is respect for the moral law." See also Kant, *The Doctrine of Virtue*, p. 164. Hegel locates his own conception of religious union at what he considers to be a still higher stage in human awareness, thus granting to the Kantian position only a subsidiary truth.

community with the divine which is unsuitable to the nature of reason and the teleology of the religious act. Consequently, he cannot accept the Kantian modality of hope as the decisive religious attitude. Hope serves as the last word of the religious man only when he remains cut off from a transcendent, inscrutable God, and can do no more than entrust himself grimly to the presumed goodness of that far-off entity.

The Hegelian theory of religion is not an answer to the question of what I may hope for, but an answer to the question: "What does love reveal me to be in my wider reality?" Kantian moral faith and religious hope are subordinated to the Hegelian theme of love and the unity of life. In this sense, Hegel takes his cue from the Pauline doctrine on the primacy of charity over the other theological virtues. His pliant image of Jesus expresses his own distinctive meaning, however, for religious love and unity with the divine. The Hegelian Jesus displays anti-Kantian features in the exact degree that Hegel emancipates love from duty and regards religion as the fulfillment of love, rather than as the extension of moral duty.

Hegel uses the figure of Jesus to point out the way whereby we can extricate ourselves from Kant's inner split between the empirical and the moral self. The Hegelian Jesus does not preach the categorical imperative and the victory of law as urgently as he does the power of love to fulfill laws and duties. He works to deprive the entire duty-sphere of its ultimacy and hostility to human inclinations. Jesus raises mankind above the spirit of Kantian morality by making the passage from "shalt" to "is," from an imposed command to the free acceptance of reality as the principle of moral action and religious loyalty. Love fulfills the commandments of the law, but does so in such fashion that the alien and coercive quality of the law is removed, and the tyranny of an external universal precept over the living individual being is broken.

Love shapes the religious attitude of Jesus, precisely because it is the sole power which reintegrates sensuous inclination and law on the higher basis of the fulfilling inclination of life itself. Religious love is

> an inclination so to act as the laws may command, i.e., a unification of inclination with the law whereby the latter loses its form as law. This correspondence with inclination is the *pleroma* [fulfillment] of the law; i.e., it is an "is," which, to use an old expression, is the "compliment of possibility," since possibility is the object as something thought, as a universal, whereas "is" is the synthesis of subject

and object, in which subject and object have lost their opposition.
. . . The correspondence of inclination with law is such that law
and inclination are no longer different; and the expression "correspondence of inclination with law" is therefore wholly unsatisfactory because it implies that law and inclination are still particulars, still
opposites.[26]

Thus Hegel assigns to a fulfilling or pleromaic love the function of overcoming the basic alienations in human existence. Any particular religion
achieves religious naturality in the degree that it embodies the unifying
power of love.

Hegel deliberately reverses the relationship between morality and religion, making the former function within the broader context of unification established by the latter. This involves a profound transformation of
the Kantian conception of the virtues and the religious reference to God.
The virtuous life does not consist any longer in maintaining the victorious
superiority of God over man or of universal moral disposition over individual inclination, but in cultivating the universal social significance of
our actual inclinations and interests themselves. "To complete subjection
under the law of an alien Lord, Jesus opposed not a partial subjection
under a law of one's own, the self-coercion of Kantian virtue, but virtues
without lordship and without submission, i.e., virtues as modifications of
love." [27] Far from denying the solidarity between the Kantian conception
of morality and theistic religion, Hegel accepts it and then spells out the
consequence that any conception of love undermining the Kantian view
of virtues and the moral principle must also undermine the Kantian
theistic view of religion.

The transformation in the meaning of religion is exhibited by Hegel
in the key instance of our love of God. On three counts, it is erroneous
to interpret the words "Love God" as a moral command, conforming to
the requirements of the Kantian imperative and of theistic religion. First,

26. *Early Theological Writings*, pp. 214–15. In this key text, Hegel joins the Pauline
term *pleroma* with the Wolffian term *complementum possibilitatis*, in order to signify
that religion achieves its existential goal through a fulfilling act of love.

27. Ibid., p. 244; the next quotation, ibid., p. 247. Walter Kern, "Das Verhältnis
von Erkenntnis und Liebe als philosophisches Grundproblem bei Hegel und Thomas
von Aquin," *Scholastik*, 34 (1959), 394–427, argues that Hegel sees the function of
love as fulfilling oneself in the other, but that he ultimately subordinates the act of
love to that of knowledge, in such fashion that the loving affirmation of the being
of the other in its own inviolable actuality is weakened.

such an interpretation would suppose that love is only a modality of duty, a disposition to do our duty willingly or with an eager heart. This may be fitted into the religious connotation of love in a secondary way, but it does not supply the primary meaning. Instead of treating love as a function of duty, the religious man treats duty as a modality of love and a particular means of realizing love's meaning.

Second, it follows that the love relationship is not properly expressed in the language of imperatives. That language does express the discrepancy between the religious man's efforts and his ideal, but the ideal itself is one of unification in which the coercive form of law and duty is left behind. Hegel argues here that man in his existential condition can commit himself to love in such a way that the imperative character of law becomes a poor thing, something superfluous and to be cast aside.

This leads to Hegel's third stricture, which is that our love for God is not a submission to the will of a personal, powerful creator who is the transcendent lord of mankind. Hence he depicts Jesus as being opposed to the thought of a personal God, whose isolative particularity of being would prevent any religious bond other than our abject submission to an object-like alien force. Such a relationship would be disruptive of the spirit of the whole, which religion seeks to nourish. If our love of God were understood primarily in imperative language and theistic categories, it would become an antimoral and antireligious principle among men.

On the more positive side, then, how can the love for God be understood in a humane and properly religious sense? Hegel's reply is that both the act and the object intended by it must be reinterpreted in accord with his own general meaning of love. "Love is a sensing of a life similar to one's own, not a stronger or a weaker one. . . . Love itself pronounces no imperative. It is no universal opposed to a particular, no unity of the [abstract] concept, but a unity of spirit, divinity. To love God is to feel one's self in the 'all' of life, with no restrictions, in the infinite."

In this description, Hegel employs several elements of the religious tradition on love. It is an original, irreducible impulse in man, not a variation of his knowledge or of his moral duty. It is not identical with, or entirely capturable in, any concept formed about it. We pursue love because it liberates and enlarges our very being, making us one with the rest of reality. Love flourishes, not in a relation of dissimilarity and distance, but in one of similarity and closeness. It brings out the likeness between one's own life and that of the beloved. It removes the disparity between superior and inferior, by disclosing a shared reality and equality between them. Our love for God must conform with this pattern. As it frees us from the shell of our individuality, it must disclose our similarity with God and our capacity to share in the total divine life.

The religion of love must not direct men toward the personal God of theism, however, but toward union with the immanent and infinite totality of life, so that they may "find peace in a nonpersonal living beauty." [28] The act of religious love is not that sort of salvific and redemptive action which would relate stranger with stranger. It is closer to an act of sympathy and harmony of spirit with spirit, but one which finds that the divine spiritual life consists entirely in an active, impersonal union among individual spirits. We develop the relation of "similarity," upon which religious love thrives, by replacing the humility-and-humiliation attitude of Kant's rational creature with the proper modesty of the finite spirit, or living particle in the organism of divine life. The religious man recognizes that he is the same in nature with the immanent whole of spiritual life, and thus is a determinate aspect of the divinity. In its Hegelian sense, the similarity required for humane religious existence consists in being an internal modification of a thoroughly intramundane divine totality.

Hegel has at last provided himself with a definite criterion for determining when there is religious alienation and when there is religious integration. A state of cleavage exists whenever the union between man and the divine fails to pattern itself upon the model of the *mode-and-totality* relationship. No matter how carefully qualified the theistic account (so that it will aim at respecting both the personal integrity and the social bond of human believers related to God), it must necessarily be adjudged by Hegel as a center of estrangement and thingification for the realities involved. Any religious outlook which refuses to accept the *component-of-the-living-whole* view of the relation between man and the divine falls short of attaining the proper religious integration.

Hegel sums up the findings of his early inquiries by specifying the rela-

---

28. *Early Theological Writings*, p. 301. In the same vein of equating the personal God with an alienating opposition, Hegel says of Christ's presence in the believing community:

> Thus specifically does Jesus declare himself against personality, against the view that his essence possessed an individuality opposed to that of those who had attained the culmination of friendship with him (against the thought of a personal God), for the ground of such an individuality would be an absolute particularity of his being in opposition to theirs. (ibid., p. 271)

tion of religion to life, reflection, and love on the one hand, and to philosophy itself on the other.[29] The language which he employs to characterize life anticipates his later teaching on spirit and the dialectic. Life is the same as pure being, but it is not an indeterminate and passive reality. It constitutes itself from within by the development of separations and oppositions, and by the recovery of union through the mastery of the oppositions. Hegel refers to this dialectical process of life as the attainment of synthesis through the growth of antitheses, or as the union reached between an original union and the differentiated factors of nonunion. This is clearly a developmental and dialectical conception of the nature of life, whose full reality as spirit is only brought out in the ultimate act of reunion or synthesis attained through struggle.

Within the life process, both reflection and love have essential roles. All the differentiating forces in the world—physical, biological, and those at the level of human intention and sociality—contribute to the work of reflection. A function of the reflective mind is to explore various forms of separation and opposition, as well as to uncover the relational principles which can bind them together. But the act of love is required for the actual binding of opposites. Love infuses us with a feeling for the totality which persists within the antagonisms of existence. It impels us to seek the reunification of extremes and the overcoming of all states of alienation.

Still, Hegel does not identify religion exclusively with either reflection or love. In both respects, religion has a fulfilling or pleromaic function to perform. Just as reflection is a fulfilling of the potentialities of life in the order of differentiation and thought, and love a fulfilling of life's practical and affective potentialities, so also is religion the distinctive realization of the conjoint capacities of reflection and love.

Religion cannot reach its proper pitch without the work of reflection, whether taken in the broad sense of life's actual differentiations, or in the more specifically human sense of achieving a rational awareness and conceptual grip upon these differentiations and their principles. Thus Hegel refers to the religious attitude as "this thinking life," in order to underscore the need for the man of religion to become deeply sensitive to the problem of life's antitheses and to seek out the bases of relational unifica-

29. This is done in the papers given the somewhat misleading editorial titles, *The Spirit of Christianity and Its Fate* (in part), *Love*, and *Fragment of a System* (ibid., pp. 253–319). Theodor Steinbüchel, *Das Grundproblem der Hegelschen Philosophie* (Bonn, 1933), pp. 229–75, sees in these fragments Hegel's first solution of the problem of the universal and the individual, in terms of a divine community among men.

tion.[30] Nevertheless, it is not enough to attain an understanding of the determinate oppositions and the tragic separations in life. The religious impulse is toward putting our rational apprehension of relations to work in healing the separations in life. This is only another way of saying that religious reflection without love is sterile, faith without works is dead. Religion must bind together the values of reflection and those of love.

Furthermore, it is the proper office of religion to render somehow visible the union which it seeks between man and the divine totality. A purely interior and unexpressed act of love is insufficient for the religious man. He must make some symbolic expression of the integration between the subjective order of feeling and particular emphasis, and the objective order of universal meaning and wholeness. Hence religious dynamism includes love, and yet surpasses it through an objectifying act of the imagination. The man of religion incarnates his activity in the credal statements, the ritual acts of worship, and the historical institutions which characterize the actual religions of mankind. He must use these sacramental means for the properly religious task of binding humanity more closely to the divine circle of being.

Hegel is at last prepared to offer a guiding *definition of religion*, one which remains operative throughout his mature philosophical investigations. Taken along with its sensible manifestations, religion is the instrument revised by men for placing their powers of reflection and love ever more fully in the actual service of the unrestricted totality of divine life.

> This self-elevation of man, not from the finite to the infinite (for these terms are only products of mere reflection, and as such their separation is absolute), but from finite life to infinite life, is religion. We may call infinite life a spirit in contrast with the abstract multiplicity, for spirit is the living unity of the manifold. . . . As connected with the animating spirit, then these single lives become organs, and the infinite whole becomes an infinite totality of life. When he [the religious man] takes the infinite life as the spirit of the whole and at the same time as a living [being] outside himself (since he himself is restricted), and when he puts himself at the same time outside his restricted self in rising toward the living being and intimately uniting himself with him, then he worships God.[31]

30. *Early Theological Writings*, p. 311.
31. Ibid., pp. 311, 312.

Both the negative and the positive results of Hegel's initial analysis of religion are summed up in this text, which will repay our closer examination on the following main points.

Religion is not a static thing or a given institution, but consists essentially in the *activity of elevating oneself*. It is a basic human operation, committing man as a responsible self to the process of searching and reaching beyond himself.

The religious movement is not accurately described as a journey from the finite to the infinite, since such a description contains a twofold defect. First, it becomes entangled in the dialectic of the ideas of the finite and the infinite, the conditioned and the unconditioned, which Kant had already shown to be inconclusive ideas, when taken by themselves. Kant himself had, therefore, returned to the theistic account of religion as a practical reference between the rational creature and the allsufficient God. Hegel, in turn, subordinates both the finite and the infinite to the more central concept of life.

In the second place, the religious attitude is not identical with taking a journey from one place to another. In moving toward the infinite whole, there can be no abandonment of its finite modalities. The religious man does not leave his finite life behind in making a search for the infinite divine life, and he does not find infinite life to be anything other than an inclusive totality within which his own finite life is an organic phase. Religion is man's elevation to the infinite community, which turns out to be the vital center of all human fellowship.

The religious man speaks of God as spirit. By this, he means that the divine reality is not a purely objective thing but has a kinship with man, the religious seeker. Furthermore, he means that the divine knits together all the manifold forms of life, all the subjective instances of spiritual reality, into an encompassing whole. To call God spirit is not to designate a separate, transcendent being but to recognize the divine quality, or sustaining fullness and freedom, within the spiritual life shared by all the active organs of the religious community.

Yet the religious act is not a purely theoretical affirmation about the being of the divine totality, but a practical relating of the human modes or partial realizations to that totality. To improve the quality of the practical bond, the man of religion ordinarily finds it useful to regard the spiritual community as a particular personal being, who is outside himself and toward whom he must move through the acts of worship. This personalizing of the divine, and projecting of it outside the believer, generates a strong form of objectification and alienation.

Nevertheless, a worshipful man is not left without recourse for correcting the personified religious relationship. He can learn to distinguish between a hardened opposition and a vital opposition, between one which simply separates God and man in their entire natures and one which regards the divine and the human as the inclusive and the partial meanings, respectively, of the same religious whole. On this basis, he can then reform his act of worship, so that it symbolizes no longer an absolute type of transcendence (where there is total otherness of being between God and man, with no oneness of spiritual life) but a relative transcendence (which distinguishes between finite life and infinite life, but only in order to affirm that the former is an integral phase within the one same reality of the latter). Religious worship can only overcome the debilitating estrangement of the divine and the human, if the believer takes a theoretical and practical hold upon these distinctions. He must reshape his relationship so that it manifests only a vital opposition and a relative sort of religious transcendence.

This latter point brings to a head the problem of *religion and philosophy.* Hegel did not resolve this issue during his early speculations, but he gradually formulated it with sufficient acuteness to see the need for a full-scale, systematic study. His first solution was to identify philosophy with the peak act of reflection and then to conclude that philosophy, like every other form of reflection, must remain subordinate to religion. Philosophy is limited in its scope by the reflective tools of the separative understanding and reason. It can determine the many oppositions in being and can make us aware of the relations which also exist. But the philosophical concept remains abstract, and hence does not itself effectively surpass the separations which it discerns.

In elevating himself to the infinite whole, therefore, the religious man cannot remain at the philosophical level, but must use love and the acts of religion to achieve a living union with the divine. He has to transcend the limits of philosophy in order to overcome his own finite partiality and distance from the divine. "This partial character of the living being is transcended in religion; finite life rises to infinite life. It is only because the finite is itself life that it carries in itself the possibility of raising itself to infinite life. Philosophy therefore has to stop short of religion." [32] To release the healing resources of life, the religious movement toward

---

32. *Ibid.,* p. 313. Here, Hegel redeemed his promise to Schelling that he would devote his thought to clarifying "what it can mean to approach God" (*Briefe,* 1, 29).

the infinite must surpass the philosophical order of oppositions and reach the supraphilosophical principle of their unity.

Although this restriction of philosophy was neat, it never seemed entirely plausible to Hegel. It made the sphere of religion quite ineffable in itself and beyond the range of philosophical criticism. But Hegel refused to draw the inference of religious indifferentism that, therefore, one form of religion is just as humane as another. He admitted that the meaning of religion can be improved, and improved precisely through a reflective clarification of the nature of the self-elevation of finite life to the infinite living totality. In practice, then, he did not regard the essential tendency of religion as moving us toward an ineffable region, lying entirely beyond reflection and the scope of philosophical examination. There can be more and less perfect forms of religious union, in proportion to our more and less adequate philosophical awareness of the nature of the relationship between finite life and infinite life.

Far from having stilled the question of philosophy and religion, then, young Hegel found his work leading toward a new set of problems. He would now have to call into question his previous restriction of the philosophical concept to the sphere of abstract oppositions. His own reflections on the unity of infinite life actually involved a new unitive concept, intended to surpass the concepts of Kantian separative understanding. Hegel was on the trail of a type of reflection which differentiates without losing sight of unification, and which generalizes without dropping out the concrete determinations of life. With the aid of some new philosophical tools, he could examine more closely the relationship between the human and the divine, thus deepening his speculative grasp on the nature of religion.

7

Religion and
Hegelian Metaphysics

Hegel's philosophical labors at the university in Jena were of immense significance for his developing conception of religion. During this period, all of his lines of research converged on the problem of metaphysics. The same reasoning that led him to remove Kantian positivity in ethical and religious matters also contained some direct implications for setting aside the Kantian moratorium upon metaphysical speculation itself. Hegel explored the new prospects for metaphysics in his Jena lectures on systematic philosophy, in his published articles on German idealism and the problem of believing and knowing, and above all in his first major book—the *Phenomenology of Spirit*. His investigations were buoyed up by a realization that the meaning and truth of religion itself would be deeply affected by his reconstitution of metaphysics. In rethinking the nature of religion apart from the antimetaphysical premises upon which Hume and Kant had operated, he was bound to introduce some radical reorientations in the emergence of philosophy of religion.

THE RESURRECTION OF METAPHYSICS

Hegel's mode of founding metaphysics is subject in our day to a widely received misunderstanding, extending also to his view of religion.[1]

1. For Heidegger's opinion that both Hegel and Nietzsche are prisoners of a non-foundational Western metaphysics, see W. J. Richardson, *Heidegger: Through Phenomenology to Thought* (Hague, 1963), pp. 331–82. But when Hegel's remarks on awareness in the *Phenomenology* are related to his conception of the totality of life and spirit, they cease to be caught in an undetected ambivalence concerning the development of truth and the subject of certitude, since the latter contrast is not ultimate for him.

His concern for historical continuity and for building upon the substance of his predecessors' thought, has led Nietzsche and Heidegger to picture Hegelian metaphysics primarily as a recapitulation and endpoint of the previous Western tradition on being, God, and man. Hegel does indeed intend to incorporate the main lines of previous discussion, but he seeks to make just as radical a reconstitution of the metaphysical tradition as he does of the religious. In both spheres, he calls for a silent but deep-going revolution which will discover the human treasures men have buried away and lost sight of, during centuries of alienation from nature and from their own reality. The metaphysical discovery of the significance of human reality in the world is a fresh birth of meaning which transforms all the traditional elements in the theory of being, as well as in the religious conviction about sharing in divine spiritual life.

What led Hegel to call into question his earlier solution of the religion-and-philosophy problem, which rather neatly subordinated metaphysics and the entire order of reflection to the religious unification of life? His doubts were aroused by a significant failure on the part of religion, by the inconclusiveness of the philosophical objections against metaphysics, and by a new lease on the problem of faith and knowledge. During his Jena years, all these points converged in Hegel's mind, encouraging him to make a new foundation of metaphysics and adapt the meaning of religion to his metaphysical standard of actuality.

His historical and theoretical studies made him increasingly aware that religion did not, in fact, fulfill the assigned task of being life's supreme unification. Looking at the religions of mankind historically in the ancient, medieval, and modern epochs, he saw their failure to achieve ultimate mastery over the conflicting forces in human society. This was not merely a factual failure but an inevitable one, bound up with the tendency of any predominating religion to make a split between the secular and the spiritual orders, between this world and the next. Whenever religion claimed to have primacy over all other modes of human life, it could not avoid such dichotomizing and hence could not bring men into a healing relationship with nature, society, and the divine whole.

What this meant theoretically to Hegel was that religion, by itself, does not have the power to realize the full potencies of life and bring them into a liberating synthesis. The religious way of uniting reflection and love is therefore not the ultimate bonding of life for which men are seeking. Religion expresses the strong urge toward such unification, but it cannot completely grip together the oppositions and estrangements in our experience. The succession of pleromaic syntheses has to be carried beyond those achieved by love and religion. The ultimate fulfillment of our quest for reconciliation is the work of philosophy alone, since the principle of unification is supplied by a philosophical view of the totality of life.

To explore and verify the meaning of a living bond among all beings is a metaphysical task, however, from which the modern philosopher seems to be permanently disbarred. Hegel regards as illusory any philosophical effort which ignores, depreciates, or otherwise fails to live through in all its intensity, the stream of modern criticism of metaphysics. There can be no return to the dreamlike paradise of Wolff and the precritical metaphysicians. And yet there can be no arresting of the human spirit at the purely critical level, which withdraws assent from naively made metaphysical assertions, but which then looks solely to the power of association, to demands of practical belief, or to the coercions of sentiment for a constructive interpretation of man's relations with the world of values and ends. Hegel looks beyond both the naive metaphysical attitude and the critico-practical one toward a new ontology, which will combine critical alertness with a careful probing into the theoretical and practical aspects of reality accessible to man. That man is not entirely cut off from the rest of reality but stands open to it, is borne home indirectly to Hegel in the course of testing the empiricist, Kantian, and skeptical objections against metaphysics.[2]

The empiricist mind prides itself upon being well grounded in the concrete order, which enables it to test and control our human assertions. But it identifies the concrete with discrete sensory data and the mass of isolated details in perception. The function of man is to bind these empiricist versions of concrete reality together and construct from them some general meanings, which will tie things together in the cognitive and the practical orders. But the task of unification is always frustrated by the empiricist predicament that every principle of relationship remains extrinsic to the concrete particulars, and eventually leads us to skepticism

---

2. This examination is started in *Differenz des Fichteschen und Schellingschen Systems der Philosophie* (in G. Lasson's ed. of Hegel's *Erste Druckschriften* [Leipzig, 1928], pp. 1–113); it is deepened in the Preface to *Phenomenology*, pp. 67–130; and the results are sharply focused in the *Encyclopedia Logic* (trans. W. Wallace, *The Logic of Hegel* [Oxford, 1892], pp. 60–142). On Hegel's criticism of these schools, see Richard Kroner, *Von Kant bis Hegel* (2d ed. 2 vols. Tübingen, 1961), 2, 142–273; John Smith, "The Relation of Thought and Being," *New Scholasticism*, 38 (1964), 22–43; G. Nádor, "Hegel on Empiricism," *Ratio*, 6 (1964), 54–60.

about their unity. The more we try to maintain the significance and pattern of human life, the more we have to move away from the concrete order and thus disrupt the very basis of living unity. Hegel regards theism as the perfect complement of this empiricist impasse, since it concedes the premise about the concrete particulars in order to advocate a divine principle of unity, residing entirely outside our world of fragmented particulars. Both Hume's human center of perception and the providential God of theism are invoked to bind together the concrete particulars, which lack any internal basis of mutual reference.

Hegel remains unconvinced by either the Humean moderate skepticism or the theistic religious solution correlated with it. The difficulty is that these positions paradoxically locate the concrete at the farthest extreme from life and its observable conditions.[3] The living order of *concrete actuality* is that of being together and growing together, whether in the case of the biological organism or that of the human community. In the light of this holistic and concrescent standard, a highly abstractive and secondary effort is required to go from the living whole of related individuals to the discrete particulars constituting the empiricist standard of inquiry. If the concrete is that which is living, original, and unitive, then it cannot be identified primarily with the separate particulars arrived at through the empiricist analysis.

Hegel's transfer of the primary meaning of the concrete from the analytic particulars of empiricism to the living whole of social agents, upon which his own philosophical reflection centers, is intimately related with his study of religion. This is a good example of the need to steer clear of the simplistic extremes which regard his view of religion either as the controlling principle of his philosophy or as a passive corollary of it. The relationship is a mutual one, with philosophy gradually assuming the lead in determining truth and actuality. Hegel is certainly encouraged by his religious investigations to keep a basic link between life and concrete reality, and thus to treat individual beings always in their aspect of mutual relatedness through action. At the same time, he refuses to make a purely global and indiscriminate reference to "the" religious stress upon a living unity. He must exercise his own philosophical judgment in assessing the

3. The differences in the ordinary meaning of the concrete as the definite and the palpable, the empiricist meaning in terms of analytic sense particulars, and the Hegelian concrescent meaning are explored by Iwan Iljin, *Die Philosophie Hegels als kontemplative Gotteslehre* (Bern, 1946), pp. 17–74, and by George Kline, "Some Recent Reinterpretations of Hegel's Philosophy," *Monist*, 48 (1964), 40–44.

various types of unification with the divine, as taught by the religions of mankind, as well as in establishing the relevance of this topic to that of concreteness in metaphysics.

To convert the possibility of metaphysics into an actuality cannot be done, as long as the Kantian ban on metaphysics still stands. There are many strands in Hegel's prolonged efforts at lifting this ban, and we will concentrate here upon those which are relevant to the problem of religion. He prolongs into the speculative order his previous line of argument, which had traced the deficiencies in Kantian moral dualism to the acceptance of theism. Now, Hegel maintains that the theistic religious view of man is also at the bottom of Kant's reluctance to admit the possibility of metaphysics in our modern scientific world. The same sharp antagonisms which enable the moral-religious attitude of hope to flourish are also the chief obstacles against allowing a metaphysical range of human knowledge. Kantian religious hope is only the reverse side of Kantian despair over metaphysical knowledge—a despair which is encouraged by moral and religious dualism.

Hegel proceeds to furnish a list of particulars in his criticism of this undue reliance upon moral theism for determining the question of a human metaphysics.[4] First, Kant refuses to recognize an intellectual kind of intuition in man, on the ground that this intuition is creative rather than receptive of the being of its objects. But this supposes a transcendent creator, a complete separation in being between the creative mind of God and the receptive human mind, and so wide a gulf between the subject and the object of knowledge that the knowing subject must produce either the very being of the object or else only its phenomenal form. These suppositions are no stronger than the theistic schema on which they rely. They are countervailed by viewing active reason as the source of all contrasts, and as the ultimate unification of being and the forms of human knowing.

Kant's second contention is that human knowledge must have a receptive side, a sensibility which can only furnish the materials for the phenomenal object and not for the noumenal reality of things. Hegel does not contest the fact and importance of human receptivity. But he challenges the view of it as a separate side of human cognition, and as a veil which prevents the human mind from attaining an immanent grasp of the active being of natural things. This phenomenalism is generated by a

4. *Differenz* and *Glauben und Wissen* are now found in Hegel's *Gesammelte Werke*: vol. 4, *Jenaer Kritische Schriften*, ed. H. Buchner and O. Pöggeler (Hamburg, 1968), pp. 5-92, 315-414.

theistic concern to keep the human mind at an unmistakable distance from the divine. Once this separatism is removed, our experience can be recognized as the way of gaining access to the meaning of being, rather than as a detour leading away from it.

Thirdly, Kant structures his critique of metaphysics by a set of contrasts between understanding and reason, categories and rational ideas, theoretical and practical reason, which he interprets as being fixed in a hard and fast opposition. Once the religious shift is made from the alienating relation between God and man to the integrating relation between the living whole and its human modes of actuation, however, the contrasts upon which Kant bases his moratorium for metaphysics need no longer be regarded as definitive. They are made by living reason itself in the course of its own development, but they are not ultimate dualisms upon which every attempt at metaphysical reasoning must founder. The Kantian contrasts represent only that stage in man's interpretation of his being and situation in the world which is determined by the abstract, dualizing understanding. Since active spiritual reason is the source of both the categorial forms and the content of experience, it has the inherent power to overcome the dualizing contrasts and achieve a metaphysical knowledge of the internal poles of experience.[5]

Hegel adds that the power of skepticism in modern philosophy and modern life will remain unbroken, as long as any absolute contrasts are presupposed. Skepticism about the religious interpretation of life draws its modern philosophical support from the Cartesian dualism between the private ego and the natural world of science, from the empiricist reduction of concrete reality to analytically isolated particulars, and from the Kantian binary theory of phenomena and noumena. After a long period of looking for noumenal reality as though it were an unchained beast behind the bush, but a beast which never heaves into sight, men finally cease to regard it as real at all. Hegel concedes to the skeptics that the bounds of credibility are overstrained by the notion of a divine noumenal entity which never appears to our theoretical reason. This is what analytic philosophers in our day call the theory of the divine gardener, who always remains invisible.

5. One of the great hinge movements in the *Phenomenology* is made from the relatively abstract standpoints of sense perception, scientific understanding, and formal-logical reason, to Hegel's increasingly concrescent metaphysics based on "actual reason" (ibid., p. 280). The great spiritual turns taken in this book are charted by Jacob Loewenberg, *Hegel's Phenomenology: Dialogues on the Life of Mind* (LaSalle, 1965).

But Hegel does not accept the skeptical conclusion that, therefore, we must suspend all metaphysical affirmations and retreat to a private region of practical prudence and perhaps some religious faith. For this skeptical advice presupposes that the separations announced by the abstractive understanding, and backed up by religious theism, constitute the ultimate natural report on our human condition. If this were so, there would indeed be no human resource left for mastering the oppositions and bringing them to a viable and verifiable unity. But when the separative understanding is related to the wider context of the life of concrete reason, these oppositions are seen to be reconcilable. They lose their ultimacy in becoming phases within a self-differentiating whole, which retains the power of life to recuperate its unity in and through the very oppositions which it brings into being. This is the Hegelian basis of confidence in affirming metaphysics in the new key of the philosophy of spirit.

Hegel can now specify more exactly the nature of the reality with which the human mind enjoys a living communion. Although the living whole is more easily understood in terms of love—which stresses the actual union between different centers of being—it is more deeply and authentically grasped in terms of spirit, which establishes how the union is realized. Hegel had been reluctant previously to equate the living whole of being with spirit, because of our customary use of "spirit" as a term of difference, as one member of an opposition between spirit and flesh, spiritual and worldly interests, or spiritual and visible reality. But his own distinctive usage is one of inclusion, not separation: spirit is the active, complex unification of all the opposing factors in experience.

Hegel is not interested in reviving some vague referent called "the metaphysical tradition," but only in founding his own *metaphysics of spirit,* to which all the elements of past speculation are subordinated in a transformational manner.[6] Spirit is the living whole which brings forth all the oppositions in experience, endures their antagonisms and separations to the utmost, and gathers them together into an enriched and dominating union. It combined the permanence of Aristotelian and Spinozistic substance with the agile reflection of Kantian and Fichtean subjectivity, the novelty of development with the fidelity of abiding purpose, and the familiar shapes of finitude with the liberation and satisfaction of their infinite pattern of reconciliation. It is to this metaphysics of

6. Hegel sets forth his central theses about spirit in *Phenomenology,* pp. 80–88; see the commentary by Wilhelm Seeberger, *Hegel oder die Entwicklung des Geistes zur Freiheit* (Stuttgart, 1961), pp. 88–180.

spirit, not to any other interpretation of experience, that the Hegelian theory of religion is adapted and by which the significance of religion is determined.

Hegel likens those who hesitate about accepting his metaphysics to the proverbial Gascon, who wanted to learn how to swim before getting into the water. To encourage at least religious believers to take the plunge and thus learn how to verify his metaphysics of spirit from within, he gives his own account of the perennial theme of believing and knowing.[7] Except for those who reduce their religion to a purely private emotive state, most religious men will follow Paul, Augustine, and Anselm in seeking to understand the faith that is in them and to give other men a good reason for adhering to it. But this striving to understand religious faith can be carried out in various ways. The usual method is to take the content of faith as an absolute, and to confine the mind's work to clarifying the parts of that content, illuminating it through our human experiences, and correlating it with our scientific and cultural understanding of the natural world.

Hegel does not propose to suppress any of these activities, but he does aim at basing them upon a more radical use of the mind in relation to the act and the content of faith. Instead of treating the realm of faith as an absolute given, an unconditioned point of departure to which every attempt at understanding religion must be referred as the norm, he treats it as a definite stage within the broader life of reason. In addition to clarifying and correlating religious faith, then, the philosopher must uncover its governing presuppositions in the life of spirit.

It is clearly necessary for Hegel to restate the problem as one concerning faith and knowledge (believing and knowing), rather than faith and reason. For if the latter couplet is taken strictly, it suggests that the realm of cognition is divided between faith, as a gift from God, and reason as the intrinsic human power of knowing. In the Hegelian context, however, reason models itself upon the holistic traits of spirit. Reason is not something partitive, and does not share its domain with any other cognitive power or act. Rather, it is the generative principle of all the human acts and powers of knowing, desiring, and willing. It is permissible to distinguish between faith and knowledge, or believing and knowing, as different

7. *Glauben und Wissen*, pp. 223–346. Contrary to Hegel, Richard Kroner's culminating chapter on him in *Speculation and Revelation in Modern Philosophy* (Philadelphia, 1961), pp. 274–301, defends both the independent rooting of revelation and its constant dialogue with philosophy.

modes and stages internal to the life of reason, but both of them are immanent to reason's own self-development.

To believe and to know are related as promise and fulfillment, as a groping cognition of the presence of divine actuality and a reflectively clarified and humanly evidenced grasp of this same actuality. The act of believing is an implicit, still undeveloped kind of knowing, ordered essentially to a direct comprehension of the metaphysical foundations of the divine totality. Faith testifies with all the substantial force and certitude of our mind to the reality of spirit, but it does so in the medium of imagery and symbol. What religion only adumbrates must then be seen in its evidential bases through the philosophical concept of spiritual actuality. Only then is knowledge found in its proper form and maturity. Thus the agelong Christian discussion about faith and reason is interpreted by Hegel as an effort at differentiating two phases in the growth of philosophical reason itself: its religious presentiment of spiritual life, as affirmed in the seedling act of faith, and its reflective metaphysical knowledge of this spiritual whole of being.

Once the right order is established between the religious and the metaphysical approaches to the spiritual whole, Hegel is anxious to utilize the former to the full extent. His most fruitful explication of religious faith centers around the great theme of *the death of God*.[8] His subtle, polyphonic elaboration of this motif sounds throughout his books and lecture series, serving as a prototype for the later reflections of Nietzsche and Heidegger, Sartre and recent American theologians. When he writes to a correspondent that philosophy has kept him strong in the Lutheran faith of his childhood, Hegel probably has in mind the continuing seminal influence which Luther's chorale on God's death exercized upon his philosophical reflections. He takes the model for a philosophical effort to

8. *Glauben und Wissen*, pp. 345–46; *Phenomenology*, pp. 780–82; *Philosophie der Religion*, 3, 157–74 (3, 86–98). There are helpful commentaries by Jean Hyppolite, *Genèse et structure de la Phénoménologie de l'Esprit de Hegel* (Paris, 1946), pp. 546–49, and by Jean Wahl, *Le Malheur de la conscience dans la philosophie de Hegel* (2d ed. Paris, 1951), pp. 69–91. Taking a Marxist approach, Roger Garaudy, *Dieu est mort: Étude sur Hegel* (Paris, 1962), takes the death of God to signify the dissolution of the pre-Revolutionary world and the passage from an abstract God to the total reality of man in nature and history, which Hegel nevertheless persists in transposing into religious terms rather than into an activist sense of work and revolution. For the American theological development of Hegel's theme, see T. J. J. Altizer and W. Hamilton, *Radical Theology and the Death of God* (Indianapolis, Bobbs-Merrill, 1966).

understand religious faith from his own personal analysis of the Passion of Christ, considered in relation to the fate of metaphysics in the modern world.

The most obvious use of the topic is to dramatize Hegel's cultural and historical report on the decline of living belief in God and Christianity. The death of God signifies the lack of conviction in people's minds, when they hear the traditional proofs given in natural theology or the strict explanations of dogmatic theology. Not even the professors of such presumed sciences are able to relate them to the going secular disciplines, which do contain some recognizable knowledge. Theism and religious creeds get cut off from the land of the living knowledges and cultural interests of modern men, and thus the living sense of being in communion with a divine basis of reality withers away.

Hegel then makes the theme of God's death yield an even more uncomfortable significance for complacent believers. For it signifies not only the strangeness of the theological mode of thinking but also its hostility toward the practical values of everyday life. God is taken as the symbol of *anti-life,* of a religious establishment which is the enemy of freedom and the natural pieties of human society. From this standpoint, God has been dissociated from humane values, and hence the death of God means the liberation of our ideals from a system of oppressive moral rules and ascetic practices, which block our understanding of nature, self, and history. This aspect of the problem underlies Hegel's own critique of religious positivity, where he argues for a reform in the meaning of religion and the divine as providing the only way to recover the values of life and human freedom.

Philosophical reflection on the death of God also helps to make more concrete the creative function of negativity in every region of being. It symbolizes the law of all being that one must die in order to live. This is a good instance where the sacred signs of religion come alive once more in Hegel's mind, and serve as guiding clues for philosophical study. Hegel looks upon the Passion story as a concrete lesson that every being must surrender its isolation, particularity, and initial self-possession, if it is to enter into the wider community of living reality. Only by differentiating itself and becoming educated to the claims of others, can it develop its own nature as a relational entity or organic member of the totality. It is the death of separative particularity, at every level of reality, which is celebrated on Calvary for all mankind to see.

Moreover, the story of God's death continues beyond Calvary to the

Resurrection. Hegel uses the directedness of the story to express his philosophical conviction that the negative or dialectical principle does not extinguish life but renews and deepens it, by forcing it to struggle with the differences and bring them to a more concrete unity. Knowledge gained through self-diremption, or the emptying process, is *"spiritualization,* whereby substance becomes subject, by which its abstraction and lifelessness have expired, and substance therefore has become *actual,* simple, and universal self-consciousness." [9] The alienations in life are meaningful, because they can become the instruments of a new and richer synthesis. Thus the religious theme of death-and-resurrection serves as concrete imagery for the dialectical law that negativity leads eventually to its own negation and to a deeper hold upon actuality as spiritual.

But does this law of life, requiring a passage through death, apply even to the God of religion? Hegel's affirmative answer marks the point at which he both enters most intimately into the Christian message and also secures its total subordination to his own philosophical principles. To determine the metaphysical significance of the death on the cross, he uses language reminiscent of St. Paul's teaching on the *kenosis* or self-emptying and humbling of God. The Christian message about the cross teaches us that "spirit is spirit only as this negating of the negative, which the negative therefore contains in itself." [10] Even God must submit to the universal law of achieving the fullness of spiritual life only by undergoing self-diremption and death.

However, Hegel regards the theological interpretation of this law in terms of the assumption of a human nature by the Son of God as being too restrictive, as failing to recognize how radically and completely the law applies to the divine reality in its every aspect. The absolute must undergo the process of estrangement in every facet of its being, so that no fiber in the divine reality fails to subject itself to internal development and reconciliation. The abstract God of theism must give way entirely before the concrete actuality of living nature and human history. The lowly death on the cross helps us to realize more vividly that the spiritual absolute comes into its own only through this course of creative self-negation, and that this truth requires us to surrender the nostalgic belief in a transcendent God, existing in aloof unchangeableness in the beyond.

Hegel's ultimate philosophical lesson is that there must literally be a death of the theistic conception of God, as providing the necessary prel-

9. *Phenomenology,* p. 782.
10. *Philosophie der Religion,* 4, 163 (3, 91 n.).

ude to the resurrection of metaphysics. Men of religious faith must be willing to recognize that the God of theism is only a waystation in the self-unfolding of the infinite spiritual reality, that this God represents the moment of separation and abstract fixation which has to be expressed and then itself negated, in favor of a more adequate view of the divine. The speculative kernel of the Good Friday message is that the divine nature contains within itself, and must eventually display itself as, all those elements of negativity and weakness, otherness and suffering, which receive their most striking image in the passion of Christ. Thus Hegel rehabilitates metaphysics only on condition that we surrender the illusion of the ultimate truth of theism. The only way to do metaphysics without illusions is to merge the grand split between the transcendent God and the isolated finite existent into the one process whereby living spiritual reality determines itself, and renders itself concrete in its own finite expressions.

Hegel intends the theory of religion to be a major beneficiary of his new metaphysics of spirit. By living through the speculative Good Friday of the death of theistic alienations, the fully reflective philosopher of religion can gain a clearer vision of the nature of religious life. He can see at once that Hegel's own preliminary definition of religion as the self-elevating of finite life to infinite life needs clarification and amplification on two counts.

First, the religious movement is not a process which begins unconditionally with the believer, as the one who is moving to the divine goal of his worship. The entire religious movement is only a phase within the broader circulatory process whereby the absolute becomes infinite actuality only by *finitizing itself*, by determining itself as the finite centers of life and desire. The religious elevation of finite life toward infinite life is only possible because finite reality itself is already a limited actualization of that infinite life, as it seeks to dirempt and recover its own being. This is the pregnant sense in which religious worship is a self-elevating of life to life. Hence religion is not primarily a practical product of man's reference to God, as Hume and Kant supposed, but an act of self-recovery on the part of the divine totality in its human manifestation.

The second emendation suggested by Hegel's metaphysical basis is that the religious movement of life can be further specified as a movement of finite spirit to infinite spirit. The significance of this point is that, whereas religion testifies by its entire presence to the reality of the spiritual and the ordination of the human spirit to the divine, it does not itself furnish a theory about spirit and a reflective method of testing the various explanations of the spiritual relationship involved in religious faith and worship. For Hegel, the ultimate principle of judgment concerning the meaning, validity, and truth of religion is found in philosophy—more precisely, in his metaphysics of spirit. The more one explores the metaphysical theory of infinite spirit and its self-finitized phasings, the more likely becomes the prospect of penetrating into the religious relationship itself and transferring its decisive interpretation from a theological to a philosophical foundation. The theme of God's death is Hegel's most dramatic way of expressing this transfer of religious meanings to the context regulated by his own metaphysical criteria.

PHENOMENOLOGY: THE TAMING OF RELIGION

A major task of the *Phenomenology of Spirit* is to develop the method for showing the primacy of philosophy over religion, and indeed for bringing about the effective recognition of this primacy in reflective minds. Hegel gets the reinterpretation of religion well under way in his particular descriptions of cultural attitudes and in his strategic use of religious language for philosophical purposes.

His examination of the transition from Greek religion to Christianity had taught him to regard the religious belief of an age as one of its shaping principles. Hence in reflecting upon any concrete cultural outlook, Hegel found it rewarding to ask whether religion was functioning there as a revolutionary force or a conservative element. One could not understand the medieval frame of mind, for instance, without taking account of the alliance between faith and theological reason, the objectification of the means of grace in sacraments and rituals, and the essential uneasiness with the world as expressed in ascetical practices and mystical states of soul.[11]

Given this sort of religious outlook, one could never regard the crusades as being exclusively either a political-military-economic venture or an otherworldly quest. Hegel cited the fundamental ambivalence of every aspect of the crusades as an indication of the unresolved dualism between the here and the beyond for the medieval religious consciousness. And in the fact that the crusaders sought to endow their great efforts with sacral significance, but found only an empty tomb in Jerusalem, he saw a powerful symbol of the failure of the objectifying attitude in religion

11. *Phenomenology,* pp. 255–67.

and a mainspring of the great march toward subjectivity in the modern era.

Hegel also carried over into his phenomenological work a linguistic peculiarity of his earlier studies: the intermingling of a very concrete and a very abstruse terminology. He served his apprenticeship by describing the Lord's Supper both in the simple language of St. John and in a technical vocabulary suited for expressing relations of alienation, community, and objectification.[12] This procedure gave linguistic backing to his contention that life must combine the singular event with the abstract law, and that the being of spirit is found only in the interplay of the two. Hegel employed this linguistic reshaping on a grand scale in the *Phenomenology*, so that he could develop the proper language and thought of spirit through the synthesis of perceptual imagery and rational concepts.

This policy involves the theory of religion in a double way. When Hegel's purpose is to integrate as closely as possible the religious beliefs and practices of an age with its particular cultural elements, he often refers to the former in a highly allusive manner by means of his technical vocabulary of alienation and integration. It comes as a shock, for instance, to find that a difficult passage, expounding the nonconceptual relation between consciousness in its particularity and an unchangeable object, really concerns the acts of religious devotion as they function in the medieval universe. Only discreet use of the cue phrase, "a cloud of warm incense," provokes the act of recognition. By this time the reader is well prepared to grant that the use of incense, bell, and candle constitutes a social symbol of an unclarified yearning for the beyond. The reader is also linguistically predisposed to concede that the key to religious symbolism is ultimately found in the philosophical dialectic of spirit.

Conversely, Hegel often uses religious language to clothe his general philosophical statements. One must be familiar with the Passion story in the Bible to capture the overtones in the statement that the life of spirit "endures death and in death maintains itself," or that a highly spiritual art form "is the night in which the substance was betrayed, and made itself subject," or that the combined historical and scientific approaches "form at once the recollection and the Golgotha of absolute spirit." [13] Hegel uses the language and rhythm of the Bible, partly to render his theory of spirit more familiar and acceptable to Christian believers and

12. *Early Theological Writings*, pp. 248–51. The cue phrase mentioned in the next paragraph can be found in *Phenomenology*, p. 259.
13. Ibid., pp. 93, 712, 808.

partly to show that philosophy appropriates the entire meaning of religion for its own doctrinal ends. Religion and its language are evoked and interiorized within the phenomenological process, thus placing their concrete resources wholly at the disposal of the philosophy which constitutes itself through that process.

The relationship Hegel establishes between religion and phenomenology is not confined to particular features, however, but reaches to the former's general nature and role in his philosophy. The same reasons which prompt him to develop his philosophy in a phenomenological form also require him to interpret religion in a way that insures its complete subordination to the life and truth of philosophy itself. In his later systematic writings and lectures, Hegel is confident about having unlocked the secret of God and the revealed Christian religion, only because he continues to work from the accepted results of his original phenomenologizing of religion. Why he regards this process as so decisive for disclosing the meaning of religion becomes clear after inspecting the relationship between religion and three central themes in the Hegelian conception of phenomenology. They are: first, its introductory function; second, its thematic pattern; and third, its power to disillusion and enlighten us. To construct a theory of religion governed by these principles is to achieve the phenomenological taming of religion, its total encapsuling as a mode of that spiritual reality whose genuine essence is constituted and interpreted by philosophy as such.

Phenomenology as Introduction and Struggle.   One of the pressing issues for Hegel during his Jena period was the seemingly obvious matter of furnishing an introduction to philosophy. All sorts of introductory manuals abounded, and the entire course in logic at the gymnasium level was credited with giving the students an entrance into philosophy. Hegel's difficulty stemmed from the fact that none of these books and courses raised the question of alienation, and hence none of them pointed students toward the resolving doctrine of the living spiritual whole. From his standpoint, then, these books and courses transmitted a vocabulary and a set of problems, principles, and theses which remained strictly prephilosophical, never getting to the generative question which really introduces us to philosophical truth.

If an effective introduction cannot be made by remaining outside the house of philosophy, then it must come from a reflective use of the mind which already leads one into that house with its first step. Hegel's *Phenom-*

enology is not a detached entrance gate or an outbuilding, but a threshold belonging to the intrinsic structure of the philosophy of spirit and already involving the experiencing mind in the life of philosophy.[14] One does not share in the philosophical life by moving to a foreign land and filling the mind with outlandish terms and definitions, but by becoming aware of the problem of separation and opposition permeating one's ordinary situation and all the actions and ideals of mankind. More precisely, the mind gains a philosophical pitch to the degree that it comes to realize the existence of a pervasive spiritual activity generating these oppositions at all levels in our experience even while it also provides a basis for reunification. The task of phenomenology is to provoke this dual awareness. It enables us to see both the alienative character of every situation in life and the reintegrating activity which also courses in us. Phenomenology is an introduction *to and within* philosophy, since it leads us into the habitual frame of mind for interrogating our experience and spiritually reconstituting it at every level of human life.

The human need is not just for philosophy, therefore, but precisely for philosophy equipped with its introductory phase of phenomenology. Hegel's philosophy is experiential in the exact measure in which it is phenomenological. For man can get his philosophical principles neither through an external indoctrination nor through appropriation of a fully elaborated system. He must generate them through his own reflection upon life's divisions and through his careful reconstruction of the unifying tendencies which shape our human experience. To follow this path is to engage in phenomenology, and such is the way of introducing oneself within philosophy.

The phenomenological education of the mind also involves a constant theoretical and practical struggle, out of which grows the meaning of experience.[15] Hegelian man is not in the position of a passive viewer, who

14. This point is established by Otto Pöggeler, "Zur Deutung der *Phänomenologie des Geistes,*" *Hegel-Studien,* 1 (1961), 256–94.

15.
> Experience is called precisely this movement wherein the immediate, the un-experienced, that is, the abstract, estranges itself, and then returns to itself from this estrangement, and thereby is only now exhibited in its actuality and truth, just as it is also a possession of consciousness. . . . This dialectical movement which consciousness exerts on itself—on its knowing as well as on its object— *insofar as out of it the new true object arises,* is that which is genuinely called experience. (*Phenomenology,* pp. 96, 142)

Cf. G. A. Schrader, "Hegel's Contribution to Phenomenology," *Monist,* 48 (1964), 18–33, on the active experiential struggle to engender philosophical principles.

can simply read off the message of experience as it unrolls before him. This visionary or spectator conception of philosophy is misleading, since it supposes that our mind is only externally related to its objects, and that the meaning of experience is already set in one unequivocal key. On the contrary, the human mind is an intimate and active participant in the very process of separation and reconciliation constituting experience, keeping its significance fundamentally ambivalent. The dominant unity of experience is not given, but is worked out as an active process by the mind engaged in living interchange with several levels of objects and values. Hegel's phenomenology is nothing other than the pattern and course of this struggle to develop the meaning of experience, and to determine its truth in the process of actively relating the mind with its objects.

Religion makes a significant contribution to phenomenological method by reinforcing Hegel's view on the need for introduction and struggle, and then by taking its place as a component in this process. Anyone who accepts the Biblical story of creation-fall-redemption, or its analogue in other religious sources, is predisposed to think of the absolute reality as manifesting itself in a realm of many, changing, and opposed entities. The believer will regard man as being somehow estranged from the divine principle, and as requiring some aid in mastering the world and coming close again to that divine source. He will look upon our present life as a testing ground, a place of preparation with which he cannot dispense in his eagerness to attain the treasures of heaven. Furthermore, he will treat his thoughts and actions in this life as orienting and setting him on the path toward union with the divine. Such religious convictions prepare the mind concretely to follow and accept Hegel's arguments for the role of phenomenology as an introductory moment within philosophy.

That the phenomenological education of the mind involves a struggle, is another position conforming to the deepest expectations of the believer. He experiences the need for making some break with the world, for detaching himself from his immediate relationships, and for winning a new order of values. Although his stress is more practical than theoretical, and although he often looks to divine help as supervening upon his own efforts at disengagement, the man of faith can readily see the point of the phenomenological reorienting of man. The religious theme of the second birth of man is a carrier for Hegel's philosophical demand that all our human relations with ourselves and the world of objects must be rejuvenated by the inquiring spirit. Nothing is left quite the same for the man of religious convictions, and this prefigures the transformation of all factors in human experience as that experience becomes renewed through phenomenological reflection.

Not content with establishing a correlation of analogy between religion and philosophy, however, Hegel presses on to deautonomize religion completely in respect to the phenomenological functions of the spiritual education and struggle of humanity. Man's education to a recognition of spirit is a social and historical process, not merely an individual affair. Although Hegel carefully avoids claiming that his philosophy can predict the future course of history, he does accord it the power of discerning the real spiritual significance of the present age and bringing that intention into actuality.[16] He maintains that the peculiar task of the modern epoch is to draw together, and synthesize for the first time, the secular and the religious traditions concerning the dignity and spiritual reality of man. By itself, neither the religious nor the secular humanist stream is sufficiently powerful to penetrate the full and proper meaning of spirit. Only philosophy can join these two traditions, release them from their one-sided emphases, and thus integrate human and divine elements in the true concept of spirit. Such is the task of the modern age and, more specifically, of Hegel's own phenomenology, acting as the interpreter and actual unifier of the partial modes of experience.

Viewed in this way, religion does not simply furnish images and dispositions of soul favoring an effort of introduction and education: it is in its entire nature a phase within the self-introductive activity of spirit. It is a major force in the spiritual formation of mankind, a powerful instrument for our self-understanding. If it were not for the religious cultivation of our minds, the philosophical interpretation of the spiritual basis of experience would not have such well prepared soil. But it is left for phenomenology to combine the religious witnessing to spirit with the witnessing to that reality coming from all the other sources in our world. Religion must be swept along into the phenomenological mainstream, wherein it becomes one of the introductory moments in preparing the mind for the philosophical truth concerning experience and spiritual reality.

Hegel uses the theme of struggle to achieve an analogous assimilation of the meaning and life of religion to his philosophy. In his lectures on philosophy of religion, he dramatically represents the religious man's grap-

16. See *Early Theological Writings*, p. 159, and *Phenomenology*, p. 75.

pling with the poles of infinite and finite life, under conditions specified by the countertendencies in our world. The man of faith expresses his attitude in this way:

> *I am the struggle*. For the struggle is precisely this opposition, which is not an indifference of the two sides as diverse but their being bound up together. I am not one of those caught up in the struggle, I am the two strugglers, I am the struggle itself. I am the fire and water which are in contact, I am the contact, the unity of that which utterly flees from itself. And precisely this contact of elements, now separated and divided, now reconciled and unified, is itself this relation which, as relation, is ambivalent and in opposition.[17]

The religious sentiment of conflict and reconciliation is a substantial embodiment of the phenomenological approach itself. The latter can draw its concrete clues from the religious recognition that life consists in the struggle itself, that the desired unification cannot be confused with an annihilation or softening of oppositions, and that there is an abiding ambiguity about how to reconcile the differences.

But whereas religion lives and executes these meanings, it does not master them through a fully reflective act. The life of religion embodies the personified struggle: the phenomenologically developed life of philosophy consists in winning the truth of this struggle. Thus religious existence ministers to the method and the content of philosophy through the mediation of phenomenology, which brings the embodied attitude of religion to its conceptual truth for reason. This is the sense in which Hegel told his student friend, Baron Boris von Yxküll, that religion is anticipated philosophy, and philosophy is religion brought to evident conscious awareness of its import.

The Thematic Pattern.   The *Phenomenology* is the log book of Hegel's voyages of discovery. As he moves from one mode of experience to another, from one cultural formation of society to another, he discerns the active presence of a recurrent pattern. The repeated lesson emerging from an analysis of our operative intentions, attitudes, and institutions is that the human spirit engages in an unquenchable search for objectivity. Uneasy with an empty interiority, man seeks to enrich himself by appropriating some reality which is entirely different, which has roots of its own

17. *Philosophie der Religion*, 1, 241–42 (1, 64).

and new treasures to offer. Whether that actuality be localized in a sensory thing, a moral law within the individual, or a vast social institution, it furnishes a horizon of resistant otherness upon which man can test his energies and draw new strength from the contact.

Yet this passion for "the alien other" is constantly being frustrated by the further discovery that objective reality is already colored by our human desires and perspectives. Man is always stumbling upon some projected fragment of himself in those looming entities, which he took to be self-sufficing and free from human touch. One particular dream of relating a pure and unmixed objective reality to the human subject may vanish, but the human spirit moves relentlessly toward another goal, toward another encounter with "the purely given" in whose constitution it has no complicity. At every level, however, the reflective mind discovers that there is no sharp boundary line between self and nonself, subject and object, finite and infinite. It learns that the components in such dualisms are self-articulations of spirit, and that the fissures of objectivity are opened up only in order to provoke new efforts of spirit for their integration.

Phenomenology educates the spirit of man by exposing him to the phases in this process at every level of desire, cognition, and social enterprise.[18] Hegel shapes his theory of religion to lend support to this view of the life pattern. With the discovery of the recurring pattern in one after another characteristic situation in life, the investigating mind breaks through the naive, natural attitude toward objectivity, enlarges its hold on the wisdom of experience, and thus actualizes the ideal of philosophical knowledge. This breakthrough is symbolized by the religious soul's passage from visible things to the invisible godhead. What the religious elevation enacts in image and symbol, the philosophical elevation achieves in reflective actuality.

Implicit in every kind of dedication of man to an alien objectivity is the master-slave relationship, which expresses unhappy consciousness. Since Hegel regards the God-man bond as the prototypal instance of the master-slave relationship, he also sees a religious significance in all the varieties of unhappy consciousness.[19] There is a common religious tie between the materialist's forlorn dedication to things and the Stoic's proud disdain of events in favor of an immutable law, between the skeptic's retreat to subjective states and the pietist's withdrawal into the interior self. All these representative individuals are trying to make bearable

18. See *Phenomenology*, pp. 88–95, 140–45.
19. Ibid., pp. 251–67; Wahl, *Le Malheur de la conscience*, pp. 119–47.

the burden imposed by the religious split between this worldly and other-worldly concerns and values. But the values of this world collapse in separation from an eternal foundation, while the values of the other world also collapse upon exposure of their all-too-human roots.

Unhappy consciousness consists in a restless and futile oscillation between these two worlds, generating a nostalgia for the divine changeless realm, which always elude our visible enshrinements. Religion orients us toward the spiritual principle for reconciling the divine and the human, but it cannot actually unify them as long as it remains attached to the God-and-man relationship, especially in its theistic version. The definitive act of detachment from this dualizing principle of unhappy consciousness does not come from religion itself but from philosophy. It takes a philosophical understanding of the nature of spiritual process to release us from the master-slave relationship at all levels, including the religious.

The Power to Disillusion and Enlighten.   The twofold effect of the phenomenological analysis is to disillusion us and enlighten us about the modes of experience which comprise our human situation. As we reflect upon the circulatory life of spirit, in its act of positing an alien reality and then finding there the traces of its own activity, we inevitably lose our original naïveté concerning the relation between the human subject and its world of resistant things and impersonal social forces. Our specific forms of illusion cease to overpower us, as we move relentlessly from one level of attachment to another. Yet as the masks fall from our relationships with men and objects, we need not become the victims of skepticism and paralyzing disbelief. For at each step, we are able to replace fantasy with the phenomenological truth about experience and its agent principles. We can exchange shadow for substance, illusion for enlightenment about the workings of spirit in the community of men and material existents.

Religion is affected in two ways by this complex process. It is indirectly co-implicated in every phase of experience, insofar as each phase involves some variation of the master-slave pattern and the anxiety of unhappy consciousness. Consequently, every instance of phenomenological reflection on an attitude in life has an implication for religion. The act of being disillusioned and enlightened concerning some specific sort of experience, includes an overtone of being disillusioned and enlightened concerning the proportionate mode and degree of the religious cleavage between the here and the hereafter, the human and the divine. This is the long-range preparation required to fortify the soul for making a direct application of the phenomenological procedure to religious experience as a whole.

Eventually, the process of disillusioning and enlightening the spirit of man must apply formally and comprehensively to the religious attitude itself. Hegel postpones this moment as long as possible in the *Phenomenology*, making it the second last step taken in his pilgrimage, the step just before entering into the plenary philosophical truth about spirit.[20] This policy of postponement is laden with significance. It is Hegel's way of telling us that the general orientation of man toward the reality of spirit is a religious act in the very broadest sense, and that it cannot be brought about on a social and historical scale apart from the contribution of the entire range of cultural forms and historical attitudes comprising our human experience. All the earlier modes of experience are recapitulated in religion, especially in modern reformed Christianity, and are then redirected by it toward the full meaning of spirit.

But the religious sphere is penultimate and not ultimate, as far as concerns a reflective understanding of the truth about the spiritual whole. There remains a residual illusion in the religious mind, an acceptance of some model of alienation between the divine and the human, some image of a separation simply existing between the other life and this one. Until this lingering illusion is removed, the investigating mind will not have attained the rational truth about the infinite-finite totality. Hence religion cannot claim the privilege of immunity from the phenomenological process of exposing and enlightening, removing the self-woven veil and thus bringing out the truth about the vital relation between the infinite whole and its finite forms of life. The scales of alienation must be removed eventually from the eyes of religious men, or at least from those among them who can master the method of phenomenology and who can endure the power of reflection. Religion's capitulation is strategically postponed, so that when at last it does occur, it will entail the total assimilation of all modes of experience to philosophical knowledge.

The specific sense can now be determined in which Hegel phenomenologizes religion. He does so by developing a conception of religion that: can be included as a phase in the introductory and self-educative work of spirit, incarnates the attitude of struggle to reconcile opposites without properly discerning its own meaning, fully exemplifies the thematic pattern of objectivication and recovery of selfhood, and is thoroughly sub-

20. *Phenomenology*, pp. 685–785.

jected to the process of disillusioning and enlightening the spirit of man.

It is true that religion retains its uniqueness and importance among the experiential formations of man. It is not just a passing incident in the education and elevation of spirit but the decisive orientation; it is not merely an instance of creative struggle but its total substance; it is the fructifying source, rather than a restricted instance, of the spirit's self-cleaving activity; and it stands out as the ultimate disenchantment, leading to a certitude which is indistinguishable from the philosophical truth concerning spirit and experience. But each of the above ways of expressing religion's distinctive nature and role only serves to reinforce its unreserved ordination to philosophy. Religion is not subordinated to philosophy in the manner in which some restricted and transient mode of experience is subordinated. For its very centrality to the life of spirit is philosophically established through the same act which assigns to philosophy the sole competence for determining the truth and certainty of all religious meanings. In this ultimate sense, the religious attitude is not entirely self-interpreting, not entirely in reflective control of its own theoretical and practical significance for humanity.

Hegel judges that "truth is the *content*, which in religion is still unlike its certainty." [21] Religion continues to rely for its certainty upon imagery and pictorial representation, which retain a separation between the infinite and the finite, the divine and the human. In principle, therefore, religious expressions of the truth about divine and human reality must remain inadequate and subject to a definitive philosophical judgment. Only in philosophy does the human spirit succeed in overcoming that gulf, by gripping both members of the religious contrast in the rational concept of the infinite-finite totality of spiritual life.

Since this reconciling view coincides with the very structure and dynamism of spiritual reality itself, the subordination of religion to philosophy is not an external, coercive relation, but an inner fulfillment of the tendency of religion itself. Hence the freedom sought by the religious believer is found ultimately in the life and truth of philosophy. Freedom is found where the spirit of the Lord is present: but that spirit enjoys its plenary presence only in the method and concept of philosophy.

This conclusion is not altered by appealing to some of the other meanings of phenomenology which, though Hegel regards them as secondary, have become popular in our day. As commonly understood today, the

21. Ibid., p. 798.

phenomenological approach is one that focuses upon the intentional character of consciousness and faithfully describes the acts and objects constituting our experience.[22] Hegel recognizes the need for the analysis of religious intentionality and the description of the various modes and structures of religious experience. The former yields an understanding of the openness of spirit to the world of objects, and the latter a disciplined grasp upon the actual shapes and historical course of our religious development. But he persists in asking about the basis of unification for the intending acts and their objects, for the described structures and our meaningful acts of belief and worship. He finds this basis in the life of infinite and self-finitizing spirit. To use Husserlian terms anachronistically, every form of phenomenological investigation of religion is teleologically ordered to an ultimate reduction to the spiritual totality. Experience is radically constituted only in the act whereby infinite-finite spirit confers meaning, truth, and being upon all the acts and objects of experience, including the religious.

What enters into Hegelian philosophy through the gateway of phenomenology is not simply religion, but religion insofar as it is completely phenomenologized. Filtered and reinterpreted in this way, religion becomes a thoroughly domesticated member of the household of the philosophy of spirit. Tamed and deprived of its potentiality, it can furnish us with no independent basis for making the religious meaning and disposition of human life ultimately decisive on questions of truth and certainty. Hegel can now proceed confidently to reconstruct God and religion entirely in terms of his own categories, because the meanings permitted entrance into his systematic philosophy of religion have been phenomenologized well in advance.

Karl Barth recognized the radical thoroughness of this methodic reformulation of all religious beliefs and practices in his striking remark that, in the Hegelian philosophy of religion, "problems are simply there in order that they may be raised and *settled* with all certainty." [23] This total control in principle over human religiousness is quite compatible with an acknowledgment of the nonrational and mystical aspects of religious life. Hegel grants the presence and importance of these aspects, but views them as moments in the self-estranging life of living reason itself. No manifestation of religious existence can escape the phenomenological

22. This is the case in the typical descriptive phenomenologies of religion discussed in chap. 10, n. 14.

23. Karl Barth, *From Rousseau to Ritschl*, p. 280.

net and still hold a significant place in the philosophy of religion. All
the modalities of religion are treated by Hegel as conforming, in principle,
with his comprehensive phenomenological pattern of infinite spirit in its
self-emptying and self-recovering rhythm. Religion pure and unstained is
present only after man's religious life has been strenuously purified by
being swept into, and completely dominated by, this dance of the absolute spirit. In thus submitting, religion furnishes philosophy with crown-
ing evidence that the world is indeed a process with a purpose aiming at
rationality, and that its purpose is properly achieved in the rational self-
awareness of the philosophical spirit.[24]

RECONSTRUCTION THROUGH ONTO-PNEUMA-LOGIC

Granted now that the mind is already installed in that reflective hold
on the life of spirit wherein the philosophical attitude essentially consists,
Hegelian logic has another set of functions to perform than that of an
introductory formal logic. It must examine the fundamental method,
concepts, and categories which are structurally and operationally inherent
in experience, and hence which hold good for actual being and not only
for the formal sphere. Kant had seen that an adequate logic must concern
an objective content, but his epistemological and ethico-religious presuppositions had prevented him from recognizing that this objective content undercuts the distinction between phenomenal objects and noumenal
reality. His transcendental logic remained prisoner to this dualism, only
because it was not founded upon that grasp of the truth of absolute spirit
which the phenomenological formation of the mind is designed to yield.
Once that foundation is gained, the method and concepts of logic are
found to be significant not only for phenomenal objects but also for the
active, constituting principle of experience and actuality in every phase.[25]
Logic cannot avoid being thoroughly metaphysical in import.

Hegel's speculative logic feeds upon the truth of absolute spirit as the
great lesson of experience, and hence his logic is also a metaphysics of
experiential being. Its method reflects and holds valid for all the developments and articulations of spirit. Hence he regards it as false humility to
refrain from claiming that his method is the one solely adequate for the

24. See F. H. Bergmann, "The Purpose of Hegel's System," *Journal of the History
of Philosophy*, 2 (1964), 189–204.
25. See *Science of Logic*, trans. W. H. Johnston and L. G. Struthers (2 vols. New
York, Macmillan, 1951), 1, 37, and *Philosophie der Religion*, 1, 171 (1, 112).

philosophical study of actuality, and that he knows this to be the case.[26] His assurance rests upon his phenomenologically generated doctrine on spirit as the organic, self-differentiating whole of actuality. A logical method which captures the pervasive pattern of this totality, and whose categories are determinations of this totality, is metaphysical by its own nature, without requiring a separate movement from the logical to the metaphysical order. These domains are indistinguishably one in the speculative logic elaborated in Hegel's *Science of Logic* and *Encyclopedia of the Philosophical Sciences*.

To express more vividly the binding principle between logic and ontology, Heidegger reformulates Hegel's philosophy as an onto-theo-logic.[27] There is ample sanction for this compound designation in Hegel's own statements that philosophy is a science and service of God, and that logic in particular is a science of God viewed in His own being, regarded prior to the formation of the worlds of nature and human consciousness. More strictly taken, however, philosophy establishes the truth about God and theism by showing their inadequacy and (to the degree that they resist transformation into the monism of absolute spirit) their inhumanity.

Hence the ruling framework of Hegel's philosophy is more precisely called an *onto-pneuma-logic*, to emphasize the centrality of his unique conception of self-developing spirit. What binds together ontology and logic is the doctrine on spirit as the living, correlating whole within which all the divisions, transitions, and unifications of thought and being arise. Only by reference to this doctrinal center does the philosopher gain assurance that thought and being stand open to each other. Our intellectual analysis has real significance and, conversely, things embody an intelligible structure, because our human minds and the things in nature participate in the common actuality of spirit. Hegel overcomes empiricism and idealism simultaneously, because he radically universalizes his conception of spirit.

There is a distinctive manner in which Hegel involves religion within

---

26. *Science of Logic*, 1, 36–37, 64–65. The application of Hegel's mediational logic to the concrete sphere of religion is studied by Henri Niel, *De la Médiation dans la philosophie de Hegel* (Paris, 1945), pp. 329–53.

27. Martin Heidegger, "The Onto-Theo-Logical Nature of Metaphysics," *Essays in Metaphysics: Identity and Difference*, trans. K. F. Leidecker (New York, 1960), pp. 35–67. One should not confuse either onto-theo-logic or onto-pneuma-logic with pneumontology, which for Hegel is confined to rational psychology, or the abstract metaphysics of subjectivity. See Hegel, *Philosophy of Mind*, trans. W. Wallace (Oxford, Clarendon Press, 1894), p. 161; this third part of the *Encyclopedia of the Philosophical Sciences* will be cited here as *Encyclopedia Mind*.

the work of ontopneumalogical reconstruction. He does not merely apply the general principles to the religious sphere, but finds there some special factors which contribute to the nature and success of the reconstructive method itself. Human religiousness affects, as well as gets affected by, the Hegelian philosophical method for reinterpreting all modes of experience. "Religion can well be without philosophy, but philosophy cannot be without religion, but rather includes the latter within itself." [28] Therefore, before examining religion in its definite kinds and systematic relation with the other domains of experience and thought, we must study its role in forming Hegel's broadest notion of onto-pneuma-logic.

Its influence is especially noticeable upon the following four aspects of his philosophical foundation: the human conditions for philosophizing, the dialectical character of philosophical method, the general theory of essence, and the concrete actuosity of spirit. Hegel does not fear that, in acknowledging the pervasive presence of a religious factor, philosophy will thereby become contaminated and founded upon something else. For his point is that the religious attitude is a concrete expression of that same spiritual actuality which philosophy alone can properly understand, and which constitutes the intrinsic, utterly autonomous foundation of philosophical knowledge itself.

The Human Conditions for Philosophizing. Religion is deeply involved in the tangled Hegelian question of whether or not philosophy makes a beginning. There is nothing in the ideal of philosophical knowledge, considered as the total self-comprehension of spiritual actuality by itself, requiring a bare start be made. The systematic philosophy of spirit operates under the sign of the closed circle, so that every move going from a logical base to a complex cultural form is completely contained within the circulating system of philosophical thought and its experiential modes. Nevertheless, this ideal must be shared by finite, human centers of reflection who, at the outset of their philosophizing, may not themselves be aware of their own status within the circle of spiritual life and philosophical activity. This is the sense in which the human mind must enter upon the path of phenomenological education, thus making at least a human beginning in the work of philosophical reconstruction of experience. Some definite religious resources are required, not only to enter this pathway but also to develop the subsequent systematic philosophy.

28. *Encyclopedia Logic*, p. xxi. The mutual impact of Hegel's philosophical logic and his theory of the Christian religion is measured in Claude Bruaire's *Logique et religion chrétienne dans la philosophie de Hegel* (Paris, 1964).

Upon becoming professor of philosophy in Berlin, in the inaugural address which he delivered in 1818, Hegel made a plea for cultivating the proper subjective conditions for philosophizing:

> At first I can only beg you to trust in science, to believe in reason, and to have confidence and faith in yourselves. The courage of truth —faith in the power of spirit—is the primal condition in the study of philosophy. Man ought to honor himself and deem himself worthy of the highest. He cannot think too much of the greatness and power of the spirit. The essence of the universe, closed though it is for itself, has no barrier to defend itself against the courage to know it. It must disclose its treasures; its depth is there for us to behold, to know, and to enjoy.[29]

Far from regarding this call for "an unswerving will to truth, and courage" as an overweening rationalism, opposed to the religious view of the universe, Hegel underlined the close affinity between the religious attitude and the one required for philosophizing.

On the side of the human investigator, the religious attitude functions as a bridge leading from the common sense and the scientific readings of reality to the philosophical.[30] It stirs the mind both intellectually and practically, by re-asking the question of truth and then by maintaining our interest in the search for a more satisfactory answer. The working conviction of the religiously motivated person is that the entire truth is not found in things as they present themselves to common sense certainty and to scientific explanation, even if these approaches are followed with methodical persistence. Religious awareness is many-levelled, and gener-

---

29. The passage is given in the G. E. Mueller translation of Hegel's *Encyclopedia of Philosophy* (New York, Philosophical Library, 1959), p. 61; the next quotation, ibid., p. 62. Unfortunately, the Mueller translation of the entire *Encyclopedia* contains too many paraphrases and editorial changes to be generally serviceable. Hegel's inaugural address of 1818 is notable for its insistence that religion is not confined to the needs and subjective feelings of the isolated individual, but that it is rather a major way in which men enter into possession of the objective truth about the natural world and their own spiritual being. "This objectivity, which is just as much [a valid sort of] subjectivity, alone constitutes religion." This text is taken from the previously unpublished second part of the *Rede zum Antritt des Philosophischen Lehramtes an der Universität Berlin*, in Hegel's *Berliner Schriften*, 1818–1831, ed. J. Hoffmeister (Hamburg, Meiner, 1956), p. 14. Hegel goes on to say that philosophy has the same goal and content as religion, and that the passage from religious representational imagery to philosophy is the final liberation and justification of that common content of spiritual truth.

30. This is the introductory theme of *Encyclopedia Logic*, pp. 3–9.

ates in us the habit of looking for a more inclusive basis for interpreting everyday objects and the whole finite world. It arouses in inquiring mankind the will to seek the unlimited truth about finite objects, as well as the recognition that such a search is of supreme importance for our lives. Without this subjective disposition and stimulation of the mind, men would never strive after that further reach of awareness in which philosophy consists.

Furthermore, Hegel attributes to the religious component in our nature the initial courage required to persist in keeping the demands of truth so stringent and yet so attractive. The courage to engage in inquiry on ultimate issues rests upon the twofold religious conviction that there is a divine spiritual reality and that our own nature is akin to it. These two certitudes are inseparable and mutually specified. Because the God of religious attitude is never purely detached: it leads us to maintain our own be called) is spiritual, there is presumptive ground for holding that the universe is intelligible and that its full significance includes its function as a pointer, leading us somehow toward the affirmation of spirit. But the religious attitude is never purely detached: it leads us to maintain our own kinship with this spiritual principle. Except when distorted by the mechanism of alienation and positivity, the religious view is that the divine idea resides in us, that we share in the divine life, and that infinite spirit manifests itself in our spirit (indeed, "in my own spirit," as Hegel likes to phrase it more personally and intensively). It is from the tireless religious formation of humanity that we learn to view our relationship to the divine as that of spirit answering to the call of spirit.

The philosopher's human confidence to will the truth and seek it unfalteringly derives from this interior witness of the spirit, from Hegel's naturalizing of the religious *testimonium internum spiritus sancti*. Such witnessing to the community of life between the divine and the human spirit is not a purely private and emotive affair (as the pietistic mind supposes), since it concerns the objective structure and basis of the experienced universe of common sense and science, no less than that of the human subject. If man could not see his own worth as being founded in the very same spiritual life of the God he worships, he would not seek out the interconnected meanings in the universe and enjoy them in the manner of a native son, working with his own heritage.

But Hegel does not conclude that philosophy is only a tributary and conceptual transcription of this sense of religious intimacy and belongingness. Religion disposes us to see the unrestricted truth, but does not furnish that insight in its own inherent form of evidence. In order to make an effective passage from the religious certitude about spiritual reality to the actual possession of its tested truth, a distinctively philosophical movement of the human mind is required. Religion furnishes the human orientation and encouragement, but it does not give the method and systematic development of knowledge in the philosophical mode. Hence the philosopher must be able to reformulate religious faith in God as an expression of the more fundamental philosophical faith in reason and the organic totality of all beings. From religious to philosophical faith is the journey taken by the fully reflective mind.

The Dialectical Character of Philosophical Method. Hegel dissociates himself firmly from the sterile triplicity of thesis-antithesis-synthesis, used as a uniform but empty logical formula for solving all problems and making all movements of inference and practice. Instead, he bases his claim for the truth and uniqueness of his ontopneumalogical method upon its fidelity to the pattern of spiritual development, a pattern which always bears reference to the interpretative acts of the mind. Every problem can be considered by the human mind from three aspects: finite abstract understanding, negative dialectical reason, and positive speculative reason.[31]

The first or *abstractly finite* viewpoint is that of immediacy and the hard-and-fast categories and contrasts of the understanding, as employed in common sense and scientific activities. The second or *dialectical* phase is characterized by the play of things as they interweave and obliterate sharp distinctions, and by the play of thought as it allows concepts to struggle and pass over into each other. Finally, the *speculative* effort is made to do justice both to the finite categorial distinctions and to the antitheses in thought and experience, while also reaching out for their immanent basis and unifying goal in the spiritual totality.

Upon which type of interpretation ought the human stress to fall, so that the inquiry will continue and our efforts will be directed, at least from afar, toward a satisfactory consummation? Human religiousness is not so constituted as to offer a theoretical answer to this crucial question of method. But the whole weight of its human reality makes it a concrete living response, which the philosopher finds instructive in weighing

31. Ibid., pp. 143–54. That the Hegelian conception of dialectic has both metaphysical and religious significance is established by Emerich Coreth, *Das dialektische Sein in Hegels Logik* (Vienna, 1952), pp. 14–17, 185–89.

the roles of the abstractive, dialectical, and speculative phases of reason. Our religious attitude inclines us to emphasize the dialectical aspect of the spiritual life, and thus to give special prominence to the dialectical moment in the rational interpretation of experience. This is not an exclusive emphasis, however, since a purely dialectical cultivation of oppositions would lead to sheer exhaustion and skepticism.

Man's religious activity cultivates the dialectical approach in such fashion that it transmutes the values of immediacy, and orders the entire struggle toward the life of blessedness. Thus the religious approach is mediatory and directional. It is a concrete expression of our characteristically human predicament of living at the swirling center of a spiritual development, which goes from the immediate and the finite and is being directed toward the full actuality of spirit. To show concern for origins and goals, and yet to do so from a distinct center of orientation, is the mark of the religious man. Through his existential mode of conducting a dialectical search, he enriches the philosophical theory of method itself.

From his methodological standpoint, Hegel can state that "religion is now itself the standpoint of the consciousness of the true," taken not in its complete purity but precisely as being shaped by the human factors of subjective spirit.[32] Thereby, he signifies that religious awareness is not to be identified simply with the truth and the life of the divine totality, but that it is essentially a seeking of this truth and this life across the horizons of our developing human consciousness and its objects. When men feel that their religious strivings after union with the divine are meaningful and worthwhile, they are substantially affirming the meaningful and valuable character of a dialectical separation itself. They are furnishing a living witness to Hegel's methodological contention that the dialectical phase of otherness, separation, and critical self-recovery is the creative motor principle in reality and in the reconstruction of experience. Thus the religious interplay between man's estrangement from God and his worshipful acts of reunion is the visible embodiment of the pattern of dialectical reason. And because dialectical reason is essentially ordered toward the speculative act of reason, there is also an ultimate superordination of the speculative method and principles of philosophy over every religious meaning and action.

On the question of how religion may confirm the theory of method, then, Hegel takes a unique position among our classical philosophers of

32. *Philosophie der Religion*, 1, 153 (1, 90–91).

religion. Whereas Hume maintains that every distinctively religious manifestation provides only the antithetic clue of being opposed to the procedure and truth of philosophy, Hegel looks to religious attitudes for
some positive guidance. Although never fully clarified at their own level
of activity, they nevertheless provide the philosophical mind with an indispensable exemplification of the dialectical moment in the process of
reconstruction. Kant would allow religion an active role, also, but it
would be mainly that of serving as a vehicle for humanizing the truth
of moral theism. The Hegelian approach moves beyond this instrumental relationship to suggest that man's religious attitude is itself a
concrete realization of the true method and import of philosophy, even
though it cannot completely clarify its own nature. Religious existence
does not simply carry some philosophical freight: its entire significance
is to actualize the life of spirit in the form of the restless passage from
human awareness to the truth of absolute spirit. In his methodological
doctrine on creative negativity and dialectical relating, therefore, Hegel
gives us the results of his philosophical reflection on this religious act
of passage.

The General Theory of Essence. On the side of the content of onto-
pneuma-logic, the counterpart to the stress upon the dialectical moment
is found in the doctrine on essence. Hegel himself remarks that this is
the most difficult part of his metaphysical logic, not only in the straightforward sense of being highly complicated, but also because it deals with
that arduous striving which constitutes all worldly actuality. In the
Hegelian logic, the life of the spiritual whole is examined from the three
standpoints of a becoming which is transpiring there (doctrine on being),
an effort at essential differentiation (doctrine on essence), and a powerful teleology toward unifying all the agencies in being and thought (doctrine on concept or the absolute idea). Without the second or mediating
order of essence, beings would perish for lack of those relationships of
opposition which enable them to define and develop themselves. And
without this same mediating function of essential differentiation, there
could be no definite structures and reflective goals to master in a telic
unity. Under the rubric of essence, all of life's forces for creative conflict
and structured growth are embraced in the most general way.

As Hegel employs the term "abstract," his theory of essence is not a
heady abstraction, but an account of those concrescent tendencies at the
heart of all actuality which make it a concretely developing whole. And

he receives encouragement on the ontopneumalogical relevance of his doctrine of essence from the fact that its main traits are exhibited before us in religious awareness. The common ground between ordinary human intelligence and philosophical analysis is furnished by man's religious attitude, which prepares the former in anticipation, and gives to the latter a common language for communicating its findings on essence.

In Pascal's haunting cry: "Nothing stays for us," the religious soul expresses its conviction that we have forever left the garden of innocent immediacy and cannot avoid making a perilous voyage.[33] There can be no direct and effortless coalescence between things as they initially are and the divine principle. Men especially must undergo a testing, in order to work out the relationships which will fit them for a union with God. They must recognize that to stand up for a principle also means to stand up against a counterprinciple, and that there is something liberating and fulfilling in such conflicts and renunciations.

Interpreted in ontopneumalogical terms, this religious witness signifies the indispensable role of the order of essence. In searching for the essential structure of anything, we are already passing beyond its unreflective condition as a being which is simply there. To ask the question of essence means to introduce a certain distance, to trace out relations of opposition and agreement, and thus to bring a being or a meaning into the sphere of mediation. Once this essential inquiry is launched as a theoretical and practical operation, the philosophical reconstruction of our experience is well underway and cannot be halted. The probing into essential correlations must go on, and in this very process the concrete actuality of beings is achieved.

There are three aspects of the theory of essence which benefit, in a special way, from Hegel's meditation upon the religious attitude. They are the correlative significance of determination and negation, the need for a manifestation of essence, and the ordering of the whole process toward a consummate actuality. On all three scores, the religious man executes in his own living belief and action that which the speculative philosopher brings to judgmental truth in his teaching on essence.

33. Pascal, *Pensées,* trans. H. F. Stewart (London, Routledge and Kegan Paul, 1950), p. 25. Hegel's basic criticism of the Spinozistic dialectic of universal determination-and-negation in the absolute is that it underestimates precisely that concrete reflective "coming to oneself" which religion affirms to be present in every spiritual development: *Science of Logic,* 1, 125–26, 2, 167–70; *Lectures on the History of Philosophy,* trans. E. S. Haldane and F. H. Simpson (3 vols. New York, 1955), 3, 267–68, 285–89.

One reason why Hegel regarded study of Spinoza as the best preparation for philosophy was the sensitivity shown by the Dutch thinker toward the metaphysical significance of religious convictions. Hegel emphasized, particularly, the correlated propositions that every determination is a negation, and that every negation is a determination. One cannot be religious, simply by laying in one's own determinate being and expanding it into the divine. Genuine religiousness requires at least a minimal act of negative reflection, sufficient to note that one's own given being is *not* the same as the other beings with which it is related. To be insistent upon one's own determinate being is not to insure one's unity with God, but rather to make oneself aware of the distance between man and God, along with the need for further efforts at achieving a religious union.

The religious outlook also sharpens the human spirit to see that meaningful negations are not hollow vacuums, but rather are the way in which man differentiates his choices and orders his values. For instance, the religious act of sacrifice would destroy a man, did it not contain a positive appreciation of eternal life and a resolve to obtain some human share in it. Bringing these religious forms of the problem of determination and negation to a critically purified, speculative condition is a major task of the Hegelian theory of essence.

The Biblical saying that by their fruits you shall know them was another point of stimulus for Hegel. Instead of interpreting it narrowly in terms of pragmatic action, he associated its primary meaning with his doctrine on the development of essential structure through its manifestation. Spiritual reality is not a treasure hidden away to rust. Its basic drive is to show itself, to shine forth in and through its works. It must take the form of actual social existence, and thus bring out the interrelatedness of our experience.

Such considerations led Hegel to take his own position on the perennial question of essence and existence. He did not regard them as different entities or even as really distinct co-principles, making their own contribution to a being. Essence is the predominate way of taking the reality of spirit itself, a spiritual reality in the throes of differentiating its own structure and manifesting that structure in the field of experience. Existence signifies precisely the manifesting phase in the essential process itself, that essential moment in which the correlational structure displays itself and assures the powerful presence of essential being. The existential manifestation is not a separate fruit of essence: it is this essential act in displayed and communicable form. This particular existence is contingent

and destined to pass away, but such is a condition for the further
presentation of new facets in the abiding spiritual actuality of the essence.

The highly general plane at which Hegel conducted his analysis of
essence and existence cannot disguise its close bearing on the actual religious and philosophical situation of his own day. His critical intent was
to challenge both a sharply dualistic religious view of this world and the
afterworld and also a Kantian phenomenalism. Both positions come to
grief in trying to make some sense out of the statement that our world
of existent things is an 'appearance. It cannot be mere illusion or a
mere shadow field or an objective sphere without noumenal significance,
since in these cases its appearing function would disappear. But if the
existing experienced world is neither pure show nor isolated phenomenal
objectivity, then it can best be interpreted as a manifesting of the essential being of spirit. The relational structure of spirit requires that it
shine forth in and as the sensible world of existents, that this world be
nothing other than an active mode of appearing and self-communication
on the part of the essential ground of all being.

Hegel does not hesitate to clothe this speculative explanation in religious terms. He invites us to regard the Christian doctrines of revelation
and the Incarnation as figurative expressions of his own theory of essence,
as the modes in which the truth about the essential being of spirit is
filtered through the religious imagination. What the religious mind grasps
is God as a revealing God, and that His revealing act consists basically in
giving Himself to the world, under the form of sensible existence.[34] But
the religious sense of there being a free gift in God's self-revealing in
creation and the Incarnation, is explained by Hegel as a consequence of
our failure to reach philosophical lucidity on the essential necessity underlying every mode of existential manifestation, including the religious.

Hegel also finds in Christianity, and in most other religious outlooks,
a ready fund of malleable materials which can be reshaped to represent
another trait of his doctrine on essence: its telic ordination to a *consummate actuality*. The religious mind is keenly aware that the present instant
and the presently existing things do not exhaust the full significance of our
lives. For the believer, the experienced world retains its continuity with
abiding spiritual principles and primal deeds of creation; it has an abyss
of meaning which can be plumbed in religious meditation; and it opens
out a prospect for personal fulfillment and not just a senseless round of

34. *Encyclopedia Logic*, pp. 252–53.

events without direction. The religious mode of consciousness is naturally eschatological. It orients men toward consideration of last things, and toward the expectation that the scattered phases of their temporal existence will be gathered together and a unifying value found for the entire human community.

This sense of purposiveness is treated by Hegel as a moving image of the truth of essence. The life of spirit must not only express its essential ground in the existent world of appearances, but must also weave them together, and achieve the mastery of essential structure over its existential modalities. The entire development of essential forms in the world of appearances is ordered toward actuality, as their unification, and toward a spiritual statement in the concept. In his expectation of an ultimate transfiguration and judgment for all things, the religious man has a presentiment of this ontopneumalogical ordering of essence and its modes of appearance toward the unifying actuality and the absolute idea. The primacy of actuality and the absolute idea is affirmed in the very attitude of the believer, even though the conceptual significance of that affirmation is only grasped by the philosopher of absolute spirit.

The Concrete Actuosity of Spirit. Hegel's chief systematic preoccupation is to insure that the metaphysical logic expounded in the *Science of Logic* and the *Encyclopedia of the Philosophical Sciences* will hold good for the realms of nature and human culture, and will regulate philosophical investigations at these levels. He secures its effective predominance through the doctrine on the actuosity of spirit, which serves not only as the binding principle but also as the universalizing basis for his onto-pneuma-logic. Living substance is not a static block, but is the energizing power constantly expressing itself through the social relations among the fluent things in our world. To designate this aspect of spiritual being, Hegel speaks about the actuosity of spirit: "its activity is its substantiality, actuosity is its being." [35] The internally directed actuosity of substance is best exhibited in the great transition from the physical universe to the world of human interiority and freedom. For the activity of substance is essentially that of a subject, a teleological agency spiritual in nature and

35. This text from Hegel's manuscript on subjective spirit is edited by F. Nicolin: "Ein Hegelsches Fragment zur Philosophie des Geistes," *Hegel-Studien*, 1 (1961), 48. In *Science of Logic*, 2, 189, Hegel refers to the movement of accidental modes as "the actuosity of substance," and throughout the *Encyclopedia* he shows a preference for the cognate active terms "religiosity" and "the religious." The operational and subject-orienting meaning of religiosity is brought out by Seeberger, *Hegel*, pp. 577–82.

tendency. The substantial power energizing our universe is that of spirit itself, which constantly aims at actualizing its own subjective nature as thinking and acting spirit, through the mediation of man's reflective and historical life.

The several levels of being and thought in our experience constitute a developing whole through the actuosity of spirit, taken as both substance and subject. But the truth of this fundamental ontopneumalogical proposition is not formally grasped by everyone, even though all modes of being must respond to it as the inner law of their activity. To bridge the gap between the concrescent actuosity of spirit and a philosophical awareness of its nature, Hegel makes use of the workings of religion among men. If religion has any common meaning for men, it is that of an actively orienting principle which enables them to grow into an operative community of spiritually concerned agents. Under the religious impetus, men move beyond their restricted bodily interests, participate in the common works of culture, and turn their hearts toward a union of spirit with spirit. In the religious shaping of humanity as a cultural development in search of the energic actuality of spirit, therefore, we have a living witness to the actuosity of spirit and its transforming work throughout the cosmos and human society. .

In order to emphasize this sign function of religious activity, Hegel rehabilitates the debased term *religiosity*. Sometimes, he uses the word pejoratively to attack an extreme subjectivism. In this sense, it means a one-sided, pietistic type of interiority which overlooks the social aspects of religion, the need for order and worship, and the presence of a reasonable factor in belief. But in a constructive sense, human religiosity is the most comprehensive and persuasive sign of the actuosity of spirit, the commonest manner in which that persistent agency is felt and expressed in ordinary human forms. It is the active balancing principle, which saves men from the excesses of both utter objectivism and utter subjectivism. Against the former, religiosity operates to recall men to themselves, lest they dedicate their lives entirely to the service and enjoyment of things, forgetting their own selfhood and spiritual vocation. And against the extreme of subjectivism, a well-balanced religiosity upholds the ideal of community service and a doctrinal tradition. Human religiosity fortifies men in the dignity of their own selfhood, but in such a manner that they also acknowledge their responsibility to the community of work and reasonable inquiry.

The dialectical nature of religiosity is seen in its function of forcing a break in our immediate attachment to the world of things and psychological states of soul. In Hegel's view, the force of religiosity erupts to disturb our untroubled commitment to anything less than the search for the spiritual absolute. We become troubled and reflective in the face of the transiency of our empirical, temporal existence, as well as in the face of the disparity between our intentions and our sharply limited deeds. At such moments, it is the working of human religiosity which moves our souls and orients us toward the divine. It gives testimony within us to the omnipresence and eternal power of spiritual actuality, thus relating us in a practical way toward this center of all life.

No matter what frames of interpretation are used by theists and other believers, Hegel sees in the religious stirring of mankind primarily the *Tun und Tätigkeit des Geistes*, the act-in-the-doing and the very activity of the spiritual totality itself.[36] The actuosity of spirit operates ceaselessly in the ordinary human mode of religiosity, irrupting in the midst of our worldly certitudes and setting us on the new path which leads toward a knowing and sharing in the life of the organic spiritual whole. When we lift up our hearts from nature to spiritual freedom, the religious act is caught up into the effort of absolute spirit to possess itself through the concentrated energy of the human spirit. In Hegelian language, the speculative truth of human religiosity becomes fully clarified only in its ultimate reference to the active doings of spirit as such.

Nevertheless, the distinctive contribution of the theme of religiosity cannot be overlooked. It enables Hegel to show that there is a "good" as well as a "bad" sort of interiority, that is, an insistence of being and thought which nevertheless stands open to the truth of infinite-finite spirit. Consequently, he maintains that the concentrated interiority marking the life of the religious believer has essentially the same import and value as that which is found in the philosopher. Precisely because an intense religious interiority is at the same time an orientation of the

36. The energic character of spiritual actuality is brought home to human religious awareness most strongly through the Christian doctrines of the Trinity, creation, and revelation (*Philosophie der Religion*, 4, 32–34, 62–64 [2, 334–35, 3, 11–13]). Compare the terminology employed in the editorial redactions, ibid., 1, 142, 258 (1, 194, 228). Hegel proposes a pneumandric labor theory of religion, as being jointly constituted by the laboring of the divine and the human spirit. In "Hegel as Panentheist," *Tulane Studies in Philosophy*, 9 (1960), 134–64, R. C. Whittemore suggests that this active view of the religious relationship is a form of panentheism and not of pantheism, Spinozistic or otherwise. But Hegel's unique theory of the developing spiritual totality can be fitted into neither pantheistic nor panentheistic categories.

whole man toward the active purposes of spirit, there is a fundamental sameness of content and intended truth in the convictions of religion and philosophy. From his analysis of religiosity as a mode of the actuosity of concrete spirit, Hegel is able to conclude that all men have a common religious vocation. However, the reflective truth about this joint searching of all men for the life of spirit comes within the competence of the philosopher alone to know and develop in all its systematic ramifications.

8

Hegel: Religion Within the Speculative System

In systematically working out the several parts of his philosophy, Hegel assigns a distinct area to the formal theory of religion. But the general meaning of religion is so intimately bound up with his fundamental judgments about spiritual development, God, and the cultural life of man that he cannot keep that meaning in an isolated pocket of his thought. The theme of human religiousness is closely intertwined with all the major steps in constructing the house of speculative wisdom. The purpose of the present chapter is to examine this interrelatedness of the religious problem with Hegel's basic position on natural theology, social and political life, art, and the sphere of revelation. Only by working out these speculative articulations can we grasp the contours of Hegel's philosophy of religion, and measure the completeness of his assimilation of religious meanings to philosophical truth.

THE RELIGIONIZING OF NATURAL THEOLOGY

Hegel steers a unique course in the seas of natural theology, but his distinctive approach often escapes notice. Ostensibly, he is engaged in a rearguard action, warding off the attacks of Hume and Kant upon the proofs of God's existence and the theory of divine attributes. At most, his originality in this region seems to consist in a bold reversal of the philosophical evaluation of the three current proofs of God's being. Hume and Kant bring all their logical criticism to bear against the so-called ontological proof from the nature of the idea of the most perfect being, and yet they allow a certain suasive force to remain in the appeal to design and order in the universe. Hegel, on the contrary, defends the on-

tological proof above all else, and assigns a secondary role to the cosmological and teleological arguments (including under the latter heading
both physical teleology and moral teleology). This is indeed a reversal
of the prevailing trend in the critique of natural theology, but its precise
significance can only be determined by replacing natural theology within
the governing context of Hegel's own conceptions of spirit and of religion. His doctrine on God is completely enclosed within this *double
context*. Every step at reconstruction reinforces the bonding and the
bondage of natural theology to the requirements of the spiritual totality
and its religious expression.

The difference between an uncontexted and a doubly contexted kind
of natural theology is decisive for Hegel. He is just as ruthlessly lucid as
his predecessors in describing the ruinous condition of the rationalist
doctrines on God, in the wake of the attacks made by empiricism and
Kantian criticism.[1] It is futile for an uncontexted natural theology to
attempt a direct passage from the perception of order in nature to God,
or from our native idea of the highest perfection to God's perfect being,
or from our natural desire for unalloyed knowledge and happiness to its
satisfaction in the divine actuality.

These attempts are vitiated by the assumption that nature and the
natural condition of man are simply there, as the starting points for a
process of reasoning which leads to God. Hegel rejects a theology which
is "natural," in this sense of a naive positing of the initial evidence. Such
a doctrine remains completely exposed to the empiricist and Kantian objections based on the limits of our knowledge of nature and man. In
developing his own doubly contexted natural theology, Hegel is not
functioning as a philosopher of the restoration but as a revolutionary
thinker, who is now extending his new order of speculation into the
sphere of our systematic thoughts about God. The resultant theology is
"natural" in the quite original sense that it exposes to view the nature of
God, reveals it to be a way of viewing the spiritual whole itself, and
thereby naturalizes the entire discourse on God as a subordinate portion
of the theory of religion.

The depth of the transformation can be measured by noting how the

---

1. Hegel describes the disarray of natural theology in *Science of Logic*, 1, 33–34,
and *Beweise*, pp. 2–3 (p. 156). Cf. Collins, *God in Modern Philosophy*, pp. 216–29,
for an analysis of *Beweise* from the specific standpoint of the theory of God rather than
of religion. See also, Q. Lauer, "Hegel on Proofs for God's Existence," *Kant-Studien*,
55 (1964), 443–65.

problem of God's existence and attributes is recast in function of three much more fundamental themes: finitude, representation, and religiosity. By prolonging these three dominating principles into the sphere of natural theology, Hegel transcends the controversies of the previous century and reduces that part of philosophy to a series of confirming theses and applications of his own metaphysical logic. There is a deliberate disintegrating of the unity of the philosophy of God. Hegel disperses the topics in natural theology by means of his metaphysical principle of finitude, his epistemological principle of representation, and his practical principle of religiosity. Our special concern is with this last way of overpowering the theological materials and making them testify to the active presence of the religious attitude at every step. But the religionizing of the science of God is a broadly conceived process, resting upon a metaphysical analysis and an epistemological clarification of the natural theologian's work.

Finitude as the Sole Basis of Demonstration.   Contrary to expectation, Hegel's first move is not to rehabilitate the individual proofs of God's existence. Instead, he submits the whole enterprise of proving God's existence to a radical reinterpretation, in which all the proofs singled out by Hume and Kant are deprived of demonstrative force and assigned a new function. This is done by means of a primary distinction between two ways of viewing the ontological, cosmological, and teleological arguments —as descriptive expressions and as a demonstration.

Looked upon as *descriptive* expressions of the religious movement of the soul, they retain a kind of validity even in the face of the Humean and Kantian criticisms of natural theology. For they do capture the religious upsurge of man, as he meditates upon the ideal of perfection and strives after those aspects of order and purpose which shine through our experience of this jagged, sensuous world of ours. The strength of the arguments in their plural descriptive form lies in the persuasiveness with which they express, and the accuracy with which they state, the religious states of soul whereby man elevates himself toward the divine actuality. Their meaning and truth can only be determined in the context of the full theory of religion, where they function as objective analyses and rational reformulations of man's inner religious activity.[2] Far from

2. "The so-called proofs of God's existence are to be regarded only as the *descriptions* and analyses of the spirit's own course, which is a *thinking* one and which

providing the foundation for a natural theology, the descriptive arguments belong among the prolonging consequences of our religious conatus.

If one inquires about the *demonstrative* character of the proofs of God,
then Hegel reduces them to a single argument, which is ontopneumalogical in nature and hence which is properly established in his science of
logic. This sharp contrast between the three descriptive-expressive arguments and the one demonstrative argument is of pivotal importance for
the transforming of natural theology. For it means that the former arguments, which lead to the God of theism and to theistic religion, are deprived of any decisive role in shaping the theory of God. The force of
demonstration is reserved exclusively for the unique ontopneumalogical
argument, which directly expresses the doctrine of spirit and furnishes
the religious principles for reforming all theistic proofs.

Hegel finds his distinctive basis of demonstration in the theory of
finitude, which is itself a portion of the ontopneumalogical doctrine on
essence. To look upon experienced beings in their effort to develop their
essential nature is to see them as already passing beyond their immediately
given condition, and as seeking to realize their full actuality. Finitude is
precisely this restless drive of all reality, its ceaseless effort to overcome
and move beyond the limits it contains. This category does not signify a
static containment within limits and an exclusion of everything else, but
rather the whole essential development, which includes not only the
inherent barriers but also the drive to go beyond them. Hence Hegel
defines finitude in logicometaphysical terms as "something, posited with
its immanent limit as self-contradiction through which it is driven and
forced beyond itself," and adds more existentially that "the determinate
has as such no other nature than this absolute unrest *not* to be what it
is." [3] The reference to self-contradiction and internal negating of limits
is ontological, rather than purely logical, in its import. Finitude is not
a simple characterization of anything, but expresses its complex union of

---

thinks the sensuous" (*Encyclopedia Logic*, p. 103). These proofs "ought to contain
the *elevation of the human spirit to God*, and express it for thought" (*Beweise*, p. 13
[p. 164]).

3. *Science of Logic*, 1, 141; *Jenenser Logik, Metaphysik und Naturphilosophie*, ed.
G. Lasson (Leipzig, Meiner, 1923), p. 31 (italics mine). The open and the closed
conceptions of finitude are contrasted, and their respective implications for theological
inference are specified in *Science of Logic*, 1, 141–50; *Encyclopedia Logic*, pp. 107–
09; *Encyclopedia Mind*, pp. 165–66.

determinate act together with an active transcendence of its own boundaries.

Before showing that finitude supplies the only demonstrative basis in natural theology, Hegel feels obliged to distinguish between two conceptions of finite beings: the closed view and the open one. In the *closed view*, a particular being vindicates its finitude by setting itself off definitively from every other finite being, and especially from the infinite being. The accent is placed simply on its internal limits, on that which keeps it apart from others and prevents it from being of the same nature with them. The previous tradition in natural theology based itself upon this closed-off conception of finite beings. On this assumption, the task of proving the existence of God amounted to one of finding ways to hurdle the Great Wall of Being which rears itself between finite things and the infinite God, and which is sustained there by the very nature of finitude.

Yet the natural theologian soon found himself to be not only based upon the finite order, but also totally and exclusively enclosed within its unyielding limits. He had no inherent resources at his disposal for making the required transition from the finite to the infinite, whether the transit was to be attempted from visible things to their efficient cause and end, or from the idea of the most perfect being to its actual existence. However subtle the inference, it was prevented by the encasing chamber of finitude from completing the passage to the infinite with any logical rigor.

Hume and Kant merely clarified this situation with admirable honesty, in declaring all such efforts at demonstrating God's existence to be failures. If men still persisted in repeating the usual arguments, it was only because they were drawing their real convictions about God from religious faith and not from theistic argumentation. The leap of faith gave them a road of access to the divine infinite reality. But this meant that the arguments in natural theology are expressions of religious faith and hence should be treated as functions of the theory of religiosity, as Hegel proposed. Their real status is that of being thematizations of religious aspiration, rather than demonstrative proofs in philosophy.

The case is quite different, however, with the *open conception* of finite beings. It is open in a twofold Hegelian sense, both methodologically and ontologically. There is methodological openness, since the theory of finitude belongs within the wider context of the theory of spirit and essence. And this in turn supposes an ontological openness, insofar as the very nature of finite beings is seen to fit within the life of the organic spiritual whole. For Hegel, an open finitude supplies the demonstrative foundation for the inference from the finite to the infinite. It is a metaphysical inference, but of the quite specific nontheistic sort required in the theory of absolute spirit. An opening is made from the finite world to the infinite, but in making the passage, the inquiring mind is forced to transmute a natural theology or philosophical doctrine on God into an ontopneumalogical doctrine on the self-developing, self-finitizing spirit.

The full surrender of natural theology to the philosophy of spirit and its religious implications is built into the peculiar Hegelian meaning for "proof of God's existence from self-transcending finitude." Each word in this key phrase is given a fresh signification, in order to guarantee in advance the unconditional ontopneumalogicizing (and hence also the religionizing) of natural theology. This semantic reformation enables Hegel to retain the language and framework of natural theology, while at the same time performing a radical transformation of that discipline into a variant statement of his own philosophy of spirit.

The kind of *proof* in question is not a purely objective logical act, which leaves the demonstrator himself unaffected, but is rather an act of reflective self-clarification on the part of the human investigator. Its entire probative force lies in bringing into the condition of lucid reflection and self-understanding, the internal dynamism of finite reality itself, as found in the life of man. To prove something from the finite order is nothing more than to permit the finite order to manifest its own nature in our philosophical thought, to show itself as being a necessary stage in the self-development of the infinite spiritual whole.

Clearly, the outcome of such proof is neither God nor His existence, except in a highly accommodated sense. For it leads the human mind to affirm the encompassing being of the infinite-finite totality, rather than the personal transcendent God. Furthermore, the inference cannot terminate in the bare assertion of divine existence. As interpreted within the Hegelian theory of essence, the existential proof is entirely provisional in status. It is a dress rehearsal for attending to the truth of the manifested divine essence itself, that is, for following out the unification of essence and existence in the distinctive actuality of the spiritual totality. Not the existential affirmation but the truth about the divine actuality, known to be the inclusive life of all finite modes of thought and being, is the proper purpose of the proving activity in Hegel's philosophy of God.

Finally, there is a directly religious connotation found in the study of *self-transcending finitude*, a connotation which every proposition in natural theology must strengthen through a drastic reinterpretation. Hegel refers to his ontopneumalogical dialectic as "the veritable, not the external, elevation above the finite."[4] Its genuine character consists in its being the immanent movement of finite being itself, as it raises itself through and beyond its own limits, toward full participation in the infinite life. In this elevation is found the truth of the religious uplifting of our hearts to God. A determinate actuality is affirmed along with the limits which interweave it into, rather than exclude it from, the wider relational life of the spiritual whole. In this spiritual unification is found the essence of religion.

Thus interpreted, religion receives its conceptual grounding and validation directly from the philosophy of spirit, without the mediation of any natural theology. The latter discipline ceases to enjoy any foundational role, or even to serve as a bridge from speculation to the practical pursuit of God. Instead, it is converted into a prismatic medium for diffracting the religious elevation of the finite to the infinite spirit. All the materials assembled in natural theology are reorganized by Hegel to furnish a conceptual reformulation, rather than a speculative proof, of the meaning of man's religious attitude.

The Religious Significance of Representation. There is a puzzling feature about Hegel's reductional approach to natural theology. It would seem as though the theories of spirit and human religiousness ought to dispense with natural theology, thus ridding themselves of its systematically misleading (unless strenuously reinterpreted) talk about the relationship between the transcendent creator and His creatures. This conclusion would indeed follow, on the contrary-to-fact condition that the human spirit were perfectly lucid about its own ontological status. Yet the actual situation is that few men can follow a philosophical analysis, not

4. *Encyclopedia Logic*, p. 148; cf. *Science of Logic*, 1, 168. In *Beweise*, pp. 107–17, 149–54 (pp. 254–61, 290–304), Hegel shows: (1) that the closed contrast of finite-versus-infinite rests upon the abstract understanding and its mutually excluding sort of concepts, (2) that speculative logic alone grasps the finite in its true being as a pulsing phase in the divine life, and nevertheless (3) that this truth is already lived for human awareness in our religious elevation to infinite life, with its attendant idea of a communion or fellowship in being and knowing between God and man. But Hegel never permits the evidence of (3) to determine the infinite-finite relationship otherwise than is dictated by the ontopneumalogical principle operating in (2).

all philosophers reach the truth about absolute spirit, and even the philosopher of spirit does not fully impregnate all his thoughts and impulses with this truth. As long as the speculative truth of spirit is present in the mode of human philosophizing, there must not only be human religiosity but a religiosity which makes good use of the style of natural theology.

Hegel brings to this problem his general doctrine on the (re-)presentational use of the human mind, because his theory of finitude accounts both for the conditions of representation and for the religious use of natural theology. The decisive category in philosophy is neither the undeveloped infinite alone nor the isolated finite entity, but their unifying principle. "The true infinite is the unity of itself and the finite; and that is now the category of philosophy." [5] This categorial union is the inherent shaper of human actuality, so that man is both determinately finite and tendentially infinite. The dynamic composition in his nature finds its proper center in *man's subjective spirit,* with its inquietude not simply to remain in any given condition but to reach out beyond any set limits. Subjective spirit is the realm in which human awareness first grasps the significance of the category of the infinite-finite, and strives to realize its implications in concrete life. Representational thinking and the religious attitude are the main expressions of this striving on the part of the human composite.

When man questions the meaning of his own being and thus arouses the life of subjectivity in himself, he tends to picture his subjective spirit as "a mean placed between two extremes, *nature* and God." This is a representational way of treating the question of what our spiritual reality is. We situate ourselves between a point of departure and a goal of arrival, so that we can describe the nature of the human spirit in terms of where it comes from and where it moves toward. What we grasp through this imagery of passage is that man comes from the natural world and heads toward his own freedom, indeed, that his reality consists exactly in the movement itself from the determinate conditions of nature to self-determining and infinite freedom.

The appropriate cognitive expression of this mediating function of

5. *Encyclopedia,* editorial redaction for paragraph 246, text given in Hegel's *Sämtliche Werke,* Jubilee Edition ed. H. Glockner, vol. 9: *System der Philosophie,* Part One: *Die Logik* (Stuttgart, Frommann, 1958), p. 46. The next quotation is from the Nicolin edition of "Ein Hegelsches Fragment zur Philosophie des Geistes," p. 48.

our human subjectivity is given in the various modes of *representation* (*Vorstellung*). By Hegel's definition, "representation is the recollected or inwardized intuition, and as such is the mediator between that stage of intelligence where it finds itself immediately subject to modification and that where intelligence is in its freedom, or, as thought." [6] Human intelligence is en route in the process of interiorizing our immediate impressions and sense intuitions, incorporating them into the general field of recollected images and signs, and thus orienting itself toward pure conceptual thought. Our representational life looks constantly backward to the realm of nature and sense immediacy, and also forward to the realm of freedom and conceptual truth. And lest this complex mediating activity simply deplete our spirit rather than enrich and orient it toward the absolute totality, we develop signs, and especially the resources of language, out of the deep mine of our intelligence. They enable us not only to hold together the intuitive content and the general reference of our experience, in a set of preliminary syntheses, but also to elevate the entire world of interiority toward the spiritual life of conceptual thought.

There is a close mutual proportionment between religion and the active means of representation. The composite, transitional, and orienting character of representational intelligence makes it the most fitting medium for developing and expressing the religious attitude. The imagery used in religious life is not a purely sensuous composition, but is imagery in the course of raising itself to the universality of rational thought. Within its synthesis are included: inadequately universal concepts of the understanding (such as the nondialectical view of God as the first transcendent cause), the provisional empirical prefigurements of genuinely dialectical relations (such as generation, the reciprocity of parts of an organism, and the inner life of the Trinity), and powerful images of the dialectical principle and its unification of the divine and the human (such as the cross, the shepherd and his flock, and the vine and its branches). In its redemptive function, religious representation interweaves all these values of subjective spirit.

It can now be seen why there always remains a subordinate descriptive task for natural theology to perform, even after its demonstrative function has been completely appropriated by onto-pneuma-logic and its

6. *Encyclopedia Mind*, p. 214. See Malcolm Clark, "Logic and System: A Study of the Transition from 'Vorstellung' to Thought in the Philosophy of Hegel" (Louvain University, unpublished doctoral dissertation, 1960), and Franz Grégoire, *Études hégéliennes* (Louvain, 1958), pp. 39–46, 153–54.

whole persuasive power has been traced back to the workings of religiosity. We can no more completely dispense with a descriptive natural theology than we can with representational thinking and religion itself. As long as the absolute totality must develop itself in the mode of the finite human spirit and its representational operations, there must be a religious relationship and a cognitive formulation of that relationship in natural theology. Religion and its prolongation in natural theology are assured a hold in being, through every act wherein we become aware of our own selfhood as finite spiritual actuality, using the synthesizing and symbolizing modes of representation.

Religiosity as Source and Goal of Natural Theology. By distinguishing between the demonstrative import and the descriptive functions of natural theology, Hegel has shattered the unity of this discipline as a demonstrative-descriptive science of God. Once the speculative truth about God has been reserved for his onto-pneuma-logic, however, he hastens to reassemble the remaining shards into a unified descriptive doctrine under the aegis of human religiosity. To those pious souls who retreat from rational criticism into a supposedly invulnerable cave of private feeling and inner testimony, he serves the reminder that religion is not merely an affair of the heart but an affair of "the heart of a spirit." [7] Religious feeling is impregnated with thought and expresses the whole man's response to reality. Human intelligence is operative at each moment in the growth of the religious attitude, thus building into it an intellectual factor which cannot be successfully repressed, and which need never be feared in its probing questions. It is the responsibility of natural theology to describe the operations of the thoughtful aspect of the religious life.

Our representational imagery in religious life encourages us to give a dualistic twist to the distinction between human finitude and the spiritual absolute. We interpret it as a contrast between man and God, time and

7. *Encyclopedia Logic*, p. xxii. Hegel agrees with Hamann and Jacobi that a feelingful elevation of the heart is desirable and necessary in religion, but it must eventually lead man into the sphere of reflective thought, where he needs a philosophical method and doctrine of truth. As stated in Hegel's preface to H. F. Hinrichs' book on religion and science (see Hegel's *Berliner Schriften*, p. 76), the decisive question is whether religious content is produced and justified by feeling or whether, on the contrary, religious feeling draws its content, determination, and justification from what Hegel regards as the intrinsically valid and self-founding philosophical truth concerning man and the spiritual totality.

eternity, the source and the goal of development. We picture God as a reality which is encountered out there, beyond our world and ourselves. Having contrasted the human self with God, however, we must then fashion the means of reconciling them in a religious union. This reconciliation is partially achieved through the power of the sacred signs and sacramental actions used in worship.

But as religious agents, we must summon all the conceptual and linguistic resources of representation to elucidate and restate the relation of God and the world. Natural theology is assigned this task, and must try to execute it within the contrary internal tendencies of religious representation toward both a dualistic separation and a familiar unification of the divine and the human. In the Hegelian system, then, natural theology is the intellectual effort of the religious mind to cope with the problem of differentiation and unity, while nevertheless remaining just this side of the speculative truth about the organic spiritual whole.

The full significance of this effort is brought out only by the philosopher of religion, who is able to view both religion itself and its intellectual expression in natural theology within the clarifying context of the life of spirit. The real nature of the proofs of God's existence becomes apparent, once the philosopher of religion submits them to his twofold analysis of symptomatic reduction and judicative reconstruction.[8] The reverse movements of these two types of analysis can be seen in this schema:

SYMPTOMATIC REDUCTION

Proofs of God's existence

Finite spirit's acts of self-elevation

Man's experience of his insufficiency and the power of spirit

Active way of spirit in total return to itself

JUDICATIVE RECONSTRUCTION

Active way of spirit in total return to itself

Man's experience of his insufficiency and the power of spirit

Finite spirit's acts of self-elevation

Proofs of God's existence as affirmations of the living totality of spirit

8. The initial five lectures in Hegel's *Beweise* serve to enclose natural theology within the phenomenology of religious consciousness (symptomatic reduction), whereas the remaining lectures evaluate the proofs in the light of his theory of spirit and man's religious elevation (judicative reconstruction).

In the method of *symptomatic reduction,* the Hegelian philosopher of religion begins with the proofs as furnished by natural theology, treats them as symptoms of the restless and striving life of the human subjective spirit, and recognizes them ultimately to be the expression of our religious experience and the underlying activity of the absolute totality. This reductive elucidation then enables him to follow the reverse path of a *judicative reconstruction.* Starting with the already established onto-pneumalogical truth about the self-dirempting and self-recovering life of absolute spirit and its finite phases of development, the investigator can trace the source of the vitality and persuasiveness of inferences about God to the life of the human spirit. He can then judge their valid speculative significance to be that of pointing toward the actuality of the infinite-finite whole, not toward the existence of a transcendent God.

While natural theology regards them as irreducible and foundational, in fact the proofs have a complex spiritual history and a gradually elaborated structure which require careful inspection. Hegel assigns this task to the philosophy of religion, since it can situate the proofs within the surging life of spirit and human religious experience. The proofs found in natural theology are formalized descriptions of the self-elevating movement of the feeling and believing religious spirit of man, who gropes toward the realm of thought or reflective spirit. And this movement is, in turn, the same as the inner way or course of the organic spiritual whole itself. It employs the self-surmounting activity of finite being to achieve its own total recovery as finitizing-infinite spiritual actuality. Hegel's systematic reduction of "proofs of God" to "the way of spirit" is symbolic of his reduction of natural theology itself to the philosophy of spirit and its religious counterpart.

New light can now be shed upon the distinction between the unique demonstration of spirit and the several descriptive proofs. There is no need to multiply the ontopneumalogical demonstration itself, once its speculative truth is grasped. But a multiplication of the descriptive proofs is unavoidable, since they are expressions of the inherently plural aspects of human experience and our modes of religious ascension toward the divine. Although the empirical priming points can be indefinitely multiplied, they tend to reinforce the reciprocal tension of religious life as a movement of the soul toward God and of God toward the soul. Hence the basic division of the proofs in natural theology is into those which go from the world to God (cosmological and teleological), and that which goes from the essential idea of God to His existence (ontological). This division reflects the duality in our religious attitude and the onesided, abstract nature of any exclusive emphasis upon one of these approaches.

The *cosmological* proof echoes our fundamental experience of contingency and dependence in being. The underlying experience is not a mere registering of empirical facts, but also a minimal reflection upon certain pervasive traits in the universe and a practical response of our human reality to them. The combination of reflective and practical acts enables us to make a religious response to our cosmic situation. Because of this religious investiture of facts, Hegel states that the point of departure for the cosmological proof is not in the bare contingent events but in contingency as a determination of thought, or in the events as somehow already subject to religious interpretation. Cosmological reasoning to God is possible only because the cosmos is first given a sacral significance by man the believer.

Furthermore, the practical aspect of the religious response means that contingency is not held in isolation, but is itself related to a supervening, necessary pattern of all things. The religious mind does not remain overwhelmed by contingent existence, but assimilates it within the divine necessity which holds good for everything. In Hegel's language, the cosmological proof serves its main function in elucidating the higher "fact of the spirit . . . in its necessity," to which our religious awareness calls attention.[9] This spiritual fact is a dynamic necessity, which includes the contingent and dependent aspects of being within its pervasive pattern.

Through the cosmological proof, the religious mind can accentuate the two divine attributes of necessity and power. Just as the starting point of the inference is not purely physical, so its conclusion does not lead to a physically qualified divinity with which we are only distantly and mechanically related. For the absolute necessity in question is that of the supremely powerful principle of all beings, their active shaper and inner law. Hegel challenges Hume's classification of necessity and power as nonmoral, natural attributes, which would overpower us but not engage our moral selfhood. The Hegelian attributes do not relate us to the divine principle in a cowed and slavish manner. Instead, they assure us

9. *Beweise*, p. 83 (p. 232). On the cosmological proof, see ibid., pp. 80–157 (pp. 228–327, 347–48); *Encyclopedia Logic*, pp. 101–09. G. E. Mueller, "Hegel's Absolute and the Crisis of Christianity," in *A Hegel Symposium*, ed. D. C. Travis (Austin, 1962), pp. 83–112, stresses the catalytic role of Hegel's criticism of the theistic proofs in resolving Christianity and other religions into his own doctrine on absolute spirit.

of the intimate presence of the Other which is sought by the soul, and invite us to find rest here from our striving. There is a religious serenity of mind in acknowledging the potent and necessary presence of the divine spiritual principle in all the events of nature and human life.

Only because our religious need is not fully satisfied by this image of the divinely necessitated course of cosmic happenings, however, does the natural theologian seek another type of proof going from the world to God. *Teleological* argumentation is generated by our religious concern to ascertain that the powerful necessity operative in the world is well ordered, that it is directed to perfective ends in our own respect. When Hume and Kant conceded the persuasive power of this type of proof, they were bearing witness to the intense concentration of religious hope which impels men to scan the physical and social worlds for traces of moral purpose and a wise ordering of things for human welfare.

Hegel distinguishes sharply, nevertheless, between the positive and the negative type of teleological proof, whether it concern physical or moral purpose. Modern theodicies violate scientific and philosophical procedure, and are also unfaithful to religious conviction, because they use the positive sort of teleological proof. This approach attempts to isolate the instances of purposive order, treat them as wholly positive phenomena, and build an inference to God solely from the aspects of the universe which they represent. Such an attempt to absolutize the evidences for design and moral purpose runs counter to the contextual treatment of all data in the sciences. It also furnishes a classic example of an evacuating abstraction, which fails to respect the relational reality of its object, and hence which fails to maintain a philosophically sound concreteness in both the point of departure and the terminus of teleological inference.

The valid teleological argument is negative, in the sense that it denies that there is or ought to be a separation in this world between happiness and sorrow, between the satisfactions of life and those failures and countertendencies which constitute the evils of existence. Just as the properly interpreted cosmological argument goes from an awareness that contingent being is *not* self-sufficient, so goes the properly constructed teleological argument from an awareness that living things taken in their immediacy, and achieved ends taken just in their finite reality, are not true actuality. "For this universal end is *not* discovered in experience." [10] Nega-

10. *Beweise*, p. 170 (p. 345), italics mine. On the teleological proof, see *Philosophie der Religion*, 1, 215–18, and *Beweise*, pp. 158–71 (3, 328–52); *Encyclopedia Logic*, pp. 345–52.

tive teleology rests upon a recognition of the dialectical split which is everywhere engendered by spirit, as a means of bringing about a more richly developed unity. The process of divine growth brings forth both the finite goods and the finite evils, both the limited ends which are reached and those which fall short or lead to disorder. This is not a literal *theo*dicy, or justification of the transcendent God, but a *pneumato*dicy in justification of the inclusion of good and evil in the purposive life of infinite spirit, which only thereby manifests itself as the absolute good in the universe.

Instead of its being religiously repugnant, this conception of an absolute teleology and pneumatodicy is recommended by Hegel for accurately interpreting the religious impulse behind all our teleological inquiries. Specifically, he finds here the explanation of that somewhat disconcerting religious combination of humility before the divine and confidant intimacy with it. Authentic religious humility does not turn around a rigid contrast between finite sinful man and the good God, as theism supposes. Rather, this state of soul is called forth by the religious presentiment that the divine spiritual totality is inclusive, rather than exclusive, of all the pain and sorrow, evil and virtue, fallibility and insight, contained in our existence. Religious humility is man's attunement with, and glad acceptance of, all the conditions of life as seen within the perspective of their divine ground and fulfillment.

What the reformed teleological proof does is to give intellectual form to our religious sense of confident trust in the spiritual purpose permeating all events. We are sure that everything will turn out well at last, because we are in the hands of the absolute good, that is, the living, wise, and purposively working spiritual principle. It is this religious confidence which robs all counterarguments of decisive force, which inclines us to look for the good outcome of every situation, and which therefore endows us with a synoptic vision of the purposive harmony of the universe.

Why, then, should men bother at all to elaborate the *ontological* argument? Hegel assigns a religious reason for now reversing the order of inference and starting with the idea of the divine essence. To rely solely upon the proofs going from the world to God would be to suggest that the vivifying religious current itself has only a one-way flow, and that religion is only a finite creation of man. But the religious believer regards God as taking His own initiative in the relationship jointly constituted by the divine and human participants. The ever resurgent at-

tractiveness of the ontological approach stems from our religious resolve
to let the divine basis manifest its own presence and power in all our
thinking.[11] Our human idea of the divine essence can then be viewed as
an expression of the self-presence of the divine principle, as a self-
affirmation of its own full actuality.

Viewed in terms of content, the ontological proof is judged by Hegel
to be both less and more significant than the cosmological and teleological proofs. It is less significant, in the sense that the ontological
passage from thought to being is only the first step in the long pilgrimage
of determining the full actuality of the spiritual whole. The cosmological
attributes of power and necessity, together with the teleological attributes
of life and purposive wisdom and harmony, carry the determination of
the divine nature beyond the bare attribution of existent being. But at
the other end of the attributive scale, one must affirm the infinite actuality of spirit as including, and yet transforming and surpassing, all the
finite determinations gathered from the cosmos and human history. Here,
the ontological proof serves to designate the spiritual totality in its infinite surplus of life.

Both evaluations of the ontological proof have a religious bearing. On
the one hand, the religious mind proclaims the value of the least existent,
simply because of the presence of God in it. Just to have being, regardless of the particular form, is to share somehow in the divine perfection
and thus to be a theophany. Hence the believer can hear with equanimity
the lesson of Hegelian logic that being is only the first and poorest determination of spirit, and that existence is always caught up in the richness of essence. But he also provides the basis for the ontological proof's
maximal function, which is to convey the surpassing richness and initiative of the spiritual whole. For the inquiring religious soul, "the being
of God" signifies this divine center of all values and active power, which
is formally symbolized in our ontological thinking.

Having surrounded natural theology by religion at all points, Hegel
formally relativizes the theory of God in respect to the philosophy of
religion.

> If we proposed to treat only the *theologia naturalis*, that is, the doc-
> trine of God as object, the object of religion, then the very concept

11. The ontological argument is rehabilitated in *Philosophie der Religion*, 1, 218–
25, and *Beweise*, pp. 172–77 (3, 353–67); *Science of Logic*, 1, 98–102; *Encyclopedia
Logic*, pp. 330–34.

of God would lead us over to religion as such, provided that this concept had been grasped in genuine speculation, not after the manner of the old metaphysics only [as] a determination of the understanding. The concept of God is its idea to become and make itself objective. This is contained in God as *spirit*. . . . Hence the concept of God leads necessarily of itself to religion.[12]

Variations in this concept of God stem from and issue in religious variations. This religious reference acts as a norm for determining the validity and completeness of all concepts of God affirmed in natural theology.

The several views of God, progressively determined by religious thought and formalized in the theological proofs, have the immediate practical effect of pluralizing and differentiating man's *general* religious response to the divine, so that it can become effective in several *special kinds* of religious action. "That which man deems he has to do in relation to God depends upon his representation of God, and conversely he cannot deem that he has to do anything determinate in respect to God, if he has or deems he can have no knowledge, acquaintance, in general no determinate representation of God." Since our representational thinking about God brings out different facets of His nature, the several descriptive proofs in which those different facets get expressed must be correlated with the specific kinds of religious actions and the religions of mankind. This practical ordering of the proofs completes the total religionizing of natural theology, as a function within Hegel's philosophy of religion.

PROOFS OF GOD AND ATTRIBUTES	RELIGIOUS ACTIONS	KINDS OF RELIGION
Cosmological: power and necessity	Revere sacred forces in nature	Religions of nature
Teleological: life, purposive mind, goodness	Respect human form and attend to conscience	Religions of spiritual individuality, art, and morality
Ontological: being, infinite actuality, spirit	Accept divine revelation and serve the human community	Absolute religion of Christian revelation, preparing men for philosophy of spirit

12. *Philosophie der Religion*, 1, 156 (1, 90, 101); the next quotation, ibid., 1, 161 (1, 69). The threefold correlation between proofs, religious actions, and kinds of definite religions is made (ibid., 1, 68–76 [1, 79–85]).

The complete enclosure of natural theology within the theory of religion is seen in the above functional correlation, which holds between the three specific kinds of descriptive proofs of God and the three definite kinds of human religion. Our present task is not to comment on the particular types of religions, but simply to notice how radical Hegel intends the religious ingestion of natural theology to be. Just as natural theology arises from the practical striving of human religiosity in general, so does it terminate in a practical act of structuring man's specific religious responses. Once the differentiated forms of religion loom into sight, human religiosity can develop its potentialities in several practical ways. Hence the main interest of the philosopher of religion now turns to the practical relations between religion and politics, the religious significance of artistic activity, and the culminating problem of Christianity and the philosophy of spirit.

POLITICS AND RELIGION

In its dialectical course of development, spirit moves from the realm of pure onto-pneuma-logic to the realms of nature and the human spirit. It reaches one climactic point in the ethical life of the state, which concentrates in itself all the energies of our subjective spiritual life of knowing and willing, as well as those energies of objective spirit which display themselves in the family and our economic and cultural values. Since religion has both a subjective side in the inner life of faith and devotion and an objective institutional side, it is intimately involved in the concrete unification achieved through the laws and power of the state. But what is the precise nature of the involvement? Does it lead to a one-way subordination of religion to the state, or of the state to religion? And do the quality and direction of religion affect the organized worldly community in a radical or a superficial manner?

In facing these questions, Hegel was able to draw upon his quite detailed historical analysis of the political evolution of the Holy Roman Empire and the modern Germanic states. In *The German Constitution,* he devoted a separate chapter to historical evidence on the important role of religion in determining the political growth of the Germanic world. During the medieval period, the political unity and activity of the Germanic people depended upon their sharing a common religious belief and pursuing common religious goals.

Religion is that wherein men's innermost being is expressed, and, even if all other external and separated things may be insignificant, men yet recognize themselves in religion as a fixed center; only thereby could they have been able to transcend the variety and mutability of their other relationships and situations and so to win the confidence in one another and become sure of one another. Here in religion at least an identity might have been thought necessary, but this identity too is something which modern states have found that they can do without. In northern Europe, religious unity has hitherto always been the fundamental condition of a state. Nothing else was known, and without this original oneness no other oneness or trust has been found possible. Occasionally this very bond has become so potent that more than once it has suddenly transformed into one state peoples which were otherwise strange to one another and national enemies.[13]

Thus in the medieval situation, when neither the economic forces nor the state power and constitution were highly developed, religion welded men in an inner connection of dispositions. It helped them to achieve that social identity, based upon mutual recognition, trust, and search for a common good, in which the life of the state essentially consists. From this phase of the Germanic political experience, it might be concluded that religious belief and practice are always foundational for the state's own reality.

But Hegel also found, in later phases of this same political history, a concrete indication of the disruptive potentialities which also stem from religion. With the modern growth of the bourgeois spirit in industry and culture, there was an individualization of dispositions and a primary concern for particular interests in society. The Germanic peoples were faced with a choice between strengthening the universal political power or subjecting it to the egoistic drives of the individual will. Not only was the latter course taken, but it carried the blessing of the Christian churches. The established churches in the modern Germanic states lent their religious sanction to the fracturing of political unity. They convinced

---

13. *The German Constitution*, in *Hegel's Political Writings*, trans. T. M. Knox (Oxford, Clarendon Press, 1964), pp. 158–59; the next quotation, ibid., p. 192. On the theological presuppositions of Hegel's political theory, cf. Günther Rohrmoser, "Die theologischen Voraussetzungen der Hegelschen Lehre vom Staat," *Hegel-Studien*, Beiheft 1 (1964), 239–45.

their adherents that the religious split at the Reformation should be reflected in a split among the centers of political power.

Thus the dispersal of the Germanic states was viewed as being merely the external consequence of the inner division of heart and conscience. Here the effect of religion was not only to induce a rupture in the broader political community, but also to weave itself into the very constitutions of the weakened particular states. Each established church regarded its type of religion as the basis of political rights, including the civil rights of all citizens within the organized territory of the state. By stressing the supreme importance of religious matters and the relative insignificance of political affairs and civil rights, the confessional leaders were able to weaken the moral importance of state law and constitutional rights, except when they were considered as reflected expressions of the divine will.

Even in the midst of this thorough débâcle of political society in the Germanic world, however, Hegel discerned a positive line of development on the part of objective spirit. The very ambivalence of particular religions, as sometimes strengthening and sometimes undermining the social dispositions of a people, brought home the point that political reality must secure its own foundation in human nature and its own rational justification. Men came to see that they could not exercise what Hegel called "the higher natural rights of freedom of conscience and the non-dependence of civil rights on faith," unless there were such a self-grounding of the political order in the moral and social tendencies of man.

Thus Hegel interpreted the modern movement toward separation of church and state as a stage in the self-clarification of human thinking about both the nature of the state and the nature of religion. This separation was a necessary condition for grasping the natural roots and the rational need for the political community, which in its perfected condition need not be mediated by a particular religious confession or an established church. Reciprocally, disestablishment helped men to realize that the potentialities of religion are never exhausted by any particular ecclesiastical arrangement, and that the freedom of religion depends upon its always remaining open to new relationships with the state, in accord with new historical conditions.

But the constitutional separation of church and state by no means resolves the problem of religion and politics today. For there is still a close and valid intermingling of religious conviction with all the phases of social life which get correlated and unified within the political order.

A philosophical analysis of the interpenetration of religious and political factors is needed, and Hegel undertakes this task in some long passages in his *Encyclopedia of the Philosophical Sciences, Philosophy of Right,* and *Philosophy of Religion.*[14] These texts provide a classic example of how he marshals the full resources of his philosophical method and system in resolving a particular issue in the philosophy of religion.

Characteristically, Hegel takes his point of departure in the common saying that the state and political life must somehow be based upon religion. Having already repudiated the theory of an established church and an ecclesiastical qualification for civil rights, he must now clarify and evaluate the several valid senses in which there can nevertheless be a close relationship between the religious and political life of a people. To clear the atmosphere of misleading suggestions, he first disposes of the view that the relationship is purely extrinsic and contingent. This is implied in the position that religion is superimposed upon an already fully constituted political community, either to shore up the latter or else to provide solace and extraterrestrial hope for its discouraged members. Hegel speaks sarcastically about those political rulers who make an apologetic use of religion, importing it by the bushel as a means of generating a sacral aura around a particular government and thus stifling any popular unrest or political reform. Such an exploitation of the sacred is degrading for both religion and the state, since it obscures the distinctive form of both these principles of social living.

In order to make some positive sense out of the common conviction that political society does somehow draw upon the resources of religious life, Hegel makes two key distinctions: (a) between the state as the full actuality of the ethico-political community ("the state proper") and as a bureaucratic organization, and (b) between the restricted ethico-political analysis of religion and the ultimate philosophical analysis of religion. The Hegelian problem of politics and religion can be more precisely stated as one which concerns the relationship between the state proper, or fully developed ethical actuality, and the religious life considered precisely from the restricted perspective of being a component

14. *Encyclopedia Mind,* pp. 281–90; *Philosophy of Right,* trans. T. M. Knox (Oxford, Clarendon Press, 1962), pp. 165–74, 283–85; *Philosophie der Religion,* 1, 302–11 (1, 246–57). Eugène Fleischmann's *La Philosophie politique de Hegel* (Paris, 1964), pp. 282–92, locates the properly political problem of religion and the state in the teaching and social welfare functions of religion, leaving the critique of the internal act of faith to the philosophy of religion and metaphysical logic.

within the ethical community which is the state. In other words, it is a problem of viewing the state in the plenary sense of being the objective actualization of spirit in its ethical form, and viewing religion precisely in its important but limited function of shaping the human materials which enter into this political actualization of spirit. Only at the end of this comparative study does religion stand forth in its full reality and transpolitical purpose.

Hegel's detailed analysis of the relationship is guided by three very general statements: first, religion serves as the basis or groundwork (*Grundlage*) for the state; secondly, religion is no more than the groundwork and hence is not the completed ethical actuality, or the state itself; and finally, the objective actuality of the state ministers in turn to the more intense actualization of the spiritual life, which is found in the area of art-religion-philosophy. Thus religion is both the basis and the outcome of ethico-political life. Or rather, religion is present in such a way as to be both an incorporated factor within the concrete ethical community and also a distinctive value which is teleologically nourished by that community.

Religious Basis of Political Life. To say that religion is basic to the political ethos of mankind is to affirm its shaping influence upon personal morality. Within the Hegelian dialectic, the state or ethical actuality includes (within itself) the more abstract moments of individual morality and public law and organization. The relative abstractness of the sphere of morality does not spell its exclusion from the concrete actuality of the state, but rather its intimate inclusion as an essentially required phase and hence a foundation or groundwork of the ethical community. Hegel agrees with Kant that the Christian religion has deeply influenced the moral order by making mankind aware of the distinctive realm of subjectivity, the inviolable freedom of the human subject, and the infinite value of personality.

These thoughts cannot be kept sealed off in the sphere of individual morality, however, since the human personal subjects in question are essentially social and strive to realize their own value within the ethico-political community. The quality of human political life itself has been indelibly modified through the growth in moral self-awareness aroused by religious belief and doctrines. In this sense the religious spirit works at the human basis of the state, strengthening the quality of political living.

Hegel emphasizes the respect owed to the interior realm of moral conscience and religious belief and doctrine. Their incorporation into the political community is not an act of surrender and loss of integrity, but one of relating one valuable aspect of human reality to another in a fruitful tension. The state must respect, not invade, the zone of free interiority where the person forms his own moral conscience and develops his religious life. It is not the state's business to dictate anything concerning the inner realm of religious belief or the distinctive content of religious doctrine. They belong within the scope of human subjectivity, which must relate itself in free and orderly fashion to our other concerns and also retain its own inviolable pattern of being.

Religion within Ethical Actuality. Within the religious perspective itself, there can be no refusal to enter into the world and accept the conditions of cooperative work in the ethical community. Restricting religion to the free inner sphere of subjectivity would be equivalent to planting a seed and then frustrating its existential manifestation and growth. An effective human religion must engage in visible worship and make a sacramental use of material things. It seeks not only to elaborate a doctrinal content within the minds of theologians but also to communicate the word, and educate generations of men in its doctrine. Furthermore, religion impels us to engage in the service of others, to mold the material resources and the community relationships so that they will aid men in fulfilling their vocation in this world. But all these requirements—worship and rite, doctrine and education, and service of the community—would be merely an ineffectual aspiration, were it not for the religious organizing of men and property in forms of worldly social power. Religion cannot satisfy its own dynamism without developing the manpower and material for realizing its actional purposes, and in the course of doing so it also implicates itself irretrievably in the common human order of property, civil laws, and worldly relations.

At this point in the argument, the religious mind may balk at its immanent political incorporation, by contending that the religious attitude is one of transcendence and orientation away from this world and its glory. Hegel meets this challenge precisely in his role as philosopher of religion; that is, as the reflective investigator who uses the norm of the doctrine on spirit to interpret and correct the self-witnessing of believers. After granting the function of religion in arousing men to break with the condition of untroubled immediacy, he then points out that religiosity is expressive of something definite, namely, the common life of spirit. But when spirit is considered in its free and essential history, it is seen to be ordered by its own nature and impetus toward an objective social actualization in the comprehensive ethical community of men. This is the more profound sense in which religion is at the basis of the state. The same spiritual current of life which inclines men toward religious belief and practice also moves them toward the objective unification of men and resources within the constitutional order and laws of the state. Fidelity of the believer to the promptings of the spirit leads to a mundane development of religious existence within the framework and opportunities of civil society, not to a flight from this world and its profane lures.

Hegel does not sidestep the problem of a conflict between religious and political judgment. When such a conflict concerns the values being objectively realized in the human ethical community, the ultimate decision must lie with the state. As he puts it, the problem is not simply to render God His due and Caesar his due, but to determine in the first place what does properly belong to Caesar. It must fall within the competence of human ethicality or the ethical community of the state to determine this issue, since men as organized within that community have their own principles, aims, and methods of action. They have the right to judge matters in accord with the ethical idea and the distinctive perspective which it opens up concerning human relationships in our world. In this sense, the state has the power and right to maintain its own conviction and objective truth, even to the ultimate point of making a definitive settlement of disputes with religion concerning the unified earthly community.

Hegel will not permit anyone to encroach upon this competence by invoking the traditional formula of the church's authority in matters of faith and morals, where "morals" may concern matters of vital interest to men joined in the ethico-political community. He appeals to the limiting principle of the representational nature of all religious thinking: all religiously grounded judgments on human society remain veiled under the form of symbolic imagery. Hence they are expressed as evaluations made on the basis of faith, authority, and inner devotional conviction. Judgments about the affairs of the ethico-political community made under these forms have not attained to the requisite reflective control over the specific problems, sources of evidence, and methods of resolution proportionate to political living. Men have developed the political order of thought and action, precisely so that they may know what they are doing when they make up their minds in this domain.

What the religious believer fails to realize, in his fascination with the realm of inner piety and subjective feeling, is "the prodigious transfer of the inner into the outer, the building of reason into the real world. . . . The divine spirit must interpenetrate the entire secular life." [15] The inward-turning soul underestimates the tremendous effort of the human spirit to master the natural world and to bring order into interhuman relationships at all levels. That this endeavor to understand and order the spheres of nature and society is basically a spiritual enterprise, fails to come home with utter seriousness to the believer who narrows down the meaning of spirituality to formally religious exercises. Although he is a follower of the spirit, he fails to notice or at least to appreciate its powerful operation in the secular human efforts oriented toward nature and social life. The spiritual, and indeed the religious, meaning of modern secularity tends to escape the believer, to the degree that he fails to submit to the discipline and order of the earthly community.

Hegel regards the political formation of the modern mind as the attainment of the standpoint of knowing, not unqualifiedly but with respect to the social development of objective spirit. Hence he can emphatically define the state's essential aim as that of working as "the self-*knowing* ethical actuality of spirit." [16] Although this or that particular state falls miserably short of realizing the goal of self-clarification about our objective social relationships, such is the internal teleology inciting men to join in the ethico-political community. Especially in the Reformed Christian view of the state as willed by God, Hegel found a symbolic glint of this truth concerning the state proper. Respect for the state can be generated either religiously, by treating it as an expression of God's will, or philosophically, by treating it as the objective social development of spirit. The former method entails all the disadvantages of the theistic conception of a transcendent God, legislating for the contingent products of His will. But at least it can dispose the mind to look for spiritual significance, and not merely the naked display of power and the mechanism of compromise, in the state.

The philosopher of spirit will always translate this religious imagery,

15. *Philosophy of Right*, p. 167; *Encyclopedia Mind*, p. 285. The main argument of Karl Löwith's *From Hegel to Nietzsche: The Revolution in Nineteenth-Century Thought*, trans. D. E. Green (New York, Holt, 1964), is that Hegel himself did not carry this prodigious transfer far enough into practical life, but remained content with "a reconciliation *not in reality, but in the ideal world*" (p. 40). It was left for Feuerbach, Marx, and Nietzsche to dissolve the ideal reconciliation of religion and the social order and to orient philosophy toward purely immanent tasks in this world.

16. *Philosophy of Right*, p. 173; cf. ibid., pp. 165, 171.

however, into the reflective truth that "the state is the divine will, in the sense that it is spirit present on earth, unfolding itself to be the actual shape and organization of a world." [17] Elsewhere, Hegel refers to the state as something *divine* which we must venerate on earth, as this actual God of our everyday existence, and as the course which God takes in our world. The theistic tone of these expressions is a persuasive but provisional way of disposing us to accept his analysis of the ethico-political community, in terms of a distinctive phase in the self-differentiation of the spiritual totality. Like every other phase in this development, the state can rightfully be called divine and infinite, somewhat in the same sense in which the Greeks spoke of every manifestation of spiritual power as divine and worthy of veneration. Yet in calling the state as such divine, Hegel raised the standard for appraising all the particular states in human history, rather than covering them over with a mantle of religious approval. Whatever hesitancies he felt about evaluating presently existing states and charting the political future were due to his general theory of spirit, rather than to the role assigned to religion in the state.

From his philosophical study of the structures involved, Hegel concludes that there can be no simple means-end relationship between religion and the state. Each one serves the other, and each one retains its own structure and finality. This is the situation which normally obtains within any living whole, where the various organs serve each other reciprocally as ends and means in a single system. Religion aids the state by arousing in the people a sense of their personal dignity, by proposing a social ideal of active service to others, and by inculcating respect for the ethico-political community and its laws. And the state in turn enables the religious spirit to move beyond the sphere of private convictions and sentiments into the actual world of rational discipline and objective fulfillment of intent.

This mutual service does not exhaust the significance of either order. Each is a final end in itself, in the sense that it retains and actualizes its own structure and values. The state is not purely instrumental to the welfare of religion, because it aids religion only in the course of realizing its own distinctive destiny as the objective ethical actualization of spirit. Similarly, the service which religion renders to the state is done in the course of executing its own task of lifting the minds and hearts of men

17. *Philosophy of Right*, p. 166. Reliable commentaries on this text are made by Grégoire, *Études hégéliennes*, pp. 330–36, and by Eric Weil, *Hegel et l'État* (Paris, 1950), pp. 44–54.

to spiritual actuality. Religion and the political order are ends in themselves, which nevertheless belong within the total human situation and minister to each other's finality. They remain distinctive, yet interrelated, formations of the striving human spirit.

The Religious Telos of Society. What remains for us to consider is the sense in which religion maintains a certain superiority over the political order, even though it cannot break loose from the total human situation wherein both of them are component members. To raise this question is to shift the perspective from religion as an internal basis within the development of political society to religion as a teleological principle, toward which our entire objective social existence is ordered. This is a move from the minimal view of religion as a social ingredient to its maximal significance for man. Religion involves itself in the ethico-political community, so that the latter can furnish the best context for bringing the religious quest itself to purposive completion.

In the introductory statement of his *Lectures on the Philosophy of History,* Hegel maintains that "religion is the sphere where a people gives itself the definition of what it regards as the true." [18] Such a definition is present initially only in the form of a prophetic vision or a social ideal, which must be explicated and tested by its power to master the material forces and organize the social relationships sustained by that people. The stuff of world history is furnished by the efforts of different peoples to express their own facet of truth, and to organize the visible world around a unifying ideal. The providential interpretation of history has always sought to show the presence of a general pattern, which fulfills the divine will through the very interplay and conflict of particular social aims and political destinies. Hegel himself offers a nontheistic version of providence at work in history, by regarding the various social ideals and their realization in particular states as so many phases in the objective social actualization of the spiritual whole.

A spiritual interpretation of world history fails to satisfy the religious mind, however, if the synthesis confines itself to the way in which spirit manifests itself in the objective social order. The life of spirit is not exhaustively expressed in the ethico-political community as such or in the historical relationships among the state powers in this world, and conse-

18. *Reason in History,* trans. R. S. Hartman (New York, Liberal Arts Press, 1953), p. 64.

quently the religious search cannot terminate itself at this point of concentration. It seeks a still richer actualization of the spiritual life, not
indeed apart from human history and the political community but within
them regarded precisely as a nourishing context, rather than as the unconditioned, ultimate purpose of man. Religion bears witness within us
to the need for the further spiritual endeavors constituting the realms of
art, religion in the formal sense, and philosophy itself.

ART AND RELIGION

Within the Hegelian system, we can distinguish three standard uses
for the term "religion." First, it is used in the most inclusive generic
sense to designate *every phase* in the restless development of finitude,
insofar as it embodies an essential ordination toward infinite spiritual
life, whether that ordination be a logical relationship, a mode of nature,
or an aspect of our conscious life and social activity. All aspects of being,
together with all stages in the analysis of being, are fraught with religious
significance to the degree that they are teleologically working out the
active relationship between finite and infinite spirit. In the second place,
the term functions as a broad but definite designation of the *entire realm
of absolute spirit* (comprising art-religion-philosophy as a complex whole),
where finite life is aware of the infinite, spiritual character of its goal
and hence grasps the absolute in its own nature as spirit. Man clarifies
his natural environment and his own historical efforts sufficiently to discover their common orientation toward spiritual actuality in its living
fullness, and thus he takes a broadly religious attitude toward all forms
of becoming and striving. Nevertheless, this clarification is actually
achieved through the three distinct modalities of art, *religion in the most
formal and determinate sense*, and philosophy. Hence in its third and
most closely qualified usage, the term refers to that particular, internal
phase of absolute spirit in which we acknowledge the absolute in its
spiritual nature, but through the medium of representational imagery
and feeling.

There are some clear systematic advantages for Hegel in maintaining
the distinction between the second and third meanings of religion.[19] For
one thing, it strengthens his claim to have incorporated all the human
roots and modalities of religion. The many facets of religious meaning in
human experience are unified and directed toward the explicit pursuit of

19. See *Encyclopedia Mind*, pp. 291–92; *The Philosophy of Fine Art*, trans. F. P.
Osmaston (4 vols. London, 1920), 1, 138–39.

spiritual actuality as such through religion, considered in its second or broadly determinant meaning. Next, the distinction in question enables Hegel to bring out the general religious significance of art, without concentrating exclusively upon sacred art. The latter is only a portion of the vast field of art, and it sometimes obscures the broader religious meaning of artistic activity as a whole, which his philosophy is fitted to underline. Another major advantage is that the dialectical overcoming of religion by philosophy can be rendered credible beforehand, by giving the name of religion to the entire order of absolute spirit. This softens the contrast between religion as a particular moment within this order and philosophy as such. Being the doctrine of infinite spiritual life, philosophy already embraces the whole content of religious existence and truth in the broader sense, and thus inevitably surpasses the more specially construed particular content of religion.

Above all, the second and mediating meaning of religion signifies the great religious turn on the part of mankind. This turn is taken not only within the context furnished by our psychic and social life but also on the basis of the experienced dissatisfactions and inadequacy of that life. Man lives through his experience of nature and history with sufficient reflectiveness to see that his capacities cannot, in principle, be satisfied by the natural forms of finitude, pursued in isolation from the infinitely differentiating life of spirit. There must be a direct relating of the world and all its physical and cultural modes of existence to spiritual actuality, taken precisely in its purposive divine unity, and this is the work of man in his broadly religious orientation. The religious turning is a distinctively human act, accomplishing itself in man's personal interiority and his community life. And as interpreted by philosophy of religion, this turning is at the same time the *re*-turning of absolute spirit to itself. The latter wins its spiritual selfhood through and across all the forms of estrangement and finitude, which now respond to the religious teleology of mankind.

Here is the basis for Hegel's claim that all men have a vocation to share in religion. Insofar as the perfecting of the human spirit involves some participation in the broad religious turning and orienting of man and his world toward the infinite spiritual totality, there is a common call to develop our human religiousness. Although not all men are called to be philosophers, they must all bring to maturity their reasonable human nature and its capacities for the spiritual life. "Religion is the kind and mode of consciousness in which the truth appeals to all men, to men of every degree of education." [20] In the second sense just enumerated, then, religiousness signifies the maturation of spiritual life precisely insofar as this is the shared responsibility and right of all men.

Art, religion in the third or more restricted sense, and philosophy share in the same *content* of truth, since they are constituted by the same comprehensive act of relating the finite modes of life to the infinite whole. They jointly acknowledge spirit to be the center of all substantial power and subjective value. But this common acknowledgment is bound to be phased and differentiated in three distinct ways, since the paths of the artist, the believer, and the philosopher to spiritual actuality remain distinct in regard to their *form*, or manner of determining the relationship and sharing it with others. [21]

The artist relies upon sensuous intuition and visible forms to develop and express his perspective on the absolute; the man of religion operates in the medium of representational thinking and feeling to capture his mode of participating in the life of spirit; and only the philosopher brings all these relational modes to their operational completion and clarification in his pure speculative thought. With the philosopher, the form of apprehension is at last perfectly suited to the content of spiritual actuality. Thus the broadly religious attitude of man demands both an essential unity of content and an internal differentiation in the forms of apprehending and expressing that content.

Hegel is very sensitive to the objection that his conception of art is too religious and spiritual in its emphasis, leaving out many elements which do not fit his perspective and cutting down drastically on the actual forms of artistic activity. Yet without claiming to give an exhaustive account of all the components and varieties of art, he nevertheless justifies his approach in function of the kind of questions he must ask about art. He wants to know what basic need of the human soul is satisfied by this activity, and how the artistic endeavor can be most effectively and generally synthesized with the other great aims of our life.

---

20. *Encyclopedia Logic*, p. xx.

21. The systematic distinction between the common content and the diverse forms of the three supreme modes of spiritual life is worked out in *Science of Logic*, 2, 466–67; *Encyclopedia Mind*, pp. 303–04; *Philosophy of Right*, pp. 216, 222–23; *Fine Art*, 1, 139–44. The co-determinate modes of artistic, religious, and philosophical actuality constitute a cultural individuality, a determinate spirit of a given people (*Die Vernunft in der Geschichte*, ed. J. Hoffmeister [5th ed. Hamburg, 1955], p. 123); cf. the approximately corresponding place in *Reason in History*, p. 63.

In seeking to determine how art serves as one of the great unifiers of our experience, he stresses its mode of acquainting us with the spiritual totality, and thus associates it closely with religion and philosophy.

Hegel maintains that art is spiritual truth existing in a sensuously perceivable form, and hence that art is broadly and essentially religious in significance. He is just as careful as Kant is to avoid reducing esthetic judgment and artistic activity to the cognitive mode found in physical science and morality. Yet he does not regard art as utterly noncognitive, as a mode of making and expressing which involves no knowing. On the contrary, it brings a new reach of vision into our lives, and helps us to apprehend the spiritual meaning of experience as an integral whole.

> Art rests upon and originates from the interest in exhibiting the spiritual idea for consciousness, and above all for *immediate vision,* precisely because man is consciousness, envisioning consciousness, not mere sensation, and more deeply because, as noted earlier, the standpoint of religion itself is not the standpoint of sensation, but a more perfectly developed standpoint. . . . It is art's function to reveal *truth* under the mode of art's sensuous or material configuration.[22]

Through its own sensuous media of apprehension and expression, then, art conveys a content of signification which is basically spiritual and religious in nature.

In his further statement that veritable art is religious art, Hegel is not making any extremist attempt to contract the whole field to the narrow closure of sacred art. Rather, his intent is to direct our attention to the intimate historical links between art and the religions of mankind. There is a religious teleology for all forms of art, in the sense that artistic activity prepares the world for a religious interpretation. The artist succeeds in gathering together the scattered moments of existence into stable, unified forms, which convince us that life does have some unity and spiritual significance. At the same time, the artist shows by his dedicated work how powerful the human urge is to incarnate our spiritual meanings in the existing material world. Thus his mediating presence in the human community testifies to the religious vocation of man to unite matter and meaning, nature and spirit, in a living community. In this respect, art serves as the evangelical preparation for the specific religious

22. *Philosophie der Religion,* 1, 281 (1, 138); *Fine Art,* 1, 77. The statement about veritable art is from *Philosophie der Religion,* 2, 225 (2, 115).

attitude, which needs encouragement in its search for the divine basis of nature and human society, as well as for the fitting sensuous expressions of spiritual reality.

Hegel would perhaps welcome, and generalize beyond the sphere ot Christian theism, this vigorous sentence from the Welsh poet, David Jones: "Something has to be made by us before it can become for us his sign who made us. This point he [Christ] settled in the upper room. No artefacture no Christian religion." [23] Religious worship as a human act depends upon the making acts which provide us with the bread and the wine, the book and the organ, the tabernacle and the scroll. Whatever may be the peculiar personal intentions of the artists who fashion these means, the making activity as such possesses a larger sacramental signification. It invites men to attend to the symbolic function of material things and artifacts, as well as to look for new ways of expressing the sacred relationships between man, the cosmos, and the divine power present in them both. There is a reconciling outcome of artistic activity, insofar as it joins the human intent with the sensuous medium, thus giving fresh momentum to the religious orientation of the experienced world to a spiritual goal.

In the development of our religious life, art performs a valuable noetic and emotive service. Its purpose is neither to expound any religious doctrines as such nor to claim to convey a special insight into their truth as religious teachings. But religion could scarcely become a communicable vision and a social power, if it could not draw upon the treasury of the human arts in order to win our assent and move the heart through song and statue, story and sacrament. These resources of human art make the difference between an abstract theological doctrine and a religion which lives in the feelings and concrete intelligence of men. Since it belongs to the very nature of human religiosity to bring the common content of spiritual actuality into our lives with emotive intimacy and force, the alliance between art and religion is essential for the latter's well-being. A religious community seeking to embody its pattern of meaning in our visible world, and to arouse the practical response of devotion and mutual service among its members, cannot regard the contribution of art as an expendable frill.

In dealing with the definite forms of religion, Hegel devotes special

23. David Jones, *The Anathemata* (London, Faber and Faber, 1952), p. 31.

attention to their various ways of employing the resources of art.[24] For him, as well as for Schleiermacher (whose discourses *On Religion* influenced his thought on the plurality of religions), this is a major way of distinguishing between the religions of nature, spiritual individuality, and revelation. In the case of the early religions of *nature*, art remains in a definitely subordinate position. Insofar as the divinity is associated with a certain place or animal, the religious energy of a people is directly centered upon the spiritual presence in these objects of perception. Art enables men to discern this presence, ornament its earthly setting, and recall the glory of the scene. Within the framework of the religions of nature, nevertheless, there is another tendency to stress the vast divine power itself and hence to notice the inadequacy of the sacred times, places, and objects which give it an earthly habitation. It is this religious straining toward infinity that accounts for the prevalence of symbolic modes of art, especially architectural works, where visible reference is made to an indeterminate spiritual reality. The great Egyptian temples enable men to manifest their religious belief in the divine power of light, but the symbolic style points transcendently beyond every sensible configuration involved in the act of worship.

It is only with the religions of *spiritual individuality* (Jewish, Greek, and Roman), however, that the urgency of the problem of art and religion is realized. The conscious and imperious need for art in the service of religion develops only when men become aware of their free subjectivity and the order of spiritual values. Believers then come to realize that religion must also concern itself somehow with this same human subjectivity. This places a severe strain upon the visible signs of the religious relationship, since they must now express a divine reality similar to our subjective life of spirit, and not merely the presence of an indefinite cosmic power. Artists must furnish the spiritually more developed sacred signs through which the new level of religious awareness is

24. For this correlation, consult *Phenomenology*, pp. 694–750; *Encyclopedia Mind*, pp. 295–97; *Philosophie der Religion*, 3, 111–91, 224–34 (2, 110–22, 224–88), on Greek religion of beauty; *Fine Art*, 1, 237–40, and the entire second part (vol. 2 of translation). Hegel usually reserves the term "symbolic" for the art form corresponding to the more developed religions of nature and applies it to religion itself only rarely and in the pejorative sense of an empty form. The term is used more broadly here to denote the signifying function of all the modes of religion, as they furnish man with a presentiment of the spiritual power in the universe. Cf. Schleiermacher's *On Religion*, pp. 139–42, 210–53, on the pluralizing of religion into its three types.

sustained. This is a good illustration of Hegel's contextual view of religion as being dependent, in its definite forms, upon all the cultural factors actually present in an age. There is a reciprocal determination between the religions of spiritual individuality and the plastic arts which flourish along with them.

Hegel's love for the Greeks breaks forth anew at this point to endow the cultural co-determination of art and religion among the Greeks with altogether special significance. He describes their outlook as being at once the religion of humanity and the religion of beauty: it is the former in such an intense fashion that it can be nothing else than the latter. The Greek people were convinced not only of the divine values found in human life but also of the adequacy of artistic renditions of the human form to express those values to our senses. Thus the poetry and statuary of this culture dwelled upon the gods in human form, so that in beholding their beauty we might also satisfy our religious quest for the actualization of the spiritual order. This was the one moment in human history when a complete fusion occurred between the religion and the art of a people. Religion did not simply employ an art form here: it found its entire meaning and purpose realized in the production and festive celebration of art works.

Hegel underscored the directly religious function of the Greek poets and artists, whose creative activity produced the gods of Greece in making the stories and statues of the divine in human form. In their imaginative productions, these creators did more than invent pleasant or awesome fictions.

> Art was the highest medium under which the community conceived its gods, and became conscious of truth. For this reason we may justly say that the poets and artists of Greece created the gods of their people. They defined for the imagination of their people the active life and energy of the divine presence, giving them the definite content of a religion.[25]

Hence in expressing their own conception of the values present in human life, the shapers of beauty were at the same time serving the creative religious force of the Greek community. The Greek gods were fashioned out of man's own imaginative and passional materials. But they were also a gift of the divine spirit working in nature and human society, and

25. *Fine Art,* 1, 140.

hence they gave men a sense of confidence in the divine basis of human and natural existence together.

Hegel located both the glory and the defect of the Greek religious attitude in the same property of its constituting a religion of humanity and beauty. The strong point in this position was the perfect correspondence between a people's religious aspirations and their conception of human nature, so that in giving worship to the divine they did not detract in any way from the honor of the human. But to achieve this serene adequation between the divine and the human, their point of union had to be conceived in an abstract way. The Greeks had to assume that there is nothing incomprehensible about the gods, that their entire reality can be understood in the act of knowing man's finite nature. This assumption betrayed a lack of awareness of the problem of relating finite to infinite subjectivity, in which concrete relationship alone the nature of the divine is properly acknowledged.

And on the human side, the Greeks achieved their calm serenity by subjecting both gods and men to the impersonal rule of rational necessity and moral law. Nothing was left for the individual will to do, except submit eventually to these universal forces of fate, and enjoy the simple grief of declaring: it is so and must be accepted. Finite subjectivity was still left fallow, for lack of placing upon it the ultimate demand of struggling toward a new reconciliation of the universal law and the suffering human person. For all its humanistic immanence, Greek religion failed to integrate into its reasonable pattern that uncertain "beyond," or contingent sphere, consisting of the concrete circumstances and individual relationships between man and the divine.

In making this criticism, Hegel is clearly preparing a transition from the natural religions and the Greek standpoint to Christianity as the *absolute revelational* religion, that is, to the religion which does wrestle with all the tensions between the infinite spirit and man's spiritual individuality. Our immediate interest is confined, however, to showing that this transition has deeply affected the relationship between art and religion. The Greek experiment shows the need to retain the distinction between these two provinces of spirit, and hence to develop art works which have a religious significance precisely because of their *in*-adequation to the divine spirit and the religious search of man. Maturation of the religious attitude depends upon our understanding that the shortcomings in the Greek religion of humanity and beauty portend not only that religion must move beyond the Greek religious position, but also that religiousness as such must firmly distinguish itself from art. Post-Hellenic religion can never expect to find its full actualization in the artistic presentation of the divine.

The Christian belief in the Incarnation does, indeed, encourage a new intensity of artistic activity to express the union of the infinite and the finite in finite form. Hegel's own preference is for the Madonna in the pietà situation and for representations of Christ surrounded by His disciples at the table, rather than for the depiction of heaven-aspiring saints or for music trailing off to an indeterminate, sentimental infinity. The pietà and Last Supper themes fill our souls with the power of love, the pattern of recovering ourselves through self-forgetting dedication to others, and the closeness of the community of believers with God. These themes direct our worship toward a union of infinite and finite spiritual life here in our midst, under the conditions and responsibilities of human existence. In this Christian religious context, art is much more determinate in its evocation of the infinite than it was in conjunction with the religions of nature. It is also much more open, than its Greek predecessor, to the hope arising from a redemptive cooperation between the divine and human agencies, working in the face of evil and suffering.

Only with the Reformation and the rise of Romantic art, however, has the relationship between art and religion been clearly articulated. We can now see that, although these two approaches do share in the medium of imagery and representational forms, religion adds the distinctive factor of *devotion*. It recovers the spiritual content from its external presentation, makes it live again more intensely in the free subjectivity of the believer, and embodies this affective and practical response in the specifically religious acts of worship and community service. Art cannot be dispensed with even here, but its religious significance does not lie any longer in its being the highest means by which a people can place itself in possession of spiritual truth, as was the case with Greek classical art. Instead, its religious function in the modern world is to express, as well as it can, the permanent *tension* between our interior life and our social obligations, the incommensurability between our finite personality and the infinite spiritual life.

Romantic art satisfies these conditions through its use of analogies and a well-contrived dissonance between content and sensuous form. Thereby, it expresses the subjective freedom of man and his yearning for an infinite spiritual fulfillment, which still eludes his grasp. There is a musical tension between the spiritual and the visible in the art works of Romanticism which suitably evokes the Christian sense of living in two worlds, and of striving to reconcile them through suffering and the service of others. At the same time, Romantic perspective has the further effect of distinguishing the art activity from the religious life it may be manifesting. It is a self-transcending signpost, using its sensuous media to direct us beyond the border of art to the specifically religious sphere as such, for our further spiritual development.

In the modern age, the appearance of Romantic art signifies that the historical growth of the human race has reached the point where we are now aware of the religious limits of art, its inherent shortness of the mark set by our religious quest.

> In the earliest beginnings of art we shall find mystery still present, a secret strain and longing which persists because art's imaginative powers are unable to envisage to sense the complete truth of its content. When once, however, the mind of man has succeeded in endowing such content with perfect outward shape in art [as is the case in Greece], it is driven inevitably away from this objective realization to its own free spiritual activity as from something repellent to it. A period such as this is our own. We may, indeed, express the hope that art will rise to yet higher grades of technical perfection; but in any case art in its specific form has ceased to meet the highest requirements of spiritual life. We may still wonder at the unrivalled excellence of the statues of the gods of Hellas, and imagine that God the Father, Christ, and the Virgin Mary have received ideal representation at the hands of more recent painters. But it is of no use. Our knees no longer bow to them.[26]

Hegel does not imply that art has become religiously meaningless in our age, and can simply be shed off by man in his spiritual activity. Nor does he freeze the development of religiously significant forms of art at the Romantic level. But he does think that there is something definitive, at least for Western consciousness, in the evolution from early symbolic art and classical forms to the romantic period.

This experience has taught us that art and religion are distinct co-determinants of human cultural life, and that there are some spiritual needs of man which can only be met by and within the religious forms of cultivating the common spiritual content. The central dynamism of

26. Ibid., 1, 142.

the human spirit now moves toward a reflective consideration of the definite forms of religion, in their own texture and operation. And within the religious domain, a focus is found in the Christian religion, rather than in the religions of nature and of beautiful humanity where the relationship between art and religion remained unclarified.

PHILOSOPHICAL EXEGESIS OF CHRISTIANITY

Hegel regards Christianity as the absolute religion, and this in several senses which contribute toward the ultimate assimilation of religion to his own philosophy. Christianity thus becomes just as central a problem in the Hegelian philosophy of religion as in the Humean and Kantian philosophies. But whereas Hume's approach to Christianity is usually oblique and aimed at showing its intellectual and moral defects, Hegel offers a more direct and constructive treatment. He formally thematizes the meaning of Christianity, and regards it as the integral religious embodiment of spiritual truth, even though he also intends to establish the final home of this spiritual truth in his speculative philosophy. Hegel also strives to overcome the residual dualism in Kant's conception of Christianity as a complex unity of moral truth and historical realization, rational pattern and mystery of grace.

In order to transform the entire Christian religious reality—human meaning and divine mystery alike—into a philosophically known and judged modality of spirit, Hegel is careful to specify the precise sense in which Christianity merits definition as the absolute religion. It is the plenary religious way of representing the absolute, but this does not constitute the ultimate human grasp of the truth concerning the absolute. To establish this point, he interprets the absolute character of Christian religious faith in these four distinctive ways: the recapitulative, probative, revelational, and thematic.

The *recapitulative* method of showing that Christianity is the absolute religion depends upon the Hegelian distinction among three main kinds of specific religions.[27] The religions of nature, spiritual individuality, and Christian revelation are not distinguished as static, separate parts of the

27. This recapitulational method is employed most effectively in the broad sweep taken in *Phenomenology*, pp. 750–90. There is an excellent account of Hegel's treatment of Christianity in Karl Löwith's essay, "Hegel and the Christian Religion," *Nature, History, and Existentialism* (Evanston, Northwestern University Press, 1966), pp. 162–203. Also H. Rondet, *Hégélianisme et christianisme* (Paris, 1965).

whole field of religion, but rather as progressively adequate interpretations of the entire meaning of religion. We learn to respond with increasing degrees of penetration to the divine reality and power, making it meaningful for ourselves first in relation to particular objects and the vast forces in nature, then in the form of the human spirit and the laws of human society, and finally in its own immanent and free spiritual life among men.

These modes of the religious interpretation and organization of life constitute respectively the natural history of religion, its moral history, and its spiritual history. Hume's reduction of every religious outlook to the passional basis in man's response to natural forces, is the philosophical theory best suited to embody the natural history phase of religious development. Kant's reference of religious meaning to our condition of hope in a morally ordered universe is proportioned to the moral history of religion. Both of these phases in the religious growth of humanity and the corresponding philosophical theorizing on religion are integrated in the Christian reality. In Hegel's view, Christianity is the absolute religion because of its recapitulative power of saving the whole content in the natural and moral history of religions, as well as its capacity to furnish guidance for his own comprehensive philosophy of religion.

The attribution of absoluteness to Christianity is an act neither of idle laudation nor of theological polemics on Hegel's part. Instead, it is an essential link in his philosophical argumentation. In effect, he is saying that Christianity is so completely recapitulative of the religious experience and reflection of mankind that it can satisfy that vast majority of men whose highest vocation is religious, and yet must inexorably force those seeking a philosophical clarification onward into his own philosophical theory of religion and our spiritual history. Just as Christianity has saved most of the religious insights and actions of the human race, so does it offer the most to be transformed by philosophical analysis of its significance. It challenges the philosopher of religion to develop a conception of religion which is adequate to this complex unification of man's spiritual dynamism.

Thus Christianity is absolute within the restricted order of religion, but that order as a whole is not the total completion of our spiritual capacities. Christianity is the ultimate synthesis in the specifically religious sphere (religion in its third or restricted meaning), yet in such a manner that it shows the penultimacy of this entire sphere in respect to the fulfillment of our spiritual life. The Christian religion stands at the borderline, and propels the questing mind of man beyond itself into the final concretion of philosophical awareness. Hence its absolute character is not purely recapitulative but also directional. It points us toward the philosophically comprehended absolute. It is the last "beyond-and-toward" formation of the human spirit, whether viewed phenomenologically or within the speculative system.

This subordinating relationship becomes clear in the *probative* method of showing the absolute character of Christian religion. In his religionizing of natural theology, Hegel had previously established a close connection between the three proofs of God's existence and the three kinds of religion. The ideas about the divine nature which underlie the informal and formal reasoning to God's existence help to shape our practical religious response in its natural, moral-esthetic, and revelational forms. But our conceptions of the divine actuality depend, in their turn, upon the way in which we conceive our human nature or the spiritual life of the human self. This accords with the Hegelian principle that "religiosity is the veritable *actuality of self-consciousness*, its veritable life, its sentient known truth." [28] The controlling source of both our reasoning to God and our definite forms of religious action lies, then, deep within the human spirit and its efforts at self-clarification. There is an originative religiosity at the basis of all natural theology and all modes of religion, and the absoluteness of Christianity can also be exhibited within this framework.

Reflection upon human religiosity, as manifested in Christian life and doctrine, prompts Hegel to formulate three basic principles of proof, around which his philosophy of religion is organized. The first fundamental proposition affirms the relational nature of religion. He defines it most compactly as the self-consciousness of God, not taken in an isolated way but precisely as achieved through the mediation of finite consciousness. Religion is a relational reality, but one in which the divine pole reaches self-awareness only in and through the work of man, as he clarifies the implications of finitude and encloses all finite beings within the infinite whole.

The second basic proposition in Hegel's theory of religion is that the perfect religion is found only where this spiritual relationship becomes objectively embodied. It is an essential law of religious life that the divine spirit finds itself actually realized in the community of faith and

28. *Philosophie der Religion*, 1, 182 (1, 205–06). For the three basic propositions, of which the theory of absolute religion is the proof, see ibid., 2, 3–6 (2, 327–28).

worship. This condition is reached only in the church, which is the religious union of a people with the indwelling divine spirit.

And the third guiding note is that the perfect religion must be a revealed religion, one in which spirit manifests itself in its own actuality and truth. This revelational quality is supplied by Christianity, which is the perfect religion or assembly of believers only because it is also the social, ecclesial response to the self-manifesting divine word. Thus Christianity is the absolute religion, precisely because it furnishes the proving reality for these three central propositions in the philosophy of religion.

Special attention must now be paid to the *revelational* nature of the absolute religion. This is a necessary rather than an optional note, one which is at least latently present in all forms of religion and which is explicitly recognized in the perfect form of religion. Hegel defends the need for revelation, in opposition both to the Enlightenment critics of the historical aspect of religion and to the theological minimizers, among orthodox believers themselves. It is striking that he accepts the requirement of a revelational element without revoking, in any way, his earlier criticism of religious positivity. There is an historically developing factor in religion, which remains distinct from positivity as such. Whereas positivity depends upon an estrangement and opposition between the divine and the human, revelation is precisely the mode in which the divine principle ferments and grows within the human community as a historical reality.

There is a definite philosophical ground for Hegel's confidence that the humanly perfect expression of religion must be revelational. In several places in his lectures on the philosophy of religion, he remarks that this discipline presupposes the phenomenological and logical knowledge about the life of spirit and the unity-in-succession of its concrete shapes.[29] It is to the findings of his own onto-pneuma-logic, rather than to the theological tradition, that Hegel turns for a confirmation of the need for revelation.

Specifically, he draws upon that section of his ontopneumalogical theory of essence which discusses the necessity for a manifestation of essential structure in the existential world. This essential law of self-manifestation can now be reformulated in properly religious language as the law of the revelatory nature of all religion, expressly of the perfect or absolute religion. Insofar as it contains the development of spiritual

29. Ibid., 1, 59; 4, 50 (1, 55; 2, 355).

reality, our religious existence must accept the essential law of embodying a divine revelation and eventually recognizing the presence of this necessary factor in our midst. Because Christianity is nothing less than this full revelational embodiment, brought to conscious acknowledgment of its own nature, it shows itself to be the absolute religion in the very insistence upon its revealed basis.

For a proper understanding of the necessity and import of revelation, however, religion must submit to the clarifying analysis of the Hegelian philosophy of spirit. The reinterpretation can be seen in some cognate texts in the *Lectures on the Philosophy of Religion* and the *Lectures on the Proofs of the Existence of God,* arranged here under four divisions.

> [1.] It is the nature of spirit itself to manifest itself, to make itself objective. This is its deed and its vitality, its unique deed, and it is endlessly its deed. . . . His [God's] being is His deed, His revealing. Spirit into spirit: only thus [is] spirit. . . . God is spirit only for spirit, and only for pure spirit, that is, for thought. . . . [2.] God must reveal Himself *in* nature, but God cannot reveal Himself *to* nature, to the stone, to the plant, to the animal, because God is spirit [and can reveal Himself] only to man, who is thinking, who is spirit. . . . [3.] The completed [perfected] religion is this, where the concept of religion has returned to itself—where the absolute idea, God-as-spirit, is the object for consciousness in accord with His truth and revealedness. . . . As previously stated, this is precisely the goal, the completed religion, that God become known as this totality which is the spirit. . . . [4.] The Christian religion is in this manner the religion of revelation. It is plain in it what God is, that He becomes known as He is, not narratively or in some other manner as in other religions, but the revealed manifestation is its very determination and content, namely, revelation, manifestation, being-for-consciousness, and [indeed] for the consciousness that it is itself spirit. . . . We have to consider the idea [of spirit in religious form] purely speculatively and justify it against the understanding, against it as rebelling against all content of religion in general. This content is called mystery, because it is something hidden to the understanding, for the latter does not attain to the process which this unity is. Wherefore, everything speculative is a mystery to the understanding.[30]

30. *Philosophie der Religion,* 1, 74–75, 158, 4, 32, 34 (1, 83–85, 2, 328–30, 3, 17); *Beweise,* pp. 13–14, 48–49, 177 (pp. 194–95, 367); italics mine.

Taken together, these passages mark the stages in Hegel's mounting argument for unconditional assimilation of the truth of revelational religion within the framework of his own philosophy of religion.

The first text squarely links the philosophical analysis of religious revelation with the theory of essence. The process of religious revelation is a more concrete and heartfelt way of grasping and expressing the essential law of spirit to manifest itself. It belongs to the very nature of divine spiritual actuality to show itself, to uncover itself in the centers of spiritual life, and thus *to be* in the very act of *being made manifest* in and to its finite modalities. Revelation is not somehow a distinct act from the nature and being of absolute spirit, but is that very being in its total spiritual process of self-manifesting development.

In the religious context, there must be an answering response on the part of a conscious, spiritual agent, to whose awareness and interest the revealing act is addressed. In the second text, Hegel specifies that the answering religious agent is man, the finite spiritual being. The primary community relationship is that which subsists between the divine and the human spirit, with the revelational act serving as the operative means for securing this social bond. In order to undercut the theistic interpretation of the revelational religious community, however, Hegel stresses that the infinite spiritual totality manifests itself to an other which belongs to it as an internal, finite determination within this totality. The revelational property of Christianity is not permitted to disrupt the onto-pneumalogical truth about the infinite-finite whole. The other spiritual nature to which the infinite spirit manifests itself is an answering point within its own historical development, and hence is, in the most pregnant metaphysical sense, the infinite spirit's own other.

Hegel's third text serves both to clarify the truth quality of the revelational relationship and to vindicate its interpretation by the rational standard of his own philosophy. Religious truth rests upon a recognition, on the part of a finite spirit, that it shares in the encompassing life of the infinite spiritual whole, and that the latter receives its modal actualization in one's own selfhood. A man gains his personal hold on religious consciousness in the act of regarding himself inalienably as this definite actualization of the total spiritual process, this nodal center in the intensive totality of spiritual life.

In plumbing the personal depths from which the religious acknowledgment of self-revealing spirit arises, the reflective individual discovers that it is an act of his own spiritual selfhood and hence an expression of the active resources of reason within him. Spirit answers to spirit, encompassing reason to encompassing reason, under the modality of faith in divine revelation. For those who have the courage to follow through the implications, this means that religious believing is perfected only through an act of philosophical knowing. Only when the meaning of revelation is reflectively comprehended by philosophical reason, can religion reach its completed condition and truth.

This consequence of the dialectic of revelation is spelled out unmistakably in the fourth text quoted above. Religion attains the revealed status, not only by enshrining the act of revealing and the content of the divine message but also by laying bare the whole religious domain to our philosophical inspection, and thus becoming exposed to the ultimate analysis and judgment of philosophical thought. Revealed religion does not simply make something else manifest: it exposes to philosophical judgment its own essential structure, as a phase in the life of spirit. Thus it makes the entire religious formation of man stand uncovered as being, in its own restricted nature, only a dispositional stage in the spiritual development of humanity. Since the absoluteness of Christianity is based on its revelational character, it can be absolute only within the religious sphere which now confesses its own essential incompleteness and ordination to philosophy.

Theologians try to avoid this conclusion by appealing to the mystery of God and the irreducible message given in the Bible. Hegel regards such religious appellations as "the hidden God," "the unknown God," and "the ineffable God," as holding good only for the limited standpoint of abstract understanding, faith, and representational thinking.[31] There is an unsoundable mystery from their perspective, precisely because that

31. Hegel refuses to accept as definitive for man the philosophical distinction between knowing the truth *that* God is and knowing *what* He is in His own essence, since his own theory of spirit is designed to give a reforming philosophical knowledge even of the divine essence as such. Moreover, he appeals to the Christian belief in divine self-revelation as a religious sign of the penetration of human reason into the essential nature of divine being. Pascal offers a contrary account of the Christian interpretation of life: "What meets our eye denotes neither total absence nor manifest presence of the divine, but the presence of a hidden God. Everything bears this stamp" (*Pensées*, Stewart trans., p. 9). Lucien Goldman, *The Hidden God*, trans. P. Thody (New York, 1964), follows the development of this theme in Pascal and Racine. On the other hand, Ernst Bloch, *Subjekt-Objekt: Erläuterungen zu Hegel* (Frankfurt, 1962), p. 330, views Hegel as transferring the objective theistic stress upon *Deus absconditus* over into the subjective sphere of *Humanum absconditum*, and then eliminating both divine and human hiddenness through the doctrine on developing spirit.

perspective is unable to reach the unifying principle of active reason, and thus to recognize in the hidden and revealing God a preliminary formulation of the infinite-finite community of spirit. What the philosophy of religion does is to spell out the consequences of the philosophical theory of spiritual actuality for the religious conception of the hidden and revealing God. Hence what does get revealed in a philosophical analysis of Christianity is the inadequacy of the mystery of God to express the life of divine spirit and its total self-revealing in human reflection and practice.

The revelatory act on the part of the Hegelian spiritual principle is absolute, in a sense which the absolute religion of Christianity cannot admit. As philosophically interpreted, revelation is the unreserved removal of every gap between infinite spirit and the act of laying itself bare in human awareness. Nothing is left under the veil in this total self-explication, nothing is left mysterious or essentially unsayable about the divine nature. Its proper accent is captured in the philosophical theory on the actuality of spirit. This doctrine does not merely interpret the mystery of God but exposes to philosophical view its entire structure, thus transforming it into a modal facet of philosophical truth. Hegel finally seals his arduously elaborated critique of theism and Christianity in his exposition of the meaning of absolute religion and divine revelation as the utter self-disclosure of the nature of spirit to our philosophical reflection.

As for the Bible, it thoroughly impenetrates Hegel's thought and language, in the theory of religion as elsewhere. Its influence is a good instance of how his philosophy presupposes religion and builds upon the concrete religious life of his own culture. Hegel treats the Biblical contribution in the same way as all other presupposed factors. It is not an unqualifiedly independent source of insight, since there are questions about its foundation and truth value which it leaves unanswered, and for the resolution of which the entire Biblical outlook must be brought under the revising judgment of philosophy of religion. In the light of the Hegelian theory on the different modes of thought and language, the Bible is recognized as a dramatic mode of expressing the common spiritual activity in representational imagery and stories.

Hegel grants that Biblical scholars can remain content with a descriptive plane of inquiry, which seeks to ascertain the actual forms of Biblical thought and the internal relationships between these various statements of belief. But it is the business of the philosopher of religion to raise certain further questions concerning these forms of thought which break through the shell of descriptive self-containment, and which force these Biblical forms of thinking out into the common marketplace of human problems and modes of inquiry.[32] Both in the original production of the Biblical texts and in their present interpretation, men bring with them to the task a concrete spirit which takes many categorial forms of thought and dramatic imagery. Philosophers of religion cannot avoid asking about the evidential adequacy of the human schemas and thought patterns which structure the Bible, and which are the operative presuppositions of Biblical interpreters themselves.

The context of modern philosophy forces the move from a descriptive use of religious categories to a critical validation of their truth claims. Hence the Biblical thought patterns raise the problem of truth, not only at the level of a faith proposal and proclamation of the word, but also at the altogether foundational level of their experiential basis of evidence and their relative capacity to illume the spiritual life in man. In Hegel's philosophy of experience and being, the Biblical meanings must be adjusted to a commanding, evidential context in the doctrine on the organic spiritual whole. Consequently, the Biblical basis for Christianity as the absolute religion does not really remove the latter from the scope of Hegelian philosophy.

Hegel now feels safe in proposing, as a final criterion of the absolute character of the Christian religion, the main dogmatic themes which constitute its doctrine and which govern its practical activities. All the other human manifestations of the religious spirit receive their *thematic* unification in the Christian doctrines of the Trinity and creation, the power of love and the community of believers gathered in the Holy Spirit. These doctrines are absolute, in the sense that they bring to credal and theological formulation the basic religious reflections of mankind. Christian doctrine carries the religious mode of thematizing our experience as far toward a comprehensive interpretation of life as is possible in that line.

---

32. *Philosophie der Religion*, 1, 37–40, 4, 23–26 (1, 31–33, 2, 341–45). Hegel defends the supreme orthodoxy of his philosophy in the sense that it studies the forms of religious representation found in the Bible and brings them to their reformed truth in his own speculative philosophical thought. For a more theological defense of Hegel as a Christian thinker, see the two articles by C. G. Schweitzer, "Die Glaubensgrundlagen des Hegelschen Denkens," *Hegel-Studien*, Beiheft 1 (1964), 237–38, and "Hegel—das grosse Missverständnis: Zur Verteidigung eines christlichen Philosophen," *Christ und Welt*, 17 (1964), 16–17.

As far as Hegel is concerned, the master theme of the absolute religion is the Trinity, around which all other topics can be organized.[33] This emphasis is not dictated by any predilection for triplicity as such, but rather by the opportunity for a general correlation of Trinitarian speculation with his own ontopneumalogical account of the growth of spiritual actuality. He usually views the theological doctrine as a pictorial way of representing the progression of spirit from abstract and indeterminate unity (Father), through a stage of differentiation and conflict (Son made man), to the ultimate concrete union (Holy Spirit in the church). The Trinitarian concretion is a reflex expression, in the medium of religious imagination and feeling, of the same pattern of spiritual development which receives its true conceptual analysis in onto-pneuma-logic.

Because of this speculative center for his interpretation of the Trinity, Hegel does not regard the doctrine as revealing the intimate life of three persons in one divine nature. Instead, he takes the three principles as modes and constituent aspects of the "absolute personality" of the spiritual whole itself. He treats the Father-moment as one perspective for viewing the infinite actuality of spirit, and makes a similar synopsis from the angles furnished in the Son-moment and the Holy-Spirit-moment. Furthermore, absolute personality does not consist of a distinctive divine life, which is imparted by the personal God to human persons. Personality is found properly in human beings, insofar as they acknowledge their mutual relations and make an interchange with each other. The divine spiritual totality is personal only to the degree that the universal life of spirit sustains the interrelational acts among human persons. Expressed in Trinitarian terms, it is only in the Father as creator, in the Son as incarnate, and in the Holy Spirit as embodied in the church, that absolute personality is effectively actualized. The personal element in religion is that which men share *with each other* on a universal spiritual basis, not that which they are pictured as sharing with a personal, transcendent God.

The kingdoms of Father, Son, and Holy Spirit are three thematic ways of viewing the internal development of absolute spirit as an illumination of our human reality. They are not the exclusive preserve of theological investigation. On the contrary, Hegel finds it philosophically

33. This is the organizing principle used to analyze Christianity in *Philosophie der Religion*, 4, 28–232 (3, 1–151); see *Phenomenology*, pp. 765–68. The Trinitarian doctrine is analyzed by J. Splett, *Die Trinitätslehre G. W. F. Hegels* (Freiburg, 1965), and by Bruaire, *Logique et religion chrétienne*, pp. 65–131.

profitable to analyze each of these kingdoms in Trinitarian thought.

The kingdom of the Father is useful as a way of illustrating what is done in speculative logic.[34] The discourse about the Father is the religious equivalent for the attitude taken by the philosopher in onto-pneuma-logic. For in both cases, the mind makes an act of abstraction from the given particulars, in order to view them in their origin and source of power. The theology of the Father is a representational means of inquiring into the actuality of spirit, taken in an as yet latent and unreleased manner, or as abstract thought and undifferentiated power. This is the standpoint of God as existing before creation and as brooding over the divine exemplar ideas, whence the world of space and time is about to spring forth. Under this imagery, the human mind is implicitly acknowledging the relevance of logic to reality, the universal presence of the categorial forms of thought and purpose throughout our experience.

The kingdom of the Son attracts Hegel's special attention, since it is the religious and theological counterpart of his theory on essence, negativity, and dialectical reconciliation. Just as his general conception of religion centers around this theoretical complex, so his exegesis of the Trinity stresses the topic of the Son. This is preeminently the perspective of religious representational thinking, whose proper atmosphere is that of struggle and reconciliation of opposing forces in the world. Under the rubric of the kingdom of the Son, Hegel organizes the religious approach to the problems of otherness, the creation of the world, and the essential nature of man as revealed in Christ.

It is only when a passage is made from consideration of the Father alone to the Father as engendering the Son that the religious mind takes the problem of otherness seriously. Hegel interprets the theological effort to maintain the Son's distinction from the Father as a spontaneous defense of the multiplicity and differentiation in our experience. To say that the Father does not dwell alone but begets the Son and creates the world in His image, is only a religious way of saying that spirit must differentiate itself, must give rise to finitudinal being, and must find its own nature in its finite expressions. The theme of the kingdom of the Son enables Hegel to coalesce the generation of the Son and the creation of the world from its divine principle. Hence the world emerges from its

34. Hegel's famous description of logic as that which *"shows forth God as He is in His eternal essence before the production of nature and of a finite spirit"* (*Science of Logic*, 1, 60) implicitly denies the mystery of God and prepares for a religious restatement of logic in terms of the kingdom of the Father.

spiritual source with the same internal necessity, freedom from external coercion, and perfect immanence to divinity, as the theologians attribute to the procession of the Son from the Father.

It is difficult for man to comprehend that the natural world does come from infinite spirit, that nature and his own finite spirit are the twin revelations of the divine ground of all being. His proofs of God's existence are an expression of man's effort to raise himself up to spiritual actuality through the mediation of nature and human society, but they are flawed by the destructive forces in nature and the evil powers rampant in human history. That is why the kingdom of the Son cannot be fully realized, without the Incarnation and death of Christ. Theodicy apart from Christology is a vain effort for the theologian. Faith in Christ generates the religious conviction in the unity of the divine and the human, through the moving story of how Christ overcomes the dualistic estrangement between the holy God and sinful man.

Hegel notes that Christian faith always views Christ's death upon the cross within the context of His resurrection and ascension into heaven. This is the concrete way in which the religious mind pictures "this death of death, the overcoming of the grave, of *sheol*, the triumph over the negative," which is essentially being signified in the confession of faith.[35] The doctrine of the resurrection is a symbol of the regenerative triumph of spiritual actuality. Its irresistible power is specially manifest in the transition from religion to philosophy, which is figuratively expressed in Hegel's reiterated phrase "the death of death." Infinite spirit recovers itself in the very negations and conflicts introduced by finite things. Philosophy of spirit leads us from the *representation of death* to the *death of representation*, that is, from an attitude of religious contrasts to the supremacy of philosophical thought over all religious representations. The philosophical meaning of faith in the resurrection is that the reign of representational thinking and hence of sovereign religion comes to an end with the assimilation of the entire process of finite life and death to the all-inclusive development of absolute spirit.

In the kingdom of the Holy Spirit, Hegel sees a ratification of his entire conception of the relation between infinite and finite spirit. That relation must become visible, objective, and social, without losing its inward spiritual significance. Religiously, this is expressed in the requirement that our bond with God not be purely private but essentially social,

35. *Philosophie der Religion*, 4, 163 (3, 91–92).

and hence that it must attain to the form of a church. The church is not a purely external organization but the assembly of believers, unified by the indwelling presence of the Holy Spirit. The people of God are constituted as such through a reconciling act, in which the world and the self, the infinite and the finite, are drawn together into a complex living community (*Gemeinde*). There are three aspects to this ecclesial form of reconciliation: doctrine is taught in a creed and explained in a theology; men worship together and share in a sacramental life binding the human to the divine; and actions are directed to service of the human community as a whole, since only in mankind's comprehensive unity does the Holy Spirit attain to full actualization. The teaching, worshipping, and serving church is the completed form of Christianity as the absolute religion.

Yet every stage in Hegel's analysis of Christian doctrine within the Trinitarian framework leads toward the conclusion that the significant content of religious conviction is not fully intelligible, within the limits set by theological interpretation. The discrepancy between the religious content and the theological explanation is especially noticeable in the order of action. There is more to man's practical devotion and dedicated social work than can be accounted for by credal and theological conceptions. What this "more" may be, can be only dimly apprehended and uneasily felt by those who remain sealed into the religious sphere as their ultimate home. But this hint at a surplus meaning is sufficiently challenging to keep the human race permanently dissatisfied with all religious outlooks, as well as to dispose some men to look elsewhere for assistance. Hegel's judgment is that there is more spiritual actuality on earth than Christianity and the specifically religious domain dream of, or at least more than they can make us the effective masters of, through their own resources.

RECONCILING RELIGION TO ITS TRUTH

The transition from religion to philosophy can be viewed both as a systematic expansion of philosophy itself and as a final fulfillment of the religious drive within men. From the former standpoint, this passage marks the ultimate explication of the meaning and power of philosophical reason, showing in actual fact its ability to analyze and transform every province in human experience. Human recognition of absolute spiritual values is a progressively self-clarifying act, which expresses itself somewhat distantly through the art work, becomes more pertinent through religious personification and practice, and at last attains the fully reflective medium of philosophical thought. Through art, religion, and philosophy, men are able to achieve that determinate rationality toward which the world's evolutionary process is actively tending.

From the fact that all three modes of relating man to the absolute share in the very same content of spiritual meaning, it cannot be argued that the relations between the three ultimate spheres are completely mutual. For although the content of spiritual life is identical, there is a genuine development from the less adequate to the more adequate manners of grasping that content of spiritual truth, and giving it formal existence. In the concrete, this means that the form of philosophical reflection is alone universal enough and reflectively penetrating enough to be exactly proportioned to the organic spiritual whole, and thus to bring its purposive actuality to an unconditionally true judgment. Whereas philosophy is inclusive enough to grasp the meaning of spirit in its artistic and religious representational forms, the latter are not reciprocally able to comprehend the speculative form of thought which is definitively taken by absolute spirit in philosophy.[36] The philosophical act of interpretation and judgment of spiritual actuality is, therefore, the ultimately decisive one.

But Hegel also looks upon the transfer of the gravamen of spiritual life as being subjectively dictated by the force and purposiveness of religiosity. By working itself out under the form of the definite kinds of religions, this spiritual impetus comes to a better understanding of its own nature. Reflective men eventually realize that the primal cleft between religiosity itself and the definite kinds of religion was a portent that the religious spirit, in the broader sense, cannot remain content with the restricted patterns afforded by the specific forms of the religions of mankind. This split can only be transcended in the act of a free surpassing of the entire

36. Ibid., pp. 230–31 (pp. 148–49). As an exoteric Hegelianism, religion has the right to maintain its faith-form against the "rationalizing" criticism of abstract understanding, but "it is another thing when religion sets herself against comprehending reason, and against philosophy in general, and specially against a philosophy of which the content is speculative, and therewith religious," in the teleological sense of showing religion to be an anticipatory mode of presenting the speculative truth of philosophy (*Encyclopedia Mind*, p. 304).

religious outlook on the part of religiosity itself.[37] We come to see its basic identity with the very actuosity of spirit, known in the form of philosophical reflection. What the internal teleology of human religiosity ultimately demands is a sharing in that spiritual truth which lives through, and sees beyond, the tears and images of the specifically religious plane of feeling and representation. To strive after a supreme philosophical synthesis is, therefore, the best way of proving one's fidelity to the broad religious orientation of the human spirit.

Indeed, this step is already in the course of being taken within the restricted sphere of human religions. Insofar as they all enjoin some sort of practical response to the spiritual power in the universe, some sort of actional recognition of its being the most important actuality for man, they are implicitly setting man on a path which leads beyond their own territory. In *the worshipping and serving aspects* of religion, Hegel discerns a spiritual disposition at work which cannot find its complete satisfaction in the religious order, and hence which effectively opens the human mind and heart outwards toward realization in philosophy.[38] Cultic transcendence is the great bridge from religion to philosophy, since it calls for a radical mastering of tensions which philosophical reason alone can secure.

Religious worship and community service are, indeed, the great practical agencies for reconciling finite life and infinite life, the subjective intent and the objective accomplishment, the demands of self and the entire universe of others. Yet they unify these poles only in the line of action, and not yet in that of reflective thought. The actional reconciliation attained through religious worship and community service remains one-sided and defective, until the structure and implications of such reconciliation are properly recognized by human awareness. The lag is only overcome when the Hegelian philosophy of the spirit artic-

37. Religiosity itself propels man toward his higher philosophical realization, since its purposive tendency is governed by the actuosity of spirit in search of the known and willed truth.

38.
   In its substance it [philosophy] is in fact rational theology, and in its service of the truth a continual service of God. . . . Here alone we are in the presence of that most intelligent form of cultus, which seeks wholly to appropriate to itself, and to grasp in concrete thought what is otherwise only the evanescent content of feeling or the imagination. In the purview of such a philosophy, art and religion, as two aspects of one truth, become related under a unifying conception. (*Fine Art*, 1, 139, 143)

ulates, in conceptual form, that organic relationship already animating our religious practice. Only then are the content and the form, the practical and the judgmental actualization of spirit, brought to a reconciling adequation. What the religious attitude ardently seeks as the presence of God-all-in-all, or the indwelling of the Holy Spirit in the worshipping human community, is actually brought about in that total concretion of spirit constituting the substance and truth of philosophy.

This throws some light upon Hegel's teaching that philosophical reason is practical as well as theoretical, and indeed that philosophy is the perduring cultic act of man. For religion to become incorporated within the speculative system, it does not have to be stripped of its actional aspect and reduced to a quietistic observation of life. The Hegelian speculative system is both theoretical and practical, not only in the sense of having a theory about practical life but also in the more intensive sense of incorporating the religiosity or actual practical strivings of the human spirit.

The guarantee for this inclusion of the whole stream of practical striving within the philosophical formation of mind comes from the philosophy of religion, which Hegel can now define succinctly and triumphantly as a "thinking, *conceiving knowledge* of religion."[39] Its mediational function is to plumb the nature of religious faith and practice, as well as their reasoned expression in natural and sacred theology, in such a way that their entire reality is preserved and elevated into philosophical thought and its conceptual synthesis. Here at its climax, Hegel's speculative philosophy manifests itself as a serpentine circle, which transformingly incorporates both the active life of religious believing and worshipping and the reflective analysis of that life, both the actuality of religion and the truth of the philosophy of religion.

Whenever he traces out the route for the final unitive assimilation of religion and philosophy of religion to the speculative system of philosophy, Hegel frankly admits to a certain disappointment in viewing the results. Our human expectations seem to remain still greater than the outcome of his study would warrant. We keep looking for a new level of

---

39. *Philosophie der Religion*, 1, 62 (1, 31). As formulated by Albert Chapelle, *Hegel et la religion*, pp. 116–17, the central conviction of Hegel's philosophy of religion is that the hour has now come for a philosophically comprehensive penetration of the entire Christian experience, history, and doctrine. See also, T. N. Munson, "Hegel as Philosopher of Religion," *Journal of Religion*, 46 (1966), 9–23, which castigates Kant from a Hegelian standpoint.

doctrinal content that will come into range, as a consequence of bringing the resources of religion within the scope of philosophy, but the enlargement of content does not occur. Hegel explains this disappointment partly in general systematic terms, such as apply to the incorporation of morality, art, and any other configuration of spirit.[40] The task of philosophy is not to generate a specifically new content, in addition to what the various domains of spiritual life develop through their proper resources, but rather to look back upon them from the peak of fully reflective and recollective thought. Its distinctive contribution is to enable men to recognize the organic spiritual whole—actualizing itself through these several modalities—and thus to secure their unification and maximum intensification within this concrete life of spirit.

Nevertheless, there is a special sense in which Hegel admits that we may be justifiably disappointed about the elevation of religion to the clarified atmosphere of active, thinking spirit. The reconciliation which the religious community attempts between faith and reason, personal need and public responsibility, is carried forward by philosophy.

> Religion must take refuge in philosophy. On the worldly side, religion undergoes a loss, but it concerns only this form of externality and contingent happening. But as was remarked, philosophy [itself] is onesided. It forms a priestly order, which is isolated and holds sway in the sanctuary. Philosophy is untroubled about how the course of the world may go, it was not permitted to mingle with it, and it has to guard this property of the truth. How things shape up in the world is not our affair.[41]

These are the closing words in Hegel's lectures on religion, but they do not still the questioning about the relation between religion and philos-

---

40. *Phenomenology*, pp. 797–808; *Encyclopedia Mind*, p. 303.

41. *Philosophie der Religion*, 4, 231 (3, 151); the text is incomplete. There is a similar mood of retrospective resoluteness and contemporary abstinence from the practical ought in the Preface to *Philosophy of Right*, pp. 11–13. Sidney Hook, "Hegel and the Perspective of Liberalism," in *A Hegel Symposium*, pp. 39–62, criticizes Hegel's double bookkeeping for the claims of the past and the present in social and political affairs. But Hegel displays a similar reluctance to offer specific directions for discerning the rose of rational truth in the cross of present experience in the case of our religious life and its practical demands. See G. R. G. Mure, "Hegel, Luther, and the Owl of Minerva," *Philosophy*, 41 (1966), 127–39, on religious finalism and retrospective philosophizing as the root of Hegel's equivocity on his systematic completeness.

ophy, any more than his account of philosophy and political life stills the questioning in that area.

Hegel regards his philosophy as being complete in one sense, and incomplete in another. It is complete in principle, that is, in the radical foundation taken in the ontopneumalogical doctrine and the proportionate method of speculative thought. These are definitive accomplishments in philosophy which are not destined to be transformed into some higher viewpoint. It is also true that, when Hegel speaks about the cultural limitations affecting every philosophy and rendering its outlook contingent, transitory, and thus incomplete, the judgment applies to his own system. But it is a self-referring type of evaluation, which draws its principles from his own philosophy of spirit. The Hegelian system is a limited configuration, yet it is such precisely within the total development of that intensive spiritual totality which furnishes the metaphysical and methodological basis of Hegel's own system. Hence the incompleteness is to be met by the same predominant method and within the same determining system of the organic spiritual whole, rather than through any revolutionary shift of mind.

This dialectic of the complete and the incomplete quality of philosophy applies to the Hegelian theory of religion, but with a not inconsiderable difference. There are some signs that the incompleteness in this case does affect the method and the systematic truth of spirit, and not merely its particular expression. One indication of this more radical sort of incomplete description and explanation is found in the fact that the reconciliation between religion and philosophy is made only by and for philosophers, in ideality and not in actuality. Hegel teaches that all men have a call to the spiritual life and hence to religion in its inclusive meaning. But not all men have the capacity and obligation to transform the religious meaning of life into its reflective philosophical form. Not even philosophers can make a total transformation of their thought and action into the philosophical mode, and hence they require the aid of religious imagery and feeling to keep a large portion of their energies focused upon the spiritual import of experience.

Thus a stubborn cleavage remains between the religious and the philosophical modes of grasping the divine actuality and power, a cleavage which reaches even into the human recesses of the philosopher. Philosophical reconciliation on Hegel's ontopneumalogical basis is not only culturally limited: it fails to satisfy the intrinsic drive of human religiosity to orient all men and every aspect of their activities toward the supreme spiritual good. There is a universal human vocation to share in the spiritual life, but this is not essentially fulfilled by submitting religion to the Hegelian kind of philosophical purification and elevation.

Hegel felt that his own age was to be the epoch for making a definitive passage from religion to philosophy, at least on the part of all adequately reflective minds. But here as well as in his theory of the state, he argued the case by painting gray upon gray, that is, by casting the relationship into the past tense of an already achieved subordination. Even the high position which he assigned to Christianity as the absolute religion of revelation was a summatory judgment, viewing it as a historical shape and spent force of the spirit, whose entire significance and power are now concentrated into that rational present constituted by the act of philosophical discernment and judgment upon religion. Hegel was able to justify the retrospective necessitizing of the relationship between religion and philosophy by noting that his philosophical method is one of reflection, re-consideration, and re-collection of what has already been developed and brought to its rational point of concentration by spirit. And yet he had to suppose that religious faith is left without further historical creativity, just as the philosophical truth about religion is itself left isolated from the present problems and uncertainties of men.

Ironically enough, Hegel's victory over an independently rooted religious position introduces into his philosophy some of those same marks of positivity and alienation for which he had previously criticized religion. There is a resurgence of hardened oppositions, due this time to the very triumph of the philosophy of absolute spirit. Hegel's synthesis of religion and philosophy leaves a gaping dualism between the ordinary man of faith and the philosopher, as well as between the needs of human action and the philosophical truth about actional reality. His philosophers of religion are isolated shepherds of truth, a separate order of priests living indeed in a privileged sanctuary, but unable to give guidance to today's world. Despite the *rational* presence of the truth of religion within the speculative system, the speculative philosophers of religion do not achieve that *human practical* religious presence which men require for making intelligent decisions about the whats and the hows of an effective course of action in our world.

In the very act of modestly foregoing any prophecy about the future, Hegel also prevents the philosopher of religion from applying his religious insight to the actual situation, upon the free determination of which depends the future shape of history. This is as inadequate a state of affairs for the believer as it is for the moralist and the statesman. Contrary to Hegel's own intention, his philosophy of spirit incorporates religion in such a fashion that the practical wisdom required for making present decisions and orientations of life is dried up. Religion is blocked from making its proper contribution to the free use of intelligence and will, in the active human present. This is not a modest recognition of limits, but a failure to comprehend the intimate link between independent religious faith and man's practical spirit precisely in respect to the demands of decisional presence.

Men must still search for a wisdom about God and the world which will guide their daily lives. The continuing religious efforts to meet a need which Hegel's theory of religion frustrates, is an index that the relation of religion to philosophy need not conform to the orthodox Hegelian pattern. There is not only a pluralism of definite kinds of religions but also a pluralism of creative modes of relating the human religious spirit as a whole to philosophy. Hegel's phenomenological and speculative reflections on religion show that philosophy can aid in clarifying its meaning, but such clarification does not lead to the deautonomizing and total assimilation of religion.[42] In the actual world from which Hegel's philosopher-priests take refuge, there still remains work for religion to do in its own irreducible manner. It makes its own response precisely in aiding men to face the whats and hows of the existing world, and the orientation of their lives toward God.

The non-phenomenologizable resources of religion become operative again at the very moment when Hegel closes the gates of his philosophical sanctuary. Their operation enforces the difference between his retrospective necessitizing of religion and a free acknowledgment of its active presence among men. Religion keeps its own rooting in human nature and continues to do its proper work in the world, even after its dissolving reconciliation with Hegelian speculative philosophy is announced and the gates are shut.

42. Theodor Litt, *Hegel: Versuch einer kritischen Erneuerung* (2d ed. Heidelberg, 1961), pp. 93–95, questions whether religion is shown to be provisional and incomplete simply from the fact of its receiving some elucidation from philosophy.

9

The Common Issues

A historical study of the emergence of modern philosophy of religion contains more than separate analyses of the three main theories. For in the course of this examination, certain topics recur from one systematic context to the next. This is an indication that the pioneer thinkers are not solely concerned with developing a view of religion consistent with each man's peculiar set of principles. They are also engaged in determining precisely those problems so central to any well-conducted, philosophical investigation of religion that they constitute the common fund of topics in the philosophy of religion. It is chiefly in terms of these basic problems that the discussions and explicit criticisms are framed, in the movement from Hume to Kant to Hegel. And hence it is through these jointly shared problems that the continuity in the whole process of emergence of philosophy of religion is realized. Although there is some agreement among the three main sources on matters of doctrinal content, their fundamental unity lies in the problematic order. It is in virtue of their recognition of the leading issues in the philosophical study of religion that they join together in charting this field in philosophy.

The present chapter seeks to identify some of the prominent questions which all three philosophers regard as unavoidable challenges in the theory of religion. Among these questions are: the manner in which religion falls within the scope of philosophy, the impact of the philosophy of religion upon natural theology, the relationship between morality and religion, the philosophical approach to religious faith, the persistent mystery of the revealing God, and the interrelation between religious belief, worship, and service to mankind. Although these six points do not exhaust the stock of common issues, they do afford an opportunity for making some significant comparisons among the philosophical positions of Hume, Kant, and Hegel. In addition, the selected topics give some determinate historical meaning to that unity of inquiry which marks the century 1730–1830 as the foundational age for modern philosophy of religion. Subsequent investigators have not been bound restrictively to these issues as a canonical pattern, but they have found in them a reliable guide for securing balance and rigor in their own theories of religion. It is a safe rule that every present day philosopher of religion should give careful consideration to these six crucial problems, and should acquaint himself with all three of the classical positions on these matters in their mutual specification.

RELIGION WITHIN THE SCOPE OF PHILOSOPHY

Man's religious life is intimately interwoven with the whole range of his interests and activities. It is not a sealed-off compartment or special mode of experience, but rather a way of interpreting and unifying all the strands in human experience, whether theoretical or practical. This close enmeshment of the religious attitude with all our other achievements and concerns is an active, reciprocal relationship. Not only does religion take the initiative in permeating the major forms of culture and bringing them to a common focus of meaning, but in turn these cultural forms include the religious factor within their own efforts at synthesis, at least to the extent that its bearing can be shown upon the enterprises of art and science, politics and economic well-being. Philosophy is one of the cultural developments of man which is involved in the religious interpretation of life and which, in turn, actively involves the religious outlook itself within its own scope of work. The more that philosophers become aware of the interlacing relationships between religion and the whole range of human concerns studied by philosophy, the more likely they are to include religion among their primary problems and thus to cultivate the philosophy of religion.

One mark of the modernity of Hume, Kant, and Hegel is their keen double awareness of the close involvement between the universalizing interpretations proposed by religion and autonomous philosophy. However they may explain and evaluate the fact, they recognize the presence of religious considerations in all phases of human meaning and value. This religious presence is specified for the intellectual order through the work of sacred theology, which sometimes uses philosophical speculations in its exploration of the meaning of religion. However, our three thinkers agree that when philosophy functions as an instrument of theology, it fails to develop its full potentialities, not only in a vast field of technical questions but also in the investigation of religion itself. Whatever may be determined about religion by theological means and by philosophy serving in the state of a handmaid of theology, there is need for a further study of religious reality by philosophy as it operates in independence of a theological framework (and hence as free from being in an ancillary status). Until religious belief and practice are examined by philosophy in accord with its own distinctively grounded principles and aims, men have failed to make full use of their capacity to explore religiousness in a philosophical manner.

The common task of the classical modern philosophers of religion is to provide the counter-initiative needed for grasping the significance of the religious attitude and its cultural permeations, insofar as that significance comes within the range of our philosophical reflection upon human experience. These philosophers of religion are not religious philosophers, in the sense of basing their inquiry upon the truth of some given religious assent or acting as an arm in the theological elucidation of such an act of faith. They set out to discover what the philosophy of religion can do, as acting on its own responsibility, that is, as freed from these instrumental preoccupations and developed for its own sake. However short they may fall of the mark in the individual instance, they do release the historical energies and exhibit the concrete advances which are being made in this sort of philosophical investigation. The separate books and sections devoted by Hume, Kant, and Hegel to the problem of religion have had an indelible effect upon the modern intelligence, which does not want to lose the insights into religion coming from an inquiry regulated in principle by the philosophical mode of judgment. Domestic disagreements, about whether or not some particular theory is sufficient for grasping religious meaning and truth, cannot obscure the general importance of making a philosophically ordered study of religion.

Disengagement from what Kant refers to as the human mind's self-incurred tutelage to theology does not guarantee by itself, however, the intellectual fruitfulness of an inquiry into religion. The predicament of the early modern freethinkers and deists was that, having completed the movement of emancipation from a governing theological context, they did not know quite what to do with their intellectual freedom in its positive uses. Their thesis about an unyielding core of rational doctrine constituting natural religion remained suspiciously similar to what many theologians and apologists then regarded as the basic natural knowledge of God. There was not too great a divide, for instance, separating Lord Herbert of Cherbury from such defenders of orthodoxy in England as

Clarke and Derham. What made the similarity less impressive and convincing than might be expected, however, was that it provided no effective answer to the more radical skeptical attack upon even a minimal rational set of truths, established by the human mind about the relation between man and God.

All shades of constructive opinion on our ability to furnish some natural evidence for the religious relationship were vulnerable to the skeptical criticism, wherever it was taken seriously. Considerable advances in our understanding of the historical variations of religion were indeed made by those seventeenth- and eighteenth-century scholars who engaged in the translation, descriptive analysis, and comparative study of the various religious scriptures. But the tendency of such researchers was to become entangled in the thicket of descriptive particulars. Either they failed entirely to reach generalization on religious meanings, or else they attained only that dialectical kind which reinforced the skeptical contentions about the weakness of the human mind in this area.

What made the century 1730–1830 such a vital period of change was the aim of its leading philosophers to insure a study of religion which would be at once free from functional dependence upon any theology, sensitive to the full power of the skeptical challenge in its religious implications, and thoroughly philosophical in nature. This last qualification was the most decisive and difficult to achieve. It meant regarding the philosophical study of religion as something distinctive in two correlative senses: negatively as being *unburdened* by extraphilosophical considerations, and positively as being an *integral phase within* the whole philosophical inquiry. For Hume, Kant, and Hegel, there could be no genuine philosophy of religion which would be lacking a general philosophical foundation and a carefully developed set of connectives between that foundation and the problems in religion. They jointly repudiated that sort of philosophy of religion which consists solely of descriptions of religious phenomena, detached reflections on the role of religion in human life, and perhaps an aura of free fantasies on the cosmic currents which sweep us along. A philosophy of religion so constructed is just as lacking in rigor and intellectual substance as any other "philosophy of" this or that, taken in splendid isolation from a general philosophical basis and method.

Underlying all the differences among these three central minds was the resolve of each to shape the theory of religion by the constitutive principles and methods of his philosophy as a whole. Their main concern was to establish a strict continuity between their foundational inquiries and those in the area of religion, and to abide by the consequences of this relationship. Hence their attitude toward the study of religion was one of prolongation, rather than of isolation and improvisation. They sought to include religious belief and practice within an ongoing process of analysis and synthesis guided by a reflective theory of the method and limits of human understanding. The arresting quality of the *Dialogues Concerning Natural Religion,* the *Religion Within the Limits of Reason Alone,* and the *Lectures on the Philosophy of Religion* stems from the resolute procedure of their respective authors, who made no privileged exception in the case of religious questions but treated them in accord with the common canons of philosophical inquiry. These treatises became landmarks in the philosophy of religion because they showed in a concrete, yet prototypal, way how the theory of religion develops internally to a general philosophical method and system. If notable differences emerged in the conception of religion presented in each of these books, it was traceable to the fundamental methodological and epistemological differences holding between their authors, and not primarily to matters of personal idiosyncrasy and prejudice.

This insistence on placing the theory of religion upon a broad basis in philosophical method and principles does not lead, however, to any mechanical and simplistic application of general premises to a particular instance. With varying degrees of emphasis, the classical modern philosophers of religion warn against relying upon an abstract definition of religion which has been unilaterally constructed out of the prior positions taken in a philosophy, and which in turn completely predetermines the issues to be faced and the evidence to be admitted. Various reasons are given for refusing to follow a purely deductive procedure in the investigation of religion. Hume points out the distinctive passional attitude of transcendence which is brought into play in the religious response, and hence which represents a new synthesis of the human elements of passion and belief. Kant deliberately follows a path of delayed exposition among the theoretical, moral, and historical factors in religion, so that the subsequent findings can be expected to have some retroactive effect upon the initial principles and thus compel some readjustment in the proposed working view of religion. And Hegel intertwines the religious attitude so closely with the springs of philosophical speculation that there are religious connotations already present in all his basic judgments about method and reality. For all three men, the relationships between the philosophical framework and the religious faith and practice of men are too complex and interacting to permit any facile deduction of the nature of religion.

The approach which they take is that of analysts, rather than creators and founders, of religion among men. Whatever their ultimate expectation of making a radical evaluation and transformation of religious meanings, they see the initial need for respecting the actual forms and shapes of their subject matter. The distinctive mode of the religious interpretation and practical ordering of life does more than impose the requirement that there must be an internal adaptation of the method and principles of inquiry. It also furnishes our three philosophers with their principal argument for the necessary inclusion of religion within the scope of their inquiry. For none of them is the philosophical study of religion a mere footnote or embellishment, whose addition or omission is indifferent to the main body of philosophy. On the contrary, the philosophical edifice is not completely structured until it includes an examination of the distinctively religious view of human life. To omit such a study would be to overlook one of the major determinations of our belief and practice, and hence to stunt the philosophical effort at understanding and weighing all aspects of human experience. The theory of religion presents a definite test for any claims of formal generalization and experiential adequacy of the methods and leading principles used in a philosophy. The use of such a test shows this theory to be an essential component in the modern philosophical enterprise, rather than an optional side issue.

It is chiefly to underline the indispensable character of the philosophy of religion that its three classical proponents insist upon the *mundanity and human footing* of the subject matter. Their insistence upon these properties is not intended in the reductive sense of claiming that religion consists of nothing other than its worldly and human aspects. Rather, their point is that the presence of these aspects makes it both possible and necessary for philosophy to study the nature of religion. It falls squarely, although perhaps not completely and exclusively, within the province of a discipline engaged in reflecting upon our modes of experiencing and interpreting the world. Religion becomes accessible to philosophy in terms of its active orientation of man in respect to the world, even though such terms may not be the central ones proposed by theologians and may not permit a complete philosophical account of religious reality. Insofar as that reality does affect the human ways of viewing the world and determining conduct therein, it comes within the philosopher's range and helps to specify his problems. The modern experience has made it clear that the philosophy of religion must investigate religiousness under the formal aspect of its mundane and human traits, whatever limitations in principle this approach may impose upon the philosophical understanding of religion.

That the approach required in philosophy of religion need not be sheerly distorting and reductive of its subject matter is evident from the descriptive minimum shared in common by the three men under study. They differ widely in their final clarification and explanation of religion. Nevertheless, Hume, Kant, and Hegel agree that they are dealing with a human reality which displays four constant traits. Human religiousness is: relational and operational, practical and enigmatic, in all its manifestations.

Religion as Relational and Operational.   Man in his religious dimension is being considered, not in artificial isolation from the rest of things, but precisely in his concrete relationships with them, in the openings which he makes and the bonds which he maintains. Such relationships become religious in character, as soon as men realize that their orientation in respect to the world is not exclusively toward the world in its experienced features. Instead, these experienced features of human existence in the world are discerned to have a leading quality about them which points to an order of reality somehow distinct from, and superior to, man in his world. We respond to our situation in a religious manner when we relate our changing, imperilled existence not only to the physical pattern of events but also to a spiritual shaping power, which is responsive to man and hence not simply reducible to the physical order. Emily Brontë concentrates this religious correlation into a single line: "Strange Power! I trust thy might; trust thou my constancy." [1] The attitude of religious transcendence consists basically in the recognition of a superior reality

1. Emily Brontë, "The Visionary," in *Complete Poems of Emily Brontë*, ed. Philip Henderson (London, Folio Society, 1951), p. 245. From the standpoint of the science of religions, Kurt Goldammer offers this description:

> Religion is the experience of a different, higher, and holy power and the enduring commerce with it, the reverential relation to a 'higher' other, which distinguishes itself basically from me, but with which I must remain in an indispensable union. This 'other,' 'higher,' 'holy,' lies in the region of the 'metabiontic,' as Karl Beth has called it, in domains which are not exhausted in and with the individual human life and with the life in nature and cosmos. (*Die Formenwelt des Religiösen* [Stuttgart, Kröner, 1960], p. 10)

whose powerful presence in the world of men and nature fills us with awe, and yet whose kinship in some respects with the human spirit also fills us with trust and hope.

Our religious relationship is thus characterized by a certain lifting up of the human mind and heart toward a spiritual reality, which is powerful over the experienced world and also responsive to our needs. This is to say that the bond in question is not a physical link, existing regardless of our response, but one whose reality depends precisely upon our personal response and hence which is essentially operational in nature. This is a crucial point upon which our philosophers concur in their preliminary description of religion and their justification of a philosophical treatment. They are not concerned to hold that the religious relationship depends solely upon our human operational response, but they do regard its operational character as necessary for showing that religion comes within the scope of philosophy.

The human act of religious recognition is complex, involving both mind and heart, both the factor of cognition and that of desire and practical acknowledgment. Kant will not deny the cognitive element; Hume will not deny the practical element in the actual religions of man; and Hegel will accept the synthesis of these factors as a major aim. In this respect, the classical modern philosophers of religion are the beneficiaries of a long human tradition of reflections on the operational nature of the religious relationship. What is distinctive about their use of that common finding, however, is their systematic inference that it justifies the independent philosophical scrutiny of religion. Philosophers can gain a foothold in the study of religion because of their competence in treating the human acts of knowing, willing, and feeling, considered in all their humanly manifested modes of operation, including the religious. And they must expand this foothold into as comprehensive and well-ordered a theory of religion as their methods and general conceptions of human knowledge and active tendency will permit.

Religion as Practical and Enigmatic. Finally, there is a working consensus about the practical and the enigmatic nature of the religious attitude. These notes follow from the type of operational relationship in question. We orient ourselves religiously toward a divine reality in whose spiritual life we seek to share, but which requires some effort on our part to attain. Whatever the emphasis placed upon the powerful action of the divine living reality, we must respond by opening our own lives to its influence and perhaps by redirecting and reforming our habitual patterns of behavior. This religious sense of responsibility for making an appropriate, practical response deeply affects our personal conduct and social institutions.

The religious motivation of action is one of the powerful shapers of human history, molding and remolding men and societies in accord with what the divine pattern seems to require at various times. Hume altogether deplores the practical impact of religious belief; Kant takes strenuous measures to regulate it by independent ethical standards; and Hegel encloses it within the double context of the ethical state and the practical life of philosophical speculation itself. But none of these thinkers depreciates the actual influence of religious belief and practice upon the whole field of human action, or sidesteps the problems which this practical influence raises for all parts of philosophy. They wrestle with the difficulties, without entirely resolving them. For the philosophical channels and dikes built to control the flow of practical religious energies are invariably flooded over in times of crisis, when a new religious message is heard and forthwith acted upon by expectant believers.

The enigmatic quality of human religiousness is frankly admitted by the three philosophers, but they regard it as a stimulating challenge rather than as a bar to philosophical analysis and judgment. Can the reality of the divine pole of the religious relationship be established by philosophical means? Does the cognitive factor in religion constitute an instance of demonstrative knowledge, a matter of belief, or a sheer delusion? Do the volitional and affective elements in the religious attitude contribute to knowledge or undermine it; do they contribute to human values or undermine them? And must the philosopher of religion remain silently helpless before the claims to have a religious revelation and mystery, or does he have at least some resources for taking a responsible stand toward them and toward their social consequences?

Such questions multiply for Hume, Kant, and Hegel, once they begin probing into that relational-operational-practical-enigmatic reality which religion manifests itself as being in human life. The questions are recurrent throughout the century of investigation, thus constituting a terrain of common issues whereon the philosophical discussion can take place. That the responses differ widely from philosopher to philosopher is due, in part at least, to the complexity of the matter under examination. And in part it is due to some radical philosophical differences in method and in the meaning of the basic conceptions concerning being, knowing, and willing. Yet there is an appropriate adaptation of the plural methods and basic conceptions to man's multiform religious reality. Throughout the period of its classical modern formulation the philosophy of religion is fortunately free from a dull and impoverishing uniformity.

RELIGIONIZING THE THEORY OF GOD

The explicit thematization of religion had a profound and somewhat surprising effect upon the philosophies at our focus. One might expect that the theory of religion would function in these systems as a relatively inert clay, whose molding forms are supplied from elsewhere. But in fact, its role was much more active than that of a receptacle for the application of broader principles. Having joined the company of independently treated philosophical themes, the study of religion began interacting and exerting a reciprocal influence upon the other parts of philosophy. And since the working meaning of religion was taken from the theistic tradition, this intellectual counterforce was exerted very strongly upon the philosophical theory of God. That theory was irrevocably transmuted in consequence of the shift taken in treating religious problems within an autonomous philosophical context (rather than in a theologically determined one), where they are nevertheless accorded central atttention (rather than regarded as distant and often only tacitly indicated corollaries of natural theology and ethics).

Once the examination of religion is admitted as a major task within a self-regulating philosophy, its close relationship with the entire theory of God cannot be ignored or deemed to be of secondary significance for the latter. The formal study of this relationship and the recognition of its decisive importance for understanding and evaluating our philosophical reasoning about God constitute the process of *religionizing* the theory of God. This process is deliberately carried through by Hume, Kant, and Hegel in such methodical fashion that it cannot now be revoked, without making a questionable detour around their philosophies. A distinction does have to be drawn, however, between two phases in this religionizing process: that of clarifying description and that of evaluating explanation. There is fairly broad agreement among the three philosophers in the former stage of the inquiry, but the specific differences between them crop out markedly in the latter stage. There is an impressive concurrence between them on the operative presence of religious considerations in our philosophizing about God, and an equally impressive disagreement on precisely what judgment should be reached about the validity of the theory of God, in view of that presence.

At the level of *descriptive* clarification, our philosophers manifest a symptomatic uneasiness about the meaning of a natural theology. Even before coming to the particular arguments, they recognize a difficulty in determining the precise sense of the adjective "natural," as used to designate this apparently quite straightforward enterprise of developing a philosophical theory of God. If that qualifier is intended to specify that the enterprise is to be carried out entirely apart from religious interests and commitments, then it serves not simply to specify a subdiscipline within philosophy but to place an artificial and hampering restriction around that subdiscipline. If the philosophy of religion were not there to argue its own case by pointing out its teleological influence upon all theistic speculations, this compartmentalizing of the theory of God and this delaying of the religious influence might seem plausible. But once the study of religion comes to the forefront in one's total conception of philosophy, the correlation between the inquiry into God and the religious concerns cannot be passed over. There is a human basis of inquiring about God, and it is permeated by man's religious tendencies. Because these tendencies are operative, the theory of God assumes great importance within a philosophical system and is repeatedly attempted, despite all obstacles and disappointments attached to previous efforts. Men care about developing a sound theory of God, not only because of its intrinsic intellectual challenge but also because of its intimate response to their religious needs.

This concrete setting of human religious needs and tendencies is one emphatic sense in which all three thinkers hold that philosophical theology is natural. Hume stresses this meaning for the naturality of the philosophical theories on God, when he treats them under the heading of natural religion and traces out their passional roots in the religious attitude of fear, curiosity, and hope concerning causal powers shaping our world. Since he distinguishes the question of human origin from that of argumentative validity, however, he does not regard the issue of natural theology as being somehow quickly settled and dismissed by the sole fact of showing its human religious context and teleology. Knowledge of these latter factors is helpful for understanding why it is so difficult to propose and weigh the theistic arguments on their evidential merits alone, but it does not rule out the evidential approach in cases where the theory of

God is controlled by a self-limiting philosophical method and a reflective awareness of the human religious interests at stake.

The meaning of religious naturality is broadened by Kant and Hegel to include some rational factors, since they widen the basis in man's active nature for the genesis of the religious attitude. Kant expands the description of the human needs underlying religious belief and theistic inquiry to include the exigencies of human reason itself, in both its practical and its theoretical aspects. And Hegel argues that the ultimate context for all the human tendencies involved in man's religious formation and search after God is the life of the spirit, which is the life of reason taken in its integral fullness. Thus the presence of the natural religious matrix for inquiries about God does not necessarily compromise the rational integrity of such inquiries, although it adds greatly to the difficulty of judging the actual evidential strength of the whole theory of God.

By retaining a distinction between the religious setting and the intellectual validity of the philosophical theory of God, the classical modern philosophers of religion are considerably more cautious than William James. His *Varieties of Religious Experience* gives ample empirical confirmation to the descriptive part of the theme of the religionizing of natural theology.[2] It furnishes many case histories showing how religious faith animates our reasoning concerning God, and how unconvincing is separation of the theistic arguments entirely from man's religious concern. But it does not follow directly from this stress on the religious context that the theory of God has no other valid function than to clarify religious feeling and belief. For a methodological distinction remains between the practical importance of the subject investigated in natural theology and the rigor of its supporting arguments. They may turn out in particular instances to be invalid, but this does not follow simply from the presence of the religious matrix and its practical motivations. That descriptive presence does not permit the philosophical critic to disregard the structure of the arguments in the theory of God.

Because they recognize the need for direct intellectual analysis of theistic argumentation from different aspects, the classical modern philosophers of religion do not move directly from a descriptive to an evaluative study of the religionizing process. Instead, they bridge the gap with the intermediate question of the *religious relevance* of the arguments for God. This question is not entirely foreign to the natural theologians themselves.

2. See the chapter on "Philosophy" in William James, *The Varieties of Religious Experience* (New York, 1958), pp. 329–47.

Although they may sometimes be reluctant to acknowledge the religious setting of their enterprise, they usually do regard its constructive outcome as a clarification helpful to those who give religious adherence to God. Thus the philosophical theory of God is encompassed on one side by the religious matrix, prompting and sustaining it, and on the other by the religious aim of rendering reasonable service to God which it is intended to promote. This latter aspect provides the modern philosophers of religion with one more significant criterion for judging the inferences concerning the existence and attributes of God. Along with their epistemological and metaphysical means of measuring the theory of God, our three thinkers also use the measure of religious relevance.

Especially where philosophy is viewed as including a study of religion, therefore, it is necessary to ask whether theistic reasoning concerns God precisely as a religious reality. Pascal's sheer dichotomy between the God of philosophers and the God of religious patriarchs cannot quiet this question, because the precise point at issue is whether or not philosophical theology does establish anything relevant for understanding the religious meaning of God. One function of the philosophy of religion is to keep this problem alive, and to press it home against both those who regard the Pascalian contrast as definitive and those who regard the religious relevance of natural theology as beyond dispute.

The latter assumption cannot easily be made within the atmosphere of modern philosophy of religion, thanks to Hume's insistent questioning on the point. The effect of his criticism of natural theology is by no means purely negative, since it leads to a salutary clarification of two types of theistic reasoning—the a priori and the empirical—and their relationship with religious faith. What he calls the a priori approach through mere reason, or the pure rational power of the mind supposedly operating apart from empirical dependencies and the context of habitual connections, is faulted on both its objective and its subjective sides. Objectively, it seeks to impose the ideal of mathematical rigor upon theistic reasoning, without respecting the existential reality and transcendence of its subject matter. Hence it deals with the being of God in the same way in which we would treat an ideal construct, whose reality is developed out of our own defining principles. Such an attitude toward God is repugnant to the religious mind, which insists upon the existential integrity, superiority, and active presence of the divine reality.

And on the subjective side, the a priori method pretends to reach conclusions about God through the bare power of reason, as though it were suddenly excused from observing the human conditions of knowledge, which include the real dependence of our existential reasoning upon the evidence and relationships slowly evolved through experience. Hume's counsel is that the religious mind cannot afford to remain epistemologically ignorant in the modern world. It can no longer indiscriminately accept just any kind of argumentation which claims to furnish it with intellectual support. Instead, it must exert enough self-discipline to demand that the intellectual approach to God respect both the divine religious reality and the human mode of existential inquiry. Hence a philosophically alert believer cannot take comfort in the a priori way to God, but must learn to disengage himself from its dubious help.

The Humean critique of empirical or design-based theism gives the religious inquirer today an even greater opportunity for self-clarification. This it does by making an epistemological challenge of the widespread claim that purely from a study of order in the visible world one can arrive at the divine ordering mind, that one attains certainty in this way without any use of religious faith, and yet that the ordering mind thus attained is the same as the God of our religious worship. Under Hume's tutelage, the reflective believer learns to avoid a routine acceptance of this claim and, more positively, to discover precisely what he is doing in the course of an examination of the visible universe for traces of divinity.[3]

This lesson is worth spelling out in some detail, in view of the fact that, in our evolutionary minded age, men are interested in discovering trends of order which indicate the active divine presence and the convergence of life upon what Teilhard de Chardin names as the Point Omega, or divine threshold of our religious longing. First, Hume presses home the distinction between discovering order *in* nature and affirming a divine source of order *for* nature. One cannot pass effortlessly from the one

3. Hume and Paley are reinterpreted from the linguistic standpoint of the religious use of purpose stories, where the "purpose" model is qualified as being "eternal" or "providential," in order to provoke a religious discernment of the divine presence in nature, but not to make either a demonstration or a probable argument. See I. T. Ramsey, *Religious Language* (New York, 1963), pp. 86–89, and J. M. Smith, "Can Science Prove That God Exists?" *Heythrop Journal*, 3 (1962), 126–38. Pierre Teilhard de Chardin has qualified the scientific model of "evolutionary process" with the religious modifier: "directional and convergent upon a goal," as furnished by his Christian faith; cf. *The Phenomenon of Man* (New York, 1959), pp. 237–308. I. T. Ramsey, *Models and Mystery* (New York, 1964), argues that the shift from picturing models to analogue models occurs both in science and religion and in both instances demands a validation of the empirical fit of the analogue.

meaning of order to the other without making some sort of inference, even though it may remain psychologically concealed. It is best to bring the inference out into the open and test its probative basis and limits. If it rests upon efficient causality or teleology, then one must be prepared either to make an epistemological and metaphysical defense of such causal and teleological inference, as reaching with certainty to the divine reality, or else clarify the sense in which the study of order is a substitutional function serving in the place of any metaphysical theory of cause and purpose.

Second, the inquirer is asked to attend to the successive expansions needed in the meaning of nature and its sphere of organization, in order to gain an intimation of the religiously relevant God. Hume and Kant express this as the difficulty of passing from the basis for the natural (metaphysical and psychological) attributes of God to that for the moral and religious attributes. To infer the reality of a powerful and purposive mind is not yet to insure that this mind has the equivalent qualities of moral goodness and concern for our personal welfare which evoke the religious response. Hume's critical caution is that these latter attributes cannot be justified solely on the basis of the scientifically described natural world. And Kant's point is that the experiential basis for affirming them of God must be taken in the human moral self and in the teleological view of natural happenings and human history. If the meaning of nature as an intimating sign or sacrament of God is enlarged to include the moral self and its purposive judgment, however, then this meaning must be acknowledged to include the factor of moral faith and to be subject to the critical limits placed upon a purposive reading of natural processes. A factor of faith is already operative in the interpretation of the evolving universe, so that it can yield a real religious significance somehow distinct from a direct acknowledgment of the immanent natural activities themselves.

All three philosophers of religion agree upon the third feature of the argument from order, namely, that it derives its persistence and strength from the religious faith which the investigator brings with him to the study of nature. The presence of this commitment prevents him from regarding dysteleological features and evil as ultimately decisive, or as impossible to reconcile with a comprehensive divine purpose for all modes of being. To avoid the charge of flagrant circular reasoning, the believing inquirer into natural processes must become aware of what he is doing and must make his situation explicit for other men. He is not placing brackets around his act of faith, starting out from scratch in the study of the natural world, and thus establishing from it alone the existence of the God of religious worship. Instead, he is trying to establish some communication between what his religious faith (however it may be obtained) tells him about the living world and what his human heritage of ordinary experience and scientific study of evolution tells him about it. His faith cannot prosper in isolation, but must be brought into determinate, unifying relationship with his other modes of interpretation. It cannot be imposed despotically upon the world as ordinarily experienced and scientifically analyzed and controlled, but it can awaken some further significance of this same world for the human agent.

Thus the meditative study of our natural world in its purposive features helps the believer to make his religious interpretation more definite and relevant to other findings about this same world. It suggests that the scientific findings at least point in the direction of an orientation of the universe which calls for a religious response. This is an intellectual work in the order of probability rather than strict demonstration, and the outcome is more likely to strengthen a religious conviction already there than to generate it in the first instance. One is left free either to move into the disclosure situation, specified by an act of religious faith in the divine source and goal of the universe, or else to plead the skeptical privilege by excluding the framework of faith from one's inspection of suffering and moral evil, order and its mechanisms. And one must be prepared also for incessant change in the content of the problem, in view of the steady increment of experience and the growth of scientific theories.

There is no monolithic way of describing the modern *evaluation* of the religionizing of the theory of God. "The" classical modern position is found only in the interchange between the individual philosophers. Hume's view of religion and the theory of God is entirely dominated by his aim of making as sharp a division as possible between popular religion and philosophical religion. From this perspective, there is no univocal meaning for the theory of God but always a systematically ambivalent one. That is, there is a difference in principle between a doctrine on God which is paired with popular religious belief and a doctrine which is paired with the philosopher's conception of religion. In the former case, there is a genuine distinction between the religious belief itself and the philosophical doctrine, but the doctrine remains totally captive and instrumental to the belief. No matter how elaborate a metaphysical fabric of principles and arguments is woven for the theory of God in this condition, it remains radically uncritical about the human origins and noetic limits of that believing act by which it is nevertheless specified and dominated. Such a theory of God achieves only an illusory transcendence of the tumultuous subjective life of human passions, dreams, and probable inferences. It is the permanent victim, and never the reflective master, of the religionizing process and its practical excesses.

Quite another situation prevails for a theory of God which is methodically correlated with the Humean philosopher's notion of religion. Here, there is a perfect identity between the theory of God and the religious relationship itself. Religion has its reality only in the reflective mind, and not in the affective, moving heart. No corruptive domination and illusion are possible, since no difference is permitted to develop between the theoretical judgment and the religious act. Hume recommends their complete adequation as the most effective way of keeping both religion and philosophical theism at the critical minimum required by his study of existential belief and inference, when they point beyond the experienced world. Such a transcendent orientation of human nature has only a slightly probable basis in evidence, not insignificant enough to deny, and yet not firm enough to serve as a guide for conduct. Hence the prudent critical mind will simultaneously limit its theory of God to a bare speculative assent to the probability of there being a superior powerful mind, and also limit its religious act to this very same assent. This theistic belief admits of no further doctrinal elaboration (apart from its justifying basis in the philosophical study of human nature and the anatomy of belief) and no valid practical consequences whatsoever.

For Hume, then, the theme of the religionizing of the theory of God means bringing men to the crossroad where they must choose between indenturing it to popular religion, with its speculative exaggerations and practical tyrannies, or else identifying it strictly with that lean, speculative assent in which the philosopher's religion wholly consists.

Kant also brings us to the crossroads, but describes the alternative in his own fashion. Combining his critique of any metaphysical knowledge of transcendent reality with his view of the moral and religious teleology of human reason, he distinguishes between two ways of taking the theoretical doctrine on God: as existential demonstrative proof and as exploration of a complex human meaning. He agrees with Hume in rejecting the former sense, both because of the phenomenal limitations upon demonstrative knowledge and because of the religious inadequacy of anything which can come within the scope of physical knowledge. He bears down with greater epistemological severity than Hume upon the religious insufficiency of that which can be demonstratively known only on condition of being itself a limited and unfree object, within our spatiotemporal world. Although we might attach the name "God" to such a known object, we could not relate ourselves to it through an attitude of respectful hope and love, and hence could not acknowledge therein the religious reality sought by men. On specifically religious as well as epistemological grounds, then, Kant refuses to integrate religion with a natural theology that claims to furnish metaphysical knowledge of the transcendent God.

But whereas Hume was content to contract religion itself to the residual theoretical belief lingering in the mind, Kant extends his analysis to include a study of the moral basis of belief in God. This move enables him to adopt the second meaning for the speculative theory of God, namely, as signifying a major phase in the exploration of the human meaning of God intended in human acts of morality and religion. Hume had shown that the religious hypothesis, or speculative entertainment of the being of God, is sterile in the sense of being incapable of aiding us to deduce further effects in the world from this premise. Kant accepts, but sharply restricts, this criticism. Precisely what is sterile is the philosophical supposition that the theory of God can be taken as a body of metaphysically demonstrated knowledge, serving as a deductive principle for reaching new objects of knowledge. This supposition is removed by noting that the moral belief in God does not function at all like a scientific hypothesis, and hence that it is not subject to the same kind of test for its fruitfulness. The appropriate test for the moral and religious conviction about God is, not that it lead deductively to new *effects*, but rather that it bring out new *aspects of personal meaning* in the ordinary things of our experience.[4] This conviction does not lead us on restlessly from one object to another; it encourages us to reflect upon the further human significance of the persons we are and the worldly situation we are already in.

Within this context, there is room for natural theology, broadly considered as a heuristic examination of the theoretical aspects contained in

4. John Wilson, *Philosophy and Religion* (New York, 1961), pp. 34–45, observes that the inconvenience of treating religious statements as predictive explanations about the world is that God is thereby reduced to another natural force or objective causal thing, thus dissolving the meaning of the religious bond rather than giving it some intellectual justification. Recent discussion on the cognivity of religious beliefs is well summarized by W. T. Blackstone, *The Problem of Religious Knowledge* (Englewood Cliffs, 1963).

the moral-religious conviction concerning God and our relationship to Him. The basic unity of human reason leads Kant to find some positive value in the human speculative doctrine on God and His attributes, as long as it foregoes the claim to demonstrate the divine existence, to penetrate the divine nature itself (rather than to uncover the human meaning of the divine essence), and to constitute the controlling foundation of ethical obligation. The speculative phase of the doctrine on God retains the important task of using the complex method of negation-eminence-analogy to assure the purity and coherence of our notions about God. It also strives to keep them relevant to human life in its scientific and practical dimensions. These services are indispensable for assuring the intellectual soundness of moral theism and the philosophy of religion.

Thus Kant's meaning for religionizing the theory of God is bound up closely with his reversal of natural theology. It is not enough for him to bar the path to transcendent metaphysics, which would give us our primary natural knowledge of God and the source of our moral and religious actions. He must also open up a positive route for appreciating the theoretical study of God. There are problems of theoretical consistency and analogical inference connected with our moral and religious approach to God. Hence if all the humanly meaningful aspects of this approach are to be investigated and synthesized into a viable pattern, there must be a speculative doctrine of God developed in the service of moral theism and religion. The intellectual needs of our nature require us to make tempered use of such a theory, in order to reach the most adequate human meaning for that reality which religious worship acknowledges to be the holy, good, and just God.

What would happen to the religionizing theme, however, if some sort of metaphysical knowledge were restored to good standing? In that case, the Humean identification of philosophically valid religion with a sliver of theoretical assent to God would seem too narrow, whereas the Kantian superordination of moral and religious theism over the speculative theory of God would seem too inflated. Hegel introduces this unsettling question into the discussion around the philosophy of religion, with predictable results. He gives much more recognition than does Hume to the distinctive structure and modalities of religious life, as well as to their detailed historical impact upon the philosophies and institutions of mankind. He looks for the philosophically justifiable meaning of religion in the very development of these modes of religion and their cultural influences, rather than in Hume's neutralizing alternation of polytheism-monotheism and his aseptic minimum of theistic assent. And yet Hegel does not permit the moral and religious view of God to dominate the speculative inquiry and to determine the ultimate truth of propositions in natural theology, after the manner of the Kantian moral theology. Having provided the speculative theory of the divine reality with an independent metaphysical foundation, he then uses it as a standard for reforming the moral and religious meanings of God.

Translated into the Hegelian frame of reference, the religionizing of the theory of God refers to but one half of the process of deliberately disintegrating the unity of natural theology. The proofs of God's existence and the study of His attributes can be treated first of all as a reflexive expression, in the order of abstract concepts, of the underlying religious acts. The theory of God formalizes the religious lifting of the heart to infinite spiritual life. This is a helpful and unavoidable work, given the human condition of a representational mélange of imagery, feeling, and idea. But the wholly functional dependence of the theory of God upon religion for its vitality and subjective persuasiveness is easily forgotten, once the formal structure of natural theology is erected. For the good health of our mind and its lucidity about the transformation processes of human life, therefore, it is necessary to restore natural theology to its existential context and thus to religionize it in a radical way.

To do this is an act of analytic description and not yet an adequate evaluation of the theory of God in truth terms. Hegel permits the philosophy of religion, acting in its own sphere, to make only a restricted, relative evaluation of the theory of God. It can trace out the transformation process whereby the religious elevation of the heart is restated as a theoretical passage either from the world to God or from the idea of God to His being. But the philosophy of religion cannot determine the ultimate meaning and truth of this passage, without turning to metaphysical logic. Hume's unincorporated theory of religion and Kant's merely morally founded theory of religion are powerless to cope with the question of the philosophical truth of the doctrine on God. For Hegel, therefore, the religionizing of the doctrine on God can be but a first stage in the reformation of natural theology.

The reforming work can be brought to completion only when natural theology and religion are themselves metaphysicized, that is, submitted to reinterpretation by the metaphysics of spirit. Only after it is established metaphysically that the religious elevation to God is a figurative mode of representing the integration of finite spirit into the infinite spirit, can a

rigorous judgment be made on the truth and significance of every speculative and practical doctrine on God. The entire theory of God expresses
the religious elevation of soul in such fashion that it raises the question
of the validity of any passage from the finite to the infinite. Nowhere
else than in his own onto-pneuma-logic does Hegel locate the speculative
answer to this question.

Hegel's most distinctive handling of the religionizing theme occurs in
the course of his exegesis of a saying which had gained currency among
pietists and intuitive philosophers of religion: "God *is* only in religion." [5]
He protests against this assertion in its bald form, as being an instance of
excessive talk about the reality of religion, made at the expense of the
reality of God and the independence of the spiritual totality of being.
It bears the implication that the only divine principle which man can
come to know is that which is the product of his own religious efforts,
divorced from any real initiative and relationship established by the
spiritual whole. Hegel's own view is that all human activities, including
those involved in religious belief and practice, are manifestations and
self-actualizations of the life of absolute spirit. Hence the latter is actively
related and known in the religious stirrings of mankind, without being
reduced to a sheer outcome of human piety and yearning.

Nevertheless, Hegel does not dismiss this saying because of its usual
meaning. Instead, he translates it into his own metaphysical idiom, so
that it will reinforce his view that the religionizing of the theory of God
is only a waystation on the road leading to the complete transformation
of every philosophical and religious conception of God into his own doctrine on absolute spirit. In its amended form, the popular saying tells us
that God is, that He is for us, and that He gives Himself a relationship
to us which originates from His side. The religious insight of mankind
assures us that God is not jealous, that He communicates His own being
to us, and that His self-revelation is indeed a manifesting and giving of
the divine reality in the religious actions of man. But Hegel is not content
merely to conclude that natural theology is a formalization and elucidation of this religious sense of God's self-communication. He presses the
exegesis of the religious commonplace to the point where it requires corrective philosophical interpretation, in three specific ways, through his
doctrine on spirit.

5. Hegel analyzes this saying in *Beweise*, pp. 46–49 (pp. 192–95). The next quotation, ibid., p. 49 (p. 195).

First, the coming of God to man in religion means that there is something special in the actualizing process of infinite spirit, when it shapes itself as the religious relationship. Although infinite spirit manifests itself *in* all modes of being as its categorial determinations, it manifests its own spiritual nature only *to* the finite but reflective spirit of man. The religious manner of expressing this recognition of spirit by spirit is found in the saying that God reserves His self-manifestation for the religious encounter. Every theory of God is thus dependent in some way upon the religious manifestation of the divine spirit to believing and worshipping man.

In the second place, Hegel maintains that the religious opening to God conveys "the more definite thought that it is not the so-called human reason with its limits which knows God, but the Spirit-of-God-in-man, it is, to use the speculative expression previously employed, the self-consciousness of God which knows itself in the knowledge of man." Infinite spirit recovers itself and achieves self-awareness of its own nature, in the very act whereby man recognizes the actuality of spirit and his modal inclusion in its developing life. Thus every human religious apprehension and correlated theory of God constitute a path which infinite spirit provides itself, for coming into its own self-knowledge of divinity.

In view of these two amendments, a third is inevitable. To maintain that God is only in religion is to confess implicitly that the religious attitude cannot entirely penetrate the meaning of spirit. The religious mind can know infinite spiritual reality only under the representational form of God, rather than in its full meaning as self-developing rational spirit. What religion discloses about the spiritual totality is unique to the religious sphere of life, but it is not formally adequate to the whole meaning and truth of spirit. The God who is found in religion and formalized in natural theology points beyond Himself to the all-inclusive life of spirit, which engulfs both man and God. Beneath the claim made for the religious apprehension of God and the religionized theory of God, consequently, there lies a demand of human nature for that closer vision of divinity which can come only from the philosophy of infinite-finite spirit.

Our classical philosophers of religion do not disappoint us in their evaluative accounts of the religionizing of the theory of God. Whatever their points of agreement, they never degenerate into a loud but thoughtless chorus of unison, sounded for its own sake. In the religionizing problem as elsewhere, they maintain a civilized philosophical discussion, in which some radical differences are brought to the fore and supported by reasonable argument.

THE RUPTURED ALLIANCE: MORALITY AND RELIGION

Although still reasonably conducted, the discussion between the three central minds becomes quite passionately intense as it moves into the area of morality and religion. This is the exposed nerve of their controversy, from which radiate all other forms of disagreement among them. It is this issue which fully establishes for them the importance of the philosophy of religion and the need to develop this theory in rigorous conformity with their respective philosophical convictions about man the knower and agent. And consequently, it is at this port of entry that we can understand most readily the urgent nature of the process whereby the philosophy of religion received its classical modern shaping and prominence.

The cultural context for the views of Hume, Kant, and Hegel on the problem of religion and morality was furnished by the eighteenth-century Enlightenment in the European countries. Whatever the tensions between the deistic, theistic, and materialistic shades of opinion, there was an impressive consensus about the deleterious social influence of religion when it exerts some control over political decisions and the disposition of public social power. For such influence does not stem from religion defined in a rarefied ideal fashion, but from the actual, particular religions which vie for a favored place in the political arena. The established religions bring with them a party spirit, dedicated to improving their special corporate interest rather than the common good of humanity. When conflicting religious motivations become entangled with the strife over social power, sincere men will eagerly engage in religious wars, persecution of minority groups, and more subtle forms of civil disability and social discrimination. Whether or not such fruits be regarded as contrary to the best aims of human religiousness, the Enlightenment leaders systematically sought the political and theoretical means for preventing their future occurrence.

Among the latter means was a concentration of fire upon the link between morality and religion, which could no longer simply be presumed to be indispensable and beneficial. The all too visible products of the union between religion and political power were inhumane, not only in the sense of being pragmatically disastrous for our worldly interests but also as being strictly immoral or opposed to the social ideals of humanity. Thus it could be argued that a more reflective understanding of the religious outlook would eventually lead believers themselves to seek disestablishment and to support a public order more in accord with social morality.

But the main thrust of the Enlightenment strategy was to make the entire morality-religion relationship a radically problematic one. Bayle and the modern skeptical tradition contributed to this movement by highlighting instances where religious motives were used (whether hypocritically or not) to deaden moral sensibility at the personal and social levels, by justifying actions which violate the dignity of other men and the common weal of society. The example of morally upright, but non-religious, men was also used to suggest that morality is detachable in principle from religion.[6] It could no longer be taken for granted that the removal of religion would mean the moral dissolution of individual and social life. There would remain a basic human respect for justice in our interpersonal relations, entirely apart from whether or not the members of a community profess religious belief. Indeed, Holbach and Diderot took the offensive in sketching a personal and social morality based solely upon this-worldly human considerations and a materialistic conception of reality.

Although such thoughts succeeded in rendering questionable the bond of religion with morality, they did not lead by themselves to a philosophical settlement. This could only be accomplished in the course of making a thorough philosophical reconstruction, which would treat the Enlightenment problems in function of a general theory of religion and morality. The difference between raising skeptical difficulties about the moral worth of religion and making a full-scale, systematic reassessment was what marked the distance between the Enlightenment background and the actual philosophical treatment of the problem by the three central philosophers of religion. The cultural context made the issue unavoidable and pressing for them, but it did not dictate the ultimate form of their philosophical judgments on the matter. Hence their teachings on religion and morality cannot be reduced merely to a chapter in the history of religious ideas.

Whatever the cultural situation, the detailed doctrinal positions of the three philosophers rest upon some dominant methods of philosophical interpretation. Hume embodies the *separatist* approach, which seeks in principle to isolate religion from morality in order to insure the integrity

---

6. R. H. Popkin, "The High Road to Pyrrhonism," *American Philosophical Quarterly*, 2 (1965), 28, points out that this example is highly ambivalent in Bayle's hands, since it may lead one either into fideism or into a wholly dereligionised morality.

and strength of moral judgments. The correlational and *completional* standpoint is taken by Kant, who stresses the ordering between the moral foundation of duty and the religious factor of sustaining hope. And Hegel proposes an *organic modalizing* of both morality and religion, considered as distinct modes of a spiritual totality which envelops and subordinates them both within its sovereign law of rationality. The archetypal solutions of separatism, completional ordering, and organic modalizing do not exhaust the philosophical ways of treating the morality-religion topic, but they do comprise the fundamental paths explored in the classical modern development of philosophy of religion. No fresh suggestion can earn the right of a hearing until it first wrestles with the problems and values represented by the participants in this dialogue.

Hume speaks to us at two levels of discourse. At the level of historical experience, his voice is a constant reminder of the actual story of human religions, with the accent falling upon the foolishness and tyranny men have imposed upon one another, under the prompting of religious beliefs. His reading of the record is highly selective, but the point is that the inhumane consequences of popular religion are there to select and cite. He turns the tables upon the apologetic argument of Charron, Pascal, and the Christian skeptics, who stressed the imbecility and misery of natural man as evidence of the need to turn toward a divine revelation. Hume's counteranalysis is that all religions feed upon this universal condition, and only intensify it with their demands for faith and obedience. They play upon the passions of terror and adulation, weakening a man by appeal to the former force and then depriving him of a sense of measure and integrity by encouraging the latter. The religious stance drains off our practical interest in achieving justice in everyday social relations, while simultaneously opening the sluices for using social power to advance the special interests of some particular church. This is only an expanded way of saying that the religions of mankind actually operate as a demoralizing force, a principle inimical to our moral interests and ideals.

But is not religion capable of reforming itself and thus of becoming a principle of comfort, hope, and harmony among men? In replying to this objection, Hume distinguishes between the necessary and the accidental consequences of religion, thus moving from the plane of historical conscience to that of strict philosophical analysis. Conceding that religion may have some beneficial social effects, he restricts them to special circumstances and traces their active origin, not to religious belief and practice as such but to some other human source, with which religion becomes temporarily allied and hence for which religion serves as a contingent carrier of benefits for man. At the level of philosophical discourse directed by his own theory of man and morals, however, Hume holds that religion is and must be antithetically related to morality. The religious spirit must function as a disruptive intrusion into the sphere of moral judgment and conduct, and any practical line of conduct primarily sponsored by religious motivations must be subversive of the self-interest and just social order of humanity. For whatever the historical permutations, the moral mind bases its judgment upon the worldly reference of the passions to oneself and other experienceable human selves, whereas the religious mind is regulated by a faith-subversive-of-moral-reasoning and by a divinity-subversive-of-the-natural-social-order.

If it be retorted that this contrast is too sharp and static, Hume will make a sober inventory of his philosophy of human nature to show that the resources are lacking for religion to reform itself and still remain a practical power, without undermining moral sentiment and reasoning. The most likely source for such an internal, reforming principle would lie in the instrumental use of philosophical theism to refine our religious conceptions and drives. But a major article in the Humean critique of natural theology and the argument from design is their inability to reach a morally qualified God, and hence to resist corruption by the passions that underlie popular religion and impede moral judgment. A philosophical theism based upon purely speculative definitions and an analogy drawn from physical nature cannot provide a basis of reform for religion, as a principle of action.

Our understanding is not entirely cut off from an obscure presentiment of a superior powerful reality, but it cannot bring its weak belief in divinity into a morally ordered relationship with our actionable world. To do so would require the cooperation of our senses, imagination, and passions, all of which are alien to the transcendent spiritual realm. There cannot be a human form of concrete reasoning which is at once concerned with the divine reality and integrated harmoniously with the practical moral relationships among men. Separatism is the only safe and reasonable policy to observe for religion and morality, just as a wholly nonpractical assent to God is the only justifiable position to retain in natural theology.

Without underestimating the corruptive tendencies in a theologico-political alliance, Kant is nevertheless dissatisfied with Hume's basic reasoning on the problem of morality and religion. He feels that the separatist solution would follow only conditionally, namely, if the intellectual basis of theism were laid in metaphysical and physico-theological arguments, and if ethics were then constructed upon this speculative basis as a means of explicating the practical consequences of natural theology. But having made a detailed criticism of this twofold condition, he rejects the conclusion on the morality-religion question which it governs. Hume's isolationist policy is tolerable only as an emergency measure, needed to liberate political order from theological partisanship, and liberate theistic inquiry itself from the overclaims made by the rationalist metaphysicians and the physicotheologians. Once this disengagement is achieved, however, some new possibilities must be investigated for the positive relating of morality and religion. For Kant, the philosophical task is to establish a proper ordering between them, rather than keeping them in permanent alienation.

The clue to determining the properly human relationship here comes from reflecting upon the nature of moral theism itself. The founding evidence for our assent to God comes from man's practical moral condition, as a composite personal agent seeking the integrity of virtue and the satisfaction of proportionate happiness, within the conditions of nature. If the fundamental assent to God is thus responsive to the moral situation of man, then every other valid conception of God and practical relationship with Him must bear a similar character. Reflection upon the moral self and the human moral community is the ordering principle for every speculative study of God and every practical response to Him, insofar as such studies and responses come within the range of philosophical critique. To observe this rule is to remove the danger of building either morality or religion upon a purely speculative conception of God, drawn from metaphysical definitions and physical analogies. At best, such definitions and analogies are nonmoral, and at worst they are antithetical to the morally qualified God. Hume's objection to the intrusion of religion into morality is telling against a mode of religion basing itself upon such theological speculation and its concomitant theological ethics, but religion thus molded is violating the rule of moral theism and its own internal constitution.

Kantian religion is never the passive victim of either the play of passions or the theoretical reasoning in natural theology, because it regulates both factors by their common reference to the moral self and the human moral community. To the degree that religion accepts this reference and meaningfully applies the rule of moral theism to religious notions and practices themselves, it does have the power of *self-reform*. It can recognize that the human foundations for religious assent and service are rooted in man's moral life, and hence that the religious attitude ought to prolong and perfect the moral strivings of our nature. Religion does not come as an invading enemy into the exclusive territory of morality: it is the further development of the same human tendencies and practical reflections which constitute us as moral agents.

Far from militating against our moral reasoning and relationships, therefore, the religious factor works toward their fuller realization. It brings to the fore of human awareness and activity the latently religious aspects of moral existence itself. Moral respect is deepened into religious reverence before the personal source of law. To the rigor of duty, religion adds the joyful performance of dutiful action and the hope of attaining the good toward which such action strains. And the reasonable bonds among men are strengthened by acknowledging God as the Lord of the entire human community, in its historical journey. By remaining true to its moral theistic foundations, religion thus achieves its own reforming passage from craven to wise fear, from terror to hope, and from despotism to free service.

The keynote of Kant's philosophy of religion is, therefore, the completional ordering between the independent moral basis and the religious consummation of our practical life. This right ordering is disturbed by the rationalists, who deduce religion from natural theology and ethical duties from our duties toward God. But it is also violated by the two kinds of *paganism*: crude and sophisticated.[7] By crude paganism, Kant means any religious attitude which respects moral conscience, but fails to reach the personal God of moral theism. The failure comes either because it does not yet have the historical maturity of seeking a personal God or because its base of analogy still lies in physical nature, rather than in the moral self. Fortunately, the active tendency of the moral seed of religion can be relied upon to bring men to eventual dissatisfaction with an impersonal religious relationship, or one in which the kinship of moral man

---

7. Crude paganism (*ethnicismus brutus*) lacks any definite conception of a personal reality transcending nature and of our human moral relation with that reality, whereas sophisticated paganism (*ethnicismus speciosus*) does have this conception, but nevertheless bases the religious relation and man's salvation upon something other than an upright moral disposition (*Streit*, p. 46). Kant holds that some paganism is present in every religious faith so that religious reform becomes an unending task.

with God is not yet recognized as central. Moral theism, along with a morally oriented religion, stands on the horizon as the proper fulfillment of this inchoative religious position.

But the case is quite different with sophisticated paganism, that is, with a religious outlook which deliberately substitutes something else for the moral basis of theistic assent and the moral measure of a man's worth before God. Christian revelation as such does not constitute such a de-ordination, but often tempts men to take a competitive and substitutional view of the relation between morality and religion. The sophisticated paganism of those who treat the creed as a replacement for moral reflection through practical reason, and who regard the rites of religion as a justification apart from observance of moral duty, is only the reverse side of the Humean attitude. To evacuate the moral grounding of religious belief and practice (the net effect of sophisticated paganism) is just as crippling to the human spirit as it is to suppress the religious implications of morality (Hume's aim). And hence Kant's counsel against theological paganism remains the same as against moral naturalism: remain close to the human ordering between foundational moral integrity and completional religious hope.

After an initial hesitation, Hegel refused to hail this Kantian imperative as the key to the peaceable kingdom, in which morality and religion would sit down amicably together for the benefit of man. For one thing, it fails to take into account the whole human reality of religion, which cannot be reduced simply to a prolongation of the moral life. Morality does have religious implications, just as the religious attitude has its moral repercussions. But they remain distinct spheres of life, whose entire meaning cannot be cramped into the area where the one overlaps the other. Religion does incorporate some basic moral elements, but in such a way that they are received into a distinctive context possessing its own rooting in the soul. Religion does not have merely a completional relationship with respect to moral striving: it constitutes a new ordering of the human soul directly toward the divine spiritual reality. The language of duty must be transposed into that of love and communion in order to express the religious attitude, and for this reason a religion of hope-as-correlative-of-duty cannot be the last word in the religious order. The Kantian exegesis of religion in terms of hope, answering to the situation provoked by moral obligation, can only be a partial and uncentered theory.

Hegel employs at least four means for taming the ethical conception of religion. His first move is to stress the plurality of the kinds of religion of mankind, repudiating the notion of an undeviating core of natural religion and hence locating the full meaning of religion in the total pattern to which each kind contributes, within its own cultural situation. He uses the threefold division into religions of nature, religions of spiritual individuality, and the absolute religion, to characterize and subordinate the work of his predecessors in the philosophy of religion. Hume's analysis is proportionate to the religions of nature, but remains blind to the ethical and revelational values in religion. Kant's approach is appropriate to the level of the religions of spiritual individuality and morality, the conditions and limits of which are brilliantly illuminated by his theory.

However, the religious spirit of mankind has some further needs and potencies, which cannot be satisfied by remaining at the plane of a morally oriented religion. Human religiosity is fundamentally ordered toward a participation in the divine spiritual life which is inwardly constitutive of everything, and, to the extent that moralistically interpreted religion erects an obstacle to this full union, it has to be surpassed. The strength of the Kantian notion of religion lies in stressing a dialectical break with the immediacy of our piety toward nature, but its weakness lies in not permitting the religious impetus to fulfill itself in man's organic union with absolute spirit. Ultimately, the ethical conception of religion must give way to the Hegelian religion of the absolute.

Secondly, the phenomenological course of life uncovers the essential instability of the moral outlook itself and the corresponding moral types of religion. One major purpose of Hegel's phenomenological analysis is to present the moral outlook as a distinctive shape of the soul and shaper of culture, but also as one which is not self-sufficient, terminal, and thus immune to painful developments beyond its own horizon. Any attempt to arrest the flow of spiritual life within a moral bastion is soon undermined by the forms of skeptical, comic, and cultic liquidation. Moral customs and certainties are called into question by the understanding, purged by artistic representation and satire, and overcome in practice by the worshipping acts of men in search of closer union with divinity. A similar fate overtakes any religious program confining itself to the implications of moral duty, and thus preventing the freest expression of human religiousness in its own right. Whereas Kant centers spiritual freedom around a morally regulated religion, Hegel locates it in the religion of the absolute or the effort to share in the developing life of the spiritual whole. The function of the phenomenology of unhappy consciousness is to impel the religious spirit to move beyond moral dualisms to such a unity as revelational religion images forth and as the philosophy of absolute spirit grasps in its truth and actuality.

In explaining why some religious minds are reluctant to make this ultimate move or to concede that the failure to do so is inhumane, Hegel must use his third instrument: the metaphysical critique of moral theism. Their reluctance is due to a freezing of the mind at the stage of moral theism, along with a refusal to accept the religious reconstruction entailed by the Hegelian onto-pneuma-logic. Because his conception of spirit and reason is practical as well as theoretical, Hegel can use it as a standard for judging the relative adequacy of moral and religious positions. The religion of moral theism retains some sharp distinctions between man and God which prevent the religious relationship from being interpreted as that between finite modes and an organic totality, realizing itself in the form of these modes. Consequently, a religious outlook structured by moral theism is bound to appear to Hegel as an instance of religious positivity and estrangement. The distinctions it fosters only serve to alienate man from nature and spiritual actuality, thus frustrating the central religious urge toward our unification with all aspects of natural and spiritual being. Morally shaped religion divides man from God, faith from knowledge, and the empirical from the spiritual self. Hence it is a basis of religious anti-humanism, until it becomes thoroughly subordinated as a waystation in man's search for the religion of the absolute.

Someone instructed in the Hegelian dialectic might reply, however, that these strictures apply only to abstract morality and right, but not to concrete ethical actuality and its corresponding religious attitude. That is why Hegel must weave a fourth strand into his argument, consisting of his study of the state and religion. Like his fellow philosophers of religion, he recognizes that religion is a powerful social force, affecting man not only in his private life and interior dispositions but also in his institutions and public forms of activity. He does not share Hume's hope that religion can eventually be quarantined in its social influence, but agrees rather with Kant that the problem is to accept its social influence, along with the competence of moral reason to determine its own affairs.

Since ethical life is realized in the state as the encompassing social order, religion must respect the integrity of political reason as operating within its own sphere of responsibility. Religion and the ethical order of the state are codeterminant modes of human reality, aiding each other but also retaining their distinct purposes within the organic whole. Religion ministers to a unique human need, one which develops within the state but which does not concern itself solely about the ethical actuality of the state. By this route as well, then, Hegel is able to distinguish between the ethical and religious facets of life, and to entrust religion with more responsibility than simply that of explicating the ethical vision of individual and social man. It must press on to a presentiment of spiritual actuality in its absolute nature and vitality for man.

After viewing these three major theories about the relation between morality and religion together, we can realize the complexity of the problem and its resistance to any simplified solution. Hume's way of separatism, Kant's completional method, and Hegel's organic modalizing—these are basic responses to the issue, even though they are not exhaustive of all the philosophical resources which can be brought to bear. They correspond, respectively, to our concern lest moral integrity be lost in the web of religious rites, to our recognition of the mutual services performed by a religious disposition sensitive to moral duty and a moral attitude leading to religious hope, and finally to our acceptance of the quite distinctive manner in which religion orients men toward the divine spiritual life.

Yet these three philosophical solutions engage our attention, not only because of their answering quality in regard to common human thoughts on religion but also because of their speculative coherence and appropriateness. Each one is suited to, and dictated by, the controlling philosophical principles from which it springs. The theoretical commitments of our philosophers concerning human nature and its capacities for action lead them ineluctably to their proper positions on how to relate morality and religion. There is no artificial leap made at this point in the argument, so that any criticism of these moral positions can become fully effective only by engaging in discussion of their philosophical underpinnings.

THE NATURAL HISTORY OF RELIGIOUS FAITH

The sources under study are in impressive agreement upon the universal need of faith, as a principal ingredient in the religious attitude. Whatever valuation they may make, the three thinkers recognize the constitutive function and power of religious faith. Although it may not directly move the Alps an inch, it does move and mold men into a distinctive frame of mind which in turn affects events in the physical and cultural worlds. And to this extent, the act of religious faith comes within the scope of philosophical analysis.

The joint claim that philosophy of religion can examine, and indeed independently evaluate, the element of religious faith was not acceptable to the principal parties in the theological discussion at mid-eighteenth century. The orthodox theologians were split internally. Some of them regarded an autonomous philosophical examination of faith as an outright denial of its supernatural character, whereas others regarded it as a timid compromise on the road to a strict and desirable demonstration of the entire content of faith. For their part, most pietists regarded the exercise as an excessively intellectual approach to the feelingful reality of faith. And at the other end of the scale, the skeptics regarded the constructive claim as being too rash and benign in its intent.

In the midst of this clash of positions, the classical modern philosophers of religion learned to steer an independent course. They conceded to the pietists that feeling has a place in religious faith, but quickly pointed out that its precise role has to be determined and related to the intellectual factor. They saw in the extremes of skepticism and theological rationalism an urgent reason for connecting one's theory of knowledge and conception of faith, in order to make a specific blend of caution and conviction in religious matters. And all three philosophers admitted that their inquiries into religion turned up serious problems for the Christian theology of supernatural faith. On this score, however, they insisted that at least some aspects of the human reality of religious faith do receive illumination from their philosophical conception of man. Even the remotest clues on such an important issue should be investigated, just as far as philosophy can reach.

Such a program leads to a philosophical sort of *natural history* of religious faith. The aim is to examine the structure of the believing act in its religious form, to ascertain the determinants in human nature for shaping this assent, and to specify the grounds in human experience for regarding it as reliable and beneficial for us. In other words, religious faith is to be investigated as a definite shaping attitude in our life, having a genesis in our active tendencies to believe and a basis of acceptance in the human situation, which it enables us to interpret and enhance.

This core purpose controls the sense in which there is a naturalizing of religious faith. The latter is inspected insofar as it bears the properties of an act and content of human belief, that is, insofar as it can be connected with the philosophical principles bearing upon human nature in its believing functions. Whether or not there is a total reduction of religious faith to what such principles can determine, depends upon how each philosopher relates himself to Christian revelation. But even apart from this latter issue, they concur in finding that some broadly human aspects of religious faith can be elucidated through their philosophical methods. Hume's method brings out the passional aspects in the natural history of religious faith; Kant's underlines the moral motif in this natural history; and the method of Hegel restores the metaphysical dimension. Between them, the three inquirers make good their claim that our understanding of religious faith is deepened and sharpened by the philosophical study of its human features.

Hume sets the tone of this classical investigation with his firm distinction between the causes and the grounds of religious belief. If the philosophy of religion is to gain any foothold, it must look into the active tendencies in our nature impelling us to believe, as well as into those traits of our experience warranting us to accept statements of belief as meaningful and in some sense well founded. The former phase of the inquiry may lead to some unexpected and disconcerting findings about the complex human factors entering into the genesis of our attitude of religious belief, but the Socratic precept of self-understanding must be honored here as everywhere else in the study of human nature. Yet, however deeply we may be shaken by the progressive uncovering of the causes shaping religious belief, we cannot legitimately permit these findings to determine, by their presence alone, the question of the validity or cognitive grounds of the statements of religious faith. The two questions remain distinct, although the causes of belief can sometimes be regarded as relevant grounds for regarding the religious assent as true or untrue.

Although he would give it a more anthropological twist, Hume could well approve of Kierkegaard's choice of a motto from Edward Young's *Night Thoughts*:

> Are passions, then, the pagans of the soul?
> Reason alone baptiz'd? alone ordain'd
> To touch things sacred? Oh, for warmer still! [8]

8. Edward Young, *The Complaint, or Night Thoughts*, IV.629–31, in *The Poetical Works of Edward Young*, ed. John Mitford (2 vols. London, Bell, 1906), 1, 71. In his customary manner, Søren Kierkegaard quotes the first half of this passage as an epigraph, but intends us to ponder the entire poetic meaning: *Either/Or*, trans. Swenson, rev. by H. A. Johnson (2 vols. New York, Doubleday, 1959), 1, 1. On Kierkegaard's notion of faith as a response of passionate subjectivity (the believer's personal heart and mind), which breaks both with unreflective immediacy and with Hegelian mediating reason, cf. Cornelio Fabro, "Faith and Reason in Kierkegaard's

Hume himself would answer this question with a resounding negative. It is utterly artificial to reduce the act of faith to the same category as the act of assenting to the conclusion of a speculative demonstration. The latter sort of assent is properly restricted to the study of abstract, nonexistential relations, whereas religious assent is decisively concrete and concerned with an existential relationship between man and God. Bare reason, stripped of its concrete matrix in the passions and habitual associations of human life, is unable to establish the religious bond between man and a superior active power. This does not spell the elimination of every cognitive factor in religious faith, but it does mean that such a factor is only one component in the concrete propensity to believe in the divine powerful mind.

Hume takes an essentially componential view of the act of religious faith. It is never the outcome of an exclusively ratiocinative process but rather of a concrete train of thinking, wherein imagination and the passions are codeterminants of religious cognition. Hence these latter factors must be "baptized," through their prominent inclusion in the philosophical analysis of religious faith. Whatever one may hold on a revelational basis about the divine aid needed for religious faith, this act owes its human origin to the joint workings of passion, habit, and imagination upon the mind. In this sense, there is a profound truth in the religious tradition which bids us turn to God with our whole soul and our whole being. Religious faith signifies this *whole turning* of man to the divine source of life, and not simply the intellectual element in the assent.

Hume also makes some headway in specifying those mighty passions which incline men to believe in the divine reality. He traces religious belief to the operation of our fear of an unknown power acting in the everyday world, our desire to know the causes of such events and relations as affect human welfare, and our unceasing hope for a quality of happiness surpassing the satisfactions supplied by technical control over nature and human cultural relations. On polemical and purgative grounds, indeed, Hume stresses the play of a debasing sort of fear and thirst for happiness. And he is loathe to concede any reforming principle within popular religion as such. Nevertheless, his distinction between popular and philosophical religion supposes that men do have some internal resources for evaluating different religious attitudes. They are able to achieve different

Dialectic," in A *Kierkegaard Critique*, ed. H. A. Johnson and N. Thulstrup (New York, 1962), pp. 156–206.

qualitative orderings of the passions which are generative of religious faith. This is the implicit Humean recognition of the question of how men of faith have striven to purify their fear, so that it is the beginning of religious wisdom and not its sorry master.

Hume's passional framework also permits the philosopher of religion to establish a juncture between the problem of faith and that of the search for happiness. The former is never a purely theoretical problem, and what keeps it thoroughly practical is its close connection with the search for happiness. In its practical and yet transcending quality, the response of religious faith is proportioned to the human search for a happiness inclusive of, and yet surpassing, our attachments with nature and human society. We are believers, because we are first of all bearers of this great hope. Fear is there to remind us of the threats to our hope; the desire for connective knowledge is there to give us orientation and daily alleviation; and philosophical criticism is there to temper the claims to knowledge and union arising from that hope. Thus the other passions do affect our act of religious faith. But it is in the pursuit of happiness that the search itself sustains our existence, and prompts us to believe in the presence and accessibility of the divine, caring mind.

In judging the validity or evidence-backed acceptance of religious belief as true, Hume and Kant agree that such belief cannot and should not be regarded as an instance of demonstrated speculative knowledge. But whereas Hume finds here nothing more for the philosophical critic than a vague hypothesis supported by a weak analogy, Kant maintains that there is a closer approximation between the factual strength of religious affirmation and the response justified by philosophical analysis. The theistic belief underlying a religious response is not a theoretical act of knowing, and cannot become such without diverting the believer away from the free spiritual reality intended by the religious relationship. And yet this belief is not to be confounded with a weak form of theoretical hypothesis, because the latter is a doctrinal type of belief remaining within the speculative order. The man of faith confronts us with a distinctive *religious practicality*. The kind of practicality belonging to theistic belief and religious hope is not that of a theoretical hypothesis or a technical tool: it is a moral and interpersonal practicality, indicating an intimate relationship with the active tendencies of man. Kantian belief in God is not a theoretical hypothesis but a moral postulate, in the quite definite sense of being recommended and required by man's total situation as a free agent, seeking to realize the moral law within the natural world.

Kant's emphasis upon the moral basis of the belief and hope in God is not dictated solely by his plan for the moral reconstitution of the doctrine on God, therefore, but also by his interest in the distinctive nature of religious practicality. He revises the natural history of religious faith in order to include the moral, along with the passional, factors inclining men to believe in God and bring religious hope into their lives. Belief and hope are revelatory of something more in the active nature of man than Hume's passional analysis was equipped to show. For they help us to see that man's search for happiness is not a hedonic sensuous impulse, but an inclination of the whole person toward the realization of all the components in our active human nature. Kant does not base moral obligation upon this ideal of the complex realization of human personality, but neither does he suppress its presence and importance in practical life. Because religion concentrates upon the mutual relationship between the integral human person and the personal God, it gives moral significance to the themes of hope and happiness, thus helping to humanize the moral order as an actional integration of virtue with happiness.

Kant adds the distinctive factor of will to the active tendencies specified by Hume as determinants of belief in God. In doing so, he does not convert theistic belief into a voluntaristic surge of blind affirmation, catering to human wishes, but helps to specify more closely the meaning of religious practicality. His insistence upon the presence of moral will in the act of theistic belief has a fourfold significance. First it is a stenographic way of stating that this act belongs in the practical order of cognition, where imagination and the passions make their contribution as integrated within the moral disposition of man. In the second place, it underlines the freedom of theistic belief, by contrast not only with any external coercion from social authorities but also with any internal compulsion from impulses and desires, which may not yet be integrated under morally reflective will. Its third function is to highlight the ordering activity requisite for having the acts of theistic belief and religious hope minister to a free personality. In his theory of religion, Kant is obliged to distinguish between will taken just as free choice and will taken maximally, as the unremitting aim of achieving the primacy of moral law and the ordering of activity around the ideal of the well-ordered personality. Will in both senses is an essential component in forming the disposition of the religious man.

And finally, the Kantian stress upon the role of will in the act of theistic belief is intended to place a demand upon the believer. Genuine belief is not just a matter of custom and upbringing, and not even a matter of stating in third-person discourse that such and such is certain or is contained in the creed. The believing and hoping individual must engage himself in a first-person affirmation: *I* am certain about this, and *I* believe that. The creed is only a retrospective impersonal formulation of the personal credo. A believer may be born into a community nourished upon a creed, but he can acquire his religious maturity only by a voluntarily directed affirmation of his credo, his personal conviction of God's existence and his bond of hope-fear-love with God.

It is within this context that Kant deals with the problem of modern *atheism*.[9] He suggests that this problem would not have arisen, or at least would not have attained to major proportions, had proper attention been paid to the moral setting for all inquiries about God and to the moral-belief character of our affirmations concerning our religious relationship with Him. Atheism takes two forms in the modern world: dogmatic or positive, and skeptical or negative. Dogmatic atheism makes the positive assertions that the idea of God is impossible, and that there is no human basis for affirming the existence of God. In Kant's analysis, both assertions depend upon taking a purely metaphysical and physical approach to the meaning and existence of God. Only when the moral self and its voluntary tendency are made central, can we grasp the real possibility or internal coherence in the morally qualified meaning of God, as well as the practical grounds for accepting His existence. In other words, dogmatic atheism is a tenable position only as long as the moral basis for belief in God and religious hope is systematically ignored by ontotheology and physicotheology.

As far as skeptical atheism is concerned, Kant distinguishes between using it as a propaedeutic method for clearing the air of epistemological confusions and then settling in it as a permanent, sufficient frame of mind. He himself withholds assent from all claims to have a metaphysical or physical demonstration concerning the existence and nature of God. But this is a preparation for discerning the grounds in our moral life for

9. *Religionslehre*, pp. 28–29; *Reflexionen*, 17, 206, 603–04, 18, 520, 556. To broaden his polemical thrust, Kant usually contrasts the religious attitude with unbelief, rather than simply with atheism. Unbelief can be founded *either* on an atheistic naturalism *or* on an attempt to replace moral theism by some physical or metaphysical reasoning as the basis of religion. Modern atheism is examined historically by Cornelio Fabro, *God in Exile: Modern Atheism* (Westminster, 1968); phenomenologically by W. A. Luijpen, *Phenomenology and Atheism* (Pittsburgh, 1964); analytico-phenomenologically by A. MacIntyre and P. Ricoeur, *The Religious Significance of Atheism* (New York, 1969); and in a Kantian perspective by James Collins, "A Kantian Critique of the God-Is-Dead Theme," in *Kant Studies Today*, ed. L. W. Beck (LaSalle, 1969), pp. 409-31.

belief in God and for religious hope, rather than a prelude to permanent skeptical suspension of assent to God and the religious reference of our lives. Once the contrast is drawn between theoretical demonstration and moral belief-with-conviction in the holy, creative, and morally good God, there is no further function for skeptical atheism. In the wake of the Kantian study of belief, it is made superfluous. To harden the skeptical negation into an ultimate way of life is to exchange an old epistemological confusion for a new one.

Characteristically, Hegel sought a way of enveloping and transcending all parties in the discussion about religious faith. Granting that the older metaphysicians and physicotheologians had failed to back up their claim to speculative knowledge, nevertheless men would simply oscillate between skepticism and moral faith until the genuine speculative basis was brought to light. Hence Hegel's intent in treating the natural history of religious faith was not merely to add an ontological strain, which can be interwoven with the passional and moral ones, in a relationship of equal footing. Rather, its presence would mean that all other elements in the act and content of religious faith are to be fundamentally relativized and reinterpreted in function of the ontological principle. Its purpose was to enable us to understand that the entire natural history of religious faith is only a modal phase within the all-embracing history of absolute spirit.

Hegel distinguishes three conditions for questing man in the modern world. The first is the *naturalistic* attitude of total concentration upon the contingent, temporal problems of everyday life. They are approached sometimes with complete forgetfulness of any further claims upon man, a deafness to any call to a vocation orienting our lives toward the divine and the eternal. Sometimes, this call is heard and causes a dim anxiety, but it is sternly quelled with a moral precept to devote oneself entirely to the secular work at hand. The second condition of modern man is essentially a transitional one. Here, the claims of the divine reality upon us are heard and honestly attended to. There is a groping apprehension of the spiritual basis of life, and a practical response through sacramental actions and community service. This *religious* attitude is the grand hinge for breaking men away from a purely naturalistic view of their destiny, and orienting them toward the divine spiritual order.

And finally, there is the purposive agency of the *philosophical* mind itself. It penetrates the alienations of the naturalistic and religious outlooks, recognizing that the spiritual whole is ceaselessly working out its own development through these partial positions. Thus philosophy achieves an internal and comprehensive unification of life's secular and religious values. Hegel sees the great task of freedom in our age to lie precisely in the effort at incorporating the first two conditions of man (the naturalistic and the religious) into the third, or philosophical, state.

Within this ontopneumalogical perspective, then, the natural history of religious faith in God constitutes the second condition of man described above. It is in the religious phase of the total process that men learn to recollect themselves, to free themselves from preoccupation with other things, and thus to win their proper share in the great community of spiritual life. It is important to take the phrase "religious faith in God" in its strongest, compositive sense. Hegel does not want it to be thought that the God of theism remains unaltered, even though He is viewed now with the eyes of faith, and now with those of the metaphysician or even the beatified soul. What men regard as the personal, transcendent God of the theistic tradition is precisely the manner in which religious faith apprehends the divine spiritual reality. There is a complete reciprocal adaptation between the act and the content of religious faith, between the believing attitude and the conception of the personal God. Both occupy an intermediate position in the growth of the human mind from a naturalistic to a philosophical interpretation of experience.

Hegel uses here the same interpretation of religious faith in God as he did previously in explaining the statement that God is given in religion. To have religious faith is to specify the only way in which the spiritual absolute appears to man under the God-form. The faith act and the God-form are perfectly proportionate to each other. That is the ultimate reason why every literal natural theology must be religionized, or restricted to a descriptive elaboration of the obscure, and still alienating, view of the absolute which comes from religious faith in God.

In his own way, Hegel makes a complete validation of religious faith and every doctrine on God, thus substantiating his claim to furnish the strongest bulwark of orthodox theology. Yet the validation is made precisely by completing the genetic account of the natural history of religious faith, thus sweeping that whole history into the autogenesis of spirit. Faith is the intermediate and transitional condition of strong conviction and muffled truth about the divine. To pass from faith to vision is a transit which need not be postponed for a future life. In principle, the passage can be made by living men, insofar as they reach the condition of philosophical reflection on the life of spirit and its encompassing ration-

ality. But philosophical truth does not simply give us the vision of the
God hailed from afar by believers. More pertinently, it gives us that
knowledge of spiritual actuality which makes us realize that the God of
religious faith is a surpassed level in the human approach to full participation in the life of absolute spirit. To validate religious faith is thus to
treat it as a meaning in search of a conceptual truth, which only the
philosophical doctrine on concrete spirit can supply.

Only after a comparison of the teachings of our three philosophers on
natural theology, morality, and religious faith, are we advantageously
placed for seeing what they did with the once vigorous argumentation in
theodicy. In the baldest terms, they challenged its claim to be an independent speculative discipline and to give an adequate treatment of the
problem of God and evil. There would be no problem here, were it not
for the comparison which men make between their religious faith in a
just and merciful God, and their dire experience of a world of misery and
rampant evils. Hence the discussion has to be methodically restored to
the context of religious faith and the philosophy of religion. Theodicists
cannot resist this change of locale, without falling victim to the skeptical
counter arguments. And once the transfer to a religious terrain is made,
the terms of the problem are reformulated, with the hardened positions
of the theodicists and their skeptical opponents being undermined.
Theodicy ceases to be a primary and legitimate discipline of its own,
since its problems are transferred to the philosophy of religion. Everything now depends upon how the relationship is conceived between
philosophy of religion and religious faith.

Hume stresses the point that either theodicy leads to a stalemate with
the skeptical covering arguments, or else the role of religious faith must
be openly acknowledged in the study of evil.[10] Leibniz had remarked that
the difficulties to which theodicy addresses itself arise a priori from comparing the concepts of God and evil, and that in the order of empirical
fact the clash can be softened. Hume replies that the relevant idea of
God is that of a good and just Father, which is basically a religious idea.
But if the theodicist claims to argue solely from speculative natural
reason, then he will have to forego the assurance of religious faith that

10. Hume's influence upon recent analytic studies of evil can be traced in the
selections edited by N. Pike, *God and Evil* (Englewood Cliffs, 1964). The phenomenology and philosophical hermeneutic of religious myths on the theme of evil are
developed by Paul Ricoeur, *The Symbolism of Evil* (New York, 1967).

there is indeed a good and merciful God. When we face the empirical world without the prior assurance from religious faith about God's moral qualities, then we are justified only in abiding by the conflicting reports in our experience. Hence skeptical reserve of judgment is the only viable position, unless we are prepared to restore the whole issue to the context of a religious faith which is concerned about the difficulties, but also assured about the divine goodness.

Whereas Hume stresses how close the theodicists and their skeptical opponents really are in recognizing the difficulties raised by evil for speculative theism, Kant moves into the offensive against a speculatively structured theodicy. He regards it as profoundly immoral that man should take it upon himself to serve as God's attorney for the defense. This violates our awareness of the limits of human reasoning on the one hand, and our sense of the divine holiness and personal mystery on the other. We are not forbidden to reflect upon the problem of evil, or to be deeply troubled by its implications. But we should deal with it philosophically in the only sphere where all the terms of the problem can be seen in focus, namely, in the philosophy of religion. Here, we can see what we are really doing in the discussion of evil. We are not making a purely speculative disquisition on order and the kinds of evil, and not defending God against accusation, but we are testing and strengthening our own religious conviction in its bearing upon the experienced world.

The theodicist is in the same position as the physicotheologian, even though the one is dealing with moral order and disorder and the other with physical. In both cases, our ordinary experience is being scrutinized for the difficulties it raises for someone who already has moral-religious belief in the wise and good Lord. The real aim of the investigation is not to establish these attributes for the first time, but to use our belief in the personal being possessing them as a guiding principle in the interpretation of the moral and physical worlds. The hoped-for result is not a juridical vindication of anyone, but an elucidation of the relationship between man's moral-religious convictions and his experience of human society and the course of physical events. Following Kant's prescription, then, the professional theodicist is rendered superfluous as a full-time intellectual worker. His functions are taken over at the technical level by the philosopher of religion, insofar as he handles the relation between human freedom and radical evil and moral rebirth, and at the level of lived experience by the conscientious believer whose steadfast action unifies belief and experience.

Hegel agrees upon the necessity of this dispersal of theodicy, taken literally as an intellectual and practical justification of the ultimacy of the theistically conceived God. The breakdown of theodicy is one phase in the general process of the death of God, or the growing realization of the inadequacy of belief in the personal, transcendent creator who is distinct from the world. Nevertheless, Hegel seeks to reassemble the functions of the theodicist upon a new metaphysical basis. Religious faith intimates that there is a reconciling principle for all events and situations in life, a way of overcoming and drawing value out of even the most wretched and malicious relationships. This religious intimation cannot be used as the basic principle for interpreting the meaning of evil, however, since it remains under the veil of pictorial imagery, which always seeks an outside ground for reconciliation of life's conflicts. Only after this imagery has been rectified by the metaphysical conception of the self-finitizing spiritual whole, can the philosopher of religion do justice to the religious conviction about a universal redemption and triumph of the divine principle.

On the Hegelian reckoning, then, Leibniz was right about a metaphysical solution, but not about its theistic principle; Hume saw the stalemate resulting from a purely theoretical approach, but not the method of making religious faith relevant; and Kant appreciated the rightful influence of belief, although he lacked the metaphysical resources for detaching moral belief and religious hope from a theistic center. Only Hegel's own onto-pneuma-logic could synthesize these views of evil by subordinating them to the immanent spiritual basis for all the splits and clashes in our experience. In the face of Hume's concern with physical evil and Kant's stress on the irreducibility of moral good and evil, Hegel gave primacy to his new metaphysical account of how the alienations and evils in experience are expressions of the very life process of absolute spirit. Pneumato-dicy, or a vindication of the course of spirit in the world, was the Hegelian instrument for simultaneously overcoming, preserving, and surpassing the tradition of theodicy.

The maturation of philosophy of religion has deeply modified all the topics related to religion. Regardless of one's theological conception of faith, one must take account of the fact that religious faith has been systematically thematized by the philosophers of religion. They have accentuated those of its aspects which depend upon our human nature and the world in which we live. They have exhibited how our conceptions of religious faith are determined in some way by our other views on the human agent, his limitations, and his relationship to worldly being and action. There are dependable correlations between the general philosophical positions of the three philosophers held in focus here and their treatment of religious faith. These correlations are now attached to the effective meaning which the problem of faith has within our historical milieu. They help to determine the manner in which the problem now presents itself as a living issue, even though they need not exclude other factors or dominate every response to it.

THE MYSTERY OF THE REVEALING
AND SAVING GOD

Since religious faith is a relational reality, the philosopher of religion is bound to consider not only the human attitude but also the divine center toward which it orients the believer. Moreover, the divine component in the religious relationship must be considered under the aspect which is designated by the faith attitude, that is, as taking the initiative in becoming present to man through revealing words and saving actions. This revelational and salvific theme runs through many religions, but it becomes the very basis of the religious bond in the theistic religions, especially the Jewish, Moslem, and Christian. What makes Christianity inevitably a major problem for the classical modern philosophers of religion is its insistence upon the revealing and saving God. Even apart from the historical circumstances of Enlightenment criticism of Christianity, these philosophers would have found it necessary to deal with religious faith precisely as claiming to be a response to the revealing God, and hence to face the problem of Christianity as thoroughly embodying this claim.

One preliminary objection which these philosophers of religion encountered in common was that the question of revelation belongs to sacred theology, and hence that they are straying beyond their proper field. They met this difficulty in two stages. Their first move was to distinguish between the problem of revelation, as signifying the study of this or that formal proposition in a credal statement or a theological system, and this same problem as signifying a personal relationship of presence of the revealing God to the human believer. Their proper concern was not so much with the particular content of statements but rather with the personal presence, insofar as the latter helps to specify the structure of the human attitude of religious faith. Where our philosophers went beyond the Enlightenment was in shifting their primary interest from the propositional statement of particular beliefs and dogmas to the general conception of the opening up of the believer's existence to the self-manifesting presence of God. To them, this was the distinctive way in which the problem of revelation belongs within philosophy of religion.

Their second move was to draw some general limits around sacred theology and its ability to handle this same problem. Here, each philosopher followed a distinctive path. Recalling his crucial distinction between popular religion, caught up in the endless flux between polytheism and monotheism, and the philosopher's form of religion, Hume assigned sacred theology entirely to the side of popular religion. Its function is to reflect upon popular beliefs as given realities, bring them to the condition of formal statement and coherent system, and exert its pressure in favor of a more refined monotheism. But in principle, it remains a prisoner within the circulating life of popular religion, and cannot liberate itself from the limitations already noted in the Humean critique of popular religion. Hence no critically decisive contribution can be expected from the theology of revelation.

For his part, Kant brought to the fore the Scriptural basis of theology. He conceived of it as an "empirical" discipline, namely, a study of the contingent historical circumstances under which men have received the message of God, particularly in the Bible. The theologians cannot be deprived of their office of viewing revelation in the context of a salvation history of God's workings with mankind. Yet neither can they be permitted to override a philosophical interpretation of revelation stemming from the reflective judgment of moral reason. As long as the philosophical account of the problem of the revealing God hugs to the shoreline of human morality and its religious consequences, it cannot be dislodged by any theological conclusion. On the contrary, should such a conclusion contradict a firm position in the morally based philosophy of religion, the theological view would have to give way in the order of formally held doctrines.

Hegel found his predecessors' solutions too dualistic, although he agreed with their use of the treatment of natural theology as a prototype for the evaluation of sacred theology. Just as he distinguished between the descriptive and the demonstrative aspects of natural theology, so did he distinguish between these two aspects of the theology of revelation. Whether it rests on a Biblical, a systematic, or a sentimental basis, the theological conception of revelation consists of a description in search of its truth signification. The description occurs in terms of dialogal images of God speaking to men and making His dwelling place among them, as well as of men's attending to the divine word and making the divine presence welcome in their midst. But the imagery calls for elucidation and determination of the truth about the revelational relationship. It is left for the philosophy of religion to reformulate the theological descriptions, in such fashion that the demand for reaching the transtheological truth concerning the meanings of the imagery becomes clear and insistent.

At this point, the demonstrative principles of interpretation contained in the ontology of absolute spirit must be applied to the religious and theological traditions concerning the revealing God. Hegel did not even concede to sacred theology the dubious autonomy which Hume accorded it as the shepherd of popular religious beliefs, let alone Kant's conception of it as the exegete of the historical conditions surrounding the gracious meeting between man and God. Instead, he took a developmental view of the theological descriptions of a revealing God as being destined for assimilation to the philosophical theory of religion. The latter is the sole heir and modern reformulation of all phases of sacred theology.

Once the possibility of interference from theology is eliminated, the three philosophers feel free to investigate, in their own manner, the intimate link between the notion of the revealing and saving God and that of religious mystery. Philosophically, it is in terms of *the human meaning of religious mystery* that an approach can be made to the problem of God the revealer and the savior of mankind. The locus of the problem in Hume is primarily anthropological; in Kant, primarily moral; and in Hegel, basically ontopneumalogical.

On the negative side, however, they all agree that the main question does not concern the claims made for this or that candidate for being a religious mystery (corresponding to the content of particular statements in a revelation or a theological system), but rather the general human recognition of something unfathomable in our religious relationship with God. This useful distinction between the mystery aspect of some particular article of belief or doctrine and the pervasive sense of religious mystery enables the philosophers to persist with the problem, even after they reject the usual apologetic appeal to miracles. Hume notes that the human historical testimony involved in the appeal to miracles is incompatible with the claim that such testimony should extort our assent, with the force of an impersonal and abstract demonstration.[11] Kant rejects the attempt to base moral belief and religious hope upon a physical occurrence, both because this argument mixes the categories and also because, if successful, it would reduce the divine to a determined phenomenal object. Hegel comes closest to placing the entire discussion on a new basis, by regarding the miracle story as one mode of recognizing the presence of divine power in the universe, as well as its benevolent intent toward man. Yet none of them will simply reaffirm the deistic slogan: "Christianity not mysterious." The question of religious mystery is not resolved forthwith, on the strength of criticism of a theological system of proposed mysteries and their miraculous warrant.

Hume prolongs his philosophy of human nature into the realm of religion, in order to dissipate a good deal of preanalytic obscurity surrounding it. Part of the darkness is due to the fact that men embrace the religious attitude in ignorance of both the passional forces at work in their nature and the basic epistemological distinctions between abstract and factual reasoning. Another portion is traceable to overlooking the religious impact of the passage from a nonscientific culture to a scientific age, with its implications for the polytheistic and monotheistic views of the universe. Such features of religious mystery are removable, provided that one engage in philosophical reflection on human passions, knowledge, and social advances. By extending the analysis of human experience into the religious sphere, part of its mystery can be dissipated.

But even after reaching the sanctuary of the philosopher's religious minimum, Hume finds that a postanalytic obscurity persists. Is the remaining religious belief founded upon even a slight evidence of divinity, or is it another instance where nature overcomes our philosophical vigilance at last, and sweeps even the critical mind along on the tide of soothing convictions? Why does religious faith persist even more strongly than might be expected, given the radical penetration of skeptical doubt and the findings of a genetic, passional analysis of man? How can such belief allowably elude the analogical rule of remaining within experienced

11. Hume's criticism led J. H. Newman to reinterpret miracle in terms of religious practicality and personal discernment of the divine power and moral purpose for man (*Two Essays on Biblical and Ecclesiastical Miracles* [New York, 1924]). The standpoints of Hume and Newman are respectively prolonged in the analytic discussion between Antony Flew (*Hume's Philosophy of Belief*, pp. 188–94, 215) and J. M. Cameron, "Miracles," *Month*, N.S. 22 (1959), 286–97. The theological reconsideration of miracle is explained by Louis Monden, *Signs and Wonders* (New York, Desclee, 1966).

instances, as well as the passional rule of restricting hope and fear to human social situations?

This cascade of questions best represents Hume's frame of mind toward religious mystery. He does not expect the beam of philosophy to transform all the recesses of human nature into a state of utter clarity. Although the religious mind does not work in total darkness, its operations remain in a glimmering dusk whenever they reach out to God. There is an incommensurability between the passional origin and the transcending reference of religious faith. What compounds the groping nature of the relationship is the believer's expectancy of a response from God, an expectancy which remains even when he is assailed by the bleak naturalistic view of life. A Jules Renard will cry out: "God, so much mystery—it is cruel, it is unworthy of you. Taciturn God, speak to us!" And yet no matter how abandoned the religious man's life may seem, he will still share Cowper's ardent hope: "Oh! for a closer walk with God." [12]

For Hume, there is sufficient mystery here in the human religious attitude of open expectancy for God's coming. This aspect of the religious mystery is permanent and ingrained in our active nature. Whatever the controversies raised over this or that form of the divine presence, and whatever the logical difficulties about confirming or disconfirming the statements of religious belief, the religious searcher stands waiting for help from a powerful, spiritual reality which will enlighten and save him. Because of the corruptive moral consequences which he assigns to action upon such belief, Hume tries to remove it from the seat of personal and social power in the practical world. Yet in deploring its effects upon us and underscoring its weak evidential basis, he does not deny entirely the real mystery in our belief in the gracious God.

To advance the discussion another step, Kant distinguishes between theoretical-technical mysteries and practical ones.[13] Men speak about the secrets of nature and those of social policy, but they are theoretical and technical, in the sense of requiring for their uncovering an act of scientific research and a policy of public disclosure, rather than a moral re-

---

12. These lines are from *The Journal of Jules Renard*, trans. L. Bogan and E. Roget (New York, Braziller, 1964), p. 137, and William Cowper, "Walking with God," in *The Poetical Works of William Cowper*, ed. John Bruce (3 vols. London, Bell and Daldy, 1867), 3, 1.

13. Kant's main discussion of mystery occurs in *Religion*, pp. 129–38. In *Vorarbeiten zum Streit*, 23, 437, he remarks that the doctrine of religion as revelation supposes a correlative doctrine of noncoercible historical faith as mystery.

sponse of the person. It is the purpose of scientific and social advances to remove such mysteries by increasing our knowledge of physical nature and of man, insofar as he is a scientifically treated object in nature and society. Such progress results in the secularization of large areas of topics, where our ignorance formerly led us to respond in the mode of belief. The advance in scientific knowledge results in the shrinking and eventual disappearance of belief based upon the mystery of man and nature, taken in this theoretical and technological sense.

Still, our moral belief and religious hope are purified and strengthened by becoming clearly distinguished from a misplaced religious response to those mysteries of nature and society which are removable, in principle, through the evolution of the physical, psychological, and social sciences. It may seem paradoxical that the tendencies of belief and unbelief should both profit by the modern secularization of our knowledge of nature and society. But Kant regards this secularization as a salutary de-believing process, which compels the man of faith to distinguish more carefully between the several kinds of mystery. He must learn to proportion his religious response more carefully to that sort of mystery which is not a temporary cover for our scientific and technological ignorance.

The mystery which persists in principle, and which alone properly motivates the man of faith, lies within the practical order. It lies in the region always designated by theistic religions as their homeland: the life shared between the free creative God and the free human agent. There is mystery here, because our minds cannot penetrate with insightful gaze into either the divine nature and its creative freedom, or into the moral freedom of the human agent. We must acknowledge the reality of both centers of freedom, but such acknowledgment retains, rather than dissipates, the mystery. In principle, the mystery of this practical relationship is a permanent presence in human life.

Kant's problem is to respect this situation, without either surrendering the task of philosophy of religion or opening the floodgates to every claim made upon our belief on a revelational basis. This he does by distinguishing, within the broad practical order, between the *moral* mystery proper (the free God and the free human agent) and those *religious* mysteries based upon claims of specific acts of revelation. Philosophy of religion is adapted to a positive treatment of the moral mystery, which includes within its scope the common human religious response of hope-love-fear with regard to God, as recognized by moral belief. All that it can do concerning the specifically revelational mysteries is to determine their contextual function of conveying the moral mystery in a historical way, and then to insist that the claims for such mysteries cannot be demonstrated in philosophy of religion, or rightfully imposed upon men through an established church. Philosophy of religion methodically limits itself in respect to revelational mysteries, so that it can more effectively oppose any efforts to impose them by philosophical and theological demonstration or by civil ordinance.

Both poles of the moral mystery dispose men toward religious faith in the revealing and saving God. In the Kantian discussion of our predications about God, a capital distinction is drawn between the divine nature itself and the idea or essential meaning of God in our experience. No matter how closely we may determine our human essential meaning of God, we can never identify it as being coeval with the divine nature in its own actuality. Thus the living God of moral belief and religious hope remains a hidden God, even though we may have moral evidence for making determinate analogical predications about Him. We cannot argue at a very general, Spinozistic level that, because God does have a nature, the natural necessity governing every agent furnishes us with a deductive foothold for determining His ways with man and the world. Kant requires every statement about the divine nature to be accompanied by the qualification that God is the free creator, recognized by theistic religious faith. God is a component in the moral mystery, in such a manner that we can place no a priori constriction upon His freedom to manifest Himself to men and to aid them in the struggle against evil.

Freedom characterizes the human partner in the moral mystery, moreover, so that the intellectual and moral integrity of the believer will not be destroyed. Kant expresses his conviction in the perfective, rather than the annihilative, quality of the moral-religious relationship with God in two remarks on the human aspect of revelation and the hope for divine aid against evil. These points are intended, respectively, to prevent any disintegration of man by claimants of the revelational mysteries, and then to keep alive the broad sense of mystery as a moral and religious reality.

First, Kant notes that on the side of the human structure into which a religious revelation is to be received, some conditions must be respected if the communication is to be made to men at all. (a) The divine revealing presence must remain a religious reality, and not get transformed into a piece of physical knowledge or metaphysical reasoning; (b) our moral reason must retain its ability to judge any religious proposals which run counter to moral truths; and (c) the specific religious mysteries may

be embraced in personal freedom, but cannot be made universal requirements of moral law or civil society. Kant does not regard these as arbitrary restrictions upon divine freedom, but as requisites for taking human freedom seriously as a component in the practical kind of mystery.
Hence a philosophy of religion based on moral theism can neither deny
the possibility of supernatural revelation nor join it to the necessary and
universal maxims of moral reason. To follow reductive naturalism in
denying the possibility of the revealing presence would contradict the
personal freedom of God. And yet to follow an uncritical supernaturalism
in treating the statement of a revelational doctrine as a strict practical
norm, which is coercive for everyone, would be to endanger both the
transcendent origin of the doctrine and the freedom of human religious
assent.

Secondly, why not eliminate all these tortuous qualifications by simply
concentrating the philosophy of religion upon a closed system of moral
theism, without any reference to the revealing and saving God, beyond
what is necessarily entailed by moral theism? Kant's answer to this suggestion is at the same time the provision he makes for encouraging a
living sense of religious mystery. The suggestion would be feasible in the
abstract, were we not concerned to preserve the human character of the
religious relationship. But this means recognizing that men develop the
religious attitude not only in response to their passions, reasoning, and
moral will, but also as a way to meet and overcome radical evil. In the
post-theodicy situation, evil is not thematized in order to induce skeptical
suspension of assent or to win a case in court, but rather to make us
reflect upon its bitter presence and the human modes of wrestling with
it. In the course of such reflection, Kant shows that the moral mystery
concerns the joint presence of a good and an evil principle of activity in
man, the rebirth of a good disposition in the face of evil tendencies, and
the persistence of men in trying to realize their ideal of the good.

Men confess the need for divine help, especially in choosing the path
of rejuvenation and reform of the personal self. This turning to God in
religious hope is correlative with the awareness of moral struggle, and
from this tension develops the moral mystery. This is the basis in human
experience for our expectant attitude in regard to the revealing and saving
God. We hope to receive aid from the word and the deed of God, coming
to us in our historical situation. The philosophy of religion cannot determine anything about the divine initiative in aiding us beyond the scope
of practical reason, but it can at least point to this source of a further
openness of the human spirit.

For his own part, Hegel regards the Kantian nuances as a provincial limitation upon the power and range of philosophy of religion. If Kantian moral theism is accorded the last word on religious mystery and revelation, men can never master the alienations in existence which their religious attitude was originally developed to heal. In arguing for the necessity of transferring human religiousness from a basis in personal theism to one in his own onto-pneuma-logic, Hegel shows just how pliant and dependent upon systematic determinants his conception of a religious humanism really is.

The believing mind, which regards revelation as a free gift coming from a transcendent God, is being held prisoner by its own sharp division between the range of human reason and that of faith in the divine. There is an inexorable depreciation and enslavement of the former in favor of the latter, so that men become incapable of judging the reasonableness and rightfulness of their religious creeds. Similarly, if the religious soul looks to the saving God for help, it estranges itself from the divine principle and consequently treats the religious relationship as an external bondage of one thing to another. The man who seeks salvation from the transcendent God admits his own abject dependence, his inner lack of worth, and his essential incapacity for attaining dignity and value through his own exertions. Thus the case against theistic religion as a devaluation of the human order, which Marx and Nietzsche will universalize so vigorously against every religious position, is for Hegel merely the first step in transmuting human religiosity in conformity with the metaphysics of spirit.

In line with this shift, the notion of religious mystery has to be reminted. Every act of religious faith is a particular modal operation of reason, and is wholly explainable in terms of the self-differentiating activity of reason. Hence there is no zone of religious mystery which our faith can acknowledge, but which our philosophical reason cannot essentially comprehend through its own resources. This does not outlaw the notion of mystery entirely from philosophy, but it does render this notion entirely subordinate to the Hegelian theory of how we come to know the spiritual totality.

There are three relevant meanings of "mystery" which Hegel brings to bear upon the present issue.[14] First, there is an epistemological meaning of mystery which is bound up with his distinction between the abstract

14. Hegel deals with mystery in *Early Theological Writings*, pp. 262, 266; *Encyclopedia Logic*, p. 154; *Beweise*, p. 177 (p. 367); and in the texts cited above, chap. 7, n. 29; chap. 8, n. 30 and 31.

understanding and concrete philosophical reason. Since the understanding is confined to the apparently hard and fast distinctions between subject and object, the finite and the infinite, it cannot grasp the concrete unifications proposed by philosophical reason. Hence all the basic speculative truths of reason concerning the ontopneumalogical unity of things must elude the grasp of understanding, and remain mysterious pronouncements for it. From the restricted standpoint of the understanding, every speculative truth of philosophical reason is a mystery. What the man of faith regards as a divine mystery is often only a speculative truth of reason concerning the infinite-finite spiritual reality, but a truth which cannot be mastered from the standpoint of theistic abstract understanding.

In the second place, the religious mind occupies a position prepared by representational thinking, which mixes the contrasts of abstract understanding and theology with the unifying images of the imagination and feeling. Religious statements about God are mysteries, in the sense that they are a representational way of indicating the infinite life of spirit, which cannot be properly known under the form of representation and feeling. In this usage, mystery signifies the disproportion which holds between the truth of absolute spirit and the religious means of expressing it.

The third meaning of mystery is proper to Hegel's own philosophy, taken in its human constitution. In order to distinguish speculative reason from both the level of abstract understanding and that of religious representation, the philosopher must make an act of faith in the unfettered power of reason to embrace all the modes and oppositions of infinite spirit within conceptual thought. The resolve with which one accepts the power of reason and its systematic consequences for experience has the aspect of mystery, in that it enables the human mind to adhere to the infinite life of spirit and its rational concept.

Nevertheless, there is a clear difference in principle between the first two kinds of mystery and the third. In the former instances, mystery signifies the inability of our abstract understanding and religious imagery to share fully in the power of rational thought, whereas in the latter instance it consists precisely in the act whereby the human mind does participate adequately in the free activity of reason and its conceptual formulation. Hence, any mystery based upon the limits of abstract understanding or of representational thinking and feeling is strictly a question of perspective. It signifies no more than the limitations of understanding and representation, when they attempt to cope with the actuality of spirit and its modalities in this world. Religious mystery presents a perspectival problem insofar as it concerns the way in which a faith based on abstract understanding and representation attempts to picture man's relationship with absolute spirit, viewed under the alienating form of a transcendent God. In principle, such a religious mystery is capable of being removed by an inquirer who attains the foundation of Hegelian speculative reason. Within the philosophy of religion, religious mystery is essentially removable and transformable into an analyzed subject.

In maintaining that such mystery is transformable into a mode of philosophical knowing, however, Hegel does not gloss over the priming sources in human life for the religious sense of mystery. But he requires that both the sources in life's conflicts and the sense of mystery which they generate must be interpeted within the ontopneumalogical frame of reference. Viewed in this context, for instance, Hume's account of the disproportion between the passional origin and the transcendent reference of religious faith is not taken as the final word about the human situation. Rather, it becomes the occasion for distinguishing between two kinds of transcendence, corresponding to two views of man's relation with the divine.

There is the calcified *absolute* notion of transcendence, as an act of stepping beyond the boundary of finite things and making contact with a separate infinite thing; and there is the vital or *relative* notion of transcendence, as an act of grasping the presence of the infinite principle operative within and as the realm of finite beings. The latter type of transcendence enriches finite actuality, by showing it to be a sharing mode in the autonomous life of infinite spirit. Religious faith and mystery need not be associated exclusively with theism's rigidly absolute sort of transcendence, but can be assimilated to the relative, self-enclosing transcendence of Hegel's own metaphysics. Here, a nontheistic interpretation can be given both to the Humean passional tension and to the Kantian conflict between the good and the evil principles in man. Hegel invites us to surpass the representational imagery of religious belief sufficiently to see that these features of human existence in the world point toward the actuality of self-generating spirit, and not to the reified God of theism.

Is every trace of mystery thereby removed from the philosophically enlightened mind? Hegel's negative reply is based on his conviction that a certain act of faith is still required at the very base of philosophizing. The ontopneumalogical doctrine of the relationship between the finite modes of being-cognition-action and the infinite totality, of which they are the realizing phases and expressions, is not conveyed in a pellucid vision. It demands an adhesion of faith on the part of the human inquirer. He must have faith and courage in reason, not taken in an indeterminate sense but considered precisely as proportioned to the relationship between self-finitizing absolute spirit and its finite actualizations.

The one holy mystery acknowledged by Hegel is found in the act of mind whereby the philosopher accepts this ultimate concretion of the infinite and the finite, in an all-inclusive totality. The mystery of the infinite-finite organic whole is not destined for any epistemological removal at a higher level of knowing. For the act of holding the infinite and the finite together, as the life of spirit, is the defining principle of philosophical reason itself, within which all other cognitive views are to be included and by whose standard of rationality they are to be adjudged. This constitutive act is philosophical, in the sense of placing us in possession of the dominant philosophical category of the infinite-finite. It is also religiously relevant, insofar as it accounts for the raising of the human spirit to the life of infinite spirit, without dissipating the effort at participation in the divine concrete actuality.

Hegel's acid test for showing that his dominant category is properly philosophical, and yet decisive for the meaning and truth of religious conviction, is provided by the problem of the revealing and saving God. True to his precept of starting with the historical religious situation, rather than with an abstract general-core definition of religion or an act of skeptical suspension, he emphasizes the Christian conviction that there is a divine revelation at the heart of religious life. But this dark affirmation of the religious soul must be illuminated by the metaphysical logic of absolute spirit and its special formulation in philosophy of religion.

The animating truth in the Christian tradition is that spiritual actuality cannot remain alone and unmanifested. Anselm's question, Why God Becomes Man? is regarded by Hegel as a theistic anticipation of the controlling ontopneumalogical question, Why Spirit Finitizes Itself? Whether the religious appeal is made to the merciful goodness of God or to the restlessness of the creative spiritual principle in the Godhead, it is a representational manner of stating the metaphysical truth that essence must articulate and develop itself completely in its contingent, existential manifestations. It is the intrinsic law of spiritual actuality to show itself in the world, to the finite minds in the world, and precisely as those reflective finite minds. This process of total self-revealing is not an optional gift, but is the necessary internal pattern for the autogenesis of divine spirit. The divine principle can achieve its infinite actuality only in and through its self-articulation, in the mode of finite reflective minds. Because the entire divine essence is involved in this self-realizing process, there can be no residue of divinity left unmanifested, no hidden God of a faith which lies beyond the range of philosophical reason.

On the strength of his logical interpretation of religious mystery and revelation, Hegel presses on to a philosophical settlement of the problem of Christianity and the other religions of mankind. Skeptical students of religion point out that the Biblical tradition is only one of many religious traditions and, consequently, that the full history of religion neither starts with, nor culminates in, the Jewish and Christian views of the revealing and saving God. Hegel accords full weight to this skeptical position, insofar as it brings out the multiplicity of human religions, their slow historical development, and the inadequacy of theism to contain all the religious aspirations of the human soul. But he also regards the skeptical argument as one-sided, because it fails to take into account the historical teleology of spirit, the universal purpose which the religious strivings of mankind seek to actualize. Their ultimate goal is to bring the spiritual totality of relationships to self-awareness and active unity, in and through the human acts of worship and service. The aim of religious developments is basically identical with that of the infinite spiritual principle itself, and indeed is the way in which that principle realizes its own potentialities within the human community.

Christianity is the absolute religion, insofar as it enables men to appreciate this teleology of spirit and hence to cooperate in the religous service of the absolute. Hegel agrees with the skeptics that the religious progress of mankind is broader than the specifically Biblical and ecclesial currents in spiritual history. Nevertheless, the basic spiritual tendencies present in the religions of nature, art, and moral perfection find their unifying fulfillment in Christianity, which weaves them into an inclusive religious pattern for mankind. This it can do, since its main task is to orient men toward the spiritual absolute as the active revealing principle, underlying all spiritual life.

Christianity carries the self-revelation of spirit as far as can be done in the blindfolded manner of religious representations.[15] It is the absolute

15. In the spirit of Hegel and Rudolf Bultmann, E. E. Harris maintains that "the essential message and value of Christianity is far from obsolete. It is, however, acceptable only in a form purified from ancient myth and thaumaturgy, and can be made intelligible only on the basis of modern scientific ideas and their philosophical

religion, in the dialectical sense of carrying the religious conception of absolute spirit to its uttermost limit, and thus of revealing the need for a more adequate form of grasping the spiritual whole. The ultimate achievement of religious revelation is to manifest, at least to philosophical minds, the inadequacy of Christianity as the *religion* of the absolute and the need for the *philosophy* of the absolute. As developed by Hegel, the theme of the revealing God culminates, not in an act of religious faith in the mystery of God, but in an act of philosophical judgment about the reduction of theistic religious meaning to the philosophical truth of the organic spiritual totality. Religion thus laid bare is then included within the processional life of absolute spirit, as a facet in its self-revealing nature.

Our three philosophers feel both fascinated and threatened by the religious stress on the revealing and saving activity of God. They are drawn to an analysis of it, since it constitutes so pervasive and constant a factor in human religious attitudes. But they stand on the alert against any attempts to transform our human religious expectancy into a philosophical premise or a practical principle, homogeneous with the other determinants of our thought and conduct. Hume prevents such mistaken use of our openness to God's saving word, by refusing to accord it any epistemological function in philosophy and any import for moral life. Kant is equally severe about any misuse of this religious conviction for metaphysical and systematic ethical purposes, but he explores with some patience its human sources in the struggle over moral evil and rebirth to a good way of life. Only Hegel is fortified by his metaphysical doctrine on the self-manifesting life of spirit to move beyond the isolational method of Hume and the correlational method of Kant to a complete assimilation of religious mystery and revelation to a philosophical doctrine about them. Still, the Hegelian engulfing of revelation into philosophy is not achieved directly, but is only as strong as the argument which favors a reduction of the revealing God of theism to the self-actualizing life of absolute spirit. The meaning of a revealing act is thereby changed from the giving of a personal presence to the unfolding of a total process.

THE RELIGIOUS CONCRETION: SYMBOL, CULT, AND COMMUNITY

Among the foundations of modern classical philosophy of religion must be counted one further theme which the three philosophers develop

---

consequences" (*Revelation Through Reason* [New Haven, Yale University Press, 1958], p. 97).

in common. They have shown the complexity of the religious reality in several ways: through the relationship of man to a somehow transcending divine principle, through the multiplicity of philosophical disciplines which must be used in analyzing this relationship, and through the interplay of natural evidence and mystery in its various senses. Within their proper terrain of a study of the human activities involved in the religious shaping of life, however, the three investigators jointly focus upon another sure indication of just how thoroughly complex our religious attitude remains, under all conditions and angles of inspection. The religious response itself is never purely cognitive, but is a cognitive act welded with an actional disposition, in a union of mutual dependence and determination. It is not even enough to view the religious bond as the child of an individual's active strivings and cognitive gropings, because such a view abstracts the individual believer from the religious community which nourishes him, and which in turn he seeks to serve. Ordinarily, one's religious creed is professed in company with other believers, and one's acts of worship are performed within the intricate actional web constituted by the convergent practices of many worshippers.

Thus every attempt to make a philosophical analysis of human religiousness must include the three factors of symbolizing belief as the mode of cognition, cultic worship as the mode of action, and community responsibility as the mode of social development in history.[16] Only in the concretion of symbol, cult, and community service does the full complexity of religion maintain itself and provide an adequate challenge for the philosopher of religion.

Hume's moderate skepticism is one way of meeting this challenge. It consists in acknowledging the overwhelming practical influence of the religious concretion, and then counterbalancing that influence through an equally complex act of philosophical critique. Viewed from this angle, there is a closeknit relationship between his passional analysis, his restriction of analogical thinking, and his divorce between religious conviction and the moral ordering of practical life. Taken together, they serve as three stages in Hume's assessment of the religious concretion and in his recommendation of a philosophical position to take in regard to the everyday, insistent presence of religion among men.

16. Using the sociology of religion, Joachim Wach, *Types of Religious Experience* (London, 1951), pp. 33 f., specifies three basic forms for expressing religious experience under widely varying cultural conditions: the theoretical (doctrinal content in the symbols of a faith), the practical (ritual action), and the sociological (social fellowship and service in the community).

By placing so much emphasis upon a study of the passional forces which shape religious belief, Hume helps to overcome an overly intellectualized approach to religion, such as is found in theological systems and apologetic tracts. He corrects the assumption that the religious attitude only becomes practical at the end of a process, which began as a purely theoretical exercise of the mind. On the contrary, the religious attitude is practical from the very start, both in its human roots and in its distinctive orientation of our life. What religion testifies primarily about human nature is its active, tendential quality, its constant striving for some sort of union with the source of power and happiness in our universe. Man's cultic acts open his awareness to a divine order of being. The religious relationship of transcendence springs from this ceaseless active searching on man's part, and is not tacked on to human reality in an extrinsic way or as a result of a speculative line of inquiry. On this issue of the primordial active inclination of man toward a practical relationship with the divine, Hume receives the full support of Kant and Hegel. They will interpret this tendency, respectively, in terms of moral will and purposive spirit, but their interpretation will only underline the intrinsically practical basis of all religious belief and cult.

Next, Hume's moderating skepticism comes into play to prevent any conversion of the natural practical propensity toward religious belief into prior assurance of the truth of such belief. There cannot be any circular appeal to axioms about the infallible workings of nature itself, since in this instance the problem concerns the very fallible passions and malleable operations of human nature. The Humean critique of the causal inference to a first sufficient reason and the design argument, is intended to show that our transcending inclination does not receive the kind of intellectual backing which might transform religious belief into the certitude of a demonstrated conclusion. Yet if the cognitive contribution does not go this far, it is not eliminated or rendered completely negligible by the objections raised against natural theology. Some cognitive assent remains operative in the religious attitude, and it is correlated with a concrete mode of thinking about man's practical situation in this world.

It is difficult for Hume to find a criterion which will distinguish the religious use of symbolic thinking from daydreaming, irresponsible hypothesizing, or sheer projection of our wishes. But he recognizes that the religious mind does reflect informally upon man's condition in the world, and does make its own integration between reason, imagination, and sensory experience. Out of this concrete, groping sort of reflection, men laboriously raise themselves to the conception of a minded being, a powerful spiritual reality distinct from the round of experienced things and the agents in human society. Their thought is guided by the analogy of a human maker and the handiwork for which he cares, but their reference of this image to a divine source of power is recognition enough that the analogy limps. There are tokens of the divine presence in ordinary human relationships, but religious belief never abandons the symbolic mode of treating these suggestions. Religious intimations resist conversion into either a proportionate insight into the divine reality or a completely mundane account of man's bonds with nature and fellow members of society. The Humean account of belief functions to thwart both the theological and the areligious ways of disintegrating the informal religious thought of mankind.

Where Hume is least able to combine criticism with constructive appraisal is in the study of social aspects of religion. Acquainted as he is with modern history, he does not underrate the actual social influence of religion. He notes with wonder how a religious symbol can unify a nation or cleave it down the middle, and how a religious aim can turn the course of national development and transfigure the national character for better or for worse. But Hume's attention is riveted to the disruptive power of religious creed and rite, when men become more scrupulous about them than about their temporal responsibilities and the demands of social justice. Hence he views the religious community as being caught up in the ceaseless alternation between polytheistic superstition and theistic fanaticism.

Since social religion cannot transcend this reflux and reach a critical standpoint toward its own practical aspects, it poses an imminent threat to the health of civil society. Whereas the other classical philosophers of religion treat these social dangers as a somber background of excess which must be countervailed within the structure of religious life, Hume regards them as the characteristic fruits of popular religion in its social expression. There is no freedom left for the religious community to reform itself, and enter into a beneficial tension with the other social centers for ordering human activity. The only way in which Hume can meet this crisis in religious sociality, is to stipulate that at least the religion of the philosopher is essentially a private and socially neutralized affair.

The Kantian and Hegelian theories of religion permit a wider range of relationships between religion and society, precisely because they treat the religious concretion as a complex, developing whole. Kant is able to view the symbol-cult-community concretion in its internal connectedness, by applying to it his general theory of the unifying schematisms which our human nature generates. And Hegel is also able to maintain a synoptic account of the elements in this concretion, because they share in the common traits of the representational mode of thought and action. Both philosophers recognize the human need to develop the religious attitude conjointly through credal symbolism, cultic action, and community institutions, rather than through a one-sided emphasis upon any single factor taken in isolation. This means not only that mankind's religious responses are as complex and varied as the combinations of the factors within the religious concretion but also that the relationships of religion to the other component forces in human society enjoy a similar capacity for variation and reform.

Kant's general approach in philosophy is to accept both the distinctions involved in human experience and also the various human ways of achieving unity between the contrasted factors. He is careful neither to push the distinct elements in experience so far apart that unification becomes hopeless nor to pretend that the humanly attainable kind of unification consists in a conflation of the contrasting principles in some higher metaphysical unity. He remains consistently loyal to this method, when he extends it to the problems of religion. Its application here does not require any multiplication of the spheres of human existence beyond the two fundamental poles of nature and freedom. Man's reality is defined by his complex and tensile sharing in these two spheres, which do not become any further multiplied by his religious experience than by his esthetic or historical modes of experience. However, religion does contribute some distinctive ways of conceiving and acting upon the human unification of nature and freedom. It aids men in interpreting the nature-freedom relationship, and does so through symbolizing thought, sacramental action, and community organization of churches. No single one of these modes of interpretation bears the main weight of the religious contribution, however, since it consists precisely in showing that the reference of the orders of nature and freedom together to God is significant for both thought and social action.

Kant's problem is to insert some principle of rigor into the analysis of the religious concretion. For assistance, he turns to the general process of unification which he has uncovered in the realm of theoretical knowing, but whose potentialities extend to other modes of unifying the diverse elements in human experience. Schematism is an active searching for the means of mutual adaptation between pure general meanings and particular sensuous conditions. As far as strict theoretical knowledge is concerned, Kant assigns this function to the inner sense of time and the mediating activity of imagination. But the work of schematism does not come to a sudden halt, with the attainment of the adaptive imagery for joining the categories with the sensuous data.

In addition to the strictly epistemic schematism for purposes of knowledge, there is a broader sphere of schematism for improving our *analogical interpretation and practical knitting* of human existence, especially in areas where the model of knowledge of physical objects is inappropriate.[17] Man's effort to achieve the effective presence of moral law and freedom within the natural world is aided by the schematism of analogies developed by religious symbolism, cult, and ecclesial relationships. Thus the religious concretion comes within the scope of a critical philosophical analysis, insofar as it can be treated as a complex schematism of analogy.

There are three considerations which recommend this approach to Kant as a method of developing a philosophical theory of religion. First, the treatment of religion in terms of the schematism of analogy entails a clear methodological limitation upon his findings. Kant can take a limited and well-controlled view of religiousness, without becoming involved in the bottomless effort to reduce the entire meaning of religion to its philosophically attainable functions of unification. The theory of religion carries along its own limits, so that every step in its elaboration need not be construed as an encroachment upon a religious mystery, which is in principle removable by philosophy. Religious mystery and philosophical theory of religion are not doomed to be unyielding antagonists.

Next, the distinction between a knowledge-yielding schematism and a schematism designed for the analogical interpretation of man's situation in the world avoids confusion about the nature of religious statements and the cognitive implications of religious actions. Direct statements of religious belief and implications drawn from the analysis of religious cult and organized activity are not operating within the context of an epistemic schematism, since they do not concern the laws and relationships determining physical objects. Once the philosophy of religion draws attention to the interpretative nature of the religious schematism for unifying our natural and moral life through a bond with God, the ground is

17. See above, chap. 5, n. 24, for the text from *Religion*, pp. 58–59 n., on the two kinds of schematism used by Kant to distinguish the cognitive model in philosophy of religion from that which prevails in the theoretical sciences of natural things.

removed from any attempt to convert religious statements into another chapter in metaphysics or into a department in any other theoretical body of knowledge. Disputes about the possibility of metaphysics do not force the conscientious thinker to suspend religious belief and practice, since religious reality is structured by another type of schematism.

As soon as this source of confusion is removed, however, a third advantage can be reaped from the approach to religion through the doctrine of schematism. For although the knowledge-generating and the interpretative kinds of schematism differ in their direct aims, they do partake of the same human activity of binding together the extremes of experience as closely as man's situation will permit. The achieved relationship may be one adapted to physical objectivity, or to moral order, or else to a reflective religious reference for both the physical world and moral law. But there is a common thread of mediating activity which permeates all these patterns. Religion is not a foreign intrusion or a questionable exception to the prevailing dynamism of human nature. Its reflective judgment and bridgemaking activity do bear a distinctive transcendent reference to God, but they also carry the marks of the common human work of unifying the ingredient principles in our life. This is Kant's basis of defense for the humanistic quality of moral theistic religion.

Of the three components in the religious concretion, symbolizing thought and ecclesial society receive the most illumination from the Kantian theory of analogical schematism, and the factor of cult receives the least. The reason for Kant's weakness on the latter point is found in his concern lest devotion to particular acts of religious worship should replace moral duty, or at least should blunt its basic demands. Although he does not regard the motives of worship and duty as being essentially antagonistic, he concentrates so much upon the inclination to substitute the former for the latter that the distinctive values of cult and prayer remain in obscurity. But in the case of religious symbolism and social life, Kant makes good use of his principle of schematism. For here, he feels free to explore the positive aid which religious symbols and community life render to the moral self and the moral interpretation of human existence.

Within the Kantian philosophy, religious imagery and social forms accomplish the essential service of *humanizing* the moral ideal and *proportioning* it to the actual world of nature and culture. Kant's moral precepts hold good for any finite rational agent, but there still remains the question of exactly how they apply to man and become effective within his actual situation. The philosophically relevant purpose of religious thought and action is to fit moral rationality to human nature in its mundane, historical condition. Religious stories about the creation and providential governance of the world enable us to interpret the natural course of events as having some community of source and goal with ourselves, and hence as being the region where freedom can display itself and moral law can achieve its operative primacy. Similarly, the religious images of the fall and redemption of mankind underline the fact that that moral order does not realize itself automatically within the human agent, any more than within physical nature. They symbolize the specifically human kind of freedom, that which is proper to a composite being who is struggling with good and evil, who is capable of rebirth in the service of the good, and whose ideal of personal order may require divine help for its realization.

Further light on the nature and practical requirements of social man is cast by the union of men in the religious community, including the visible church. This is a way of rendering concrete the moral conception of the kingdom of ends and personal agents. It brings home the point that the good sought by human agents is not purely individual, but is a social and historical good. The religious notion of the people of God, marching and suffering through time, guides our reflective judgment to discern that the temporal, cultural sphere is not amoral, but ought to be made responsive to our moral and religious purposes. Kant's theory of religion is mundane, in this specific sense of enabling our reflective judgment to see the grounds for maintaining the moral and religious significance of the natural world and human history.

There is a close resemblance between the Kantian teaching on the religious schemata and the Hegelian theory of religious representation. For Hegel also views the words and acts of religion as mediational principles between the sensuous and the spiritual orders, between particular objects and general notions. Whereas all modes of human language and action share in this mediational work, it is most effectively executed by religious language and cult. For they not only furnish the imagery and deeds which unify the poles of tension in our experience: they also orient us expressly toward the spiritual basis of all oppositions and activities. It is not accidental that the religious mind dwells upon the image of the divine Father and His children, the shepherd and his flock, the vine and its branches, the people in passage and its savior. Through such pictures, religious sensibility expresses its conviction in the living union of all beings and the divine nature of the bond which gathers all modes of reality into a whole. The problem of modern times is precisely to reconcile this religious symbolism for the unity of all things with the tremendous techniques developed for exploring and exploiting the differentiated structures and opposing forces in the universe.

In meeting this difficulty, however, Hegel parts company with Kant on the nature of the religious concretion and its synthesizing role in modern culture. His metaphysical commitment requires him both to intensify that role and also to deprive it of any ultimacy. The unification between nature and human moral-religious aims need not be restricted to the Kantian sphere of reflective judgment, which maintains that there is a meaningful practical relationship, but not one based on metaphysical insight into the essence of either term in the relationship. One striking consequence of Hegel's metaphysics of spirit is that the dynamism in man's moral and religious life is known to be a distinct expression of the same dynamism operating throughout the physical world and human culture. The Kantian schematism of analogy is thereby reduced to the schematism of knowledge, and hence the Kantian reflective judgment is converted into a metaphysically constitutive judgment about the meaning of religion. Instead of referring the religious union of nature and freedom to the practical requirements of the moral self, Hegel treats it as a metaphysically grounded instance of the variformed workings of absolute spirit. In the degree that religious language, thought, and action convey the lived truth of this spiritual process of differentiation and recovery, they give stronger assurance of the practicability of religious purposes than is possible through the critically restricted, reflective judgment of Kant.

Furthermore, Hegel wants to establish this conclusion, not only as a systematic application of his metaphysics but also as a truth to which the very nature of the religious concretion testifies. Hence he stresses the importance of precisely that middle component in the concretion which gets the least treatment from Kant: cultic action.[18] For it is here that the unremitting actuosity of spiritual substance brings religious belief and

18. Ernst Cassirer, *The Philosophy of Symbolic Forms* (3 vols. New Haven, 1953–57), 2, 199–231, acknowledges Hegel's pioneer work on the role of cult and seeks to show, through a descriptive phenomenology of religion, that cultic action is the supreme form of religious symbolic expression. That the phenomenology of cult provides a ground of comparison between Christianity and our natural religious awareness of the sacredness of our universe is the theme of Louis Bouyer's *Rite and Man* (Notre Dame, 1963).

feeling to active expression, within the community of men. Men engage in worship to express their religious conviction in appropriate actions, as well as to transcend the limitations of religious imagery. Our cultic acts have a reforming significance which moves beyond our explicit religious beliefs, even though we may be unable to give speculative formulation to the more adequate relationship.

Hegel regards the whole order of worship as an actional response to the dim presentiment that our union with the divine is much more intimate and abiding than the religion of theism and revelational mystery dares to acknowledge. Through our acts of worship, we do more than bring man and God together, in terms of atonement and adoration. We transform the relationship itself, so that it will no longer really express a *theistic contrast*, but will image forth the *ontopneumalogical union* of all human agents with the divine spiritual whole. Cult is the disturbingly creative, dialectical factor in the religious concretion, forcing a reinterpretation of both the religious symbols and the meaning of the religious community or people of God. Hegel permits neither the symbols nor the community structure to support the theistic-revelational conception of the religious life alone, since their cultic expression is at the same time a transformation of religious meanings to signify the intensive totality of spiritual relations.

Still, the cultic recasting of religious life remains enigmatic and conceptually inarticulate. The direction toward which it orients the believer must be actually followed through and examined, in the reflective mode of philosophical thought. It is in this sense that Hegel attaches less ultimacy (than does Kant) to the religious attitude. In the Kantian view, the confines of the human interpretation of existence are reached with the reflective judgment and practical response of the religious man; but Hegel seeks to transcend this position by incorporating it within the ultimate context of philosophical truth and reflection. Religious representation *is* the life of mediational activity, but that life must still be brought from the representational mode to its full actuality and known truth. This comes only when the entire religious concretion is reconstructed in the fully adequate form of philosophical thought.

To speak paradoxically, the religious concretion is itself somewhat abstract, is not yet concrete enough to satisfy the entire drive of spirit toward its total concretization. For Hegel, the ultimate gripping-together of all components and relationships in experience is reserved for the speculative act of philosophizing, which joins the values of theory with those of practice. The concept and the actuality of spirit fully impenetrate each other only in the act of philosophical knowing and willing. The religious concretion is not lost, but finds here the final actualization of all the ties between man and the world, as well as between one historical community of men and another, of which it makes us aware and toward which our concern is directed.

Given the presence of the religious concretion among men, then, what should be the philosopher's evaluation of it? The sources under consideration provide quite diverse responses to this question. Hume advises a separational and disintegrative view of it. Insofar as symbol, cult, and community cohere together as a practical unit, they must be restricted entirely to the popular mode of religion. The only element which the philosopher should try to detach, disinfect, and reformulate in a purely theoretical manner is the symbolizing mode of religious thought, which can be assimilated to a weak analogy without entailing any morally warranted response. The assent to this analogy is cult enough and social commitment enough for the cautious mind.

Kant's position is that the religious concretion must be respected as a whole and at its own human level, since it furnishes a common meeting ground for both the ordinary believer and the philosopher who marries belief with critique. The main caution to observe is against treating the concretional religious attitude either as a pathway to a metaphysical vision of the cosmos or as a substitute for plain acceptance of moral duty. Finally, Hegel draws a distinction between respecting the internal integrity of the religious concretion and attending to its broader spiritual significance and ordination. His philosophical judgment about religion is governed by his primary dedication to the inclusive spiritual concretion itself, of which the religious concretion is the living image and penultimate expression.

THE THREEFOLD PATTERN

One inductive lesson flowing from this comparative study is the advisability of maintaining all three philosophies of religion at full strength, as the broad classical basis for any further work in the theory of religion. The situation here is similar to the one confronting us in the general history of modern philosophy, as soon as we attempt to determine its central figures. Depending upon whether we make a naturalistic, a critical, or an idealistic reading of the main themes in modern philosophy, we are inclined to regard either Hume or Kant or Hegel as the climactic thinker. But when we look again at the historical realities, we recognize that the central plateau is composed of the speculative achievements of the three men taken in conjunction. To become thoroughly schooled in the modern way of philosophizing, we have to ground ourselves in the methods and systematic approaches taken by all three philosophers, and reflect upon their mutual relationships.

The same requirement holds in regard to the modern development of philosophy of religion.[19] Indispensable spadework was done during the formative years by a broad range of minds, extending from Montaigne and Hobbes to Spinoza, Leibniz, and Berkeley. They showed that the nature of religion can be clarified by skeptical questioning, by empirical examination of religious belief, and by the systematic metaphysical reconstruction of religion as well as all other elements in experience. Guided by these pioneer efforts to gain a philosophical understanding and evaluation of religion, the three central thinkers in the years 1730–1830 were able to make the study of religion an integral and prominent portion of their own thought, and henceforth a major task for philosophy in the modern spirit. The philosophy of religion received its classical modern foundation through the joint efforts of Hume, Kant, and Hegel, who showed by their example that its problems are as fruitful as they are unavoidable for open inquirers. It was their convergent witness on this issue that brought the philosophical study of religion to the thematic forefront, and it was precisely in the interplay between their distinctive elaborations of the theme that this discipline found its living basis.

The philosophy of religion presents itself to us historically as a complex, threefold pattern. It makes the definite demand upon our mind of attending to the skeptical and naturalistic approach taken by Hume, the critical and moralistic conception proposed by Kant, and the phenomenological and dialectical speculation done by Hegel. The classical modern doctrine on religion is a conspectus involving these three components. Hence any present day theory of religion which attends to the issues raised by only one or two of these interpretations is bound to be one-sided, since it has not met the full challenge of the classical modern development. One's ultimate position on the meaning and truth of religion may well accord more closely with one strand than with the others in the modern pattern

19. The broad current of Western theories of religion is described by G. F. Thomas, *Religious Philosophies of the West* (New York, 1965), and some key texts for situating our three sources within a continuing historical tradition are presented by Ninian Smart, *Historical Selections in the Philosophy of Religion* (London, 1962).

of philosophy of religion. But at least it must grow out of an effort to provide an adequate response to the whole classical situation. Since the concrete point of departure is only found in the interplay of the three approaches, there is a responsibility to weigh the entire complexus in the course of reaching a personal position.

Specifically, this means that there is something historically and doctrinally unbalanced about the practice of shaping a philosophy of religion exclusively in the Humean tradition or exclusively in the German tradition of Kant and Hegel. As far as philosophy is concerned, this customary split is not sufficiently justified by an appeal to theological precedent or national preference. The adequacy of a philosophy of religion must be judged at least partly by its capacity to deal with the problems raised by some other major methods and traditions. One reasonable test for a theory of religion is to submit it to intimate criticism by the strongest presentation of another classically important and relevant theory.

Thus someone working in the Kantian framework should take systematic steps to examine the Humean and Hegelian conceptions of religion. He should pay special attention to the arguments of Hume against any alliance of religion with morality, as well as to the effort of Hegel to absorb the moral view of religion within his own phenomenologizing process. Similarly, an inquirer into religion whose doctrinal ties are mainly with Hume or Hegel should expose himself deliberately to the bite of the Kantian criticism of a nature-based theism and (by anticipation) of an idealistic metaphysical surpassing of the human standpoint in religion. Only by remaining open to the entire range of the classical modern discussion and by listening to the arguments of all three central participants in their full intensity, can the contemporary philosopher of religion understand the limitations of his own approach and the value of other methods.

It is not difficult to detect the consequences of having an imbalanced historical foundation in a theory of religion. If such a theory fails to nourish itself upon the Humean component, for instance, then it is apt to regard the skeptical challenge to religious belief as something remote and purely academic. And it is likely to be unprepared for assimilating the thoroughly genetic approaches now being taken in the psychiatric, anthropological, and sociological studies of religion. One mark of an adequate philosophy of religion today is its keen awareness of the radical nature of skeptical questioning on all matters of religious belief and practice, as well as its methodical exploration of all the scientific avenues for the genetic and social analysis of human religiousness. For these purposes, Hume remains a master to consult and retain.

On the other hand, if a theory of religion fails to give due weight to the Kantian and Hegelian components in its historical basis, then it develops blind spots with respect to their unique contributions. It will be inclined to dismiss the moral rooting of religion as a concession to the tender minded, and to judge that the dialectical and speculative account of religion is a concession to obscurity. But the real test of a properly tough-minded approach to religious attitudes lies in the individual philosopher's ability to combine Hume's unblinking report on the naturalistic aspects with what Kant uncovers about the religious implications of human moral agency, and what Hegel urges about the phenomenology and systematic relatedness of religion. Only when all these reports are in, and the arguments made as strongly as possible for the three classical modern conceptions of religion, can the philosopher of religion have some assurance of developing his own theory with the aid of a humanly complex enough groundwork of diverse methods and valuations.

Sometimes, the historical study of philosophy of religion is itself responsible for overlooking one portion of the threefold modern pattern, or at least for regarding it as minor in significance. This happens when the procedure of following the historical order of investigation and comparison is converted into an argument for the necessary superiority of the subsequent to the antecedent phases in the process. In philosophy, however, the temporal sequence of thinkers cannot be identified with an inherent movement of doctrinal improvement. Philosophers do not replace each other in a linear series of ever more adequate minds, but rather take their own place at the open conference table. The dialogue grows more complex and the later thinkers do have the advantage of leisurely acquaintance with previously presented arguments, but there is a remarkable staying power exhibited by every participant, regardless of his time of entry into the discussion.[20] The philosopher of religion must remain vigilant against the fallacy of converting a temporal sequence of thinkers into a victory march, rendering each successive theory obsolete and insignificant for the next generation.

Applied to the present case, this caution means that Hume's view of religion is not overcome or rendered relatively insignificant, simply because of its temporal anteriority and its fate of becoming the subject of Kantian criticism and Hegelian transformation. His account of religious belief and

20. "The history of philosophical ideas is both cumulative and original. . . . The intellectual edifices that the great philosophers of the past builded have a way of enduring" (J. H. Randall, Jr., *How Philosophy Uses Its Past* [New York, Columbia University Press, 1963], pp. 20, 30).

practice retains a certain independent basing in our experience of man's religious life. It also accords with his general conception of philosophical method and of human nature, which furnishes a broader basis for his analysis of religion. Within his teaching on human knowledge and action, there are some critical principles which continue to challenge Kant's moral theism and Hegel's onto-pneuma-logic, and hence which still supply a continuing intellectual support for the Humean theory of religion.

Similarly, the theories of religion espoused by Hume and Kant together are not rendered wholly functional to the Hegelian dialectic, by the sole fact of their being subordinately incorporated therein by Hegel himself, working as the latest thinker in the group. Hume and Kant are not reducible simply to the role of forerunners and intermediate stages in the process of building the Hegelian philosophy of religion, any more than Hegel himself is merely the summation of his predecessors. There is a resilient basis for the Kantian conception of religion in man's moral experience, and this basis remains in force even after Hegel accomplishes his act of surpassing the Kantian waystation. Each philosopher must be studied in terms of his own approach to human experience and its religious interpretation, and not solely in the incorporated role he may be assigned in some subsequent ordering of theories about religion. This applies also to Hegel's own philosophy. It has to be examined on its own merits and for its own sake, rather than just as an historical springboard for reaching the religious theories of Feuerbach and Marx. Each contributor to the modern foundation of philosophy of religion can still communicate his own argued position directly to us, whatever its historical transformation may be within the minds of later philosophers.

Only after trying to grapple with the complexity of this historical pattern, can we realize that the philosophy of religion rests at every moment upon a double dependency. It is sustained on the one hand by human *religious reality* itself, and on the other by the *distinctive methods and conceptions of man* developed by the central philosophers. Without the nourishing presence of human religiousness in our experience, there would be neither sense nor need in the project of a philosophical study of religion. It is man's insistent religious actuality which insures the presence of a nucleus of common problems, around which the discussion and dissent among the classical modern philosophers of religion can intelligently revolve.

These philosophers join in examining a practical human relationship involving cognition and action, a mode of belief within which the theme of God is firmly enclosed, a searching operation of the inquiet heart combining the mundanity of its basis with the transcendence of its aim, and an orientation of the whole man and his community toward sharing in the life of a powerful, spiritual reality which remains somehow distinct from everyday experience. And yet each philosopher must explore human religiousness with the aid of his own method and his guiding conception of human nature and its activities. Hence the philosophy of religion receives its diverse forms of emphasis and systematic development partly from the complexity of its human subject matter, and partly from the general philosophical context of procedure and principle, which each major investigator brings to the study of our religious reality.

Out of this double dependency, modern philosophy of religion takes its proper shape. It is thereby assured of a firm rooting both in the relationships constituting our human experience and in some basic philosophical modes of interpreting that experience. Because they bring this dependency from the condition of a latent tendency to that of an explicit and major philosophical task, Hume and Kant and Hegel cooperate in laying the groundwork for philosophy of religion as an integral modern discipline.

Neither the human attitude of religiousness nor the philosophical methods and general conceptions bearing upon it can remain frozen, however, at some classical moment of expression. There has been ceaseless historical development both in man's religious awareness and activities and in his philosophical instruments, in the years since 1830.[21] During the frantic decade and a half after Hegel's death, his philosophy of religion was submitted to radical naturalization by Feuerbach, Hess, and Marx. The genetic approach to religion taken by Hume was given some powerful tools of analysis and factual information, as soon as Darwin's theme was applied to the cultural order and an evolutionary interpretation made of all present forms of religious belief and practice. In diverse ways, evolutionary naturalism served as a background for the interpretations of religion proposed by Nietzsche and Freud. The former sought to combine the Hegelian message of God's salutary death with the evolutionary affirmation of the sacredness of this life, in order to achieve an attitude of total religious immanence and reconciliation. But Freud judged that the religious way of compensating for life's alienations and conflicts must itself eventually give way before man's scientifically generated knowledge of nature, self, and society.

Could there still remain a distinctively religious mode of perfecting

21. The nineteenth-century developments are set forth in Karl Löwith's *From Hegel to Nietzsche*, and the more recent theories of religion are historically analyzed by John Macquarrie, *Twentieth-Century Religious Thought* (New York, 1963).

human existence and deepening our education to reality? An affirmative answer was given from an evolutionary standpoint by Bergson and Teilhard de Chardin, and from an interpersonal, existential standpoint by Kierkegaard, Jaspers, and Buber. They agreed that life retains its creative openness through the religious efforts to relate man with God and with other selves in the free community of men. Their lead was followed by the phenomenological analyzers of the structures and aims of religious existence.

The classical philosophers of religion, with whom we have been mainly concerned in this book, do not exert any causal determinism upon these tumultuous, later developments in the theory of religion. Rather their influence lies in the order of problems and thematic meanings, where there remains a basic continuity even in the midst of the flood of new methods and new conceptions of nature and man. Perhaps their most pertinent function is to insist upon relating particular investigations of religion to the most radical questions about meaning, truth, and human conduct. In this way, the philosophical status of every statement made about religion continues to be the living issue. Hume, Kant, and Hegel keep us in their debt by refusing to diminish the standard of evidential connectivity between religious research and one's general philosophical method and doctrine. Their own achievements form a splendid, interwoven pattern which continues to stimulate work being done in the philosophical interpretation of man's religious ordering of life. We retain our freedom of inquiry and judgment, but our work in the philosophy of religion is bound to be all the more rigorously conceived and fruitfully developed for having pondered their argumentation.

IO

Tasks for Realistic Theism

The common heritage of problems which slowly emerged with the classical modern philosophies of religion has continued to disturb reflective men and illumine their religious inquiries ever since. This long-range fertilization is detectable in all contemporary efforts at developing a philosophical theory of religion, whether or not these efforts are made in close dependence upon the teachings of Hume, Kant, and Hegel. No exception need be made in the case of a philosophy which is realistic in its metaphysical and epistemological bases, and theistic in its ultimate interpretation of human experience. To achieve relevance and to grapple with the most urgent issues in the philosophy of religion, realistic theism has to function within the present intellectual situation. This means that it must develop a theory of religion which will at once deepen the basic realistic and theistic orientation and also take account of the issues raised by the great modern philosophers of religion. The objective of this final chapter is to determine the general conditions which will permit such a confluence to occur, as well as to gauge some of the major modifications which such a meeting is likely to effect in our understanding of the nature of philosophy of religion.

In order to develop an adequate theory of religion, realistic theism has to accomplish three kinds of tasks: cultural, methodological, and doctrinal. Its *cultural* problem is that of achieving self-clarification concerning the role of religion in modern society and the significance of modern intellectual concern about the nature of religion. Essentially, this is a problem of learning to understand the secularization process and to appreciate the values enshrined in modern secularity. What makes this task relevant to the development of a realistic philosophy of religion is the fact that human religiousness is deeply involved in the secularization process and is included among the values affirmed in modern secularity.

To recognize this mutual implication of religion and secularity is a primary condition for doing any pertinent work today in the philosophy of religion.

The second challenge confronting the realistic theist is to gather a *methodological* equipment sufficient to meet the contemporary complexities in the theory of religion. What will be called here the method of integrative analysis is intended to provoke an awareness of the wide scope of the investigation and to suggest a way of bringing the available resources into play. No careful inquirer can afford to dispense with a direct personal acquaintance with the human fonts of religious life: he must examine the sacred writings, creeds, cultic acts, and social efforts of the great religions of mankind. To an understanding of these expressive realities, he must bring whatever aids are furnished by the social and psychological sciences, the formal theologies, and the contemporary approaches of analytic and phenomenological procedures in philosophy. In addition, the philosophical investigator is well-advised to ground himself in the history of philosophical theories about religion. And if he himself is a realistic theist, then he has the added obligation of unifying the various portions of his philosophy which bear properly upon the nature of human religious belief and action. This last facet in the method of integrative analysis may prove to be the most difficult to develop, from the very fact that the need for making a specific unification on the question of religion is often underestimated.

The urgency of making a new synthesis becomes evident as soon as realistic theism begins its *doctrinal* work. For a well-elaborated theory of religion does not spontaneously form itself, as the fruit of the efforts made in other regions of philosophy. There are some fundamental difficulties raised by the classical modern philosophers of religion which can only be resolved through a new and creative use of the mind, working deliberately in the framework of the philosophical theory of religion. In what sense is the realistic philosophy of God included in the religionizing process? What sort of difference persists between a moral view and a religious view of human activity? Realistic theism cannot reasonably expect to meet these grave issues simply by prolonging the theory of God and that of moral conduct by one more step. Rather, it must be prepared to restructure its other doctrinal resources in terms of the distinctive requirements of the philosophy of religion. The latter is only achieved through a fresh interrogation of our experience and a judgment which responds to the religious acts involved in that experience.

Only after a genuine start is made in meeting these three kinds of tasks can there be any substantive discussion of the humanistic quality of the conception of religion toward which realistic theism points. It is best to postpone any discussion of an open religious humanism until the end of our entire journey. To have placed it at the beginning would have been to engage in an idle claim. To save it until the end is the only way in which its defining traits can be specified, and its congenial relationship with realistic theism brought modestly to notice.

PHILOSOPHY OF RELIGION AND HUMAN SECULARITY

It might be expected that theists in the realistic tradition would be in the forefront of philosophical investigations of the meaning and truth of religion. But at least those theists who are also believers in revealed religion often find themselves hindered at the very threshold from sharing wholeheartedly in the modern developments in philosophy of religion. They are held back from the enterprise by long ecclesial memories of the Enlightenment conflict and its attempt to emancipate mankind from the encumbering rites and ordinances of positive religion. Within this particular historical frame of reference, philosophy of religion is viewed as the chief intellectual instrument for the notion of a natural religion which stands opposed to revealed faith and the church community, or at least which has no constructive significance for a religious life structured around this faith and community basis. Thus many believing theists feel obliged by their commitment either to underscore the essential incompatibility between revealed religion and the modern philosophical approaches to religion, or else to deprive the latter of their autonomy and decisive relevance for our human religious existence.

Some of the grounds for this theological opposition are bound to be modified, however, in the light of historical and methodological studies of the classical modern philosophies of religion and the larger secularization process, to which they belong. It is sometimes supposed that Spinoza and the radical deists have irrevocably committed modern philosophy of religion to a certain course of thought. They are supposed to have built into this discipline a claim that the philosophical conception of religion exhausts the entire significance and truth of religion, leaving no room for the supernatural order, mystery, and revelation.[1] The notion of natural

1. Gaston Rabeau, *Introduction à l'étude de la théologie* (Paris, 1926), p. 45. The entire chapter on "The Solutions of the Philosophers" (pp. 45–70) turns around an antithesis between modern autonomous philosophies of religion and a theology of revelation.

religion regulated by this claim is a closed and absolute totality, which excludes the message and work of the free saving God of revealed faith, except in the sense of a popular imagery which requires philosophical rectification through natural religion. If this be the essential law of every philosophical theory of religion, then clearly the theist must bracket or cancel out his faith in the revealing God, in order to have a share in the investigation. He is caught in the dire choice of: suppressing one view of religion, of enduring a cleavage between the two utterly disparate views, or else weakening the independence of the one conception of religion and making it an instrumental tool in the service of the other.

Yet this predicament clearly rests on the assumption that there is but one graven law for all modern philosophers of religion, one path which all must follow. This premise runs clearly counter to the rule, emerging from our historical studies, that we should avoid erecting one particular approach to religion into a rigid prototype, to which all modern philosophies of religion must conform. Among the classical thinkers, agreement on the common issues and some matters of substance coexists with the sharpest disagreement on those methodological and epistemological questions which really govern the work being done in the theory of religion.

It is noteworthy, for instance, that Hume, Kant, and Hegel remain relatively indifferent to the demand of furnishing a uniform and exhaustive definition of religion. They do not permit their investigations to revolve around any set definition, whose phrases they are to parse and whose systematic consequences they are to work out, as their chief aim. Their analyses are not aimed primarily at the definitional level, even though they readily employ working definitions at various stages. Definitions do serve a descriptive function in respect to the human beliefs and practices under analysis, and they help to guide the kinds of questions belonging in the theory of religion. Another function for them is to crystallize the results of a long series of investigations, but this is done more for the sake of orienting some further work than for unbaring the unchanging essence of religion. The classical modern philosophers of religion are too intensely aware of the distinctive religious life of man and the conflicting requirements of their own methods to permit the problems of religion to be regulated basically by some uniform definition of the essence of religion. That this was indeed the main preoccupation of many Enlightenment and nineteenth-century writers on religion should be taken only as an indication of their polemical zeal, not of their creative power and archetypal influence in the philosophy of religion.

Specifically, our three thinkers do not permit any predetermined concept of "natural religion" to be imposed upon their speculation. Instead, they prefer to call this concept into question, bringing out the unsuspected ambiguities in its actual usage and thus establishing its thoroughly problematic status. This is what forces Hume to summon the resources of the dialogue form in treating the theory of religion. The Humean dialogue brings out the complexity and clashes concealed in the notion of natural religion, and thus sets in motion a philosophical reform of conventional thinking on the issue. Kant also balks at accepting the usual contrast between natural religion and supernatural faith, as an adequate and unavoidable framework for his philosophizing on religion. His sometimes tortuously developed distinctions between pure and historical-empirical religion serve the main purpose of suspending the protocols of religious naturalism and deism, thus forcing each philosopher to rethink the meaning of religion in terms of his own method and general view of knowledge and reality.

With Hegel, the alternatives are clearly spelled out for making sense of the idea of natural religion. It may refer to the religious veneration of nature and its sacred forces, but then it has a sharply limited range and historical period of dominance. Or, it may signify man's inherent religious tendencies, which are notoriously multifarious and always developing new forms and relationships. Finally, it may be a way of talking about whatever the philosopher can determine concerning human religiousness, in which case everything depends upon the method he uses. No one who follows this intensive modern criticism of the notion of natural religion can hold, on historically ascertainable grounds, that the philosopher of religion is precommitted to some essentially determined law favoring one of these standard meanings of natural religion.

That philosophy is omnicompetent to ascertain the full meaning and truth of our religious beliefs and practices does not belong among the stipulations for doing modern philosophical research into religion. If Hegel reaches this position, it is not dictated by any intrinsic requirement in the philosophy of religion, but rather by the distinctive method and ontology found in his own general philosophical foundations. He does not assimilate religion to philosophy simply because he is following a philosophical order in the study of religion, but because it is a consequence of his peculiar doctrine of spirit and rational knowing. This same doctrine dictates his view of the complete reducibility of religious mystery, revelation, and the supernatural to representational modes of expressing philosophical truths. Their reducibility in principle is not a

necessary entailment of the philosophy of religion, although it is unavoidable when such an inquiry is conducted in accord with the Hegelian
speculative method and its phenomenologizing treatment of all religious
aspects of our experience. The closed naturalism which Feuerbach, Marx,
and Nietzsche suggested as being the last chapter in the philosophy of
religion as such, was in fact no more than the last chapter in the Hegelian
strain within the classical modern philosophies of religion. It could not
be accepted as canonical by Hume and Kant, precisely because of their
different conceptions of philosophical method and the nature of human
knowledge, God, and the religious relationship.

Such internal differences are indicative of the modern philosopher's
freedom in his study of religion. His research is not necessarily regulated
by the aim of determining a minimal truth, in respect to which every
other aspect of religion is at best incidental and at worst a positive burden. Nor is he committed to the search for a maximal essence of religious
meaning, to which every actual view of religion must be resolutely
adapted. The philosophy of religion is not a prisoner of this *minimax*
way of framing the issues, since the minimax approach treats religion as
though it were a separate entity which can be isolated and defined, apart
from its human context and the methods of investigation.

In point of fact, the term "natural religion" does not designate an
entity at all, but rather a complex and operational relationship, indeed,
a relationship considered precisely as being somehow examined and
known through definite human methods of inquiry. There is a double
openness involved in any philosophical study of religion, an openness
dependent upon human relationships with the divine which continue to
be actively determined in freedom, and dependent also upon the definite
methods of analysis and inference being employed by the investigator.
This twofold openness belongs to the human situation in question, and
the only way to achieve a minimax closure would be to transform that
situation into something other than a philosophically regulated inspection
of an active ordering of our existence toward eternal life. But then the
meaning of philosophy of religion itself would be altered from a humanly depending and developing discipline into something quite different.

Whenever they consider the minimax closure to be the standard for
every philosophical study of religion, many theologians feel obliged to
defend the integrity of faith in the revealing God through rather desperate measures. The philosophical conceptions of religion are then regarded as being totally unrelated to revelational faith, or as related to it
only by way of raising questions for which purely Scriptural and theo-

logical replies must then be sought. This policy of achieving purity of faith through separation from philosophical findings may even be pushed to the extreme point of abandoning the field of "religion" entirely to philosophy and the other disciplines concerned with these human manifestations, and concentrating theological work entirely upon "faith" in the revealed word and upon "community" modes of responding to the divine message and saving activity.[2] A systematic split develops between the philosophically ascertainable reality of human religiousness and the whole realm of divine faith and communion. The complete cleavage thus introduced into the language, thought, and eventually the practice of religion, is a counterpart to the equivocity introduced into the philosophy of religion by those who view its task as the ascertainment of either the minimal truth or the comprehensive maximal essence of an entity. But there is no need for either philosophers of religion or theologians to conform their work to this all too closely adaptive rule of minimax thinking in philosophy and in theology.

A theologian who refuses to confine himself within this adaptive circle may nevertheless hold that the revealing act of God and faith in revelation belong at the beginning of the theological inquiry into religion, and that if they are not there from the outset, they will not be found or reconstructed at the end. This is his way of maintaining the distinctive character of the theological approach to religion, since it must take its start with God and with the human recognition of the divine act of revealing and saving. But no wall is thereby built around man's religious

---

2. W. C. Smith, *The Meaning and End of Religion* (New York, Macmillan, 1963), cites Barth, Brunner, and Bonhoeffer on the equivalence between human religion and unbelief, and hence on the need for a literally religionless Christianity (p. 125). Smith's own proposal is that

> the study of man's religious life has in the past been inadequate in so far as its concept of religion has neglected either the mundane or the transcendent element in what it has studied, and has been confused in so far as its concept has attempted to embrace both. I ask whether these studies may not proceed more satisfactorily in future if, putting aside the concept "religion" or "the religious" to describe the two, we elect to work rather with two separate concepts. I propose to call these "cumulative tradition," on the one hand, and "faith," on the other. The link between the two is the living person. (p. 156)

But the classical modern philosophers of religion and contemporary realism will reply that a philosophical study of this linkage in the human person enables us to take a clarifying mundane view of the transcendent element itself and thus to acquire a balanced framework for philosophy of religion. This approach is distinct from the reductive analytic naturalism proposed by A. Flew, *God and Philosophy* (New York, 1966).

life, excluding the philosopher from making his own examination of it or confining him to a series of interrogations, which lead to no positive philosophical findings on man's religious relationships. Without subverting the theologian's work, the philosopher has his own tasks to perform in regard to these relationships. He can examine them insofar as they are human modes of interpreting and ordering our experience, and must do so in the manner and depth allowed by the reflective methods which he finds to be generally effective for understanding human experience. The philosopher of religion makes an independent appraisal, whose competence and autonomy are founded upon the general methods and interpretative concepts of his philosophy as a whole. He does not carry water for any other master, even though his questions and findings may help any theologian who cares to use them on his own initiative.

The essential maxim for the philosopher of religion to respect is that religion is to be investigated by means of the same general methods and guiding principles which govern his philosophy as a whole. By adhering to this rule, he can assure both the rigor and the freedom of his inquiry. He will be able to prolong into the study of religious relationships some broadly tested procedures and concepts, rather than invent particular explanations at every step. There will still be need to take account of the distinctive experiential traits and difficulties found in man's religious beliefs and practices. But the problems will be met through a responsible adaptation of the general principles of inquiry, and not by making a privileged exception of the religious sphere.

Rigorous philosophical thinking on religion requires a clear distinction between fitting the common canons of reasonable inquiry and one's own methodic principles to the religious sphere and making special exceptions, which can be given no general philosophical justification. With the aid of this distinction between proportioning a philosophical method to religious reality and dispensing with any general rules of inquiry, the proper role of descriptive analysis of religious statements, beliefs, and actions can be recognized. No adaptation of a general method and principles can be made without having a direct descriptive apprehension of the subject under specific investigation. Faithful description of the religious attitudes of men serves as a guide for the proportioning of general methods, and the latter in turn help to preserve the descriptive work from declining into sheer rhapsody or apologetics for a particular conviction.

There is a rather trivial truth stating that a philosophy of religion reveals the religious position of the philosopher in question. But the point is that a well-conducted investigation of religion does not reveal only the investigator's own religious views. It also brings to light both the defects and the strength of his underlying philosophical premises and procedures, as involved in a major test of their capacity for analytic description and inferential explanation. The individual philosopher of religion is not merely expressing his own cultural context and personal convictions, even though there is indeed an expressive factor in all his statements. He is also manifesting the disciplinary power of his method and fundamental judgments over his own religious standpoint, as well as over the broader field of other religious positions which come within range.

In religious problems as well as in metaphysical and ethical and aesthetic ones, the conscientious inquirer strives to abide by the same standard of reasonable inquiry which he asks other investigators to observe, and which he admires in their approach. And to the common standard he adds those conceptions of human reality which he regards as most sound and fruitful. What is at stake in a theory of religion is primarily the claim to soundness and fruitfulness made for a philosopher's own conception of the complex reality of man, taken now in his religious aspects. Consequently, any criticism of a theory of religion remains superficial until it grapples with the controlling principles which shape the entire philosophy. The only intrinsically satisfactory critique of a philosophy of religion is one which keeps in sight this relationship between the specific position taken on religion and the foundational conception of method and human reality.

By bearing in mind this operative connection, one is in a better position to evaluate instances of confining the entire meaning and truth of religion to the content of a given philosophical theory of religion. This tendency to absolutize the philosophical findings is not peculiar to the theory of religion, since it manifests itself in other philosophical conceptions of being, conduct, and social order. In all these areas, it is difficult to refrain from equating the entire reality with what is discovered about it by means of a particular philosophical study. Reflection upon the whole situation of the inquiry is required, in order to recognize that the rounding-off is due to the influence of the method in use and marks the limits of its helpfulness, at least within the present situation. That is why philosophers continue to devise fresh methods and uses of method, as well as to take account of new ways in which freedom shapes our experiences at every level.

In the case of philosophy of religion, any claims to have an exhaustive theory of the nature and validity of religion must be referred back to the general methodology structuring the theory in question. Sometimes, the philosopher who proposes the theory of religion is also careful to make this methodological reference, and thus to introduce a definite qualification upon the sense in which his view of religion is complete. He recognizes that his theory of religion may exhaust the potentialities of his own method, without exhausting those of human religiousness. But where the methodological reference is left implicit, a contribution can be made to the critical side of the philosophy of religion by rendering it explicit and reinterpreting the note of comprehensiveness. Methodological absolutizing cannot be left permanently uninterpreted in the philosophy of religion, any more than in the psychological, anthropological, and sociological approaches to religion.

From the stress on method and human reality which is common to all philosophical modes of studying religion, the conclusion is often drawn that they concern themselves only with a human artifact, which has nothing in common with religion as a living communion with the saving Lord. Insofar as the restrictive words "only" and "nothing" may derive from stipulations laid down within some particular theological perspective, they refer back to the structure of that theology, but without destroying the philosophical accessibility of man's religious life. Nevertheless, the suggestion that religion is being viewed by the philosopher as a human artifact does hold some direct philosophical interest. For it can serve to focus upon the formal context within which the modern philosophies of religion have been elaborated.

One theme which the classical modern philosophers of religion sound persistently is the mundanity of their enterprise. They are studying human religiousness insofar as it signifies relationships and activities which develop in our world, and which can be studied through the intellectual means proportioned to our human experience. The expressions "natural religion" and "religion as a human artifact" do not refer to any special kind or segment of religion. They designate our human religious language, acts, and beliefs precisely insofar as they are: (a) aspects of our world, (b) ways of interpreting and orienting our experience, and (c) thematic subjects for investigation by our humanly elaborated methods and principles. Although this connotation is complex and somewhat cumbersome, it serves to correct the tendency to treat human religiousness as an idolatrous, alienating thing, simply on the basis of its natural source and its focusing of human energies. The philosophy of religion is a mundane approach, because it is concerned with those qualities of religious existence which belong within our human experience and can be inspected through our humanly developed concepts and procedures.

For accomplishing the cultural task of self-clarification which faces realistic theism, it is now necessary to point out the connection between the classical theme of the mundanity of philosophy of religion and the general process of secularization of modern life.[3] An awareness of the mundane character of the philosophical approach to religion develops within the modern age, precisely because both the philosophical approach and the awareness of its mundane significance are aspects of the wider movement toward achieving *secularity* in every phase of human existence. There is nothing paradoxical in this relationship of inclusion of the philosophical study of religion within the march toward human secularity, as long as the difference in principle between the secularization process itself and doctrinaire secularism is recognized. The former is a general effort to grasp and develop the reality of nature and human society in their own structure, value, and capacity for change. In order to proportion our intelligence and activity to the natural and social world in their own presence, modern man has found it necessary to make two strategic negations. The fluent reality of nature and society is *not* merely the instrument of an otherworldly purpose, since it offers its own values and opportunities for realization; and it is *not* enclosed within a sacral regime, where it would attain footing and dignity only on condition of being specially reserved for the formal service of God. Thus the modern secularization process is negatively characterized by its effort at de-instrumentalizing and de-sacralizing the reality of nature and man in his social relationships.

At this point, secularism arises in the form of a suggestion that a third negation be added. It seeks to eliminate all faith in the revealing and saving God and, when more radically pursued, seeks to uproot human religiousness in every mode. Thus the mark of secularism is found in its

3. The mutual clarification and purification of religion and philosophy within the modern secular climate are defended by L. W. Beck, *Six Secular Philosophers* (New York, 1960), and by John Smith, *Experience and God* (New York, 1968). On the concern of theologians to find effective forms of communication in our era, consult Paul van Buren, *The Secular Meaning of the Gospel* (New York, 1963), and Harvey Cox, *The Secular City* (New York, 1965); Paul van Buren and others, "Linguistic Philosophy and Christian Education," *Religious Education*, 60 (1965), 4-42, 48; Harvey Cox and others, "The Phenomenon of Secularization," *Christian Scholar*, 48 (1965), 9-57. A critique of van Buren is made by E. L. Mascall, *The Secularization of Christianity* (New York, Holt, Rinehart, and Winston, 1966). See *The Secular City Debate*, ed. D. Callahan (New York, 1966).

proposal for the complete de-religionization of human life, a step which it seeks to make mandatory for the secularization process as such. Whether or not this step is possible and desirable cannot be determined a priori, simply by manipulating the meaning of the secularization process. Once this suggestion is made, the philosopher has no other recourse than to renew his study of natural being and human reality, at the very radical plane of inquiring about the humanly available evidence bearing upon the meaning and ground of human religious relationships. The classical modern philosophies of religion thus emerge in response to the question of whether secularism represents the fulfillment or the deviation of the secularization process.

The stress in Hume, Kant, and Hegel upon the naturality and human rootedness of religion can now be seen in its cultural setting. This stress, along with the correlative theme of the mundanity of the philosophy of religion, is a way of conveying the finding that secularism is an important alternative which it is well to consider, and well to keep firmly distinct from the ideal of human secularity. The later is sought by the classical philosophers of religion quite apart from, and indeed in contradistinction to, any form of secularism.

The attainment of secularity depends upon an appreciation and always fresh creation of natural and human values, among which are to be counted those of human religiousness. Our understanding of nature and man is enhanced by the inclusion of their religious aspects, which make a positive call upon our freedom. Hence the growth of secularity demands that man's power of interpretation and action be permitted to develop in its religious modality, as well as its other modalities. There is a discovery of man's religious tendencies within the heart of his dedication to the work of achieving integral secularity. And the philosophy of religion is the most proper manner in which this discovery is given intellectual recognition and development in technical depth.

There are three specific considerations which suggest that believing theists should develop the philosophy of religion precisely as a discipline in the mode of human secularity. First, the secularization process furnishes a common ground of activity for believers and nonbelievers alike, in all areas of human interest. It is only through their joint participation in the study of man and his natural world that the process of secularization is not identified simply with secularism, or the total removal of theism and religious belief from the region of effective human values. To keep alive the alternative interpretations of the secularizing exploration of reality, men who are theists and religious believers must contribute their share of the work.

Second, it is essential that modern secularity continue to concern itself explicitly with the problem of religion, and not simply with such other problems as may be posed by religious thinkers. The most convincing testimony that the cultivation of human secularity does not mean ignoring or repudiating the religious theme in human existence is found in the inclusion of this theme among the proper subjects of discussion. Religion continues to remain central in man's evolutionary development, because the working methods in psychology, anthropology, and philosophy are normally applied to our religious life.

And finally, it is in the philosophy of religion, cultivated in the framework of modern secularity, that this abiding concern for the religious view of man is brought to a climax. It is a formal acknowledgment of the centrality of the study of religion in the entire modern tendency toward secular values. The evolutionary strength and generality of the religious theme led in the past to the emergence of the classical modern philosophies of religion. And in the present, the philosophy of religion is the probing point where the evolving methods in the various sciences and arts can show their religious significance in a unified manner. Thereby, our human religiousness can freely submit itself to scrutiny and evaluation, in terms of all the instruments developed in the secularization process. One condition for recovering a sense of the relevance of revelational faith for our age is found in that real meeting between religious actuality and the entire range of human reflective procedures which it is the business of philosophy of religion to secure.

INTEGRATIVE ANALYSIS OF RELIGION

Unlike Blake's sun and moon, we are the kind of beings who would go out, if we did *not* doubt in some fashion all our existential convictions, including the religious. Our hold upon the latter would not be humanly honest and living, if we failed to consider the difficulties and to search constantly for new evidence bearing upon them. This law of unremitting inquiry holds good for all elements in the religious relationship (for our view of both man and God, as brought into a religious bond) and for all modes of affirming it (the faith assent as well as the philosophically developed judgment). The obverse side of the uniform witness of religious souls to their condition of groping in darkness toward the divine light is the human obligation always to test the grounds of religious assent, reexamine the presently available evidence, and make pertinent use of those newly evolving disciplines which bear upon our religious situation. Although this obligation to bring one's convictions about religion to a more reflective condition must be adjusted to individual ability and opportunity, it remains in force as a principle of restless search affecting believers and nonbelievers alike.

This human condition of ceaseless inquiry on religion has to be borne in mind, when the various uses for the term "the philosophy of religion" are examined. There are many variants registered under this name, extending from sporadic, informal reflections to scientific investigations of the subject, and reaching to full-blown philosophical treatises. Such a wide variation of meanings is to be expected here, as well as in the case of any other "philosophy of" this or that. But the opportunity for participating in some kind of reflection on religion is much broader than in other fields, due to the wide range of religious issues and the widely felt demand to attain some clarification of them for oneself. Often, that clarification will be sought today through a combination of one's personal reflections with what can be learned from the history of religions, the comparative study of religions, and the phenomenological description of religious attitudes. This informal synthesis provides the inquirer with some patterns of religious symbolism and action, on the basis of which he can then make a generalized statement about the meaning and validity of human religion. In practice, this is the philosophically *uncontexted* sense in which people are in possession of a theory of religion.

Our attention must be directed, however, principally to the philosophically *contexted* sense in which one has a theory of religion. It includes the contributions of personal reflection, comparative religion, and the phenomenological analysis of religion, but it includes them precisely as components incorporated into a functioning philosophical context. Their ultimate significance and use will depend upon the kind of philosophical method and guiding principles under which they are subsumed. But the reception of such elements will also depend upon the internal manner in which the topic of religious belief and practice is treated within the incorporating philosophy. Nothing specific can be ascertained about how the personal, comparative, and phenomenological findings are being used, simply by remarking upon their transition from a philosophically uncontexted to a contexted condition. For philosophies take decisively different views of how to treat the problems of religion, and hence of how to employ the valuable findings made in a nonphilosophical manner.

One helpful question to ask is whether or not the philosophy assigns a distinct treatise to the study of religion. Since the emergence of the modern philosophies of religion, this question does pose a genuine alternative. Is a unified phase of the philosophical inquiry reserved for detailed exploration of the language, beliefs, and actional developments of religion? Or are religious questions scattered around within the philosophy, being considered only in function of other topics and having a legitimate standing only on the strength of association with those other topics? This is the difference between an integral, systematic approach to the theory of religion and an incidental, unfocused approach. The former is the path opened up by modern philosophy, as exemplified in the classical treatises written by Hume, Kant, and Hegel. And for the most part, the latter approach is the one still being taken by realistic theists toward the problems of religion. Whatever may be done about religion on the part of realistic theists still remains incidental and dispersed, especially by comparison with the massive philosophical analyses accorded to this subject by the classical modern philosophers of religion.

Looking at typical presentations of realistic philosophy today, one is hard put to find the explicit treatment of religion.[4] It is likely to be mentioned in passing in connection with several standard topics, but it is seldom analyzed in depth and for its own sake as an important part of the work in philosophy. At the outset of such a presentation, a distinction is made between philosophy and theology, pointing out the need for divine revelation and the founding of theology upon man's response to the revealing and saving God. Insofar as religion consists in this personal and community response to God, including as it does some reflective grasp of the whole situation, its human aspects are recognized from the

---

4. A sampling of the references to religion in recent English presentations of the Thomistic type of realism might include A. J. Benedetto, *Fundamentals in the Philosophy of God* (New York, 1963), pp. 10–17; V. J. Bourke, *Ethics* (New York, 1951), pp. 396–412; E. Gilson, *The Christian Philosophy of St. Thomas Aquinas* (New York, 1956), pp. 333–50; T. Gornall, *A Philosophy of God* (New York, 1963), pp. 34–42, 155–66; M. R. Holloway, *An Introduction to Natural Theology* (New York, 1959), pp. 21–23; S. M. Thompson, *A Modern Philosophy of Religion* (Chicago, 1955); and John Wild, *Introduction to Realistic Philosophy* (New York, 1948), pp. 252–73. See St. Thomas Aquinas, *Summa Theologiae*, II–II, 80–91: vol. 39, *Religion and Worship*, trans. K. D. O'Rourke (New York, 1964); V. de Couesnongle, "La Notion de vertu générale chez saint Thomas d'Aquin," *Revue des Sciences Philosophiques et Théologiques*, 43 (1959), 601–20, on religion as a special virtue and as a general virtue which can order all our commanded acts to God and thus permeate all other virtues.

outset. But the formal task of examining religion, in this meaning of a sustained communion between man and God, is assigned preponderantly to theology. The methodological problem of whether philosophy is competent to make its own inspection of man's religious life is seldom formally raised or acknowledged to be urgent.

Nevertheless, the realistic philsopher clearly recognizes that his doctrine on God and man does, in fact, concern the two poles of the religious relationship. The religious implications of his speculative discussion of the being of God and the nature of man are never far from his mind. This does not mean that they will inevitably exert a corruptive influence over his reasoning, prejudicing it beforehand in a certain direction and destroying the theoretical rigor of its course. He will employ whatever methodic safeguards are available for preserving the integrity of his analysis and keeping his conclusions carefully within the limits prescribed by the discovered evidence. Along with this methodic control, however, will go a constant awareness of the significance of his investigation for a philosophical appraisal of religion. In developing the philosophy of God, he realizes that his findings concerning propositions on the being and attributes of God have a direct bearing upon the intellectual quality of the religious response made by reflective minds. And similarly, the difference between discerning and denying a free spiritual principle in man's nature will not be lost upon the realistic philosopher, not only with regard to his theory of man but also with regard to the factor of self-appraisal involved in making the religious commitment.

Sometimes, the realist will identify the philosophy of religion with a natural theology which gives special room to the description of religious experience and the problem of evil. The religious implications of the philosophy of God may be noted, in discussing whether the demonstrated proposition about the uncomposed first causal existent concerns the being whom men call God. This can be restated as a problem about whether the propositional truths established by inference concern the same divine reality affirmed in the religious meaning of God. To answer in the affirmative is to point the direction of the subsequent inquiry toward a treatment of those divine names which are most prominent in the religious approach to God: the good, just, and provident spiritual reality.

Some of the difficulties encountered in considering these attributes have a religious provenance, which the alert theistic philosopher will indicate. Thus a purely metaphysical approach to the divine goodness is incomplete, since we are concerned about attributing to God a meaning of goodness which will respond to our human sense of personal moral goodness. That is also why a purely speculative treatment of evil is also unsatisfactory, since we have in view the difficulties raised by religious belief in the good and powerful Lord. There is an operative religious intentionality present throughout the speculative doctrine on God, not undermining and suborning it, but definitely comparing its restricted findings with the religious dimension of the same issues. The positive effect of such comparison is to keep our religious discontent alive in the search for more philosophical light than the metaphysical theory of God can shed, however helpful its speculations are to the religious inquirer.

A similar situation develops in the course of the speculative doctrine on man. Some portions of it have a special bearing on religion, apart from the general proposition that the religious bond involves an orientation of man's entire being. This is the case with the analysis of the interplay between intellect and will, as well as the entire discussion of the passions of man. Among the many particular instances of the cooperation between the knowing and the willing operations, that involved in any act of religious belief holds special interest. Whether the question be treated psychologically or epistemologically, the theistic philosopher must ponder the experience of religious belief, and realize that his analysis affects the interpretation made of that act by thoughtful believers themselves. He is also aware that his study of the basic passions of love, hope, and fear is not conducted in a vacuum, but retains its experiential links with the notable instances furnished by the religious attitude. Especially if he takes cognizance of the Freudian theory of religion as a compensatory cultural neurosis associated with these passions under certain social conditions, he will find it difficult to avoid making an explicit bridge between his theory of man and the religious sphere.[5]

Once more, however, there will be a disproportion between the incidental and distributive manner in which such bridges are built, in the process of working out a theory of man, and the need for a unified formal analysis of the religious aspects of human nature. The realistic philosopher will eventually have to gather together the threads of religious meaning in his thoughts about man, so that they may constitute a steady

5. Alden Fisher, "Psychoanalysis and Religion," *Insight,* 1 (1962), 27–36, suggests that Freud's classical analysis of religion in *The Future of an Illusion* should now be modified in the light of the psychiatric theory of conflict-free relations of the ego to reality, thus opening the way for a more constructive conception of human religiousness as a permanent actuation and education of man.

and well-ordered pattern for the philosophical interpretation of religion.

He may even think that his intellectual obligation toward the study of religion can be fully discharged within the existing framework of ethics. For this is the one place, within the customary presentation of a realistic philosophy, where the topic of religion is formally and explicitly treated for its own sake. It finds a systematic place within the doctrine on justice, one of whose potential parts is the special virtue of religion. There is an aspect of justice about the religious relationship, since it disposes us to perform the acts of prayer, worship, and service due to God, from whom man derives all that he is and has. Yet once this conception of our bond with God is stated, it evokes a stream of questions comparable to the interrogative surplus raised in the wake of the speculative philosophy of God and man.

Here in the practical order, the inquirer can guide himself by his own direct acquaintance with religious beliefs and practices. To approach religion in terms of a relation founded upon justice does express the obligation to worship God. But the complex significance of religion cannot be reduced to this special relationship, or shown to be only an elaborate entailment from it. There are more general religious responses based upon a sacral interpretation of nature or upon love for the personal God which may be joined with a sense of religious duty, but which nevertheless remain distinctly motivated modes of relating man to God in a religious union. And even within a justice-oriented notion of religion, there are some unanswered questions about how the particular duty of worshipping God is connected with the general basis of moral obligation. In a word, man's religious life has an internal generality of meaning which prevents it from being condensed into, and entirely pivoted around, the claim owed in justice by man to his source of life. Philosophy of religion shifts the center of inquiry from the special virtue of religion to the general virtue of religiousness, which permeates all our dispositions and actions with a striving reference toward life with God.

The purpose of the above description, of how religion is usually treated in a realistic philosophy, is to point up the inadequacy of this piecemeal way of handling the problem. Its shortcomings are evident, both by comparing this scattered treatment with the concentrated treatises constituting the modern philosophies of religion and also by considering the internal questions which do arise within a realistic context, but which are not dealt with there in a thorough manner. In our day, it is no longer sufficient to say that there are religious implications in the realistic philosophy of knowing and being, of God and man, of conduct and valuation. These points must be made more explicit, worked out in more careful detail, and (above all) brought to systematic unity as a distinctive philosophical treatise. Otherwise expressed, the makings of a realistic philosophy of religion must be brought together for the formal development of such a doctrine.

To carry out the explicit thematization of religion, under the present conditions, requires the adoption of what I will call *the method of integrative analysis*. Its purpose is to knit together the available resources which can be used for working out a realistic philosophy of religion. There are four essential operations involved in this method: an historical study of the philosophical theories of religion, especially the development of the modern philosophies of religion; a distinctive unification of those factors in a realistic philosophy which bear upon the meaning and truth of religion; a direct and continuing inspection of the religions of mankind in their scriptural statements and their practical expressions; and a deliberate use of the findings and procedures in the present day sciences and arts concerned with the study of religion, including the theological interpretations and the nonrealistic philosophical theories.

The four components in the integrative method are not to be regarded as temporally successive stages, one of which must be worked through completely, before starting on the next. Instead, they are joint prongs in one complex probing operation, and hence should be simultaneously pursued by an entire generation of researchers working in the realistic tradition. Only by pressing the investigation along all these fronts together, can there be a reasonable expectation of achieving a realistic philosophy of religion.

The Historical Guidance. The historical study of philosophical reflections on religion, particularly the emergence of modern philosophies of religion, has to be pursued for its own sake. This historical development possesses its own intrinsic structure, which must be examined and respected in its own right. Yet such a study does help to define the actual intellectual situation within which any realistic discussion of religious matters occurs. Unless the realistic analysis is to be conducted in a self-isolating way to which no one will attend, it must work within the modern conditions for the philosophical inquiry into religion.

Perhaps the most basic condition instituted by the work of Hume,

Kant, and Hegel is that the latent strains of a philosophy of religion must be explicitly worked out and unified in an organized theory. These three thinkers owe their classical stature in the philosophy of religion to their ability to become sustained integrators of a theoretical structure, each one achieving the kind of synthesis which his own general position requires. The realistic philosopher of religion is not asked to duplicate any one of these theories, but he is expected to make a similar integration of whatever philosophical resources he possesses for determining the meaning and truth of religion.

The Doctrinal Focus. A realistic philosophy cannot permit itself to remain the prisoner of the divisions of topics which it uses. There are good reasons for the traditional divisions of philosophy, but they should not be converted into a rigid straitjacket, preventing the growth of new philosophical areas of study. The mind must retain its freedom and initiative to develop a distinctive phase of philosophical inquiry, whenever the historical circumstance and the doctrinal potentialities conspire to make it feasible and urgent.

Such is the case with the philosophy of religion. For its optimum development, it cannot be treated simply as a descriptive analysis of some special region of religious experience, or as a name for the religious consequences of work done elsewhere in speculative and practical philosophy. The analysis of some specially denominated religious experience is likely to run dry abruptly. This happens either because the supposedly privileged character of the experience itself may prevent the rest of us from examining its evidential claim or because it turns out to be a religious mode of interpreting our entire experience, and hence to require a general philosophical theory of human experience as its intellectual basis.[6] And the view that philosophy of religion is an outlying depository for inferences drawn from other departments of philosophical work simply fails to do justice to the requirements of the subject and the present stage of the philosophical discussion of religion.

6. Daya Krishna, "Religious Experience, Language, and Truth," in *Religious Experience and Truth*, ed. Sidney Hook (New York, 1961), p. 240, stipulates the autonomous validity of religious experience, but a realistic philosophy of religion treats it critically as an interpretative act which can be assessed and related to other modes of human experience. See J. B. Lotz, "Metaphysical and Religious Experience," *Philosophy Today*, 2 (1958), 240–49, and Emerich Coreth, *Metaphysik* (Innsbruck, 1961), pp. 619–33, on the correlation between metaphysical knowing and religious loving.

The subject matter of the philosophy of religion is the active relationship—conative as well as cognitive, social as well as individual—between man and the living spiritual reality wherein he seeks fulfillment. Within the context of realistic theism, the relationship can be understood as man's worship, love, and community service for the personal God, who is distinct from the natural and social worlds and yet intimately and powerfully present in them. This relationship is determinate enough and yet complex enough to require a distinctive, systematic treatise of its own, within one's total philosophy. The general methods must be adjusted to its structure, and the connections between the different doctrinal positions bearing upon the religious ordering of life must be shown in patient detail and common focus. The philosophy of religion cannot result incidentally from a series of appendices to the other parts of philosophy. Such an approach fails to make the necessary methodological adaptation and the integration of doctrinal analyses, which the subject matter calls for.

The integrative method proceeds gradually to gather together the philosophical resources for a unified interpretation of religion. It respects the realistic requirements of knowledge, as being based upon a reflective study of man's living relationship with the natural world. Without prejudging the nature of religious knowledge, it does require that all philosophical judgments about the nature of religion be deeply qualified by the order and limits involved in man's bond with natural being. This method exercises similar care in incorporating the speculative doctrines on God and man. Although it is not led by the modern critique of metaphysics to abandon the metaphysical approach to God, it does proceed with a more sensitive awareness of the existential religious context for all inquiries into the existence and attributes of God, as well as the importance of examining the nonmetaphysical ways of reaching Him. The realistic theist must recognize that every aspect of the speculative theory of God and man undergoes a functional modification, when it becomes incorporated into the study of religion.

The religious relationship is itself a practical one, so that all speculative doctrines must be adapted to the interpretation of a practical reality. On this score, there is already a close affinity between the ethical account of religion and the proper theory of religion. Yet even here, the integrative analysis of religion calls for a fresh consideration of the moral, and also the esthetic, aspects of the religious relationship. For those aspects have to be viewed now as components within man's religious existence, and hence they have to be proportioned to the unifying philosophical study of the life of belief, worship, and reverent service to other men.

Religious Experiences and Scriptures. It would be disastrous to think, however, that the realistic philosophy of religion could be constituted merely by the sum of the prolongations and adaptations made from the rest of one's philosophy. Anyone who operated on this assumption would be unlikely to feel the need for undertaking the radical work of developing a theory of religion. There is no portion of a realistic philosophy which grows through a pure deduction from other premises, or through a sheer application of findings made elsewhere and for other formal purposes. At every significant stage in the elaboration of a realistic philosophy, some direct and sustained inspection must be made of our human experience in its determinate aspects. Making this experiential return is as necessary in the theory of religion as in any other phase of our philosophizing.

Without ruling out in any way the mystical experience of man, however, we are not obliged to found the philosophy of religion upon some special sort of religious experience. Instead, we can find a source in reflection upon the religious orientation of human experience as a whole. The ways in which religious men interpret all facets of their experience, in the course of their search for divine spiritual life, comprise the experiential basis for the philosophy of religion.[7] That basis is essentially complex, due both to the components in the determinate relationship of man-toward-God and to the other aspects of human life, which can be given a religious interpretation and thus be incorporated into the active relationship. By constantly consulting the determinate complexity of the religious mode of orienting human existence in the world, we gain an existential warrant for having a full-fledged philosophy of religion, as well as a guide to the content of the integrative analysis of religion.

The philosopher of religion can be no more satisfied with a purely second-hand theory of religion, constructed out of philosophical inferences made elsewhere and descriptive studies made by someone else, than can the philosopher of science be content with a relationship always at one

7. The method of studying man's experience of God along with his other ways of experiencing and valuing is exhibited in E. S. Brightman, *A Philosophy of Religion* (New York, 1940), pp. 1–26, 108–31; H. D. Lewis, *Our Experience of God* (New York, 1959), pp. 104–19; John Baillie, *The Sense of the Presence of God* (New York, 1962), pp. 41–68; and J. M. Bochenski, *The Logic of Religion* (New York, 1965), pp. 46–48, 58, 94–96, 108–17. Also, Thomas McPherson, *The Philosophy of Religion* (Princeton, 1965), pp. 101–24, against an exclusive private experience view.

remove from the actual methods and concepts of the sciences. The philosophical realist is pledged to penetrate the actual configurations of religious life, through a personal study of the religious scriptures of mankind, the existing religious beliefs, and the practical manifestations. His task is to achieve a convergence between the religious reality and the interpretative principles of philosophy, but one which rests upon his independent examination of both poles in the relationship. Without gaining his own understanding of human religiousness, he would lack an *experiential* measure for adapting the general philosophical principles. And without gaining his own hold upon the method and guiding principles, he would be unable to reach any distinctively *philosophical* judgment upon the religious reality.

The Full Range of Studies. As an aid in the assessment of man's religious relationships, the philosopher of religion must retain his effective membership in the community of human research on religious matters. He must seek the aid of all the sciences which concern themselves with this aspect of human life. The integrative analysis of religion includes a methodic use of whatever illumination comes from the history of religions, the comparative study of religious patterns and symbols, the psychological and anthropological concepts of religious origins and forms, and the sociological research on religious communities and organized structures.[8] A systematic study of their findings is indispensable for assurance of a sound footing in the humane understanding of religion. And because of religion's close and continuous association with art, special attention should be given to the artistic forms employed to express, evoke, and enact the religious life of mankind.

A realistic philosopher of religion draws into his integrative movement,

8. For example, the following three books of Mircea Eliade have their special pertinence for the integrative analysis of religion. *The Sacred and the Profane* (New York, 1961) clarifies the meaning of religions of nature, describes the sacral attitude toward the cosmos, and thus helps to establish a difference between the profane (as the counterpart to the sacral) and the modern secular view of the world. *Patterns in Comparative Religion* (Cleveland, 1963) studies man's common symbolic forms of religious response under diverse cultural conditions and the religious permeation of all aspects of human living. *Myth and Reality* (New York, Harper and Row, 1963) suggests how to achieve demythization without outlawing the religious use of images, how to treat sacred history within the frame of reference of secular man, and how to interpret cultic enactments without destroying their relational sense. In addition to Eliade, the integrative philosophical study of religion is enriched by the pioneer phenomenology of sacred art done by Gerardus van der Leeuw, *Sacred and Profane Beauty: The Holy in Art* (New York, 1963).

therefore, all the scientific and artistic insights which bear upon his major themes. He cannot passively ingest them, however, since his prime responsibility is to reach a philosophically informed judgment about the significance of religion. Hence he must make sure both that his reflection will take the scientific and artistic views of human religions into account and also that his ultimate interpretation will accord with his philosophical analyses of man-and-God-in-living-relationship.

A study of religion conducted in the integrative manner will also lead the realistic philosopher to consult with the theologians and the non-realistic philosophers. He cannot afford to cripple his investigation by failing to weigh their contributions. There is a long Christian theological tradition of treatises done on the true religion, which is conceived as being one with Christianity. In developing the topic of the true religion, theologians have found their own way to deal with the question of the diversity of religions of mankind. They have had to specify some common traits of human religiousness which relate Christianity in significant ways to the other religions, and which enable the latter to bear genuine religious qualities. These theological generalizations have to be explored in the process of building a realistic philosophy of religion, which remains open to all the religions and theologies of mankind.

It must also consider the religious insights of the nontheistic and non-realistic philosophies. Fundamental disagreements at the epistemological and metaphysical levels do not lead to any global rejection of another kind of philosophy, whether taken in its historical growth or in its present forms of argument. One working test of the adequacy of a realistic philosophy of religion is its concern for the well-evidenced views on religious matters which are imbedded in other philosophical positions. All such philosophical achievements of man have a peremptory claim upon the attention and judgment of the realistic theist.

Like any other method, that of integrative analysis is intended for the logical guidance of some definite investigations of doctrinal problems. Its nature and capacity are best exhibited in the course of treating some actual issues in the philosophy of religion. That is why there must be added to the cultural and methodological tasks of realistic theism, a specifically doctrinal task of developing the intrinsic content in the realistic theory of religion. Out of the many doctrinal issues which must be faced, two major ones have been chosen here to indicate how the method of integrative analysis works in practice, and what differences are introduced into the theory of religion by taking the path of realistic theism.

The next two sections will concentrate upon some systematic problems taken respectively from the metaphysical order and the ethical order, insofar as these problems now become incorporated within the context of the philosophy of religion.

THE METAPHYSICAL DIFFERENCE

To avoid syncretism, the incorporated elements in the realistic theory of religion must submit to an epistemological and metaphysical reinterpretation under realistic principles. There is an experiential base of reference for all propositions on religion which gain our philosophical assent, and hence which become assimilated into the growing body of a realistic philosophy. As far as their philosophical acceptance is concerned, it depends upon showing that their referents have a determinate presence in our experience of man, as related to the world through operations of feeling and acting, knowing and willing, personal and social effort. That presence is specified either by way of being directly involved within the total situation of man in his world or by way of being inferentially implied by the actually experienced traits.

The philosophical examination of religious reality is thus conducted in accord with a composite method, which is both analytically descriptive of the relevant factors in the man-world relationship and also inferentially interpretative of whatever religious implications are warranted by reflection upon that relationship. This *analytico-inferential* approach is not designed to exhaust the full significance of human statements made about religion, or those made in the religious mode. But it is the controlling principle for determining the basis of assent for their acceptance within an experiential philosophy, and hence the precise manner in which they contribute to the meaning and truth of the realistic theory of religion.

The propositions about God which are developed and warranted by means of this analysis and inference constitute a metaphysical doctrine on God. Because the metaphysical theory of God directly affects our understanding of the religious relationship between man and God, it has to be incorporated into the realistic philosophy of religion. One major office for a realistic theism, therefore, is to show what difference it makes to include, in the theory of religion, a view of God worked out in this fashion. That it will make a considerable difference can be safely predicted from both terms in the comparison. For a realistic metaphysics of God is not usually examined from the standpoint of its religious context and of the modifications required so that it can serve as part of a philosophical theory of religion. And on the side of the modern philosophies of religion, there are no major precedents to follow in showing how the integration can be made. A fresh act of the inquiring mind is needed in order to give the philosophy of religion this distinctive form of a contribution made to our human conception of religion by the realistic metaphysical approach to God. Both from the standpoint of developing some further capacities in such a metaphysics and from that of broadening the range of modern philosophical theories of religion, the attempt is worth making.

To trace the effects of such a refashioning of the philosophy of religion, we can consider the differences it introduces into the meaning of at least one central modern theme: *the religionizing of the theory of God.* The modifications will be pointed out here, first of all with respect to our three classical philosophies of religion, and then with respect to two contemporary positions: the analysis of religious language and the phenomenology of religion.

As far as Hume and Kant are concerned, the religionizing of the theory of God is an outgrowth of their criticisms of metaphysics. They understand the religionizing process to be the substitution of another basis of thinking about God for that proposed in rationalistic metaphysics, especially the mélange of reasoning used in the a priori proof and the design argument. Hume seeks a new foundation in the theoretical analysis of the operation of human passions and the formation of existential beliefs, whereas Kant enlarges it to include the implications of the moral life. But for both thinkers, the religionizing of our conception of God is only the positive side of an inquiry which begins with the elimination of nonexperiential, metaphysical assertions about the transcendent order of being. If the theory of religion is to have any theistic character, the conception of God must be drawn from those nonmetaphysical analyses of human nature and its practical tendencies, from which religious belief itself springs. Whatever significance the theory of God possesses in their philosophy must be drawn from its function within the encompassing theory of man, and solely from there.

The realistic philosophy of religion is part of the broad revision of the positions of Hume and Kant on the nature and limits of human knowledge. Realism agrees with these thinkers in being dissatisfied with rationalistic metaphysics and the jumble of principles invoked in popular natural theology. However, it suggests that metaphysics can be developed through an analysis of the general factors present in human experience, and through an inferential study of the implications which these factors bear concerning the reality of God. The few carefully grounded and qualified propositions about God which this experiential metaphysics yields, do have some bearing upon man's understanding of the goal of the religious search. For whatever light they may shed upon the bond between man and God, they should be included within the philosophical theory of religion. They do not surrender their full yield, until they are considered specifically in their function as interpretants within the theory of religion.

In the realistic context, then, there is no mutual exclusion between the metaphysical theory of God and the philosophy of religion. The latter is not born out of the former's failure to furnish any knowledge about God, and hence is not essentially intended to serve a substitutional function at all. Rather, these two respective phases in philosophy embody two distinct concerns of the human mind: to determine some true propositions about God from a study of our experienced world, and to explore the complex modes in which man actively relates himself to the divine reality. In the metaphysical theory of God, the emphasis is placed upon finding the speculative warrant for statements concerning the existence and attributes of God, whatever the consequences may be for man's response to the divine reality. And in the philosophy of religion, the analysis centers directly upon the human search for and response to God, the ways in which the communion between man and God is actively sustained in human beliefs and practices. Thus these two philosophical disciplines respond to distinct intentional aims of the inquiring mind, whose guiding purpose is not to displace the one by the other, but to insure the evidential soundness of each and also to work out their integrating relationships.

For although the theory of God and that of religion are distinct, they are not utterly discrete and unrelated areas in philosophy. One of the major goals for a realistic philosophy of religion is to examine the various types of relationship which do obtain between the two areas, when the theories of God and religion are developed upon realistic principles.[9] The

9. On efforts to combine a realistic and personalist approach to God with a theory of religion which includes historical and phenomenological elements, see August Brunner, *Die Religion* (Freiburg, 1956), and Paul Ortegat, *Philosophie de la religion* (2 vols. Paris, 1948). Whitehead's theory of God in process supplies the base for the interpretation of religion proposed in J. B. Cobb's *A Christian Natural Theology* (Philadelphia, 1965). However, because the revealed word of God seems thereby to

connection between them is not a simple one-way relationship, in which the doctrine on God would be considered merely as a speculative reflection of the religious bond, or in which the religious bond itself would be regarded merely as a practical application of the metaphysical doctrine of God. The actual interlinkings are too various, continuous, and mutual to permit any oversimplified schema to capture their real nature and significance for man. The fact of these mutual linkages does not destroy the integrity of either discipline. For the intellectual distinctness and rigor of the one theory do not depend upon its total isolation from the other theory, but upon its intrinsic fidelity to the proper object and method demanded by its own interrogation of human experience.

The realistic meaning for religionizing the theory of God consists in becoming reflectively aware of these jointly maintained bonds between the philosophical study of God and that of human religiousness. It includes a crucial distinction between the religious context and the verification of the metaphysical doctrine on God. The distinction in question is required in order to respect the difference between showing the existential *setting*, within which the metaphysical study of God is carried on, and establishing the *validity* of the statements which constitute the metaphysical theory of God. The inquirer may well be impelled by his religious belief to engage in theistic investigation. The religious context may well contribute toward the language he uses, the specific issues he faces, and the evidence he weighs. But he also has the methodological responsibility of referring all these contributions to the general standards of evidence and verification obtaining within his realistic metaphysics. Otherwise, his reflections on God are those of a man shaped by his religious beliefs, indeed, but not also shaped by the intentional aims of the metaphysical inquiry. To religionize the theory of God is to bring out explicitly this distinction between the religious setting and the metaphysical canons of argument and verification, lest there be any inadvertent confusion of the two or any artificial disqualification of the one, simply through an act of indicating the operative presence of the other.

Analysis of the modifications required in the theory of religion, through its assimilation of the metaphysical findings on God, is a complex affair.

---

be judged by an extrinsic standard, many theologians will concede God's manifestation in nature and even a natural religious belief in Him, but yet refuse to acccept any natural philosophical theology, as noted by G. B. Matthews, "Theology and Natural Theology," *Journal of Philosophy*, 61 (1964), 99–108.

One way to appreciate its importance, however, is to note some specific differences which the presence of such assimilated factors makes to us in rethinking the Humean and Kantian theories of religion. Hume himself recognized that the rigid distinction between popular religion and his own philosophical notion of religion rested on the assumption that there is no sound metaphysical basis of theism. If there were a metaphysical theory of God which could meet the requirements of experiential thinking, then there would be an intellectual means of criticizing polytheism and thus breaking out of the perpetual cyclic reflux between this position and monotheism. The metaphysical theory of God would not be merely a formalization of this reflux movement generated by human passions, and hence there might be a philosophically acceptable development of the conception of religion itself beyond Hume's own skeptical minimum. Similarly, he acknowledged that the entire dialectic of evil, as counting against any expansion of the theistic minimum, would have to be modified, were the experiential study of our world aided by a metaphysically established theory of the divine attributes.

In Kant's case, there would be profound modifications aroused by two features in the realistic doctrine on God: its existential character, and its methodic refusal to treat moral obligation as a sheer deductive conclusion from the speculative view of God. The existential judgment made about God in a metaphysical theism would remove the as-if qualification placed upon prayer and upon the moral view of divine commands. The refusal of a deductivist founding of morality would eliminate the fear that the religious acknowledgment of God might become a purely speculative act, having no basis in man's moral nature and no need to engage his moral freedom. These issues help to forecast the other differences which follow from incorporating into the theory of religion some metaphysical statements about God, established along realistic lines.

Hegel readily admits the need for joining the theory of religion with metaphysics, as well as the decisive effects which follow for the former in the wake of this union. Here, the problem of the metaphysical difference is not to show what results from having the presence, rather than the absence, of a metaphysical approach to God, but what results from taking radically different metaphysical approaches to God. The Hegelian theory of religion is completely dominated by the phenomenologizing process which religion must first undergo, as well as by the onto-pneuma-logic by whose doctrinal standard it is interpreted and judged. Religion can present itself for philosophical examination only in the degree that it is regarded as a phenomenologized mode of spirit, an aspect of the self-unfolding experience of absolute spirit.

Within this Hegelian framework, the religionizing of the theory of God can only mean its necessary submission to a dichotomizing procedure. Insofar as the theory of God concerns the demonstrated truth about God, it belongs entirely to the metaphysical doctrine on spirit; insofar as it concerns the description of the human soul's elevation toward spirit under the form of God, it belongs entirely to the philosophy of religion. There is still a metaphysical truth concerning God, but it is the truth about absolute spirit, of which theism is an alienating and one-sided expression. And there is an analytic religious conception of God as the goal of our religious aspiration, but this stands in need of a fundamental correction and reformulation in terms of the superior philosophical mode of conceiving the true actuality of spirit. Thus the religionizing theme spells the dismemberment of the doctrine on God in the speculative order, as a prior condition for having a philosophy of religion.

In part, realism can define itself historically by its critical refusal to accept the Hegelian epistemological distinction between representational thinking and thought conducted at the pure level of the rational concept. The two poles of this distinction are undercut by the realistic account of the human modes of knowing, which permits an inference to be made about spiritual reality, but always on the basis of our composite experience and hence always by means of an analogical reference from the existing things in that experience. Because of the analogical mode of all inferentially based judgments about spiritual actuality, there can be no humanly accessible sort of pure rational thought, and hence no humanly verifiable ground for maintaining the truth of Hegel's pure rational concept of absolute spirit. Philosophy is under no essential requirement to regard every notion of spiritual actuality as a variant of the Hegelian absolute spirit, or to regard every developing act of the human soul toward spiritual being as a phase in the internal articulation of that absolute.

The consequence of this realistic critique of the theory of absolute spirit is liberational for the philosophy of religion, in particular. It is freed from the need to make a split between the demonstrative truth and the descriptional analysis of the theory of God. There is both descriptional analysis and demonstrative explanation to be sought at every place in philosophy where the theory of God is treated. Hence the realistic metaphysical approach to God is precisely a descriptive and inferential doctrine *about God*, not a doctrine *about absolute spirit*, into which everything said in the theistic mode must be reductively translated. And in turn, the philosophy of religion is also a descriptive and inferential study of the relationship between existing men and the existing, saving God, rather than a theory about our modal enclosure within absolute spirit.

Religion does not turn out to be a preliminary way of envisaging the internal process within a spiritual totality. Hence religionizing the theory of God is not a step taken toward robbing the latter of an ultimately theistic significance. It is a step toward discovering how our human speculation on God receives new practical values, as a component within man's religious search after God. Enrichment in the line of theistic meaning itself, rather than transformation of theistic meaning into something else, is the aim of the realistic sort of religionizing process. This constitutes another mark whereby the metaphysical difference, introduced by realistic theism into the theory of religion, can be recognized in a philosophical inquiry.

Turning now to the two fruitful contemporary developments of the theory of religion along the paths of linguistic analysis and phenomenology, the realistic philosophy of religion is deeply indebted to them both. For they help to shape the actual situation within which that philosophy must grow, and they provide it with welcome nourishment. Due to their influence, a contemporary philosophy of religion in the realistic spirit cannot prudently ignore the problems raised by religious language and by the intentional description of religious attitudes among men. The resources contained in the study of linguistic expressions and structures constitutive of meaning in the religious sphere must be assimilated by the realistic philosopher of religion.

At the same time, he must be prepared to raise here some questions similar to those which are pertinent in his historical study of the classical modern sources. The problem of determining the metaphysical difference recurs within the contemporary situation. There is still the attractive alternative of either regarding the philosophy of religion as a substitute for any metaphysical doctrine on God or else of making the theory of religion serve the ends of a nonrealistic, and perhaps even a nontheistic, metaphysics. This alternative cannot be met effectively through a stereotyped repetition of the historical discussion of Hume, Kant, and Hegel. However, that historical investigation does help to identify the issues and to show that the present day positions are not being shaped solely by the methods of linguistic analysis and phenomenology themselves. The influence of the classical developments upon these recent movements is clearly discernible. Nevertheless, the analytic and phenomenological theories of religion remain creatively open, since they are still undergoing development by many different minds and in many different directions.

At first, the analysis of religious language was conducted for the most part without any formal appeal to metaphysics. This did not exclude an implicit dependence upon the conclusions reached in various kinds of metaphysical theism, but there was not any widespread facing of metaphysical issues or any adoption of metaphysical methods of interpreting religious discourse. The reluctance to make use of such methods was traceable sometimes to a theological judgment that metaphysical reasoning is an interloper upon religious soil, and sometimes to a philosophical judgment that the objections raised by logical positivism against metaphysics still retain sufficient force to prevent any effective use of metaphysical principles.[10] The direct alliance between an analytic way of doing philosophy and the world of religious statements would seem to be disturbed and weakened by introducing metaphysical considerations. Hence the analytic approach to religious language was taken to be a workable route for developing a philosophy of religion in close conjunction with the expressions of faith, while yet avoiding the intellectual entanglements of the agelong controversies over metaphysics.

During the formative stage of the analytic study of religious language, this attitude of closure to metaphysical questioning was useful. It enabled investigators to make a direct and undistracted study of the structure of religious talk and the defining features of the religious mode of bringing conceptual meanings to a unity of outlook. But there are indications that this initial closure is being outgrown, and that the discussion is reaching the point where metaphysical questions are clearly pertinent. That the metaphysical difference counts for an analytically constructed philosophy of religion is now being brought home from both sides of the relationship. From the internal standpoint of the analysis of religious language, some issues are being unturned which can benefit from a metaphysical interpretation. And conversely, realistic theism is beginning to appreciate the philosophical significance of such analysis, and to include it among those factors in the philosophy of religion which noticeably affect the metaphysical component.

One linguistic convention, employed by I. M. Crombie and other analytic theists and their opponents, is to use the term "theological state-

10. See James Collins, *Crossroads in Philosophy* (Chicago, 1969), Chapter 13, "Analytic Philosophy and Demonstrative Theism"; and John Macquarrie, *God-Talk* (New York, 1967).

ments" in so broad a way that it covers both the God talk of believers and the God talk of philosophical theologians, whether they be believers also or not.[11] This is a crucial usage, since it suggests that the only evidential warrant for the use and placing of the divine names comes from the believer's confession of faith or religious experience. Here is a clear instance where the inclusion of a philosophically founded theistic realism within one's philosophy of religion forces a reconsideration of a linguistic convention. If one's use of the divine names is regulated at least in part by findings obtained through a philosophical method in the theory of God, then this regulation by philosophically founded evidence must be made to count in the study of God talk.

The difference cannot be glossed over between *religious* language, in the sense of statements made within the religious mode itself, and *theological* language in the sense of statements made on the basis of a philosophical theory of God, and yet which also concern the religious relationship of man with God. Statements which terminate a confession of faith remain distinct from statements which terminate a course of philosophically evidenced argument. To respect this difference in the methodic structure and evidential grounding, it is necessary to distinguish among the several modes of man-and-God talk which are to be analyzed in the philosophy of religion. This does not rule out the effort toward an ultimate unification of the several ways of talking about God and our bond with Him, but it does rule out any initial confusion of the plural modes of discourse relevant to religion. This is not a grammatical question, but one concerning the controlling method of one's God talk.

The fact that the metaphysical method employed in realistic theism is of an analytico-inferential nature also affects the problem of determining the relevant meaning for the term "God." If the theological discourse examined in the philosophy of religion requires the above distinction between religious testimony to God and a philosophical theory of God, then the content and range of the term "God" cannot be determined

11. I. M. Crombie, "The Possibility of Theological Statements," in *Faith and Logic*, ed. Basil Mitchell (Boston, 1957), pp. 31–83. On the contrary, J. A. Hutchison, *Language and Faith* (Philadelphia, 1963), pp. 227–47, distinguishes firmly between first-order religious statements, which are directly expressive of faith, and reflective theological statements intended to yield a conceptual understanding of religion. This is a helpful distinction, but it still leaves undifferentiated the different methods (philosophical and theological) whereby reflective knowledges about religion are obtained.

solely from a study of the passage from religious metaphor to literal meaning, from image to fact. Insofar as the God talk is also regulated by an inferential situation which remains permanently relational and inferential, there can be no simple dichotomy between metaphor and literal meaning, as though the former were the religious husk and the latter the philosophical kernel. To frame the problem of theistic meaning in this bifurcational way is to transfer, on to the linguistic plane, that same hankering after a noumenal backdrop which is indeed affected by the epistemological criticism of our three classical philosophers of religion.

Instead of searching for a linguistic noumenon, or pure literal meaning of "God," the realistic philosophy of religion retains in their integrity both the theistic discourse of the religious man and the theistic discourse governed by the analytico-inferential method in philosophy of God. The philosophically determinate content and range of meaning do not come from making a total passage from the former to the latter source of discourse, but rather from the mutual interpretation of the two ways of governing our God talk. What theistic realism seeks is not an ideal literal meaning, shorn of metaphor and imagery, but a progressively determined understanding of the whole situation of man searching after God. Only by reference to this relationship does the philosopher of religion find the human meanings proper to his approach.

Another prominent theme in the analytic study of religious language is the deliberately odd use of words.[12] This odd religious usage is inevitable, given the twofold situation in which the direct meaning of words is taken from our experience of man in the world, and yet in which these words are used to express something about the transmundane spiritual reality of God. The believer employs ordinary human language in order to bear witness to his acceptance of a religious bond with this divine reality and, if possible, to provoke a similar acknowledgment on the listener's part. The sharing of religious understanding is not attempted through the use of unusual words, but through an unusual use of the common words of mankind. They are woven into a definite pattern, usually through sentences which tell a story and lead to a climax. The discussion may begin with the language proportioned directly to the tending of flocks, but its orientation will be toward conveying the message about God's loving concern and care for men. Or, the resources of the talk which enlivens

12. On the deliberately intended peculiarities in religious discourse, cf. I. T. Ramsey, *Religious Language*, pp. 20–54, and John Hick, *Philosophy of Religion* (Englewood Cliffs, 1963), pp. 78–93.

human familial relationships will be reshaped in a direction pointing toward a bond of friendship between God and man. The ordinary language is given an extraordinary tension, enabling the human self to share by linguistic enactment in the word and work of God for mankind.

Once this trait of directed religious discourse is brought to the fore, it raises enough questions to cut through the temporary and artificial barriers between the analytic approach and metaphysics. Internal to the analytic study of religious language is the problem of whether the linguistic oddness is warranted or not. This problem is not settled by declaring that the odd use of language is appropriate to the purpose of the believer. It may well be shown that there is an adaptation between the believer's intent and his use of language in religious fashion, but philosophical questioning will not stop at this level of what is fitting to one's subjective intent. It will press on to inquire into the validity of the religious purpose itself, to which the religious discourse is appropriately fitted.

The philosopher is one who asks about the commonly available grounds for having a religious aim in discourse, and to do so is to keep the question of the *intellectual warrant* for religious talk distinct from that of its *expressive appropriateness*. What keeps this odd talk from being simply queer, in the sense of an idiosyncratic quirk of the tongue? If the answer comes back that the talk is intended to dispose the listener to take a look for himself in the linguistically pointed direction, then the nature of that act of seeing and its evidence remain to be determined. Either the act will be identified exclusively with religious faith, excluding those inquirers who do not share in it, or else its humanly ascertainable structure and evidential basis will come under consideration. The latter part of this alternative involves a recognition of the religious bearing of a metaphysical study of human experience and its implications concerning God.[13]

At the same time, the analysis of religious language enables a realistic philosophy of religion to make a significant adaptation of theistic metaphysics itself. As it becomes incorporated within the context of philosophy

13. For the view that metaphysics is a descriptive elaboration of some sort of faith or basic perspective on things (not necessarily of the Christian revealed story), a conceptual development of a root metaphor or religious model of reality, see F. Ferré, *Language, Logic and God* (New York, 1961), pp. 159–66; F. Ferré and Kent Bendall, *Exploring the Logic of Faith* (New York, 1962), pp. 163–81; F. B. Dilley, *Metaphysics and Religious Language* (New York, 1964). A realistic theism attains its metaphysical character, however, *directly* from its methodic analysis of human experience and from the inferences it makes concerning the implications found in the existent beings of our experience.

of religion, realistic theism discovers some new problems for itself and some new resources for meeting them. This is evident in the very theme of directed religious talk. The concrete words employed in this talk belong in the same family as the metaphysical terminology of cause-substance-relation, as Kant had already pointed out in adapting his relational class of categories to the topics in philosophy of religion. There is a closer affinity between the meaning found in religious discourse on the powerful Lord, the searching human self, and the people of God respectively, and in metaphysical analyses of cause, substance, and relation than realistic theists sometimes recognize.

Although a metaphysical approach is itself in the speculative order, it should take account of all the human sources of meaning for these three central conceptions, including that source which is furnished by the religious relating of man to God. Only if the personal meaning of cause and substance, together with the interpersonal community meaning of relation, is included in the metaphysical doctrine, can that doctrine become relevant to religious inquiry. Thus the analysis of religious language helps metaphysics to proportion itself to the context of the philosophy of religion. The latter need not divest itself of all speculative elements, but it must take steps to proportion such elements to the specific, practical relationships in religious life, and here linguistic analysis is helpful.

Furthermore, the incorporation of the metaphysical doctrine requires that a personal and communitarian meaning be specified for these three conceptions of cause-substance-relation taken together, in order to respect their mutual reference. Their solidarity within the religious perspective suggests that all three of them must be reoriented from a primarily physicalistic basis to one which is fitted to the full scope of our human experience of man, in his natural and social world. Here is an important instance where there is a reciprocal influence of philosophy of religion upon metaphysics, so that the latter can function as a component in the study of religious reality, rather than remain an alien and deforming element. In this case, the metaphysical difference signifies the specific modifications which must be made in realistic metaphysics itself, in order to prepare it for some pertinent use in philosophy of religion. Under prodding from the analysis of religious language, then, realistic theism is just as intimately affected by the incorporative process as is the theory of religion which it helps to determine.

As far as phenomenology is concerned, the first task of a realistic philosophy of religion is to gain an adequate understanding of the present situation in phenomenological studies of religion. That situation is marked by a wide diversity of opinions concerning the precise relationship between the phenomenology and the philosophy of religion.[14]

14. One end of the phenomenological spectrum is occupied by W. B. Kristensen, *The Meaning of Religion: Lectures in the Phenomenology of Religion* (Hague, 1960), and E. J. Jurji, *The Phenomenology of Religion* (Philadelphia, 1963). They correlate the phenomenology of religion chiefly with the history of religions, which phenomenology is able to render more systematic by describing the recurrent forms in a more general and systematic fashion. Kristensen situates the phenomenology of religion midway between the historical data, which it orders and compares, and the philosophy of religion, whose ideas it renders concrete. But he formally refuses to assign to phenomenology of religion the task of determining the essence of religion, leaving this work to a quite distinct and otherwise founded philosophy of religion. That this task *does* come within the competence of phenomenology of religion is the postulate upon which Gerardus van der Leeuw operates in *Religion in Essence and Manifestation: A Study in Phenomenology* (2 vols. New York, 1963). The phenomenological comprehension (*Verstehen*) of religion is not an act of causal explanation or evolutionary gradation of religions, but it is a grasp upon the complex essential meaning of the object of religion (sacred, superior power) and its subject (sacred, worshipping man). Van der Leeuw (2, 671–95) locates the phenomenal reality of religion in a structural meaning or ideal type, which the inquirer grasps through an act of intellectual suspense (a phenomenological *epoché*) and one of interpretative comprehension. Although he sees no conflict between retaining the act of faith and engaging in the phenomenological suspension, he does continue to differentiate phenomenology of religion from philosophy of religion, conceiving the latter in a vaguely Hegelian sense as an intent to transform the intentional structure of religion by submitting its meaning to the dialectical movement of spirit. Max Scheler, *On the Eternal in Man* (New York, 1960), pp. 107–356 ("Problems of Religion"), subordinates every sort of descriptive phenomenology of religion to the essential phenomenology of religion, which he then identifies with the essential philosophy of religion. The latter develops an eidology, or intentional analysis of the forms of the object and act of religion, which is the ultimate philosophical foundation for every type of study of religion. Although Scheler begins by accepting a correlational conformity between revelational religion and the eidological structures determined by his essential phenomenology, he eventually completes the phenomenological reduction of the entire truth of revealed religion to philosophical anthropology and a theory of God in process. See Scheler, *Man's Place in Nature* (New York, 1962), pp. 88–95, and Maurice Dupuy, *La Philosophie de la religion chez Max Scheler* (Paris, 1959). Inspired partly by Blondel, an effort to treat the phenomenology of religion as a categorial discipline which is open to revelation, but not totally assimilative of it, is made in Henry Duméry's books, *The Problem of God in Philosophy of Religion* (Evanston, 1964), and *Philosophie de la religion* (2 vols. Paris, 1957). On Duméry's theory of religion, cf. Louis Dupré, "Philosophy of Religion and Revelation: Autonomous Reflection vs. Theophany," *International Philosophical Quarterly*, 4 (1964), 499–513; H. van Luijk, *Philosophie du fait chrétien* (Paris, 1964). A similar attempt to combine

Some investigators maintain a sharp distinction between them, restricting the phenomenology of religion to a descriptive understanding of historical configurations of the religious attitude. Particular religious patterns of thought and action are analyzed with delicate attention to structure and shading, but systematic generalizations about the human religious patterns and forms are cast in a tentative, hypothetical mode. General philosophical conclusions on the essence of religion and religious values are avoided.

The properly philosophical character of phenomenological analyses of religion is defended by other workers, who nevertheless refrain from maintaining that the phenomenological findings constitute the totality of the philosophical theory of religion. Proponents of this view tend to use not only the descriptive techniques but also some degree of phenomenological reduction. Their aim is to uncover the essential meanings which converge together in the human religious attitude, thus furnishing philosophy with an essential understanding of the religious relationship. However, they usually place some restrictions upon the phenomenological investigation. The intentional meanings of religion do not yield a univocal definition of the nature of religion, since the essential pattern lives only in and through the various modes of religious relationship. Moreover, the aim is to determine religious meanings as structures in our experience, but not as a rigid standard for settling on the truth of religion, amid the diverse religions of mankind. This distinction between religious meanings and the truth about religion leaves the door open for contributions from other philosophical methods, as well as from nonphilosophical sources of enlightenment on religious issues.

The question raised by these two interpretations of the phenomenology of religion is how to control the passage from description to philosophical judgment, and from intended meaning to founding truth, in religious matters. The difficulty is not lessened by regarding the religious attitude as a fulfilling expression of man's pre-philosophical understanding of his condition in this world. For when the transfer is made to the level of man's pre-understanding of his situation, still another view of the relation between phenomenology and philosophy of religion becomes relevant.

---

revelational openness with phenomenological techniques and an Augustinian view of man's religious life is made by Johannes Hessen, *Religionsphilosophie* (2d ed. 2 vols. Munich, 1955), esp. 1, 243–304. Phenomenologists of all shades acknowledge dependence upon Rudolf Otto's *The Idea of the Holy* (New York, 1958), which is guided by the theme of the codetermination of religious acts and their intended objects in the holy. See A. Vergote, *Psychologie religieuse* (Brussels, 1966).

Husserl himself maintains that, once we enter upon the path of reduction to the constituting source of meaning, there can be no stopping short of the intending life of the transcendental ego. From this radical basis, the phenomenological method is viewed as the comprehensive method of philosophy, adequate for determining precisely those founding acts of meaning in which the truth of our intending patterns of thought and action consists. The intending and constituting activity of the transcendental ego is as comprehensive as our experience, leaving no privileged forms of meaning which are there, but are not included in the primordial founding work. Thus all religious modes of human pre-understanding are included, in principle, within the operational scope of the active constitution of self and world together. If human religiousness is correlated with these modes, rather than with a divine initiative entirely beyond philosophical consideration, then it cannot escape an ultimate reduction to the founding operations of the transcendental ego. Thus Max Scheler identifies the essential phenomenology of religion ultimately with a philosophical anthropology, which excludes revelation and accepts an evolving God.

This diversity among phenomenologists gives a provisional leeway to the realistic philosopher of religion. If he takes the most restricted view of phenomenology, he can make good use of the rich field of phenomenological descriptions of human forms of religion. Such descriptions will deepen his comprehension of the actual structures of belief, rite, and community service brought forth in human societies. An adequate realistic theory of religion cannot ignore or run counter to what is thus ascertained about the shapes of religion in human history. And if the philosopher of religion learns to make use of the more generalized phenomenological studies of religious meanings, he will widen his basis still more. For these studies call attention to the common patterns constituting the unity of the human family, on religious grounds. They also emphasize the correlation between our intending act and the intended object in the religious situation. Here, we can affirm the co-reality of both the numinous religious attitude and the sacred order of life toward which it orients us.

Having availed himself of these levels of phenomenological research, however, the philosopher of religion must eventually face the challenges coming from Husserl, the great source of contemporary phenomenology, and from Scheler's phenomenological reconstitution of all the acts and objects of religion. Husserl forces the inquirer to consider, at the most radical level, whether he is really working as a philosopher or only exploiting a philosophical schema for extraneous ends. If the investigator is not merely using the terms and schemas of phenomenology to restate his theological convictions, then he has to recognize that all the conceptions of man and his situation used in a religious exegesis are affected by the Husserlian doctrine on the transcendental ego's universal constitution of meaning, truth, and being.

The metaphysical question is as inescapable in the phenomenological context as in the analytic, with the same effect of breaking up any circular relationship between a particular conception of human nature and a given religious view of life. The truth of these correlated meanings is brought into question, in the sense that the evidence in experience for holding them and giving them a practical unification must be formally shown. To refer our human situation ultimately to the intending consciousness of the transcendental ego is to seek a different philosophical foundation for religious meanings and religious truth than is given by realistic theism. This different basis might perhaps be supplied either by Husserl's co-constituting ego or by the later Scheler's co-evolution of man and deity. Becoming aware of this metaphysical difference is the clear responsibility of any philosopher of religion who intends to use the phenomenological analyses of religion, and yet retain the metaphysical component of realistic theism.

ETHICS AND RELIGIOUS ETHOS

There is no more controversial part of the philosophy of religion today than that section concerned with the relation between religion and morality. Our interest and passion are likely to be aroused by this topic, since it affects matters of personal concern and the disposition of great social power. Hence it is doubly important here to follow the rule of developing one's theoretical position with maximum attention to the historical study of the emergence of classical modern philosophies of religion.

At least three preliminary observations can be made on the basis of our historical investigation of this issue. First, although the problem of morality and religion has always troubled reflective men, it gains new urgency during the formative modern centuries from the presence of some social factors, which are even more active today. Preeminent among these is the fact of religious diversity among men who nevertheless belong to the same civil society, and stand under the same necessity of reasoning together and reaching a common practical policy. Whether the social context be found in the nation state or in the one world of today, there is great practical pressure to envisage the morality-religion relationship in such a way that we can reach moral agreement, even though we enjoy no religious unity. Indeed, this practical motive underlies the modern drive to elaborate the philosophy of religion itself, with the hope that it will enable us to clarify the meaning of religion and its connections with morality, under the improved conditions of religious pluralism and liberty.[15] This discipline responds to a definite practical need of modern man, and not solely to the exigencies of theory.

The second pertinent historical finding is that the classical modern trio is widely split over how to relate religion and morality. We have already seen that Hume follows the separational path, Kant the completional, and Hegel the organic modalizing. Yet the function of the historical portion in philosophy of religion is not simply to register this division but also to provoke some reflections, which can guide our contemporary efforts. The contrasts between the three classical philosophers of religion on the morality-religion issue are not traceable solely to their different positions in epistemology and metaphysics. These contrasts stem also from the direct estimates which these thinkers made of man's very complicated practical situation, within which the moral and religious factors must interact. Hume directs his attention to the corruptive effects of such inter-action; Kant emphasizes the need for an ordering of the two elements which will preserve moral maturity; and Hegel defends the distinctness of the religious attitude and the relationship of love for the spiritual goal of life. From the example of these great minds, a realistic philosophy of religion can learn to respect the internal complexity of the problem and the difficulty of reconciling the different insights which men have into its several facets. It is better for a present day theory of religion to sin on the side of being sensitive to the conflicting sides in the issue than on the side of a drastic, doctrinaire simplification, which will achieve unity at the cost of the human multiplicity of considerations.

Somewhat distinct from the stress upon complexity is a third point: that human religiousness is likely to enter into several different relationships with morality. Account must be taken not only of a *multiplicity of*

---

15. Thus the semantic investigation in W. A. Christian, *Meaning and Truth in Religion* (Princeton, Princeton University Press, 1964), has the aim of distinguishing between the open and the closed types of religious concepts and truth predications. "While, if truth-claims are admitted, some truth-claims in religion would be incompatible with others, admission of true religious propositions does not entail the kinds of exclusiveness which characterize insensitivity, intolerance, obsessiveness, and idolatry" (p. 261).

components in the practical situation but also of a *variety of ways* in which they can stand related to each other.[16] Hence the oversimplification to be avoided concerns both the content of religious and moral meanings and also the several kinds of relationship between these meanings. The realistic philosopher of religion cannot permit himself to conclude, from the backing which he may discover for one conception of the relationship, that this is the only valid way to conceive the connections between morality and religion. There is special need here for a forewarning about exercising methodic self-discipline against premature closure of the inquiry around one well-founded view of the ordering of these factors. The depth and persistence of the modern conflict on the issue suggest that a realistic approach should deliberately prepare to explore, and at least try to integrate, several different relationships found in our experience.

Some clarification, but no ultimate solution, can be obtained from examining the classical extremes of the religious man who does immoral deeds, and the moral man who does not act upon religious motives. The former case would be quite trivial, if it were supposed that a man is religious simply by subscribing to a certain religious creed or attending a church. He can do these things and still not have a firm enough grasp upon religion to see its consequences for his conduct, or at least to care about reshaping his conduct in accord with those practical implications. This insensitivity tells primarily against the quality of his religious apprehension, without informing us definitely about the nature of the consequences of religion for the active life.

The problem becomes much more acute when a man is knowledgeable and sincere in his religious profession, but acts in ways which most men regard as immoral. Here, several possibilities open up. It may be a case of personal conflict, where the agent knows what should be done and yet omits to do it (or acts contrariwise), out of malice or weakness. This raises the question of whether it makes any effective difference in his moral conduct that he should engage himself in religious belief and practices. Another possibility is that he acts precisely in conformity with the

16. Some dialectical problems in determining the various senses of dependence and independence for the relationship between religion and morality are brought out in the course of two recent discussions: (a) A. MacIntyre, *Difficulties in Christian Belief* (London, 1959), pp. 102–08, and Kai Nielsen, "Morality and God: Some Questions for Mr. MacIntyre," *Philosophical Quarterly*, 12 (1962), 129–37; (b) Kai Nielsen, "Linguistic Philosophy and 'the Meaning of Life,'" and Ralph Sleeper, "Linguistic Philosophy and Religious Belief," *Cross Currents*, 14 (1964), 313–59.

law and spirit of his religion, and hence that there is a conflict between what his particular religion prescribes for practical life and the ordinary moral judgments of men. Such a conflict usually involves many cultural and interpretative factors which have to be analyzed with patience, instead of summarily outlawing the religion and its adherents from the human moral community. Often, the conflict is an expression of failure on the part of all parties to make the requisite analysis, and to develop some fresh views of the religious and moral grounds of disagreement.

Still another factor in this pure position is the appraisal made by a third party, not directly involved in the situation. When he observes a person or a social group making some overt religious commitment and also engaging in immoral action, he is likely to judge that something has gone astray. Without necessarily impugning anyone's integrity, he may nevertheless regard the co-presence of the commitment and the action as an anomaly and a defect. Perhaps the observing critic will then take a satirical attitude, directed either toward the individual and group in question (hypocritical discrepancy between their belief and practice) or toward the religious position as such (inhumanity of its teachings and irreconcilability with our moral ideals). Underlying this critical response is the realization that the meaning of religion includes both some doctrine about the superior divine reality and a way of life for men. Religion does not consist solely in an affirmation of an eternal order of being, but also in an effort to achieve man's practical relationship to it. What makes that relationship practical is its purposive ordering of all our temporal actions and social relations. They are all somehow touched by the religious reorientation of man, since that operation occurs in our world and by means of the actual qualities and expressions of human life.

If a believing community remains true to its human religious vocation, it is committing itself to a practical way of life and conduct.[17] For that community to strive after no detectable reordering of conduct in conformity with its religious profession, or for it to embrace a way of life which spells the death of many human values and moral ideals, is to expose itself to justifiable satire. But the satirical response is itself witness to

17. In the wake of Josiah Royce's theory of religious community, Peter Bertocci, *Introduction to the Philosophy of Religion* (New York, 1961), pp. 497–516, weighs the influence of religion on the wider community of practical action, whereas Paul Weiss, *The God We Seek* (Carbondale, 1964), pp. 99–122, 227–41, stresses that the religious group itself constitutes the dedicated community, which gives an ethico-religious shaping to practical life.

the intimate connection which men ordinarily expect to find between the religious and the moral shaping of life.

What sense can be made, then, of that other pure position occupied by the morally upright man who does not base his conduct on religious motives? In part, his standpoint may be generated as a protest against the hypocrisy and inhumanity found among men who do appeal to such motives. But many other considerations can enter into the attitude of moral separatism. Negatively, it sometimes arises as an emergency measure for purging social life of religious superstitions and debasing fears. To deprive them of any influence over personal and policy decisions, a person may declare himself to be a nonreligious man in respect to the principles used in reaching practical decisions. He means that superstition and fear will not be permitted to interfere with the operation of his moral judgment. Often, the meaning of morality itself is altered to denote only those issues which concern a man's actions in this world, and those rules of conduct drawn from his direct relations with fellow men. By stipulation, then, a moral man is one who attends to such actions and rules, regardless of his position on religious matters. To call such a morally formed agent nonreligious, is a negative way of directing our own attention to the experienced content of mundane social action and the intrinsic norms it conveys.

The actual religious view of the moral man so defined cannot be determined in a uniform, univocal sense. He may be repudiating any religious ordering of life, or he may regard the two practical orderings as real but unrelated spheres. Often his purpose in disconnecting them is to discover some intrinsic basis of practical evidence for his moral ideals and virtues. He wants to accept them on their own merit, not merely on religious recommendation. Their constant reception in a religious context may have induced a skeptical crisis about whether they have any foundation in human experience and in man's actual relationships with the world and society. By methodically searching out a nonconventional basis, he can personally grasp the grounds of assent to moral law and can communicate them to fellow members of society from whom he may be otherwise divided, in regard to religious creed and worship. The practical consensus which they all need will be achieved more solidly, because of this interrogation of their common experience for the clues to morally regulated decisions.

At least one more interpretation of moral autonomy must be reckoned with, since it involves a reordering, rather than a total divorcement, between the moral and religious spheres. The theme of autonomous morality sometimes adds to the affirmation that moral obligation rests upon a human condition, which we can apprehend in its own structure, the further clause that reflection upon this structure provides a distinct route toward determining the religious relationship itself. The human foundations of morality may have some religious implications, which cannot be discovered in any other way or confounded with anything else having a religious connotation. Here, the thinking is that the duty to believe and to worship God cannot have its basis solely in the conventional religious setting where such duty is first heard of.

Eventually, a person must discover a proportionate ground of obligation for the duty of religion itself, and this means that he has to trace it as flowing from the common human source of all moral obligation. Viewed in this way, the conscientious man would be morally defective, both if he were to fail to search for the practical foundation of morality in man and if he were to fail to engage in the religious acts included in that moral duty. The autonomizing of morality gives religion an opportunity to flourish as a humanly rooted relationship, the overlooking of which would leave an individual or a community morally impaired.

The descriptive factors in the problem of morality and religion become even more complicated, when the investigation moves from the abstractly defined extremes to the actual positions worked out by concrete individuals and by group decisions. To cope with such complications and thus do more justice to this tangled issue, a philosophy of religion responding to theistic and realistic principles must adhere closely to its method of integrative analysis. It will avoid pitting one of the descriptively encountered standpoints against the other, since its aim is not to reach a solution based on the suppression of alternatives, but rather to find an adequate human basis for including and ordering the several interpretations. Integrative analysis suggests the existence of at least five basic aims of the human spirit, which must be respected and woven together in the present inquiry. These aims are: to retain the ethical view of morality, to stress the ethical view of religion, to safeguard the religious meaning of religion, to bring out the religious conception of morality, and thus to unite an ethically sanctioned religious act with a practically effective religious ethos. In trying to weigh these several considerations, we can appreciate the difficulty and delicacy of the problems in philosophy of religion.

Ethical View of Morality. A realistic philosophy of religion developed through integrative analysis will include ethical elements, just as it includes metaphysical and psychological ones. There will be a closer affinity between the ethical sources and the theory of religion, since they are both located in the practical order. But just as philosophy of religion incorporates metaphysical and psychological components without destroying their proper nature, so does it incorporate ethical ones without destroying their distinctive basis. Indeed, it supposes that the ethical factors which are relevant to the understanding of religious life do have their own proper founding in the practical order, since otherwise they would not be assimilated relevantly to the theory of religion but created arbitrarily by it. The intent of philosophy of religion is to include some ethical truths bearing on the religious relationship, not to become a part of ethics or to take the place of ethical reasoning on the evidence furnished by our moral life itself. The relationship is one of adaptive inclusion, not one of substitutive rivalry. This is a particular application of the general method of integrative analysis in the theory of religion, which draws upon the resources of the other parts of philosophy without becoming confused with them or undermining their proper autonomy.

It is to the ultimate advantage of an honestly constructed philosophy of religion that the immanent, human foundation of morality be acknowledged and studied for its own sake. The seed of morality is present, when the agent considers something more than impulse and private convenience, in determining his course of action. His acts begin to take on a moral quality, insofar as they admit of some measure and demand placed upon them. He takes into account not only his flow of likes and dislikes but also a pattern of active relationships with other persons and things. The active self recognizes that it belongs in a wider community, that it has a good to achieve in and through the relationships with others, and that there is some fruitful demand being placed upon itself to act in accord with this fuller measure of practical life. In thus opening itself up, the human self learns what it means to judge and act in a moral way.

When the bases of moral life are considered at this stage in the analysis, there may perhaps be no explicit reference to God and our bond with Him.[18] Viewing his own situation, the moral agent may feel unable to specify any definite referent for his measuring pattern of action and his

18. The question of whether or not God's existence matters for our moral life is not really decisive for the problem of theism, since one can establish an intrinsic human basis of morality without having resolved the ultimate relationships which God may have to human activity. For a nontheistic and a Kantian theistic treatment of this question, respectively, see W. I. Matson, *The Existence of God* (Ithaca, 1965), pp. 219–49, and H. J. Paton, *The Modern Predicament* (New York, 1962),

wider good, beyond the human community. He may express his moral commitment simply as a permanent concern to act as he should, to realize his selfhood in its full and demanding measure, and thus to share in the beneficial practical relationships which bind all personal agents together. The philosopher of religion cannot impose a theistic interpretation from without. He can only point out that there is nothing in the situation excluding the theistic reference, and that the developing life of the moral self actively leads toward such an interpretation as its fulfillment. But there is also nothing in the logic of moral growth and fulfillment to warrant a judgment that, without the formal recognition of the God of theism, the intrinsic human ground of morality is worthless and ineffective. Quite to the contrary, part of the methodic discipline of a philosophy of religion developing in the spirit of realistic theism is to repudiate such a judgment. This theory of religion builds upon the positive tendencies in moral man, not upon a denigration of them or an artificial recasting of them in premature molds.

Ethical View of Religion. There are many ways in which religion is rooted in the soil of moral life, and hence many ways of working out an ethical perspective on religion. As Georg von Wright observes, we are sometimes overwhelmed by the complexity of the relationships entering into the pattern of moral living.

> It is a deeply impressive fact about the condition of man that it should be difficult, or even humanly impossible, to judge confidently of many things which are known to affect our lives importantly, whether they are good or bad for us. I think that becoming *overwhelmed* by this fact is one of the things which can incline a man towards taking a religious view of life. "Only God knows what is good or bad for us." One could say thus—and yet accept that a man's welfare is a subjective notion in the sense that it is determined by what *he* wants and shuns.[19]

We are conscientiously aware that we cannot judge firmly about many things that are good for us, and cannot determine all the consequences of even our most carefully meditated courses of action. And yet our intention

---

pp. 58–64, 322–42. Anthropological evidence on both the independence of the moral foundation and its complex interrelation with religion in primitive societies is examined by A. Macbeath, *Experiments in Living* (New York, 1952), pp. 291–350.

19. G. H. von Wright, *The Varieties of Goodness* (New York, Humanities Press, 1963), p. 110. J. H. Newman, *Grammar of Assent* (New York, Doubleday, 1955),

is to make responsible moral judgments and to enrich, rather than disrupt, the actional community among persons. These considerations can lead us to open out our freedom to the aid and guidance of God, thus engaging in a religious response to our practical situation.

Such a religious response is not based upon despair over the powers of man, but upon an enlargement of the interpersonal community to include the good and caring God, with whom we can become related in ways which bear upon man's moral realization. This leads to a moral conception of religion, since our bond of divine worship and service is viewed primarily as a component within the search for the full measure of well-patterned human activity. When the moral view of religion is assimilated to the philosophy of religion, its distinctive value is preserved. There would be a loss in the human meaning of religion, if the sense in which religion serves for the perfecting of man's moral life were not respected and indeed accented.

Reflection upon this moral aspect of religion leads to the ethical judgment of the worth and duty of worshipping and serving God. Religion receives an ethical sanction, insofar as men discern an effective relationship between their religious acts and their basic moral effort to meet a demanding pattern and achieve a fulfilling good for themselves. When this connection is grasped, religious acts take on the quality of being both morally good for man and required for his responsible participation in the interpersonal community. Once again, a loss would be sustained in the full human meaning of religion, if it did not include the mode of engaging in the religious life on the prompting of moral motivations. Religion depends upon morality, in the specific sense that religious acts are judged to be morally important and obligatory. This specific aspect exhausts neither the meaning of morality nor that of religion, but it does determine one specific relationship between the moral foundation of human action and the religious ordering of life, acknowledged to be a moral requirement.

The ethician treats the moral aspects of religion under the virtue of justice. Depending upon the narrower or the broader conception of justice itself within which he operates, he will develop a narrower or a broader

---

examines obligating moral conscience, not only as a path to conviction about God's personal existence, but also as "the creative principle of [natural] religion . . . our great internal teacher of religion" (pp. 101, 304) and a reforming basis "making it a necessary point to adjust the religions of the world with the intimations of our conscience" (p. 307). See H. D. Lewis, *Philosophy of Religion* (New York, 1965), pp. 254–71, on the pluriform relations between morality and religion.

ethical view of religion. When the virtue of justice is considered in a restricted way, as rendering to another what is his due, then the acts of religion are viewed as the practical means of rendering to God the worship and service owed by man to his divine source and goal. The meaning of God and the creative way in which He imparts life to man will depend upon the several sources of theism available to the moral agent. But however the bond of dependence upon God is specified, it can be viewed morally as entailing for man the obligation in justice to make a proportionate response with his mind and actions. Seen in this light, the religious man is one who is careful to return to God the personal and social response which is His due, as the Lord of all life.

It is important to notice, however, that when justice is given a broader meaning, it also deepens the quality of the morally rooted religious response to God. It belongs to the office of justice to assure that the several virtues and actions of man are working toward his good and self-fulfillment. The just man seeks to engage in all those actions and relationships which will achieve his maximal realization as a person and member of the human community. To the degree that he acknowledges the theistic interpretation of his personal and interpersonal life, he also sees that the pursuit of God is central to that life. The virtue of justice keeps him dispositionally mindful of his bond with God, and prompts him to engage in those human acts of belief, adoration, and service whereby he can enliven and strengthen that bond, from the human side at least. The general religious response to God does not cease to be an act of rendering due service to Him, but this aspect is included within the wider frame of meaning set by our due regard for achieving free selfhood and social interrelatedness. Thus the narrower conception of religion as a duty owed in justice is incorporated within the broader moral conception of religion, as a mode of realizing the just man's concern for sharing in the goods of personal and interpersonal existence.

The ethical judgment about religion as a good, a virtue, and a duty for man culminates in this broader conception of religious acts. For here, the several moral strands in the religious attitude can be brought together in a moral unity. The morally reflective theist accepts a religious orientation of his conduct, on all these grounds. He finds in such orientation a meaningful way to interpret the demanding pattern manifested in his actions, to give practical expression to the theistic relationship with the good and caring Lord, and to find free self-fulfillment in all the personal centers of value which are open to his human searching. Ethically sanctioned religion is the religious relationship viewed precisely in this complex fashion, as a component in man's efforts toward practical realization. Religion has an ethical basis and backing, insofar as it is structured by those tendencies of the human agent which interweave his good and his dignity with a sharing in divine life.

Religious View of Religion. But philosophy of religion cannot confine itself to the ethical tendencies, any more than to the psychological and metaphysical ones, which incline men toward the religious relationship and which help to shape its actual forms. It must view religion not only as one of the climaxes in ethical life itself but also as being distinctively structured by the habitudes and acts constituting its own reality. Whatever the various rootings of human religiousness and the various motivating principles behind its development, it nevertheless constitutes a unified active pattern of human engagement with the divine source of our life. At some point in the examination of religion, this pattern must be reflectively acknowledged and considered for its own sake.

The religious shaping of the human spirit draws *upon* many sources in our experience, but it also draws them *together*, so that they may contribute to the specifically religious focus and practical ordering of our existence. One task of philosophy of religion is to insure that sort of appraisal of the nature and import of religion which comes reflectively from within the religious relationship itself. It is evident that if religious values were to be viewed only from within their own perspective, the philosophical theory of religion would be impoverished and corrupted by the lack of common canons of evidence. But if there were no recognition at all of human religiousness, as seen in its own intrinsic unity, then its distinctive reality would vanish. The philosophical theory of religion would never attain to that form of human activity and relatedness which originally called forth this specific sort of inquiry.

A major aim of the method of integrative analysis is precisely to insure the specificity of the philosophical inquiry into religion. The relevant factors drawn from the theory of man, the theory of being, and ethics, are incorporated into a definite line of analysis aimed at understanding and evaluating the religious life of man. Taken in this functional way, these several factors always remain helpful means for clarifying the human meanings of religion, and for testing the values enshrined in the religious attitude. They cannot be converted from tools of analysis into reductive bases, however, to which the order of religious beliefs and practices might simply be resolved. They are integrated together, so that the philosophical examination of religion will not destroy the integrity of its subject, in the course of uncovering the many roots it relies upon in all the modes of human experiencing and valuing.

Whatever the motivating considerations, religion engages the individual and the group in some characteristically patterned order of activities. Religious men come to direct themselves toward the divine for its own sake, and thus to find in their active communion with the divine reality a primary center of reference, not a sheer entailment from anything else. Realistic theism serves the philosophy of religion, to the degree that it acknowledges this distinctive texture of the religious relationship and of the revaluations which it prompts men to make. It sees in the love of God a unifying center, around which all other religious factors become organized.

There are powerful grounds in human nature, in the general purposiveness of being, and in the ethical search for human good, which orient men toward God. Viewed in terms of a realistic theism, what these grounds dispose men toward is a life of searching after God, through the acts of believing, loving, and serving Him. Such acts draw men into an interpersonal religious community, in which God's initiative is disclosed and man's response is freely given. The interpersonal religious community has a structure of its own, which can be studied by the different sciences, and yet which never dissolves under scrutiny and never ceases to display fresh resources. In unifying the different intellectual approaches to man's resilient religious life, the philosophy of religion respects the structure upon which it is focusing. It furnishes an effective method for self-examination of the religious bond on the part of its active participants, as well as for presentation of the religious interpretation of all other facets of human existence.

Religious View of Morality. In the course of fulfilling this latter work, the philosophy of religion is bound to consider the religious view of moral actions. Especially within a theistic context, the distinctive structuring of the religious relationship is not construed as an isolation of it from the rest of human life. Since religious search and communion are specifically directed toward the Lord of all life, there is a universal significance to the bonds that hold men in responsive engagement with God. A reflective religious interpretation reaches out far beyond the formal structures of belief and service, which directly concern our intercourse with God. It encompasses all the active relationships of man with his fellow men and with the universe, including the moral ones. There is a properly religious manner of envisaging the basis and nature of moral relations, and this also must find its detailed analysis within the philosophy of religion.

The religious interpretation of the moral life usually takes two basic forms: divine precept and religious ethos. Within the theistic religious community, God maintains a creative initiative in respect to the motives and goals of human actions. These practical qualities do not remain indifferent to Him or beneath His consideration, but rather they capture His concern and come within the range of divine providence, acting in human hearts and in human history. The divine providential concern finds expression not only in saving actions but also in the divine *precepts* themselves. God's commands are a basic way in which His personal intent concerning the uses of human freedom is effectively communicated to men. These commands are not confined to matters of formal religious belief, ritual, and service of the altar. The commandments reach out to moral phases of human activity: to one's use of goods, to one's communication with others, to family and other societal relationships.

Thus many specific features in the moral ordering of life become matters of divine commandment. For the religious community, they are regulated by God's precept and not only by man's direct moral reflection. Hence for religiously motivated agents, the enjoined actions will be performed or omitted in response to the demands placed by God upon human freedom, along with whatever grounds in human nature there are for so conducting themselves. Indeed, such agents are likely to interpret the proximate grounds for moral action which are discoverable in human relationships and dynamisms as one further mode of communication, used by God to convey to all mankind the quality and purpose of moral living in His presence.

In addition to explicit commands having a moral import, however, there is another way in which religion helps to specify morality. Theistic and nontheistic religions alike regard themselves as a way of life, not simply on the strength of certain specific laws of conduct but on account of their *ethos*, or pervasive orientation of our whole existence.[20] An individual or a community will act differently, for having been permeated by a religious interpretation of the origin and destiny of the human

20. Using the phenomenological concepts of Otto and the early Scheler, Bernard Häring, *Das Heilige und das Gute* (Krailling, 1950), pp. 46–58, observes that the religious act always involves a sacral ethos (disposing us actively toward God), but that it must be developed in its interpersonal significance so that it can entail a sanctioned ethos or morality (setting certain moral duties concerning interhuman relations).

family and its place in the living universe. This difference is expressly affirmed in the theistic stress upon God as the creator of all beings and as the common father of the human race. To enter into constant religious communion with God as so qualified, is to develop a practical interpretation of our relationships with other men and the universe which deeply affects our conduct. The religious man is always mindful of the divine source, basis, and goal of things in this world. His relationships with other men, as persons and as personal members of the human community, are marked by this same religious mindfulness. He may well run roughshod over such considerations, but he does so with an uneasy conscience and a sense of betraying some differences which should count importantly in his conduct.

The practical transformation worked by religion in man's interpretation and response to his total situation in this world constitutes the religious ethos. It may add nothing to the specific content of moral precepts, but it permeates all moral decisions with a further measure of awareness. It exerts a dispositional power over reflective religious minds. They are prompted to make their moral action consonant with the universal range of God's loving concern for mankind and with the quality of fraternity which should permeate all human relationships, in virtue of our common ordination to life with God. These considerations are effectively related to moral judgments through a well-sustained religious ethos. The latter serves as a living principle of communication and mediation between the religious and the ethical orders. Its function is to assure that the pertinent religious convictions will not be relegated to some nonmundane attic of our lives, but will noticeably affect the course and quality of our practical conduct in this world.

Whenever we invoke the pragmatic criterion for the soundness and sincerity of religious belief, we are acknowledging that such belief ought to be accompanied by an operative religious ethos. What we believe in religious matters affects our total interpretation of existence and the pattern of working values, involved in the decision process. To be persistently aware of the practical difference made in our frame of action by the presence of a religious factor, is to respond to an operative religious ethos. A personal agent thus animated is impelled not only toward the doing of specific good works but also, and perhaps more importantly in the long run, toward moral carefulness. He recognizes that there are also religious grounds for his responsible moral action: to the other reasons for being conscientious, he adds that of being religiously committed to the pursuit of the moral good itself. This same strengthening of our moral carefulness is found in the social order of human secularity, insofar as the religious ethos permeates the whole community.

Ethico-Religious Teleology. A clear course is set out for the philosophy of religion in this complicated issue of morality and religion. It must enter into, and sympathetically develop from within, each of the four perspectives just outlined. Its strength as a realistic theory of religion comes from accepting all the factors in the human practical situation, and at their full strength. No one of them can be diluted or simply made the tool of another aspect, without denying its own kind of evidence and demand upon human freedom. There is a moral view of morality and religion which is not reducible to anything else in our experience, just as there is a religious view of morality and religion which retains its original hold upon experience. The two views do not tend to cancel each other out, unless some exclusive claim is made in favor of one, or unless one is reduced to a sheerly instrumental standing. By respecting each approach, we can discover experientially and theoretically the meaning of the finitude of human action. Human individuals and communities have to cultivate a certain sustained tension between the morally based and the religiously based interpretations of both morality and religion.

There is no perfect merger and synthesis of the two within human experience, but there is a helpful discipline emerging from their mutual scrutiny and stimulus. We are better persons for having our human acts compounded, both of those aspects flowing from ethical motives and sanctions and those reflecting the power of a religious ethos. The only theory of religion commensurate with realistic theism is one which makes methodical provision for this interplay between the ethical good and the religious ethos, so that human action can benefit from both strands in our practical relationships.

Although no perfect fusion is either desirable or to be expected, a theistic philosophy of religion does establish a purposive order for the several factors in religiously oriented human action. Without depriving them of their own bases in meaning, it nevertheless unifies them around its primary teleological theme of man's search for and love of God.[21] In

21. Henri Bergson, *The Two Sources of Morality and Religion*, trans. R. A. Audra and C. Brereton (New York, 1935), pp. 240–46, 255–64, 300, assigns a common destiny to closed morality and closed religion (based on motives of social conformity and survival) and a distinct common destiny to open morality and open religion (responding to broad motives of human freedom and growth in love).

this loving search for God, there is a convergence of the distinct approaches to religious acts taken in terms of their moral worth and obligation and their sharing in the divine life. These are the actual routes for understanding and motivating man's free intercourse with God, and hence they contribute jointly toward the philosophical interpretation of the religious relationship, grounded in our practical activity. The unification achieved in philosophy of religion on this issue remains deliberately at the level of a reflective analysis of the distinct components which man, the religious searcher, requires in his active striving toward God. This purposive unity does not permit any one-way reduction of either the moral or the religious paths to God.

AN OPEN RELIGIOUS HUMANISM

Realistic theism generates a conception of religion which is an open religious humanism. This is a descriptive designation, without any honorific connotation. It affords an opportunity to elucidate the sense in which the operative terms "humanistic" and "open" are applicable to this theory of religion, but even after that sense is determined, a self-laudatory use of the terms has to be systematically avoided. They are bound up too closely with the whole network of issues and analyses constituting the realistic philosophy of religion to serve, all by themselves, as an obvious means of recommendation for this philosophy. Only after examining the cultural, methodological, and doctrinal tasks in detail, can one see that the position in which they ultimately terminate is an open and humanistic view of religion, distinguished on specific grounds from some other philosophical notions of religion. This is the kind of theory of religion toward which the realistic mind is led, as it tries to meet its three main tasks in cultural self-clarification, methodology, and doctrinal development.

To designate this theory of religion as humanistic is not to classify it under a neatly defined category, but rather to launch it into a turbulent sea of contemporary discussion concerning the meanings of humanism and the compatibility of religious attitudes with these meanings. There is no predetermined, authoritative definition, by agreement with which, or by entailment from which, it can easily be shown that the realistic view of religion has a humanistic character. Rather, the theme of its humanistic quality is part of the continuous argument whereby this theory builds itself, and determines its relations with other accounts of religion. It must reckon with the fact that the Marxian and Sartrean types of humanism exclude any distinctively religious response, that American naturalistic humanism admits a form of religiousness but purified of any theistic traits, and that many theologians conclude from the humanistic basis of a theory of religion that it must remain closed to, and perhaps inimical toward, faith in the revealing God. In declaring its humanistic character, the realistic theory of religion is only fortifying its close involvement in the going discussion of these contended issues. It is not using an honorific label to close off the critical argument or somehow elevate itself above the fray.

There is some profit to be gained from underlining the thoroughly problematic nature of realism's claim to constitute a type of religious humanism. That claim could not be sustained, within the actual framework of inquiry and argument today, by a philosophy of religion which would declare its complete independence from an undergirding of other speculative and practical reasonings. If a theory of religion were to autonomize itself as a field of specialized meanings which requires no epistemological, metaphysical, anthropological, and ethical supports, it would be unable to join issue with the other philosophical conceptions of religion and humanism. For the contending views on religion and man do draw upon methodology and the other portions of philosophy. Some definite theory of knowing, being, or conduct is invoked to show that one cannot take a humane view of man and still be religious, or cannot accept God without drawing mortiferous consequences upon man, or cannot build upon the human foundations of religion without falling into idolatry and an antirevelational outlook. These are definite critical positions, by reference to which a realistic philosophy of religion must work out its own humanistic meaning. Since the force of the argument is drawn in each instance from some general philosophical considerations, it can be met properly only by examining the underlying doctrines in themselves and not merely in their particular application.

The general philosophical sources for the realistic theory of religion must continue to animate it, at every phase in its growth. Without these roots, there would be only a regional discipline which could perhaps describe itself as humanistic, but which could not examine the grounds of dissent from this description and the arguments for taking a divergent position on the humanistic quality of theism. It could attach labels to itself, but it could not show in practice that it has a philosophical grasp upon the meaning of religion and man. It would not strictly qualify as a philosophically constituted and explicated sort of religious humanism.

There are two basic senses in which a theory of religion can be called humanistic: because it stresses the sources in human nature for religious belief and practice, and because it judges that the religious response enriches human nature and its grasp upon reality. These constitute respectively the *genetic* and the *valuational* meanings of religious humanism. On both counts, the realistically developed conception of religion has a humanistic cast. Its characteristic approach is to search out the roots of the religious attitude in man's own structure and experience, as involved in active relationships with the physically and historically evolving universe. It gradually specifies a philosophical meaning for religion, from a study of man's implication in natural being and his discernment of the presence there of God. Thereupon, realistic theism judges that the search after God is well founded in our human experience, and hence that the religious orientation enhances the values and interpretative range of human life. Religion not only rests upon man's active nature and relationships in the world but also helps to develop them further, by actualizing their reference to God. In the intensive sense of the method used and the valuations attained, then, a humanistic pattern is woven in the realistic philosophy of religion.

The weaving does not go on in a cultural vacuum, of course, but in full awareness of the strong countertendencies to dissociate humanism from any religious view, or at least from religious theism. The heroic pathos surrounding this program of dissociation is voiced in Sartre's remark that "atheism is a cruel and long-range affair: I think I've carried it through. I see clearly, I've lost my illusions, I know what my real jobs are. . . . I do not occupy myself with God, I occupy myself with man." [22] Sartre and the Marxists hold that religion is well lost, since in the process of losing it they have gained a hold upon a more authentic humanism today, whatever religion's past contributions to man may have been.

Sartre's declaration evokes the concrete attitude of nonreligious man, who regards it as his moral duty to refuse transcendence and all religion. He seeks an ascetic purification of religious inclinations and any allegiance to the divine, because he regards them as hindrances now to his freedom

22. Jean-Paul Sartre, *The Words*, trans. B. Frechtman (New York, Braziller, 1964), p. 253; the last part of the quotation is a personal remark made by Sartre to Wilfrid Desan and reported in the latter's book, *The Marxism of Jean-Paul Sartre* (New York, Doubleday, 1965), p. 32.

and hence as a betrayal of his total commitment to the human good. If humanism consists in the affirmation of man-in-nature as the sole active reality and the sole agent and goal of history, then there is no room for theism and a religious way of life within the humanistic perspective. It is this powerful linking of the future of mankind with emancipation from all religious ties, especially in the theistic mode, which furnishes the actual setting and significance of the problem of realistic theism and humanism.

It is sometimes thought that the secular city, constructed to contain the clash between religious man and nonreligious man, as well as between various modalities of religion, is surrounded by high walls. These walls of civil living loom high enough to prevent any communication between God and man, thus effectively silencing the religious man and depriving him of that living intercourse with the divine which made his message credible and moving in the past. Consequently, our age is taken by Heidegger to be one in which the human names for God are lacking in meaning and conviction, and by Buber to be one in which God keeps a purifying silence.[23] We must wait patiently until the positive values of the atheistic protest are fully explicated and assimilated by human existence. This is the dark interval between the religiously meaningful cosmos of the past, and whatever new religious awareness may yet dawn upon mankind.

Realistic theism takes instruction from both the atheistic humanists and the self-silencing believers in the eclipse of God, but it remains ultimately critical of the interpretations proposed by both these groups of thinkers. There are precious human and religious values underlying both readings of the religious situation, and sufficient cultural motives to make each one strive to compensate for the other's shortcomings. And yet they share a tacit premise, which has to be called into question. Both interpretations suppose that, as far as the present opportunities for freedom and human creativity are concerned, man's religious tendencies have been caught up into a condition of *stasis*, a fixed state deprived of real present initiative.

From the standpoint of atheistic humanism and its image of nonreligious man, religion has been captured in its quintessential form and definitively revealed to be an obstacle to our development. Its inhumane essence is now brought to frozen stability for our inspection, and nothing

23. Cf. J. M. Robinson and J. B. Cobb, *The Later Heidegger and Theology* (New York, 1963), and Martin Buber, *Eclipse of God* (New York, 1952), on the obscuring of God in our age.

more can be expected from it except by those who have not yet attained to this lucid insight, or who cannot endure its findings about man and religion. The predicament of God-seeking men is somewhat relieved by those who await a renewing word from God, and who look for an enlivening human word about God. But they also immobilize the present situation, subject it to an essential law of noncommunication between the divine and the human, and thus preserve the separation between religion and humanistic aims during the noncommunicatory interval. It is this immobilist premise which subjects an open religious humanism to the crossfire of the atheistic humanists and the self-silencing believers alike.

What has happened is that, once more, religion is made an exception to the common rules of inquiry, and this time to its clear detriment and paralysis. Whereas all other aspects of human experience and practical relating are seen to develop in conjunction with each other in a ceaseless historical process, religion is treated as though it terminates in some isolated essence or encloses itself in some ahistorical interspace. What comes to a standstill in the effort to interrelate religion and humanism is not precisely human religiousness but this particular method of viewing it as a static essence, embodied in "the" religious man of a given philosophical definition, and as a timeless condition of silence between man and God. It is just such a methodological overpowering of our ever evolving religious reality which classical modern philosophy of religion sought to avoid, and which a realistic philosophy of religion calls into question today.

To prevent an essentializing separation of religion from human life and intelligence, the realistic theory of religion adheres to the method of integrative analysis. It stresses the mundanity of religion, the need for investigating it through the common modes of inquiry, and the development of a philosophical theory of religion only within a broader context of principles and evidences. By these methodic measures, the doors are kept open between all other findings about man and the actual universe and the religious response to our always freshly shaping experience. Instead of foredooming religion to a separatist approach, tyrannized by a stipulated essential definition of the religious outlook or by a metaphor of high walls around the city of man, the realistic method permits it to be examined in its firm human texture. Religiousness can be studied in its open historical development, therefore, along with our other ways of interpreting man's relationships with natural and cultural being.

The philosophy of religion is itself one of man's effective modes of speaking about his orientation toward God, within the conditions of the contemporary secular city. Realistic theism uses the resources of both the historical growth of classical modern philosophy of religion and the doctrinal work of integrative analysis to show that our present situation is not an anomalous *interval*, but rather a directional *phasing* in the religious history of mankind.[24]

From the study of Hume-Kant-Hegel, it is clear that there has been no rigid sequestration of religious beliefs and practices, in order that they will not infect the genuine meaning and values of man. Rather, the Humean critique of superstition, the Kantian critique of amoralism, and the Hegelian critique of positivity, are all directed toward removing those constructions of religion which would keep it entirely apart from our evolving human destiny and from a continuing integration with the other factors in human action. The intent of these philosophers is to cleanse and improve the human conception of religion, not to isolate it or snatch it somehow out of the context of an incessant deepening of all modes of human response to our world. Moreover, the naturalistic efforts to detheize religion and then to eliminate any transcendent reference to a divine spiritual reality depend upon a quite one-sided lineage of theories about the meaning of God and the spiritual order. The natural resources of human reflection upon God and the religious relationship are not confined to the targets of naturalistic criticism, that is, to the particular views of God, religion, and human history which Comte and Feuerbach, Marx and Nietzsche, found it necessary to attack on humane grounds.

On the historical side, therefore, the view that religion has either reached its terminus or entered a wordless interval cannot be supported. For this estimate is itself the outcome of a traceable historical genesis; it embodies only a partial unification of the interpretative resources of mankind up to the present; and it is ordered toward critical integration with all the other meanings and evidences for religion. The only inhumane aspect of this situation would be found in so doctrinaire an insistence upon the terminalist and intervalist positions, that the directional dynamism toward a more adequate conception of religion and its social role would go unrecognized.

A similar shift from the intervalist to the open phasing interpretation

24. "Martin Buber suggests that this is an age when God is 'silent.' It might be more accurate to say that it is an age in which man is silent about God, in great part because man has not assimilated to his knowledge of God the new knowledge of the physical universe which has been recently given him" (W. J. Ong, *In the Human Grain* (New York, Macmillan, 1967), p. 180).

of the problem of religion and humanism is generated by the doctrinal use of integrative analysis. All the factors in the doctrinal investigation indicate that the realistic theory of religion is still very much in the making, that its capacities for interpretation are still being developed in a gradual, forward thrusting manner. The general project of achieving a confluence between the classical modern theories of religion and realistic philosophy as a whole is being explored in stages, without there being any blueprint of how to join these two currents of thought.

First steps are being taken in the methodological order, where realistic theism is learning to use the resources of the analytical study of religious language and the phenomenological study of religious meanings and attitudes. Similarly, there are groping efforts underway to discover precisely what metaphysical difference is made in the speculative interpretation of religion by employing a realistic theory of knowing and being, as well as a realistically elaborated doctrine on the existing God. This approach is bound to affect such a religiously sensitive topic as the manner in which to conceive of the divine transcendence without having a far-off extrinsic deity, and to recognize the divine intimate presence in man without converting man into a mode of a spiritual totality. And in the ethical sphere, realistic theism is beginning to grasp the full complexity of viewpoints involved, and the need to respect all components in the relationship between ethically grounded conduct and the religious ethos. In a word, all the tasks so far cited in the present chapter point toward a philosophical development going on in the theory of religion, aided by the continuous evolution of views on man and religion in the social sciences.

Our age is not a season of becalming, when religion can be contemplated as a fixed mechanism of alienation belonging to man's past or as a discipline of neutralized self-silencing, but rather a time of transition and rapid growth in our understanding and evaluation of religion, as well as all other aspects of human nature. We do have to attach a prudent qualifier of tentativeness to a good many of our philosophical statements on religion, but this is an affair of methodological precision and not of silence or past-tense treatment of man's religious acts. There is solidarity here between the exact phrasing of statements about religion, in an age of discovery and ever more complexly related findings, and the exact phrasing of statements on other aspects of our existence. Such solidarity manifests the humane quality of religion and the study of religion, in both the genetic and the valuational senses of humanism. A realistic philosopher of religion will prize this quality as a sign of the human experiential nature of his method. It also serves as a salutary check upon the tendency to declare himself in possession of the definitive and comprehensive meaning of religion.

Along with this ingrained openness to its own potentialities in inquiry, the religious humanism developed by realistic theism is open in four other significant directions. First, it never cuts itself off from the pluralism of many philosophical methods and doctrinal systems. The illusion of theoretical self-sufficiency and aloneness is greatest, whenever the theory of religion is treated as an autonomous specialty in philosophy or as a reflective arm of some religious group. To combat that illusion, the historical and philosophical roots and the methodological rules of one's theory of religion must constantly be retraced, so that the continuity of the analysis will be retained and the more general conditions of philosophical inquiry borne in mind. In this way, the realistic approach to the nature of experience, the analytico-inferential method of inquiry, the judgments of existence, process, and structure, will be seen to be continually relevant to every statement made in this theory of religion.

The realistic philosopher of religion can never cease to inquire into the fundamental differences on method and metaphysics which divide great thinkers, and which ultimately generate quite different conceptions of the nature of religion and its role in human life. He has to keep searching not only into the different historical angles of vision directly concerned with religion but also into the underlying diversity of philosophical principles. His purpose must be to enlarge his own apprehension of religious meanings by trying to appropriate the still elusive gleams of experience, to which the other doctrines on method and reality are somehow responsive. His interpretation will not fuse with theirs, but it will become a degree less impoverished for having been forced to attend to some overlooked or underestimated facet of man's bond with natural being. Insofar as this other aspect illuminates our orientation toward the divine, it demands a proportionate resonance in the realistic theory of religion, whatever the method and metaphysical context of its initial presentation.

In the second place, the realistic philosopher of religion must submit to the constant discipline of the ideal of humanity. That is, he has to measure any actual statement of his view of religion by the requirement that it be communicable to the rest of mankind, verifiable in other men's experience, and capable of expressing and enhancing their own religious values. This respect for the religious search of other men and the interhuman capacity for sharing in religious values calls for a ceaseless purifying and deepening of one's entire theory of religion. It must be kept open to the comparative study of the different religions of mankind, just as it is kept open to the different philosophical interpretations of method and the theory of man in general.

Karl Jaspers and Paul Weiss have pointed out the dangers arising from a philosophical theory of religion which is nothing more than a speculative transcription of some particular religious position.[25] When the theory of religion is regarded as merely a reformulation of a particular confession in philosophical terms, it cannot correct the tendency to claim a monopoly upon the theoretical truth of religion and to exclude other views as being defective in principle. Yet the remedy does not come from dissolving one's relationship with a faith and a church, or from any other kind of severance. Rather, it comes from a reflective realization of the distinctive procedure of the realistic philosopher of religion. He accepts suggestions about the meaning of religion from all the available human sources, including his own faith and the faiths of other men. But he is bound by his method to shape his philosophical assent and the structure of statements in his philosophy of religion by the evidence which belongs in his experience of natural being and the inferences sustained by it. And he is also bound by his practical intent, in the philosophy of religion, to keep developing a meaning of religion which will help men to realize their full and common vocation. In this sense, the realistic theory of religion accepts responsibility for working toward the continuing education of humanity to its own potentialities, stressing those which involve a common sharing in God's spiritual life.

Realistic theism carries with it a third sort of openness: to the free, personal God, present in the universe and distinct from it through His creative presence. Being open to the personal God has a humanistic connotation, because of the close tie between man's self-estimation and his view of God. It is precisely in the philosophy of religion that this relationship is examined in itself, thus calling attention to a religious context for philosophical anthropology as well as for natural theology. Although the philosophical theories of man and God remain formally distinct in their methods and principles, nevertheless there are some significant

25. See Weiss, *The God We Seek*, pp. 136–59, and the following works by Karl Jaspers: *The Perennial Scope of Philosophy* (New York, 1949), pp. 75–117; *Philosophy and the World* (Chicago, 1963), pp. 141–51; and his entire book, *Philosophical Faith and Revelation* (New York, 1967).

correlations between their problems. Especially in the meaning of personal selfhood, freedom, and interpersonal community, there is a noticeable relationship between the way a man views his own reality and the position he takes on God.[26] A common destiny binds together the quality of our acknowledgment of God and that of our comprehension of the personal self and the living society of men.

This mutual ordering between the meaning of man and the meaning of God becomes an explicit theme in the philosophy of religion. Here, some common ground can be found between these two central problems, without supposing that the meaning of the personal God is only an alienated form of man's self-reflection, or that this meaning is only a projection of revelation into the zone of philosophy. The philosopher has to weigh all the aspects of his meaning of man and God by the methods and guiding judgments proper to human experience of natural being. From this standpoint, there is a shared destiny for our human apprehension of the free, interpersonal community among men and the free, interpersonal community between men and God. By reflecting upon this interrelation of meanings as being essential for a religious interpretation of experience, realistic theism specifies its own humanistic basis.

Fourthly, the realistic philosophy of religion remains open in several ways to the revealing and saving God. This type of openness is already remotely prepared for, in the way in which this philosophy views the secularization process and its goal in human secularity. The secularization process does not exclude religion, the modern developments in philosophy of religion, and scientific studies of religion, but includes them as part of the human reality which is undergoing development. Not only is there no total de-religionizing of man within human secularity, but he is positively conceived as including an awareness of being under a call. The religious relationship is not an isolated construct on man's part, but develops within a twofold human context: that of seeking to fulfill our human vocation, and that of waiting in expectation of God's help. The religious attitude arises in man as a response to a call, at least a call to realize his own nature in active relationships.

In a theistic perspective, man regards his religious acts as already in-

26. "The belief in the self follows a curve which is determined or at least influenced by the current ideas of God, and belief or disbelief in him" (M. C. D'Arcy, *No Absent God: The Relations Between God and the Self* [New York, Harper and Row, 1962], p. 24). Cf. John Macmurray, *Persons in Relation* (New York, 1961), pp. 151–65, 214–24, on religion as the celebration of the interpersonal community among men and between men and God.

volved in an interplay, wherein God takes His own creative initiative. The disposition toward believing, worshipping, and serving God is interpreted as a participation in a community of persons, where there is expected a reciprocal act from all the fee agents involved. Whatever restrictions of methodology and epistemology are placed upon a philosophical study of the divine creative initiative and religious message, the human attitude of responding to some call and awaiting some aid and light belongs in the philosophically determined meaning of human religiousness. That meaning is a word spoken by man concerning his search for God, but it does not exclude from the secular city a word coming from God to man thus waiting.

Nevertheless, the word of human religiousness and that of divine revealing and saving faith remain distinct. In the hands of the theologian Karl Rahner, the philosophy of religion becomes a study of human reality precisely insofar as man is a hearer of the divine word.[27] This theologian treats man as a being who can open himself to the revealing and saving word, which comes in a free act from the personal God. Hence Rahner conceives of the philosophy of religion as a personalist metaphysics of man, the existent who can be lifted by God's power to the hearing of His word and the sharing in His supernatural life. In this context, the

27. Karl Rahner, *Hörer des Wortes: Zur Grundlegung einer Religionsphilosophie* (Munich, Kösel-Pustet, 1941; quotations are from this original text, rather than from the reformulated 1963 ed. by J. B. Metz).

> The philosophy of religion which we seek is an inner moment of the general theory of being itself and simultaneously a metaphysical anthropology. . . . Man is the being of a receptive spirituality, which in freedom stands before the free God of a possible revelation which, when it comes, occurs in his history in the word. Man is the one who is penetratingly heedful in his history to the word of the free God. A metaphysical anthropology is at its goal, at that moment when it has been conceived as the metaphysics of an obediential potency for the revelation of the supramundane God. . . . Consequently, philosophy of religion was not for us the construction of a self-grounding and self-completing natural religion, but the constitution of man as a finite spirit ordered by virtue of his nature to a possible revelation. (Ibid., pp. 25, 205, 209)

Rahner does not rule out natural religion entirely, but requires that the open philosophical concept of it be developed within his perspective of a fundamental theological anthropology. Man's natural religiousness is adapted to his capacity for hearing and responding practically to the word of God, as it comes in a historical revelation. This provides Carlos Cirne-Lima with the reference points for interpreting the supernatural act of faith itself as a personal and historical response to the word and power of God (*Personal Faith* [New York, 1965]). The 1963 Rahner-Metz volume is translated as *Hearers of the Word* (New York, 1969).

theory of religion becomes a fundamental theological anthropology. This is a case where the philosophy of religion is positively developed within a theological milieu, and for ends ultimately specified by the actual presence of revelation. Rahner retains the distinction between human religion and divine faith, but he does not regard the former as an idol and the latter as unrelated to the expectancy of the man of human religion. Revealed faith can come to man through the processes used to develop human religion, even though the use of such means does not identify the two formations of the human spirit.

The realistic philosophy of religion can profit by studying this example of a theory of religion in the theological mode, just as it does from a study of theories of religion in the philosophical mode. But it retains its own internal philosophical structure, differing from the theological approach to the nature of religion. This is due to the decisive influence of the method of integrative analysis in developing a realistic conception of religion. That method requires the investigator to incorporate the historical study of the classical modern philosophies of religion, including those in the Humean naturalistic line. It also imposes an obligation of referring all analyses back to our reflective experience of man's bond with natural being. The realistic approach does not seek out a set of a priori structural forms of religious apprehension, but centers upon our experienced relationships with nature and human society, along with whatever inferences about God are warranted by such experience.

Furthermore, the use of integrative analysis prevents any identification of the philosophical theory of religion with the metaphysical component, or with a view of man specified as a fundamental theological anthropology. The integrative path includes metaphysical and anthropological aspects, but it brings them into an orderly relation with the practical experience of our moral life, rather than directly specifying them as an obediential potency for revelation and the supernatural. The purposive unity of the realistic theory of religion arises from organizing all relevant contributions around the philosophically inspectable patterns of human religiousness, considered as a growing concretion of belief, worship, and community service within human experience. This conception remains open in principle to some further interpretation and use in a theologically directed theory of religion, but such use is the responsibility of theologians and does not absolve the philosopher from taking his own soundings on the religious interpretation of our experience. The realistic philosophy of religion draws its integrity from its own method and intent in examining the evidence for the human meanings of religion, even though its findings may also prove helpful to theological inquirers.

THE UNIVERSITY MATRIX

In conclusion, it is important to specify the social setting within which the tasks in the philosophy of religion can best be pursued. The work is carried on with maximal effectiveness in the university, and perhaps it is only in the university that the proper intellectual and moral climate exists for such an enterprise. Historically, the modern development of the philosophy of religion has been bound up with the university, which furnishes the conditions of freedom within the arts faculty for an independent examination of religion. Kant made this point clearly in *The Strife of the Faculties*, when he observed that the well-being of a philosophical approach to religion depends upon our having the opportunity to inspect religion in terms of the liberal disciplines, taken in their autonomous organization as distinct from a divinity school. His distinction between a creative strife and a destructive battle between the faculties in the university concerning the meaning of religion also remains valid.[28] The different interpretations of religion made by theologians, philosophers, and other investigators are not intended to obliterate each other, but rather to bring out distinct estimates which together will enlarge our human understanding of the same complex reality.

It is not a question here of whether it is good for the university to include the study of religion from various sides. Newman made this point forcefully enough in *The Idea of a University*, but the converse proposition should gain an equally broad assent. It is good for the quality and course of religion itself to be examined by all the relevant disciplines represented in the university community. Like every other human reality, it benefits from the long and systematic scrutiny accorded it from different standpoints. Only in this way can its full complexity and impenetration of human life be brought out, and measures be suggested for improving its quality and practical influence upon our action. There is no need to strive after a perfect integration of the theological, philosophical, sociological, and psychological conceptions of religion which emerge from a university-wide investigation of it. A condition of "strife," of creative ten-

28. The insistence of both Kant and Hegel on the freedom of university inquiries into religion is given a contemporary restatement by Karl Jaspers, *The Idea of the University* (Boston, 1959), pp. 2–3, 67, 85–88.

sion and uneasiness, between the several accounts of religion is best suited
to our human ways of being religious. In our actual condition of pilgrimage, a certain jostling between the different methods and practical
recommendations for human religiousness helps the latter to remain
alive, and open to all the other advances in our relationships with the
universe. And this enmeshment of religion in the several methods of human inquiry is systematically assured by its inclusion in university research. Such inclusion saves all students of religion from the illusion of
having attained a perfect synthesis and rounded-off comprehension of the
religious relationships of mankind.

It is certainly to the advantage of the realistic philosophy of religion
to be cultivated within the university situation, and specifically within the
philosophy department. It is the university which furnishes the normal
climate encouraging a philosophical theory of religion to become an open
religious humanism. The realistic philosopher of religion is obliged to
remain open to findings by men in the other humane fields, by participating
in the interdisciplinary programs and conferences on religion. And as a
member of the philosophy department rather than of the theology department or the divinity school, he is kept aware both of his distinctive approach to religion and of the value of discussing fundamental issues with
philosophers taking other approaches.

The realistic inquirer into religion will ultimately determine his own
procedure and propositional account of religion by the internal conditions
for work within philosophy itself. He must conduct his research and
shape his philosophical assent in accord with the common requirements
of inquiry, governing all analysis and interpretation in philosophy. This
will keep the realistic theory of religion open to the investigator's own
views on method, knowing, and being. And it will also insure reception
of the strenuous criticism and divergent judgments on religion supplied
by his colleagues in philosophy. The realistic philosopher of religion is
constantly reminded by the university situation that he is not an isolated
specialist but simply a philosophical worker, prolonging his inquiry into
the religious ordering of the meanings and values in our existence, and
doing so along with a wider, cooperating community of interpreters of
human religiousness.

Within the university matrix, a systematic effort is made to listen to all
the voices engaged in the continuing discussion of the significance of
the religious response. This educational situation of reflective dialogue
on religion from many quarters of research can be represented by the

question and response of a Russian dramatist and an English poet:

> Look out there, it's snowing. What's the meaning of that?
> Anton Chekhov
> Mine, O thou lord of life, send my roots rain.[29]
> Gerard Manley Hopkins

Along with the rest of the company of investigators in the university, the philosopher of religion must attend to the always renewed questioning on religion, adding his own word in accord with whatever the method and evidence determining his philosophical judgment will permit him to say.

29. Anton Chekhov, *Three Sisters*, in *Chekhov Plays*, trans. E. Fen (Baltimore, Penguin Books, 1959), p. 282; G. M. Hopkins, "Thou art indeed just, Lord, if I contend," *Poems of Gerard Manley Hopkins*, ed. W. H. Gardner (3d ed. New York, Oxford University Press, 1961), p. 113.

Bibliography

BOOKS

Altizer, T. J. J., and W. Hamilton, *Radical Theology and the Death of God,* Indianapolis, Bobbs-Merrill, 1966.

Antonopoulos, Georg, *Der Mensch als Bürger zweier Welten,* Bonn, Bouvier, 1958.

Aquinas, St. Thomas, *Summa Theologiae,* II-II, 80–91: vol. 39, *Religion and Worship,* trans. K. D. O'Rourke, New York, McGraw-Hill, 1964.

Asveld, Paul, *La Pensée religieuse du jeune Hegel,* Louvain, Publications Universitaires, 1953.

Baillie, John, *The Sense of the Presence of God,* New York, Scribner, 1962.

Barth, Karl, *From Rousseau to Ritschl,* London, SCM Press, 1959.

Baumgarten, Alexander, *Metaphysica,* 4th ed. Halle, Hemmer, 1757.

Bayle, Pierre, *Historical and Critical Dictionary,* selected and trans. by R. H. Popkin, Indianapolis, Bobbs-Merrill, 1965.

Beck, Lewis, *A Commentary on Kant's Critique of Practical Reason,* Chicago, University of Chicago Press, 1960.

———, *Six Secular Philosophers,* New York, Harper, 1960.

Benedetto, A. J., *Fundamentals in the Philosophy of God,* New York, Macmillan, 1963.

Bergson, Henri, *The Two Sources of Morality and Religion,* New York, Holt, 1935.

Bertocci, Peter, *Introduction to the Philosophy of Religion,* New York, Prentice-Hall, 1951.

Bewkes, E. G., and J. C. Keene, *The Western Heritage of Faith and Reason,* rev. ed., New York, Harper and Row, 1963.

Beyer, Kurt, *Untersuchungen zu Kants Vorlesungen über die philosophische Religionslehre,* Halle, Klinz, 1937.

Billicsich, Friedrich, *Das Problem des Übels in der Philosophie des Abend-landes*, 3 vols. Cologne, Verlag Sexl, 1952–59.

Blackstone, W. T., *The Problem of Religious Knowledge*, Englewood Cliffs, Prentice-Hall, 1963.

Bloch, Ernst, *Subjekt-Objekt: Erläuterungen zu Hegel*, Frankfurt, Suhrkamp, 1962.

Bochenski, J. M., *The Logic of Religion*, New York, New York University Press, 1965.

Bohatec, Josef, *Die Religionsphilosophie Kants in der "Religion innerhalb der Grenzen der blossen Vernunft,"* Hamburg, Hoffmann and Campe, 1938.

Bourke, Vernon, *Ethics*, New York, Macmillan, 1951.

Bouyer, Louis, *Rite and Man*, Notre Dame, University of Notre Dame Press, 1963.

Brightman, E. S., A *Philosophy of Religion*, New York, Prentice-Hall, 1940.

Brontë, Emily, *Complete Poems of Emily Brontë*, ed. Philip Henderson, London, Folio Society, 1951.

Bruaire, Claude, *Logique et religion chrétienne dans la philosophie de Hegel*, Paris, Seuil, 1964.

Brunner, August, *Die Religion*, Freiburg, Herder, 1956.

Buber, Martin, *Eclipse of God*, New York, Harper, 1952.

Buren, Paul van, *The Secular Meaning of the Gospel*, New York, Macmillan, 1963.

Burgelin, Pierre, *La Philosophie de l'existence de J.–J. Rousseau*, Paris, Presses Universitaires, 1952.

Butler, Joseph, *The Works of Joseph Butler*, ed. W. E. Gladstone, 2 vols. Oxford, Clarendon Press, 1896, vol. 1: *The Analogy of Religion*.

Callahan, Daniel, ed., *The Secular City Debate*, New York, Macmillan, 1966.

Cassirer, Ernst, *The Philosophy of Symbolic Forms*, 3 vols. New Haven, Yale University Press, 1953–57.

Castelli, Enrico, ed., *Demitizzazione e morale*, Rome, Istituto di studi filosofici, 1965.

Chapelle, Albert, *Hegel et religion*, 3 vols. Paris, Editions Universitaires, 1964-67.

Chappell, V. C., ed., *Hume: A Collection of Critical Essays*, New York, Doubleday, 1966.

Chekhov, Anton, *Chekhov Plays*, trans. E. Fen, Baltimore, Penguin Books, 1959.

Christian, W. A., *Meaning and Truth in Religion*, Princeton, Princeton University Press, 1964.

Cirne-Lima, Carlos, *Personal Faith*, New York, Herder and Herder, 1965.

Clarke, Samuel, A *Demonstration of the Being and Attributes of God*, London, Knapton, 1705; reproduced, Stuttgart, Frommann Verlag, 1964.

Clark, Samuel, A *Discourse Concerning the Unchangeable Obligations of Natural Religion and the Truth and Certainty of the Christian Revelation*, London, Knapton, 1706; reproduced, Stuttgart, Frommann Verlag, 1964.

Cobb, John B., A *Christian Natural Theology*, Philadelphia, Westminster Press, 1965.

Collins, James, *God in Modern Philosophy*, Chicago, Regnery, 1959.

————, *The Lure of Wisdom*, Milwaukee, Marquette University Press, 1962.

————, *Three Paths in Philosophy*, Chicago, Regnery, 1962.

Coreth, Emerich, *Das dialektische Sein in Hegels Logik*, Vienna, Herder, 1952.

————, *Metaphysik*, Innsbruck, Tyrolia-Verlag, 1961.

Costello, W. T., *The Scholastic Curriculum at Early Seventeenth-Century Cambridge*, Cambridge, Harvard University Press, 1958.

Cowper, William, *The Poetical Works of William Cowper*, ed. John Bruce, 3 vols. London, Bell and Daldy, 1867.

Cox, Harvey, *The Secular City*, New York, Macmillan, 1965

Crocker, L. G., *An Age of Crisis*, Baltimore, Johns Hopkins Press, 1959.

————, *Nature and Culture*, Baltimore, Johns Hopkins Press, 1963.

D'Arcy, Martin, *No Absent God: The Relations Between God and the Self*, New York, Harper and Row, 1962.

Delekat, Friedrich, *Immanuel Kant*, Heidelberg, Quelle and Meyer, 1963.

Deleuze, Gilles, *Empirisme et subjectivité: Essai sur la nature humaine selon Hume*, Paris, Presses Universitaires, 1953.

Desan, Wilfrid, *The Marxism of Jean-Paul Sartre*, New York, Doubleday, 1965.

Dibon, Paul, *La Philosophie néerlandaise au siècle d'or*, 1, Amsterdam, Elsevier, 1954.

Dillenberger, John, *Protestant Thought and Natural Science*, New York, Doubleday, 1960.

Dilley, Frank B., *Metaphysics and Religious Language*, New York, Columbia University Press, 1964.

Duméry, Henry, *Philosophie de la religion*, 2 vols. Paris, Presses Universitaires, 1957.

————, *The Problem of God in Philosophy of Religion*, Evanston, Northwestern University Press, 1964.

Dupuy, Maurice, *La Philosophie de la religion chez Max Scheler*, Paris, Presses Universitaires, 1959.

Eberhard, J. A., *Vorbereitung zur näturlichen Theologie*, Halle, Waisenhaus, 1781.

Eliade, Mircea, *Myth and Reality*, New York, Harper and Row, 1963

————, *Patterns in Comparative Religion*, Cleveland, World Publishing Company, 1963.

————, *The Sacred and the Profane*, New York, Harper, 1961.

Fabro, Cornelio, *Introduzione all'ateismo moderno*, Rome, Editrice Studium, 1964.

Fairweather, E. R., trans., *A Scholastic Miscellany: Anselm to Ockham*, Philadelphia, Westminster Press, 1956.

Ferré, Frederick, *Language, Logic and God*, New York, Harper, 1961.

———, and Kent Bendall, *Exploring the Logic of Faith*, New York, Association Press, 1962.

Finance, Joseph de, *Essai sur l'agir humain*, Rome, Gregorian University Press, 1962.

Findlay, J. N., *Hegel: A Re-Examination*, New York, Macmillan, 1958.

Fleischmann, Eugène, *La Philosophie politique de Hegel*, Paris, Plon, 1964.

Flew, Antony, *God and Philosophy*, New York, Harcourt, Brace and World, 1966.

———, *Hume's Philosophy of Belief*, New York, Humanities Press, 1961.

Forster, L., ed., *The Penguin Book of German Verse*, rev. ed., Baltimore, Penguin Books, 1959.

Franken, Johannes, *Kritische Philosophie und dialektische Theologie*, Amsterdam, J. H. Paris, 1932.

Freud, Sigmund, *The Future of an Illusion*, New York, Doubleday, 1957.

Garaudy, Roger, *Dieu est mort: Étude sur Hegel*, Paris, Presses Universitaires, 1962.

Gilson, Etienne, *History of Christian Philosophy in the Middle Ages*, New York, Random House, 1955.

Glasenapp, Helmuth von, *Kant und die Religionen des Ostens*, Kitzingen, Holzner-Verlag, 1954.

Goldammer, Kurt, *Die Formenwelt des Religiösen*, Stuttgart, Kröner, 1960.

Goldmann, Lucien, *The Hidden God*, New York, Humanities Press, 1964.

Gornall, Thomas, *A Philosophy of God*, New York, Sheed and Ward, 1963.

Gray, J. G., *Hegel's Hellenic Ideal*, New York, King's Crown Press, 1941.

Grégoire, Franz, *Études hégéliennes*, Louvain, Publications Universitaires, 1958.

Greig, J. Y. T., *David Hume*, New York, Oxford University Press, 1931.

Grimsley, Ronald, *Jean d'Alembert, 1717–83*, New York, Oxford University Press, 1963.

Haering, Theodor, *Hegel: Sein Wollen und sein Werk*, 2 vols. Leipzig, Teubner, 1929–38.

Hanson, N. R., *Patterns of Discovery*, London, Cambridge University Press, 1958.

Häring, Bernard, *Das Heilige und das Gute*, Krailling, Wewel, 1950.

Harris, E. E., *Revelation Through Reason*, New Haven, Yale University Press, 1958.

Hatfield, Henry, *Aesthetic Paganism in German Literature from Winckelmann to the Death of Goethe*, Cambridge, Harvard University Press, 1964.

Hegel, G. W. F., *Berliner Schriften, 1818–1831*, ed. J. Hoffmeister, Hamburg, Meiner, 1956.

———, *Briefe von und an Hegel*, ed. J. Hoffmeister and R. Flechsig, 2d ed. 4 vols. Hamburg, Meiner, 1961.

———, *Early Theological Writings*, trans. T. M. Knox and R. Kroner, Chicago, University of Chicago Press, 1948.

———, *Encyclopedia of Philosophy*, trans. G. E. Mueller, New York, Philosophical Library, 1959.

———, *Enzyklopädie der philosophischen Wissenschaften*, ed. F. Nicolin and O. Pöggeler, 6th ed. Hamburg, Meiner, 1959.

———, *Erste Druckschriften*, ed. G. Lasson, Leipzig, Meiner, 1928.

———, *Hegel's Philosophy of Mind*, trans. W. Wallace, Oxford, Clarendon Press, 1894.

———, *Hegel's Political Writings*, trans. T. M. Knox, Oxford, Clarendon Press, 1964.

———, *Hegels theologische Jugendschriften*, ed. H. Nohl, Tübingen, Mohr, 1907.

———, *Jenenser Logik, Metaphysik und Naturphilosophie*, ed. G. Lasson, Leipzig, Meiner, 1923.

———, *Lectures on the History of Philosophy*, trans. E. S. Haldane and F. H. Simpson, 3 vols. New York, Humanities Press, 1955.

———, *Lectures on the Philosophy of Religion, Together with a Work on the Proofs of the Existence of God*, trans. E. B. Speirs and J. B. Sanderson, 3 vols. London, Routledge and Kegan Paul, 1962.

———, *The Logic of Hegel*, trans. W. Wallace, Oxford, Clarendon Press, 1892.

———, *The Phenomenology of Mind*, trans. J. Baillie, 2d ed. New York, Macmillan, 1931.

———, *The Philosophy of Fine Art*, trans. F. P. B. Osmaston, 4 vols. London, Bell, 1920.

———, *Philosophy of Right*, trans. T. M. Knox, Oxford, Clarendon Press, 1962.

———, *Reason in History*, trans. R. S. Hartman, New York, Liberal Arts Press, 1953.

———, *Science of Logic*, trans. W. H. Johnston and L. G. Struthers, 2 vols. New York, Macmillan, 1951.

———, *System der Philosophie*, Part One: *Die Logik*, in the H. Glockner Jubilee Edition, Stuttgart, Frommann, 1964.

———, *Die Vernunft in der Geschichte*, ed. J. Hoffmeister, 5th ed., Hamburg, Meiner, 1955.

———, *Vorlesungen über die Beweise vom Dasein Gottes*, ed. G. Lasson, Hamburg, Meiner, 1966.

————, *Vorlesungen über die Philosophie der Religion*, ed. G. Lasson, 4 vols bound in 2, Hamburg, Meiner, 1966.

Heidegger, Martin, *Essays in Metaphysics: Identity and Difference*, trans. K. F. Leidecker, New York, Philosophical Library, 1960.

Hendel, Charles W., *Studies in the Philosophy of David Hume*, new ed. Indianapolis, Bobbs-Merrill, 1963.

Hessen, Johannes, *Religionsphilosophie*, 2d ed. 2 vols. Munich, Reinhardt, 1955.

Hick, John, *Philosophy of Religion*, Englewood Cliffs, Prentice-Hall, 1963.

Hintikka, Jaakko, *Knowledge and Belief*, Ithaca, Cornell University Press, 1962.

Hirsch, Emanuel, *Geschichte der neuern evangelischen Theologie*, 5 vols. Gütersloh, Bertelsmann, 1949–54.

Hobbes, Thomas, *Leviathan*, ed. M. Oakeshott, Oxford, Blackwell, 1946.

Hölderlin, Friedrich, *Sämtliche Werke*, ed. F. Beissner, 6 vols. Stuttgart, Cotta, 1944–62.

Holloway, M. R., *An Introduction to Natural Theology*, New York, Appleton-Century-Crofts, 1959.

Hook, Sidney, ed., *Religious Experience and Truth*, New York, New York University Press, 1961.

Hopkins, G. M., *Poems of Gerard Manley Hopkins*, ed. W. H. Gardner, 3d ed. New York, Oxford University Press, 1961.

Hume, David, *Dialogues Concerning Natural Religion*, ed. N. K. Smith, Indianapolis, Bobbs-Merrill, 1963.

————, *Essays Moral, Political and Literary*, New York, Oxford University Press, 1963.

————, *An Inquiry Concerning Human Understanding*, ed. C. W. Hendel, New York, Liberal Arts Press, 1955.

————, *An Inquiry Concerning the Principles of Morals*, ed. C. W. Hendel, New York, Liberal Arts Press, 1957.

————, *The Letters of David Hume*, ed. J. Y. T. Greig, 2 vols. Oxford, Clarendon Press, 1932.

————, *The Natural History of Religion*, ed. H. E. Root, London, Black, 1956.

————, *New Letters of David Hume*, ed. R. Klibansky and E. C. Mossner, Oxford, Clarendon Press, 1954.

————, *A Treatise of Human Nature*, ed. L. A. Selby-Bigge, Oxford, Clarendon Press, 1946.

Hurlbutt, R. H., *Hume, Newton, and the Design Argument*, Lincoln, University of Nebraska Press, 1965.

Hutchison, J. A., *Language and Faith*, Philadelphia, Westminster Press, 1963.

Hyppolite, Jean, *Genèse et structure de la Phénoménologie de l'Esprit de Hegel*, Paris, Aubier, 1946.

Iljin, Iwan, *Die Philosophie Hegels als kontemplative Gotteslehre*, Bern, Francke, 1946.

James, William, *The Varieties of Religious Experience*, New York, New American Library, 1958.

Jansen, Bernhard, *Die Religionsphilosophie Kants*, Berlin, Dümmler, 1929.

Jaspers, Karl, *Philosophical Faith and Revelation*, New York, Harper and Row, 1967.

——, *The Idea of the University*, Boston, Beacon Press, 1959.

——, *The Perennial Scope of Philosophy*, New York, Philosophical Library, 1949.

——, *Philosophy and the World*, Chicago, Regnery, 1962.

Jeffner, A., *Butler and Hume on Religion*, Stockholm, Aktiebolaget Tryckmans, 1966.

Johnson, Howard, and Niels Thulstrup, eds., *A Kierkegaard Critique*, New York, Harper, 1962.

Jones, David, *The Anathemata*, London, Faber and Faber, 1952.

Jurji, E. J., *The Phenomenology of Religion*, Philadelphia, Westminster Press, 1963.

Kant, Immanuel, *Critique of Judgment*, trans. J. H. Bernard, New York, Hafner, 1951.

——, *Critique of Practical Reason and Other Writings in Moral Philosophy*, trans. L. W. Beck, Chicago, University of Chicago Press, 1949.

——, *Critique of Pure Reason*, trans. N. K. Smith, New York, Macmillan, 1933.

——, *Der Streit der Fakultäten*, ed. K. Reich, Hamburg, Meiner, 1959.

——, *Die Religion innerhalb der Grenzen der blossen Vernunft*, ed. H. Noack, 7th ed. Hamburg, Meiner, 1961.

——, *The Doctrine of Virtue*, trans. M. J. Gregor, New York, Harper, 1964.

——, *Gesammelte Schriften*, Prussian Academy ed. 24 vols. Berlin, Walter de Gruyter, 1902–66.

——, *Introduction to Logic*, trans. T. K. Abbott, New York, Philosophical Library, 1963.

——, *Lectures on Ethics*, trans. L. Infield, New York, Harper, 1963.

——, *The Metaphysical Elements of Justice*, trans. J. Ladd, Indianapolis, Bobbs-Merrill, 1965.

——, *On History*, ed. L. W. Beck, Indianapolis, Bobbs-Merrill, 1963.

——, *Prolegomena To Any Future Metaphysics*, trans. P. G. Lucas, New York, Barnes and Noble, 1953.

——, *Religion Within the Limits of Reason Alone*, trans. T. M. Greene and H. H. Hudson, rev. Torchbook ed. with an Introduction by J. R. Silber, New York, Harper, 1960.

———, *Vorlesungen über die Metaphysik*, ed. K. Pölitz, Erfurt, Keyser, 1821; reproduced, Darmstadt, Wissenschaftliche Buchgesellschaft, 1964.

———, *Vorlesungen über die philosophische Religionslehre*, ed. K. Pölitz, Leipzig, Franz, 1817.

———, *Vorlesungen über philosophische Enzyklopädie*, ed. G. Lehmann, Berlin, Akademie-Verlag, 1961.

Kaufmann, Walter, *Hegel*, New York, Doubleday, 1965.

Kierkegaard, Søren, *Attack upon "Christendom,"* 1854–1855, trans. W. Lowrie, Princeton, Princeton University Press, 1944.

———, *Either/Or*, trans. D. F. and L. M. Swenson, rev. by H. A. Johnson, 2 vols. New York, Doubleday, 1959.

Kristensen, W. B., *The Meaning of Religion: Lectures in the Phenomenology of Religion*, Hague, Nijhoff, 1960.

Kroner, Richard, *Speculation and Revelation in the History of Philosophy*, 3 vols. Philadelphia, Westminster Press, 1956–61; vol. 3: *Speculation and Revelation in Modern Philosophy*, 1961.

———, *Von Kant bis Hegel* 2d ed. 2 vols. Tübingen, Mohr, 1961.

Laird, John, *Hume's Philosophy of Human Nature*, London, Metheun, 1932.

Lasson, Georg, *Einführung in Hegels Religionsphilosophie*, Leipzig, Meiner, 1930.

Leeuw, Gerardus van der, *Religion in Essence and Manifestation: A Study in Phenomenology*, 2 vols. New York, Harper, 1963.

———, *Sacred and Profane Beauty: The Holy in Art*, New York, Holt, Rinehart and Winston, 1963.

Leibniz, G. W., *Theodicy*, New Haven, Yale University Press, 1952.

———, and Samuel Clarke, *The Leibniz-Clarke Correspondence*, ed. H. G. Alexander, New York, Philosophical Library, 1956.

Leroy, André, *David Hume*, Paris, Presses Universitaires, 1953.

———, *La Critique et la religion chez David Hume*, Paris, Alcan, 1930.

Lewis, H. D., *Our Experience of God*, New York, Macmillan, 1959.

———, *Philosophy of Religion*, New York, Barnes and Noble, 1965.

Litt, Theodor, *Hegel: Versuch einer kritischen Erneuerung*, 2d ed. Heidelberg, Quelle and Meyer, 1961.

Locke, John, *An Essay Concerning Human Understanding*, ed. A. C. Fraser, 2 vols. New York, Dover Press, 1959.

Loewenberg, Jacob, *Hegel's Phenomenology: Dialogues on the Life of the Mind*, Lasalle, Open Court, 1965.

Lovejoy, A. L., and G. Boas, *Primitivism and Related Ideas in Antiquity*, Baltimore, Johns Hopkins Press, 1935.

Löwith, Karl, *From Hegel to Nietzsche: The Revolution in Nineteenth-*

Century Thought, trans. D. E. Green, New York, Holt, Rinehart, and Winston, 1964.

Löwith, Karl, *Nature, History, and Existentialism*, Evanston, Northwestern University Press, 1966.

Luijk, H. van, *Philosophie du fait chrétien: L'Analyse critique du christianisme de Henry Duméry*, Paris, Desclée, 1964.

Luijpen, W. A., *Phenomenology and Atheism*, Pittsburgh, Duquesne University Press, 1964.

Lukács, Georg, *Der junge Hegel*, Berlin, Aufbau-Verlag, 1954.

Macbeath, A., *Experiments in Living*, New York, Macmillan, 1952.

MacIntyre, Alasdair, *Difficulties in Christian Belief*, London, SCM Press, 1959.

Macmurray, John, *Persons in Relation*, New York, Harper, 1961.

McPherson, Thomas, *The Philosophy of Religion*, Princeton, Van Nostrand, 1965.

Macquarrie, John, *Twentieth-Century Religious Thought*, New York, Harper, 1963.

McRae, Robert, *The Problem of the Unity of the Sciences: Bacon to Kant*, Toronto, University of Toronto Press, 1961.

Manuel, Frank E., *The Eighteenth Century Confronts the Gods*, Cambridge, Harvard University Press, 1959.

Mascall, E. L., *The Secularization of Christianity*, New York, Holt, Rinehart, and Winston, 1966.

Matson, W. I., *The Existence of God*, Ithaca, Cornell University Press, 1965.

Metzger, Hélène, *Attraction universelle et religion naturelle chez quelques commentateurs anglais de Newton*, 3 vols. Paris, Hermann, 1938.

Mitchell, Basil, ed., *Faith and Logic*, Boston, Beacon Press, 1957.

Monden, Louis, *Signs and Wonders*, New York, Desclee, 1966.

Mossner, E. C., *The Life of David Hume*, Austin, University of Texas Press, 1954.

Mueller [Müller], G. E., *Hegel: Denkgeschichte eines Lebendigen*, Bern, Francke, 1959.

Mure, G. R., *The Philosophy of Hegel*, London, Oxford University Press, 1965.

Newman, John Henry, *An Essay in Aid of a Grammar of Assent*, New York, Doubleday, 1955.

———, *Two Essays on Biblical and Ecclesiastical Miracles*, New York, Longmans, 1924.

Niel, Henri, *De la Médiation dans la philosophie de Hegel*, Paris, Aubier, 1945.

Nietzsche, Friedrich, *The Portable Nietzsche*, trans. W. Kaufmann, New York, Viking, 1954.

————, *Thus Spoke Zarathustra*, trans. R. J. Hollingdale, Baltimore, Penguin Books, 1961.

Oates, Whitney, ed., *The Stoic and Epicurean Philosophers*, New York, Random House, 1940

Orr, John, *English Deism: Its Roots and Its Fruits*, Grand Rapids, Eerdmans, 1934.

Ortegat, Paul, *Philosophie de la religion*, 2 vols. Paris, Vrin, 1948.

Otto, Rudolf, *The Idea of the Holy*, New York, Oxford University Press, 1958.

Pascal, Blaise, *Pensées*, text and trans. H. F. Stewart, London, Routledge and Kegan Paul, 1950.

Passmore, John, *Hume's Intentions*, London, Cambridge University Press, 1952.

Paton, H. J., *The Modern Predicament*, New York, Collier Books, 1962.

Peperzak, Adrien, *Le Jeune Hegel et la vision morale du monde*, Hague, Nijhoff, 1960.

Philipp, Wolfgang, *Das Werden der Aufklärung in theologie-geschichtlicher Sicht*, Göttingen, Vandenhoeck and Ruprecht, 1957.

Pike, N., ed., *God and Evil*, Englewood Cliffs, Prentice-Hall, 1964.

Pomeau, René, *La Religion de Voltaire*, Paris, Nizet, 1956.

Popkin, Richard, *The History of Scepticism from Erasmus to Descartes*, New York, Humanities Press, 1960.

Price, J. V., *The Ironic Hume*, Austin, University of Texas Press, 1966.

Rabeau, Gaston, *Introduction à l'étude de la théologie*, Paris, Bloud and Gay, 1926.

Rabel, Gabriele, *Kant*, New York, Oxford University Press, 1963.

Rahner, Karl, *Hörer des Wortes: Zur Grundlegung einer Religionsphilosophie*, Munich, Kösel-Pustet, 1941; new ed. by J. B. Metz, 1963, trans. as *Hearers of the Word*, New York, Herder and Herder, 1969.

Ramsay, Andrew, *The Philosophical Principles of Natural and Revealed Religion*, 2 vols. Glasgow, Foulis, 1748–49.

Ramsey, I. T., *Models and Mystery*, New York, Oxford University Press, 1964.

————, *Religious Language*, New York, Macmillan, 1963

Randall, J. H., Jr., *How Philosophy Uses Its Past*, New York, Columbia University Press, 1963.

Raven, C. E., *Natural Religion and Christian Theology*, 2 vols. London, Cambridge Press, 1953.

Redmann, Horst-Günter, *Gott und Welt: Die Schöpfungstheologie der vorkritischen Periode Kants*, Göttingen, Vandenhoeck and Ruprecht, 1962.

Reese, W. L., and E. Freeman, eds., *Process and Divinity*, La Salle, Ill., Open Court, 1964.

Renard, Jules, *The Journal of Jules Renard*, trans. L. Bogan and E. Roget, New York, Braziller, 1964.

Richardson, W. J., *Heidegger: Through Phenomenology to Thought*, Hague, Nijhoff, 1963.

Richter, Liselotte, *Immanenz und Transzendenz im nachreformatorischen Gottesbild*, Göttingen, Vandenhoeck and Ruprecht, 1955.

Ricoeur, Paul, *Fallible Man*, Chicago, Regnery, 1965.

———, *Finitude et culpabilité*, vol. 2: *La Symbolique du mal*, Paris, Aubier, 1960.

Robinson, J. M., and J. B. Cobb, *The Later Heidegger and Theology*, New York, Harper, 1963.

Rohrmoser, Günther, *Subjektivität und Verdinglichung: Theologie und Gesellschaft im Denken des jungen Hegel*, Gütersloh, Mohn, 1961.

Rondet, Henri, *Hégélianisme et christianisme*, Paris, Lethielleux, 1965.

Rosenkranz, Karl, *Georg Wilhelm Friedrich Hegels Leben*, Darmstadt, Wissenschaftliche Buchgesellschaft, 1963.

Salmony, H. A., *Kants Schrift "Das Ende aller Dinge,"* Zurich, EVZ-Verlag, 1962.

Sartre, Jean-Paul, *The Words*, trans. B. Frechtman, New York, Braziller, 1964.

Scheler, Max, *Man's Place in Nature*, New York, Noonday Press, 1962.

———, *On the Eternal in Man*, New York, Harper, 1960.

Schleiermacher, Friedrich, *On Religion*, trans. J. Oman, New York, Harper, 1958.

Schmalenbach, Herman, *Kants Religion*, Berlin, Junker and Dünnhaupt, 1929

Schultz, Werner, *Kant als Philosoph des Protestantismus*, Hamburg, Reich, 1961.

Seeberger, Wilhelm, *Hegel oder die Entwicklung des Geistes zur Freiheit*, Stuttgart, Klett, 1961.

Selby-Bigge, L. A., ed., *British Moralists*, 2 vols. bound in one, Indianapolis, Bobbs-Merrill, 1964.

Shaftesbury, Anthony, Earl of, *Characteristics of Men, Manners, Opinions, Times*, ed. J. M. Robertson, 2 vols. bound in one, Indianapolis, Bobbs-Merrill, 1964.

Smart, Ninian, ed., *Historical Selections in the Philosophy of Religion*, London, SCM Press, 1962.

Smith, N. K., *The Philosophy of David Hume*, London, Macmillan, 1941.

Smith, R. G., *J. G. Hamann, 1730–1788: A Study in Christian Existence*, New York, Harper, 1960.

Smith, W. C., *The Meaning and End of Religion*, New York, Macmillan, 1963.

Spink, J. S., *French Free-Thought from Gassendi to Voltaire*, London, Athlone Press, 1960.

Splett, J., *Die Trinitätslehre G. W. F. Hegels*, Freiburg, Alber, 1965.

Steinbüchel, Theodor, *Das Grundproblem der Hegelschen Philosophie*, Bonn, Hanstein, 1933.

Stephen, Leslie, *English Thought in the Eighteenth Century*, 3d ed. 2 vols. New York, Peter Smith, 1949.

Stewart, John B., *The Moral and Political Philosophy of David Hume*, New York, Columbia University Press, 1963.

Teilhard de Chardin, Pierre, *The Phenomenon of Man*, New York, Harper, 1959.

Thomas, G. F., *Religious Philosophies of the West*, New York, Scribner, 1965.

Thompson, S. M., *A Modern Philosophy of Religion*, Chicago, Regnery, 1955.

Tillich, Paul, *Systematic Theology*, 3 vols. Chicago, University of Chicago Press, 1951–63.

Toynbee, Arnold, *An Historian's Approach to Religion*, New York, Oxford University Press, 1956.

Travis, D. C., ed., *A Hegel Symposium*, Austin, University of Texas Press, 1962.

Vancourt, R., *La Pensée religieuse de Hegel*, Paris, Presses Universitaires, 1965.

Vico, Giambattista, *The New Science of Giambattista Vico*, trans. T. G. Bergin and M. H. Fisch, Ithaca, Cornell University Press, 1948.

Wach, Joachim, *Types of Religious Experience*, London, Routledge and Kegan Paul, 1951.

Wahl, Jean, *Le Malheur de la conscience dans la philosophie de Hegel*, 2d ed. Paris, Presses Universitaires, 1951.

Watson, R. A., *The Downfall of Cartesianism*, Hague, Nijhoff, 1966.

Weil, Eric, *Hegel et l'État*, Paris, Vrin, 1950.

Weiss, Paul, *The God We Seek*, Carbondale, Southern Illinois University Press, 1964.

Westfall, R. S., *Science and Religion in Seventeenth-Century England*, New Haven, Yale University Press, 1958.

Whitehead, A. N., *Religion in the Making*, Cleveland, World Publishing, 1960.

Wild, John, *Introduction to Realistic Philosophy*, New York, Harper, 1948.

Wilson, John, *Philosophy and Religion*, New York, Oxford University Press, 1961.

Wolff, Christian, *Preliminary Discourse on Philosophy in General*, trans. R. J. Blackwell, Indianapolis, Bobbs-Merrill, 1963.

Wright, G. H. von, *The Varieties of Goodness*, New York, Humanities Press, 1963.
Wundt, Max, *Die deutsche Schulmetaphysik des 17. Jahrhunderts*, Tübingen, Mohr, 1939.
Yolton, John, *John Locke and the Way of Ideas*, New York, Oxford University Press, 1956.
Young, Edward, *The Poetical Works of Edward Young*, ed. John Mitford, 2 vols. London, Bell, 1906.

ARTICLES

Bergmann, F. H., "The Purpose of Hegel's System," *Journal of the History of Philosophy*, 2 (1964), 189–204.
Buren, Paul van, and others, "Linguistic Philosophy and Christian Education," *Religious Education*, 60 (1965), 4–42, 48.
Butler, R. J., "Natural Belief and the Enigma of Hume," *Archiv für Geschichte der Philosophie*, 42 (1960), 90–100.
Cameron, J. M., "Miracles," *Month*, N.S. 22 (1959), 286–97.
Couesnongle, V. de, "La Notion de vertu générale chez saint Thomas d'Aquin," *Revue des Sciences Philosophiques et Théologiques*, 43 (1959), 601–20.
Cox, Harvey, and others, "The Phenomenon of Secularization," *Christian Scholar*, 48 (1965), 9–57.
Dupré, Louis, "Philosophy of Religion and Revelation: Autonomous Reflection vs. Theophany," *International Philosophical Quarterly*, 4 (1964), 499–513.
———, "Toward a Revaluation of Schleiermacher's Philosophy of Religion," *Journal of Religion*, 44 (1964), 97–112.
Fackenheim, Emil, "Kant and Radical Evil," *University of Toronto Quarterly*, 23 (1953–54), 339–53.
———, "Kant's Concept of History," *Kant-Studien*, 48 (1956–57), 381–98.
Fisher, Alden, "Psychoanalysis and Religion," *Insight*, 1 (1962), 27–36.
Hendel, Charles W., "The Eighteenth Century as an Age of Ethical Crisis," *Ethics*, 72 (1962), 202–14.
Kaufmann, Walter, "Hegel's Early Antitheological Phase," *Philosophical Review*, 63 (1954), 3–18.
Kern, Walter, "Das Verhältnis von Erkenntnis und Liebe als philosophisches Grundproblem bei Hegel und Thomas von Aquin," *Scholastik*, 34 (1959), 394–427.
King-Farlow, John, "Justifications of Religious Belief," *Philosophical Quarterly*, 12 (1962), 261–63.

Kline, George, "Some Recent Reinterpretations of Hegel's Philosophy," *Monist*, 48 (1964), 34–75.

Lauer, Q., "Hegel on Proofs for God's Existence," *Kant-Studien*, 55 (1964), 443–65.

Lotz, J. B., "Metaphysical and Religious Experience," *Philosophy Today*, 2 (1958), 240–49.

Matthews, G. B., "Theology and Natural Theology," *Journal of Philosophy*, 61 (1964), 99–108.

Merlan, Philip, "From Hume to Hamann," *Personalist*, 32 (1951), 11–18.

Mitchell, Basil, "The Justification of Religious Belief," *Philosophical Quarterly*, 11 (1961), 213–26.

Mossner, E. C., "Hume's Early Memoranda, 1729–40: The Complete Text," *Journal of the History of Ideas*, 9 (1948), 492–518.

Munson, T. N., "Hegel as Philosopher of Religion," *Journal of Religion*, 46 (1966), 9–23.

Mure, G. R. G., "Hegel, Luther, and the Owl of Minerva," *Philosophy*, 41 (1966), 127–39.

Nádor, G., "Hegel on Empiricism," *Ratio*, 6 (1964), 54–60.

Nicolin, F., "Ein Hegelsches Fragment zur Philosophie des Geistes," *Hegel-Studien*, 1 (1961), 9–48.

Nielsen, Kai, "Linguistic Philosophy and 'the Meaning of Life,'" *Cross Currents*, 14 (1964), 313–34.

———, "Morality and God: Some Questions for Mr. MacIntyre," *Philosophical Quarterly*, 12 (1962), 129–37.

Noxon, James, "Hume's Agnosticism," *Philosophical Review*, 73 (1964), 248–61.

Ong, Walter, "American Culture and Morality," *Religious Education*, 58 (1963), 1–13.

Pöggeler, Otto, "Zur Deutung der Phänomenologie des Geistes," *Hegel-Studien*, 1 (1961), 256–94.

Popkin, R. H., "The High Road to Pyrrhonism," *American Philosophical Quarterly*, 2 (1965), 18–32.

———, "Hume and Kierkegaard," *Journal of Religion*, 31 (1951), 274–81.

Ricoeur, Paul, "The Symbol: Food for Thought," *Philosophy Today*, 4 (1960), 196–207.

Rohrmoser, Günther, "Die theologische Voraussetzungen der Hegelschen Lehre vom Staat," *Hegel-Studien*, Beiheft 1 (1964), 239–45.

Schrader, George, "Hegel's Contribution to Phenomenology," *Monist*, 48 (1964), 18–33.

Schüler, G., "Zur Chronologie von Hegels Jugendschriften," *Hegel-Studien*, 2 (1963), 111–59.

Schweitzer, C. G., "Die Glaubensgrundlagen des Hegelschen Denkens," *Hegel-Studien*, Beiheft 1 (1964), 237–38.

———, "Hegel—das grosse Missverständnis: Zur Verteidigung eines christlichen Philosophen," *Christ und Welt*, 17 (1964), 16–17.

Sleeper, Ralph, "Linguistic Philosophy and Religious Belief," *Cross Currents*, 14 (1964), 335–59.

Smith, J. M., "Can Science Prove That God Exists?" *Heythrop Journal*, 3 (1962), 126–38.

Smith, John, "Philosophy and Religion," *Thought*, 39 (1964), 20–36.

———, "The Relation of Thought and Being," *New Scholasticism*, 38 (1964), 22–43.

Wheeler, M. C., "The Concept of Christianity in Hegel," *New Scholasticism*, 31 (1957), 338–63.

Whittemore, R. C., "Hegel as Panentheist," *Tulane Studies in Philosophy*, 9 (1960), 134–64.

Index